Donation

INTERNATIONAL

We work with leading authors to develop the
strongest educational materials in business,
bringing cutting-edge thinking and best learning
practice to a global market.

Under a range of well-known imprints, including
Financial Times Prentice Hall, we craft high quality
print and electronic publications which help
readers to understand and apply their content,
whether studying or at work.

To find out more about the complete range of our
publishing please visit us on the World Wide Web at:
www.pearsoneduc.com

INTERNATIONAL BUSINESS

A Strategic Management Approach

Second Edition

ALAN M. RUGMAN

Templeton College
University of Oxford

RICHARD M. HODGETTS

Florida International University

FINANCIAL TIMES
Prentice Hall

An imprint of **Pearson Education**

Harlow, England · London · New York · Reading, Massachusetts · San Francisco
Toronto · Don Mills, Ontario · Sydney · Tokyo · Singapore · Hong Kong · Seoul
Taipei · Cape Town · Madrid · Mexico City · Amsterdam · Munich · Paris · Milan

Pearson Education Limited
Edinburgh Gate
Harlow
Essex CM20 2JE
England

and Associated Companies throughout the world

Visit us on the World Wide Web at:
http://www.pearsoneduc.com

First published by McGraw-Hill, Inc. 1995
Second edition 2000

© Pearson Education Limited 2000

ISBN 0 273 63897 1

British Library Cataloguing in Publication Data
A CIP catalogue record for this book can be obtained from the British Library.

Library of Congress Cataloging-in-Publication Data
Rugman, Alan M.
    International business : a strategic management approach / Alan M. Rugman, Richard
M. Hodgetts.—2nd ed.
        p. cm.
    Includes bibliographical references and indexes.
    ISBN 0-273-63897-1
        1. International business enterprises—Management.   I. Hodgetts, Richard M.   II. Title.
    HD62.4.R843   2000
    658′.049—dc21
                                                                                    99-088956

10 9 8 7 6 5 4 3 2
04 03 02 01 00

Typeset by 35 in 9.25/12pt Stone Serif
Printed and bound by Rotolito Lombarda, Italy

Contents in Brief

Contents

Contents

Contents

Contents

List of Maps

Preface

Students of international business are fortunate enough to be living in a laboratory where the principles in this book can be used on a daily basis. Virtually every management decision being made today is influenced by global events, and naive thinking about international politics, economics, cultures, exchange rates and foreign competitors can have quick and adverse effects on a firm's bottom line. The objective of this introduction to international business is to provide relevant theoretical and practical insights to management students so that the real world of global business is better understood. We do this in three ways.

First, the text has an extremely strong emphasis on *relevance*. In each of the 20 chapters there are at least five "cases", so the book has a total of over 100 real-world examples of international business issues to provide insight and perspective.

Second, this text incorporates the latest *theoretical* advances in a manner easily comprehensible for university and college students, from BA to MBA level. For example, the text discusses such important material as Michael Porter's "diamond" theory of international competitiveness, the latest work on the theory of multinational enterprises and new research on organizational learning within corporations.

Third, and most important, the text integrates both the practical and theoretical issues through a sustained use of the concepts of *strategic management*. Indeed, this is the first text to have a strategic management focus in the teaching of introductory international business. This unique feature helps students choose from the extraordinarily broad menu of events in the international environment by building confidence in understanding which ones are useful for strategic management analysis at the firm level.

The three elements – relevance, strong theoretical foundation and strategic synthesis – reinforce each other and provide the student with the opportunity to gain deep and lasting insights into the management of international business. In short, this book paints a broad yet detailed picture on the canvas of the global practice of international business.

Distinctive features of *International Business: A Strategic Management Approach*

There are six distinctive features, in particular, that make this book different from competing textbooks.

First, the book examines international business with an integrative framework, using the strategic management viewpoint. The strategic management approach gives the text the integrative theme of "how to manage an international business" and ties the chapters together into a relevant framework.

Second, many of the excessively technical or mechanistic concepts found in other international business textbooks are de-emphasized. For example, we select relevant aspects of foreign exchange rate management, but we leave technical issues, such as the details of "currency swapping" for the purpose of financing international trans-actions, to a specialized course in international finance. Similarly, absolute and comparative advantage is covered, but these are examined in terms of their relevance to managers of multinationals in formulating and implementing strategy. We have one chapter on international economics, not an entire course. In short, the technical concepts that business majors are learning in their discipline courses are not reinvented in this book; instead, we select analysis that is of relevance to international business students.

Third, each chapter has an opening "Active Learning Case" that is revisited throughout the chapter. The purpose of this "real life" case is to illustrate how the chapter material is used by multinational enterprises in implementing their strategies. The case also breaks the chapter into subparts and helps to reinforce student learning.

Fourth, there are two "Real Cases" at the end of each chapter. These cases are drawn from recent newspaper and journal sources and provide the student with an opportunity to apply the chapter concepts to real-world situations. The cases also offer additional information on subjects covered in the chapter.

Fifth, throughout each chapter there are two "International Business Strategy in Action" boxes. These are drawn from the current literature and provide specific strategy applications of the material being discussed.

Sixth, Part Four of the book is devoted to doing business in particularly important geographic regions of the world, especially in the "triad" of North America, the European Union (EU), and Japan. In this unique feature, the focus is on illustrating how the concepts already presented in the previous parts are being used by multinationals to establish market positions worldwide.

Listening to the market

Our vision of a practical, thematically integrated text built upon a solid theoretical foundation was further refined through an extensive market research effort. We queried the international business market in several important ways:

1. Hundreds of international business instructors participated in a detailed editorial survey during the formative stages of the project. Our survey revealed many important market trends, including some useful insights about international business professors. In recent years, the international business course has grown in popularity and is now often taught by professors with degrees in areas other than international economics or finance. At many universities, professors of management (especially business strategy and general management) are responsible for the course. We believe that our unique strategic management focus will appeal to traditional economics professors as well as management professors; indeed, international business now combines these approaches.

We also learned that numerous professors with "real-world" experience were finding that older text offerings do not "tell it like it is". In recent years there has been a dramatic increase in the number of international business professors who travel to international meetings and engage in joint international research and dialogue with colleagues from other countries. This book, with its macro-oriented approach, will appeal to this market niche.

2. Our manuscript was subject to a rigorous editorial review process at key stages in its development. We are grateful for the incisive comments and critical suggestions by our colleagues in the profession. In particular, we appreciated assistance from:

Bharat B. Bhalla, Fairfield University
Gary N. Dicer, University of Tennessee – Knoxville
Prem Gandhi, State University of New York – Plattsburgh
J. Leslie Jankovich, San Jose State University
Robert A. Kemp, Drake University
Rose Knotts, University of North Texas
Michael Kublin, University of New Haven
Stephen Luxmore, St. John Fisher College
John L. Lyons, Pace University
David L. Mathison, Loyola Marymount University
Stanley D. Nollen, Georgetown University
Moonsong David Oh, California State University – Los Angeles
Lee E. Preston, University of Maryland
John Stanbury, Indiana University – Kokomo
Robert Vichas, Florida Atlantic University

Acknowledgments for the First Edition

The high quality of this book was greatly enhanced by the dedicated secretarial assistance of Amy Ho at the Faculty of Management, University of Toronto. In addition, invaluable research assistance was provided by Samuel He, Bill Mohri, and Bill Gottlieb. Useful comments have been received from Michael Gestrin, Andrew Anderson, Michael Scott and others associated with the Center for International Business at the University of Toronto.

While Professor Rugman served as the Ross Distinguished Visiting Professor of Canada–US Economic and Business Relations at Western Washington University, he received valuable secretarial assistance from Ms Kathleen Finn and useful comments from members of the faculty, especially Robert Spich.

Professor Hodgetts is grateful for the suggestions and continued assistance from Fred Luthans; George Holmes, Professor of Management, University of Nebraska, Lincoln; Gary Dessler and Constance Bates, Management and International Business Department, Florida International University; Jane Gibson, Nova Southeastern University; and Regina Greenwood, Kettering University.

Acknowledgements for the Second Edition

Invaluable research assistance has been provided by Cecilia Brain of the Rotman School of Management, University of Toronto, especially over the three summers of 1997–99 period when the tables, cases and Instructor's Manual were revised and updated. At Templeton College, University of Oxford, exceptional support has been provided by Denise Edwards.

We are pleased to have worked with members of the Pearson Education team in London, from Publisher Jane Powell to Commissioning Editor Sadie McClelland to Editors Nikki Bowen and Claire Brewer.

Distinctive features of the Second Edition

This second edition of an already well-established international business text maintains its unique strategic focus and the use of the triad (US/Europe/Far East) as a framework within which international business is explored. There is an emphasis on the economic environment facing business and the strategies of multinationals throughout. The real strength of this book lies in its relevance, secured by the use of case material, most of which has been revised or replaced, which now offers balanced coverage of each of the triad regions. All data have been revised to be fully up to date. Each chapter retains a common pedagogy, which includes objectives, active learning cases, international business strategy in action, key points, key terms, review and discussion questions, and real cases.

The relevance of the book has been enhanced by the inclusions of 47 brand new "cases" out of the 100 which form the bedrock of the book. The other 53 cases have been updated and expanded. New cases include: Benetton, Upjohn Pharmacia, Thames Water, P&O, Nortel, IKEA, Daewoo, Nokia, Ericsson, Arthur Anderson, McKinsey, Kingfisher, HKSB, Kiwifruit, Acer, Nike, Enron, Philips, Matsushita, Fuji Xerox, Mitsubishi, Lufthansa, Tate & Lyle, Hewlett Packard and environmental capabilities, Japanese FDI in Scotland, APEC, and EMU.

These 100 real world case examples of actual multinational businesses and their operations and strategies offer balanced coverage of the "triad" regions of North America, Europe, and Asia. This is the only major international business textbook to go beyond and "American" or alternatively an "European" perspective, and offer equal treatment of all parts of the triad.

Features of the second edition:

- strategic management approach to international business topics;
- unique triad framework means that each region is given balanced coverage;
- full updated tables and figures;
- 47 new cases and the other 53 expanded and updated;
- new material on World Trade Organization, North American Free Trade Agreement and other international institutions;
- new material on environmental regulations and corporate "green" strategies;
- website of all MNEs and international organisations, which have been added to the case discussions;
- expanded coverage of China, emerging economies, and the Asian financial crisis;
- new theoretical material on the firm-specific advantages and country-specific advantages approach.

An instructor's manual is available, which is the best in the field, with over 100 multiple choice questions for each of the 20 chapters, and with extra test banks.

Alan M. Rugman
Richard M. Hodgetts

A Companion Web Site accompanies
International Business by Rugman and Hodgetts

Visit the **International Business** Companion Web Site as *www.booksites.net/rugman* to find valuable teaching and learning material including:

For students:
- Study material designed to help you improve your results
- Links to valuable resources on the web
- Multiple Choice Questions to help you check your understanding and build confidence
- Search for specific information on the site

For lecturers:
- A secure, password protected site with teaching material
- Links to articles and resources on the web
- A syllabus manager that will build and host a course web page
- An electronic, downloadable version of the Instructor's Manual

About the Authors

ALAN M. RUGMAN is Thames Water Fellow in Strategic Management at Templeton College, University of Oxford. Previously he was a professor at the University of Toronto 1987–98, Dalhousie University 1979–87 and the University of Winnipeg 1970–78. He has also taught international business as a visiting professor at Columbia Business School, London Business School, UCLA, Brandeis University, Warwick Business School and the University of Paris-La Sorbonne.

Dr Rugman has published over 200 articles dealing with the economic, managerial and strategic aspects of multinational enterprises and with trade and investment policy. These have appeared in such leading refereed journals as *The American Economic Review, Strategic Management Journal, Journal of International Business Studies, California Management Review* and *The World Economy*. His many books include: *Inside the Multinationals* (Columbia University Press, 1981); *Administered Protection in America* (Routledge, 1987); *Global Corporate Strategy and Trade Policy* (co-author) (Routledge, 1990); *Foreign Investment and North American Free Trade* (ed.) (University of South Carolina Press, 1994); *International Business* (co-author) (McGraw-Hill, 1985, 1995); *The Theory of Multinational Enterprises* and *Multinational Enterprises and Trade Policy* (Elgar, 1996); *Trade and the Environment* (co-editor) (Elgar, 1998); and *Environmental Regulations and Corporate Strategy* (co-author) (Oxford University Press, 1999).

As a leading authority in international business, Dr Rugman served as Vice-President of the Academy of International Business in 1989–90 and was elected a Fellow of the Academy in 1991. He is also a Fellow of the Royal Society of Arts, elected 1998. He has been identified as one of the five most cited scholars in International Business. He has lectured widely across North and South America, in Western Europe and in Australia and East Asia.

Born in England in 1945, Dr Rugman became a Canadian citizen in 1973. He earned his BA in economics from Leeds University in 1966, MSc in economic development from London University's School of Oriental and African Studies (SOAS) in 1967 and his PhD in economics from Simon Fraser University in 1974. He was elected to an MA (Oxon) in 1998.

Dr Rugman served as an outside advisor on international competitiveness to two Canadian Prime Ministers over the 1986–93 period. He was the only academic member of Canada's business International Trade Advisory Committee from 1986–88 while the Canada–US Free Trade Agreement was being negotiated. Subsequently he served on the sectoral trade advisory committee for forest products from 1989 to 1993, as NAFTA was negotiated. He has been a consultant to major private sector companies, research institutes and government agencies. These include Exxon/Imperial Oil, Kodak, Royal Bank of Canada, Northern Telecom and other multinational enterprises. He has also been a consultant to international organizations such as the United Nations (UNCTAD), NAFTA's Commission on Environmental Co-operation, the Organization for Economic Co-operation and Development (OECD) and the Commonwealth Secretariat.

RICHARD M. HODGETTS is a Professor of Management in the Department of Management and International Business at Florida International University (FIU). He was born and raised in New York City and earned his BS in management at New York University in 1963, his MBA at Indiana University in 1964, and his Ph.d. at the University of Oklahoma in 1968. He then joined the faculty at the University of Nebraska, Lincoln (1966–1975) where he taught strategic mangement. After accepting a visiting professorship at Texas Tech University (1975–1976), he joined Florida International University (FIU) in 1976 where he teaches the international business in both the Executive MBA program and the Graduate Diploma Series program and the strategic management course at the MBA level.

Dr. Hodgetts has published over 125 articles and research papers in a wide variety of areas including international strategy, international compensation, the development of metrics for world class organizations, and the role of quality in creating sustainable advantage in the 21st century. He is also the author or coauthor of 49 different books including *International Management*, 4th edition (Irwin/McGraw 2000) which is the best selling international management textbook in the world; *Entrepreneurship*, 4th edition (Dryden, 1999) which is the leading entrepreneurship book in the US market; and a series of quality-focused management books including *Measures of Quality and High Performance: Simple Tools and Lessons from America's Most Successful Firms* (Amacom, 1998).

Professor Hodgetts has also served as a trainer and consultant for a wide variety of organizations and firms including Advanced Micro Systems, AT&T Technologies, Digital Equipment, Eastman Kodak, General Electric, General Motors, Hewlett Packard, Motorola, Procter & Gamble, Wal-Mart, and the US Federal Reserve System.

Dr. Hodgetts is the editor of the *Journal of Leadership Studies* and the book review editor for *Organizational Dynamics*. He is also a member of the review boards of the *Journal of Economics and Business* and the *Journal of Business Research* and he is the author of the "business" and "corporation" section of the *Microsoft Encarta Encyclopedia* (1998) and the "mergers," "management information systems," and "office work" sections of the *World Book Encyclopedia* (1998). Dr. Hodgetts writes a biweekly column titled "Minding Your Business" for the *Ft. Lauderdale Sun Sentinel*. He is also a past member of the Academy of Management Board of Governors (1993–1996) and a member of the Fellows of the Academy since 1983.

In recent years Professor Hodgetts has been the recipient of a number of awards including the Outstanding Educator Award, National Academy of Management (1999), the John F. Mee, Management Contribution Award, Management History Division, Academy of Management (1998), and the Professorial Excellence Program Award, FIU (1997).

THE WORLD OF INTERNATIONAL BUSINESS

PART ONE: THE WORLD OF INTERNATIONAL BUSINESS

Chapter 1	Chapter 2	Chapter 3
Introduction	MNEs	Triad

PART TWO: THE ENVIRONMENT OF INTERNATIONAL BUSINESS

Chapter 4	Chapter 5	Chapter 6	Chapter 7
Political Environment	Cultural Environment	Economic Environment	Financial Environment

PART THREE: INTERNATIONAL BUSINESS STRATEGIES

Chapter 8	Chapter 9	Chapter 10	Chapter 11
Strategic Planning	Organizing Strategy	Production Strategy	Marketing Strategy

Chapter 12	Chapter 13	Chapter 14
Human Resource Strategy	Political Risk/Negotiation	Financial Strategy

PART FOUR: INTERNATIONAL BUSINESS STRATEGIES IN ACTION
To do Business in International Markets Including:

Chapter 15	Chapter 16
Corporate Strategy/National Competitiveness	EU

Chapter 17	Chapter 18	Chapter 19
Japan	North America	Non-Triad Nations

PART FIVE: INTERNATIONAL BUSINESS HORIZONS

Chapter 20
Future of International Business

CHAPTER 1

The Challenge of International Business

OBJECTIVES OF THE CHAPTER

In the twenty-first century we are seeing dramatic global developments that are changing the nature of international business. The political and economic changes in Eastern Europe and Russia are opening the doors for a wide variety of business activity, and multinational enterprises are hurrying to take advantage of these new opportunities. Japan is leading the Asia Pacific area in becoming an economic power and the dream of a unified European Union is now a reality. A similar development is occurring in North America where the United States, Canada, and Mexico are creating their own free trade area. By the year 2010 we will likely see three major economic markets in the world: North America, Europe and Asia Pacific. Many firms and countries outside these regions are also improving their economic status and becoming more active in international business. This chapter examines some of the latest international developments. We then ask: What conditions are necessary for creating and maintaining an international competitive advantage? The last part of the chapter presents the philosophy and model that we will use throughout our study of international business. The specific objectives of this chapter are to:

1. **Define** the term "international business" and provide examples of current international business activity.

2. **Discuss** the two primary ways in which international business occurs.

3. **Examine** the four major determinants of national competitive advantage and relate how each can be used effectively.

4. **Describe** the role of government and trade regulations in the conduct of international business.

5. **Discuss** the significance of the multinational enterprise to international business.

6. **Present** the model that will be used in this text for studying international business.

ACTIVE LEARNING CASE

Coke takes control in Europe

Coca-Cola is the largest selling soft drink in the world. But sales vary by nation. The average American consumes almost 291 12-ounce servings of Coke annually, while in Iceland consumption is a whopping 333 servings. On the other hand, many Europeans are not big Coca-Cola drinkers. The average annual number of 12-ounce servings in Germany, Spain, Belgium and Austria is 166; in Great Britain, Ireland and Switzerland it is about 110; France, Italy and Portugal lag behind with consumption at an average of 65. However, all of this is in the process of changing. Coke has undertaken a vigorous campaign to dramatically increase consumption in Europe.

One of the first strategic steps has been to replace local franchisers who had become too complacent and turn their franchises over to more active, market-driven sellers. In France, Pernod, a Coca-Cola franchisee, was forced to resell some of its operations back to Coke and a new marketing manager was appointed for the country. Coke's prices have now been lowered and advertising for the product increased. As a result, per capita consumption in France has increased by over 65 per cent since the early 1990s.

In England, Beecham and Grand Metropolitan used to be Coke's national bottlers but that has been turned over to Cadbury Schweppes, most famous for its Schweppes mixers. The new marketer began to run contests and sponsor events all over the country. In the first three years since Schweppes took over, sales tripled.

In Germany the pace has been even faster. As people poured across the border from East to West Germany in 1990, they were greeted by Coca-Cola representatives giving out free samples, and Coca-Cola invested in distribution networks to package and sell Coke locally. In the rest of the country, marketing efforts have been even more dramatic. A new bottling plant has replaced the inefficient bottling network that was inhibiting growth, and marketing efforts are paying off handsomely. As a result, Germany is now Coca-Cola's largest and most profitable market in Europe, and the company has the largest soft-drink market share in every country in Eastern Europe.

Some government agencies and companies are concerned about the way in which Coca-Cola is pushing aside those who are unable to lower costs and generate more business. The European Union's DG-IV Competition Department, based in Brussels, is investigating possible anti-competitiveness in Coke's bid to purchase CCSB, a British bottler. In Britain, the British Monopolies and Mergers Commission investigated Coke on its joint venture with Schweppes; and San Pellegrino, the mineral water company, filed a complaint with the Commission of the European Communities, contending that Coca-Cola has abused its dominant position by giving discounts to Italian retailers who promised to stock only Coke.

None of this is stopping Coca-Cola's efforts to establish a strong foothold in Europe. As the European Union eliminates all internal tariffs, it will be possible for a chain store with operations in France, Germany, Italy and the Netherlands to buy soft drinks from the lowest-cost supplier in the continent and not have to worry about paying import duties for shipping them to the retail stores. So low cost and rapid delivery are going to be key strategic success factors in what is likely to be a major "cola war." Coke believes that its current strategy puts it in an ideal position to win the war.

Sources: Adapted from Patricial Sellers, "Coke Gets Off Its Can in Europe," *Fortune*, August 13, 1990; Susan E. Kuhn, "Are Foreign Profits Good for Stocks," *Fortune*, November 16, 1992; John Huey, "The World's Best Brand," *Fortune*, May 31, 1993; Howard Banks, "Stomach Share," *Forbes*, November 11, 1996; Patricia Sellers and Wilton Woods, "Where Coke Goes From Here," *Fortune*, October 13, 1997; and "Coca-Cola Map: Next Year, The French-Fry Index," *The Economist*, December 12, 1997.

1. Why is Coca-Cola making foreign direct investments in Europe?

2. How is Coke improving its factor conditions in Europe?

3. How is local rivalry helping to improve Coke's competitive advantage?

4. Is Coca-Cola a multinational enterprise?

INTRODUCTION

International business is the study of transactions taking place across national borders for the purpose of satisfying the needs of individuals and organizations. These economic transactions consist of trade, as in the case of exporting or importing, and direct investment of funds in overseas operations. About 80 per cent of all direct investment is conducted by the 500 largest firms in the world; these firms also account for over half of all international trade. Thus the study of international business is heavily focused on the activities of large **multinational enterprises** (MNEs), which are headquartered in one country but have operations in other countries. MNEs account for the majority of the world's investment and trade.

In the past decade alone MNEs have directly invested billions of dollars overseas to buy or create businesses. Most of these foreign investments have been two-way: the United States investing in the European Community and the European Community investing in the United States; Japan investing in the United States and the United States investing in Japan; Canada investing in the United States and the United States investing in Canada.

More recently MNEs have been turning their attention to developing countries, many of which are emerging from communism.[1] Eastern Europe, for example, is becoming an attractive market for foreign investment. For example, Volkswagen (VW) has invested billions of dollars in the Czech automaker Skoda; Opel has built a multi-million dollar car plant in East Germany; and General Electric has purchased Tungsram, Hungary's giant light bulb manufacturing plant.[2] At the same time Bertelsmann AG, the German media conglomerate, has holdings in both Hungary and Slovakia's largest daily newspapers and a television station in Poland, and is manufacturing compact disks, audio tapes, and CD-ROMS in Russia.[3] Automakers are also actively pursuing the Eastern European market. Daewoo, Ford, General Motors, Kia Motors, and VW all have operations in the former Soviet Union.[4]

What makes these investments particularly interesting is the fact that while most Eastern European economies are undergoing very difficult economic and political turbulence, these countries are also viewed as generating high enough profits to attract foreign investors. Privatization in other parts of the world, from Mexico to the Pacific Basin, is also attracting attention.[5] For example, US air carriers are now working hard to create lucrative alliances in Latin America,[6] and a growing number of automakers from Europe, North America, and Asia are now producing cars in Brazil and Argentina for domestic buyers as well as for export.[7]

Another popular area of international business activity has been the **international joint venture**, which is an agreement between two or more partners to own and control an overseas business.[8] For example, General Motors and Toyota jointly produce cars in the United States; Ford and Volkswagen have a similar arrangement in South America; Motorola and Toshiba are now developing computer chips for high-definition television sets;[9] and Nissan and Hitachi have teamed up to create a "mobile office" that will develop, produce, and sell mobile telephones, facsimile machines, television sets, videocassette recorders, and navigation systems.[10] Other firms, such as the seven US regional telephone companies, are finding that their local markets do not provide sufficient growth opportunity and thus are turning to joint ventures in overseas markets.

INTERNATIONAL BUSINESS STRATEGY IN ACTION

American Airlines and British Airways alliance delayed by three sets of regulators

On June 1996, American Airlines (AA) and British Airways (BA) announced their plans to create a transcontinental alliance. The company was reacting to a wave of partnership creations by their competitors. Since 1991, the Lufthansa–United–SAS, KLM–Northwest, and Delta–Sabena–Swissair–Austrian alliances have been formed. AA and BA felt that their partnership would allow them to compete better globally. The new alliance would provide better flight services, with increased destinations, less stopover time and a direct luggage service, which the other alliances already offer. The AA/BA partnership, which was to come into effect in April 1997, would allow both companies to coordinate their flights, share pricing information, use a common coding system and consolidate their frequent flyer programs. As there was to be no exchange of equity or any other form of cross-shareholding involved, the companies would continue to be two separate entities, maintaining their nationalities, their employees, and their logos. Two years later, the partnership has still not come into effect because US, British and EU regulators have not come to an agreement on a variety of antitrust issues.

Both regulators and competitors are concerned about the dominance of an AA/BA alliance in the US–UK market. Together, AA and BA control 58 per cent of the available seats between the US and the UK, and this poses a threat to competitors who fear they will be completely eliminated from the market. Regulators are also concerned about a monopolistic situation in

which the strong dominance of the alliance might lead to an increase in prices.

For approval, the proposed alliance had to undergo a never ending review by the US Department of Justice, and is presently awaiting the decision of the Department of Transportation. However, even if the Department of Transportation rules in favor of the alliance, the US government will only consider the alliance if the British government deregulates its airports to allow for freer competition. Both airlines have decided to endorse the "open skies" concept of free market access. However, the US and Britain don't seem to agree on what signifies "open skies." As if the difficulties the carriers face were not enough, the EU has threatened to sue the British government if it allows the alliance.

AA/BA are ready to give up 12 slots at Heathrow airport, the British government has requested 168, and a judge in the US has ruled that the divestment of slots need not be a condition for allowing the partnership. The EU is opposed to the dominance of AA/BA on 13 specific routes. The competitors, many of which are part of a similar alliance, have lobbied and sued to prevent the alliance. As a result of these problems, the proposed deal has almost ceased to exist on a variety of occasions. Recently, BA's executives announced that they will continue to press for the deal as long as there seems to be some progress. However, with lawsuits, delays, and governmental conflicts, it is not clear whether there will be such an alliance in the near future.

Sources: Richard Evans, "A US–UK Alliance Comes Apart," *Fortune*, March 3, 1997; Geoff Colvin, "A Grand Alliance," *Fortune*, February 10, 1997; Ronald B. Lieber, "Flying High, Going Global," *Fortune*, July 7, 1997; *http://www.amrcorp.com/amr/aa_ba_oct1496a.htm; http://www.amrcorp.com/amr/aa_ba_news.htm; http://www.legislate.com/xp/p-daily/l-8998060401/a-89691761/article.view.*

THE ROLE OF SMALL BUSINESS

International business is not limited to giant multinational enterprises. Many small and medium-sized businesses are also involved in this arena. These include service industries, which currently employ about 70 per cent of all workers in the United States, Canada, and Europe. Traditionally economists have thought of services and small business as part of the "nontraded" sector. But today we live in a globally integrated business system. The information technology revolution and the advances in transportation mean that knowledge, skilled people, goods, and services are extremely mobile. The world is now a global village, where the producers of goods and services often compete both domestically and internationally. A good example is provided by small export firms that are now finding there is a market niche for their goods and services. In fact, some companies are so successful that they are now doing more business overseas than they are domestically.[11]

Today small businesses account for the majority of jobs; when you graduate, you are more likely to work in a service industry or small business than in a multinational enterprise. But the study of international business will be relevant whether you work in a small business or in a multinational enterprise because they function together in the global economy. The large multinational enterprises tend to influence the success of smaller businesses because they rely on small businesses for goods and services. In addition, workers in the public sector (national, state, and local government) are indirectly involved in the success of global firms since the economic performance of a nation's multinational enterprises helps to generate the revenues for these services and the government purchases billions of dollars of goods and services annually.

The primary focus of this book is on the large MNEs which dominate world trade and investment. However, we also need to consider the vital role played by small- and medium-sized businesses, which account for a growing amount of world trade and investment. As a result, consideration will be given to international enterprises of all sizes.

WORLD BUSINESS: A BRIEF OVERVIEW

The majority of international business is conducted by MNEs. This activity is carried out in several ways. One is through international trade such as importing and exporting. Another is through foreign direct investment. A third is through licensing, joint ventures, and other forms of FDI. We shall focus on the first two at this time, and address the third later in the book.

Exports and imports

Exports are goods and services produced by a firm in one country and then sent to another country. **Imports** are goods and services produced in one country and brought in by another country. In most cases people think of exports and imports as physical goods (cars, shoes, food) but the latter also include services such as those provided by international airlines, cruise lines, reservation agencies, and hotels. Indeed, many international business experts now recognize that one of the major US exports is its entertainment and pop culture such as movies, television, and related offerings.

Table 1.1 provides a breakdown of worldwide trade in a recent year. A close look shows that the European Union (EU) is the world's single largest trading unit, followed by Asia and North America. The majority of this export and import activity is in the area of manufacturing such as industrial machinery, computers, cars, televisions,

Table 1.1 World trade, 1996

Country/region	Exports		Imports	
	Billions of US $	% of total	Billions of US $	% of total
United States	622.9	11.8	817.8	15.1
Canada	200.1	3.8	187.8	3.5
Mexico	96.0	1.8	98.4	1.8
North America	919.0	17.5	1,104.0	20.4
European Union	2,041.6	38.8	1,953.2	36.2
Japan	411.2	7.8	349.5	6.5
Other Asia	975.5	18.5	1,044.4	19.3
Asia including Japan	1,386.7	26.3	1,393.9	25.8
All others	918.5	17.4	949.9	17.6
Total	5,265.8	100.0	5,401.0	100.0

Source: Adapted from International Monetary Fund, *Direction of Trade Statistics Yearbook*, 1997.
(Washington D.C., IMF, 1997).

Table 1.2 The top ten trading partners of the United States, 1996

Rank	Importing country	US exports (in millions of US $)	Exporting country	US imports (in million of US $)
1	Canada	132,584	Canada	159,746
2	Japan	67,536	Japan	117,963
3	Mexico	56,761	Mexico	74,111
4	UK	30,916	China	54,409
5	Germany	23,474	Germany	39,989
6	Korea	23,297	Taiwan	31,023
7	Taiwan	18,413	UK	29,700
8	Singapore	16,686	Korea	23,297
9	Netherlands	16,614	Singapore	20,648
10	France	14,413	Malaysia	18,331
	Other	222,251	Other	248,568
	Total Exports	622,945	Total Imports	817,785

Source: Adapted from IMF, *Yearbook, Direction of Trade Statistics*, 1997.

VCRs, and other electronic goods. However, as will be seen later, an increasing proportion of world trade is in services.

Data on exports and imports are important to the study of international business for two reasons. First, trade is the historical basis of international business and trade activities help us understand MNE practices and strategies. For example, in 1996 the United States' largest export partners were Canada, Japan, Mexico, the United Kingdom, and Korea (see Table 1.2 and the map, using 1997 data). Some of the major products that are shipped abroad include computers, farm machinery, machine tools, and electronic goods. The table also reveals that the United States' largest import

Table 1.3   Foreign direct investment in the United States, 1996

Country/region	Millions of US $	% of all countries
All countries	630,045	100.0
Canada	53,845	8.5
Europe	410,425	65.1
France	49,307	7.8
Germany	62,242	9.9
Netherlands	73,803	11.7
United Kingdom	142,607	22.6
Latin America and other Western Hemisphere	24,627	3.9
Brazil	591	0.1
Mexico	1,078	0.2
Africa	717	0.1
Middle East	6,177	1.0
Asia and Pacific	134,255	21.3
Australia	9,747	1.5
Japan	118,116	18.7

Source: US Department of Commerce, *Survey of Current Business*, March 1998.

markets have been Canada, Japan, Mexico, the People's Republic of China and Germany. In addition to automobiles, other major imported products have included footwear, consumer electronics, machine tools, and apparel. Note that most of the United States' 10 largest import partners are also the country's largest export partners. The United States sells and buys a large percentage of its goods and services among a small number of countries. (See also Appendix 1A–1D for information on major exporters, importers, and the direction of world trade flows.)

Information about exports and imports also helps us to understand the impact of international business on the economy. For example, how does being a major exporter affect a country's economy? How does relying on imports affect the economy? We can explore these questions by looking at the effect of exports and imports on the United States. International business activity is critical to the success of the US economy because it provides additional markets for our goods.

Foreign direct investment

Foreign direct investment (FDI) is equity funds invested in other nations. Industrialized countries have invested large amounts of money in other industrialized nations and smaller amounts in less developed countries (LDCs) such as those in Eastern Europe or newly industrialized countries (NICs) such as Hong Kong, Korea, and Singapore. Most of the world's FDI is in the United States, the EU,[12] and Japan.

By 1990, the United States had become such a major investment target that foreign holdings in the United States amounted to approximately $1.5 trillion. At the same time US holdings abroad totaled around $1.2 trillion.[13] Table 1.3 shows the stocks of FDI in the United States in 1996, and Table 1.4 reports FDI by the United States in other countries in this same year.

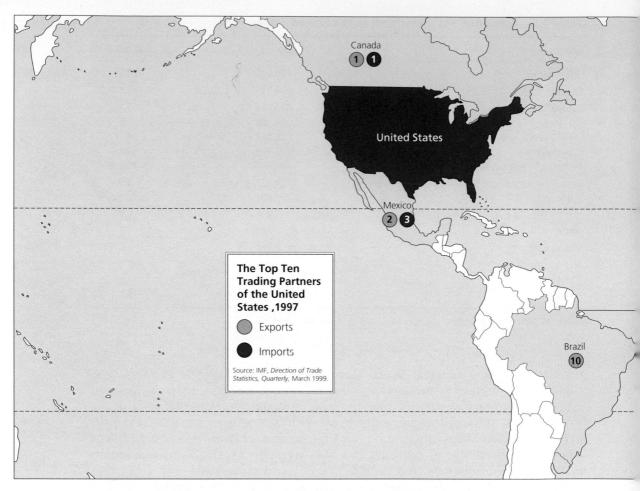

The Top Ten
Trading Partners
of the United
States ,1997

 Exports

 Imports

Source: IMF, *Direction of Trade
Statistics, Quarterly,* March 1999.

Table 1.4   Foreign direct investment by the United States, 1996

Country/region	Millions of US $	% of all countries
All countries	796,494	100.0
Canada	91,587	11.5
Europe	399,632	50.2
France	34,000	4.3
Germany	44,259	5.6
Netherlands	44,667	5.6
United Kingdom	142,560	17.9
Latin America and other Western Hemisphere	144,209	18.1
Brazil	26,166	3.3
Mexico	18,747	2.4
Africa	7,568	1.0
Middle East	8,743	1.1
Asia and Pacific	140,402	17.6
Australia	28,769	3.6
Japan	39,593	5.0
International	4,352	0.5

Source: US Department of Commerce, *Survey of Current Business,* March 1998.

The largest investors in the United States in 1996 were Britain, Japan, the Netherlands, Germany and Canada. Collectively they accounted for over 70 per cent of all FDI in the United States. Despite increased activity in foreign investment, FDI constitutes less than 5 per cent of the entire wealth of the United States.

At the same time the United States is a major worldwide investor. Table 1.4 reports the stock of US FDI in other countries for 1996. The major stake was in the EU, followed by Canada and Japan.[14] This table reveals how the United States is conducting two way FDI with other major industrialized nations. This balance in two-way trade and investment is a key aspect of international business.

As nations have become more affluent, they have pursued FDI in geographic areas that have economic growth potential. The Japanese, for example, have been investing heavily in the EU in recent years and from 1985 to 1995 they more than tripled the percentage of their total FDI there.[15] A large percentage of these funds is in manufacturing, but there are also substantial holdings in the banking and the insurance sectors. One reason for this strategy was the forecasted growth for the EU during the 1990s. A second is the import barriers and perceived entry barriers that surround the EU market, which make it much more profitable to be on the inside than on the outside. For similar reasons, American and Canadian MNEs have been investing heavily in the EU. (For more on FDI see Appendixes 1E and 1F.)

ACTIVE LEARNING CHECK

Review your answer to Active Learning Case question 1 and make any changes you like. Then compare your answer to the one below.

1. Why is Coca-Cola making foreign direct investments in Europe?

Coke is making these investments in order to improve its market position. This is being done in three ways. First, the construction of new bottling plants is helping the company produce a low-cost product. Second, marketing expenditures are helping the company to gain the product recognition needed for growth. Third, direct investments in facilities closer to the market are reducing delivery time and eliminating import duties.

MEETING THE INTERNATIONAL BUSINESS CHALLENGE

What must nations do to gain and hold strong international trading and investment positions? There are three areas in which they must excel. First, the country must maintain economic competitiveness. Second, it must influence trade regulations so that other countries open their doors for its goods and services, being willing to buy from as well as sell to the country. Third, its businesses must develop a global orientation that allows them to operate as MNEs, not just as local firms doing business overseas.

Maintaining economic competitiveness

During the 1980s the United States saw some of its economic competitiveness weakened by Japanese and European imports, although the late 1990s saw a strong resurgence as the US once again became the world's most competitive nation. Japanese cars that during the 1970s were regarded as mediocre quality now proved to be better than those produced by the US auto giants. Leather goods and ceramic tiles from Italy gained world renown, and the German printing press industry proved to be the best in the world. At the same time the United States maintained its lead in mainframe computers and microprocessor chips; continued to be regarded as the best in the world in manufacturing passenger aircraft; and started to make serious headway in the development of high-definition television, an area in which many had believed the Japanese were too far ahead to be caught. In the international service industries the picture was also mixed, with some countries dominating one area and other countries clearly ahead in different areas. For example, Britain was now the leader in specialty retailing; Italy was in front in design services; and the United States held sway in fast-food service, entertainment, financial services, and information services.[16]

Quite clearly, economic competitiveness is in a continual state of flux. The United States has lost its position in some industries but leads in others.[17] What accounts for the competitive advantage that nations enjoy? Many experts have contended that the most important determinants of competitiveness are labor costs, interest rates, exchange rates, and economies of scale.[18] The problem with this thinking is that it fails to take into consideration the true sources of international competitive advantage.

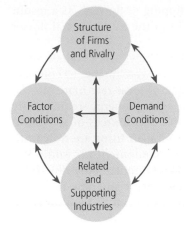

Figure 1.1   Porter's determinants of national competitive advantage

Source: Adapted from Michael E. Porter, *The Competitive Advantage of Nations* (New York: Free Press, 1990), p. 72.

Research shows that the best way for companies to achieve competitive advantage is with innovation. Quite often this is accomplished through ongoing improvement of goods or services. For example, Volvo, the Swedish automaker, has continually striven to improve auto safety; as safety has become a more important factor in the consumers' car-buying decisions, Volvo has increased its competitive advantage.

International competitiveness

Why are some firms able to innovate consistently while others cannot? According to Porter, the answer rests in four broad attributes that individually and interactively determine national competitive advantage: factor conditions, demand conditions, related and supporting industries, and the environment in which firms compete.[19] The relationships among these determinants are illustrated in Figure 1.1.

Factor conditions   According to basic international trade theory, a nation will export those goods that make most use of the factor conditions with which it is relatively well endowed. These **factor conditions** include land, labor, and capital. For example, if a country has a large, relatively uneducated work force, it will seek to export goods that are highly labor-intensive. In this way the country can use its people effectively. On the other hand, if the work force is highly educated, the country will seek to produce goods and services that tap the intellectual abilities of these people. Nations attempting to compete with these countries may find themselves at a distinct disadvantage because they lack either the supply of labor or the educational achievement of the work force.

However, there is more to international trade theory than merely capitalizing on one of the basic factors. In order to maintain a competitive position, a country must continually upgrade or adjust its factor conditions. For example, Denmark has two hospitals that specialize in studying and treating diabetes; Denmark also is a world leading exporter of insulin. By creating specialized factors and then working to upgrade them, the country has maintained its premier position in the health-care field. Similarly, the Netherlands, the world's leading exporter of flowers, has created research institutes in the cultivation, packaging, and shipping of flowers. As a result, no one has been able to dislodge that country's foothold in the international flower industry.

Sometimes nations may develop the factor conditions they need. Italian steelmakers in northern Lombardy, for example, found that they were unable to compete because of high energy costs, high capital costs, and lack of local raw materials. So they pioneered technologically advanced minimills that use less energy, require only modest capital investment, permit producers to locate close to sources of scrap and end-use customers, and are efficient at small scale. These Italian firms are now both important minimill operators and world leaders in selling equipment for minimills. The Japanese are another good example. The country has to import many raw materials, but by developing just-in-time production methods, major Japanese manufacturers have been able to reduce the amount of resources they need to keep on hand and to increase their overall productivity at the same time. This has helped them gain world market share in the auto and consumer goods sectors.

Gaining competitive advantage depends on an ability to use one or more of the four determinants in tandem. For example, to be innovative, a company must often have access to people with the necessary skills (factor conditions) as well as domestic competitors who create pressure to innovate (rivalry), customers who want a better or less expensive product (demand conditions), and/or suppliers (supporting industries) who can provide both innovative suggestions and low-cost materials. It is also necessary for a firm to commit itself to the industry (firm strategy) and to be determined to find a way to solve the problem through innovative effort rather than to look for an easy way around the disadvantage. Otherwise the outcome may be disastrous, as Porter has illustrated with this example:

> Faced with high relative labor costs, for example, American consumer electronics firms moved to locate labor-intensive activities in Taiwan and other Asian countries, leaving the product and production process essentially the same. This response led only to labor cost parity, instead of upgrading the sources of competitive advantage. Japanese rivals, facing intense domestic rivalry and a mature home market, set out instead to eliminate labor through automation. Doing so involved reducing the number of components which further lowered cost and improved quality. Japanese firms were soon building assembly plants in the United States, the place American firms had sought to avoid.[20]

ACTIVE LEARNING CHECK

Review your answer to Active Learning Case question 2 and make any changes you like. Then compare your answer to the one below.

2. How is Coke improving its factor conditions in Europe?

Coke's factor conditions include land, labor, and capital. The company is using land and capital to build new bottling plants that are more efficient and better situated to meet market demand. It is working to improve the effectiveness of the labor force by getting the personnel to become more market-oriented and to sell the product more vigorously throughout Europe.

Demand conditions   Porter states that a nation's competitive advantage is strengthened if there is strong local demand for its goods and services. This demand provides a number of benefits. First, it helps the seller understand what buyers want. Second, if changes become necessary, such as customer desires for a product that is smaller, lighter, or more fuel efficient, the local seller has early warning and can adjust or innovate for the market before more distant competitors can respond. In fact, the more sophisticated the local buyers, the greater the advantage to the local seller. For example, one reason the Japanese firms pioneered small, quiet air-conditioning units is that many Japanese live in small houses and apartments where loud noise can be a problem. The firms also developed units that were powered by energy-saving rotary compressors because customers complained that the price of energy was very high and they wanted a more fuel-efficient unit. As a result, the Japanese now dominate the world market for small air conditioners. Similarly, Sweden, long concerned with helping the disabled, has now spawned a competitive industry that focuses on the special needs of these people, and Denmark's environmental concern has resulted in Danish companies developing highly effective water-pollution control equipment and windmills. In the United States, consumers helped to develop a highly efficient fast-food industry, and as the desire for this cuisine spread worldwide, US franchisors like McDonald's and Pizza Hut have been able to tap international demand for their products.

Related and supporting industries   Porter's third major determinant of national competitive advantage is the presence of related and supporting industries that are internationally competitive. These are mainly service industries. When suppliers are located near the producer, these firms often provide lower-cost inputs that are not available to the producer's distant competitors. In addition, suppliers typically know what is happening in the industry environment and are in a position to both forecast and react to these changes. By sharing this information with the producer, they help the producer maintain its competitive position. The Italian shoe industry is an excellent example. Shoe producers interact on a regular basis with leather manufacturers, exchanging information that is useful to each in remaining competitive. This interaction is mutually beneficial to both parties.[21]

The advantages of this interaction show us that manufacturers should not create "captive" suppliers who are dependent on them. If suppliers do business with competitors, they are in a better position to learn more about the business environment of a particular industry and so provide useful information about future industry developments and trends. This information is particularly important because information flow and technical interchange often speed the rate of innovation and quality improvements in the industry. So captive suppliers actually limit the manufacturer's ability to innovate and meet competitive pressures.

Firm strategy, structure, and rivalry   Porter's fourth broad determinant of national advantage is the context in which the firms are created, organized, and managed, as well as the nature of domestic rivalry. No one managerial system is universally appropriate. Nations tend to do well in industries where the management practices favored by the national environment are suited to their industries' sources of competitive advantage. In Italy, for example, successful firms typically are small or medium sized;

operate in fragmented industries such as lighting, furniture, footwear, and packaging machines; are managed like extended families; and employ a focus strategy geared toward meeting the needs of small market niches. Germany, in contrast, tends to have hierarchical organizations that emphasize technical or engineering content (optics, chemicals, complicated machinery) that demand precision manufacturing, a careful development process, after-sale service, and a highly disciplined management structure. In Japan, successful firms are often those that require unusual cooperation across functional lines and that demand management of complex assembly operations. Auto production, television manufacturing, and computer assembly are examples of such industries.

National goals are also important. Some countries want rapid results. Others tend to do best in industries where long-term development is valued more. In the United States, for example, investors like fast financial return. So US firms are more likely to invest in new industries such as software and biotechnology where success can come quickly. In Germany and Switzerland, investments are held for long-term appreciation and are rarely traded. These countries are more likely to invest in mature industries where ongoing investment in research and development and new facilities are important but return on investment is only moderate.

Another important area of consideration is the career choices people make, which are often influenced by the nation's value system. For example, in Switzerland, where banking and pharmaceuticals are regarded as important, outstanding young people seek careers in those fields. In Israel, agriculture and defense-related fields are given high priority. In Germany, the chemical sector is prestigious, while in Japan, it is the consumer electronics field. In the United States, finance, entertainment, and professional sports are regarded as highly prestigious.

Another area of importance is domestic rivalry. Researchers have found that vigorous domestic rivalry and competitive advantage are related. Nations with leading world positions often have a number of strong, local rivals. For example, in Switzerland, the pharmaceutical firms of Hoffman-LaRoche, Ciba-Geigy, and Sandoz help the country to maintain its internationally competitive edge. In Germany, BASF, Hoechst, and Bayer help the country to keep ahead in chemicals. In the United States, rivalry among IBM, Digital Equipment, Hewlett-Packard, and other computer makers help them to hold their own against foreign competitors.

Another important aspect of domestic rivalry is the location of the competitors.[22] Quite often successful firms are located near each other. For example, in Italy, successful jewelry firms are located near two towns: Arezzo and Valenza Po. In Switzerland, the major pharmaceutical firms are in Basel; in Japan, motorcycle and musical instrument companies are in Hamamatsu; in Germany, cutlery companies are in Solingen; in the United States, advertising agencies are clustered on Madison Avenue in Manhattan, New York City, and minicomputer firms are located off Route 128 in Boston.

When the importance of local rivalry is examined, it becomes clear that world leadership is not a result of one or two firms capturing the home market and then going international. Rather, competitive global success is a result of vigorous competition at home that pressures the companies into improving and innovating. This in turn builds up the companies' strengths and puts them in an excellent position to compete internationally.

ACTIVE LEARNING CHECK

Review your answer to Active Learning Case question 3 and make any changes you like. Then compare your answer to the one below.

3. How is local rivalry helping to improve Coke's competitive advantage?

Coke faces strong competition in Europe. Europeans do not drink as much Coke as do Americans; drinks like coffee and tea are more popular. Coke is using this situation to help formulate its strategy. This includes new bottling plants that are driving down costs and making Coke more price competitive, and marketing campaigns designed to draw customers away from competitive products. The firm is also entering into joint ventures with local partners, and these groups are helping the firm to understand national tastes and how to formulate local response strategies.

Porter's determinants as a system   As noted earlier, each of the determinants in Figure 1.1 often depends on the others. For example, even if a country has sophisticated buyers that can provide a company with feedback about how to modify or improve its product (demand conditions), this information will not be useful if the firm lacks personnel with the skills to carry out these functions (factor conditions). Similarly, if suppliers can provide the company with low-cost inputs and fresh ideas for innovation (related and supporting industries) but the firm clearly and easily dominates the industry (firm strategy, structure, and rivalry) and does not feel a need to upgrade the quality of its products and services, it will eventually lose this competitive advantage.

Research shows that of the four determinants in Figure 1.1, domestic rivalry and geographic clustering are particularly important. Domestic rivalry promotes improvements in the other three determinants and geographic concentration magnifies the interaction of the four separate influences.[23] The box "International Business Strategy in Action: The Italian Tile Industry" illustrates how these influences helped Italy develop a premier place in the ceramic tile industry. In the millennium these determinants served as the bedrock for formulating and implementing strategy. This activity begins at home, where the strategy is set, the core product and process technology are created, and the production facilities are established. Then, working off the interaction of the four determinants, the company will develop the necessary expertise to go international.

Government and trade regulations

Porter notes that government and chance influence the four determinants in Figure 1.1. These are examined in more detail in Chapter 14. Here we will take a first look at how government activity influences international business.

Government policies can have serious consequences for international trade. For example, government intervention for the purpose of protecting home industries usually results in less competitive national companies. But there is often strong domestic pressure to provide such protection.[24]

Congress and local government   Over 300 members of Congress were presented with three economic scenarios for the United States: (1) regulated free enterprise such as that which exists currently; (2) guided free enterprise such as that used by Japan and

INTERNATIONAL BUSINESS STRATEGY IN ACTION

The Italian tile industry

The Italian ceramic tile industry is an excellent example of how regional manufacturers gained national and then international prominence. The heart of the industry is in Sassuolo near Bologna in northern Italy. Tile has been produced here for over 700 years. So when Italy started rebuilding after World War II, the area began to flourish. Within 15 years the number of local tile companies had increased sevenfold and Sassuolo began to attract engineers and skilled workers.

At first the tile manufacturers had to import raw materials and machinery. There was no white clay in the region, so it was brought in from England. There were no tile equipment manufacturers, so kilns were purchased from Germany, the United States, and France and presses for both forming and glazing tiles were bought overseas. However, the Italian tile producers soon learned how to modify the equipment to better fit their needs, and technicians began leaving the tile companies to set up their own equipment firms. By 1970 companies in the region were exporting tile kilns and presses. At the same time, the local equipment producers were competing fiercely for the business of the tile companies, thus keeping down the cost of making tile; and supporting companies began to establish businesses in Sassuolo region to offer molds, packaging materials, glazes, and transportation services. Specialized consulting companies soon emerged to give advice to tile producers on plant design, logistics,

and commercial, advertising, and fiscal matters. The ceramic tile industry association, Assopiastrelle, started offering services of common interest to the firms: bulk purchasing, foreign market research, and consulting on fiscal and legal matters. A consortium consisting of the University of Bologna, regional agencies, and the ceramic industry association was founded to conduct process research and product analysis.

As these developments occurred, Italian customers continued to give the manufacturers feedback on product quality and ideas for innovative designs and features. This led to intense rivalry in the form of product offerings. The tile companies also began working to improve their equipment and to lower production costs. A rapid single-fire process for tile making was developed. The system reduced the number of workers by 60 per cent and the cycle time by 95 per cent, so more tiles could be made by fewer people. This new equipment was also smaller and lighter than its predecessor and found an eager international market. The manufacturers also developed a continuous, automated production system to replace the batch process and this, too, drove down costs and increased productivity.

Today the Italian ceramic tile industry is the world leader. In recent years Sassuolo has accounted for 30 per cent of world production and 60 per cent of world exports. As a result, the country's annual trade surplus from this industry alone is over $1 billion.

Sources: Adapted from Michael J. Enright and Paolo Tenti, "How the Diamond Works: The Italian Ceramic Tile Industry," *Harvard Business Review*, March–April 1990; *http://www.assopiastrelle.it/welcome.html; http://www.itse.com/exhibitor_pages/467.html.*

Germany; and (3) managed capitalism such as that employed by Sweden.[25] The politicians were asked which scenario they preferred and which they believed would be dominant in the United States during the next 10 years. Seventy-five per cent of the respondents said that the regulated free enterprise system was the best and slightly less than 75 per cent said that this system would dominate during the next decade. The results were consistent across the group and were not influenced by age, political affiliation, business experience, or geographic region. These findings suggest that Congress is not likely to try changing the US economic system.

However, there is support among the politicians for cooperative efforts among businesses, universities, and government research laboratories. At the state and local level there is growing interest in guided free enterprise similar to that in Japan and

Germany. For example, the Michigan Strategic Fund, a state agency guided by a private sector majority board, offers seed capital to fledgling entrepreneurs and startup businesses. The Small Business Enterprise Center in Ohio coordinates support for emerging businesses from local companies, chambers of commerce, universities, and vocational institutes. The businesses are offered managerial, legal, technical, and export-trade counseling assistance. The Corporation for Indiana's International Future consists of business, government, labor, and education officials. The corporation's job is to identify and promote local industries with export potential. It also works to improve relations with prospective foreign investors, to identify language training needs, and to strengthen ties with important educational and cultural groups. These efforts are designed to help small and local businesses develop competitive advantages and compete internationally.

World trade negotiations   A government's major role in international business may well be that of world trade negotiator. Many people believe that their government should limit competition from foreign goods because sales of foreign goods take jobs away from local businesses. In the United States, people question why the Japanese are allowed to set up auto plants there, while US farmers cannot sell rice in Japan even though imported rice would cost less than Japanese-produced rice.

Negotiations among countries to ease such restrictions and prevent unfair trade practices are ongoing. The **General Agreement on Tariffs and Trade (GATT)** is a major trade organization that was established to negotiate trade concessions among member countries.[26] The members met periodically and, from time to time, there had been very significant progress. For example, the Tokyo round in 1979 resulted in a 35 per cent reduction in tariffs between the United States and the EU and a 40 per cent reduction of tariffs on US imports into Japan. In 1986 member countries met in Uruguay for another major round of negotiations.[27] However, these were less successful.[28] Follow-up meetings in Montreal in 1988 and Brussels in 1990 were also unsuccessful.[29]

The **World Trade Organization** (WTO) was established on January 1, 1995. It is the umbrella organization governing the international trading system. The WTO oversees international trade arrangements and provides the secretariat for the GATT.

Contrary to popular belief, the WTO does not replace the GATT. An amended GATT remains as one of the legal pillars of the world's trade and, to a lesser extent, investment system. The other pillars were set up in the Uruguay Round's Marrakesh agreement of 1994 and include the General Agreement on Trade in Services (GATS) and the Agreement on Trade-Related Aspects of Intellectual Property Rights (TRIPS). The membership of the WTO has increased from the 76 founding members of 1995 up to 132 members by 1998. Members include virtually all the developed and most of the developing countries. A notable nonmember of the WTO is the People's Republic of China, whose entry has been blocked by the United States on the grounds that its economy is not open enough and that intellectual property rights are not sufficiently protected. The members of the WTO account for well over 90 per cent of the world's trade and virtually all of its investment.

The origins of the WTO can be traced back to the Atlantic Charter of 1941 developed by US President Franklin Roosevelt and British Prime Minister Winston Churchill. In order to counter US isolationism, the principle of the Atlantic Charter was for an international trading system with equal access to trade for all nations. This was seen as a complement to an effective world political forum, the United Nations, established in 1946, with its permanent headquarters in New York City. The United States organized an international conference on trade and employment which resulted in the Havana

Charter of 1948, in which it proposed to establish the International Trade Organization (ITO). Concurrently 23 countries agreed to a set of tariff cuts and these were ratified by the GATT, which was set up as a transition arrangement to be subsumed under the ITO. However, the ITO was never ratified and the GATT continued for 47 years until the WTO finally emerged in the last stages of the Uruguay Round to take on the powers originally designed for the ITO. The WTO now stands with the World Bank and the International Monetary Fund as the third leg of the global economic system.

The WTO carries on the key GATT principle of nondiscrimination, i.e., any barrier to trade should be applied equally to all member countries. If also keeps the most favored nation (MFN) principle, i.e., any liberalization measures, with some exceptions, should also be granted to all members. To understand what these principles mean it is fruitful to think of the WTO as a club whose membership rules require that all members receive the same treatment and if one member rescinds a trade concession then other affected members can withdraw their reciprocal concessions or receive compensation to equivalent commercial effect. If trade disputes arise, they can be settled by the unified dispute mechanism of the WTO, which can ensure timely compliance in contrast to the basically voluntary procedures of the GATT. Now decisions of a WTO dispute panel can no longer be blocked by the disputant party, as was possible under the GATT. Panel findings can be subject to review by an Appelate Body of the WTO. In addition, the publication of trade policy reviews and the activities of the Trade Policy Review Body (which regularly monitors the trade policies of member countries) complement the WTO dispute settlement activities by contributing significantly to enhanced transparency.

There are four important exceptions to the key GATT principle of nondiscrimination. First, developed countries can give tariff preference to developing countries. Second, countries entering into regional free trade agreements do not need to extend the preferences negotiated in this context on an MFN basis. Third, a country can invoke temporary "safeguard" protection to one of its industries suffering serious injury due to a surge of imports. Fourth, temporary quantitative restrictions can be invoked by a country with serious balance of payment problems. In the latter two cases, these measures are temporary exceptions to the member's commitment to the GATT and a public investigation has to be undertaken to allow for limited relief from GATT obligations.

Another important principle of the WTO, which is a significant improvement on the GATT, is the "single undertaking." WTO members must accept all the obligations of the GATT and any other corollary agreements. This ends the "free ride" of some developing countries under the old GATT, when they could receive the benefits of some trade concessions without having to join and undertake their full obligations. For most developed countries in North America and Western Europe the single undertaking was already being made and the meant few new obligations.

The major tensions in the WTO relate to the issues of agriculture, trade in services, and trade-related investment measures. None of these issues were included in the original mandate of the GATT, which dealt with trade in goods. Agriculture is a sector which most governments subsidize and it was left out of the original GATT. One technical advance which helps to increase the transparency of subsidies is the calculation of producers' subsidy equivalents. As a result, in the Uruguay Round some progress was made towards the future reduction of the most egregious agricultural subsidies through a process of "tarification," i.e., the translation of existing subsidies and other barriers to trade into tariff equivalents. Much work remains to be done in future rounds to liberalize agricultural trade.

Today, services account for 70 per cent of the employment and value added in advanced industrialized countries, and also for at least half the world's trade and investment. The Uruguay Round started to address issues of trade in services with the establishment of GATT. Trade-Related Investment Measures (TRIMS) were also considered and a substantive agreement that prohibits a number of investment requirements affecting cross-border trade in goods was reached, e.g., the TRIMS agreement restricted the imposition of export requirements on foreign investors. Future negotiations at the WTO (following upon the last Uruguay Round of the GATT) will need to develop a deeper and more comprehensive set of rules for multinational investment than in TRIMS. These may well be based upon the model of NAFTA, using the national treatment principle as the basic logic. National treatment states that foreign investors should not be discriminated against, but receive the same treatment as domestic firms in the application of domestic laws.

The WTO millennium round could build upon a multinational agreement on investment which was partially negotiated by the Paris-based Organization for Economic Cooperation and Development (OECD) over the 1995–98 period. Currently, investment issues are being discussed at the WTO in the context of the Working Group on the Relationship between Trade and Investment, established and given a two-year mandate at the 1996 Ministerial meeting in Singapore. Another important Working Group established during the WTO Singapore meeting is that which is examining the interaction between trade and competition policy.

Over a fifty-year period, the GATT has moved forward to the extent that today's new constitution for international trade, embodied in the WTO, includes an even fuller agenda of policy issues than envisaged by its pioneering founders. These issues include: further reduction of tariffs; a set of rules for multinational investment and competition policy; and the development of increased linkages between trade and issues of social policy, such as the environment and labour policy. The hurdles to achieving these three sets of objectives are lowest for tariff cuts, higher for investment, and highest of all for environmental and other social issues.

Developing an international perspective Many companies do business in other countries, but they have not developed the needed international perspective. This requires attention in three areas: experience, focus, and attitude.

Experience One way to create an international perspective is to hire individuals with international experience. A company cannot become a true MNE without sending its managers overseas, and research shows that many US chief executive officers (CEOs) lack this experience. As seen in Table 1.5, a classic study found that US CEOs had much less foreign experience than their European, Japanese, or Pacific Rim counterparts. One of the primary benefits of such experience is that it helps managers learn how to evaluate situations, and this process is often *different* from that used at home. For example, one of the most frequent criticisms of US managers is that they rely too heavily on scientific strategic planning; overemphasize quantitative models; and overlook the artistic, diplomatic, and humanistic aspects of international business.[30] Greater international experience would help managers avoid such tendencies.[31]

Focus A second way to develop an international focus is by emphasizing the importance of international activities. Unfortunately, these activities often rank quite low on a company's list of priorities and there are few rewards associated with them. Tung and Miller surveyed 123 US executives about selection criteria for senior management, programs for grooming senior executives, performance evaluation of senior

Table 1.5 International experience profile*

Experience profile	Chief executive officers from			
	United States (%)	Europe (%)	Japan (%)	Pacific Rim (%)
No foreign experience	14	3.10	1.10	2.60
Travel abroad only once or twice a year	23	1	15	18
Travel abroad more than twice a year	56	80	78	75
Studied abroad	16	28	13	54
Worked abroad	32	47	19	46
Managed a company abroad for current company	16	37	5.3	21
Firm has foreign directors	21	34	3.1	41

* Based on data from 433 chief executive officers from around the world.

Source: Adapted from George Anders, "Going Global: Vision vs. Reality," *Wall Street Journal*, September 22, 1989, p. R21.

management personnel, and incentive programs for senior management.[32] They found the following:

1. Over 93 per cent of the respondents did not consider "international experience or perspective" as a criterion for promotion/recruitment into the ranks of senior management. Over 80 per cent of the respondents indicated they had no intention of increasing the international focus in the future.

2. While most (56.1 per cent) of the companies provided training programs to groom candidates for top management positions, few of the firms gave any attention to international management training.

3. Respondents were asked to rank the importance of criteria that determined the size of the incentive package needed to retain people at the senior management level. Not one executive ranked increase in international market share as the most important criterion and 78.9 per cent of the respondents did not consider it at all in their determination of the size of the incentive package.

4. Respondents were asked to identify the functional area in which they held their first job, where they were currently employed, how fast their upward progress had been, and the functional area in which they would concentrate if they could start their career again. Less than 1 per cent had begun in the international area and only 5 per cent reported that they would concentrate here if they could start again. Only the computer/information and the research and development areas were less popular.

These findings illustrate that many US firms do not have an international orientation. The managers are focused on domestic operations, feeling little need to spend any time overseas because they believe that the best opportunities are available to those who stay at home. This serious problem is one of the reasons that more US managers need to study international business. In Chapters 9, 12, and 20 we discuss ways in which this inward-looking managerial mindset may be overcome.

Attitude   A third way to develop an international perspective is by changing the attitudes that many US managers have toward their work. In addition to the overemphasis on scientific/rational strategic planning noted above, they tend to have a short-term orientation, to be overly materialistic, to lack subtlety, to be informal and frank, and to be impatient. In comparison to European and Pacific Rim managers,

American managers working overseas have been found to be too focused on doing things the way they are done back in the States. In dealing with this problem, companies need to screen candidates carefully for international assignments and to provide more appropriate training. In later chapters of this book, we shall examine some of the steps that are being taken to address these managerial challenges.

ACTIVE LEARNING CHECK

Review your answer to Active Learning Case question 4 and make any changes you like. Then compare your answer to the one below.

4. Is Coca-Cola a multinational enterprise?

Coke is an MNE because it conducts production and distribution activities in nations other than its home country. In terms of strategy and management orientation, the firm does three things that further illustrate its multinational nature. First, Coca-Cola adjusts its operations to meet local needs. The firm markets on a country-by-country basis. Second, Coke has international partners who help to run the operation and do not report directly to the company on day-to-day matters. Third, the organization relies heavily on teamwork by all involved parties and serves more as a coordinator and cheerleader for the product than as an on-site manager.

THE STUDY OF INTERNATIONAL BUSINESS

In recent years the international trade environment has changed dramatically. In this section we examine some of the important changes that have taken place and then describe the model that we will use to present the material.

From general to strategic emphasis

The field of modern international business began to develop in the 1950s. At this time there was not a great number of MNEs, and most of them were American. World War II had ended less than a decade before and many nations, including Japan and the EC countries, were more concerned with rebuilding than with overseas investing. Early textbooks tended to be written by American professors and to offer a general, descriptive approach to the field. There were few international research studies to provide substantive information. International companies that served as teaching examples were often those with international divisions, rather than true MNEs. Professors teaching international business were frequently educated in areas such as economics or general business and relied on an interdisciplinary approach to address the varied needs of the course. (Table 1.6 provides additional comparisons.)

During the 1970s and 1980s the field of international business changed dramatically. The economic growth of EC countries and Japan, coupled with great strides by a number of newly industrialized countries (NICs), resulted in tremendous attention being focused on international business. Professors became much more research oriented and the number of PhD granting institutions offering at least a minor in international business increased. Articles and books by Canadian, European, and Asian professors began to appear and US research sophistication gained markedly. International economics and finance became primary areas of interest and the general

Table 1.6   Comparative differences in the study of international business, 1950–2010

Topic	1950–1969	1970–1989	1990–2010
Focus of interest	General information	Functional areas of development	Strategic emphasis
Approach to studying international business	Descriptive	Analytical	Integrative
Method of explanation	Heavily historical	Functional	Multidisciplinary
Research emphasis	Interdisciplinary	More quantitative research methods and overseas travel	Quantitative research methods, overseas travel, and international assignment
Enterprise viewpoint	US enterprises	Global enterprises	Multinational enterprises
Countries examined	Industrialized	Industrialized, NICs, and LDCs	Industrialized, NICs, and LDCs
Number of journals	Some	Many	Ever increasing
Journal emphasis	General international topics	Functional	Functional and strategic
Amount of joint research	Some	Much more	Ever increasing

research approach of the 1950s and 1960s was supplanted by more rigorous quantitative and methodological designs. More and more research studies were conducted and the number of journals in the field rose dramatically. In the latter part of the 1980s we also saw the beginning of efforts to bring together much of what was happening into a meaningful composite. How could we understand what was going on in the world of international business, when so much seemed to be occurring at the same time? The rise of *perestroika* and the decline of command economies in Eastern Europe and the Soviet Union only added to the problem. It was becoming evident that many of the developments of the 1970s and 1980s were being studied in too micro a fashion and a more macro approach to the field was in order.

Now we are seeing the emergence of a strategic management focus for drawing together the field of international business. The descriptive ideas of the 1950s and 1960s and the analytical ideas of the 1970s and 1980s are being combined into an integrative approach for the millennium and beyond. Historical and quantitative research is now being incorporated into models that describe, explain, and help predict what is happening in the international business arena. The earlier interdisciplinary and functional approaches are being supplemented by a multidisciplinary approach that draws on information from a wide variety of disciplines that affect international business. New journals in the field are also taking a more strategic management view of developments. This theme of strategic management, managerial actions that include strategy formulation, strategy implementation, evaluation, and control, encompasses a wide range of activities, including environmental analysis of external and internal conditions and evaluation of organizational strengths and weaknesses. This theme provides the basis for the framework that will be used in this text.

Framework for this book

This book employs a strategic management approach to the study of international business. There are five major parts in the text. Part One is an introduction and encompasses this chapter and Chapters 2 and 3, which address the nature and scope of MNEs

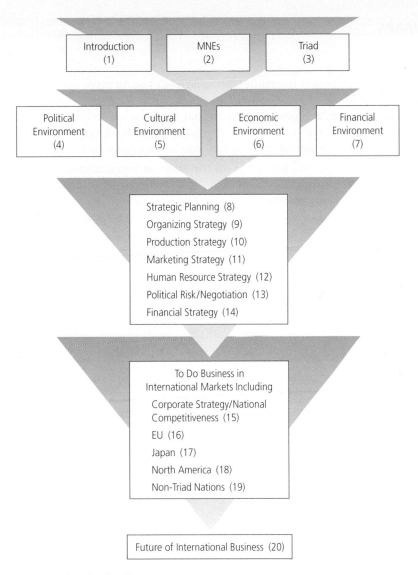

Figure 1.2 Model for this book

and the triad (United States, Japan, and the EU). Part Two examines the environments of international business: political, cultural, economic, and financial. Part Three focuses on the strategic planning of MNEs and the major components of their overall strategy: planning, organizing, production/sourcing, marketing, human resource development, political risk and negotiation, and the integration of firm strategy and international competitiveness. Part Four examines the ways in which the information presented thus far can be used in actually doing business throughout the world. In this part we look specifically at the EU countries, Japan, North America, and non-triad markets. Finally, Part Five examines the future of international business.

Figure 1.2 presents an illustration of the model that will be used throughout this book. The current chapter has set the stage for the study of international business. Now, in Chapter 2 we will examine the key actor on the stage: the MNE.

SUMMARY

Key points

1. International business is the study of transactions taking place across national borders for the purpose of satisfying the needs of individuals and organizations. Two of the most common types of international business are export/import activities and foreign direct investment (FDI). In recent years both have been on the rise. In particular, FDI is of interest as it is conducted by multinational enterprises (MNEs).

2. Although the MNE is the key actor on the stage of international business, small- and medium-sized firms and services are also involved in international business, but in a more indirect manner.

3. Countries and companies must take a host of steps to meet modern international business challenges. One is to maintain economic competitiveness. This is done by (a) creating the necessary factor conditions; (b) having strong local demand for the goods and services that are being produced; (c) having related and supporting industries that are internationally competitive; and (d) having a suitable strategy and structure and domestic rivalry that encourages continued innovation. A second important step is a knowledge of the government rules and regulations that affect international operations. A third is the development of an international perspective.

Key terms

- international business
- multinational enterprise (MNE)
- international joint venture
- exports
- imports
- foreign direct investment (FDI)
- factor conditions
- General Agreement on Tariffs and Trade (GATT)
- World Trade Organization (WTO)
- strategic management

Review and discussion questions

1. What is international business all about? In your answer be sure to include a definition of the term.
2. What are the two primary ways in which world trade can be described?
3. Will foreign direct investment increase or decrease in the future? Why?
4. How can a country or business make effective use of factor conditions to maintain economic competitiveness? Cite two examples.
5. Why are demand conditions and related and supporting industries important to the maintenance of economic effectiveness? In each case, cite an example.
6. In what way are firm strategy, structure, and rivalry important to the maintenance of economic effectiveness? In each case, cite an example.
7. Each of the four determinants of national competitive advantage depends on the others. What does this statement mean?
8. How can companies go about formulating a proper international perspective?

REAL CASES

THE UPJOHN COMPANY

Founded in 1886, Upjohn Company is a large pharmaceutical company based in the US. The company began operations abroad in the early 1900s when it received an order from Egypt to deliver "Quinine" and other pills. The company responded by delivering the order accompanied by a catalog written in Arabic. While this venture was not successful, it was the company's initiation into the international market, and was followed by thirty years of careful exporting. The company soon exported to South America its anti-malaria pill "Quinine." The pill filled the demand from travelers visiting this area. The 1930s saw company representatives establishing contacts all over South America and exports to Asia began. Meanwhile the first foreign branch was established in Canada in 1935. In 1957, an international division was created in Kalamazoo, Michigan; this strengthened the position of the pharmaceutical company in South America, where offices began to be built.

Perhaps the most interesting part of Upjohn's international strategy is its late entry into the European market. By the time the company considered entering Europe in the 1950s, its competitors had a strong hold on the market. The company's name was quite famous in the US market, but the European consumers were better acquainted with Merck, Pfizer, and Parke/Davis. A head-to-head battle in that market might have resulted in serious losses for Upjohn. Instead, the company decided to consider strategic alliances as a means to enter the European market. The position of Upjohn in the US market made it a good partner for any European company considering marketing its product in the US. Its first such alliance occurred in 1953 with Boots Drug Company in England. This partnership set the ground for what would become Upjohn's strategy for the rest of Europe.

The company's strategy was so successful that by the 1960s the company had manufacturing plants in Canada, the UK, Australia and Mexico. During the 1960s the company opened manufacturing plants in seven other European countries, and by the 1980s nine other countries had manufacturing plants. Belgium became the European headquarters, responsible for operations in Asia and Africa. Puerto Rico serves as South American headquarters. This new strategic structure permitted Kalamazoo to concentrate on the US domestic market.

Strategic alliances have helped Upjohn enter markets where competitors were already well established. Additionally, alliances with companies well acquainted with foreign markets helped Upjohn overcome cultural barriers that it might have had to face were it to enter these foreign markets itself. The company became global due to its efforts and those of its partners.

In August 1995 the Upjohn Co. and Pharmacia AB, a Swedish company, announced a merger that made the new company, Pharmacia & Upjohn, the ninth largest pharmaceutical company in the world. The new company employs over 30,000 people and in 1997, its revenues surpassed $7 billion. The merger was of benefit to Upjohn because of Pharmacia's new line of products. Meanwhile Pharmacia can tap into the marketing network Upjohn has developed.

1. What factors might have influenced Upjohn to choose alliances as a way to enter the European market? Why were these alliances less likely in non-European markets?

2. How does the merger with Pharmacia fit in Upjohn's global strategy?

3. Is Pharmacia & Upjohn a true MNE?

Source: Adapted from Erminio Fina and Alan Rugman, "A Test of Internalization Theory and Internationalization Theory: The Upjohn Company," *Management International Review*, vol. 36, 1993, pp. 199–213; *http://sddt.com/files/librarywire/DN95_08_21_07.html; http://www.pnu.com/business/textcorpinfo.asp.*

PIZZA HUT IN RUSSIA

As Eastern Europe and Russia have started opening their doors to capitalistic ventures, a host of firms have begun investing in these countries. One is Pizza Hut, which is a major US force that started operations in Russia by opening two outlets in Moscow and which hopes to capture the Russian market in the long run. However, the firm is learning that good intentions are not always enough to guarantee success. The Russians are used to doing business in a different way and between rules, negotiations, and threats from local officials, a store manager can find him or herself developing a negative attitude toward the business climate.

The two first Moscow units began as joint ventures between PepsiCo, the previous owner of Pizza Hut (in 1997 Pizza Hut became a member of Tricon Global Restaurants), and the city of Moscow. However, this arrangement did not guarantee smooth sailing. One Friday afternoon, soon after the units opened, a local sanitary inspector showed up, announced that the unit had failed to file all the necessary papers, including venereal disease tests for every employee, and wired the doors shut. The manager made a frantic call to local health authorities and was told to see them at 4 p.m. that day. When he arrived, they had left for the weekend. He then made an urgent call to the president of PepsiCo who was bicycling in France. The president called the Russian ambassador to the United States and by the next afternoon Pizza Hut in Moscow was back in business.

On the positive side, the restaurant is very popular with the customers and the company is managing to keep prices under control by negotiating carefully with local suppliers. The manager of the overall operation has found that by traveling south of Moscow to small farms he has been able to purchase food of better quality. The farmers were initially unaccustomed to cleaning and boxing their produce carefully before shipping it, but because Pizza Hut pays more for food that is cleaned and prepared, the farmers are now providing higher quality than ever.

The company is also learning from experience how to increase operating efficiency. Pizza Hut has also learned that Russian customers prefer US food over their own, so initial attempts to create cuisine with a "Moscow taste" have been abandoned. The unit manager is also learning that the fastest way to get things done in Russia is often to bypass the system and take matters into one's own hands. For example, when truck drivers are late in coming to pick up supplies, the manager goes out in the street and hires trucks. And there are a few things that the Russians are learning about the way Pizza Hut does business. For example, despite Russian arguments that trained cooks make the best pizzas, the truth is that eager, inexperienced youngsters are usually superior and within a few weeks they are turning out pizzas that trained cooks cannot match. As time goes by it is likely that both sides will continue to learn from each other.

1. Why is Pizza Hut making a direct investment in Russia? Would they not make more profit by putting these funds into a new, US-based unit?

2. How does Pizza Hut use demand conditions to help revise operating strategy?

3. How important is an understanding of government regulations to the success of the Moscow operation? Why?

Sources: Adapted from Allen R. Myerson, "Setting Up an Island in the Soviet Union," *New York Times*, December 30, 1990, Section 3, pp. 1, 6; Lois Therrien, "The Hunger Pangs Let Up a Little," *Business Week*, January 11, 1993, p. 97; and Sunita Wadekar Bhargava, "Gimme a Double Shake and a Lard on White," *Business Week*, March 1, 1993, p. 59; *http://www.triconglobal.com.*

ENDNOTES

1. James B. Treece et al., "New Worlds to Conquer," *Business Week*, February 28, 1994, pp. 50–52.
2. Shawn Tully, "GE in Hungary: Let There Be Light," *Fortune*, October 22, 1990, pp. 137–142.
3. Cacilie Rohwedder, "Bertelsmann, Divinely Guided, Enters Russian Market," *Wall Street Journal*, March 30, 1998, Section B, pp. 1, 11.
4. Carol Matlack, Keith Naughton, and David Woodruff, "Ready to Burn Rubber in Russia," *Business Week*, March 31, 1997, pp. 52–53.
5. Richard Molz, "Privatization in Developing Countries," *Columbia Journal of World Business*, Spring/Summer 1990, pp. 17–24; R. Molz, "Privatization of Government Enterprise: The Challenge to Management," *Management International Review*, vol. 29, no. 4, 1989, pp. 29–44; Richard W. Peterson, "The Pain of British Privatization Has Yielded a String of Successes," *New York Times*, February 22, 1994, pp. A1, C5; and Mary Speck, "Private Group to Run Peru Phone," *Miami Herald*, March 1, 1994, p. 7A.
6. Wendy Zeller and Andrea Mandel-Campbell, "The Battle of Argentina, Brazil, Chile, Venezuela . . . ," *Business Week*, May 19, 1997, p. 56.
7. Keith Bradsher, "In South America, Auto Makers See One Big Showroom," *New York Times*, April 25, 1997, Section C, pp. 1, 4.
8. Peter Lorange, Johan Roos, and Peggy Simcic Bronn, "Building Successful Strategic Alliances," *Long Range Planning*, December 1992, pp. 10–17.
9. Christopher J. Chipello, "Motorola, Toshiba Near Pact to Develop Chip for High-Definition Television Sets," *Wall Street Journal*, December 11, 1990, p. B5.
10. Jacob M. Schlesinger, "Nissan and Hitachi Team Up to Create a 'Mobile Office,'" *Wall Street Journal*, December 13, 1990, p. A11.
11. See, for example, Robert L. Rose and Carl Quintanilla, "More Small US Firms Take Up Exporting, With Much Success," *Wall Street Journal*, December 20, 1996, Section A, pp. 1, 8.
12. The European Community (EC), or Common Market as it is sometimes called, was founded in 1957. The six initial members were Belgium, Germany, Italy, France, Luxembourg, and the Netherlands. Since then Denmark, Ireland, the United Kingdom, Greece, Portugal, and Spain have joined. In 1995, Austria, Finland and Sweden joined and the European Union (EU) replaced the EC.
13. Richard M. Hodgetts and Fred Luthans, *International Management*, 3rd ed. (New York: McGraw-Hill, 1997), Chapter 1.
14. Also see Mark Mason, "United States Direct Investment in Japan: Trade and Prospects," *California Management Review*, Fall 1992, pp. 98–115.
15. Bernhard Heitger and Jurgen Stehn, "Japanese Direct Investments in the EC – Response to the Internal Market 1993?" *Journal of Common Market Studies*, September 1990, p. 3.
16. Michael E. Porter, *The Competitive Advantage of Nations* (New York: Free Press, 1990), p. 255.
17. See, for example, George Lodge and Richard Walton, "The American Corporation and Its New Relationships," *California Management Review*, Spring 1989, pp. 9–24.
18. Michael E. Porter, "The Competitive Advantage of Nations," *Harvard Business Review*, March–April 1990, p. 74.
19. The following section is an abbreviated version of the model and the ten-country empirical analysis of Michael Porter, *The Competitive Advantage of Nations* (New York: Free Press, Macmillan, 1990), especially Chapters 3 and 4.
20. Porter, *The Competitive Advantage of Nations*, ibid., p. 85.
21. Porter, *Harvard Business Review*, op. cit., pp. 80–81.
22. Porter, ibid., p. 82.
23. Porter, ibid., p. 83.
24. See, for example, Jennifer Lin, "Dusting Off a Weapon," *Miami Herald*, March 4, 1994, Section C, pp. 1, 3.
25. David A. Heenan, "Congress Rethinks America's Competitiveness," *Business Horizons*, May–June 1989, pp. 11–16.
26. Sylvia Ostry, "Governments & Corporations in a Shrinking World: Trade & Innovation Policies in the United States, Europe & Japan," *Columbia Journal of World Business*, Spring/Summer 1990, pp. 10–16.
27. Lee Smith, "What's at Stake in the Trade Talks?", *Fortune*, August 27, 1990, pp. 76–77.
28. Robert J. Samuelson, "World Trade on the Brink," *Newsweek*, December 10, 1990, p. 59; Marc Levinson, Scott Sullivan, and Ann McDaniel, "Free Trade Loses a Round," *Newsweek*, December 17, 1990, p. 44; and Christopher J. Chipello, "Japanese Trade Official Blames U.S., Exporting Nations for GATT Impasse," *Wall Street Journal*, December 14, 1990, p. A15.
29. "No Gains on GATT," *New York Times*, January 4, 1993, p. C3.
30. Ashok Nimgade, "American Management as Viewed by International Professionals," *Business Horizons*, November–December 1989, p. 100.
31. Also see Christopher A. Bartlett and Sumantra Ghoshal, "What Is a Global Manager?" *Harvard Business Review*, September–October 1992, pp. 124–132.
32. Rosalie L. Tung and Edwin L. Miller, "Managing in the Twenty-first Century: The Need for Global Orientation," *Management International Review*, vol. 30, no. 1, 1990, pp. 5–18.

ADDITIONAL BIBLIOGRAPHY

Beamish, Paul W. and Calof, Jonathan L. "International Business Education: A Corporate View," *Journal of International Business Studies*, vol. 20, no. 3 (Fall 1989).

Becker, Fred G. "International Business and Governments: Issues and Institutions," *Management International Review*, vol. 32, no. 4 (Fourth Quarter 1992).

Caves, Richard E. "Research on International Business: Problems and Prospects," *Journal of International Business Studies*, vol. 29, no. 1 (First Quarter 1998).

Daniels, John D. "Relevance in International Business Research: A Need for More Linkages," *Journal of International Business Studies*, vol. 22, no. 2 (Second Quarter 1991).

Dunning, John H. "The Study of International Business: A Plea for a More Interdisciplinary Approach," *Journal of International Business Studies*, vol. 20, no. 3 (Fall 1989).

Hax, Arnoldo C. "Building the Firm of the Future," *Sloan Management Review*, vol. 30, no. 3 (Spring 1989).

Kline, John M. "Trade Competitiveness and Corporate Nationality," *Columbia Journal of World Business*, vol. 24, no. 3 (Fall 1989).

Lecraw, Donald J. "Review of World Investment Report 1992: Transnational Corporations as Engines of Growth," *Journal of International Business Studies*, vol. 24, no. 3 (Third Quarter 1993).

Mulligan, Thomas M. "The Two Cultures in Business Education," *Academy of Management Review*, vol. 12, no. 4 (October 1987).

Nehrt, Lee C. "The Internationalization of the Curriculum," *Journal of International Business Studies*, vol. 18, no. 1 (Spring 1987).

Rugman, Alan M. and Stanbury, William. *Global Perspective: Internationalizing Management Education* (Vancouver BC: Centre for International Business Studies, UBC, 1992).

Rugman, Alan M. and Verbeke, Alain "Multinational Enterprises and Public Policy," *Journal of International Business Studies*, vol. 29, no. 1 (First Quarter 1998).

Yip, George S., Loewe, Pierre M., and Yoshino, Michael Y. "How to Take Your Company to the Global Market," *Columbia Journal of World Business*, vol. 23, no. 4 (Winter 1988).

APPENDIX TO CHAPTER ONE

Appendix 1A   The top 25 importers in the world, 1996

Rank	Country	Value of world imports (in millions of US $)
1	United States	817,785
2	Germany	445,015
3	Japan	349,508
4	United Kingdom	283,590
5	France	275,973
6	Italy	207,002
7	Hong Kong	198,551
8	Canada	187,042
9	Netherlands	160,990
10	Belgium-Luxembourg	154,940
11	Korea	150,370
12	China	138,822
13	Singapore	131,506
14	Spain	121,865
15	Taiwan	101,276
16	Mexico	98,411
17	Switzerland	78,176
18	Malaysia	77,797
19	Thailand	73,484
20	Austria	68,674
21	Australia	67,666
22	Sweden	66,584
23	Brazil	58,907
24	Russia	43,318
25	Indonesia	42,945

Source: Adapted from International Monetary Fund, *Direction of Trade Statistics Yearbook 1997* (Washington DC: IMF, 1997).

Appendix 1B   The top 25 exporters in the world, 1996

Rank	Country	Value of world exports (in millions of US $)
1	United States	622,945
2	Germany	513,472
3	Japan	411,242
4	France	289,555
5	United Kingdom	258,291
6	Italy	250,732
7	Canada	200,146
8	Hong Kong	180,526
9	Netherlands	177,444
10	Belgium-Luxembourg	157,251
11	China	151,093
12	Korea	130,526
13	Singapore	125,118
14	Spain	102,090
15	Mexico	95,991
16	Sweden	84,472
17	Russia	81,438
18	Switzerland	79,503
19	Malaysia	78,246
20	Australia	60,967
21	Saudi Arabia	57,300
22	Thailand	55,789
23	Norway	48,660
24	Ireland	48,076
25	Indonesia	48,059

Source: Adapted from International Monetary Fund, *Direction of Trade Statistics Yearbook 1997* (Washington DC: IMF, 1997).

Appendix 1C Direction of world trade flows, 1990–96

	With industrial countries		With developing countries		With other countries n.i.e.*		Total	
	Exports	Imports	Exports	Imports	Exports	Imports	Exports	Imports
			Billions of US dollars					
Industrial countries								
1990	1,868.0	1,913.5	561.9	649.4	1.8	0.9	2,431.7	4,994.6
1991	1,872.3	1,922.6	614.4	667.2	1.6	1.0	2,488.3	5,078.1
1992	1,963.2	2,009.7	676.0	691.2	1.2	1.1	2,640.4	5,341.3
1993	1,801.8	1,797.4	725.9	702.4	1.2	0.8	2,528.9	5,028.7
1994	2,041.3	2,036.1	809.0	812.4	1.4	1.1	2,851.7	5,700.2
1995	2,407.9	2,393.2	975.7	966.2	1.8	1.1	3,385.4	6,744.8
1996	2,434.6	2,445.6	1,011.3	1,035.0	1.8	1.2	3,447.7	6,928.3
Developing countries								
1990	571.0	573.8	335.4	335.3	2.4	1.3	907.7	1,816.8
1991	598.9	636.8	370.9	367.1	2.2	0.8	970.6	1,974.5
1992	639.5	720.6	429.0	426.2	1.6	0.9	1,069.4	2,216.2
1993	663.5	761.0	464.0	465.1	1.9	1.2	1,128.7	2,354.8
1994	753.7	854.2	563.2	546.0	1.9	1.2	1,318.1	2,718.3
1995	892.3	1,027.4	713.8	695.6	2.5	1.1	1,607.2	3,330.2
1996	961.5	1,084.2	769.7	775.4	3.4	1.7	1,732.9	3,592.5

* n.i.e. (not included elsewhere) refers to Cuba and North Korea.

Source: Adapted from International Monetary Fund, *Direction of Trade Statistics Yearbook 1996* (Washington DC: IMF, 1997).

Appendix 1D World trade flows by major countries and regions

Countries/regions	1996 (in billions of US $)	% of world	Countries/regions	1996 (in billions of US $)	% of world
Exports to			Imports from		
World	5,401.0	100.0	World	5,265.8	100.0
Industrial countries	3,503.9	64.9	Industrial countries	3,481.3	66.1
Developing countries	1,891.8	35.0	Developing countries	1,781.5	33.8
Africa	112.0	2.1	Africa	110.8	2.1
Asia	1,044.0	19.3	Asia	975.5	18.5
Europe	254.6	4.7	Europe	245.0	4.7
Middle East	175.3	3.2	Middle East	190.1	3.6
Western hemisphere	305.4	5.7	Western hemisphere	260.0	4.9

Note: numbers might not add up due to rounding.

Source: Adapted from International Monetary Fund, *Direction of Trade Statistics Yearbook 1997* (Washington DC: IMF, 1997).

Appendix 1E   Inward stocks of world foreign direct investment, 1985–96

Countries/regions	1985 (in billions of US $)	% of total	1996* (in billions of US $)	% of total
Developed countries	537.70	72.2	2,269.3	70.3
United States	184.60	24.8	644.7	20.0
Western Europe	245.00	32.9	1,302.5	40.3
EU	226.60	30.4	1,219.2	37.8
Austria	6.10	0.8	19.9	0.6
Belgium/Luxemburg	8.80	1.2	100.8	3.1
Denmark	3.60	0.5	23.4	0.7
Finland	1.30	0.2	9.4	0.3
France	33.40	4.5	168.4	5.2
Germany	36.90	5.0	171.0	5.3
Greece	8.30	1.1	20.3	0.6
Ireland	4.60	0.6	14.0	0.4
Italy	19.00	2.5	75.0	2.3
Netherlands	25.10	3.4	118.6	3.7
Portugal	1.30	0.2	6.7	0.2
Spain	8.90	1.2	105.0	3.3
Sweden	5.10	0.7	42.0	1.3
United Kingdom	64.00	8.6	344.7	10.7
Other Western Europe	18.30	2.5	83.3	2.6
Switzerland	10.10	1.4	59.6	1.8
Norway	8.00	1.1	23.1	0.7
Others	0.20	0.0	0.6	0.0
Canada	64.60	8.7	129.2	4.0
Australia and New Zealand	27.10	3.6	156.8	4.9
Japan	4.70	0.6	18.0	0.6
Other developed countries	11.70	1.6	18.1	0.6
Developing countries	207.30	27.8	960.0	29.7
Africa	21.30	2.9	59.5	1.8
Asia	107.50	14.4	535.7	16.6
Latin America and the Caribbean	76.80	10.3	316.1	9.8
Developing Europe	0.50	0.1	2.3	0.1
Central and Eastern Europe	0.20	0.0	46.4	1.4
Total	745.20	100.0	3,229.3	100.0
Addenda:				
Outward stock	690.40		3,178.2	
Inward stock	745.20		3,229.3	
Difference	−54.80		−51.1	

* 1996 numbers are estimates.
Numbers might not add up due to rounding.
Source: Adapted from UN, World Investment Report, 1997.

Appendix 1F   Outward stocks of foreign direct investment, 1985–96

Countries/regions	1985 (in billions of US $)	% of total	1996* (in billions of US $)	% of total
Developed countries	664.2	96.2	2,893.4	91.0
United States	251.0	36.4	794.1	25.0
Western Europe	312.4	45.2	1,585.8	49.9
EU	286.5	41.5	1,404.6	44.2
Austria	1.9	0.3	13.5	0.4
Belgium/Luxemburg	4.7	0.7	73.3	2.3
Denmark	1.8	0.3	22.4	0.7
Finland	1.8	0.3	18.3	0.6
France	37.1	5.4	206.4	6.5
Germany	59.9	8.7	288.4	9.1
Greece	—	—	—	—
Ireland	0.2	0.0	4.5	0.1
Italy	16.3	2.4	118.5	3.7
Netherlands	47.8	6.9	184.7	5.8
Portugal	0.2	0.0	3.5	0.1
Spain	2.1	0.3	38.2	1.2
Sweden	12.4	1.8	76.3	2.4
United Kingdom	100.3	14.5	356.3	11.2
Other Western Europe	26	3.8	181.2	5.7
Switzerland	21.4	3.1	153.3	4.8
Norway	4.6	0.7	27.8	0.9
Canada	40.9	5.9	111.3	3.5
Australia and New Zealand	8.5	1.2	56.5	1.8
Japan	44.3	6.4	330.2	10.4
Other developed countries	7.0	1.0	15.6	0.5
Developing countries	26.1	3.8	282.2	8.9
Total	690.4	100.0	3,178.1	100.0

*1996 numbers are estimates.
Numbers might not add up due to rounding.
Source: Adapted from UN, *World Investment Report*, 1997.

CHAPTER 2

The Multinational Enterprise

Most of the best-known companies in the world are multinational enterprises, and many of their names are easily recognized because their products and services are so popular. This is true not only for US multinationals, such as General Motors, Exxon, and IBM, but for others as well. Consider, for example, some of the largest overseas industrial multinationals headquartered in European and Pacific Rim countries: Unilever (Britain/Netherlands), Fiat (Italy), Volkswagen (Germany), Philips (Netherlands), Peugeot (France), Nestlé (Switzerland), Toyota Motor (Japan), and Samsung (South Korea). The primary objective of this chapter is to examine the nature and operations of these enterprises. In doing so, we will devote particular attention to the characteristics of multinationals and to studying how they manage their operations. The specific objectives of this chapter are to:

1. **Describe** the characteristics of multinational enterprises.

2. **Explain** why firms become multinational enterprises.

3. **Discuss** the strategic philosophy of these firms.

4. **Examine** select multinational enterprises in action.

5. **Study** some of the ways in which these firms use strategic management.

Euro Disney or Disneyland Paris

Between 1988 to 1990 three $150 million amusement parks opened in France. By 1991 two of them were bankrupt and the third was doing poorly. However, this track record did not scare off the Walt Disney Company's plan to open Europe's first Disneyland in 1992. Far from being concerned about the theme park doing well, Disney executives were worried that Euro Disneyland would be too small to handle the giant crowds. The $4.4 billion project is located on 5,000 acres in Seine-et-Marne 20 miles east of Paris. And the city seemed to be an excellent location; there are 17 million people within a two-hour drive of Euro Disneyland, 41 million within a four-hour drive, and 109 million within six hours of the park. This includes people from seven countries: France, Switzerland, Germany, Luxembourg, the Netherlands, Belgium, and Britain.

Disney officials were optimistic about the project, especially after the success of Tokyo Disneyland, where the amusement park could not accommodate the large number of visitors. The company's initial share of the European venture was 49 per cent, at a cost of $160 million. Other investors put in $1.2 billion, while the French government provided a low interest $900 million loan, banks loaned $1.6 billion, and the remaining $400 million came from special partnerships formed to buy properties and to lease them back. The Walt Disney Company was to receive 10 per cent of Euro Disney's admission fees, and 5 per cent of food and merchandise revenues in addition to management fees, and 49% of all profits.

The location of the amusement park was thoroughly considered. France and Spain, the two principal locations being considered, conscious of the park's capacity to create jobs and stimulate the economy, wooed the company. France offered both a central location in the heart of Europe and considerable financial incentives. Additionally, the French government promised to build a train line to connect the amusement park to the European train system. Thus, France was chosen as the site.

Unfortunately, things started to look gloomy from the first day. The inauguration was expected to attract 500,000 visitors but a mere 50,000 showed up. This was partly a result of French sentiments against the park. Vandalism during the first days of the operation and media criticism against the American operation began to upset investors. Furthermore, the company received complaints about high prices, labor policies, and operating policies that conflicted with European practices. Prices were so high due to the Franc exchange rate that it was cheaper for the English to go to Florida than to Euro Disney. Labor policy was in contradiction with French law, which led to a high turnover of staff. By May 1992, only a month after the amusement park opened, 3,000 employees had quit over pay and working conditions. Worker complaints ranged from managers having to speak English in meetings, even if most people at the meeting were French, to policies on personal grooming. Other conflicting policies were a result of Disney's previous experiences. In the United States, liquor was not sold outside of the hotels or specific areas. The general park was kept alcohol free, including the restaurants. This was to maintain a family atmosphere. In Japan, the policy was accepted and worked out very well. However, Europeans were used to having outings with alcoholic beverages. In particular, the French were accustomed to wine while the Germans wanted beer.

In 1994, after three years of heavy losses, the company was in such bad shape that it was expected it would have to be shut down. A variety of measures were taken to save the company. Prince Walid Talal purchased 24.6 per cent (reducing Disney's share to 39 per cent) of the company, injecting $500 million of much needed cash. Furthermore, Disney waived its royalty fees and worked out a new loan repayment plan with the banks; additionally, new shares were issued. These measures allowed Euro Disney to buy time while it restructured its marketing and general policies to fit the European market.

In October 1994, Euro Disney officially changed its name to "Disneyland Paris." This made the park more French, while it capitalized on the romanticism that the word Paris conveys. Most importantly, the new name allowed for a new beginning, disassociating the park from the failure of Euro Disney. This was accompanied with measures to remedy past failures. The park changed its most offensive labor rules, reduced prices, and began being more culturally conscious. Now, alcohol beverages are served in most areas of the park.

The company began operations by stressing the European origins of its founder, Walt Disney, and of many of the firm's fairy-tale characters. It also produced European-specific attractions (such as European history movie shows, and a science fiction tour inspired by Jules Verne's stories). Now the company is increasing its efforts even further in this area. The reason is very simple: the firm does not want to be seen as an American company, but one that can appeal to Europeans, especially the French.

It seems that things might have begun to turn around for the ailing park. In 1995, for the first time, the company reported a slight profit. The trend continued for 1996 with profits doubling and no further losses have been reported. However, critics say that the signs are misleading and that these profits are not so much a result of an improvement in the general profitability of the company, but a result of Disney's waiving of royalty fees and the favorable payment plan from the banks. Nonetheless, prices have started to rise in the amusement park, and anti-Disney hostility has cooled off. Investors are hoping that the future will be much brighter than the past.

Sources: Adapted from Steven Greenhouse, "Playing Disney in the Parisian Fields," *New York Times*, February 17, 1991, Section 3, pp. 1, 6; "Euro Disney Resignation," *New York Times*, January 16, 1993, p. 19; William Heuslein, "Travel," *Forbes*, January 4, 1993, p. 178; Stewart Toy and Paula Dwyer, "Is Disney Headed for the Euro-Trash Heap?," *Business Week*, January 4, 1994, p. 52; Theodore Stanger et al., "Mickey's Trip to Trouble," *Newsweek*, February 4, 1994, pp. 34–39; "International Briefs: Revenue for Euro Disney Up by 17% in Quarter," *New York Times*, January 22, 1998; "Euro Disney Theme Park Cuts Loss, Shares Fall," *Yahoo News: Reuters*, April 22, 1998; Charles Fleming, "Euro Disney to Build Movie Theme Park Outside Paris," *Wall Street Journal*, September 30, 1999, pp. 18, 21.
(*http://www.clubblue.com/text/headlines/9 . . . nment/stories/industry_eurodisney_1.html*); *http://www.informatik. tu-muenchen.de/~schaffnr/etc/disney/his8891.htm*; *http://www.informatik.tu-muenchen.de/~schaffnr/etc/disney/finhist.htm*.

1. **What are some of the characteristics of multinational enterprises that are displayed by the Walt Disney Company?**

2. **Why did Disney take an ownership position in the firm rather than simply licensing some other firm to build and operate the park and settling for a royalty on all sales?**

3. **In what way does Euro Disney reflect the strategic philosophy of Walt Disney as a multinational enterprise?**

4. **Did Disney management conduct an external environmental analysis before going forward with Euro Disney? Explain.**

INTRODUCTION

A **multinational enterprise** (MNE) is a company that is headquartered in one country but has operations in other countries. Sometimes it is difficult to know if a firm is an MNE because multinationals often downplay the fact that firms are foreign held. For example, many people are unaware that Bayer, the drug company, is German-owned; Nestlé, the chocolate manufacturer, is a Swiss company; Northern Telecom is Canadian; and Jaguar, the British-based automaker, is now owned by Ford Motor.

Similarly, approximately 25 per cent of banks in California are Japanese-owned, but that is not often evident from their names. Simply put, many large MNEs have world holdings far beyond that which is known to the casual observer. Yet these companies have a dramatic impact on the quality of goods and services that are being produced around the world. A closer look at the nature of MNEs will make this clear.

THE NATURE OF MULTINATIONAL ENTERPRISES

The United Nations has identified over 45,000 MNEs, but the largest 500 account for 80 per cent of all the world's foreign direct investment.[1] Of these, 443 are from the "triad" blocs of the United States, European Union (EU), and Japan. Table 2.1 shows the world's largest 500 MNEs by country/bloc. There are 176 from the United States, 112 from Japan, and 155 from the 15 member countries of the EU. Total annual sales of these 500 firms are in excess of $11 trillion and they collectively employ over 35 million people. These firms are engaged in operations such as autos, chemicals, computers, consumer goods, financial goods, industrial equipment, and oil and steel production. Clearly, the large industrial MNEs have a significant impact on international business and the world economy. The names of the largest triad-based MNEs, as well as those from Canada and the third-world countries, are listed in Appendixes 2A through 2E.

Table 2.1 The World's largest 500 multinational enterprises

Country	Number of MNEs
United States	176
European Union	155
Japan	112
South Korea	12
Switzerland	12
Canada	8
Australia	7
Brazil	5
China	4
Norway	2
Hong Kong	1
Taiwan	1
Malaysia	1
Mexico	1
Venezuela	1
Russia	1
India	1
Total	500

Source: Adapted from *Fortune*, "The Fortune Global 500," August 3, 1998

Home Country	Stakeholders	Host Countries
Competitors		Competitors
Customers		Customers
Domestic Affiliates	Multinational Enterprise	Foreign Affiliates
Suppliers		Suppliers
Government		Government
	Banks	

Figure 2.1   The multinational enterprise and its environment

Characteristics of multinational enterprises

One way of identifying the characteristics of MNEs is by looking at the environment in which they operate. Figure 2.1 shows some of the major forces in this environment. Notice that an MNE has two major areas of concern: the home country of its headquarters and the host countries in which it does business. Stakeholders are not included within these two areas of Figure 2.1 because they can come from anywhere in the world. For example, an investor in Switzerland can purchase stock in Sears Roebuck even though the company does not do business in Switzerland.

One characteristic of MNEs is that their affiliates must be responsive to a number of important environmental forces, including competitors, customers, suppliers, financial institutions, and government (see Figure 2.1). In some cases the same forces are at work in both the home and host country environments. For example, many of General Motors' competitors in the US market are the same as those in Europe: Ford, Chrysler, Honda, Volkswagen, and Volvo, among others. Similarly, the company often uses the same suppliers overseas that it employs domestically.

A second characteristic of the MNE is that it draws on a common pool of resources, including assets, patents, trademarks, information, and human resources. Since the affiliates are all part of the same company, they have access to assets that are often not available to outsiders. For example, both Ford and General Motors compete vigorously in Europe and many of the design and styling changes developed for their European cars have now been introduced in US models. The flow of information and technology between European and US affiliates has led to successes in the worldwide market. Similarly, if an affiliate in Japan needs expansion funds, an MNE can see if the money can be obtained in the local market at a lower cost. If not, the MNE will work with the affiliate to raise the money. Since the company will back the loan, the affiliate is likely to find many financial institutions that are willing to provide the funds.

A third characteristic of an MNE is that its affiliates are linked by a common strategic vision. Each MNE will formulate its strategic plan so as to bring the affiliates together in a harmonious way. Such plans will, of course, vary by MNE. Sometimes a very centralized plan is drawn up; other times a decentralized plan is employed. General Electric uses a combination of both types of plans to set major sales and profit goals for all operations worldwide.[2] The strategic plan will also address the financial and human resource needs of the affiliates, transferring funds and assigning people as needed.

ACTIVE LEARNING CHECK

Review your answer to Active Learning Case question 1 and make any changes you like. Then compare your answer to the one below.

1. What are some of the characteristics of multinational enterprises that are displayed by the Walt Disney Company?

One of the characteristics of a multinational enterprise is that affiliated firms are linked by ties of common ownership. In this case the Walt Disney Company holds a substantial interest in Euro Disney, in addition to its ownership of Disneyland and Disneyworld in the United States. A second characteristic is that the MNE draws on a common pool of resources. One way Euro Disney does this is through the use of Disney trademarks and characters (Mickey Mouse, Goofy, Donald Duck) and the experience of the Disney team in setting up and running similar theme parks in the United States. A third characteristic is that MNEs have a common strategy for linking together the affiliates. The Walt Disney Company does this through its overall plan such as the one it used for deciding where to set up Euro Disney and how to manage the park.

Why firms become multinational enterprises

Companies become MNEs for a number of reasons. One is to protect themselves from the risks and uncertainties of the domestic business cycle. By setting up operations in another country, they can often diminish the negative effects of economic swings in the home country. This is a form of international diversification.

A second reason is to tap the growing world market for goods and services.[3] This is part of the process of globalization, the rapid growth of similar goods and services produced and distributed by MNEs on a world scale. For example, many foreign MNEs have targeted the United States because of its large population and high per capita income. It is the world's single largest market in terms of gross national product. Americans have both a desire for new goods and services and the money to buy them. For the same reason, US MNEs have been targeting Europe and Asia as primary areas for the twenty-first century.

Firms also become MNEs in response to increased foreign competition and to protect world market shares. Using a "follow the competitor" strategy, an MNE will set up operations in the home countries of competitors. This approach serves a dual purpose: (1) it takes away business from competitors, and (2) it lets others know that if they attack the MNE's home market, they will face a similar response. This strategy of staking out global market shares is particularly important when MNEs want to communicate the conditions under which they will retaliate.

A fourth reason to become an MNE is the desire to reduce costs. By setting up operations close to the foreign customer, MNEs can eliminate transportation costs, avoid the expenses associated with having middlemen handle the product, respond more accurately and rapidly to customer needs, and take advantage of local resources. This process, known as "internalization" of control within the MNE, can help to reduce overall costs.

A fifth reason is to overcome tariff walls by serving a foreign market from within. The EU provides an excellent example. Firms outside the EU are subject to tariffs on

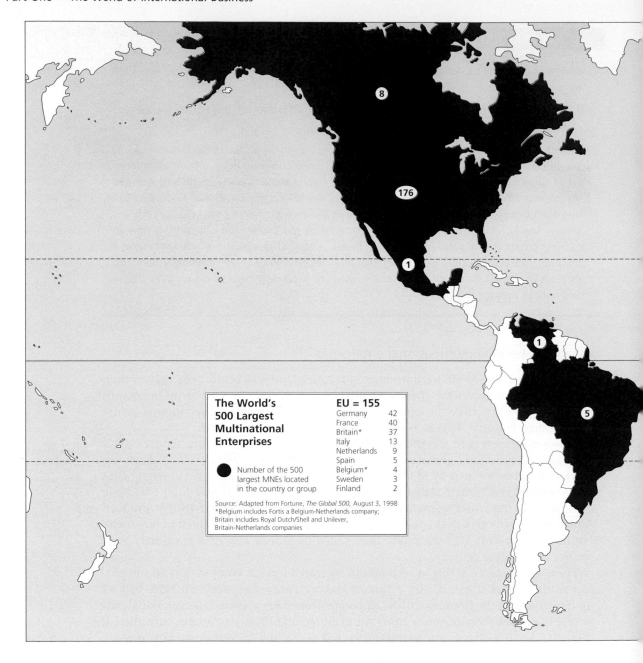

The World's 500 Largest Multinational Enterprises

● Number of the 500 largest MNEs located in the country or group

EU = 155

Germany	42
France	40
Britain*	37
Italy	13
Netherlands	9
Spain	5
Belgium*	4
Sweden	3
Finland	2

Source: Adapted from Fortune, *The Global 500,* August 3, 1998
*Belgium includes Fortis a Belgium-Netherlands company;
Britain includes Royal Dutch/Shell and Unilever,
Britain-Netherlands companies

goods exported to EU countries. Firms producing the goods within the EU can transport them to any other country in the bloc without paying tariffs. The same is now occurring in North America, thanks to the North American Free Trade Agreement (NAFTA), which eliminates tariffs between Canada, the United States, and Mexico.[4]

A sixth reason for becoming an MNE is to take advantage of technological expertise by manufacturing goods directly rather than allowing others to do it under a license. A **license** agreement is a contractual arrangement in which one firm, the **licensor**, provides access to some of its patents, trademarks, or technology to another firm,

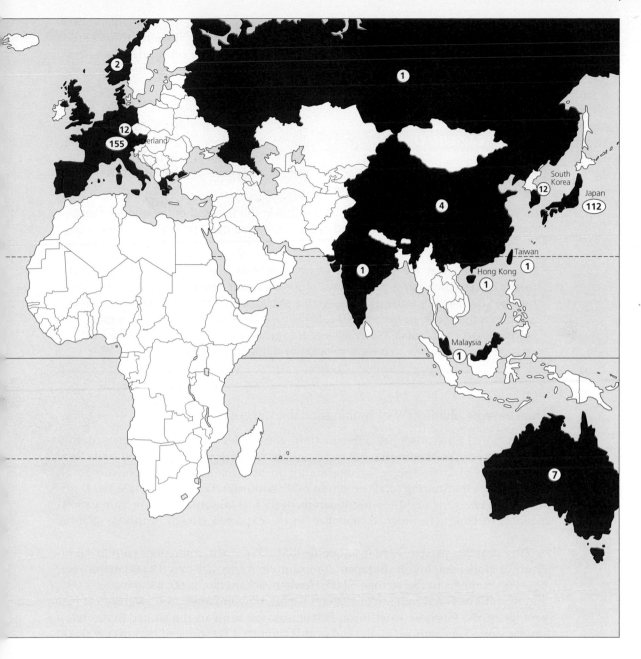

the **licensee**, in exchange for a fee or royalty. This fee often involves a fixed amount upon signing the contract and then a royalty of 2 to 5 per cent on sales generated by the agreement. A typical licensing contract will run five to seven years and be renewable at the option of either or both parties. Although the benefits of a licensing agreement are obvious, in recent years some MNEs have concluded that it is unwise to give another firm access to proprietary information such as patents, trademarks, or technological expertise, and they have allowed these arrangements to lapse. This allows them to reclaim their exclusive rights and then to manufacture and directly sell the products in overseas markets. This direct involvement in foreign markets brings the company closer to emerging technological developments, helping to prepare it to respond by acquiring the new technology or by developing substitutes. As a result, MNEs are better able to protect their international competitiveness than companies that have license agreements.

ACTIVE LEARNING CHECK

Review your answer to Active Learning Case question 2 and make any changes you like. Then compare your answer to the one below.

2. **Why did Disney take an ownership position in the firm rather than simply licensing some other firm to build and operate the park and settling for a royalty on all sales?**

Disney believed that the theme park was too lucrative a venture to settle for just a royalty on sales. Not only is the potential of the park extremely high, but Disney's investment of $160 million is extremely low given the amount of control it maintains and the fees and profits that would be generated should the park prove as highly attractive as company executives were forecasting. Disney also needs to retain control over its brand name products and services in order to prevent imitation by substandard rivals.

The strategic philosophy of multinational enterprises

Multinational enterprises are different from companies that confine their activities to the domestic market in that MNEs do not see the company as confined to its local roots. MNEs make decisions based primarily on what is best for the company, even if this means transferring funds or jobs to other countries. For example, IBM has transferred 120 executives and the headquarters of its $10 billion a year communications business to Europe in order to capitalize on the expected growth in this geographic region.[5]

This strategic pattern is not unique to IBM. US-owned companies employ thousands of global employees. In Japan, for example, Xerox has over 12,000 employees, Texas Instruments has more than 5,000, Hewlett-Packard has 3,000, 3M has over 2,000, and Bristol Myers has more than 1,000.[6] Overall, US companies hire a significant percentage of the Japanese work force. Foreign-owned firms in the United States tell a similar story. For example, by the end of this century it is estimated that over 800,000 Americans will be working for Japanese firms.[7] In all, foreign-owned firms now employ more than 3 million Americans.[8] So there is a great deal of economic interaction in the international arena, giving business firms headquartered in one country a significant impact on the economies of other countries.

Sometimes these projects involve workers from a host of countries. For example, Mazda's sportscar, the MX-5 Miata, was designed in California, had its prototype created in England, was assembled in Michigan and Mexico using advanced electronic components invented in New Jersey and fabricated in Japan, and was financed from Tokyo and New York. Similarly, Chevrolet's best-selling Geo Metro was designed in Japan and built in Canada at a factory owned by Japan's Suzuki. Simply put, MNEs

INTERNATIONAL BUSINESS STRATEGY IN ACTION

US firms in Japan

For years Japan has bought or borrowed US technology and then sold it back to the United States in the form of finished products. In one recent year Japanese firms paid American companies $2.5 billion in royalties and licensing fees, while also selling $33 billion of high-tech products to the United States. Now American firms are beginning to tap the Japanese technology market by setting up operations in Japan and hiring leading Japanese scientists away from locally based MNEs such as Toshiba and Nissan, as well as from elite universities and laboratories run by the ministry of International Trade and Industry (MITI). Why would a Japanese R&D scientist be willing to work for a US firm? One reason is the financial remuneration. A senior scientist in his mid-40s can earn approximately 50 per cent more at a US company. A second reason is the intellectual freedom and the opportunity to plug into the research networks that the corporation has set up worldwide.

Japan has now become a favorite target of high-tech US firms. One reason is that the Japanese are originating many of the most advanced breakthroughs in areas such as high-definition television, liquid crystal displays, semiconductors, biotechnology, and manufacturing technology. By locating near the source of these ideas, US firms are in an ideal position to hire knowledgeable people, to keep up with recent developments, and to monitor the competition. For

example, many high-tech developments that occur in Japan are reported in the local papers, but not elsewhere in the world. One US firm with a presence in Japan recently discovered 15 cases of patent infringements by Japanese firms.

US firms with R&D operations in Japan read like a "Who's Who" in US industry: American Cyanamid, Dow Corning, Eastman Kodak, Hewlett-Packard, IBM, Pfizer, Procter & Gamble, Texas Instruments, and Pharmacia & Upjohn, among others. Their research goals vary widely. For example, IBM is doing basic research in image recognition systems, multiprocessor computing, and computer applications; Kodak is working on molecular beam epitaxy, a method of growing crystals for making gallium arsenide chips; Texas Instruments is making chips for high-definition television sets; and Pharmacia & Upjohn is developing high-tech antibiotics for combating cancer, central nervous system disorders, and cardiovascular diseases.

At the same time US companies are funding research by prominent Japanese professors and are luring top students with scholarships. They are also licensing technology from Japanese firms. In 1982 US firms spent $89 million for such licensing; in 1990 they spent almost $500 million. US MNEs clearly realize that if they are to remain on the cutting edge of R&D, they have to go where the action is.

Sources: Adapted from Susan Moffat, "Picking Japan's Research Brains," *Fortune,* March 25, 1991, pp. 84–96; Brenton R. Schlender, "Japan: Hard Times for High Tech," *Fortune,* March 22, 1993, pp. 92–104; Carla Rapoport, "How Clinton Is Shaking Up Trade," *Fortune,* May 31, 1993, pp. 103, 108.

make whatever agreements are in their best interests, even if this means bringing in firms from three or four different countries. This is as true among small MNEs as it is among large ones.

Research and development (R&D) is particularly important in high-tech industries, and in recent years the Japanese have made significant market gains in autos and computers because of emphasizing R&D. Much of this success has been a result of Japanese MNEs hiring highly capable R&D people from other countries. Foreign MNEs are now doing the same, as seen in the box "International Business Strategy in Action: US firms in Japan."

Review your answer to Active Learning Case question 3 and make any changes you like. Then compare your answer to the one below.

3. In what way does Euro Disney reflect the strategic philosophy of Walt Disney as a multinational enterprise?

One way in which Euro Disney reflects the strategic philosophy of the company as an MNE is that Disney is willing to modify the park to meet the preferences of local visitors by catering to their markets. Euro Disney is not identical to Disneyland in California. The focus on European roots and culture are an integral part of the park. In addition, notice how the company used an international approach to funding the project. The monies were not all raised in France. The government helped, but so did banks, private investors, and Disney itself.

MULTINATIONALS IN ACTION

There are many multinationals, large and small, that sell a wide variety of goods and services. In this section we will see how MNEs operate by looking at sales and profits of several of the largest MNEs and then taking a closer look at the operations of some smaller MNEs.

Sales and profits

Most MNEs are not giant corporations, but the giants are almost all MNEs. Some exceptions are major utilities, banks, and retailers that restrict their operations to the home country. For example, the Wal-Mart Corporation is the largest and fastest-growing retailer in the United States. However, Wal-Mart has only recently begun tapping the international market and international sales are still a small per cent of overall revenues.

Some examples of MNEs in action

MNEs range from extremely large to fairly small in terms of both sales and employment, and they can be found in a variety of different industries. The following are five examples of MNEs in action.

Cemex SA   Cemex SA is Mexico's largest cement maker. In fact, it is the third largest cement maker in the world and in recent years has been highly profitable thanks to a series of well-executed strategies. In particular, since the early 1990s Cemex has spent billions of dollars to acquire and fix up smaller cement companies, mainly in Latin America and the Caribbean. Typically the firm has focused on low-income markets where cement is still sold one bag at a time to retail customers and where the economy still needs to build a great many highways, bridges, and harbors.[9]

When Cemex embarked on this strategy, many bankers were concerned that the company would still be making most of its money in Mexico, and a devaluation of the peso would severely impact on its international operations. In late 1994 when the Mexican government suddenly devaluated its currency, Cemex was generating only 25 per cent of its earnings from overseas operations and the firm was highly leveraged in dollars. However, instead of pulling back, Cemex convinced the bankers that the best strategy was to press forward and buy cement companies in Colombia and Venezuela. The decision was fortuitous. Venezuela soon devalued its own currency, but as its economy went into a tailspin Cemex sent in some of its own executives to straighten out the operation, reorganize the administrative and information systems, integrate the cement and concrete production operations, put in a new distribution system, and cut the work force. By the end of the year Cemex had doubled the unit's annual cash flow to $200 million. Meanwhile in Mexico, where the firm still generates 50 per cent of its income, a stronger economy has resulted in higher sales and profits. As a result, Cemex is now paying down its debt and expanding operations in Europe and Asia where it is both buying and building plants; and the company estimates that by the first decade of the twenty-first century sales will be in excess of $5 billion and profits will be higher than ever.

Kodak   Kodak is internationally known for its cameras and film production and has been a leading-edge competitor for decades. Recently, however, the firm has been hard hit by competitive pressures. Fuji, in particular, has been gaining US market share by cutting prices and offering quality products that some regard as superior to Kodak's. In turn, the giant American MNE is fighting back. One of its recent strategies in the film area has been the creation of more aggressive marketing programs designed to prevent further encroachment by Fuji. The company is also narrowing its focus and developing products that are simpler for consumers to use.

At the same time Kodak is working to cut overhead expenses, thus allowing it to lower prices and be more competitive. One way it is accomplishing this is through layoffs. Another is by carefully eliminating bureaucracy and waste. Coupled with these efforts, the firm has also been spinning off marginal businesses such as microfiche and microfilm and outsourcing some of its production.

The biggest challenge, however, is that of maintaining technological leadership. For example, competitors such as Hewlett-Packard, Canon, and Epson are producing competing products at ever-lower prices. However, Kodak is fighting back. One strategy that the firm is counting on to pay off handsomely is the development of "Image Magic." This is a network of digital printing stations that are being installed in retail stores worldwide. Now consumers will be able to access photos they store on the Internet, manipulate them in various ways, and print them. It will be a while before Kodak knows how successful this strategy will be, and one of the biggest risks is that this approach will not become profitable before alternative digital imaging technology replaces it. Additionally, competitors are rapidly producing lower-cost photo-quality printers which some marketing experts believe will be more than a match for Kodak's new "Image Magic" offering. Only time will tell whether Kodak will prevail.[10]

Mercedes-Benz   Mercedes-Benz is one of the world's best-known auto firms. For years it has produced some of the finest European cars. However, as costs began to rise in Europe during the 1990s, Mercedes realized that it could no longer rely strictly on a strategy of producing cars in Germany and exporting them to world markets. The company had to begin setting up operations in foreign markets. This is when Mercedes decided to establish production operations in the United States. The company's choice was Vance, Alabama, a small town in a rural part of the state. Labor costs here were 50 per cent lower than they were back home and Mercedes was convinced that it could find and train the work force it needed to build its new M-class sport utility vehicle.[11]

After poring through over 45,000 applications, Mercedes hired 1,500 workers. Two of the primary hiring criteria were the ability to get along with others and the willingness to follow orders. The reason for the latter is that Mercedes builds its cars to precise specifications. All factory-floor jobs are carried out in accordance with SMPs (standard methods and procedures) which spell out the exact, proper, and only way to do the task. These SMPs are drawn up by German engineers and are posted at every work station so that each employee can see exactly what needs to be done, right down to the official way to tighten a lug nut.

It will be a while before the company knows how well its Mercedes M-class cars will fare in the marketplace because they will have a great deal of established competition from the Jeep Grand Cherokee and the Ford Explorer. However, Mercedes is certain about one thing. The cars that roll off its Alabama production line will be the equal of the quality driving machines that the firm offers back home.

Levi Strauss   Levi Strauss is one of the few companies that pulled out of China during the mid-1990s because it felt that the government was guilty of pervasive human rights violations. Now the company is back, expanding its manufacturing facilities, and selling its products locally.[12]

The company stopped manufacturing jeans in China after it found evidence of child labor, forced labor, and a military presence at factories that were producing clothing for the firm. The company did not own any of these factories on the mainland; it relied on local subcontractors to perform the manufacturing. However, company guidelines prohibited the suppliers from using child labor, forced labor, or excessive work hours. So when Levi Strauss learned of these violations, the company concluded that its association with the contractors would damage its reputation and it began a phased withdrawal from China.

Now Levi Strauss is coming back into the marketplace and even has plans to start a direct-marketing operation on the mainland. The firm has promised to carefully monitor its new Chinese factories to ensure that they comply with human rights guidelines. At the same time, however, Levi's is glad to be back because, like many other MNEs, the company believes that China is a marketplace of the future. One senior executive in the company put it this way, "You're nowhere in Asia without being in China."

Canon   Canon is one of the world's leading photo and printer firms. This has not always been the case. For many years Canon followed the leaders and worked to improve its technology. However, in recent years the firm has taken the lead against firms such as Leica in cameras and Xerox in photocopiers. Now the company's strategy is directed at remaining ahead.[13]

Today Canon is in the top three in all of its major business lines; and its original product line, cameras, now accounts for less than 10 per cent of sales. However, the firm is the world leader in both single-lens reflexes and compacts, and earns almost one-third of its income from copiers. And to maintain its momentum, Canon has adopted a two-pronged strategy. First, it is seeking to maintain profits by cutting costs in its core business by making suppliers more efficient or by shifting work to factories in Taiwan, in order to reduce the high cost of building some of its products in Japan.

Second, Canon is moving into the digital age by cultivating alliances with companies that know the networking and computer world better than it does. For example, Canon has teamed up with Hewlett-Packard, one of its major competitors, to build laser printers. The company is also looking into developing smart printers with personal computer-like abilities including electronic mail; and it is looking at the market for digital cameras, while continuing to develop printers that produce high-quality photo prints on plain paper. Quite clearly, Canon believes that its future rests with the continued development of innovative products that draw on its core competencies in the optical field.

STRATEGIC MANAGEMENT OF MULTINATIONAL ENTERPRISES

As noted earlier, one of the characteristics of MNE affiliates is that they are linked by a strategic plan. As a result, units that are geographically dispersed and/or have diverse product offerings all work in accord with a strategic vision. The formulation and implementation of strategy will be discussed in detail in Chapter 8. Here we will look at the basic nature of the strategic management process and how select MNEs use strategic planning in managing their far-flung enterprises.

Strategic management of MNEs: an introduction

The strategic management process involves four major functions: strategy formulation, strategy implementation, evaluation, and the control of operations. These functions encompass a wide range of activities, beginning with an environmental analysis of external and internal conditions and an evaluation of organizational strengths and weaknesses. These activities serve as the basis for a well-formulated strategic plan. Then by carefully implementing and controlling this plan, the MNE is able to compete effectively in the international arena. Figure 2.2 illustrates the five specific steps in this overall process.

Figure 2.2   The strategic management process in action

Steps in the strategic management process Strategic planning typically begins with a review of the company's **basic mission**, which is determined by answering the questions: What is the firm's business? What is its reason for existence? By answering these questions, the company reaffirms the direction in which it wants to go. Shell Oil, BP Amoco, and Texaco see themselves as being in the energy business, not in the oil business, and this focus helps to direct their long-range thinking. AT&T, Sprint, and MCI view themselves as in the communications business, not in the telephone business. Coca-Cola and PepsiCo are in the food business, not in the soft-drink business.[14]

In recent years many MNEs have revised their strategic plan because they realized that they had drifted too far away from their basic mission. During the 1980s Unilever, the giant Anglo-Dutch MNE, concluded that it needed to adopt a "back to the core" strategy.[15] The firm reassessed its capabilities and skills in all areas of business and then sold a whole range of peripheral operations, including transport, oil, milling, wallpaper, floor coverings, and turkey breeding. Today Unilever confines its business to such areas as consumer products and industrial operations in specialty chemicals and agribusiness. The firm's strong R&D labs continue to develop new products in each of these areas, thus helping Unilever maintain its worldwide market shares.[16]

After determining its mission, the MNE will evaluate the external and internal environment. The goal of external environmental analysis is to identify opportunities and threats that will need to be addressed.[17] Based on opportunity analysis, for example, the Deutsche Bank, Germany's largest, has started a network of 250 branches in what used to be East Germany. Allianz, the giant insurance company, has bought a 50 per cent interest in Staatliche Versicherung, the former East German insurance company. BMW is investing there in small startup companies to produce components and tools for its auto manufacturing business. McDonald's is going to open 100 fast-food restaurants in the region, and Woolworth is moving to establish general merchandise stores there.[18] These companies all see the region as having tremendous financial potential.[19]

However, these expansion decisions were made only after the respective companies had analyzed the potential pitfalls, and there are many of them. One is that eastern Germans have lived in a centrally planned bureaucracy for 45 years. Can they adapt to a free-market economy? Will they be able to accept individual responsibility in a country where the state will no longer be the major provider? Will they be able to upgrade their inefficient factories and improve the quality of output? Western firms believe that with an influx of capital, the country can improve. However, there are a number of problems that eastern Germany faces and investors must be aware of them. These include the need to increase worker productivity, improve the local infrastructure, and bring in qualified managers to run the operation.[20]

The purpose of internal environmental analysis is to evaluate the company's financial and personnel strengths and weaknesses. Examining its financial picture will help the MNE decide what it can afford to do in terms of expansion and capital investment. Examining its financial picture will also help it to identify areas where cost-cutting or divestment are in order. For example, in recent years some major US airlines have sold partial ownership to overseas carriers in order to increase the size of their fleet and better position themselves for competing in the market. However, since the US government currently limits foreign ownership of domestic airlines to 25 per cent, these carriers are finding that they must now generate expansion funds through either loans or profits that are poured back into the operation.[21] An evaluation of personnel will help the company determine how well the current work force can meet the challenges of the future and what types of people will have to be hired or let go.

Internal and external analyses will help the MNE to identify both long-range goals (typically two to five years) and short-range goals (less than two years). The plan is then broken down into major parts, and each affiliate and department will be assigned goals and responsibilities. This begins the implementation process. Progress is then periodically evaluated and changes are made in the plan. AN MNE might realize that it must stop offering a particular good or service because the market is no longer profitable or might create a new product in order to take advantage of an emerging demand. The box "International Business Strategy in Action: CNN" provides an example of this.

ACTIVE LEARNING CHECK

Review your answer to Active Learning Case question 4 and make any changes you like. Then compare your answer to the one below.

4. Did Disney management conduct an external environmental analysis before going forward with Euro Disney? Explain.

The company conducted a thorough external environmental analysis. First, the location of the European population was examined in order to identify how far people would have to travel to visit the park. Second, the company examined the cost of building the park and identified potential sources of funds. Third, the firm determined how the park was to be built and where it would find the necessary contractors. Fourth, the company made a forecast regarding the number of visitors to the park each year, how much they would spend, and what the firm's profit would be on the venture.

Strategic management in action

There are a variety of ways that MNEs use the strategic management process. In this section we examine the way each of three multinationals emphasizes a particular segment of the process.

Goodyear: strategic planning and reformulation   The worldwide tire industry generates approximately $70 billion in annual revenues. However, because of strong competition, profitability is very small. Nevertheless, Goodyear Tire & Rubber, which is currently the world's third largest tire manufacturer (behind Michelin and Bridgestone), has plans to increase both market share and profitability over the next decade.

One way it intends to do this is by carefully reformulating its strategic plan to cut costs and gain market acceptance. Part of this success is tied to its new "run-flat" tire that is designed to let air out of a punctured tire but still retain its shape. This is possible thanks to special steel cords that the company has developed which hold the tire rigid even with zero air pressure, thus allowing the driver to continue for 50 miles at 55 miles per hour.

Another of the firm's strategies is to reduce costs by shifting production to lower-wage countries. Labor currently accounts for about one-third of a tire's factory cost,

INTERNATIONAL BUSINESS STRATEGY IN ACTION

CNN

When United Nations forces liberated Kuwait from the invading Iraqi forces in 1991, people all over the world tuned into the Cable News Network (CNN). In Europe 5.1 million people had access to the CNN channel. By the time hostilities ended, the network had garnered 1.1 million new subscribers. In Japan, broadcasters relied heavily on CNN footage and analysis to provide news from the war. The same was true in the United States where the major networks were not as well positioned as CNN to cover the story. Realizing that there is an international demand for global television news, networks in a host of countries are now scurrying to create new offerings.

The one in the best position to take on CNN is the British Broadcasting Company (BBC) which in 1997 launched a 24-hour local news channel in Britain. This move is a stepping stone to the company's plan to offer up to 18 hours per day of news and entertainment programs worldwide. The BBC has some formidable strengths, including the fact that its World Service radio reaches 120 million people globally. In fact, US Marines first heard Saddam Hussein's withdrawal orders on the BBC, and Iraqi troops learned about it from the BBC's Arabic service. The company now uses their previous network of radio correspondents to file television reports and an Internet service called BBC Online News. If all goes according to plan, BBC World Service Television and BBC Online News will dominate their respective markets in a few years.

The BBC may find itself facing some very strong competitors. One is Rupert Murdoch's Sky News, which is offering a 24-hour, London-based news channel to European satellite and cable companies. Another is a group of ten state-owned European broadcasters operating out of Switzerland, who are pooling their resources to spearhead a 24-hour, multilingual news program called "Euronews." A third is a French group consisting of two all-news French-language stations. A fourth is UFA, the film and television unit of German publisher Bertelsmann, which is considering an all news station for Germany, Switzerland and Austria and which recently merged with Cie. Luxembourgeoise de Télédiffusion (CLT). Bertelsmann and Murdoch's Sky News are also part of a four-partner alliance, with Canal Plus and Havas as the other partners. A fifth competitor is Nihon Hoso Kyokai (NHK) of Japan that wants to add an 8-hour global service to news and business programs sold in the United States.

Will these competitors be able to mount a real threat to CNN? Some observers warn that the risks associated with this venture are great, and if too many companies get into the market, there will be very little profit for them.

Clearly, CNN has the inside track and is working to exploit it, despite the firm's heavy debt load and low profitability. CNN is now opening bureaus across the Middle East and is developing programming for the overseas market. Furthermore, CNN's World Report allows itself to be used as a news board for a variety of local news sources. Chinese and Cuban news are broadcast from CNN unfiltered, which provides for a variety not always found in other news sources. Nevertheless, the profit potential from global television news is so great that many communications MNEs cannot resist the temptation to enter the market. As a result, strategic alliances are beginning to be formed as companies position themselves for a battle for the market.

Sources: Adapted from Richard A. Melcher et al., "Everybody Wants to Get into the Act," *Business Week*, March 19, 1991, p. 48; Elizabeth Comte, "The 45th Annual Report on American Industry: Entertainment and Information," *Forbes*, January 4, 1993, p. 143; and Walter Kiechel III, "How We Will Work in the Year 2000," *Fortune*, May 17, 1993, pp. 38–52; *http://www.scripps.ohiou.edu/cnnbook/press-r.htm*; Jay Branegan, "Bertelsmann Bets Big," *Times International*, April 15, 1996; "Turner sees BBC as threat to Murdoch" (*http://www.nando.net/newsroom/ntn/biz/110597/biz11_8118_noframes.html*).

and Goodyear has found that workers in Slovenia and Mexico are just as productive as those in the US, while the hourly labor rate is almost 50 per cent less.

A third part of the firm's strategic plan is tied to developments in technology and manufacturing. The new steel cord that the company has created for use in its "run-flat" tire is 40 per cent stronger than the wire now used in steel-belted tires. And the new cord is thin enough to be used in the body of the tire as well as in the sidewalls without compromising ride quality, thus paving the way, hopefully, for a very successful new product.

Still another development being implemented at Goodyear plants is a new manufacturing system known as Impact. While tires are typically made on an assembly line that can stretch for more than half a mile and have hundreds of feet of conveyors moving items from one process to the next, Goodyear plans on eliminating half the intermediate steps by reducing floor space by 25 per cent, improving uniformity, and reducing labor costs by 35 per cent. This new approach could significantly increase productivity.

Goodyear's new plan also calls for an increase in revenues of more than 50 per cent over the next five years, while increasing return on sales by 25 per cent and cutting overhead by 15 per cent. If the firm can achieve these targets, it will be well on its way to become the number two tire manufacturer in the world![22]

Statoil: scenario-based decision making Statoil is a Norwegian oil and gas company.[23] One of Statoil's biggest challenges has been developing an effective research and development strategy. This strategy is critical because R&D plays such a major role in oil and gas exploration. For example, if a competitor develops a radically new process for finding, recovering, or processing oil, Statoil could be in big trouble. On the other hand, the chances of this happening may be slim and the company might be better off investing its R&D funds in making incremental improvements in the current state of technology. In an effort to deal with this problem of forecasting the future and deciding what course of action to take, Statoil employed a common strategic management forecasting tool: scenario analysis.

Scenario analysis involves a formulation and analysis of events that are likely to happen. After analyzing each of the scenarios, the company will decide how to allocate resources. In the case of Statoil, four scenarios were formulated: (1) Norway's future will continue to be dominated by the oil and gas economy, in which case it would be a seller's market and oil companies would continue developing national oil and gas resources; (2) the worldwide economy will improve but European countries and the United States will continue to be dependent on oil producers, so Norway will continue to develop its energy resources and diversify the economy; (3) the worldwide economy will turn down, energy prices will drop, countries will try to become self-sufficient, and Norway will have to use its energy resources to survive economically; and (4) there will be high-technology breakthroughs in areas such as information technology and biotechnology, the demand for gas will go up but that for oil will decline, it will become a buyer's market, and Norway will have to restructure its economy.

Each of these scenarios was developed in detail. In the process, consideration was given to a wide range of possible developments including economic growth in Western and Eastern European countries. From an evaluation of these scenarios the company decided on an R&D strategy that would help it address the most likely and most serious future events.

Nissan: evaluating and controlling operations   For a number of years the Nissan Motor Company had been predicting that it would hold 25 per cent of the Japanese auto market by the turn of the century. The company also forecasted continued growth in the US auto market. However, recent results show that these predictions were all highly optimistic. In fact, Nissan is currently in the process of evaluating and controlling its operations in order to ensure that developments do not get any worse than they are already. What went wrong? A number of things.

First, by the late 1990s many Asian economies began to encounter problems, thus reducing Nissan's sales potential in that region. At the same time, the US market became much more competitive and the firm, which had almost surpassed Honda and become the second largest Japanese firm in America, suddenly found itself falling back.

Second, the company's production efficiency began to slip badly. Costs per auto increased to the point where they were much higher than those of its two major rivals, Toyota and Honda. So Nissan started making far less money per unit on sales.

Yet the firm's major problem may well be its inability to develop a vehicle that provides a clear image in the minds of buyers. While its main offering, the Nissan Altima, is judged to have high quality, the company has not been able to compete successfully with the Honda Accord or Toyota. The primary reason, in the view of industry analysts, is that the car lacks flair. Moreover, the company does not have the financial resources to design and develop the models that it needs to overtake its two main competitors.

In dealing with these problems, Nissan is currently evaluating its operations and introducing a variety of changes. One is the decision to build vehicles on fewer platforms and thus cut costs. Current plans call for a reduction in the number of platforms from 25 down to 10 within five years. Nissan also plans to eliminate marginally profitable models and to sharply reduce inventories. It also intends to reduce some of its massive debt. If these control efforts can be properly carried out, the company will again become a major player in both the Japanese and the US automotive markets.[24]

SUMMARY

Key points

1. A multinational enterprise is a company that is headquartered in one country but has operations in two or more countries. There is a series of characteristics that are common to multinational enterprises. These include: (a) affiliated firms that are linked by ties of common ownership, (b) a common pool of resources, and (c) a strategic vision that guides all the affiliates.

2. Multinationals, especially large industrial enterprises, account for a large percentage of world sales and employment. MNEs, large or small, also engage in a wide variety of business activities, ranging from manufacturing to retailing to consulting services.

3. Companies become MNEs for a number of reasons: (a) a desire to protect themselves from the risks and uncertainties of the domestic business cycle, (b) a growing world market for their goods or services, (c) a response to increased foreign competition, (d) a desire to internalize in order to reduce costs, (e) a desire to overcome tariff barriers, and (f) a desire to take advantage of technological expertise

by manufacturing goods directly rather than allowing others to do it under a license agreement.

4. Multinational enterprises have a strategic philosophy that is different from that of home country businesses. MNEs do not see their company as an extension of their domestic roots. They hire, fire, and transfer personnel to meet global needs, even if this means laying off home country employees. They also combine their talents with those of other MNEs in creating, financing, and managing joint ventures.

5. Successful MNEs rely on the strategic management process, which has five major phases: (a) identification of the firm's basic mission, (b) external and internal environmental analysis, (c) formulation of objectives and overall plans, (d) implementation of these plans, and (e) evaluation and control of operations.

Key terms

- multinational enterprise (MNE)
- license
- licensor
- licensee
- basic mission
- scenario analysis

Review and discussion questions

1. What is a multinational enterprise? Is it likely that the number of MNEs will increase during the next decade? Why?

2. What are the three common characteristics of an MNE? Identify and briefly describe each.

3. Why do firms become multinational enterprises? Identify and discuss four reasons.

4. In what way is the strategic philosophy of an MNE different from that of a domestic firm?

5. How successful are the large industrial MNEs? What accounts for this?

6. If Kodak proves to be very successful, what strategic moves will have accounted for this? If the company loses money and has to retrench, what decisions will have caused this?

7. Why is Mercedes so successful? What can other firms looking to go international learn from Mercedes' success?

8. Why is Canon so successful? What can other firms looking to go international learn from Canon's success?

9. What are the five basic steps in the strategic management process? Identify and briefly describe each.

REAL CASES

LAPTOP COMPUTERS

Over the last decade laptop computers have continued to gain market share. In the last few years demand for these machines has increased dramatically. In 1994, 8.6 million mobile computers were shipped worldwide. In 1996, this rose 46 per cent to 12.6 million units. As they become lighter and more powerful, laptops will be replacing desktop computers more frequently.

A number of MNEs are currently vying for position in this market. The Japanese have the inside track because of their expertise in areas such as liquid crystal display (LDC) screens, floppy drives, memory chips, and miniaturization techniques. As a result by 1995, Japanese firms such as Toshiba, NEC, and Fujitsu controlled 29 per cent of the worldwide market. However US firms relying heavily on their marketing expertise (an area where Japanese firms are particularly weak) have control of over 31 per cent of the worldwide market.

In an effort to ensure that they do not lose this battle, many US manufacturers are entering into agreements with Japanese firms. For example, Compaq worked with Japan's Citizen Watch Company to miniaturize Compaq's laptop components to fit into an $8^1/_2$ by 11-inch package. IBM joined Toshiba to develop color laptop screens. Meanwhile Texas Instruments is trying to get back into the market by selling laptops designed with a Japanese partner. Others are simply having Japanese firms produce the machines for them.

The US market, while large, is not the only important market. In Japan laptops account for about 50 per cent of all personal computers. Demand in Europe is also quite brisk. This certainly helps to explain why Italy's Olivetti built a new line of laptops in its Nuremberg, Germany factory and has signed a deal with Digital Equipment to provide the firm with machines for the US market.

The biggest challenge in this market will be staying on the cutting edge of technology. There are now so many firms in the industry that those who do not offer state-of-the-art machines can expect their share to drop quickly. What types of breakthroughs will these MNEs have to make if they hope to be major players? Some of the most likely developments will include improved graphics quality; color LCD screens; smaller and more sophisticated chips that allow the emergence of sophisticated notebook computers; smaller

(1.8 inch) hard-disk drives that can store more information; nickel-hydride batteries that will have 50 per cent more life than those currently operating; flash memory cards that will be used in place of a hard-disk drive and reduce both power consumption and weight; durable materials that will be resistant to possible accidents; and flexible circuit boards that, combined with tape-automated bonding techniques, will be more reliable and take up less space.

Clearly, a variety of laptop options will be available in the future. This trend has begun to emerge as companies like Toshiba have all sizes of laptops. Typing and reading comfort, durability, and weight might not be complementary, so the laptop of the future will be tailored to consumers' needs. Technology to decrease size and weight will be developed to both improve the general quality of the product (most people will like light laptops) and to be able to increase the amount of choices available. The demand is huge and the profits attractive. Unfortunately, the market is crowded and those who hope to prosper will have to remain flexible and alert to changing market conditions.

1. Why are the major competitors in the laptop computer industry MNEs? Could a domestic firm do well in this market?

2. How does the coordination of effort and creation of partnerships with foreign companies fit into the strategic philosophy of US MNEs? Explain.

3. What phase of the strategic management process is most important to MNEs in the laptop market? Which phase is second in importance? Defend your answer.

Sources: Adapted from Deidre A. Depke et al., "Laptops Take Off," *Business Week*, March 18, 1991; Alan Deutschman, "Stress Jobs' Next Big Gamble," *Fortune*, February 8, 1993; Brian Zajac, "The Forbes 500s Annual Directory: Sales," *Forbes*, April 26, 1993; Peter Burrows, Gary McWilliams, and Robert D. Hof, "Cheap PCs," *Business Week*, March 23, 1998, pp. 28–32; http://orion.adnc.com/~websites/kmarcus/iomega/Channel.htm; http://www.pctoday.com/editorial/tips/970234a.html.

ACER TAIWAN

Acer Taiwan is the third largest PC manufacturer worldwide. It has 80 branch offices worldwide and distribution networks in over 100 countries. By 1998 the Acer Group had over 23,000 employees. It is the best known brand in Asia, and a large player in Latin America. In the United States, where IBM, Compaq, and Dell dominate, Acer has earned the number two position in the PC consumer electronic market. By 1997, the company owned over 400 patents. Not bad for a company no one knew about prior to 1986.

In 1976, CEO Stan Shin and some of his friends managed to put together $25,000 to start Multitech. With seven employees, the company began to develop small electronics such as pocket calculators and games. Slowly the company began to grow. Its initial entrance in the PC market was not direct. Multitech produced computers to be sold under other brand names. It was only in 1986 that the company launched its own brand name computer: Acer. While the company still supplies under other brand names such as Hitachi and Siemens, Acer has become the seventh best known brand in the world. In 1994, the company's revenues totaled $3.2 billion.

The question is how a small company from Taiwan could gain market share on the more established computer manufacturers. The answer is niches. Shin summarizes his philosophy with the following proverb: "It is better to be a big fish in a small pond than a small fish in a big pond." Small markets which were not yet captured by the likes of IBM were a driving force behind Acer's success. Additionally, Shin is planning to develop tailored PCs. Instead of a computer that can do everything, a more task-specific computer can be build at a low cost.

Acer's distribution system is also a novelty. With the product life of computer components at about three months, exporting overseas becomes a problem. Acer has manufacturing and assembling plants all over the world. The company distributes parts with long product lives by ship, while highly volatile products like semiprocessors, PCB, and memory are shipped by plane. This allows for just-in-time production which Shin compares to the distribution system of a fast-food chain with perishable and non-perishable ingredients.

The success of the company is highly correlated with the management structure created by Shin. Unlike traditional Chinese business, where management is highly hierarchical and controlled by the owning family, Shin has decentralized management. Autonomy is important. Managers should think like owners, so as to take advantage of all profit opportunities. Additionally, Acer has gone public. The Shin family stake is only about 10 per cent. Employees have the option of buying shares at extremely low prices. Acer functions as a top co-ordinator for the group member, which themselves have the flexibility to implement the goals of the headquarters.

To succeed in the long term the company has built alliances. To enter the United States the company formed a joint venture with Texas Instruments. To acquire specific technology, in 1987 Acer bought Counterpoint Computers, a US maker of multiuser systems. In 1990, Altos (US) and Kangaroo Computer (Dutch) were also purchased to acquire needed technology. Lately the company has been using a different strategy. Acer has cross-licensing agreements with IBM and Intel.

Acer is well positioned for the future. Its market share has been increasing steadily and the company has ventured well outside its borders to become a multinational enterprise. Investors seem to be optimistic about the future as the market value of Acer shares is constantly increasing. The company is an excellent example of a wealth creator.

1. Why would a joint venture between Acer and Texas Instruments be beneficial to Acer? What does Texas Instruments gain from such a partnership?

2. Do you see any strategic reason that might have influenced Acer to negotiate deals with IBM and Intel? Why are these deals different from those negotiated with smaller companies?

3. Who are the stakeholders of the Acer group? How are incentives tied into the organizational structure of Acer?

Sources: Adapted from Stefan Simmons, "Lessons from the Village Shop," *Spiegel*, November 4, 1997; Brian Dumaine, "Asia's Wealth Creators Confront a New Reality," *Fortune*, December 8, 1997; Catherine Shepherd and Alejandro Reyes, "Lords of High Tech," *Asiaweek*, November 7, 1997; Charles Goldsmith, "Russia's Plane Makers Reverse Free Fall," *Wall Street Journal*, June 17, 1997, p. A14; *http://www.acer.com.tw/ai/factsht/fs_reen2.htm*; *http://www.acer.com.tw/ai/newsrel/apifdab4.htm*; *http://www.acer.com.tw/ai/newsrel/pribmlc2.htm*.

ENDNOTES

1. United Nations, *World Investment Report*, 1997,
2. See, for example, Eduardo Lachica, "GE Sees Asia Placing More Than 45% of Global Orders for Power Equipment," *Wall Street Journal*, February 4, 1994, p. A5.
3. Gale Eisenstodt, "Bull in the Japan Shop," *Forbes*, January 31, 1994, pp. 41–42.
4. Clyde H. Farnsworth, "Trade-Talk Role Seen for Canada," *New York Times*, December 31, 1990, pp. 21, 28. Also, see Alan M. Rugman, *Multinationals and the Canada–United States Free Trade Agreement* (Columbia, SC: University of South Carolina Press, 1990).
5. Robert B. Reich, "Who Is Them?" *Harvard Business Review*, March–April 1991, p. 77.
6. James C. Morgan and J. Jeffrey Morgan, *Cracking the Japanese Market* (New York: Free Press, 1991), Appendix A.
7. Ibid., p. 45.
8. Robert H. Reich, "Who Is Us?" *Harvard Business Review*, January–February 1990, p. 55.
9. Jonathan Friedland, "Mexico's Cemex Wins Bet on Acquisitions," *Wall Street Journal*, April 30, 1998, p. A14.
10. Geoffrey Smith et al., "Can George Fisher Fix Kodak?" *Business Week*, October 20, 1997, pp. 116–128; Edward W. Desmond, "What's Ailing Kodak? Fuji," *Fortune*, October 27, 1997, pp. 185–192; and Bob Davis and Laura Johannes, "Kodak and US Government Team Up for New Drive on Japan's Film Market," *Wall Street Journal*, February 4, 1998, p. A4.
11. Justin Martin, "Mercedes: Made in Alabama," *Fortune*, July 7, 1997, pp. 150–158.
12. Mark Landler, "Reversing Course, Levi Strauss Will Expand Its Output in China," *New York Times*, April 9, 1998, pp. 1, 5.
13. Edward W. Desmond, "Can Canon Keep Clicking?" *Fortune*, February 2, 1998, pp. 98–104.
14. Also, see Gail E. Schares and Neil Gross, "Siemens is Starting to Look Like a Chipmaker," *Business Week*, February 7, 1994, pp. 43–44.
15. Floris A. Maljers, "Inside Unilever: The Evolving Transnational Company," *Harvard Business Review*, September–October 1992, pp. 46–52.
16 F. A. Maljers "Strategic Planning and Intuition in Unilever," *Long Range Planning*, April 1990, pp. 63–68.
17. See, for example, Herman Daems, "The Strategic Implications of Europe 1992," *Long Range Planning*, June 1990, pp. 41–48.
18. Heinz Weihrich, "Europe 1992 and a Unified Germany: Opportunities and Threats for United States Firms," *Academy of Management Executive*, January 1991, p. 94.
19. Also, see Carla Rapoport, "The New US Push to Europe," *Fortune*, January 19, 1994, pp. 73–74.
20. Ibid., p. 95.
21. John H. Cushman, Jr., "For US Airlines, a Sudden Lust for Foreign Entanglements," *New York Times*, December 30, 1990, Section F, p. 10.
22. Alex Taylor III, "Goodyear Wants to be No. 1 Again," *Fortune*, April 27, 1998, pp. 131–134.
23. This information comes from P. R. Stokke, W. K. Ralston, T. A. Boyce, and I. H. Wilson, "Scenario Planning for Norwegian Oil and Gas," *Long Range Planning*, April 1990, pp. 2–17.
24. Stephanie Strom, "No. 2 and Not Enjoying the Ride," *New York Times*, May 21, 1998, Section C, pp. 1, 4.

ADDITIONAL BIBLIOGRAPHY

Beamish, Paul W. and Banks, John C. "Equity Joint Ventures and the Theory of the Multinational Enterprise," *Journal of International Business Studies*, vol. 18, no. 2 (Summer 1987).

Birkinshaw, Julian and Hood, Neil. "Multinational Subsidiary Evolution: Capability and Charter Change in Foreign-Owned Subsidiary Companies," *The Academy of Management Review*, vol. 23, no. 4 (October 1998).

Buckley, Peter J. "The Frontiers of International Business Research," *Management International Review*, vol. 31 (1991).

Buckley, Peter, J. and Casson, Mark C. "Models of the Multinational Enterprise," *Journal of International Business Studies*, vol. 29, no. 1 (First Quarter 1998).

Chernotsky, Harry I. "The American Connection: Motives for Japanese Foreign Direct Investment," *Columbia Journal of World Business*, vol. 22, no. 4 (Winter 1987).

Cho, Kang Rae. "The Role of Product-Specific Factors in Intra-Firm Trade of US Manufacturing Multinational Corporations," *Journal of International Business Studies*, vol. 21, no. 2 (Second Quarter 1990).

Dunning, John H. "The Eclectic Paradigm of International Production: A Restatement and Some Possible Extensions," *Journal of International Business Studies*, vol. 19, no. 1 (Spring 1988).

Hennart, Jean-François. "Can the New Forms of Investment Substitute for the Old Forms?: A Transaction Cost

Perspective," *Journal of International Business Studies*, vol. 20, no. 2 (Summer 1989).

Kim, W. Chan and Hwang, Peter. "Global Strategy and Multinationals' Entry Mode Choice," *Journal of International Business Studies*, vol. 23, no. 1 (First Quarter 1992).

Kim, Wi Saeng and Lyn, Esmeralda O. "Foreign Direct Investment Theories, Entry Barriers, and Reverse Investments in US Manufacturing Industries," *Journal of International Business Studies*, vol. 18, no. 2 (Summer 1987).

Kimura, Yui. "Firm-Specific Strategic Advantage and Foreign Direct Investment Behaviour of Firms; The Case of Japanese Semiconductor Firms," *Journal of International Business Studies*, vol. 20, no. 2 (Summer 1989).

Madura, Jeff and Whyte, Ann Marie. "Diversification Benefits of Direct Foreign Investment," *Management International Review*, vol. 30, no. 1 (First Quarter 1990).

Moore, Karl and Lewis, David. "The First Multinationals," *Management International Review*, vol. 38, no. 2 (1998).

Rugman, Alan M. *Inside the Multinationals: The Economics of Internal Markets* (New York: Columbia University Press, 1981).

Rugman, Alan M. "The Multinational Enterprise," in Ingo Walter (ed.), *Handbook of International Management* (New York: Wiley, 1988), pp. 1–18.

Rugman, Alan M. *The Theory of Multinational Enterprises* (Cheltenham: Elgar, 1996).

Rugman, Alan M. and Verbeke, Alain. "A Note on the Transnational Solution and the Transaction Cost Theory of Multinational Strategic Management," *Journal of International Business Studies*, vol. 23, no. 4 (Fourth Quarter 1992).

Sabi, Manijeh. "An Application of the Theory of Foreign Direct Investment to Multinational Banking in LDCs," *Journal of International Business Studies*, vol. 19, no. 3 (Fall 1988).

Yoshida, Mamoru. "Macro-Micro Analyses of Japanese Manufacturing Investments in the United States," *Management International Review*, vol. 27, no. 4 (Fourth Quarter 1987).

APPENDIX TO CHAPTER 2

Appendix 2A   The 25 largest US MNEs, 1997

Rank	MNE	Industry	Sales (in millions of US $)
1	General Motors	Motor vehicles	178,174
2	Ford Motor	Motor vehicles	153,627
3	Exxon	Petroleum	122,379
4	Wal-Mart Stores	General merchandisers	119,299
5	General Electric	Electronics, electrical equipment	90,840
6	Intl. Business Machines	Computers, office equipment	78,508
7	Chrysler	Motor vehicles	61,147
8	Mobil	Petroleum	59,978
9	US Postal Service	Mail, Package, Freight Delivery	58,216
10	Philip Morris	Tobacco	56,114
11	AT&T	Telecommunications	53,261
12	Boeing	Aerospace	45,800
13	Texaco	Petroleum	45,187
14	State Farm Insurance Cos.	Insurance	43,957
15	Hewlett Packard	Computers, office equipment	42,895
16	E.I. Du Pont De Nemours	Chemicals	41,304
17	Sears Roebuck	General merchandisers	41,296
18	Travelers Group	Financial	37,609
19	Prudential Insurance	Insurance	37,073
20	Chevron	Petroleum	36,376
21	Procter & Gamble	Soaps, cosmetics	35,764
22	Citicorp	Banks	34,697
23	Amoco	Petroleum	32,836
24	K-Mart	General merchandisers	32,183
25	Merrill Lynch	Securities	31,731

Source: Adapted from *Fortune*, "The Fortune Global 500," August 3, 1998.

Appendix 2B The 25 largest European MNEs, 1997

Rank	MNE	Country	Industry	Sales (in millions of US $)
1	Royal Dutch-Shell	Britain-Netherlands	Petroleum	128,142
2	Axa	France	Insurance	76,874
3	Daimler-Benz	Germany	Motor vehicles	71,561
4	British Petroleum	Britain	Petroleum	71,193
5	Volkswagen	Germany	Motor vehicles	65,328
6	Siemens	Germany	Electronics, electrical equipment	63,754
7	Allianz	Germany	Insurance	56,785
8	Fiat	Italy	Motor vehicles	52,569
9	Unilever	Britain-Netherlands	Food	48,761
10	Nestlé	Switzerland	Food	48,254
11	Credit Suisse	Switzerland	Banks	48,242
12	Veba Group	Germany	Trading	43,881
13	Elf Aquitaine	France	Petroleum	43,572
14	Deutsche Bank	Germany	Banks	40,792
15	RWE Group	Germany	Utilities, gas and electric	40,233
16	Royal Philips Electronics	Netherlands	Electronics, electrical equipment	39,188
17	Deutsche Telekom	Germany	Telecommunications	38,969
18	ING Group	Netherlands	Insurance	38,673
19	HSBC Holdings	Britain	Banks	37,474
20	ENI	Italy	Petroleum	36,962
21	Electricité De France	France	Utilities, gas and electric	36,673
22	Renault	France	Motor vehicles	35,624
23	BMW	Germany	Motor vehicles	34,692
24	Crédit Agricole	France	Banks	34,015
25	Metro	Germany	Food	32,790

Source: Adapted from *Fortune*, "The Fortune Global 500," August 3, 1998.

Appendix 2C   The 25 largest Japanese MNEs, 1997

Rank	MNE	Industry	Sales (in millions of US $)
1	Mitsui	Trading	142,688
2	Mitsubishi	Trading	128,922
3	Itochu	Trading	126,632
4	Marubeni	Trading	111,121
5	Sumitomo	Trading	102,395
6	Toyota	Motor vehicles	95,137
7	Nissho Iwai	Trading	81,894
8	Nippon Telegraph & Telephone	Telecommunications	76,984
9	Nippon Life Insurance	Insurance	71,388
10	Hitachi	Electronics, electrical equipment	68,567
11	Matsushita Electric Industrial	Electronics, electrical equipment	64,281
12	Sony	Electronics, electrical equipment	55,033
13	Nissan	Motor vehicles	53,478
14	Honda	Motor vehicles	48,876
15	Dai-Ichi Mutual Life Insurance	Insurance	47,442
16	Toshiba	Electronics, electrical equipment	44,467
17	Tomen	Trading	43,400
18	Tokyo Electric Power	Utilities, gas and electric	42,997
19	Sumitomo Life Insurance	Insurance	42,279
20	Fujitsu	Computers, office equipment	40,613
21	NEC	Electronics, electrical equipment	39,927
22	Bank of Tokyo-Mitsubishi	Banks	34,750
23	Nichimen	Trading	31,362
24	Meiji Life Insurance	Insurance	31,047
25	Mitsubishi Electric	Electronics, electrical equipment	30,967

Source: Adapted from Fortune, "The Fortune Global 500," August 3, 1998.

Appendix 2D   The largest Canadian MNEs, 1997

Rank	MNE	Industry	Sales (in millions of US $)
1	BCE	Electronics, electrical equipment	23,974
2	Royal Bank of Canada	Banks	12,810
3	Seagram	Beverages	12,560
4	CIBC	Banks	12,289
5	Transcanada Pipelines	Energy	10,288
6	George Weston	Food	10,055
7	Bank of Nova Scotia	Banks	9,594

Source: Adapted from Fortune, "The Fortune Global 500," August 3, 1998.

Appendix 2E   The 25 largest third-world MNEs, 1997

Rank	MNE	Country	Industry	Sales (in millions of US $)
1	Daewoo	South Korea	Motor vehicles	71,526
2	PDVSA	Venezuela	Petroleum	34,801
3	SK	South Korea	Petroleum	33,816
4	Pemex	Mexico	Mining	28,565
5	Hyundai	South Korea	Trading	27,838
6	Samsung	South Korea	Trading	25,804
7	Samsung Electrics	South Korea	Electronics, electric equipment	23,810
8	Bank of China	China	Banks	22,478
9	Banco Do Brasil	Brazil	Banks	20,310
10	Samsung Life Insurance	South Korea	Insurance	20,269
11	Petrobras	Brazil	Petroleum	18,050
12	Sinochem	China	Trading	17,853
13	LG International	South Korea	Trading	16,359
14	LG Electronics	South Korea	Electronics, electric equipment	14,699
15	Telebras	Brazil	Telecommunications	14,666
16	Indian Oil	India	Petroleum	14,299
17	Korea Electric Power	South Korea	Utilities, gas and electric	14,064
18	Cofco	China	Trading	13,526
19	Banco Bradesco	Brazil	Banks	12,662
20	Hyundai Motor	South Korea	Motor vehicles	12,392
21	Pohang Iron & Steel	South Korea	Metals	12,090
22	Itausa-Investimentos Itau	Brazil	Banks	12,046
23	Jardine Matheson	China	Food and drug store	11,521
24	Petronas	Malaysia	Petroleum	10,995
25	Chinese Petroleum	Taiwan	Petroleum	10,729

Source: Adapted from *Fortune*, "The Fortune Global 500," August 3, 1998.

Appendix 2F   The top 100 economies, 1996

Rank	Country/Company	Millions of US $	Rank	Country/Company	Millions of US $
1	United States	7,433.5	11	Spain	563.2
2	Japan	5,149.2	12	South Korea	483.1
3	Germany	2,364.6	13	Netherlands	402.6
4	France	1,533.6	14	Australia	367.8
5	UK	1,152.1	15	India	357.8
6	Italy	1,140.5	16	Russian Federation	356.0
7	China	906.1	17	Mexico	341.7
8	Israel	903.0	18	Argentina	295.1
9	Brazil	709.6	19	Belgium	268.6
10	Canada	569.9	20	Sweden	227.3

continued overleaf

Appendix 2F (cont'd)

Rank	Country/Company	Millions of US $	Rank	Country/Company	Millions of US $
21	Austria	226.5	61	**Volkswagen**	**66.5**
22	Indonesia	213.4	62	**Daewoo**	**65.2**
23	Thailand	177.5	63	Egypt, Arab Republic	64.3
24	Turkey	177.5	**64**	**Siemens**	**63.7**
25	Denmark	168.9	65	Pakistan	63.6
26	**General Motors**	**168.4**	66	Ireland	62.0
27	Hong Kong, China	153.3	**67**	**Chrysler**	**61.4**
28	Norway	151.2	68	Ukraine	60.9
29	**Ford Motor**	**147.0**	**69**	**Nissan Motor**	**59.1**
30	**Mitsui**	**144.9**	70	Peru	58.7
31	**Mitsubishi**	**140.2**	71	New Zealand	57.1
32	**Itochu**	**135.5**	**72**	**Allianz**	**56.6**
33	South Africa	132.5	**73**	**US Postal Service**	**56.4**
34	Switzerland	131.7	**74**	**Philip Morris**	**54.6**
35	**Royal Dutch/Shell Group**	**128.2**	**75**	**Unilever**	**52.1**
36	Poland	124.7	**76**	**Fiat**	**50.5**
37	**Marubeni**	**124.0**	**77**	**Sony**	**50.3**
38	Greece	120.0	**78**	**Dai-Ichi Mutual Life Insurance**	**49.1**
39	**Exxon**	**119.4**	**79**	**IRI**	**49.1**
40	**Sumitomo**	**119.3**	**80**	**Nestlé**	**48.9**
41	Finland	119.1	81	Czech Republic	48.9
42	**Toyota Motor**	**108.7**	**82**	**Toshiba**	**48.4**
43	Portugal	100.9	**83**	**Honda Motor**	**47.0**
44	Singapore	93.0	**84**	**Elf Aquitaine**	**46.8**
45	Malaysia	89.8	**85**	**Tomen**	**46.5**
46	Philippines	83.3	**86**	**Bank of Tokyo-Mitsubishi**	**46.5**
47	Colombia	80.2	**87**	**Veba Group**	**45.2**
48	**General Electric**	**79.2**	**88**	**Tokyo Electric Power**	**44.7**
49	**Nissho Iwai**	**78.9**	**89**	**Texaco**	**44.6**
50	**Nippon Telegraph & Telephone**	**78.3**	90	Hungary	44.3
51	**Intl. Busines Machines**	**75.9**	**91**	**Sumitomo Life Insurance**	**44.1**
52	**Hitachi**	**75.7**	**92**	**Sunkyong**	**44.0**
53	**AT&T**	**74.5**	**93**	**NEC**	**43.9**
54	**Nippon Life Insurance**	**72.6**	94	Algeria	43.7
55	**Mobil**	**72.3**	**95**	**Electricite de France**	**43.7**
56	**Daimler-Benz**	**71.6**	**96**	**State Farm Insurances Cos.**	**42.8**
57	Chile	70.1	97	United Arab Emirates	42.7
58	**British Petroleum**	**69.9**	**98**	**Deutsche Telekom**	**41.9**
59	**Matsushita Electric Industrial**	**68.1**	**99**	**Philips Electronics**	**41.0**
60	Venezuela	67.3	**100**	**Union des Assurances de Paris**	**40.7**

Data for the countries is GNP (GDP for Hong Kong) and data for companies is measured by sales.
Source: Adapted from World Bank, *1998 World Development Indicators*, and *Fortune*, "The Global 500," August 4, 1997.

CHAPTER 3

The Triad and International Business

▼

OBJECTIVES OF THE CHAPTER

A small number of countries account for a large portion of international investment and international trade. These countries include the United States, the European Union (EU) and Japan, and are often referred to collectively as the **triad**. The objective of this chapter is to examine the role and impact of the triad nations on international business activity. We will examine trade and investment – especially the foreign direct investment (FDI) – conducted by members of the triad, looking at examples of how each member of the triad pursues target markets in other triad countries. We will also look at how current trade relationships have caused some politicians and businesspeople to call for greater protectionism. The specific objectives of this chapter are to:

1. **Describe** the major reasons for FDI.

2. **Discuss** the role of triad nations in worldwide FDI.

3. **Relate** select examples of inter-triad business activity.

4. **Explain** some of the reasons for protectionism concerns of triad members and how these concerns are being addressed.

Boeing vs. Airbus

In 1970 a European consortium consisting of Germany, France, and Great Britain (today Spain is also a member) created Airbus Industrie. The objective of the consortium was to build commercial aircraft. Airbus has achieved this objective with enormous success. By 1990 the company had back orders for 1,100 planes; by 1997 the number reached 2,300. In the process Airbus has captured over 30 per cent of the world market. The battle over the aircraft market took a turn in late 1996 when Boeing and McDonnell Douglas announced a merger creating a duopoly with Airbus.

The success of Airbus is crucial to the EU because over the last two decades a number of ventures have been designed to create a worldwide competitiveness industry in Europe, but none of them has done as well as Airbus – and the future looks promising. The consortium is planning to merge by the year 1999 into one independent corporation. This will allow Airbus greater flexibility on decision matters regarding the location of production and costs. The consortium's manufacturing arrangement put Airbus at a disadvantage against its competitors. It guaranteed every member country a part of the production. This made it impossible for management to choose the most cost-effective alternative. Additionally, the security of the relationship made suppliers less efficient. The new corporation will do without these structural problems.

Airbus's goal is to have 50 per cent of the market by the year 2002. Its operations are growing rapidly. In 1997 production increased by 32 per cent. One reason for this success has been new fuel-efficient aircraft. Airbus started out by producing two wide-body medium-range models, the A300 and A310. As commercial airlines began to realize that the Airbus planes were reliable and that the consortium would survive, orders started flowing in. What does the future hold? One possibility is the development of superjumbo planes that would carry up to 1,000 passengers, competing directly with Boeing's 747 in the over 400 passenger market. The Airbus project could force Boeing to spend billions of dollars in developmental costs rather than risk losing this lucrative market niche.

Another basis for success is the fact that the consortium is strongly oriented towards marketing. The group started out by making aggressively priced offers both to struggling carriers such as Braniff, Eastern, and Northwest, and to solid performers like American Airlines.

Airbus's impact is being felt in the US aircraft industry, which has been demanding that Congress take protective action. Boeing officials, for example, contend that they are competing not just against a company called Airbus, but against the French, German, British, and Spanish governments, which are subsidizing Airbus's operation.

The EU governments that are part of the consortium contend that the US aircraft manufacturers have also had a great deal of support from their government; much of the funding used to develop airplanes such as the C-5A cargo plane (the key research, development, and other forms of assistance needed to design large passenger aircraft) was provided by the military. Additionally, these governments argue that: (1) without such support, Europe could never have developed a competitive aircraft industry; (2) such support has declined in recent years; and (3) the aid is really more like a loan than a subsidy since Airbus pays a predetermined sum to the governments for each aircraft it sells. The Americans do not accept these explanations and argue that if the Airbus governments do not greatly limit subsidies, Washington will have to take action to protect the US commercial aircraft manufacturing industry. At present, discussions are continuing between the two groups.

Sources: Adapted from Steven Greenhouse, "There's No Stopping Europe's Airbus Now," *New York Times*, June 23, 1991, Section 3, pp. 1, 6; Agis Salpukas, "Northwest Cancels Jet Order," *New York Times*, December 8, 1992, p. C1; Dori Jones Yang and Andrea Rothman, "Reinventing Boeing," *Business Week*, March 1, 1993, pp. 60–67; Charles Goldsmith, "Airbus Partner Countries are Seeking Strict Enforcement of 1992 Subsidy Pact," *Wall Street Journal*, June 17, 1997, p. B9A; Charles Goldsmith, "After Trailing Boeing for Years, Airbus Aims for 50% of the Market," *Wall Street Journal*, March 16, 1998, pp. A1, 8; Frederic M. Biddle and John Helyar, "Behind Boeing's Woes: Clunky Assembly Line, Price War with Airbus," *Wall Street Journal*, April 24, 1998, pp. A1, 16.

1. What are three reasons for the Europeans creating the Airbus consortium?
2. How will Airbus help the EU compete in the United States?
3. How will Airbus help the EU compete in Japan?
4. In what way does the Airbus consortium use a "keiretsu" approach to building the aircraft? Why do you think it opted for this approach?

INTRODUCTION

During the 1990s international business activity increased dramatically, especially among the triad nations (the United States, Japan, and the EU). In fact, the most active countries in the international arena remained basically the same throughout the 1980s and 1990s: the United States, Japan, and major EU members, including Germany, France, the Netherlands, and Great Britain. During the upcoming decades it is likely that Canada and Mexico; non-EC countries in Europe; and a number of Pacific Rim nations, such as Hong Kong, Singapore, South Korea, and China, will become more economically involved with the triad leaders. In the meantime, however, a small number of countries will continue to account for most of the world's international business activity. For this reason, every student of international business should be familiar with the triad and its impact on both FDI and trade.

It is also important to realize that triad members would like to protect their current position and, if possible, enhance it by increasing their FDI and trade. In particular, international competitiveness is often measured by export dominance and there is national pressure to keep exports growing. Such growth can often be achieved only at the expense of other countries, which are inclined to retaliate or demand some form of economic reciprocity. This reaction can vary from the protectionism of quotas or embargoes to degrees of managed trade, in which exports to a particular country are offset by imports from that nation; that is, Japan will have to buy more goods from the United States in order to eliminate or drastically reduce annual trade imbalances. While these approaches fly in the face of free-trade ideals, they represent political and economic reality and will continue to be widely used in the international arena of the coming decade. Before we examine data on the nature of triad activity, it will be helpful to define and review the concept of FDI since FDI is becoming as important as trade in the conduct of international business operations.

REASONS FOR FOREIGN DIRECT INVESTMENT

Foreign direct investment (FDI) is the ownership and control of foreign assets. In practice, FDI usually involves the ownership, whole or partial, of a company in a foreign country. This equity investment can take a variety of forms, from the purchase of an established firm to setting up a new overseas operation as either a joint venture or a totally owned enterprise. FDI is different from **portfolio investment**, which entails the purchase of financial securities (especially bonds) in other firms for the purpose of realizing a financial gain when these marketable assets are sold.[1] In short, the objective

Table 3.1 US firms with the largest foreign revenues, 1996

Rank	Firm	Foreign revenues (in millions of US $)	Foreign sales as % of total sales
1	Exxon	96.9	79.6
2	Mobil	48.4	65.9
3	General Motors	47.8	29.2
4	IBM	45.1	62.7
5	Ford Motor	41.9	30.6
6	Philip Morris	27.7	41.9
7	Du Pont	20.6	48.8
8	Texaco	18.2	51.1
9	Hewlett-Packard	17.6	55.9
10	General Electric	17.1	24.4
11	Motorola	17.0	63.0
12	Procter & Gamble	16.8	50.3
13	Coca-Cola	12.7	70.6
14	Chevron	11.9	32.8
15	Dow Chemical	11.2	55.4
16	United Techologies	10.3	45.2
17	Johnson & Johnson	9.7	51.6
18	Xerox	9.2	55.4
19	AT&T	8.7	16.9
20	PepsiCo	8.7	28.6

Source: Adapted from the "Top 100 TNCs Ranked by Foreign Assets," of the United Nations, *World Investment Report 1997* (New York: United Nations, 1997).

of FDI is active participation in and control of a foreign firm's activities, while the objective of portfolio investment is growth in the value of financial holdings.[2]

There are a number of reasons for FDI. In Chapter 2 we noted several motives for FDI and that a multinational enterprise (MNE) needs to acquire a firm-specific advantage. In this section we examine some of the most important ways in which FDI can provide firm-specific advantages.

Increase profits and sales

When a company develops and markets a new product, it initially promotes the product in a local market. Eventually the company's focus will turn to the export opportunities. These new markets often help to sustain sales growth while generating increased profits.

In fact, global markets frequently offer more lucrative opportunities than do domestic markets. This helps to explain why Mitsubishi,[3] BMW, and Mercedes[4] are now pushing hard to increase their share of the profitable US automobile market, while Ford, General Motors, and Chrysler are striking hard in Europe. Similarly, Coca-Cola is earning more sales revenue and profits overseas than in the United States,[5] and PepsiCo has become Mexico's largest consumer products company.[6] Table 3.1

Table 3.2   Leading foreign direct investment in Eastern Europe, 1990–97

Investor	Host country	Industry	Amount (in millions of US $)
Fiat (Italy)	Poland	Automotive	1,841
Telesource (Netherlands)	Czech Rep.	Telecommunications	1,400
Daewoo (South Korea)	Poland	Automotive	1,100
Ameritech (USA) and Deutche Budespost Telecom (Germany)	Hungary	Telecommunications	875
PepsiCo (USA)	Poland	Beverages	792
Asea Brown Bovery (Switzerland)	Poland	Manufacturing	540
General Motors (USA)	Hungary	Automotive	500
VW/Audi (Germany)	Hungary	Automotive	420
ING (Netherlands)	Poland	Banking	403
International Paper (USA)	Poland	Paper	370
US West International (USA)	Hungary	Cellular phones	330
Daewoo Automobile (South Korea)	Romania	Automotive	156
Shell (Netherlands)	Romania	Petroleum	91
Boeing (USA)	Czech Rep.	Aircraft	32

Note: Investment amounts are the sum of realized and committed investment.

Sources: Hungary, Investment and Trade Development Agency; *http://homepage.interaccess.com/~comconpl/top20int.htm*; *http://www.czech.cz/washington/newslet/c11-0697.html*; *http://www.washtimes.com/internatlads/romania/8.html*.

shows the US firms with the largest foreign revenues in 1996. A close look at the table shows that a very high percentage of the income and profits of these firms comes from foreign sales. Obviously, FDI is paying off handsomely for many US companies.[7]

Enter rapidly growing markets

Some international markets are growing much faster than others, and FDI provides MNEs with the chance to take advantage of these opportunities. For example, the laptop computer market in Japan in the early 1990s was booming;[8] more than 40 per cent of all personal computers sold there were laptops. As a result, IBM introduced its new laptop in Japan.

Many MNEs also use FDI to gain footholds in emerging markets such as Eastern Europe, where a large number of companies are acquiring firms or setting up joint ventures (see Table 3.2),[9] and Australia,[10] which is gaining greater international prominence. Another region that continues to attract attention is Russia, which is actively encouraging foreign investment. Japanese FDI in China and in the countries of Southeast Asia is growing rapidly and is now well ahead of US FDI in the Pacific.

Reduce costs

An MNE can sometimes achieve substantially lower costs by going abroad than by producing at home (see the box "International Business Strategy in Action: Japanese FDI in Scotland"'). If labor expenses are high and represent a significant portion of overall costs, an MNE may be well advised to look to other geographic areas

INTERNATIONAL BUSINESS STRATEGY IN ACTION

Japanese FDI in Scotland

American computer MNEs, such as IBM, Honeywell, and NCR, have been active in Scotland since the 1950s. The MNEs were attracted to Scotland because of the availability of low-cost skilled labor and the government's incentives to attract FDI. By the 1990s, Scotland produced one-third of all branded personal computers (PCs) sold in Europe, which represents about 7 per cent of world output. It also accounts for 12 per cent of European production of semiconductors. The foreign-owned electronics sector is quite important in Scotland since it accounts for one-third of all jobs in foreign-owned companies in Scotland. While some EU MNEs have settled in Scotland, the sector is dominated by US and Japanese firms that chose Scotland as an entry port into the EU.

The electronic sector is divided into five sub-sectors: information systems (processing systems, peripherals, support products); semiconductors; telecommunication electronics; consumer electronics (TVs and VCRs); and software and others. Today IBM is the only one of the three information systems producers to remain active in the region. However, ten other information systems manufacturing companies have settled in Scotland. These companies, which together employ over 6,500 people, include: Compaq (US), Digital (US), Sun Microsystems (US), OKI Electric (Japan), AT&T (US), Apricot (Japan – owned by Mitsubishi Electric), Elonex (UK), Tandem (US), Exabyte (US), and Escom (Germany). Furthermore, two US MNEs, Motorola and Hewlett-Packard, have major telecommunication electronics facilities in Scotland. Together they employ over 3,000 people and completely dominate the telecommunications electronics sub-sector.

While the production of information systems and telecommunications is heavily dominated by US companies, the production of semiconductors, which today accounts for more than 5,000 jobs in Scotland, is more highly influenced by Japanese MNEs. US MNEs such as Motorola and National Semiconductor established silicon production in Scotland in the 1960s and were followed by Digital and Hughes. Subsequently, Japanese MNEs such as NEC and Fuji Electric chose

Scotland as their first European manufacturing location. The initial NEC Scottish facility for the assembly and testing of semiconductor components was upgraded to house the first Japanese wafer fabrication in Europe. There has been a program of continuous investment by NEC to remain competitive in semiconductor manufacturing technology. Fuji Electric started the production of power transistor modules for use in control systems in 1991, the company's first European location. For both NEC and Fuji Electric, it is clear that Scotland provides a low-cost production platform for entry into the EU market.

The Japanese also dominate the consumer electronics sub-sector. MNEs such as Mitsubishi Electronic and Matsushita Panasonic produce color television sets in central Scotland, attracted by the relatively low labor costs, government assistance, and access to the European market. Mitsubishi first located in Scotland in 1979 and now has two plants employing 1,200 people in manufacturing TVs and VCRs. Production of television sets includes 37-inch sets, the largest models in the world. The video cassette recorder plant is Mitsubishi's principal manufacturing facility for sales outside Japan. Matsushita Panasonic opened in 1993 and manufactures flyback transformers for use in television and computer monitors.

The challenges that face the Scottish electronics sector are many. In spite of the continued growth of the sector since the 1950s, the electronics sector failed to develop the higher value-added end of the industry and it now faces a serious competitive threat from lower-cost producers in Southeast Asia, such as Taiwan and Singapore. The sector also failed to develop key supplier linkages or university research infrastructure. The Scottish electronics sector is seeking to transform itself to become more competitive. The creation of the Scottish Electronics Forum may help to foster better linkages with nonbusiness infrastructure. Furthermore, the Alba Centre, a collaborative project between the electronics industry, the public sector and academia, is expected to increase the autonomy of the Scottish industry, while creating key domestic linkages. The centre is expected to be ready by mid-1999 and will include an independent trading house for semiconductor design and an academic centre.

Scotland has key advantages for the industry to develop, one of which is an already existing infra-structure, labor, and access to the EU market. It is in the success of the new steps the Scottish electronics industry is taking that the chance of becoming truly competitive in the world electronics market really lies.

Sources: Alan M. Rugman, "The Five Partners/Flagship Model and the Scottish Electronics Cluster", in Jean-Louis Mucchielli (ed.), *Research in Global Strategic Management*, vol. 6, 1998 (Greenwich, Conn: JAI Press), pp. 165–181; *http://www.hotecho.org/archive/se20/features/electronics.html*; *http://www.hotecho.org/news/news.html*.

where the goods can be produced at a much lower labor price. In recent years some Canadian manufacturers have been moving operations across the border to take advantage of lower US labor unit costs.[11]

A second important cost factor is materials. If materials are in short supply or must be conveyed a long distance, it may be less expensive to move production close to the source of supply than to import the materials.

A third critical cost factor is energy. If the domestic cost of energy for making the product is high, the company may be forced to set up operations overseas near sources of cheaper energy.

A fourth important factor is transportation costs. Japanese steel firms are no longer able to produce and deliver steel at prices lower than those of US manufacturers. US steelmakers have improved their efficiency to the point where the cost of shipping steel from Japan brings the overall price above that of the domestically manufactured product.

In recent years many US firms have used all four of these reasons to justify moving assembly operations to other countries. Wage rates are much lower in Mexico than in the United States, Korea, Hong Kong, Taiwan, or Singapore, so Mexico has become a prime target for the manufacture of labor-intensive products. In fact, some US firms have even set up **twin factories**, or **maquiladoras**, which involve production operations on both sides of the border and the shipment of goods between the two countries. US components are shipped into Mexico duty-free, assembled by Mexican workers, and reexported to the United States or other foreign markets under favorable tariff provisions. (We discuss this arrangement further in Part Four). A similar approach is used under the Caribbean Basin Initiative: the US apparel industry sends precut pieces to Haiti and other countries in the region for assembly and return of finished goods to the United States.

Consolidate economic blocs

In the 1990s we saw the consolidation of powerful economic blocs. The United States–Canada Free Trade Agreement of 1989 started to fashion a giant North American market. In January 1994 this agreement was expanded into the North American Free Trade Agreement (NAFTA) to include Mexico, which added to the economic strength of this market. Furthermore, NAFTA member countries have been considering the integration of Chile and other Latin American nations into the economic bloc.[12] The EU's agreement with the European Free Trade Association (EFTA) is creating a major economic force in western Europe, called the European Economic Area (EEA).

Additionally, since the end of the Soviet bloc, many Eastern European countries have applied to enter the EU. We have already noted that Japan is increasing its trade and investment in the Asia Pacific Region, also helping to create a growing economic bloc there.

For a variety of reasons, companies are in a better position to do business with trade bloc countries in which they have a presence. As noted in Chapter 2, one important reason is that businesses located in countries outside an economic union are subject to various tariffs.

Protect domestic markets

Many companies will enter an international market to help weaken potential competitive moves against their domestic business; they reason that a potential competitor is less likely to enter a foreign market when it is busy defending its home market position. Conversely, a company may choose to enter a foreign market in order to bring pressure on a company that has already challenged its own home market. For example, 10 days after Fuji began building its first manufacturing facility in the United States, Kodak announced its decision to open a manufacturing plant in Japan.

Sometimes the decision to go international helps a firm to protect its position with current clients who are going international. For example, when Honda Motors set up operations in Indiana, Nippodenso, a producer of automobile radiators and heaters, established a plant nearby. So did Mitsubishi Bank, the primary bank for Honda. In addition to the extra business it generates, this strategy helps to combat local competitors, such as Indiana manufacturers and banks, who might otherwise gain inroads and perhaps even threaten domestic business should they decide to set up in Japan.

Protect foreign markets

Sometimes MNEs will increase their FDI in order to protect foreign markets. For example, in the 1990s British Petroleum (BP) invested heavily in its US operations. From 1981 to 1991 the total number of service stations in the country had declined by over 50 per cent, and BP realized the need to upgrade its stations in order to increase market share. Since BP refines and markets petroleum products, this strategy also helps the firm to move its goods downstream to the final consumer. In 1998, BP merged with Amoco to form BP Amoco, with sales of $5.5 billion. Similarly, many international manufacturers are moving operations to the United States because US manufacturing productivity now matches that of most world competitors and because these MNEs can best protect their US market with on-site facilities.[13]

Acquire technological and managerial know-how

In addition to conducting research and development (R&D) at home, another way of obtaining technological and managerial information is to set up operations near those of leading competitors. This is why some US firms have moved R&D facilities to Japan. They find it is easier to monitor the competition and to recruit scientists from local universities and competitive laboratories. Kodak is an excellent example.

In 1987 the company began building a 180,000-square-foot research center and started cultivating leading scientists to help with recruiting. Kodak used all the same approaches that Japanese firms employ in the United States: financing research by university scientists and offering scholarships to outstanding young Japanese engineers, some of whom will later join Kodak. In addition, the company hired internationally known scientists to help attract experienced colleagues from leading Japanese companies and to recruit young graduates from the host universities such as the Tokyo Institute of Technology. As a result, Japan is now the center of Kodak's worldwide research efforts in a number of high-technology areas.[14]

ACTIVE LEARNING CHECK

Review your answer to Active Learning Case question 1 and make any changes you like. Then compare your answer to the one below.

1. What are three reasons for the Europeans creating the Airbus consortium?

One of the reasons for the Europeans creating the Airbus consortium was to enter a rapidly growing market. As can be seen from the data in the case, hundreds of billions of dollars will be spent on aircraft between now and the year 2010. A second reason is to help build a stronger EU economy. The Airbus industry will provide thousands of jobs and billions of dollars to the member countries. A third reason is to protect the domestic market by making it less reliant on foreign competitors such as Boeing.

FOREIGN DIRECT INVESTMENT BY TRIAD MEMBERS

Of all foreign direct investment made annually, more than 80 per cent occurs among triad members: the United States, the European Union, and Japan.

The triad's domination of FDI

Over the past decade the triad has accounted for an extremely large percentage of both FDI *and* world trade. For example, as seen in Table 3.3, triad countries make billions of dollars of investments in one another. The data in this figure reveal that in 1995 total US FDI was $315.4 billion in the EU and $39.1 billion in Japan.[15] In turn the EU countries and Japan had total investments in the United States of $317.4 billion and $194.4 billion, respectively. There is also a large amount of FDI among the members of the EU. Moreover, as seen in Table 3.4, the percentage of global

Table 3.3   FDI in the triad, 1995, $bn.

Outward/inward	EU	US	Japan
EU	—	317.4	7.7
US	315.4	—	39.1
Japan	84.3	194.4	—

Note: Data for Japan are 1994, 1995 data are not available.

Source: Organisation of Economic Co-operation and Development, *International Direct Investment Statistics, 1997* (Paris: OECD, 1997).

Table 3.4 Ten years of triad FDI

Country/region	1985 FDI stock (in billions of US $)	1985 % of world	1994 FDI stock (in billions of US $)	1994 % of world
United States	251.0	36.4	610.1	25.7
EU*	286.4	41.5	1,074.1	45.2
Japan	44.3	6.4	277.7	11.7
Triad	581.7	84.3	1,961.9	82.5
All others	108.7	15.7	416.1	17.5
World	690.4	100.0	2,378.0	100.0

* EU numbers are outward stocks of FDI by every EU member. Thus intra-EU FDI stock is included.
Source: Adapted from United Nations, World Investment Report 1997 (New York: United Nations, 1997).

Table 3.5 Trade in the triad, 1995, $bn.

Outward/inward	EU	US	Japan
EU	—	127.2	49.5
US	123.6	—	64.2
Japan	70.4	122	—

Source: International Monetary Fund, Direction of Trade Statistics Yearbook, 1996 (Washington DC: IMF, 1996).

FDI accounted for by triad countries during the last decade remained approximately the same at over 80 per cent, even though the amount of worldwide FDI more than tripled in that decade.

This dominance by the triad is also seen in the amount of trade done by triad members. Table 3.5 shows much the same picture for trade patterns in the triad as we saw for FDI; there are very strong two-way trade flows in the triad. Also note that there is a huge amount of trade within the EU. Table 3.6 reports the trade of the triad and shows that it accounted for about 57 per cent of world trade imports and exports in 1996. As a result of such trade (and FDI), it is clear that the triad is the major economic force in the international arena.

Triad FDI clusters

The triad's impact on international business extends well beyond the FDI and trade that takes place among its members. In recent years triad members have also become major investors in poorer countries. The United Nations Centre on Transnational Corporations (UNCTC) reports that triad members accounted for over 40 per cent of the FDI in 25 of the 37 developing countries being studied.[16] Typically, recipients of FDI are part of an **FDI cluster**, which is a group of developing countries that are usually located in the same geographic region as the triad member and having some form of economic link to it. For example, the United States tends to be a dominant investor in Latin America, Eastern Europe is a favorite investment target for EU countries,[17] and Japan has major investments in the Pacific Rim.[18]

Table 3.6   Ten years of triad trade

	Exports to				Imports from			
Country/region	1987 (billions of US $)	% of total	1996 (billions of US $)	% of total	1987 (billions of US $)	% of total	1996 (billions of US $)	% of total
United States	252.9	10.5	679.5	12.7	424.1	17.1	791.2	15.0
EU*	1,049.1	43.7	1,926.6	36.0	1,049.6	42.3	1,882.1	35.6
Japan	231.3	9.6	456.9	8.5	150.9	6.1	317.6	6.0
Triad	1,533.3	63.9	3,063.0	57.3	1,624.6	65.5	2,990.8	56.5
All others	867.2	36.1	2,284.7	42.7	854.9	34.5	2,299.9	43.5
Total	2,400.5	100.0	5,347.7	100.0	2,479.5	100.0	5,290.7	100.0

* EU numbers are for exports and imports of every member to the rest of the world. Thus, EU exports and imports include intra-EU figures. Triad: United States, EU and Japan.

Sources: IMF, *Direction of Trade Statistics Report*, 1994; IMF, *Direction of Trade Statistics*, Quarterly, June 1997.

Not all developing countries have been successful in attracting triad investment. Much of this money has been used by multinationals to build regional networks, often starting near their home base and then working outward. The UNCTC found that 61 per cent of all FDI in Mexico comes from US firms and 52 per cent of FDI in South Korea is generated by Japanese firms. At present the UNCTC found that more than half of all investment into developing countries is going to five nations: Brazil, China, Hong Kong, Mexico, and Singapore.

Such investment policies appear to help reinforce the triad's dominance of regional economic clusters. In the future, triad members may well continue to strengthen their FDI in specific regions, as in Europe, where the EFTA and EU joined together to form the EEA. This will restrict trade and investment opportunities for some developing countries.

THE TRIAD AND INTERNATIONAL BUSINESS STRATEGY

During the upcoming decade the triad will continue to dominate the international business scene. In particular, members will pursue market opportunities in other areas of the triad. The following discussion provides some examples.

Triad activity in the United States

Automobiles and electronic equipment are two important areas of the US market that have been the target of EU and Japanese activity.

Automobiles in the United States   The American auto market for cars and light trucks, in recent years, has been in the range of 15 million units, a number which is down substantially from the 18 million car market of the mid–late 1980s. Competing in this market are General Motors, Ford, Chrysler and Daimler-Benz, other European car makers including BMW, Saab, Volvo, and Audi, and Asian manufacturers including Honda, Toyota, and Nissan.[19]

In the case of EU-based auto firms, these companies have been selling cars in the US market for decades and the future promises to see a strong continuation of this trend. For example, over the last decade German automakers have started again gaining US market share and more than holding their own against Japanese competition. In particular, BMW, Audi, Mercedes, Porsche, and Volkswagen all saw turnarounds in sales beginning by the mid-1990s. One of the primary reasons accounting for this success was that German producers began building cars that appealed to American buyers. This was in sharp contrast to their earlier strategy where they offered products that were attractive to Europeans, who were far more interested in engineering quality and road handling than were American customers. Now German cars, especially for the luxury market, are sportier and more nimble than their predecessors. They also offer conveniences that US buyers look for in their cars including such mundane things as coffee cup holders. Commenting on this fact, a BMW board member noted that in the past German car makers had traditional disdain for such "petty" offerings and as a result found that US buyers responded "by buying the other guys' cars." Now the Mercedes M-Class model being built in Alabama offers no fewer than five cup holders.[20]

European car makers have also found that their Japanese competitors were able to undercut them in two key areas – quality image and price. Many American customers felt that cars such as the Lexus and Infiniti were better products than not just local offerings such as Cadillacs and Lincolns, but BMWs and Mercedes as well. In particular, the Japanese offerings had few quality problems and their prices were more competitive.

Faced with these challenges, the European car manufacturers made a series of strategic decisions that have tilted the playing field more in their favor. First, they began setting up production facilities in the US and thus reduced the cost of manufacturing their cars. At the same time they found that, like buyers worldwide, Americans prefer to purchase locally made products rather than imports. This is clearly seen in the case of the BMW 7-series where US demand from the early to the late 1990s tripled, while sales of its other models doubled. Second, the German automakers sharply cut the time to market. So when one of their cars became very popular, they could quickly meet the demand. Third, they began catering more to US buyers. For example, while European luxury cars are built to be "driving machines," most Americans do not buy these cars because of their superior handling. Rather they are looking for cars that are reliable and comfortable. Fourth, the German car makers kept stressing technical innovation and quality workmanship, two factors that many Americans found attractive when conducting comparison shopping with other luxury cars.

Not all European automakers have been highly successful in the US market. Volvo and Saab are examples. Both have found that while their worldwide auto sales increased beginning in the mid-1990s, their performance in the American market was stagnant and their market shares were lower than a decade previously. One reason is because they were slow to add options such as electric windows and other conveniences that are valued in the US market. A second reason is that the two automakers have had trouble producing cars efficiently. Their costs are sharply higher than those of other luxury car makers and, as a result, their selling prices tend to limit market demand. A third problem has been their market niche which is dominated by firms such as BMW, Mercedes, and Lexus, so they are having difficulty maintaining market share. A fourth problem is their limited model offerings. Finally, there is the problem of how to change these cars without losing their image in the marketplace. For example, Volvo has now begun offering sportier models and industry analysts wonder if this strategy is the correct one for a market niche that typically is interested in a family sedan that offers safety and reliability. Similarly, one of the more recent Saab offerings arrived in the US with a hatchback instead of a trunk, a style associated in the American market with inexpensive economy cars. Nevertheless, it appears that during the next decade both Volvo and Saab are going to be adopting more international designs and trying to establish themselves as key players in the American premium-car market. Whether this will work or their previous image as manufacturers of family automobiles will prove their undoing is yet to be determined.[21]

The Japanese are also competing very vigorously in the US market. In fact, in recent years Toyota and Honda have both expanded their presence despite the fact that this market is now moving into the maturity phase and it is becoming increasingly more difficult to gain and hold market share. In particular, the two automakers have increased their output capacity and are planning additional major expansions. Collectively, they are able to produce approximately 2.5 million cars in the US, giving them a very strong local presence. Additionally, as the demand for their autos has increased in recent years, they have been able to respond more quickly to the market and ensure adequate dealer inventories. Toyota and Honda have also been focusing attention on the light truck market. Importing these units from Japan has meant paying a 25 per cent tariff, but producing them locally gives the manufacturers a strong competitive position.

In addition, Japanese car makers have found that the downturn in the Asian economy has produced some benefits for their import operations. For example, as the yen continued to slide against the dollar and fell from 110 to 140, the cost of imports declined, making it more economically feasible to export additional cars to the American market. One of the reasons why the Japanese had begun setting up operations in North America was to deal with the strong yen of the early 1990s which threatened to sharply reduce its ability to sell high-ticket items in competitive worldwide markets. Now that this threat has subsided, Japanese activity in the US auto market is coming from both overseas as well as domestic production.[22]

Electronics and the US market   EU and Japanese firms also do well in many areas of the US electronics industry. For example, Braun (a German firm, now owned by Gillette) is well known for its electric shavers and coffee makers, and Sony of Japan owns a significant share of the US television market. However, the electronics field changes very quickly, so the future will see vigorous competition for new markets in the United States during the next decade.

One area of strong competition is telecommunications equipment, in which lesser-known companies are doing quite well. For example, while AT&T is the best-known manufacturer of telephone equipment, Alcatel Alsthom, a French firm, is one of the world's largest, and the company is making strong inroads into the United States. The company has purchased Rockwell International Corporation's telephone transmission equipment business and is focusing very intently on the industrial market. The company's telecommunications division is now the leader in worldwide sales. Alcatel also supplies satellite equipment, competing directly with General Motors' Hughes Space and Communications Group. The company also has a line of broadband switches that enable phone companies to carry and route vast amounts of voice, video, and computer data.[23]

An even hotter battle is likely to be waged between US and Japanese competitors for the home entertainment electronics business in the United States. In 1961 Ampex, a US firm, invented the videotape recorder for industrial use. Japanese manufacturers figured out how to reduce Ampex's $20,000 price to $250 and mass market the product for home use. The Japanese now dominate the US home entertainment equipment market. However, new developments are occurring that could make the US home entertainment market a major battleground for triad competitors and force the current market leaders to completely revamp many of their product offerings.

Specifically, two major products are converging: the home computer and the television. The result will be a single unit computer with a high-quality display screen. Inside the box there will be digital instructions for receiving all sorts of signals from broadcasting and media firms. This development will revolutionize the present home entertainment industry and create a worldwide electronics market worth hundreds of billions of dollars.

A number of Japanese computer companies such as Sony, Fujitsu, and Matsushita are very strong in consumer electronics. However, today's television sets, VCRs, cassette tapes, and laser-disc movies use analog technology, which directly mimics the sound and image that are being copied. New developments in digital technology allow information to be stored, compressed, corrected, edited, and manipulated. The Americans currently lead in digital technology. If US companies can apply this technology to home entertainment ahead of the competition, they will make profitable inroads for such products as high-definition, interactive television sets, telecomputers, and graphic work stations.

ACTIVE LEARNING CHECK

Review your answer to Active Learning Case question 2 and make any changes you like. Then compare your answer to the one below.

2. How will Airbus help the EU to compete in the United States?

Airbus will open up markets in the United States by offering alternative aircraft to those being produced by Boeing. These Airbus offerings are not only reliable but fuel efficient and, as noted in the case, are often provided at very competitive prices. As a result, Airbus has been able to tap a US market that had been closed to the EU because no European company could compete effectively with US firms.

Triad activity in the EU

US FDI is greater in the EU than in any other area of the world (see Table 3.3). The EU is also a favorite target of the Japanese. Two of the major industries where triad competition in the EU is particularly strong are automobiles and computers.[24]

Automobiles in the EU   Triad competition in the EU auto industry is different from that in the United States. US firms such as General Motors and Ford are well established in Europe. In fact, they have been the fourth and fifth largest auto firms, respectively, in the EU market in recent years, with Volkswagen, Fiat, and Peugeot leading the pack.[25] In contrast, the Japanese share of the European market has been quite small.

Another characteristic of the EU auto market is the wide use of strategic alliances with other European manufacturers, as well as among all the triad members.[26] For example, Renault and Volvo have an agreement to jointly make and exchange parts to be used in autos and commercial vehicles. Volvo sells its 1.4-liter-engine series to

Renault, and Renault supplies Volvo with engines and transmission components for its new models. Meanwhile, Ford and Volkswagen have an agreement to manufacture minivans in Portugal; Toyota and VW have a joint agreement to make light commercial vehicles for sale on the continent; GM Europe is operating a joint-venture assembly plant with Isuzu; and Ford and Nissan have a deal to assemble and distribute four-wheel-drive all-terrain vehicles throughout the bloc.

Another recent development has been the acquisition or merging of firms. For example, Volkswagen has bought Rolls-Royce and VW's Audi unit has acquired Lamborghini.[27] Meanwhile, Daimler-Benz has merged with Chrysler to form a company that is now almost as large as Ford Motor and promises to make the collective firm much more competitive in the worldwide market.

Triad members are also building or expanding their production facilities.[28] Volkswagen is implementing a multi-billion-dollar investment strategy that involves setting up new operations in Eastern Europe. General Motors has bought Lotus, and Ford Motor has acquired Jaguar.[29] In addition, both GM and Ford are spending billions of dollars on upgrading and expanding operations throughout the EU.[30] At the same time Japanese auto producers such as Daihatsu, Honda, Isuzu, Mitsubishi, Nissan, and Toyota are all increasing their vehicle production in Europe.[31] The result is that there now is more automaking capacity in Western Europe than in either Japan or the United States. This expansion is likely to bring increased competition and to put strong pressure on the EU automakers, some of which are not able to compete with their triad counterparts in terms of quality and price.

The strongest triad competition comes from American automakers. Ford has been revamping its worldwide strategy and focusing more and more on increased profitability. As a result, the old days of producing marginally profitable cars in order to maintain market share are coming to a close. Now the firm is concentrating on increased production efficiency such as assembling cars worldwide with identical parts. The company has also been stretching its investment dollar by becoming a leader in what is called platform engineering. Designing and tooling a basic set of automotive components such as suspensions, floor pans, and struts can cost $400 million or more. In Europe Ford has managed to pull six different models, ranging from a two-door minicar to a small pickup truck, from one small-car platform.[32] The firm has also installed computer work stations throughout the company. As a result, now that engineers are all wired to the same network, the company is able to integrate engineering, manufacturing, and testing into one system. These developments are designed to prevent the company's European market share from further erosion, while simultaneously increasing the firm's profitability.

General Motors is also pushing very hard in the EU marketplace. A good example is the firm's competitive offerings in the small car market. Volkswagen dominates this area with its Golf, the top-selling line which accounts for almost one-third of its sales in Europe. GM is hoping that its Astra, which has consistently run second to the Golf, will help it gain market share. At the same time, Renault is working to mount a competitive challenge in this market.

The Japanese, meanwhile, have fallen on hard times in Europe. During the early 1990s there was concern that when restrictive import quotas were removed the Japanese would increase their market share sharply. By 1993, for example, they held over 12 per cent of the EU market. However, in the next five years this share dropped below 11 per cent and many European automakers felt that the Japanese were going to have a hard time rebuildingx share because many buyers found these cars to be bland and uninteresting.[33] Another reason why European automakers appeared unconcerned was that they have sharply increased both the quality and the productivity of their offerings. During the 1980s they had a myriad of operational problems. However, as they increased their efficiency, they were able to cut costs and become more price competitive with the Japanese. At the same time, they continued to focus on an area where they have always been leading edge – auto design. By now producing stylish and sporty cars that appeal to European buyers, they have found that these cars maintain their resale price, in contrast to many Japanese models which do not. In fact, the strategy used by Japanese luxury car makers has not proven effective in Europe. Many buyers feel that models such as the Lexus and the Infiniti are poor imitations of a Mercedes or other high-quality European offering.

In response to this increased competitiveness, the Japanese are fighting back. They have begun shifting more manufacturing to Europe and tailoring new cars to match local tastes. In particular, they are pumping more and more money into research and development and spiffing up their current offerings. For example, Toyota engineers have introduced a Corolla with over head- and tail lights, and they have given the car sturdier brakes and a stiffer suspension than the previous model. At the same time the Japanese are beefing up their dealer networks.[34] If these efforts are successful, the EU car market is going to get even more competitive over the next decade. In 1998, Daimler-Benz of Germany merged with Chrysler, with joint sales of $130 billion. The new firm, Daimler Chrysler, has joint-CEOs and co-headquarters, and is the fifth largest car maker in the world, behind GM, Ford, Toyota and Volkswagen.

Computers in the EU   Triad competition in the EU computer market is also different from that in the United States. The EU computer market is characterized by market fragmentation that has created many small markets. As a result, computer products that sell well in one country often have a difficult time establishing strong market position in another. One reason for this is a result of preferential treatment given to local firms. In particular, many governments support their own national champions, which they feel merit both formal and informal assistance.[35] As a result, Groupe Bull does quite well in France, Olivetti is the market leader in Italy, and Siemens dominates the German market.

The strongest competition in the EU comes from those US firms that have a long-standing presence in Europe and, in many cases, are regarded as European firms by the local populace. IBM is the best example. The company has a dozen factories throughout Europe and earns a substantial portion of its profits from this market. Digital Equipment is another well-entrenched competitor, and its recent acquisition of Philips' computer business puts the company in a position to offer strong competition to IBM.[36]

Japanese computer firms are relatively weak in Europe,[37] primarily because of the difficulty of breaking into local markets. Some firms have attempted to circumvent this problem through acquisitions. For example, by acquiring Britain's International Computers, Ltd., Fujitsu has become the second largest computer firm in Britain. Overall, however, Japanese firms have had slow growth in the EU. Most of their efforts have been in the mainframe computer sector, which is growing only slowly, and in peripheral markets such as matrix printers, diskette drives, and optical storage.

During the millennium the EU market is likely to expand rapidly, and computers, especially micros, are going to gain market share. As this happens the Americans and Japanese are likely to offer greater competition to their European rivals.

Aflac

The insurance industry is dominated by many well-known names: Prudential, Aetna, Northwestern, etc. Few people have ever heard of Aflac Inc. of Columbus, Georgia. However, the company is the most successful in Japan, with annual revenues in excess of $5 billion and profits well over $500 million in 1996. Aflac is the world's leading seller of cancer insurance, which helps to pay the cost of treating the disease, and it holds 90 per cent of the Japanese market for this coverage. The Japanese subsidiary accounts for over 70 per cent of Aflac's pretax earnings.

The firm began doing business in Japan in 1974. Initially Aflac approached big Japanese insurers as potential joint-venture partners; none of them was interested. Eventually the Ministry of Finance gave the company a licence to sell insurance, primarily because no Japanese insurer was in the business so that there would be no competition for local firms.

A key to Aflac's rapid growth and profitability is its system of selling through corporate agencies. The firm has set up in-house subsidiaries in Japanese corporations to handle the sale of its insurance. These subsidiaries would be illegal distributors in the United States, but they are very common in Japan. As a result, Aflac eventually ended up with over 40,000 Japanese companies offering its policies to their employees.

From Hitachi to Sony, Toyota to Nissan; and Mitsui to Mitsubishi, policyholders throughout the country pay premiums of approximately $21 a month through an automatic payroll deduction plan. Moreover, once they are signed up, few Japanese drop out. In contrast to the United States where only 25 per cent of health and accident insurance policyholders remain with the same company for a decade or more, in Japan 75 per cent of Aflac policyholders have been with them for ten or more years.

Will Aflac be able to continue its success in the market? In many countries such as the United States, cancer insurance is declining in popularity because coverage is now provided by basic policies. In Japan, however, the first stage of cancer treatment can cost up to $50,000. Even though the Japanese government is expected to introduce national care insurance, it has made clear that it will not be able to cover the full cost. Furthermore, about four years ago the company began to diversify their product. Today over 30 per cent of all sales in Japan are for noncancer-related insurance. As a result of the costs associated with cancer, Aflac's supplemental coverage remains very popular. The additional success of its new products makes Aflac find the Japanese market to be profitable.

Sources: Adapted from Steve Lohr, "Under the Wing of Japan, Inc., a Fledgling Enterprise Soared," *New York Times*, January 15, 1992, pp. A1, C5; *Forbes*, January 4, 1993, p. 167; *Fortune*, May 31, 1993, p. 218; *http://www.reportgallery.com/aflac/japan.htm*; *http://www.oecd.org/publications/figures/money.html*.

Triad activity in Japan

Many people complain that Japan keeps its trade doors closed to the rest of the world, but this is not true. Firms such as Coca-Cola, Exxon, IBM, and Mobil earn billions of dollars annually in the Japanese market[38] and often earn higher profits there than anywhere else.[39] (The box "International Business Strategy in Action: Aflac" describes an example from the field of cancer insurance.) Some of the areas where there is growing triad activity include automobiles and retail trade.

Automobiles in Japan   While Japanese cars sell very well in North America and moderately well in Europe, US and EU manufacturers are discovering that they are now able to make in-roads in Japan. Firms such as BMW, Mercedes, General Motors, Ford, and Chrysler all have growing operations there.

One of the biggest problems in this market, unfortunately, has been the recent downturn in the economy.[40] Firms such as Mitsubishi Motors have suffered large annual losses and most Japanese automakers have been finding that there is less local demand for cars than was expected.[41] As a result, the Japanese automarket in the late 1990s was encountering slowing demand coupled with a growing number of competitors that were offering a wide array of new products. Some industry analysts believe that this scenario is the same one that will confront automakers in North America and Europe in the near future: a maturing market and a proliferation of product offerings.

In the case of Japan, the outlook appears even gloomier. The government has increased the consumption tax to 5 per cent from 3 per cent and this has served to dampen new car demand. In order to offset this problem and to compete more effectively, Japanese car makers have begun introducing autos with sporty designs and more environmentally friendly engines, including a hybrid car that can get 66 miles per gallon on a combination of gas and electricity. These new offerings are designed to protect market share and to serve as a testing ground for the world market. If the cars do well in Japan, automakers such as Toyota intend to market them in North America and Europe. And firms such as Honda are creating smaller and more fuel-efficient recreational vehicles with the same objective in mind.[42] So competition in the Japanese market is going to increase over the next decade as US and EU firms enter the market and compete for share against Japanese offerings of cars designed for both the local and the international markets.

Retail in Japan   The Japanese retail market is difficult to penetrate because thousands of regulations have been imposed to limit foreign competition. For example, the Large-Store Law places restrictions on store size, location, and business hours. However, in recent years the law has been modified to accommodate a degree of competition, and a number of foreign firms have flocked into Japan.[43] A noteworthy recent example is Toys "R" Us, with a store 40 miles north of Tokyo that opened in 1991 after "three years of heavy slogging through the swamps of Japanese bureaucracy, local vested interests, labyrinthine real estate practices, and heavy, often hostile Japanese press coverage."[44] The company's success in opening the unit is partially explained by the fact that it followed some of the most important rules for doing business in Japan: (1) get a local partner, (2) be prepared for bureaucratic delays, (3) offer a product or service that has high quality and a competitive price, and (4) design the product for the tastes of the local market.

In contrast to the local competition, which stocks 1,000 to 2,000 kinds of toys in each store, Toys "R" Us Japan stocks 8,000 different toys and has plans to raise the number to 15,000. Most of these toys are produced locally, although one-third of them are imports. One of the company's major coups has been to convince Nintendo to sell directly to it. Toys "R" Us believes that it will eventually persuade many other toy manufacturers to follow suit. The company is off to a very good start and has plans to open ten stores a year, making it a major competitor.

Will other toy retailers follow this example and begin opening outlets in Japan? This is unlikely among small toy companies because of the supplier relationships and expertise needed to succeed in the market. However, giant toy retailers are likely to enter because competition is not as great or strong as it is in the United States and in the EU, and the Japanese toy market is growing at a rapid annual rate of 10 per cent.

Another retailer that has succeeded in Japan in Amway, which has found a way to circumvent Japan's restrictive and costly distribution system: direct selling.[45] However, rather than going door-to-door as it does in most countries, Amway salespeople work through networks of family and friends. This approach is effective in Japan because the Japanese notion of obligation makes it difficult for acquaintances to refuse to buy. In addition, in recent years Amway has redesigned its products to suit Japanese tastes. The company is also spending a great deal more money on training the work force for increased productivity and efficiency and on inducing them to stay with the firm. Today over 500,000 Japanese belong to Amway's sales force and the firm grosses over $1.5 billion in this market, accounting for approximately one-third the company's worldwide business.[46]

ACTIVE LEARNING CHECK

Review your answer to Active Learning Case question 3 and make any changes you like. Then compare your answer to the one below.

3. How will Airbus help the EU to compete in Japan?

Japanese airlines will continually need to replace and expand their current stock of planes. This demand had previously been satisfied by US aircraft manufacturers. However, thanks to Airbus the EU now has an industry that can offer Japan a competitive product. Moreover, until Japan creates its own worldwide competitive aircraft industry. Airbus will be able to continue to tap this market potential.

ECONOMIC RELATIONS WITHIN THE TRIAD

A close look at the data in Table 3.5 and Table 3.6 reveals that the Japanese are net exporters, while other members of the triad import more from Japan than they export. This trade pattern helps point up one of the areas of ongoing concern with the Japanese. At the same time the recent and sharp economic decline in Japan has resulted in all the other major economic powers carefully evaluating their relationship with the country. The primary reason is because the economic health of Japan influences not only the other economies of Asia but those of the triad as well. If Japan were to enter a major recession, the strong US economy could eventually be dragged down and European economies as well, thus resulting in problems worldwide. At the same time, however, this latest development has an upside in that it is forcing the Japanese to review their economy and introduce much-needed changes.

The Japanese downturn

Beginning in the mid-1990s the Japanese economy began encountering serious problems. One of major reasons was the large number of bank loans that had been given to businesses which now found themselves unable to repay them. This was particularly true in the case of firms that had borrowed large sums while using their real estate holdings as collateral. In many cases the appraised value of these assets was far higher than the resale value. And when the banks began writing down the loans to reflect the losses, the amount of capital they had available for lending decreased sharply. In turn, this meant that many businesses needing capital for expansion were unable to get it. At the same time, international competition began to increase and markets where Japanese firms once earned healthy profits now generated lower returns on investment.

Coupled with these developments, in 1998 Asian currencies came under attack as speculators unloaded them in favor of more stable currencies. In the process the Japanese yen began to slip precipitously. In the early 1990s the yen stood at 95 to the American dollar, making it one of the strongest currencies in the world. By 1998 the yen had fallen to 145 to the dollar and many Japanese businesses were finding it difficult to purchase goods and equipment in the international marketplace because prices were too high.

Small Japanese businesses, in particular, were finding it difficult to stay afloat because the banks were being hard pressed by stiff new regulatory requirements that the government was mandating to prevent a collapse of the banking system.[47] So rather than lending more money to small firms that were seeking to expand, a growing number of banks moved in the opposite direction and began pushing to collect these loans as they became due. In the process, the banks started pushing many of these firms over the edge. One local analyst for a large credit-research agency estimated that roughly 16 per cent of all bankruptcies were small low-tech suppliers.

Fortunately, not all small and medium-sized companies were facing financial crises that prevented them from expanding operations. Some had sufficient assets to continue to meet the growing demands from their customers for higher quality output at lower prices. However, many firms were finding that they were being squeezed harder to lower their costs because the large Japanese MNEs were under pressure from their own customers to sell products at lower prices. This was particularly true in the personal computer and auto markets, where the multinationals were trying to maintain their profit margins. As a result suppliers from low-cost countries such as China were beginning to make in-roads into the Japanese market.

At the same time unemployment began to increase, rising above 4 per cent for the first time in decades. This, in turn, resulted in greater pressure on the yen, and the American and EU governments began considering approaches they could take to help strengthen the Japanese currency and reduce the chances that their own economies would be adversely affected by Asian economic conditions.[48]

The economic troubles of Japan were also resulting in two other developments. The most heralded was the increasing interest by outsiders who were eager to buy Japanese assets. American investors, for example, spent more than $7 billion in the first five months of 1998 to purchase Asian properties, most of them in Japan. Table 3.7 provides some examples. Part of this development was a result of the weak Japanese economy. Many companies there had no capital for expansion and were facing declining demand for their goods and services. So they were willing to unload some of their assets as well as take on foreign partners who could provide funds and growth opportunities. At the same time, the impact of Japanese deregulation was beginning to take effect. For a long time both the US and the EU have been encouraging Japan to reduce its protectionist policies and allow greater opportunities for foreign investors. In the early 1990s the government promised to open up its markets to more foreign goods

Table 3.7 Asian acquisitions

Investor	Company being purchased	Purchase price
Travelers and Salamon Smith Barney	Nikko Securities (25% stake in Japanese operation)	$1.6 billion
Associates First Capital	DIC Finance, 90% stake (Japan)	$995 million
AES	Hanwha Energy power plant (South Korea)	$870 million
Adaptec	Symbios (South Korea)	$775 million
Investment group including George Soros, Enron, and Steel Dynamics	Nakornthal Steel Mill (Thailand)	$650 million
GE Capital	Toho Mutual Life Insurance (Japan) New business, sales network	$594 million
Zions Bancorp	Sumitomo Bank of California	$544 million
Goldman Sachs	Office building/Yamato Mutual Life (Japan)	$455 million
Coca-Cola	Doosan Beverage facility (South Korea)	$441 million
NCR Corporation	NCR Japan, 30% stake	$304 million
American Skiing	Steamboat and Heavenly ski resorts (Japan)	$288 million

Source: Reported in *USA Today*, June 10, 1998, p. 4B.

and even agreed to buy more cars, auto parts, and computer equipment from outside vendors. Now as the local economy began to falter and the rules and regulations that used to stymie foreign investors began to come down, the result was a rush by foreign MNEs into this marketplace.

The other development that was occurring in both Japan and Asia was an interest by local investors to buy assets in the US and the EU. The turmoil in the Asian markets was having a fundamental impact on the way these investors were now acting. In particular, they were concerned with protecting their capital. Investors who had long believed that the Asian market would continue its upward growth now began to realize that they had to diversify. The plunging stock markets and the decline in the value of local currencies against the dollar resulted in some investors losing 50–75 per cent of their assets in just a few months. And as these economies began to encounter problems, investors started looking to protect their assets. One Templeton Franklin global fund marketed in Asia reported that within the first five months of 1998 its assets had multiplied from under $100 million to $750 million.[49]

At the same time, American and EU firms continued to emulate some of the Japanese business practices that were proving so successful in the international market. In the US, for example, the chairman of the Federal Reserve System expressed the belief that US antitrust practices were out of date and that competitors should be allowed to acquire and merge with each other in order to protect themselves from world competition. This idea has long been popular in Japan where *keiretsus*, or business groups which consist of a host of companies that are linked together through ownership and/or joint ventures, dominate the local environment and are able to use their combined wealth and connections to dominate world markets. Today this form of cooperation is being copied by many firms including Deere & Company, Ford, IBM, and Harley-Davidson, to name but four.

ACTIVE LEARNING CHECK

Review your answer to Active Learning Case question 4 and make any changes you like. Then compare your answer to the one below.

4. In what way does the Airbus consortium use a "keiretsu" approach to building the aircraft? Why do you think it opted for this approach?

A *keiretsu* is a business group, which often consists of a host of companies that are linked together through ownership and/or joint ventures. In the case of Airbus, notice how Germany, Great Britain, and Spain build the aircraft and France assembles it. This is the same approach used by keiretsus that coordinate their operations in such a way that each provides products and services to the group at a lower price than any one could provide individually. Another reason that the consortium undoubtedly opted for this approach is that each participant benefits because of the money pumped into its economy for doing this work.

SUMMARY

Key points

1. Foreign direct investment (FDI) is the ownership and control of foreign assets. This usually means the ownership, whole or partial, of a company in a foreign country. Foreigners have invested over $600 billion in FDI in the United States, and Americans have about $800 billion of FDI invested overseas.

2. There are a number of reasons for FDI. These include increased profits and sales, a chance to enter rapidly growing markets, lower costs, economic unions, protection of domestic markets, protection of foreign markets, and the acquisition of technological know-how.

3. While there is a great amount of FDI made every year, most of it (over 80 per cent) occurs within or between triad countries. Much of the remaining FDI is in countries that are members of triad-based FDI clusters.

4. The triad nations dominate world trade and investments, and a great deal of this activity takes place both among and within triad countries. For example, the United States and Japan do approximately $186 billion of trade annually, the United States and the EU account for over $250 billion of trade, and the EU and Japan do $120 billion of business annually. EU intra-trade is even greater with members of the European Union doing over $1 trillion of trade with each other each year. Some of the major areas of triad trade include automobiles, computers, and retail selling.

Key terms

- triad
- portfolio investment
- twin factories
- maquiladoras
- FDI cluster
- keiretsu

Review and discussion questions

1. Which countries are the biggest investors in the United States? In which countries does the United States have the largest FDI? What conclusions can be drawn from these data?

2. Why do companies make FDI? Identify and describe four reasons.

3. How dominant are the triad countries in terms of FDI and world trade? Explain.

4. What is an FDI cluster? Why are certain countries such as Mexico and Venezuela more likely to be in the US cluster than in the EU cluster?

5. Is the US auto industry likely to be the target of foreign automakers during the coming decade? Why?

6. How is the EU trying to hold back the onslaught of Japanese auto competitors? Is this a wise strategy? Should the Americans follow a similar strategy?

7. How successful have the United States and the EU been in breaking into the Japanese market? Be objective in your answer and cite some examples.

8. How dominant have the Japanese become in the international arena? Cite three examples to support your answer.

9. When President Bush went to Japan early in 1992, he was able to extract agreements to buy more US autos, auto parts, and computer equipment. Some critics point out that such agreements show that the Japanese really could open their markets, but they will not do so unless strong pressure is brought to bear. Are the critics right? Defend your answer.

10. In what way can a keiretsu approach be of value to US and EU companies in becoming more competitive worldwide? Explain.

REAL CASES

MATSUSHITA BEATS PHILIPS

In terms of triad-based competition, the 1980s saw the emergence of Japanese firms in the consumer electronics industry. One of the major companies was Matsushita. The firm was initially successful with colour TVs, but its best known product has been the video cassette recorder (VCR), a field which it dominates by using the VHS system instead of the Sony "betamax" format VCR and others produced by European and American rivals. Paradoxically, the VCR was developed in California in 1956 by a US firm, Ampex, but the product development and distribution was captured by the clever global strategy of Matsushita.

In order to dominate world business in VCRs Matsushita managed to make the VHS format the industry standard. The company achieved this not just by its own massive production and worldwide sales, but by licensing the VHS format to other MNEs such as Hitachi, Sharp, Mitsubishi, and even the major European-based rival, Philips. Other companies such as GE, RCA, and Zenith (which sold VCRs under their own brand names) were tied into the VHS format because of the production and process technology retained by Matsushita in its strong Japanese home base. The company's massive global economies of scale enabled it to cut VCR prices by 50 per cent over its first five years.

In contrast, Philips was in desperate trouble by the 1980s. Built up in the interwar period of protectionism and strong government regulations, the company had developed a very highly decentralized organizational structure. Individual national country managers held the power in Philips and they were slow to respond to the Japanese threat in the postwar period. As a result, Philips lacked economies of scale and its radios, TVs,

▶

and VCRs were too expensive compared to comparable Japanese products. Philips had more than 600 manufacturing plants across the world, all developing products for local markets. However, the challenge facing the firm was how to restructure its entire business away from locally responsive national organizations toward a more integrated and leaner manufacturer capable of reaping the necessary economies of scale through standard global production.

In essence, the Japanese changed the rules of the game in the consumer electronics business. Matsushita, as a centralized, high-quality, low-price and innovative company was able to beat the decentralized and nationally responsive European firm. One tactic used by European firms was to lobby their governments for protection in the form of antidumping actions and tougher customs inspection of Japanese products. But such "shelters" only bought some breathing room before MNEs such as Philips restructured and fit their organizational capabilities to the required industry strategy.

Finally, the response of Matsushita to more protection has been to switch overseas sales from export to foreign direct investment (FDI). With FDI

the firm has been able to evade European trade barriers such as antidumping actions. For example, today it manufacturers in a number of European countries including the United Kingdom, where it has a major plant in Cardiff, Wales. At the same time this means that Matsushita must make its foreign subsidiaries as effective as possible by encouraging local initiatives, and this strategy can conflict with its internationally centralized Japanese-based management culture. In short, the very government regulations which have made Philips too decentralized are now being reapplied half a century later to make Matsushita less global and more local.

1. What type of globalization strategy was followed by the Japanese firm, Matsushita?

2. Why could the European firm, Philips, not compete well with its Japanese rival by the 1980s?

3. How can a government help its own firms against triad rivals?

Source: Adapted from Chris Bartlett and Sumantra Ghoshal, *Managing Across Borders*, 2nd ed. (Boston, Mass: Harvard Business School Press, 1995).

MERCEDES-BENZ AND BMW

In the early 1990s, the luxury car market was shaken. BMW and Mercedes-Benz were redesigning their cars only once every eight to ten years. So when their latest models reached the showroom floors, everyone looked to see what was new from Germany's premier automakers and whether these cars would be able to hold their own against the Japanese models that were proving so popular in this market niche.

In the past both BMW and Mercedes had found an eager market in the United States. However, in the early 1990s buyer demands changed. J. D. Power & Associates, the leading automotive market research firm, reported that car owners appreciated status and prestige, but they were now buying based on reliability. So while BMW and Mercedes are considered very fine cars, many consumers felt they were too expensive when compared

with competing models that gave more value for the dollar. Lexus and Infiniti were at the top of customer satisfaction, and Mercedes had fallen to third and BMW was in tenth place.

At this time both German automakers were making far more than the average $500 per car earned by the Big Three in the United States. BMW's profit was over $1,300 per vehicle and Mercedes' was around $3,000. However, given that there were six competitors in the 1980s and 15 in the 1990s, things were bound to change. Most new competition was coming from Japan, and the German manufacturers were being forced to review the way they did business. Additionally, while Mercedes and BMW led the foreign luxury car market in 1986, by 1991 the Japanese had taken over.

What did BMW do to turn things around? First, the firm began to focus on engineering improvements that would increase quality and mileage, as well as push up factory productivity. The company was also moving more production overseas by putting cars together from preassembled kits in South Africa, Taiwan, India, Brazil, and other countries, while keeping the manufacturing in Germany. Mercedes followed a similar strategy. At the same time, Mercedes merged with Chrysler and was seeking a stake in Nissan's truck subsidiary.

As a result, things began to turn up by the mid-1990s as both BMW and Mercedes regained market share. This was heavily influenced by the strong yen, which made Japanese car prices skyrocket. Additionally, BMW led the way cutting prices in Europe. Yet, whatever the Germans do, one thing is clear: the United States is the major world market for luxury cars and BMW and Mercedes must continue to do well here to wrest market share from the Japanese luxury competitors. As one observer put it, "The current battle in the United States is a prelude to war in Europe. If the Germans cannot win in America, it will be only a matter of time before they are forced to defend their home market from the Japanese."

1. Why are BMW and Mercedes interested in competing in the US market? Identify and describe three reasons.

2. How much of a battle will the two German automakers face in the United States from Japanese competition? Explain.

3. Will the Japanese be as successful in the luxury car market in the EU as they have been in America? Explain.

Sources: Adapted from Alex Taylor III, "BMW and Mercedes Make Their Move," *Fortune*, August 12, 1991; Patrick Oster, "Buying an Import over There," *Business Week*, March 29, 1993; and Keith H. Hammonds, "Made-in-the USA Mercedes," *Business Week*, April 12, 1993; Alex Taylor III, "A New Boost for Japan's Automakers," *Fortune*, October 16, 1995; Alex Taylor III and Ani Hadjian, "Speed! Power! Status!," *Fortune*, June 10, 1996; Dave Phillips, "DaimlerChrysler to be Official Sept. 18," *The Detroit News*, Friday, June 26, 1998; Sue Zesiger, "The Most Improved Wheels," *Fortune*, November 24, 1997; Alex Taylor III and Luis Fernando Llosa, "So You Want to Buy a Luxury Car . . . Or Truck," *Fortune*, November 13, 1995.

ENDNOTES

1. See Dyan Machan, "Buy France and Spain, Sell Germany," *Forbes*, April 15, 1991, p. 72; and John Marcom, Jr., "The New Face of Spain," *Forbes*, March 4, 1991, pp. 43–44.
2. For a discussion of an interesting combination of FDI and portfolio investment, see John Philips and Karen Woolfson, "Franco-German Banking Link-Up Ignore Sceptics," *The European*, April 12–14, 1991, p. 20.
3. Karen Lowry Miller, Larry Armstrong, and James B. Treece, "Mitsubishi Pulls Out the Stops," *Business Week*, May 6, 1991, pp. 64–65.
4. Alex Taylor III, "BMW and Mercedes Make Their Move," *Fortune*, August 12, 1991, pp. 56–63.
5. Susan E. Kuhn, "Are Foreign Profits Good for Stocks," *Fortune*, November 16, 1992, p. 27.
6. Claire Poole, "Pepsi's Newest Generation," *Forbes*, February 18, 1991, p. 88.
7. Also, see James B. Treece et al., "New Worlds to Conquer," *Business Week*, February 28, 1994, pp. 50–52.
8. See Deidre A. Depke et al., "Laptops Take Off," *Business Week*, March 18, 1991, pp. 118–124.
9. Ferdinand Protzman, "Rebuilding East German Industry," *New York Times*, February 14, 1991, pp. C1, C5; and Richard A. Melcher et al., "Bankrolling the Rebirth of the East," *Business Week*, April 29, 1991, pp. 45–46.
10. Jack Lowenstein, "Foreigners Weather Aussie Onslaught," *Euromoney*, April 1991, pp. 39–42.
11. William C. Symonds, "Shufflin' Off to Buffalo," *Business Week*, April 8, 1991, pp. 47–48.
12. Keith Bradsher, "House Vote Backs Bush's Authority on Trade Accords," *New York Times*, May 24, 1991, pp. A1, C2.
13. Sylvia Nasar, "American Revival in Manufacturing Seen in US Report." *New York Times*, February 5, 1991, pp. A1, C17.
14. Susan Moffat, "Picking Japan's Research Brains" *Fortune*, March 25, 1991, p. 92.
15. Mark Mason, "United States Direct Investment in Japan: Trends and Prospects," *California Management Review*, Fall 1992, pp. 99–115.
16. "Foreign Investment and the Triad," *The Economist*, August 24, 1991, p. 57.
17. In addition, the EU is trying to expand its economic influence by enlarging the European trading bloc, as was seen in Alan Riding, "Europeans in Accord to Create Vastly Expanded Trading Bloc," *New York Times*, October 23, 1991, pp. A1, C18.

18. Also, see Bill Powell and Peter McKillop, "Sayonara, America," *Newsweek*, August 19, 1991, pp. 32–33.

19. Kathleen Kerwin and Bill Vlasic, "Manufacturing Autos: Prognosis 1998," *Business Week*, January 12, 1998, pp. 102–103.

20. Brandon Mitchener, "German Car Horns are Tooting Again," *Wall Street Journal*, January 7, 1998, p. 18.

21. For more on this see Alex Taylor III, "Too Slow for the Fast Lane? Volvo and Saab," *Fortune*, July 21, 1997, pp. 68–72.

22. Valerie Reitman, "Japanese Car Makers Plan Major Expansion of American Capacity," *Wall Street Journal*, September 24, 1997, Section A, pp. 1, 12.

23. Jacques Neher, "A French Giant Stalks US Telephone Market," *New York Times*, November 25, 1991, pp. C1, C5.

24. For additional examples, see Bernhard Heitger and Jurgen Stehn, "Japanese Direct Investments in the EC – Response to the Internal Market 1993?" *Journal of Common Market Studies*, September 1990, pp. 3–15.

25. Tony Riley, "Investing in US Positioning in the EC: Which US Companies Will Be the Winners?" *Journal of European Business*, November/December 1991, p. 10.

26. Robert Porter Lynch, "Building Alliances to Penetrate European Markets," *Journal of Business Strategy*, March/April 1990, pp. 4–8.

27. "VW's Audi Agrees to Buy Lamborghini," *Houston Chronicle*, June 13, 1998, Section C, p. 2.

28. See, for example, John P. Wolkonowicz, "The EC Auto Industry Gears Up for Greater Competition," *Journal of European Business*, November/December 1991, pp. 12–14.

29. Richard A. Melcher and John Templeman, "Ford of Europe: Slimmer, but Maybe Not Luckier," *Business Week*, January 18, 1993, pp. 44–46.

30. See David Lei, "Building US Presence in European Markets," *Journal of Business Strategy*, July/August 1990, p. 33.

31. Richard A. Melcher and Stewart Toy, "On Guard, Europe," *Business Week*, December 14, 1992, pp. 54–55.

32. Alex Taylor III, "The Gentlemen at Ford are Kicking Butt," *Fortune*, June 22, 1998, p. 74.

33. David Woodruff and Heidi Dawley, "Japanese Cars Spin Their Wheels on the Continent," *Business Week*, October 13, 1997, p. 50.

34. Ibid.

35. Carol Every, "A Chip Off the Old Trade Bloc: US Companies Storm the European Computer Market," *Journal of European Business*, September/October 1991, p. 19.

36. Jonathan B. Levine, "Grabbing the Controls in Mid-Tailspin," *Business Week*, January 17, 1994, pp. 44–45.

37. For more on this, see John Verity, Neil Gross, and Gary McWilliams, "The Japanese Juggernaut That Isn't," *Business Week*, August 31, 1992, pp. 64–65.

38. Carla Rapoport, "You Can Make Money in Japan," *Fortune*, February 12, 1990, pp. 85–90.

39. Hilary Clarke, "Taking the Road to Japan," *International Management*, March 1991, pp. 34–35.

40. Joji Sakurai, "Japan's Recession Weighs Heavily on Economically Needy Neighbors," *Houston Chronicle*, June 13, 198, Section C, p. 3.

41. Neil Weinberg, "A Setting Sun?" *Forbes*, April 20, 1998, pp. 118–124.

42. Emily Thornton, "Too Many Cars, Too Few Buyers," *Business Week*, October 20, 1997, p. 56.

43. For some reasons why, see Andrew Pollack, "Myths Aside, Japanese Do Look for Bargains," *New York Times*, February 20, 1994, Section E, p. 5.

44. Robert Neff, "Guess Who's Selling Barbies in Japan Now?" *Business Week*, December 9, 1991, p. 72.

45. Gale Eisenstodt and Hiroki Katayama, "Soap and Hope in Tokyo," *Forbes*, September 3, 1990, p. 62.

46. Norihiko Shirouzu, "Amway's Glitzy Man in Japan Cleans Up," *Wall Street Journal*, June 9, 1998, Section B, pp. 1, 4.

47. Emily Thornton, "The Other Japan," *Business Week*, February 9, 1998, p. 53.

48. Sheryl WuDunn, "Japan Says Unemployment Has Reached Record High," *Wall Street Journal*, May 30, 1998, Section B, p. 2.

49. Andrew Tanzer, "Change of Heart," *Forbes*, December 15, 1997, p. 144.

ADDITIONAL BIBLIOGRAPHY

Agarwal, Sanjeev and Ramaswami, Sridhar N. "Choice of Foreign Market Entry Mode: Impact of Ownership, Location and Internalization Factors," *Journal of International Business Studies*, vol. 23, no. 1 (First Quarter 1992).

Andersen, Otto. "On the Internationalization Process of Firms: A Critical Analysis," *Journal of International Business Studies*, vol. 24, no. 2 (Second Quarter 1993).

Buckley, Peter J. "Problems and Developments in the Core Theory of International Business," *Journal of International Business Studies*, vol. 21, no. 4 (Fourth Quarter 1990).

Contractor, Farok J. "Contractual and Cooperative Forms of International Business: Towards a Unified Theory of Modal Choice," *Management International Review*, vol. 30, no. 1 (First Quarter 1990).

Dunning, John H. "The Study of International Business: A Plea for a More Interdisciplinary Approach," *Journal of International Business Studies*, vol. 20, no. 3 (Fall 1989).

Dunning, John H. *Alliance Capitalism and Global Business* (London: Routledge, 1997).

Dunning, John H. "Location and the Multinational Enterprise: A Neglected Factor?" *Journal of International Business Studies*, vol. 29, no. 1 (First Quarter 1998).

Haar, Jerry. "A Comparative Analysis of the Profitability Performance of the Largest US, European and Japanese Multinational Enterprises," *Management International Review*, vol. 29, no. 3 (Third Quarter 1989).

Harrigan, Kathryn Rudie. "Strategic Alliances: Their New Role in Global Competition," *Columbia Journal of World Business*, vol. 22, no. 2 (Summer 1987).

Kim, Wi Saeng and Lyn, Esmeralda O. "FDI Theories and the Performance of Foreign Multinationals Operating in the US," *Journal of International Business Studies*, vol. 21, no. 1 (First Quarter 1990).

Kotabe, Masaaki. "A Comparative Study of US and Japanese Patent Systems," *Journal of International Business Studies*, vol. 23, no. 1 (First Quarter 1992).

Li, Jiatao and Guisinger, Stephen. "The Globalization of Service Multinationals in the 'Triad' Regions: Japan, Western Europe and North America," *Journal of International Business Studies*, vol. 23, no. 4 (Fourth Quarter 1992).

Ostry, Sylvia. "Governments & Corporations in a Shrinking World: Trade & Innovation Policies in the United States, Europe & Japan," *Columbia Journal of World Business*, vol. 25, nos. 1, 2 (Spring/Summer 1990).

Parkhe, Arvind. "Interfirm Diversity, Organizational Learning, and Longevity in Global Strategic Alliances," *Journal of International Business Studies*, vol. 22, no. 4 (Fourth Quarter 1991).

Rugman, Alan M. "A New Theory of the Multinational Enterprise: Internationalization Versus Internalization," *Columbia Journal of World Business*, vol. 15, no. 1 (Spring 1980).

Rugman, Alan M. (ed.) *New Theories of the Multinational Enterprise* (London: Croom Helm and New York: St. Martin's, 1982).

Rugman, Alan M. "The Comparative Performance of US and European Multinational Enterprises," *Management International Review*, vol. 23, no. 2 (1983).

Rugman, Alan M. and Boyd, Gavin (eds) *Euro-Pacific Investment and Trade* (Cheltenham: Elgar, 1997).

Rugman, Alan M. and Boyd, Gavin (eds) *Deepening Integration in the Pacific Economies* (Cheltenham: Elgar, 1999).

Rugman, Alan M. and Verbeke, Alain. "Multinational Corporate Strategy and the Canada–US Free Trade Agreement," *Management International Review*, vol. 30, no. 3 (Third Quarter 1990).

Sullivan, Daniel and Bauerschmidt, Alan. "The Basic Concepts of International Business Strategy: A Review and Reconsideration," *Management International Review*, vol. 31 (1991).

Vernon-Wortzel, Heidi and Wortzel, Lawrence H. "Globalizing Strategies for Multinationals from Developing Countries," *Columbia Journal of World Business*, vol. 23, no. 1 (Spring 1988).

Yip, George, *Total Global Strategy* (Englewood Cliffs, NJ: Prentice-Hall, 1995).

PART TWO

THE ENVIRONMENT OF INTERNATIONAL BUSINESS

▼

PART ONE: THE WORLD OF INTERNATIONAL BUSINESS

| Chapter 1 Introduction | Chapter 2 MNEs | Chapter 3 Triad |

▼

PART TWO: THE ENVIRONMENT OF INTERNATIONAL BUSINESS

| Chapter 4 Political Environment | Chapter 5 Cultural Environment | Chapter 6 Economic Environment | Chapter 7 Financial Environment |

▼

PART THREE: INTERNATIONAL BUSINESS STRATEGIES

| Chapter 8 Strategic Planning | Chapter 9 Organizing Strategy | Chapter 10 Production Strategy | Chapter 11 Marketing Strategy |

| Chapter 12 Human Resource Strategy | Chapter 13 Political Risk/Negotiation | Chapter 14 Financial Strategy |

▼

PART FOUR: INTERNATIONAL BUSINESS STRATEGIES IN ACTION
To do Business in International Markets Including:

| Chapter 15 Corporate Strategy/National Competitiveness | Chapter 16 EU |

| Chapter 17 Japan | Chapter 18 North America | Chapter 19 Non-Triad Nations |

▼

PART FIVE: INTERNATIONAL BUSINESS HORIZONS

| Chapter 20 Future of International Business |

CHAPTER 4

International Politics and Economic Integration

OBJECTIVES OF THE CHAPTER

Politics and economics are closely linked and each can affect the other. A good example is the economic changes that are sweeping Eastern Europe today. As these countries abandoned their communist ideologies, their centrally driven economies started changing toward market-driven economies. This latter development would have been impossible had it not been preceded by the requisite political change. The purposes of this chapter are to examine the linkage between political forces and economic change and then to review some of the major forms of economic integration that are being used to create regional trade areas and common markets. In future chapters these topics will be developed in more depth. The specific objectives of this chapter are to:

1. **Compare** and **contrast** major political and economic systems and to note the linkage between these systems.

2. **Examine** the primary reasons for the current privatization movement, and the economic impact that this movement is having on selected countries.

3. **Describe** the major forms of economic integration and the benefits to be gained from each.

4. **Relate** some of the steps that multinational enterprises take to benefit from changes in economic integration.

Is investment in Russia risky?

When Mikhail Gorbachev began changing the economic policies of the USSR in the late 1980s, many foreign businesspeople viewed this as the beginning of new opportunities in what was then the Soviet Union. By the time Gorbachev resigned in late 1991 no one seemed to know how profitable or risky an investment in Russia might be. The new union that was being created was given the name of Commonwealth of Independent States and was to be a loose economic and political alliance consisting of any of the former Soviet republics that wished to join in. Most signed an agreement that called for open borders and economic cooperation, but no central government.

At the same time the Russians began to implement western-style economic concepts. The prices on many goods were deregulated and people soon found themselves paying five to ten times as much for some products. The value of the ruble quickly sank to around 1 cent and the government-owned foreign exchange bank denied many requests for withdrawals. However, no one wanted to close the bank because this would have meant defaulting on nearly $85 billion of foreign debt. Gross national product during the early 1990s fell by 10 per cent.

In an effort to help the newly-formed Russian republic, a number of prominent businesspeople and politicians called for aid in the form of grants, technological assistance, and direct investments. The Bush administration urged that the country be admitted to full membership in the International Monetary Fund (IMF) and the World Bank. The US Secretary of the Treasury explained this position by noting that, "Membership in the IMF and World Bank will further market-oriented economic reforms in these newly independent nations. We will work with them to assure that their applications are considered as quickly as possible." After months of discussion Russia and 12 former soviet republics were admitted in 1992.

At the same time there were diverse opinions regarding the benefits of investing in Russia. Many western diplomats were arguing that new investment should be minimal until stability returned. By the mid-1990s the outlook was more optimistic. A prospective market of 150 million had begun luring investors. Tetrapak, a Swedish food-packing company, invested $60 million in three Russian plants. PepsiCo and McDonald's were locking their positions before other competitors had a chance to do so. Ford was investing $150 million in a car venture and had over 60 dealerships in the country.

The severe reforms which turned over 70 per cent of public companies to private hands, deregulated prices and foreign trade, eliminated central planning, and created a new banking system have changed foreign opinions on the Russian economy. The process of transformation is virtually irreversible. However, the government has to be timely in its future reforms. Presently, many foreign companies doing business in Russia must pay protection money to the mafia. Additionally, corruption and the lack of a legal structure to protect foreign investments have contributed to the near crash of the Russian economy in 1998, when the IMF, the World Bank, and the Japanese government had to provide the country with a relief loan.

The IMF's loan is expected to buy the government some time to enact reforms that will make investors more comfortable about the economy. The Russian government must meet specific conditions under which the loan was negotiated. Optimism is still in the air, and some believe that the Russian economy is bound to become a strong power in less than 20 years.

Sources: Adapted from Paul Hofheinz, "Russia Starts All Over Again," *Fortune*, January 13, 1992; Barbara Crossette, "US, in Reversal, Urges Russian Link to Global Lenders," *New York Times*, January 4, 1992; Paul Hofheinz, "Let's Do Business," *Fortune*, September 23, 1991; James B. Hayes, "Wanna Make a Deal in Moscow?" *Fortune*, October 22, 1990; Vladimir Kvint, "Siberia: A Warm Place for Investors," *Forbes*, September 16, 1991; Ralph Frasca, "The Russians Are Coming," *Forbes*, February 1, 1993; http://www.dfait-aeci.gc.ca/english/NEWS/NEWSLETR/CANEX/960429ae.htm#titleA; John Thornhill and Robert Chote, "IMF Leads $12.6bn Support Package," *Financial Times*, Tuesday, July 14, 1998; Charles Clover, "Russia Waits on Investor's Judgement," *Financial Times*, Tuesday, July 14, 1998; Martin Walker, "Investing in Russia not for the Weak at Heart," *Europe*, March 1997; Michael J. Mendel and Dean Foust, "How to Reshape the World Financial System," *Business Week*, October 12, 1998, pp. 112–116.

1. What type of economic system now exists in Russia: market-driven, centrally determined, or mixed?

2. Would Russia benefit by gaining admission to one of the major economic unions such as the EU? Why?

3. Is Russia a good potential investment for western business? Explain.

INTRODUCTION: CHANGING POLITICAL SYSTEMS

Over the past two decades there has been a dramatic change in the political systems of many countries. In the Americas both Chile and Nicaragua have seen a return to democracy. Many former communist countries in Eastern Europe are now building free-market systems. In Africa, the Marxist government of Ethiopia has fallen. Political and economic changes abound, opening new opportunities in many economies and closing others in countries experiencing political unrest.

International business has been particularly affected by the movement of Eastern European countries toward market-driven economies. These nations include Poland, Hungary, Czech Republic, Romania, Bulgaria, and the Balkan countries, as well as the former East Germany – now merged into the former West Germany. Ten years ago the former Soviet Union would not have permitted these satellite nations to abandon the command economy advocated by communist ideology for a free-market system. Under Mikhail Gorbachev, however, the USSR revised its political and economic thinking.

The current economies of the former Soviet republics are extremely weak and outside investment is required in order to prevent economic collapse. The only practical way for the republics to get this investment is by adopting market-driven capitalistic theory. Certainly no large western firms are going to make major investments in the former Soviet Union without guarantees ensuring repatriation of their funds and protection of their assets against government seizure.

At the same time as the former Soviet republics face this major economic challenge the European Union (EU) is merging into a single, internal economic market. In order to take advantage of this development, major political and economic changes are taking place in Eastern Europe, helping to speed the movement toward free enterprise economies that can effectively compete in this new environment. If they hope to improve their economies over the next few decades, even countries like Cuba will also have to abandon their adherence to old-line communism. All political systems eventually are affected by the pressures of international business and the nature of global economic competition.

Political ideologies and economics

An **ideology** is a set of integrated beliefs, theories, and doctrines that helps to direct the actions of a society. Political ideology is almost always intertwined with economic philosophy. For example, the political ideology of the United States is grounded in the Constitution, which guarantees the rights of private property and the freedom of choice. This has helped to lay the foundation for US capitalism. A change in this fundamental ideology would alter the economic environment of the United States. The some is true, for example, for China and the former USSR republics. Simply put, the political and economic ideologies of nations help to explain their national economic policies.

Political systems In the extreme, there are two types of political system: democracy and totalitarianism. **Democracy** is a system of government in which the people, either directly or through their elected officials, decide what is to be done. Good examples include the United States, Canada, England, and Australia. Common features of this system include (1) the right to express opinions freely, (2) election of representatives for limited terms of office, (3) an independent court system that protects individual property and rights, and (4) a relatively nonpolitical bureaucracy and defense infrastructure that ensure the continued operation of the system.

Totalitarianism is a system of government in which one individual or political party maintains complete control and either refuses to recognize other parties or suppresses them. There are a number of types of totalitarianism that currently exist. The best known is **communism**, in which the government owns all property and makes all decisions regarding production and distribution of goods and services.[1] The best example is Cuba. Another form is **theocratic totalitarianism**, in which a religious group exercises total power and represses or persecutes nonorthodox factions. Iran and some of the sheikdoms of the Middle East are good examples. A third form is **secular totalitarianism**, in which the military controls the government and makes decisions which it deems to be in the best interests of the country. An example is Iraq. Political systems typically create the infrastructure within which the economic system functions.

Economic systems There are three basic economic systems: capitalism, socialism, and mixed. However, for purposes of our analysis it is more helpful to classify these systems in terms of resource allocation (market-driven versus centrally determined) and property ownership (private versus public). In a **market-driven economy** goods and services are allocated on the basis of demand. If consumers express a preference for cellular telephones, more of these products will be offered for sale. If consumers refuse to buy dot-matrix printers, these goods will cease to be offered. The United States and EU nations have market-driven economies. In a **centrally determined economy** goods and services are allocated based on a plan formulated by a committee that decides what is to be offered. Cuba, and to a large degree China, are examples. The people are able to purchase only what the government determines should be sold.

Market-driven economies are characterized by private ownership. Most of the assets of production are in the hands of privately owned companies that compete for market share by offering the best quality goods and services at competitive prices. Centrally determined economies are characterized by public ownership. Most of the assets of production are in the hands of the state and production quotas are set for each organization.

In recent years market-driven economies have become more popular. An example is Russia, which has begun introducing aspects of free enterprise such as allowing people to start their own businesses and to keep any profits that they make.[2] Eastern European countries are another example.

In examining economic systems, it is important to remember that most economies of the world are **mixed economies**, characterized by a combination of market- and centrally driven planning. For example, the United States, a leading proponent of market-driven economic policies, plays an active role in providing health care and other social services. Other countries with mixed economies, such as Great Britain, Sweden, and Germany, have even stronger social welfare systems. Similarly, in recent years the United States has become a more active partner in promoting business and in ensuring that US firms gain or maintain dominance in certain market areas.[3] The box "International Business Strategy in Action: Washington's New Approach" provides some examples. The governments of many other mixed economies support various industries through incentives and financial assistance to firms that they believe produce goods and services that are considered important to the long-run growth of the economy.

As a result of such developments, there has been a blurring of the differences between market-driven and centrally determined economies. The biggest change has been the willingness of the latter to introduce free-market concepts. At the same time, however, many market-driven economies are making greater use of centrally determined ideas, such as studying the benefits of business–government cooperation in order to fend off external competitors. An example is the use of political force to limit and restrain the ability of overseas firms to do business in their country. In the United States, for example, the government is being urged to play a more active role in monitoring foreign business practices, including lobbying efforts.[4] On balance, however, in the millennium we are seeing a move from central planning to market-driven and mixed economies. One prominent example is provided by the privatization movement that is taking place worldwide.

Government control of assets

Over the last decade an increasing number of countries have begun moving toward **privatization**, the process of selling government assets to private buyers. To understand the reasons for and the economic impact of this process, it is helpful to examine the potential benefits of government ownership and the advantages of moving to privatization.

There are six common, and sometimes interdependent, reasons for countries to control business assets, a process known as **nationalization**. These include (1) promoting economic development, for example by coordinating the assets of many businesses into one overall master plan; (2) earning profits for the national treasury; (3) preventing companies from going bankrupt and closing their doors; (4) enhancing programs that are in the national interest; (5) increasing the political or economic control of those in power; and (6) ensuring goods and services to all citizens regardless of their economic status.[5]

The opposite situation, privatization, can take two forms. The most common form is **divestiture**, in which the government sells assets. The other is **contract management**, in which the government transfers operating responsibility of an industry without transferring the legal title and ownership. The major trend today is toward divestiture.

Some of the primary reasons for privatization include (1) it is more efficient to have the goods and services provided by private business than by government-run companies; (2) a change in the political culture brings about a desire to sell off these assets; (3) the company has been making money and the government feels that there is more to be gained by selling now than by holding on; (4) the purchase price can be used to reduce the national debt; (5) the company is losing money and the government has to assume the losses out of the national treasury; (6) the company needs research and development funds in order to maintain a competitive stance, and the government is unwilling to make this investment; and (7) international funding agencies are making assistance to the country conditional on a reduction in the size of the government.[6]

INTERNATIONAL BUSINESS STRATEGY IN ACTION

Washington's new approach

US firms have long tried to prevent foreign competitors from gaining a foothold in the US market by using the government to block such expansion. On the other hand, for a long time the US government played a passive role in promoting US business overseas. Now, faced with trade deficits and growing concern that countries selling billions of dollars in goods in the United States are not opening their own markets to US firms, the government appears to be playing a more active role. Even US presidents have been pitching in. In one case Indonesia was about to give a $3 billion project to the NEC Corporation. After receiving a letter from President George Bush and doing additional reflecting on the decision, the country split the contract between NEC and AT&T. In another case Saudi Arabia was on the verge of signing a major contract with Alcatel of France, but following a letter from President Bush, the country announced that it was going to rethink the matter.

These actions are nothing new in other countries. For years European leaders have been helping their companies to sell merchandise abroad. President Mitterand of France talked to the Saudis on behalf of Alcatel; Chancellor Kohl led groups of German businesspeople to Moscow to scout opportunities; and within ten days of the time British troops entered Kuwait, Prime Minister Major was in the country talking to officials about contracts for British businesses.

The United States is also using its embassies to help promote business. New ambassadors are given special lectures on trade as part of their two-week seminar preparing them for an overseas assignment. In addition, the US Commerce Department now hires and assigns commercial officers to foreign outposts. The job of these officers is to promote US business in those countries. (Similarly, in Canada in the early 1980s the Trade Commission Service moved from the old Industry Department to External Affairs with the objective of improving the trade and economic knowledge of Canadian diplomatic officials posted abroad.)

The United States still relies most heavily on its ambassadors to provide on-site support. Michael Armacost, recent US ambassador to Japan, repeatedly urged Japanese companies to buy American and did not hesitate to criticize the web of local relationships that tended to exclude foreign suppliers. Commenting on his role, the ambassador once noted, "Other countries' embassies are aggressive in support of their corporations, and our companies have every right to expect comparable support." The ambassador made it a point to be visible to US businesses in the country. For example, when Applied Materials, a California producer of semiconductor manufacturing equipment, built a research facility outside Tokyo, the ambassador went to the grand opening; previous US ambassadors maintained a low business profile and would not have attended such an event. However, that is all part of the past. Today Washington has a new approach.

Sources: Adapted from Edmund Faltermayer, "The Thaw in Washington," *Fortune*, Special ed., Spring/Summer 1991, p. 52; Edmund L. Andrews, "AT&T and British Rival Clash," *New York Times*, April 16, 1993, pp. C1–C2; and Keith Bradsher, "Europe, US Reach Partial Pact," *New York Times*, April 22, 1993, pp. C1, C10.

Privatization in action   Many nations have privatization programs.[7] These include countries with moderate per capita gross domestic products, such as Argentina, Brazil, Chile, Mexico, and China, as well as economically advanced nations such as the United States, Japan, Germany,[8] and the United Kingdom. All feel that their economies can be strengthened through privatization programs.

In the case of Argentina, for example, the government has now begun ending the nation's phone monopoly and opening up this $10 billion market to outside investors. Previously the two telephone companies that monopolized all long distance and local phone services had their territories firmly established and neither could compete with the other. Now they can, and additional telephone companies will be granted licences to operate throughout the country. The government believes that as competition increases, phone rates will drop and service will increase sharply. The two firms that had the monopoly positions are owned and managed by French, Spanish, and Italian phone companies and they will have to work very hard to remain competitive. At the same time, however, these firms will be allowed to bid on new cellular phone licences, thus giving them additional potential sources of revenue.[9]

In the case of the United Kingdom, privatization and deregulation have proven to be a national boon. A few years ago British Telecommunications began downsizing its operations so as to increase its competitiveness and profitability. The firm slashed 100,000 jobs, and critics said that privatization and deregulation were hurting the economy. However, just the opposite occurred. Many of the workers who were laid off began finding jobs with small telecommunications firms that were springing up throughout the country. At the same time, there has been an influx of large foreign competitors such as AT&T, the giant American telecommunications company, and AB L. M. Ericsson, the Swedish telecom-equipment maker, that have hired thousands of people. As a result, between 1990 and 1999 the number of jobs in the United Kingdom's telecommunications industry increased, while prices decreased and service improved sharply.[10]

Another major group of nations that is turning to privatization is Russia and Eastern European countries. At the grass roots in Russia a market economy is evolving. Despite the lack of national or local laws to guide them, hundreds of small factories and service businesses are privatizing themselves. Enterprises are pushing ahead with Russian-style versions of leveraged buyouts, employee stock ownership plans, and private spin-offs.[11] At the same time commercial banks are sprouting up across the country. However, there will also have to be an influx of more western capital if privatization efforts are to be successful in Russia.

Among the Eastern European countries, there is also a flurry of privatization activity. However, firms looking to invest face a myriad of problems. The German government, in an effort to alert investors to some of the roadblocks they are likely to face when making direct investments in the eastern part of the country, has published a long list of impediments, including the following:

● There is a considerable lack of suitable industrial sites, and prices for the few good ones are exploding. Rents for new offices in eastern Berlin are already higher than those in Dusseldorf and Cologne.

● Administrative authorities in many places still obstruct, or are unable to handle and organize, the purchase of real estate.

● A lot of red-tape still persists in the regional subsidiaries of the Treuhandanstalt – the holding company set up to control and privatize the formerly state-owned companies.[12]

● Investors have great difficulties obtaining legal information about the costs and responsibilities they must accept when they buy heavily polluted properties. Companies must cope with a poor telephone network, inadequate transport systems, and slow payment transactions.[13]

Another problem facing investors in Eastern Europe is the difficulty of determining how much a business is worth. As one observer put it, "To aggravate matters, popular and political opinion often thinks state companies are worth more than they are, given their generally obsolete capital stock, overstaffing, poor management, absence of marketing orientation, uncompetitiveness, and so forth."[14] Some individuals have suggested that instead of selling all these businesses to private firms for cash, the stock in some of them should be transferred to pension funds, municipalities, and educational institutions. Then these enterprises can use the dividends and capital gains from the businesses rather than rely on treasury handouts. In this way there would be a reduction in government spending and the creation of new ownership.

Private firms that are willing to invest in Eastern Europe are finding these countries prepared to offer a wide variety of subsidies and grants. The German government, for example, has announced that it will support investment and economic activities in the eastern sector by direct or indirect subsidies. In addition, companies doing business in Eastern Europe are able to recruit managers who have had experience dealing with other Eastern European countries, are fluent in their languages, and can help to pry open markets in these countries. So the privatization trend in Eastern Europe is likely to continue.

Government–business cooperation

While governments are privatizing assets, this does not mean that they are distancing themselves from business firms. Both in the EU and in Japan there has been a large amount of business–government cooperation. Perhaps the best-known example in the EU has been the subsidized development of the Airbus (discussed later in Chapter 14.) In Japan, after World War II the Japanese government gave responsibility for implementing the country's trade and industrial policy to the **Ministry of International Trade and Industry (MITI)**. The initial focus of the ministry was on both providing protection to Japanese companies and marketing the products of four major industries: electric power, steel, shipbuilding, and fertilizers. Incentives were created to encourage investment in these industries and to help successful firms export their products. In recent years MITI's focus has been on targeting less energy-intensive industries for Japanese investment and growth. Prime examples include computers and chemicals, where MITI works cooperatively with Japanese businesses to help ensure success. The focus of MITI has changed from a proactive to a much more cooperative agency in the last decade; its role now is mainly in funding export markets for Japanese businesses.

The American response   The results of such cooperative efforts have not been lost on Washington, which is now considering what may well be the beginning of an industrial policy similar to that of the old-fashioned MITI. This is a marked change for the US federal government, which is worried about the competitiveness of the United States in the international arena. In 1990 a special White House panel of experts from industry, academia, and the government released a list of 22 technologies that it deemed as essential to the national defense and economic prosperity of the United States. The list includes composite materials, flexible computer-integrated manufacturing, and high-definition electronic displays. This list is intended to guide the Critical Technologies Institute, created by Congress in 1990 to conduct long-range strategic planning and to work closely with the private sector in developing critical technologies.

This idea has worked well in Japan and in Europe, and now research consortia are springing up in the United States. Table 4.1 provides a comparison of selected consortia from each of the three major groups. At the same time individual states are

Table 4.1 Select research consortia: United States, Japan, and Europe

Organization	Year formed	Budget (% from gov't)	Areas of investigation
United States			
Sematech	1987	$200 million a year (50%)	Methods, materials, and equipment for making advanced semiconductors
National Center for Manufacturing Sciences (NCMS)	1986	$80 million a year (35%)	Improved machine tools, software, better machine methods, new materials
Microelectronics & Computer Technology Corp. (MCC)	1983	$60 million a year (10%–15%)	Advanced computing, software, computer-aided design, semiconductor packaging
Japan			
Advanced Telephony Project	1986	$70 million a year (70%)	Hardware and software for telephones capable of translating languages
Synchrotron Orbital Radiation Technology Center (SORTEC)	1986	$15 million a year (70%)	X-ray lithography for advanced semiconductors; includes development of small atom smasher
Optoelectronics Technology Research Corp. (OTRC)	1986	$7.5 million a year (70%)	Optoelectronic parallel processor, 10-gigabit-per-second switch for communications networks
Europe			
Europe Strategic Program for R & D in Information Technology (ESPRIT II)	1987	$4.2 billion through 1992 (50%)	More than 400 projects in information technologies, microelectronics, computer-integrated manufacturing.
R & D in Advanced Communications in Europe (RACE)	1987	$1.6 billion through 1992 (under 50%)	Integrated broad-band telecommunications network
European Research Cooperation Agency (EUREKA)	1985	$8 billion committed (30%)	Encompasses 370 industrial technology projects, including a chip initiative called "Jessi"

Source: Adapted from *Fortune*, Special Issue, Spring/Summer 1991, p. 49.

creating consortia to help underwrite some of the costs associated with new technology development, and the results are quite promising.[15]

Moreover, in recent years the states have collectively spent over $550 million annually on technology development, with companies typically picking up at least half the cost of participating in the programs. In return, companies gain information about new manufacturing technology, links to university experts, and, sometimes, "seed" money.

On February 22, 1993 President Bill Clinton unveiled an industrial policy in which the government would explicitly strengthen the US economy by promoting innovation in high technology. The president's high-tech program would shift billions of dollars from military research funds to civilian research and development, for an increase of about 31 per cent. This would accelerate investment in advanced manufacturing technologies that promote US industrial competitiveness, reestablish the technological leadership and competitiveness of the US auto industry, and create a so-called computerized information superhighway to link the nation's businesses, schools, libraries, hospitals, and government agencies. President Clinton also emphasized that the government has an important role not only in researching new technology, but also in turning it into commercially useful products.

At the federal level the government has relaxed antitrust laws, thus permitting companies in the same industry to band together and conduct research that can lead to a host of new high-tech products. Once this research is completed, the companies take the information, go their own way, and develop competitive products for domestic and worldwide use.[16] This is the purpose of the consortia described in Table 4.1.

In the case of Sematech (see Table 4.1), a group of 14 semiconductor manufacturers, members match the $100 million that is given to them annually by the Defense Advanced Research Projects Agency. These funds are used to pursue a variety of objectives, including shoring up the chipmaking equipment industry. The consortium is also working on the development of reliable methods for making the world's most densely printed chips. The National Center for Manufacturing Sciences (NCMS) consortium (see Table 4.1) membership ranges in size from General Motors to small family-owned firms. The group gets $80 million annually from the US Air Force and parcels out these research monies to outside contractors. As a result of these investments, NCMS has achieved some major breakthroughs, including a method for hardening cutting tools by coating them with diamond film. The Microelectronics and Computer Technology Corporation (again, see Table 4.1) was founded in 1983 as an answer to Japan's fifth-generation computer project. Consortium members have achieved developments in computer-aided design programs, artificial intelligence systems, and the packaging of semiconductors.[17]

Following an approach that has been popular in both Europe and Japan for many years, these consortia are designed to improve US competitiveness in world markets. Results so far show the success that effective government–business cooperation can create.

ACTIVE LEARNING CHECK

Review your answer to Active Learning Case question 1 and make any changes you like. Then compare your answer to the one below.

1. What type of economic system now exists in Russia: market-driven, centrally determined, or mixed?

At the present time a mixed system exists. The country is moving away from a centrally determined economy, but there is a long way to go. As can be seen from the information in the case, this transition is causing a great deal of economic upheaval. This may result in a regression toward some of the previous central-determination decision making, but the country is not likely to go back to the old way of doing things. A mixed economic system will probably remain in place because, as seen from the text material, this is really the only way the Russians can save their economy.

ECONOMIC INTEGRATION

Economic integration is the establishment of transnational rules and regulations that enhance economic trade and cooperation among countries. At one extreme, economic integration would result in one worldwide free trade market in which all nations had a common currency and could export anything they wanted to any other nation. At the other extreme is a total lack of economic integration, in which nations were self-sufficient and did not need to trade with anyone. (The theory of these polar extremes will be discussed in Chapter 6.)

The concept of economic integration is attractive, but there are many implementation problems. For example, in order to form an economic union, the participants have to surrender some of their individual economic power, such as the authority to set tariffs and quotas. Complete integration requires a common currency or permanently fixed exchange rates; neither is easy to initiate or maintain.

There are a number of regional economic efforts that have been undertaken over the last 30 years, although none of them has attained total economic integration. The most successful has been the EU. Less developed countries (LDCs) have also made integration efforts, but these have not been as successful.

Trade creation and trade diversion

Regional economic integration brings about a shift in business activity. This shift can result in trade creation and/or trade diversion, depending on the economic efficiency of member countries in relation to nonmember countries.

Trade creation occurs when members of an economic integration group begin focusing their efforts on those goods and services for which they have a comparative advantage and start trading more extensively with each other. Trade creation results in efficient, low-cost producers in member countries gaining market share from high-cost member producers, as well as generating increased exports. These results occur because the efficient regional producers are able to offer lower-price and higher-quality output than can their competitors inside and outside the group. For example, Mexico, a low-cost producer, is now producing more cars for the US market as well as for Latin America.

Trade diversion occurs when members of an economic integration group decrease their trade with nonmember countries in favor of trade with each other. One common reason is that the removal of trade barriers among member countries makes it less expensive to buy from companies within the group, and continuing trade barriers with nonmember countries makes it more difficult for them to compete. Thus trade diversion can lead to the loss of production and exports from more efficient nonmember countries to less efficient member countries that are protected by tariffs or other barriers.

The formation of an economic integration group is not always beneficial to international trade. The creation of these integration groups is beneficial only if trade creation exceeds trade diversion. Otherwise the economic union impedes international trade.

Levels of economic integration

There are five levels of economic integration. Let us look at each.

Free trade area   A **free trade area** is an economic integration arrangement in which barriers to trade (such as tariffs) among member countries are removed. Under this arrangement each participant will seek to gain by specializing in the production of those goods and services for which it has a comparative advantage and importing those goods and services for which it has a comparative disadvantage.

One of the best-known free trade arrangements is the **North American Free Trade Agreement (NAFTA)**, a free trade area currently consisting of Canada, the United States, and Mexico. The United States and Canada created a free trade area with the United States–Canadian Free Trade Agreement of 1989. This arrangement has now been expanded to include Mexico.[18] While trade diversion can occur under free trade arrangements, the North American Free Trade Agreement (NAFTA) has also resulted in a great amount of trade creation.

Customs union   A **customs union** is a form of economic integration in which all tariffs between member countries are eliminated and a common trade policy toward nonmember countries is established. This policy often results in a uniform external tariff structure. Under this arrangement, a country outside the union will face the same tariff on exports to any member country receiving the goods.

Under a customs union member countries cede some of the control of their economic policies to the group at large. None of the regional integration groups in existence today has been formed for the purpose of creating a customs union; many of them have sought greater integration in the form of a common market or economic union. However, because of the difficulty of attaining this degree of integration, some have effectively *settled* for a customs union. The Caribbean EC and the Andean Pact are two examples.

Common market   A **common market** is a form of economic integration characterized by (a) no barriers to trade among member nations, (b) a common external trade policy, and (c) mobility of factors of production among member countries. A common market allows reallocation of production resources such as capital, labor, and technology, based on the theory of comparative advantage. While this may be economically disadvantageous to industries or specific businesses in some member countries, in theory it should lead to efficient delivery of goods and services to all member countries. The best example of a successful common market is the EU although it has now progressed beyond this economic integration and is focusing on political integration.

Economic union   An **economic union** is a deeper form of economic integration characterized by free movement of goods, services, and factors of production between member countries and full integration of economic policies. An economic union (1) unifies monetary and fiscal policy among the member nations, (2) has a common currency (or a permanently fixed exchange rate among currencies), and (3) employs the same tax rates and structures for all members. Most of the national economic policies of the individual countries are ceded to the group at large.

Political union   A **political union** goes beyond full economic integration, in which all economic policies are unified, and has a single government. This represents total economic integration, and it occurs only when countries give up their national powers to leadership under a single government. One successful example is the United

States, which combined independent states into a political union. The unification of West and East Germany in 1991 has also created a political union; the two countries now have one government and one set of overall economic policies. In contrast, Canada's constitution gives substantial economic powers to the provinces, so it is more of a federation than a political union. The former USSR has dissolved into a loose federation, rather than the political union held together by the Communist party.

Economic integration: an overall perspective

Before concluding our discussion of levels of economic integration, four points merit consideration. First, it is not necessary for a country to pursue economic integration by starting with a free trade area and then working up to a common market or economic union. For example, Great Britain was a member of a free trade area before deciding to leave and enter the EU Simply stated, countries will choose the appropriate level of economic integration based on their political[19] and economic needs.

Second, economic integration in the form of free trade typically results in a winning situation for all group members, since each member can specialize in those goods and services it makes most efficiently and rely on others in the group to provide the remainder. However, when a bloc of countries imposes a tariff on nonmembers, this often results in a win-lose situation. Those outside the bloc face tariffs, are thus less competitive with group member companies, and lose market share and revenue within the bloc. Among group members, however, increased competition often results in greater efficiency, lower prices, and increased exports to nonmember markets.

Third, and complementary to the above, bloc members often find that their business is able to achieve **internal economies of scale** brought about by lower production costs and other savings within a firm. So while a firm in France may have found that its plant was only moderately efficient when producing 1,000 units a week for the French market, it is now highly efficient producing 4,000 units a week for countries throughout the EU. The elimination of tariffs and trade barriers and the opening up of new geographic markets allow the company to increase production efficiency. In addition, since factors of production in a common market are allowed to flow freely across borders, the firm may also achieve **external economies of scale** brought about by access to cheaper capital, more highly skilled labor, and superior technology. In short, in-group companies can draw on resources in member countries to help increase efficiency.

Finally, in the short run, some bloc countries may suffer because other members are able to achieve greater increases in efficiency and thus dominate certain industries and markets. This may result in an adjustment period that lasts as long as a decade, as poorer bloc countries scramble to improve their technology, retrain their work force, and redirect their economies to markets where they can gain and sustain an advantage *vis-à-vis* other group members.

The European Union (EU)

In Europe from 1920 through World War II, there was fierce nationalism and economic trade was often characterized by isolationism and protectionism. After World War II the **Organization for European Economic Cooperation** was established to administer the Marshall Plan and to help with the reconstruction of Europe. It now consists of 22 advanced economies, mostly in Western Europe plus Japan, the United States, and Canada. In 1952 six European countries (Belgium, France, Italy, Luxembourg, the Netherlands, and West Germany) established the **European Coal and Steel Community (ECSC)** for the purpose of creating a common market that would revitalize the efficiency and competitiveness of these industries. The group's success was notable and set the stage for further cooperative efforts.

Formation   The foundation of the European Union was laid in 1957 by the Treaty of Rome. The six nations of the ECSC were the original founders of the European Economic Community, and by 1991 six others had joined them (Great Britain, Denmark, Greece, Ireland, Portugal, and Spain). In 1995, Austria, Finland and Sweden joined the European Community (EC), which was renamed the EU after the Treaty of Maastricht in 1992. The main provisions of the founding treaty of 1957 were:

1. Formation of a free trade area among the members would be brought about by the gradual elimination of tariffs, quotas, and other trade barriers.
2. Barriers to the movement of labor, capital, and business enterprises would eventually be removed.
3. Common agricultural policies would be adopted.
4. An investment fund to channel capital from the more advanced regions of the bloc to the less advanced regions would be created.
5. A customs union characterized by a uniform tariff schedule applicable to imports from the rest of the world would be created.

These were ambitious goals and some countries felt that the objectives went beyond what they wanted to do. These countries formed the European Free Trade Association (EFTA), whose primary goal was to dismantle trade barriers among its members. Austria, Denmark, Norway, Portugal, Sweden, Switzerland, and the United Kingdom were the founding members. Over the years the distinctions between EFTA and the EC had blurred, as some of the former members (Great Britain, Denmark, Portugal, Austria and Sweden) have joined the EC. In 1992 EFTA signed a treaty which formally gives EFTA members an economic association with the EU. In addition, most EFTA members are applying for admission to the EU.[20]

Growth and challenges   Over the years the EU made vigorous headway in pursuit of its objectives. For example, during the 1970s formal barriers to the free flow of labor and capital were gradually dismantled. The **Single European Act**, which effectively prevents a country from vetoing any EU decision it deems to be in conflict with its vital interests, was enacted in the 1980s. In the past this veto power had been continually used by EC members to protect their respective economic advantages and made it difficult for the group to make decisions. Now veto power is based on a total of 87 votes which are allocated among the 15 members, and 62 votes are needed to pass a proposal.

Other major breakthroughs are occurring in the political and financial areas. With the EC 1992 measures, the EU has transformed itself into a political, economic, and monetary superpower that can speak with one powerful voice about everything from interest rates to defense. In moving in this direction, the EU political leaders negotiated and put into process a method for ratifying two new treaties that would extend the community's powers from their present largely economic role to foreign and

INTERNATIONAL BUSINESS STRATEGY IN ACTION

EU trade restrictions

One of the basic underpinnings of a common market is that all member countries engage in free trade with each other. Outsiders who want to benefit from this free trade must set up operations within the market or be subject to quotas or other trade barriers. Now it seems that some EU countries are concerned that this arrangement does not provide sufficient protection against foreign competition. Of primary concern are the Japanese automakers.

Both Italy and France have maintained quotas on Japan's auto imports, thus helping to restrict the latter's European market share to around 10 per cent. These quotas were supposed to be abolished after the EU became a single European market. However, the Italians and French are lobbying for new restrictions.

There is ongoing support for restricting Japanese sales in Europe until the year 2000. These restrictions are in the form of quotas that would allow Japanese unit sales to increase from 1.2 million vehicles in 1990 to a maximum of 2.5 million in 1999. This means that at the turn of the century Japanese automakers would hold around 16 per cent of the European market. While this is a fairly healthy market share increase, it is much less than the Japanese would be likely to gain if the restrictions were lifted. In the mid-1990s it seemed as if the increase in the yen could change the luck of European producers, but the recent Asian crisis threatens to increase the strength of the Japanese. With quotas in place, cheap exports from Asia cannot go over the limit, but the profits for producers will be higher, strengthening the overall position of Japanese competitors.

Perhaps worst of all, European protectionists want the quota limits to include Japanese autos made in Europe as well as those that are imported. This will severely handicap the Japanese since they have spent billions of dollars buying and building auto plants in Europe. For example, the Nissan plant in Britain can assemble 200,000 cars annually and there are plans underway to double this output.

One of the major arguments protectionists make is that without some form of quota, the Japanese will dominate the European market which will then be difficult to recapture. They point to Denmark, Greece, and Ireland, which have no quotas and where Japanese cars already hold more than 35 per cent of the market. Those in favor of strict quotas want a transition period that will allow European car makers to strengthen their product quality and reliability and to be in a position to compete more effectively with the Japanese. For their part, the Japanese wonder if this new wave of protectionism sentiment is not simply a way of sidestepping the spirit of the EU agreement in order to prevent them from gaining a major foothold in Europe.

Sources: Adapted from Mark Maremont, Karen Lowry Miller, and Stewart Toy, "Protectionism Is King of the Road," *Business Week*, May 13, 1991; Howard Gleckman et al., "Clinton's Agenda," *Business Week*, January 25, 1993; Keith Bradsher, "Europe, US Reach Partial Pact," *New York Times*, April 22, 1993; *http://www.automotive.co.uk/teetnews/pages-2/news1297/nf1857.htm*; "When Horrid for Car Makers is Smashing for Customers," *The Economist*, September 30, 1995.

security policy and monetary affairs and, eventually, to defense.[21] The effect of such actions would be the creation of a "United States of Europe." (These EU 1992 measures, and the Maastricht Treaty of 1991, are discussed in more detail in Chapter 15.)

However, the EU still faces a number of problems. One is disagreement among the members regarding the relationship that should exist between the community and the rest of the world. The box "International Business Strategy in Action: EU Trade Restrictions" provides some examples. A second problem is the protection that countries give to their own industries, which is in direct contrast to the spirit of EU rules.[22] A related area is the community's agriculture policies, which provide subsidies and rebates to farmers and have resulted in charges of unfair trade practices. A third problem is the disagreement among the members regarding the amount of protection that poorer countries (Spain, Portugal) should be given before all trade barriers are dismantled.[23]

One of the key goals of EU integration is the free flow of capital, and the single European currency will help to bring this about. Closely linked to this goal is the establishment of a central European bank that will regulate the money supply and thus be able to stabilize interest rates throughout the EU.[24]

Even if this goal is not fully attained during this decade, the EU is going to be an increasingly powerful economic force in the international arena.[25] A close look at the community's organizational arrangement helps to explain why.

Organization   There are four major institutions that manage the EU: the Council of Ministers, the European Commission, the European Parliament, and the Court of Justice.

The **Council of Ministers** is the major policy decision-making body of the EU. These 15 individuals are the foreign ministers of their respective countries and, with the exception of the budget, they are responsible for final EU decisions.

The **European Commission** has 20 members who are chosen by agreement of the member governments. France, Germany, Italy, Spain and the UK have two representatives each, and the other members one each. The Commission, the executive branch of the EU, handles a great deal of the technical work associated with preparing decisions and regulations. The group is responsible for drafting legislation for proposal to the Council of Ministers, overseeing the implementation of EU policies, and carrying out studies on key policy issues.

The **European Parliament** has approximately 630 members who are elected directly by the voters in each member country. The Parliament serves as a watchdog on EU expenditures in addition to evaluating other decisions of the Council.

The **Court of Justice** has one judge appointed from each EU member country; this Court serves as the official interpreter of EU law. In most cases this requires the justices to rule on the meaning or application of the Treaty of Rome, based on the actions of member countries, companies, and individuals. Because EU rules are becoming more closely interwoven with national laws in the member countries, in recent years the Court has been serving increasingly as a court of appeal for national courts on issues that are EU-related. The Court sits in Luxembourg.

The future   The EU is a powerful economic union. Empirical studies show that the community has created much more trade than it has diverted from the rest of the world. Moreover, this market has a greater combined gross domestic product than any of the two other major markets: North America or Japan and the industrialized Orient. At the same time it is likely that EU-generated projects will offer major competition to other worldwide industries. For example, Airbus Industries, a consortium formed by some of the EU countries, now offers substantial competition to major aircraft manufacturers such as Boeing. Quite clearly, the common market concept promises tremendous economic gains for member countries.

Other economic alliances

The EU is the most successful economic union, but there are a host of others. The following briefly examines three others.

Andean Pact   The **Andean Pact** (sometimes known as Ancom, which stands for Andean common market) is an economic union that now consists of Bolivia, Colombia, Ecuador, Peru, and Venezuela. These five countries were members of the original Latin American Free Trade Association (now called ALADI) but were not satisfied with the progress of this group and so broke away. The original objectives of the Ancom countries were to integrate themselves economically, to reduce internal tariffs, to create a common external tariff, and to offer special concessions to the two smallest members, Bolivia and Ecuador. The group also agreed that no foreign direct investment (FDI) would be allowed in sectors such as banking, telecommunications, and retail sales, and foreign investors in all other sectors would be required to sell at least 51 per cent of their holdings to local investors over a 15-year period. There also are restrictions on annual profit remittance. These regulations have been enforced with a variety of exceptions being allowed. They have also proved to discourage FDI. Chile, an original member of Ancom, left the group because it wanted to attract more FDI. The other members of Ancom have had varying degrees of economic success. The group has not been able to achieve tariff-free trade or a common external tariff, and economic development has been far short of expectations.

ASEAN   The **Association of Southeast Asian Nations (ASEAN)** was founded in 1967 and includes Brunei, Indonesia, Malaysia, the Philippines, Singapore, Thailand, and Vietnam. This economic bloc is different from most others in that the primary emphasis is not on reducing trade barriers among the members, although this has been done, but rather on promoting exports to other countries. With the notable exception of Singapore, which has offshore manufacturing assembly plants, the group relies heavily on exports of raw materials. Members have been particularly successful in promoting exports to the Japanese market and to the EU. Until the late 1990s members of ASEAN have experienced rapid economic growth, thanks in no small part to the efficiency and productivity of their members as well as to their impressive marketing skills. However, the economic downturn in Asia in recent years has stalled many of these economies, especially Indonesia.

Free trade agreement   Not all integration efforts are designed to create an economic union. In the case of the United States and Canada free trade has proven to be the most beneficial route. The United States–Canada Free Trade Agreement (FTA) of 1989 was designed to remove most trade barriers between the two countries by the end of the 1990s. A similar pact (NAFTA) was negotiated with Mexico in 1993.[26] From 1990 to 1996 US exports to Canada and Mexico increased from $111.3 billion to $189.3 billion annually. As a result of these initiatives, exports among the three countries have reached dramatic new highs during the 1990s. This will be particularly important to the United States, which would like to see a strong North American economy that can compete effectively with the EU and the Pacific Rim. An earlier free trade agreement was signed between Australia and New Zealand in the late 1980s. In addition, Mexico has signed several free trade agreements with Central and South American nations. These arrangements are discussed in more detail in Part Four.

ACTIVE LEARNING CHECK

Review your answer to Active Learning Case question 2 and make any changes you like. Then compare your answer to the one below.

2. Would Russia benefit by gaining admission to one of the major economic unions such as the EU? Why?

Russia certainly would benefit by gaining admission to one of these economic unions. Such a development would make it possible for the country to take advantage of a wide variety of benefits, including free movement of goods and services across borders, trade creation, possible development of internal economies brought about by the huge market that would then be available for Russian goods, and a strengthening of the nation's currency. Of course, admission into the EU or one of the other major economic unions is unlikely to occur, at least within the next few years. However, it would offer a very big boost to the nation's economy.

ECONOMIC INTEGRATION AND STRATEGIC MANAGEMENT

How can MNEs use strategic planning to benefit from worldwide economic integration efforts? A number of strategic steps have proved particularly helpful. These include the use of joint ventures and acquisitions and the localization of business focus.

Joint ventures and acquisitions

One of the easiest ways of benefiting from economic integration is by establishing a joint venture with a company that is a member of that union. In Europe, in recent years, there have been numerous examples ranging from telecommunications to automobiles to breweries.

Telecommunications Lucent Technologies recently ended more than a century of independence in the telephone manufacturing business when it agreed to merge its consumer phone unit with that of Philips Electronics NV. The two firms, acting in consort, will produce a wide range of products from corded and cordless telephones to answering machines and a variety of types of digital cellular phones. In particular, this arrangement will give Philips's consumer phone business a strong boost. At the same time it will help Lucent, which is very strong in network gear and high tech chips and software that are used in switches and phones but which has been having trouble remaining competitive in the face of stiff competition from European suppliers.[27]

Another example is Microsoft and Sony which have now teamed up to link personal computers and consumer electronics devices, thus moving closer together on technology standards for digital television and other consumer products. The two firms have endorsed a technology that can connect videocassette recorders, camcorders, personal computers, and other devices. Microsoft intends to license software from Sony used with the networking technology and use this software with versions of an operating system that it is trying to make a standard for non-personal computer (PC) products. If things work according to plan, the joint venture will result in a technology that consumers can use to easily plug a camcorder to a PC or television set-top box for sending video mail over the Internet.[28]

Still another example is the recent $24 billion acquisition of MCI Communications by British Telecommunications (BT). This merger is the largest acquisition of a US company and opens a major market to BT. At the same time, under the terms that were hammered out with the US Justice Department, BT will not be allowed to use its dominance in the British market to keep American competitors such as AT&T from competing there. The result is likely to be increased competition, lower prices, and better service for customers in both the US and the United Kingdom.[29]

Automobiles   The largest automobile firm in the world is General Motors which in a recent year sold approximately 9 million cars and trucks. Daimler-Benz's recent acquisition of Chrysler does not put the firm in the same league as GM, but it does catapult the new company, DaimlerChrysler AG, into fifth place behind Ford, Toyota, and Volkswagen. More importantly, it provides both of the parties with an opportunity to exploit what it does best, while also gaining more access to the other's primary market. Daimler's Mercedes-Benz passenger cars are synonymous with luxury and superb engineering. Chrysler is known for its low-cost production of trucks, minivans, and sport-utility vehicles. Mercedes is a global company that has been heavily confined by its luxury car niche. Chrysler is almost wholly domestic in its sales coverage. Now, by spreading Chrysler's production expertise to Daimler's operations and merging both product development forces, the new firm hopes to cut costs by $3 billion annually and become an international competitor in all major markets from Europe and North American to Asia. In particular, the merger is allowing both companies to move into markets where they could not go alone. For example, neither had much presence in either Latin America or Asia, although Daimler did sell heavy trucks there. Now, Chrysler's inexpensive small cars will give Daimler a vehicle to sell in emerging markets, since its Mercedes is far too expensive to gain a major foothold here. At the same time, Daimler will provide Chrysler with strong entry into the EU and Asian markets. The company will also give Chrysler assistance in improving its auto quality, and with its diesel engines, Daimler could help Chrysler in its efforts to sell subcompacts and minivans in Europe. For its part, Chrysler, which has the best supplier relations in the US auto industry, can help Daimler negotiate better prices on its parts and supplies. Additionally, working together the two can save on warehousing and logistics for cars and spare parts in both Europe and the US. The two will also be able to jointly make internal components such as air conditioning systems and door latches and pool their resources in developing basic technology. As a result, DaimlerChrysler AG is likely to become a growing competitor for GM, Ford, Toyota, and Volkswagen worldwide.[30]

Breweries   Many brewers have found, to their regret, that it is difficult to get customers to change brands. This is particularly true in countries such as Germany, England, and the Netherlands, where beer is popular. Customers are often fiercely loyal to local brands, and the only way of tapping into these markets is by purchasing the brewery. Major European brewers have long realized this and have not hesitated to buy operations in other countries. A good example is the purchase of La Cruz del Campo, Spain's largest brewery, by Britain's Guinness. However, the company has a long way to go before it will catch Heineken, which for years has been buying small brewers on the continent. As a result of such strategies, many of Europe's largest brewers earn a considerable percentage of their income from foreign sales.

Localization of business operations

MNEs cannot conduct business overseas in the same way that they do at home. Assuming that they can often results in serious problems. Successful localization efforts typically focus on four areas: products, profits, production, and management.[31]

Products   Localization of products requires the development, manufacturing, and marketing of goods best suited to the needs of the local customer and marketplace. This typically requires modification of products that have sold well in other geographic regions. For example, in North America, buyers use motorcycles primarily for leisure and sports, so they look for high horsepower output and speed. In contrast, Southeast Asians use motorcycles as a basic means of transportation, so they look for low cost and ease of maintenance; in Australia, where shepherds use motorcycles to drive sheep, low-speed torque is more important than either high speed or ease of maintenance.[32]

MNEs commonly localize production by investing in research and development, so they can produce the product that fits the specific needs of that market. This is sometimes more difficult than it appears, especially if the MNE has been successful with a product in the home market and is unwilling to change.

A good example is provided by the Whirlpool Corporation, which dominated the US market before going to Europe in the late 1980s. The firm believed that the giant $20 billion European appliance market with dozens of marginally profitable companies was on the verge of consolidation and it wanted to be one of the major players. So it bought a majority stake in a struggling appliance operation belonging to NV Philips, the Dutch electronics giant. Then, two years later, it acquired the rest of the operation for $1.1 billion. Whirlpool believed that the European market was highly regionalized because there were so many diverse consumer preferences. For example, the Swedish liked galvanized washers that could withstand salty air; the British washed their clothes more often than many others, so they wanted quieter washing machines. Stoves provided even greater examples of product diversity. However, Whirlpool believed that the market was ready for product consolidation as seen by its support for a "world washer," a single machine that could be sold anywhere on the continent. As product diversity was reduced, Whirlpool believed, the marginal producers would be driven from the market and its own share would climb. What the company found was that the European market was a lot more competitive than it realized. Sweden's AB Electrolux and Germany's Bosch-Siemens Hausgeraete GmbH proved to be excellent competitors. In particular, they have revamped their factories and driven costs down sharply. They also began introducing new products that kept customers coming back. By thus appealing to local tastes, Electrolux and Bosch-Siemens managed to keep Whirlpool's profits to a minimum, while preventing the firm from gaining market share.[33]

Localization of profits   Localization of profits is the reinvestment of earnings in the local market. MNEs do this by taking their earnings and using them to expand operations, set up new plants and offices, hire more local people, and make the investment more self-sufficient. In the United States, for example, Honda started out with an initial investment of $250,000 and has gradually reinvested its US profits. Today the company has almost $2 billion in its motorcycle, auto, and engine manufacturing plants in Ohio. At the same time the company has reinvested almost $200 million in Honda Canada, a manufacturing plant making Honda Civics.

Localization of production   Localization of production involves the manufacture of goods in the host market.[34] Many MNEs, upon entering a foreign market, handle this function by exporting from the home country. For a successful relationship, however, this often is only a short-run strategy and is eventually replaced by a local manufacturing base.[35] One strategy for localizing production is by increasing the amount of local content in the product, for example by producing more and more of the subunits in the host country. The ultimate step, of course, is to produce the entire product locally. In the case of Honda, for example, the company decided in 1987 to make its auto manufacturing facility in Ohio a fully integrated, self-reliant entity. This strategy entailed five steps:

1. The company decided that by 1991 the plant would be exporting 70,000 cars to international markets, including Japan.
2. The number of engineers engaged in research would be increased from 200 up to 500 between 1989 and 1991 and another 200 engineers would be hired for designing and developing new production equipment and machinery.
3. The Ohio engine plant would be expanded to produce 500,000 units annually.
4. A new auto production facility would be set up next to the existing factory so that Ohio plant production would rise to over 500,000 annually.
5. The domestic content of Ohio-built cars would be at least 75 per cent.[36]

Toyota provides another good example of product localization. The company recently increased capacity at its Georgetown, Kentucky plant from 380,000 vehicles up to 500,000, doubled its Corolla production to 200,000 units at its Ontario, Canada facility, and is now building a plant in Evansville, Indiana to turn out 100,000 T100 pickup trucks powered by V-8 engines. Toyota has also doubled production at its Burnaston, Britain plant where Carina E sedans and wagons are made and is considering the construction of a new passenger-car factory on the continent. At the same time the company is increasing auto production in its Thailand plant and negotiating with the government to build an engine factory in Tianjin, China.[37]

A second way in which production is localized is by providing added value in operations by modifying the imported product and adapting it to local conditions and tastes. This approach is used when a product requires country-by-country (or regional) changes.

Localization of production is often carried out in conjunction with a home country partner, who provides the plant and personnel while the MNE is responsible for the initial product and the technology needed in assembling or modifying the goods. Sometimes, however, the MNE will own the total operation and depend on local management to help run the organization.

Localization of management   There are a number of ways that MNEs localize the management, that is, trying to develop a polycentric (host-country-oriented) attitude. One way is by encouraging home office managers to learn the local culture and become part of the community. Research reveals that companies that staff their subsidiaries with older, mature senior managers from the home country who are fluent in the local language are often more highly productive than are MNEs that staff operations with younger, less experienced managers.[38] A second way of localizing management is by delegating authority to host country managers and developing and promoting them wherever possible. This strategy helps to create a bond between the host and the home country management. As one MNE spokesperson put it:

> . . . we have become convinced that good communication between management and labor, as well as delegation of authority, elevate the employees' sense of participation in decision making. This, in turn, gives the employees a stronger sense of responsibility and motivation, which leads to improved productivity and maintenance of high quality standards.[39]

115

ACTIVE LEARNING CHECK

Review your answer to Active Learning Case question 3 and make any changes you like. Then compare your answer to the one below.

3. Is Russia a good potential investment for US business? Explain.

Arguments can be made for each side. Untapped natural resources and potential consumer demand could provide billions of dollars of annual sales. On the other hand, the economy is currently in terrible shape, and it is likely to take many more years before Russia begins to provide an adequate return on investment for many current projects. One of the major reasons for getting in now, of course, is to try and gain a strong foothold in the market and to use this to effectively block out the competition. If this should happen, those coming later would find slim pickings. However, this is unlikely to happen and in most cases investors are best off proceeding with caution and waiting for the current uncertainty and turmoil to settle.

SUMMARY

Key points

1. Political ideologies and economic systems are interwoven. Democracies tend to have market-driven economies; totalitarian governments tend to have centrally determined economies. However, there are few nations that fit totally into one of these two paradigms. Most use a mixed economic model such as that of the United States, which is mainly a market-driven economy with some central planning, or Russia, which still relies on central planning but is moving fast to allow some degree of free enterprise.

2. Another current economic development is the trend toward privatization. Many countries are selling off state-owned enterprises, and there are a variety of reasons that can be cited for these actions. In most cases these are economic in nature, including (a) increased efficiency, (b) reduction in government outlays, and (c) generation of funds for the national treasury.

3. Economic integration is the establishment of transnational rules and regulations that permit economic trade and cooperation among countries. Effective integration brings about trade creation, although in some cases these efforts have resulted in trade diversion. There are five levels of regional economic trade integration: free trade areas, customs unions, common markets, economic unions, and political unions. The most successful examples have been the EU and the North American Free Trade area.

4. Multinational enterprises use a variety of strategies to benefit from integration efforts. One is joint ventures and acquisitions by which they are able to surmount the economic wall and gain an inside position in the economic alliance or free trade area. The other strategy is through the localization of operations by focusing on products, profits, production, and management. MNEs typically use both of these strategic approaches.

Key terms

- ideology
- democracy
- totalitarianism
- communism
- theocratic totalitarianism
- secular totalitarianism
- market-driven economy
- centrally determined economy
- mixed economies
- privatization
- nationalization
- divestiture
- contract management
- Ministry of International Trade and Industry (MITI)
- economic integration
- trade creation
- trade diversion
- free trade area
- European Free Trade Association (EFTA)
- customs union
- common market
- economic union
- political union
- internal economies of scale
- external economies of scale
- Organization for European Economic Cooperation
- European Coal and Steel Community (ECSC)
- Single European Act
- Council of Ministers
- European Commission
- European Parliament
- Court of Justice
- Andean Pact
- Association of Southeast Asian Nations (ASEAN)

Review and discussion questions

1. As political systems change, economic systems follow. What does this statement mean?
2. How does a centrally determined economy differ from a market-driven economy? Explain.
3. What are the benefits of privatization? Why will the trend toward privatization continue?
4. Why are government–business cooperative efforts beginning to increase? What benefits do they offer?
5. What is the purpose of research consortia? What is their future likely to be? Why?
6. How does trade creation differ from trade diversion? Compare and contrast the two.
7. There are five levels of economic integration. What is meant by this statement? Be complete in your answer.
8. How does the EU function? Identify and describe its organization and operation.
9. What is the purpose of the following economic alliances: North American Free Trade Agreement, the Andean Pact, and ASEAN.
10. One of the primary ways that MNEs use strategic planning to benefit from economic integration efforts is through joint ventures and acquisitions. How do MNEs do this?
11. How do MNEs seek to localize their business focus? Describe three steps that they take.

HOW ENVIRONMENTAL REGULATIONS CAN BE USED AS TRADE BARRIERS

With free trade areas evolving around the globe, many protected industries are now facing unwelcome competition. Free trade agreements generally include a principle of national treatment under which a country must treat all producers, domestic or foreign, equally. However, some seemingly neutral environmental regulations pose a greater burden on foreign producers than on their domestic competitors. Thus, they act as trade barriers under the disguise of environmental regulations.

For example, while environmental groups lobby for newsprint to contain a determined amount of recycled material and domestic producers of newsprint support the regulation, foreign newsprint companies, which have no recycling facilities in the host country, face a competitive disadvantage. This is what has been called a "baptist-bootlegger" coalition. During the US prohibition era, Baptists were opposed to alcoholic consumption on moral grounds, while bootleggers actually benefited from prohibition by the sale of illegal alcoholic beverages. Today, environmental groups and domestic producers often form coalitions to promote their respective interests.

In the newsprint case, the foreign company would have two options if it were to continue to supply material from its home country. It could either open recycling plants in the host country and transport pulp from its country to be processed there so as to meet the environmental regulations or take the recycling material to its home country to be processed. Both alternatives pose significant transportation costs to the foreign producer.

A similar case is presented by the Ontario Beer Can Tax. In the early 1990s the province of Ontario levied a tax of $0.10 on each aluminum beer can. The province argued that these cans were not environmentally friendly and that the tax was designed to encourage the use of refillable glass bottles. US producers of beer and aluminum cans contended that this was a protectionist move, and that the Ontario government was singling out the competition with its beer industry since it had no similar tax for soft drinks and juice cans. Moreover, research studies found that the aluminum can and the glass bottle both affect the environment equally, and 80 per cent of all the cans were being recycled. Additionally, it was found that the larger, heavier glass required more energy than did the lighter aluminum cans.

1. How can a health and safety regulation become a trade barrier? Provide examples.

2. How can different environmental circumstances make one country's regulations inefficient in another country?

3. What are some reasons why the government might not be willing to make allowances for different countries?

Sources: Adapted from Alan M. Rugman, John Kirton and Julie Soloway, *Environmental Regulations and Corporate Strategy: A NAFTA Perspective* (Oxford: Oxford University Press, 1999) M. Trebilcock and R. Howse, "Trade Policy and Domestic Health and Safety Standards," *The Regulation of International Trade*, 2nd ed. (London: Routledge, 1999); Julie Soloway, "Environmental Trade Barriers in NAFTA: The MMT Fuel Additives Controversy," *Minnesota Journal of Global Trade*, vol. 8, no. 1, 1998; David Vogel and Alan M. Rugman, "Environmentally Related Trade Disputes between the United States and Canada," *The American Review of Canadian Studies*, Summer 1997, pp. 271–292.

THAMES WATER GOES INTERNATIONAL

Thames Water plc is the largest British water company, established in 1989 after Prime Minister Margaret Thatcher privatized the water industry. The company supplies the water and sewage services to over 11 million people in the Thames Valley, from the quaint university city of Oxford to one of the world's largest urban agglomerations in London.

The activities of the core water utility division of Thames Water are still subject to regulation by OFWAT, the UK water regulator, which sets price controls and regulatory standards over water and sewage services every five years. The OFWAT policy is to force the British regional water monopolies to make price cuts to the water bills of their customers. The managerial paradox is that any increases in operating efficiency in the water utility essentially are taxed away every five years. In the intervening period there is some incentive for the overall company to use economic efficiency improvements in the utility division to help fund development of its nonregulated commercially-based business.

Thames Water is no exception to this policy. Whereas some water utilities have moved into other sectors (such as electricity and gas), Thames Water has decided against the multi-utilities approach, adopted by other British water companies such as United Utilities and Hyder. Instead Thames Water's strategy is two-fold. First it has expanded into commercial aspects of the water business. Half of its 11,000 employees now work in water-related businesses, such as the design, engineering and maintenance of water membrane systems and related water treatment products, or in the servicing and marketing of water-related business.

Second, the company has engaged in international diversification. It has major projects in Australia, Turkey, Indonesia, Ukraine, Malaysia, the Philippines and Thailand. This is a geographic extension of its firm-specific advantage in water production and supply. The international market for water is worth over $1 billion dollars a year and profit potential abroad is much greater than in Britain. The major global rivals are the two giant French water companies, CGE (compagnie Générale des Eaux) now called Vivendi, with sales of $30 billion, and Suez-Lyonnaise des Eaux with sales of $20 billion. There are few North American commercial water companies due to the fragmented and regulated nature of the US municipal and Canadian provincial markets.

In Indonesia, Thames Water has a 25-year contract to supply fresh water to half the population of the capital city, Jakarta. In March 1998 this contract was temporarily rescinded by the new President as he alleged that it was signed with the son of the former President Suharto. Despite being the first western business to be disrupted by this type of political risk, within a month Thames Water had signed up with the new government of Indonesia.

In the Australian project in Adelaide, Thames Water supplied the technical expertise in collaboration with a French partner. The French did the political lobbying, and their skill in this was reflected by winning the contract shortly after the French government conducted a series of nuclear tests in the Pacific which were strongly opposed by the Australian and New Zealand governments. The political image of Thames Water in Asia was not affected by this association and the British company tends to have "neutral" political risk exposure.

Thames Water has already learned some harsh lessons in international business. Former CEO, Mike Hoffman, took a bath by acquiring an East German design and contracting business (UTAG) in 1992. This firm lost money as the effective demand for water market infrastructure post-reunification did not expand in Germany as much as expected. Thames Water also did not research the local politics, where there remained strong local municipal regulations. So Thames Water sold off its German venture and under new CEO, Bill Alexander, it built up a new portfolio of international operations which rest on its core skills. The board and new CEO also decided to closely integrate all the international operations with its basic British utility business.

Over the next OFWAT regulatory period (2000–2005) Thames Water will need to further build up its international operations to contribute to profits and to continue moving from a regulated utility to an international business.

1. How has Thames Water dealt with the ongoing British regulation (despite privatization) of its core water utility?

2. What is your assessment of the political risk associated with Thames Water's international projects, especially that in Indonesia?

3. In what way can international trade agreements help to reduce such political risk?

Sources: Annual Reports of Thames Water plc.

ENDNOTES

1. Fred Luthans and Richard M. Hodgetts, *Business*, 2nd ed. (Hinsdale, Ill.: Dryden Press, 1992), pp. 11–12.

2. Also, see Steven Greenhouse, "Soviet Economists Say Shift to Free Market Is Inevitable," *New York Times*, February 18, 1991, p. 21; and Allessandra Stanley, "Mission to Moscow: Preaching the Gospel of Business," *New York Times*, February 27, 1994, Section F, p. 4.

3. See, for example, David E. Sanger, "US–Japan Talks at Impasse on Access to Building Jobs," *New York Times*, June 1, 1991, pp. 17, 19.

4. Doron P. Levin, "Big 3 Charge Mini-Van Dumping," *New York Times*, June 1, 1991, p. 20.

5. R. Molz, "Privatization of Government Enterprise: The Challenge to Management," *Management International Review*, vol. 29, no. 4, 1989, pp. 29–30.

6. Ibid., pp. 32–33.

7. For excellent coverage of privatization, see Dennis J. Gayle and Jonathan N. Goodrich (eds.), *Privatization and Deregulation in Global Perspective* (New York: Quorum Books, 1990).

8. Ferdinand Protzman, "Bonn, Scouting for Cash, Hopes to Sell Autobahn," *New York Times*, February 10, 1993, p. C2.

9. Clifford Krauss, "Argentina to Hasten End of Phone Monopoly," *New York Times*, March 11, 1998, Section C, p. 4.

10. Gautam Naik, "Telecom Deregulation In Britain Delivered A Nice Surprise: Jobs," *Wall Street Journal*, March 5, 1998, pp. A1, A6.

11. Rose Brady, Rosemarie Boyle, and Peter Galuszka, "Going Private: The Soviets Can Hardly Wait," *Business Week*, June 10, 1991, p. 49.

12. See, for example, Thomas Sommerlatte, "Six Months After the Merger of the Two Germanys," *International Executive*, March–April 1991, pp. 7–9.

13. Klaus Wieners, "Responding to German Reunification: Opportunities for US Companies in the (Former) GDR," *Journal of European Business*, January/February 1991, p. 5.

14. Richard W. Judy, "Privatization in Eastern Europe: Opportunities and Pitfalls," *International Executive*, July–August 1990, p. 9.

15. Edmund Faltermayer, "The Thaw in Washington," *Fortune*, Special Issue, Spring/Summer 1991, p. 48.

16. For one development, see Andrew Pollack, "Technology Links Will Be Discussed by Apple and IBM," *New York Times*, June 10, 1991, pp. A1, C2.

17. Faltermayer, op. cit., p. 51.

18. Larry Reibstein et al., "A Mexican Miracle?" *Newsweek*, May 20, 1991, pp. 42–45; and Paul Magnusson et al., "The Mexico Pact: Worth the Price?" *Business Week*, May 27, 1991, pp. 32–35.

19. Germany is a good example, and some people are discussing similar possibilities for Korea as seen in Ford S. Worthy, "Can the Koreas Get Together?" *Fortune*, February 11, 1991, pp. 126–132.

20. Also see "Europe's Long Stride on a Road to Unity That Reaches the Horizon," *New York Times*, January 1, 1993, p. A5; and "A Business Guide to the New Europe," *New York Times*, January 2, 1993, p. 13.

21. Philip Revzin, "EC Leaders Adopt 2-Year Plan to Forge Political, Monetary Unity in Europe," *Wall Street Journal*, December 17, 1990, p. A6.

22. Peter Fuhrman, "Aidez-moi," *Forbes*, April 15, 1991, p. 43.

23. Jeff Madura and Francis W. Wright, "What Are the Real Prospects for Total EC Integration?" *International Executive*, March–April 1991, p. 16.

24. For more on this, see Jacques Groothaert, "The Implications of 1991 for Financial Management," *International Executive*, January–February 1991, pp. 17–23.

25. For example, the EU is beginning to look into cutting subsidies and forcing companies to compete in a freer market environment, as explained in Jonathan B. Levine, "European High Tech Tries to Do Something Drastic: Grow Up," *Business Week*, March 25, 1991, p. 48.

26. Keith Bradsher, "Trade Pact Signed in 3 Capitals," *New York Times*, December 18, 1992, pp. C1–C2.

27. John J. Keller, "Lucent, Philips to Produce Phones Jointly," *Wall Street Journal*, June 18, 1997, p. A3.

28. Don Clark and David Bank, "Miscrosoft, Sony To Cooperate on PCs, Devices," *Wall Street Journal*, April 8, 1998, p. B6.

29. John R. Wilke, "British Telecom Purchase of MCI Is Cleared by Justice Department," *Wall Street Journal*, July 8, 1997, p. B4.

30. Bill Vlasic et al., "The First Global Colossus," *Business Week*, May 18, 1998, pp. 40–43; "Gentlemen, Start Your Engines," *Fortune*, June 8, 1998, pp. 138–146; and Alex Taylor III, "Neutron Jurgen Ignites a Revolution at Daimler-Benz," *Fortune*, November 10, 1997, pp. 144–152.

31. Hideo Sugiura, "How Honda Localizes Its Global Strategy," *Sloan Management Review*, Fall 1990, pp. 77–82.

32. Ibid., p. 78.

33. Greg Steinmetz and Carl Quintanilla, "Whirlpool Expected Easy Going in Europe, And It Got A Big Shock," *Wall Street Journal*, April 10, 1998, pp. A1, A6.

34. Ferdinand Protzman, "Rewriting the Contract for Germany's Vaunted Workers," *New York Times*, February 13, 1994, Section F, p. 5.

35. "Pepsi Investing $350 Million in China Plants," *New York Times*, January 27, 1994, p. C3.
36. Sugiura, op. cit., p. 80.
37. Brian Bremner et al., "Toyota's Crusade," *Business Week*, April 7, 1997, pp. 104–114.
38. See Robert O. Metzger and Ari Ginsberg, "Lessons from Japanese Global Acquisitions," *Journal of Business Strategy*, May–June 1989, p. 35.
39. Ibid., p. 79.

ADDITIONAL BIBLIOGRAPHY

Averyt, William F. "Managing Public Policy Abroad: Foreign Corporate Representation in Washington," *Columbia Journal of World Business*, vol. 25, no. 3 (Fall 1990).

Calingaert, Michael. "Government–Business Relations in the European Community," *California Management Review*, vol. 35, no. 2 (Winter 1993).

Cheit, Earl F. "A Declaration on Open Regionalism in the Pacific," *California Management Review*, vol. 35, no. 1 (Fall 1992).

Dunning, John H. *Governments, Globalization and International Business* (Oxford: Oxford University Press, 1997).

Eden, Lorraine "The Emerging North American Investment Regime," *Transnational Corporations*, vol. 5, no. 3 (December 1996).

Eiteman, David K. "Political Risk and International Marketing," *Columbia Journal of World Business*, vol. 23, no. 4 (Winter 1988).

Geringer, J. Michael. "Strategic Determinant of Partner Selection Criteria in International Joint Ventures," *Journal of International Business Studies*, vol. 22, no. 1 (First Quarter 1991).

Globerman, Steven. "Government Policies Toward Foreign Direct Investment: Has a New Era Dawned?" *Columbia Journal of World Business*, vol. 23, no. 3 (Fall 1988).

Gomes-Casseres, Benjamin. "Firm Ownership Preferences and Host Government Restrictions: An Integrated Approach," *Journal of International Business Studies*, vol. 21, no. 1 (First Quarter 1990).

Goodman, John B. and Loveman, Gary W. "Does Privatization Serve the Public Interest?" *Harvard Business Review*, vol. 69, no. 6 (November/December 1991).

Hillis, W. Daniel; Burton, Daniel F.; Costello, Robert B.; White, Robert M.; Weidenbaum, Murray; Georghiou, Luki; Colombo, Umberto; Schnieder, Leslie; Lee, Thomas H.; and Gorte, Julie Fox. "Technology Policy: Is America on the Right Track?" *Harvard Business Review*, vol. 70, no. 3 (May/June 1992).

Howell, Llewellyn D. and Chaddick, Brad, "Models of Political Risk for Foreign Investment and Trade: An Assessment of Three Approaches," *Columbia Journal of World Business*, vol. 29, no. 3, (Fall 1994).

Johnston, Russell and Lawrence, Paul R. "Beyond Vertical Integration – The Rise of the Value-Adding Partnership," *Harvard Business Review*, vol. 66, no. 4 (July/August 1988).

Kim, W. Chan. "Competition and the Management of Host Government Intervention," *Sloan Management Review*, vol. 28, no. 3 (Spring 1987).

Lieberman, Ira W. "Privatization: The Theme of the 1990s – An Overview," *Columbia Journal of World Business*, vol. 28, no. 1 (Spring 1993).

MacDonald, Kevin R. "Why Privatization Is Not Enough," *Harvard Business Review*, vol. 71, no. 3 (May/June 1993).

Magee, John F. "1992: Moves Americans Must Make," *Harvard Business Review*, vol. 67, no. 3 (May–June 1989).

Moore, John. "British Privatization – Taking Capitalism to the People," *Harvard Business Review*, vol. 70, no. 1 (January/February 1992).

Ostry, Sylvia. "Governments & Corporations in a Shrinking World: Trade & Innovation Policies in the United States, Europe & Japan," *Columbia Journal of World Business*, vol. 25, nos. 1, 2 (Spring/Summer 1990).

Pound, John. "Beyond Takeovers: Politics Comes to Corporate Control," *Harvard Business Review*, vol. 70, no. 2 (March/April 1992).

Ramamurti, Ravi. "Why Are Developing Countries Privatizing?" *Journal of International Business Studies*, vol. 23, no. 2 (Second Quarter 1992).

Rugman, Alan M. (ed.) *Foreign Investment and NAFTA* (Columbia, SC: University of South Carolina Press, 1994).

Rugman, Alan M. "Towards an Investment Agenda for APEC," *Transnational Corporations*, August 1997.

Rugman, Alan and Gestrin, Michael. "US Trade Laws as Barriers to Globalization," *The World Economy*, vol. 14, no. 3 (1991).

Rugman, Alan and Gestrin, Michael. "The Strategic Response of Multinational Enterprises to NAFTA," *Columbia Journal of World Business*, vol. 28, no. 4 (Winter 1993).

Rugman, Alan and Gestrin, Michael. "The Impact of NAFTA Upon North American Investment Patterns," *Transnational Corporations* vol. 3, no. 1 (February 1994).

Rugman, Alan M. and Verbeke, Alain. "Strategic Responses to Free Trade," in Maureen Farrow and Alan Rugman (eds.), *Business Strategies and Free Trade* (Toronto: C. D. Howe Institute, 1988).

Rugman, Alan M. and Verbeke, Alain. "Multinational Corporate Strategy and the Canada–US Free Trade Agreement." *Management International Review*, vol. 30, no. 3 (Summer 1990).

Rugman, Alan M. and Verbeke, Alain. "Multinational Enterprise and National Economic Policy," in Peter J. Buckley and Mark Casson (eds.), *Multinational Enterprises in the World Economy: Essays in Honour of John Dunning* (Aldershot, UK: Edward Elgar, 1992).

Rugman, Alan M.; Verbeke, Alain; and Luxmore, Stephen. "Corporate Strategy and the Free Trade Agreement: Adjustment by Canadian Multinational Enterprises," *Canadian Journal of Regional Science*, vol. 13, no. 2/3 (Summer/Autumn 1991).

Safarian, A. E. *Multinational Enterprise and Public Policy* (Cheltenham: Elgar, 1993).

Trebilcock, Michael and Howse, Robert *The Regulation of International Trade*, 2nd ed. (London: Routledge, 1999).

Whisenand, James D. "Cuba's Legal Structure: How it Affects Foreign Investment and Trade," *Columbia Journal of World Business*, vol. 30, no. 1 (Spring 1995).

CHAPTER 5

International Culture

OBJECTIVES OF THE CHAPTER

Across the globe people behave differently, even when faced with similar situations. For example, in the United States and the EU drivers automatically stop at a stop sign, but in many third world countries, drivers stop only if there is traffic in the other direction. When the president gives a speech in Mexico, everyone listens on television or radio; in the United States, most people switch to a different station and depend on a newscaster to fill them in with the news later. In France, meetings start on time; in Peru, they often begin late. In Japan, politeness is very important, so people frequently say "yes" when they mean "no." In the United States, most people say what they really mean.

What accounts for these differences? Part of the answer is culture. This chapter examines the nature of culture, key elements of culture, cultural and attitudinal dimensions, and the role that culture plays in strategic international management.

The specific objectives of this chapter are to:

1. **Define** the term "culture" and relate why culture creates problems for firms doing business internationally.

2. **Examine** some of the key elements of culture, including language, religion, values and attitudes, customs and manners, material culture, aesthetics, and education.

3. **Describe** the four dimensions that help to explain cultural differences among countries and geographic regions.

4. **Present** three of the most important culturally related concepts that affect the strategic management decisions of multinational enterprises.

ACTIVE LEARNING CASE

US pop culture

US business may be having trouble selling their hardware – cars, steel, electronic products – in overseas markets, but it is having little trouble selling US software in the form of culture: movies, music, television programming, and home video. Pop culture is so popular that only the sale of aircraft and related equipment account for more US exports. And if one expands the definition of pop culture to include licensed consumer products such as Levi's jeans and Coca-Cola's soft drinks, the export picture looks even better. For example, the American music industry earns about 70 per cent of its profits outside the United States with sales of US television programming to Europe accounting for over $600 million a year. Many people in Europe watch old *Dallas* and *Dynasty* programs and now just about everyone watches the *X-Files*. And one of the most popular films of all time in Israel and Sweden was *Pretty Woman*, which grossed more than $360 million worldwide even before it opened in the two biggest overseas markets, Japan and France. There are also record stores everywhere that sell the latest international hits, many of them by such well known US celebrities as Michael Jackson, Whitney Houston, and Madonna. In fact, US pop culture is so pervasive that it influences the lifestyle of people worldwide.

In an effort to get on the bandwagon, foreign transnationals are now buying into US pop culture. For example, Sony purchased Columbia Pictures; Pioneer Electronics bought 10 per cent of Carolco Pictures, maker of *Rambo*, *Total Recall*, and *Terminator II*; and Japan Victor has invested $100 million in Largo Entertainment, producers of *Die Hard*, *Predator*, and *48 Hours*. And investors are flocking to Disney as limited partners in film productions.

Despite these developments, a lot of pop culture remains solidly in US hands. A good example is Turner Broadcasting, with CNN in 101 countries and territories. While the network broadcasts in English, the most popular language in the world, in non-English-speaking nations it is also extremely popular. And CNN broadcasting has been able to expand into the international market with the same format used at home. Simply put, US pop culture is proving to be a worldwide phenomenon that can transcend national boundaries.

Sources: Adapted from John Huey, "America's Hottest Export: Pop Culture," *Fortune*, December 31, 1990; John Huey, "What Pop Culture Is Telling Us," *Fortune*, June 17, 1991; Christopher Power, "Sweet Sales for Sour Mash-Abroad," *Business Week*, July 1, 1991; Melanie Warner, "TV Exports," *Fortune*, November 25, 1996; Douglas A. Blackmon, "Forget the Stereotype: America Is Becoming A Nation Of Culture," *Wall Street Journal*, September 17, 1998, pp. A1, A18.

1. In what way does pop culture help to overcome language as a cultural barrier?

2. How does pop culture help to change country customs and develop universal customs and manners? Give an example.

3. How can pop culture in the form of movies, for example, affect the cultural dimensions of a society? Give an example.

4. Can pop culture help to encourage achievement motivation in people? How?

INTRODUCTION

Culture is the acquired knowledge that people use to interpret experience and to generate social behavior.[1] Culture is shared by members of a group, organization, or society.[2] Through culture we form values and attitudes that shape our individual and group behavior. Culture is learned through both education and experience. Culture is also passed from one generation to another, so it is enduring. At the same time cultures constantly undergo change as people adapt to new environments. In most countries, the culture of the twenty-first century is not the same as that of the 1960s.

To be successful in multinational businesses, one must understand the cultures of other countries and learn how to adapt to them. To an extent, all individuals are home country oriented; the challenge in international business is learning how to broaden one's perspective to avoid making business decisions based on misconceptions.

One cause of these misconceptions is **ethnocentrism**, the belief that one's way of doing things is superior to that of others. There are a number of forms of ethnocentric behaviors. Some of the most common include patronization, disrespect, an aura of superiority, and inflexible behavior.[3] Ethnocentric behavior can be found among both people and organizations. In the case of individuals in a society, it often takes the form of "we're better than anyone else." In the case of organizations it is typified by an MNE that uses the same strategies abroad that it employs at home because it is convinced that the way business is done in the home country is superior to that used by the competition overseas. Other examples include (1) not adapting a product to a particular market's special needs, (2) bringing profits back to the home country without any reinvestment in the foreign market, and (3) filling key positions of overseas units with national managers who have done well at home but have no international experience. Ethnocentric behavior can be avoided by learning about the culture where one will be doing business. This can be done by studying the elements of the culture. A good example is provided in the box "International Business Strategy in Action: A Universal Soft Drink."

ELEMENTS OF CULTURE

Culture is a complex, multidimensional subject. In understanding the nature of culture, we need to examine its elements: language, religion, values and attitudes, manners and customs, material elements, aesthetics, education, and social institutions.

Language

Language is critical to culture because it is the primary means used to transmit information and ideas (see Table 5.1). A knowledge of the local language can help in four ways. First, it permits a clearer understanding of the situation. With direct knowledge of a language, a businessperson does not have to rely on someone else to interpret or explain. Second, language provides direct access to local people who are frequently more open in their communication when dealing with someone who speaks their language. Third, an understanding of the language allows the person to pick up nuances, implied meanings, and other information that is not being stated outright. Finally, language helps the person to understand the culture better.

One of the best examples of the value of language is knowing the meaning of everyday idioms and clichés. For example, a doctoral student from China discussed her class schedule with fellow doctoral students and expressed some concern over a course she would be taking in multivariate analysis. The US students assured her that if she studied hard, the course would be "a piece of cake." Confused by the unfamiliar idiom, the student soon went to ask her advisor what "a piece of cake" meant

INTERNATIONAL BUSINESS STRATEGY IN ACTION

A universal soft drink

From 1981 to 1996 Coca-Cola's market value increased from $4.3 billion to $147 billion, and many people still consider it a good investment given the success the firm is having in capturing developing markets. What accounts for this success? One answer is that the firm has learned how to market Coke internationally. The late company president, Roberto Goizueta, put it this way, "We used to be an American company with a large international business. Now we are a large international company with a sizable American business." Today Coke earns more than 80 per cent of its profits internationally, and the firm has clearly staked its future on rapid growth in the multicultural environment. Some of Coke's recent international marketing campaigns help explain this success.

The company currently is the largest selling soft drink in every Eastern European country, a market that used to be dominated by Pepsi. When the Berlin Wall came down Coca-Cola was readily waiting to enter these markets. The firm decided to sell its product in risky local currency in order to be first in the market. Furthermore, Coca-Cola purchased distributors and bottlers to reinforce its management, and by 1996 the company had garnered 40 per cent of the market compared to Pepsi's 21 per cent.

Other geographic areas of the world from Latin America to the Far East provide similar growth statistics. In Latin America, Coca-Cola set up distribution networks around mega-bottlers that control regional areas of the market. This initiative has led many coun-tries previously dominated by Pepsi or local brands to increase their consumption of Coca-Cola. In Mexico and Brazil, Coke has over 50 per cent of the soft-drink market. In Venezuela, a market long dominated by Pepsi, Coke bought Pepsi's main bottler, literally putting the competition under siege.

In China, an innovative marketing strategy shows the company's willingness to adapt to its new environment. A country with less than 1 Coke per capita consumption, China has immense potential due to its population and future prospects for economic growth. The problem of how to reach the average Chinese consumer was approached by using the ruling party's spies. Neighborhood Committees were staffed with senior citizens to act as informants to the government. Then Coke got an idea. These senior citizens with nothing to do could be the distributors of Coca-Cola. This allowed the Neighborhood Committees to have some income while it provided an intense distribution network for Coca-Cola products.

As a result of Coca-Cola's global strategy, the company is the world's largest beverage company, with 46 per cent of the world market for carbonated drinks. However, Coke is not satisfied with this statistic and it looks forward to achieving 50 per cent of the market. The company's new ventures inside the Arab markets, its continued stress on less developed countries, and particularly its multicultural mindset, all point to a bright future for the firm.

Sources: John Huey, "The World's Best Brand," *Fortune*, May 31, 1993; Howard Rudnitsky, "Why Warren Buffet Still Likes Coke," *Forbes*, May 24, 1993, and *Forbes*, April 26, 1993; "Next Year, The French-Fry Index," *Fortune*, December 10, 1997; Betsy Morris, "Dough Is it," *Fortune*, May 5, 1998; "The China Card," *Fortune*, May 2, 1998; Patricia Sellers and Patty Llosa, "How Coke is Kicking Pepsi's Can," *Fortune*, October 28, 1996; "Sipping the Fizz in Coca-Cola's Profit," *Wall Street Journal*, May 1, 1997, p. C1; Nikhil Deogun, "A Coke and a Perm? Soda Giant is Pushing Into Unusual Locales," *Wall Street Journal*, May 8, 1997, pp. A1, A8.

in this context. In other cases the meanings of idioms and clichés differ from one country to another. Similarly, in Britain, "tabling a proposal" means taking action on it immediately, whereas in the United States it means delaying a decision.

A knowledge of language is also important because direct translation may be inadequate or misleading. For example, in many countries of the world, the word "aftertaste" does not exist. To convey this meaning would require an extensive,

Table 5.1 Language distribution of the world

Rank	Language	Primary country	Population
1	Chinese, Mandarin	China	885,000,000
2	Spanish	Spain	332,000,000
3	English	United Kingdom	322,000,000
4	Bengali	Bangladesh	189,000,000
5	Hindi	India	182,000,000
6	Portuguese	Portugal	170,000,000
7	Russian	Russia	170,000,000
8	Japanese	Japan	125,000,000
9	German	Germany	98,000,000
10	Chinese, Wu	China	77,175,000
11	Javanese	Indonesia, Java, Bali	75,500,800
12	Korean	South Korea	75,000,000
13	French	France	72,000,000
14	Vietnamese	Vietnam	67,662,000
15	Telugu	India	66,350,000
16	Chinese, Yue	China	66,000,000
17	Marathi	India	64,783,000
18	Tamil	India	63,075,000
19	Turkish	Turkey	59,000,000
20	Urdu	Pakistan	58,000,000

Source: Adapted from Barbara F. Grimes (ed.), *Ethnologue Languages of the World, Thirteen Edition* (Dallas: Summer Institute of Linguistics, 1996).

detailed translation. In other cases literal translations are not accurate. Advertising is a good example:

> Ford . . . introduced a low cost truck, the "Feira," into some of the less-developed countries. Unfortunately, the name meant "ugly old woman" in Spanish. Needless to say, this name did not encourage sales. Ford also experienced slow sales when it introduced a top-of-the-line automobile, the "Comet" in Mexico under the name "Caliente." The puzzling low sales were finally understood when Ford discovered that "caliente" is slang for a street walker.
>
> One laundry detergent company certainly wishes now that it had contacted a few locals before it initiated its promotional campaign in the Middle East. All of the company's advertisements pictured soiled clothes on the left, its box of soap in the middle, and clean clothes on the right. But, because in that area of the world people tend to read from right to left, many potential customers interpreted the message to indicate the soap actually soiled the clothes.[4]

One of the most common ways of dealing with language barriers is through the use of translators. This is particularly important in the case of written communications, where some people recommend a double translation of the information. First, the material is translated into the second language and then it is translated back to see if the original material and the retranslated material are the same. However, the use of "back-translation" is not perfect. Researchers have found that even when bilingual experts are employed, there are problems in translation.[5] There is no substitute for being able to speak and write the language fluently.

ACTIVE LEARNING CHECK

Review your answer to Active Learning Case question 1 and make any changes you like. Then compare your answer to the one below.

1. In what way does pop culture help to overcome language as a cultural barrier?

Pop culture helps to overcome language as a cultural barrier in two ways. First, this culture is so popular that everyone worldwide understands it. Language is not necessary for people throughout the world to enjoy Coca-Cola or to appreciate Disneyland theme parks in Japan and France. Second, even if the product or service is presented in English, like a Bruce Springsteen record, young people in Germany, Chile, and Taiwan can understand the music just as well as a teenager in Atlanta, Georgia, can.

Religion

There are a number of major religions in the world, including Catholic, Protestant, Jewish, Islamic, Hindu, Buddhist, and Confucian. Religions influence lifestyles, beliefs, values, and attitudes and can have a dramatic effect on the way people in a society act toward each other and toward those in other societies.

Religion can also affect the work habits of people. In the United States, it is common to hear people talk about the **Protestant work ethic**, which holds that people should work hard, be industrious, and save their money. This work ethic helped to develop capitalism in the United States because of the importance it assigned to saving and to reinvestment of capital. However, Americans are not the only people who work hard. In Asian countries where Confucianism is strong, this attitude is known as the **Confucian work ethic**. In Japan, it is called the **Shinto work ethic**. Simply put, religious beliefs can influence people's work habits.

Religion also affects work and social customs from the days of the week on which people work to their dietary habits. Even major holidays are often tied to religion. On December 25, Christmas Day, many Americans and Europeans exchange gifts. However, the Dutch exchange gifts on St. Nicholas Day (December 6), the Russians do it on Frost Man's Day (January 1), and in many Latin countries, as well as in Latin-oriented communities in the United States such as Miami, this activity is often carried out on Wise Men's Day (January 6).

Religion also affects politics and business. For example, when the Ayatollah Khomeini assumed control of Iran, western businesses soon left the country because of the government's attitude toward them. Over the next decade Iran plunged into a major war with Iraq and the economy weakened significantly. Khomeini's policies also caused trouble with other world governments, most noticeably that of the United States, whose embassy personnel in Tehran were seized and held hostage by the Iranians. Even today the country's religious beliefs continue to affect its political and economic decisions.

Values and attitudes

Values are basic convictions that people have regarding what is right and wrong, good and bad, important and unimportant.[6] An **attitude** is a persistent tendency to

Table 5.2   Value scales

One set of values	A second set of values
A view of people as essentially bad	A view of people as essentially good
Avoidance or negative evaluations of individuals	Confirming individuals as human beings
A view of individuals as fixed	Seeing individuals as being in process
Resisting and fearing individual differences	Accepting and utilizing individual differences
Utilizing an individual primarily with reference to his/her job description	Viewing an individual as a whole person
Walling off the expression of feelings	Making possible both appropriate expression and effective use of feelings
Maskmanship and game playing	Authentic behavior
The use of status for maintaining power and personal prestige	The use of status for organizationally relevant purposes
Distrusting people	Trusting people
Avoiding facing others with relevant data	Making appropriate confrontation
Avoidance of risk taking	Willingness to risk
A view of process work as being unproductive	Seeing process work as being essential to effective task accomplishment
A primary emphasis on competition	A much greater emphasis on collaboration

Source: Adapted from Alfred M. Jaeger, "Organizational Development and National Culture: Where's the Fit?" *Academy of Management Review*, January 1986, pp. 178–190.

feel and behave in a particular way toward some object. Values influence culture, as seen, for example, by the value Americans now assign to equality in the workplace that is resulting in legislation and action against sexual discrimination. This value change is also reflected in new attitudes toward dealing with those guilty of such discriminations.

One way of examining value differences among cultures is through the use of value scales. Table 5.2 provides an example. Notice that these 13 value scales are presented in terms of polar lists. The values on the left are markedly different from those on the right. In examining country cultures in terms of these values, we find it likely that no country fits entirely on one side or the other. There will be a combination of the two lists in the table. Moreover, in many cases cultures are in a state of transition. For example, in recent years the United States has been moving toward the right side of Table 5.2, as seen by legislative and social efforts to provide equality for everyone in the workplace.

The attitudes that emanate from values directly influence international business. For example, Russians believe that McDonald's cuisine is superior to their own (value judgment) and are thus willing to stand in long lines in order to eat at these units (attitude). In Japan, Borden has found that its products are regarded by customers as superior to those of the competition (value), so it sells Lady Borden ice cream and Borden cheese packaged and labeled in English and consumer demand (attitude) remains high. In France, General Foods sells a chewing gum called Hollywood that has a picture of teenagers riding bicycles on a beach because it has found that customers like the direct association with America (value) and this results in high sales (attitude). Similarly, Swiss chocolate manufacturers know that US customers believe Swiss chocolate products are of high quality (value), so that companies emphasize their Swiss origin and thus generate high sales (attitude). And in Japan, the Levi Strauss company touts its brand name because it knows that the Japanese view Levi's as prestige jeans (value) and buy accordingly (attitude). In short, by being aware of the values and attitudes of the people in the culture, a business firm can effectively position its product.

In other cases there are negative attitudes toward foreign-made goods, causing firms to deemphasize their origin. For example, while there are many foreign-owned businesses in the United States, their names give no indication of their foreign ownership: Firestone Tire & Rubber is owned by Bridgestone, a Japanese firm; Ponds (hand cream) is owned by Unilever, a British/Dutch company; the Celanese Corporation is owned by Hoechst, a German firm; and Standard Oil is owned by British Petroleum.

Customs and manners

Customs are common or established practices. **Manners** are behaviors that are regarded as appropriate in a particular society. Customs dictate how things are to be done; manners are used in carrying them out. For example, it is customary in the United States to eat the main course before having dessert. In carrying out this custom, people use knives and forks, finish all the food on their plate, and do not talk with food in their mouth.

In many countries of the world, social customs and manners are quite different from those of the United States. For example, in Arab countries, it is considered bad manners to attempt to shake hands with a person of higher authority unless this individual makes the first gesture to do so. In Latin countries, it is acceptable to show up late for a party, whereas in England and France, promptness is valued. In many western countries, it is acceptable to talk business when golfing since this is often the underlying reason for the golf match, but in Japan, business is never discussed over golf. In the United States, it is acceptable for a boss to give a secretary roses to express appreciation for helping to close a big deal; in Germany and in many Latin countries, such action would be seen as a sign of romantic attachment and therefore inappropriate. When dealing with the Russians and east Europeans, typically we find that they begin with large demands and offer very little in return, but as the negotiations wind down, they will make a large number of concessions. This is in contrast to the US style of making early concessions and trying to get the other party to make early counter-concessions.

Customs also dictate the way companies advertise and market their products.[7] For example, in the United States, orange juice is touted as a breakfast drink, but in France, it is sold as a refreshment because the French do not drink orange juice with breakfast. In Japan, Maxwell House coffee is simply called Maxwell because the word "house" is confusing to the customers. In Japan, talc products such as baby power are sold in the form of powder puff rather than in containers because the Japanese do not like the way loose talc shakes out of a container. Moreover, Americans will often use a talc powder after bathing, but the Japanese feel it makes them dirty again. In Mexico and other Latin countries, soup manufacturers sell cans that are large enough to serve four or five people, while in the United States, a typical can serves one or two people. This is because families in Latin countries tend to be larger. In the United States, men buy diamond rings for their fiancées, but in Germany, young women typically buy their own diamond ring; advertising practices by diamond merchants in the two countries differ significantly. Unless business firms understand the customs and manners of the country, they are likely to have trouble marketing their products.[8]

Material culture

Material culture consists of objects that people make. When studying material culture, we consider how people make things (the technologies that are involved) and who makes them and why (the economics of the situation). In examining this element of a culture, we consider the **basic economic infrastructure** such as the country's transportation, communications, and energy capabilities; the **social infrastructure**, which consists of the country's health, housing, and education systems; and the **financial infrastructure**, which provides banking, insurance, and financial services in the society.

A society's technology is important because it influences the national standard of living and helps to account for the country's values and beliefs. If a country is technologically advanced, the people are less likely to believe that fate plays a major role in their lives and are more likely to believe that they can control what happens to them. Their values are also more likely to be materialistic because they have a higher standard of living.

When doing business in technologically advanced countries, businesses need to have up-to-date products that are either less expensive than current offerings or which provide more benefits. In less technologically advanced nations, these goods may be too advanced because the infrastructure will not support their use or because there is no need for them. For example, one of the major computer products for the next couple of years will probably be the laptop computer. However, the demand for this product in third world countries is limited because these nations cannot fully benefit from this product. Similarly, while more fuel efficient, price competitive cars are gaining market share in the United States, they have not made major inroads in third world countries because of the limited infrastructure (road and highways) and the need for new automobiles.

Aesthetics

Aesthetics relates to the artistic tastes of a culture. For example, the aesthetic values of Americans are different from those of the Chinese as reflected by the art, literature, music, and artistic tastes of the two peoples. In understanding a culture, we need to study how such differences affect behaviors. For example, opera is much more popular in Europe than in the United States. That is why some great US opera stars first made their mark in Europe before they achieved successful careers at home. On the other hand, in the area of movie making the United States sets the international standards, while films produced by Europeans often enjoy only limited success. This, as seen in the box "International Business Strategy in Action: The Japanese in Hollywood," helps to explain why Matsushita has purchased MCA. Movies also help to explain how, in some cases, cultural values are becoming international. The impact of movies is felt worldwide and movie stars are international celebrities.[9]

However, there are many aspects of aesthetics that make cultures different. For example, in the United States, sex is not used in advertising as much as in Europe.

INTERNATIONAL BUSINESS STRATEGY IN ACTION

The Japanese in Hollywood

While movies are made by companies all over the world, Hollywood continues to be the leader, as seen by the blockbusters it produces annually. The income earned by producers, directors, and stars helps to reinforce this fact. In a recent two-year period Steven Spielberg, best known for such movies as *E.T., Jaws*, and *Raiders of the Lost Ark* and its sequels, grossed $87 million, and major movie stars did quite well: Sylvester Stallone, $63 million; Arnold Schwarzenegger, $55 million; Jack Nicholson, $50 million; and Eddie Murphy, $48 million.

In an effort to get into this market, Japanese firms have been buying movie studios. In 1989 Sony purchased Columbia Pictures and, more recently, Matsushita acquired MCA for almost $7 billion in cash. This deal provides Matsushita with an excellent complement to its own product lines. The giant Japanese firm produces audio and video equipment, electronic components, and communication equipment. MCA's lines run to filmed entertainment, music, book publishing, and other businesses such as a television station and studio tours. More importantly, MCA provides Matsushita with an international market where entertainment transcends cultural barriers. Most blockbusters in the United States do even greater business in the foreign market. In fact, Hollywood makes more money in overseas sales than it does nationally. Moreover, movie films tend to have universal appeal so that successful offerings in the United States are often well accepted by international audiences. Movies also offer the opportunity to filmmakers to make different versions of the same film. The length of the film can be adjusted to the market taste of the audience, as can the story itself. Many of the steamy sex scenes in Hollywood movies are cut out of the version marketed in the United States but are shown in Europe. Even the ending of the movie can be altered so that it appeals to audience taste.

The economic value of entertainment holdings has not been lost on firms such as Seagram's which has long been a major competitor in the alcoholic beverage industry. In 1995 Seagram's purchased MCA from Matsushita and renamed it Universal. More recently the company bought PolyGram, the largest music firm in the world. This addition to Seagram's other holdings, which include Universal Studios Inc., which is the basis of the firm's film and theme park empire, makes Seagram's a major competitor in the entertainment industry. Additionally, the company's combined music empire now boasts a distribution system that contains a collection of talented veteran record executives and superstar artists from rap star LL Cool J to Country-and-Western songstress Shania Twain to pop veteran Elton John. The purchase price of $10.6 billion for PolyGram, mostly in cash and the rest in Seagram's stock, may well turn out to be one of Seagram's best investments. The company's revenues, which were initially generated by sales of alcoholic beverages, will now come mostly from the entertainment side.

Sources: Adapted from Ronald Grover and Judith H. Dobrzynski, "Lights, Camera, Auction," *Business Week*, December 10, 1990, pp. 27–28; John Huey, "Why Matsushita Bought MCA," *Fortune*, December 31, 1990, pp. 52–53; Peter Newcomb and Matthew Schifrin, "Golden Boys and Girls," *Forbes*, October 1, 1990, pp. 143–146; Johnnie L. Roberts, "He Owns The Songs," *Newsweek*, June 1, 1998, pp. 52–53.

An advertisement for the Electrolux vacuum cleaner in the United States touts its "power," whereas in England, advertisements note that "nothing sucks like an Electrolux." In Germany, Commodore International, the US computer manufacturer, has used a naked young man in ads that ran in the German version of *Cosmopolitan*. This ad is unlikely to run in the US version of the magazine. Another aesthetically related area is color. In many western countries, the color black is used for mourning, while white is used for joy or purity. In many Oriental countries white is the color for mourning. Quite clearly, aesthetic values influence behavior and we need to understand aesthetic values if we are to appreciate another culture.

Education

Education influences many aspects of culture. Literate people read widely and have a much better understanding of what is happening in the world. Additionally, higher rates of literacy usually result in greater economic productivity and technological advance. Education also helps to provide infrastructure needed for developing managerial talent. Simply stated, education is a critical factor in understanding culture.

One of the most common gauges of education is formal schooling. In most countries of the world schooling is increasing. This helps to explain why the literacy rate in most countries is on the rise. However, these raw data do not relate the quality of education nor do they provide information regarding how well the supply of graduates meets the demand. On the other hand, the data do provide insights regarding the overall level of education and, at the university level, the areas of specialization.

For example, in Japan and South Korea, there is a very strong emphasis given to engineering and the sciences at university level. In Europe, the number of MBAs has increased sharply over recent years. These data provide insights regarding the market potential of the country, as well as the types of goods and services that will probably be purchased by these people. For example, educationally advanced countries like England, France, and Germany are more likely to be markets for computers and other high-tech equipment than are poorer countries such as Poland, Czech Republic, and Romania. It is also likely that MNEs doing business in these countries will find it easier to recruit and train local managers in Western Europe than in Eastern Europe.[10]

ACTIVE LEARNING CHECK

Review your answer to Active Learning Case question 2 and make any changes you like. Then compare your answer to the one below.

2. How does pop culture help to change country customs and develop universal customs and manners? Give an example.

Pop culture influences and develops universal customs in a number of ways. One is by changing lifestyles. For example, because of McDonald's, many people around the world now eat fast food as part of their regular diet, and Coca-Cola has changed their drinking habits. Movies and television programs have also introduced what is now a universal language. For example, thanks to Dirty Harry movies, the saying, "Make my day," is part of the international lexicon. Levi jeans are another example of a trend that has helped to change the dress habits of people throughout the world.

CULTURAL AND ATTITUDINAL DIMENSIONS

Language, religion, values and attitudes, manners and customs, material goods, aesthetics, and education are elements of culture that explain behavioral differences among people. In recent years researchers have attempted to develop a composite picture of culture by clustering these differences. This has been done in two ways. Some researchers have looked at cultural dimensions that reflect similarities and differences among cultures. Other researchers have used these findings to group countries into clusters of nations with similar cultures.

Cultural dimensions

Geert Hofstede, a Dutch researcher, has found four cultural dimensions that help to explain how and why people from various cultures behave as they do. His initial findings were gathered from over 116,000 questionnaires completed by respondents from 70 different countries.[11] This is the largest organizationally based study ever conducted, and researchers are continuing to investigate and extend the findings.

Hofstede's four dimensions are (1) power distance, (2) uncertainty avoidance, (3) individualism, and (4) masculinity.

Power distance **Power distance** is the degree to which less powerful members of organizations and institutions accept the fact that power is not distributed equally. People in societies where authority is obeyed without question live in a high power distance culture. Hofstede found that many Latin and Asian countries such as Malaysia, the Philippines, Panama, Guatemala, Venezuela, and Mexico were typified by high power distance. In contrast, the United States, Canada, and many European countries such as Denmark, Great Britain, and Austria had moderate to low power distance.

In countries with high power distance, managers make autocratic and paternalistic decisions and the subordinates do as they are told. Often these societies have business structures that are typified by close control of operations and a fairly weak work ethic. Organization structures tend to be tall and managers have relatively few subordinates reporting directly to them. In countries with moderate to low power distance, people put a high value on independence, managers consult with subordinates before making decisions, and there is a fairly strong work ethic. Organization structures tend to be flat and managers directly supervise more subordinates than do their counterparts in high power distance enterprises.

Uncertainty avoidance **Uncertainty avoidance** is the extent to which people feel threatened by ambiguous situations and have created institutions and beliefs for minimizing or avoiding these uncertainties. Countries with high uncertainty avoidance try to reduce risk and develop systems and methods for dealing with ambiguity. Hofstede found strong uncertainty avoidance in Greece, Uruguay, Guatemala, Portugal, Japan, and Korea. He found weak uncertainty avoidance in countries like Singapore, Sweden, Great Britain, the United States, and Canada.

Countries with high uncertainty avoidance tend to formalize organizational activities and depend heavily on rules and regulations to ensure that people know what they are to do. There is often high anxiety and stress among these people, they are very concerned with security, and decisions are frequently a result of group consensus. Low uncertainty avoidance societies have less structuring of activities and encourage managers to take more risks. People who are less stressed have more acceptance of dissent and disagreement and rely heavily on their own initiative and ingenuity in getting things done.

Individualism   **Individualism** is the tendency of people to look after themselves and their immediate family only. This dimension is in direct contrast with **collectivism**, the tendency of people to belong to groups that look after each other in exchange for loyalty. Hofstede has found that economically advanced countries tend to place greater emphasis on individualism than do poorer countries. For example, the United States, Great Britain, the Netherlands, and Canada have high individualism. In contrast, Ecuador, Guatemala, Pakistan, and Indonesia have low individualism. Although Hofstede did not measure changes in individualism along a time continuum, he did find that Japan has a higher individualism score than any other country in the Orient. Given the fact that collectivism is very important in this part of the world, it is likely that individualism is increasing in Japan as that nation has become a major force in the international economic arena.

Countries with high individualism expect people to be self-sufficient. There is a strong emphasis on individual initiative and achievement. Autonomy and individual financial security are given high value, and people are encouraged to make individual decisions without reliance on strong group support. In contrast, countries with low individualism place a great deal of importance on group decision making and affiliation. No one wants to be singled out for special attention, even for a job well done. Success is collective and individual praise is embarrassing because it implies that one group member is better than the others. Countries with low individualism emphasize belongingness and draw strength from group affiliation.

Masculinity   **Masculinity** is the degree to which the dominant values of a society are "success, money, and things." Hofstede measured this dimension in contrast to **femininity**, which is the degree to which the dominant values of a society are "caring for others and the quality of life." He found that countries with high masculinity included Japan, Austria, Venezuela, and Mexico. Countries with low masculinity (or high femininity) included Norway, Sweden, Denmark, and the Netherlands. The United States had a moderate to high score on masculinity, as did other Anglo countries.

Countries with high masculinity scores place a great deal of importance on earnings, recognition, advancement, and challenge. Achievement is defined in terms of wealth and recognition. These cultures often tend to favor large-scale enterprises and economic growth is viewed as very important. In school, children are encouraged to be high performers and boys are expected to think about work careers where they can succeed. Less emphasis is given to this for girls because the number of women in upper-level jobs is limited. Countries with low masculinity scores place great emphasis on a friendly work environment, cooperation, and employment security. Achievement is defined in terms of human contacts and the living environment. There is low stress in the workplace and workers are given a great deal of freedom.

Integrating the dimensions   The four dimensions described earlier influence the overall culture of a society and result in a unique environment. No culture is identical

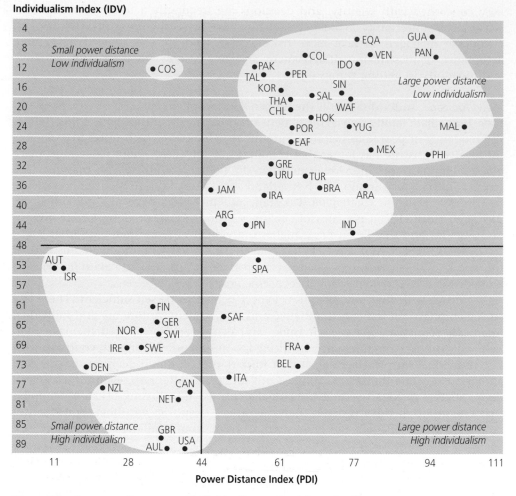

Figure 5.1 A power distance and individualism–collectivism plot (for 50 countries and 3 regions)

Source: Geert Hofstede, "The Cultural Relativity of Organizational Practices and Theories," *Journal of International Business Studies*, Fall 1983, p. 82.

to another; however, there are similarities. Hofstede illustrated this when he examined the effect of pairs of dimensions on culture. Figure 5.1 shows the effect of power distance and individualism–collectivism as an example. (See Table 5.3 for the names of the countries and regions used in Hofstede's research.) The United States (USA) is located in the lower left-hand quadrant. It has high individualism and moderate power distance. US culture is characterized by a desire to do things personally (individualism) and people are not overawed by individuals in authority. Notice that other Anglo cultures are also located nearby, including Australia (AUL), Great Britain (GBR), and Canada (CAN). In the same quadrant, directly above this group, there are a host of western European countries, including Sweden, Switzerland, Denmark, and Ireland. In the lower right-hand quadrant there are some of the other western European countries, including Italy, Belgium, France, and Spain. They have cultures that are sim-

Table 5.3   Countries and regions used in Hofstede's research

ARA	Arab countries (Egypt, Lebanon, Libya, Kuwait, Iraq, Saudi Arabia, UAE)	JAM	Jamaica
		JPN	Japan
		KOR	South Korea
		MAL	Malaysia
ARG	Argentina	MEX	Mexico
AUL	Australia	NET	Netherlands
AUT	Austria	NOR	Norway
BEL	Belgium	NZL	New Zealand
BRA	Brazil	PAK	Pakistan
CAN	Canada	PAN	Panama
CHL	Chile	PER	Peru
COL	Colombia	OHI	Philippines
COS	Costa Rica	POR	Portugal
DEN	Denmark	SAF	South Africa
EAF	East Africa (Kenya, Ethiopia, Zambia)	SAL	Salvador
		SIN	Singapore
EQA	Equador	SPA	Spain
FIN	Finland	SWE	Sweden
FRA	France	SWI	Switzerland
GBR	Great Britain	TAI	Taiwan
GER	Germany	THA	Thailand
GRE	Greece	TUR	Turkey
GUA	Guatemala	URU	Uruguay
HOK	Hong Kong	USA	United States
IDO	Indonesia	VEN	Venezuela
IND	India	WAF	West Africa (Nigeria, Ghana, Sierra Leone)
IRA	Iran		
IRE	Ireland	YUG	Yugoslavia
ISR	Israel		
ITA	Italy		

Source: Geert Hofstede, "The Cultural Relativity of Organizational Practices and Theories," *Journal of International Business Studies*, Fall 1983, p. 79.

ilar to those of their European neighbors. Most of the remainder of the countries and regions examined by Hofstede are in the upper right-hand quadrant. This includes Latin countries, oriental nations, east and west African countries, and Arab nations. They are characterized by moderate to low individualism and moderate to high power distance. It is particularly interesting to see that of all the Oriental nations, Japan is closest to the United States. This similarity indicates that the effect of technology and affluence may cause a culture to change in a direction that makes it more like others with a similar economic/technologic environment.

A second example of pairs of cultural dimensions is provided in Figure 5.2, where masculinity–femininity and uncertainty avoidance are plotted. In this case the United States is in the upper right-hand quadrant. US culture encourages uncertainty

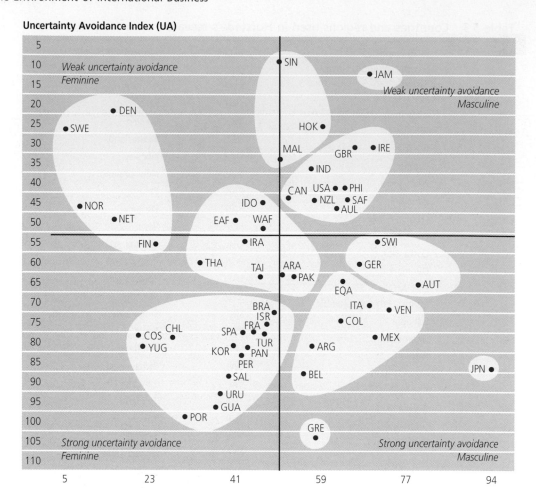

Figure 5.2   A masculinity–femininity and uncertainty avoidance plot (for 50 countries and 3 regions)

Source: Geert Hofstede, "The Cultural Relativity of Organizational Practices and Theories," *Journal of International Business Studies*, Fall 1983, p. 86.

avoidance, with moderate emphasis on masculinity. Once again some of the countries surrounding the United States are Anglo nations that are characterized by similar religion, history, and economic development and that speak the same language. In the upper left-hand quadrant there are most of the Scandinavian countries, while Latin and oriental nations are located in the lower half of the figure, characterized by high uncertainty avoidance and varying degrees of masculinity. Notice that Japan is by itself in the lower right-hand quadrant, characterized by high uncertainty avoidance and high masculinity.

Figures 5.1 and 5.2 are only two of the six figures that can be constructed by using Hofstede's four cultural dimensions. However, they are sufficient to illustrate the effect of culture on behavior. We see that some countries tend to cluster, thus indicating the effect of similar cultural values. In recent years other researchers have used Hofstede's work to study attitudinal dimensions and country clusters.

Review your answer to Active Learning Case question 3 and make any changes you like. Then compare your answer to the one below.

3. How can pop culture in the form of movies, for example, have an effect on the cultural dimensions of a society? Give an example.

Movies influence culture in that people learn the way things are done in other societies and, in many cases, want to emulate what they see on the screen. For example, to the extent that movies have presented the middle-class lifestyle of Americans, they have helped to increase the drive for materialism among many people and, in the process, increased the society's masculinity score. US movies have also depicted US values of democracy and helped to influence power distance scores. The same can be said for individualism and uncertainty avoidance. Simply put, movies can help to change a country's culture by showing the viewers alternative lifestyles that they may want to pursue.

Attitudinal dimensions

Based on the data in Figures 5.1 and 5.2, it would be difficult to make an overall assessment of the similarities and differences among the 50 countries and three geographic regions. The relationships among them change from one figure to the next. But these types of findings have helped researchers to investigate similarities and differences in work values and attitudes. Ronen and Kraut concluded that "countries could be clustered into more or less homogeneous groups based on intercorrelations of standard scores obtained for each country from scales measuring leadership, role descriptions, and motivation."[12] The two researchers then sought to cluster countries by using a mathematical technique that allowed them to identify how close countries were to each other in terms of overall culture. They found that there were five different country clusters: Anglo, Nordic, South American, Latin European, and central European. Since their research, additional multicultural studies have been conducted and the number of countries and clusters has been expanded.

Ronen and Shenkar reviewed the literature and found that eight major cluster studies had been conducted in the previous 15 years. These studies had looked at four major cultural areas: (1) the importance of work goals, (2) need deficiency, fulfillment, and job satisfaction, (3) managerial and organizational variables, and (4) work role and interpersonal orientations. Although each of the eight studies examined different countries and regions, Ronen and Shenkar were able to identify eight country clusters and four countries that did not fit into any of the clusters. Their findings are presented in Figure 5.3.

Each of the countries in Figure 5.3 that has been placed in a cluster has similar values, attitudes, and beliefs to those of the other countries in that cluster.

Not everyone agrees with the data in Figure 5.3; some researchers have formulated different international clusters. However, the figure does provide a basis for investigating the international cultural environment, and it is particularly useful to the study of international business. After all, a multinational firm must understand the nature of the culture where it will be doing business; this is critical to the firm's strategic management choices. In particular, MNEs can benefit from a knowledge of the impact of local culture on business attitudes and practices.

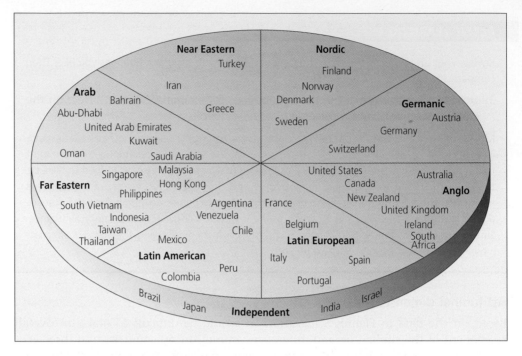

Figure 5.3   A synthesis of country clusters

Source: Simcha Ronen and Oded Shenkar, "Clustering Countries on Attitudinal Dimensions: A Review and Synthesis," *Academy of Management Journal*, September 1985, p. 449.

CULTURE AND STRATEGIC MANAGEMENT

In deciding where to invest overseas and how to manage the operation, MNEs are particularly interested in those aspects of culture that will directly affect the performance of the unit.[13] Here we will look at three of the most important aspects – work attitudes, achievement motivation, and time – and then relate the value of cross-cultural training to these management efforts.

Work attitudes

Work attitudes are important to MNEs because they can influence both the quality and quantity of employee output.[14] Americans are taught to believe in the work ethic, but this ethic is not unique to the United States. As noted earlier, many people around the world believe in hard work and it shows in their attitudes. In many Oriental countries, job attendance is viewed as a major responsibility and everyone comes to work every day. One researcher, commenting on the Japanese, has noted that 100 per cent work attendance is critical, and "men and women, in whatever role or rank, must make a commitment to the things they do and show it by being there."[15] Another common cultural work attitude among Orientals is that they remain on the job for the entire workday, in contrast to many Americans who believe that if people can get their work done early, they should be allowed to go home.[16] In Japan, if someone were to do this, it might well be misinterpreted. Here is an example reported by a US researcher:

A student of mine from Japan told me the story of his good friend who worked at . . . a major bank and had been kept exceptionally late at work for a period of months in order to complete a major project. When the project was complete, the section chief sent the staff home early every day for a week. After two days of coming home in the afternoon, the young man was confronted by his mother, with whom he lived. "Please," she asked him, "go to bar, go play *pachinko*, but don't come home so early. The neighbors are stopping me on the sidewalk to ask whether you are having troubles at work, and it is embarrassing to have to explain to everyone."[17]

Another example of the importance of work attitudes and culture is provided by the Upjohn Company of Kalamazoo, Michigan merger with Pharmacia AB of Sweden, which also has operations in Italy. Despite the carefully prepared approach to the merger, the Americans failed to realize some of the cultural differences between themselves and their new European partners. As the *Wall Street Journal* noted, "Swedes take off the entire month of July for vacation, virtually en masse, and Italians take off August. Everyone in *Europe* knows, that is, but apparently hardly anyone in Kalamazoo, Mich., does."[18] As a result, a linkup that was supposed to give a quick boost to the two companies, solving problems such as aging product lines and pressure from giant competitors, never got off the ground. Things had to be rescheduled and both partners ended up having to meet and talk about their cultural differences, so that each side better understood the "dos and don'ts" of doing business with the other.

When the two firms first got together, they never expected these types of problems. Upjohn, with household names such as Rogaine and Motrin, had no likely breakthroughs in its product pipeline, so it was happy to merge with Pharmacia. The latter had developed a solid roster of allergy medicines, human-growth hormone, and other drugs, but its distribution in the United States was weak and its product line was aging. So a merger seemed ideal for both firms. The big question was how to bring the two companies together. Given that Pharmacia had recently acquired an Italian firm, there was a proposal by the European group that there be three major centers – Kalamazoo, Stockholm, and Milan – as well as a new headquarters in London. However, this arrangement had a number of built-in problems. For one, the executives in Italy and Sweden were accustomed to reporting to local bosses. For a second, the people in London did not know a great deal about how to coordinate operations in Sweden and Italy. American cultural values added even more problems in that at Upjohn workers were tested for drug and alcohol abuse, but in Italy waiters pour wine freely every afternoon in the company dining room and Pharmacia's boardrooms were stocked with humidors for executives who liked to light a cigar during long meetings. Quite obviously there were cultural differences that had to be resolved by the companies. In the end, Pharmacia & Upjohn said it would meld the different cultures and attitudes and get on with its growth plans. However, one thing is certain: the different cultures created a major challenge for the merging companies.

Another important aspect of work attitude is organizational commitment. Research shows that US factory workers are very committed to their companies; so, too, are Japanese workers. Although many people would have anticipated this finding, they are unlikely to have realized two additional facts: (1) worker commitment among US factory employees is almost as high as that of their counterparts in Japan, and (2) job satisfaction is higher among US factory workers than among Japanese factory workers.[19] These data are presented in Table 5.4 and help to

Table 5.4 Organizational commitment and job satisfaction among US and Japanese factory workers

	United States	Japanese
Organizational commitment		
(1 = strongly agree; 5 = strongly disagree)		
Willingness to work harder than is necessary in order for the company to succeed	3.91	3.44
Willingness to take any job in order to continue working for the company	3.12	3.07
Perceived similarity between personal values and those of the company	3.15	2.68
Pride in working for the company	3.70	3.51
Willingness to turn down another job for more pay in order to stay with the company	2.71	2.68
Feeling of very little loyalty to the company	3.45	3.40
Job satisfaction		
Overall satisfaction with the job (0 = not at all; 4 = very)	2.95	2.12
Willingness to recommend this type of work to a friend (0 = no; 2 = yes)	1.52	0.91
Willingness to take this job again, if starting all over (0 = no; 2 = yes)	1.61	0.84
How well the job measures up to the type of work that was desired when starting out this job (0 = not what was wanted; 2 = exactly what was wanted)	1.20	0.43

Source: Adapted form James R. Lincoln, "Employee Work Attitudes and Management Practice in the United States and Japan: Evidence from a Large Comparative Survey," *California Management Review*, Fall 1989, p. 91. Copyright © 1989 by The Regents of the University of California. Reprinted from the *California Management Review*, vol. 25, no. 1. By permission of the Regents.

shed light on the similarities of work attitudes in the two countries. It is likely that both Americans and Japanese would be surprised by the results of this research, which involved over 8,300 workers from both countries and is the largest and most detailed body of survey information on US and Japanese factory workers undertaken to date.

International research reveals that work is important to many people. This has been clearly illustrated through research on work goals and what individuals are looking for in their jobs. Table 5.5 reports on the importance of a series of work goals among workers in seven different countries. A close look at the table shows that interesting work, on average, is the most important objective. Moreover, the researchers found that this was consistent internationally and held true for different organizational levels, for men and women, and for all age categories.[20] People want interesting work.

Commenting on this research, Harpaz has noted that the major findings have a number of practical implications. For example, the emphasis that the employees give to interesting work points to the need for challenging, meaningful jobs.

Table 5.5 Average and intracountry ranking of work goals: a seven nation comparison

Work goals	Belgium	Britain	Germany	Israel	Japan	Netherlands	United States
Opportunity to learn	5.8*	5.55	4.97	5.83	6.26	5.38	6.16
	7**	8	9	5	7	9	5
Interpersonal relations	6.34	6.33	6.43	6.67	6.39	7.19	6.08
	5	4	4	2	6	3	7
Opportunity for promotion	4.49	4.27	4.48	5.29	3.33	3.31	5.08
	10	11	10	8	11	11	10
Convenient work hours	4.71	6.11	5.71	5.53	5.46	5.59	5.25
	9	5	6	7	8	8	9
Variety	5.96	5.62	5.71	4.89	5.05	6.86	6.10
	6	7	6	11	9	4	6
Interesting work	8.25	8.02	7.26	6.75	6.38	7.59	7.41
	1	1	3	1	2	2	1
Job security	6.80	7.12	7.57	5.22	6.71	5.68	6.30
	3	3	2	10	4	7	3
Match between the people and the work	5.77	5.63	6.09	5.61	7.83	6.17	6.19
	8	6	5	6	1	6	4
Pay	7.13	7.80	7.73	6.60	6.56	5.27	6.82
	2	2	1	3	5	5	2
Working conditions	4.19	4.87	4.39	5.28	4.18	5.03	4.84
	11	9	11	9	10	10	11
Autonomy	6.56	4.69	5.66	6.00	6.89	7.61	5.79
	4	10	8	4	3	1	8

* First row shows average rank on a scale of 1 to 10.
** Second row shows ranking of work goals within each country, with a rank of 1 being *most* important and 11 being *least* important.
Source: Adapted from Itzhak Harpaz, "The Importance of Work Goals: An International Perspective," *Journal of International Business Studies*, vol. 21, no. 1, 1990, p. 81.

Additionally, when the work is interesting and challenging, the personnel are willing to exert greater effort. This has led Harpaz to conclude that "intrinsically motivated employees are concerned with the expressive aspects of work life (i.e., interesting work, autonomy, advancement), not necessarily for the purpose of securing more financial rewards, but because these very rewards are associated with intrinsically motivating jobs."

Achievement motivation

A second cultural factor, closely linked to work attitudes, is achievement motivation. How achievement-driven are people across the world? Recent research reveals that achievement drive in Eastern Europe is not very high.[21] Industry managers in the former Czechoslovakia, for example, had much lower achievement drive than US managers. As Eastern Europe makes the transition from a command economy to a market economy, this could change. After all, the need for achievement is a learned need, largely determined by the prevailing culture.

Table 5.6   Standardized scores on work goals for managers from four countries

Variable	People's Republic of China	Hong Kong	Taiwan	Singapore
Making a contribution	671	n/a	n/a	n/a
Coworkers who cooperate	635	579	571	624
Autonomy	603	512	480	532
Training	583	596	657	611
Challenge	515	548	548	571
Working relations with manager	483	522	524	551
Earnings	454	567	442	552
Security	450	452	506	437
Recognition	446	487	487	442
Benefits	439	323	363	439
Favorable physical conditions	n/a	477	438	362
Promotion	364	640	630	593
Time for nonwork activities	345	307	372	348

Sources: Oded Shenkar and Simcha Ronen, "Structure and Importance of Work Goals Among Managers in the People's Republic of China," *Academy of Management Journal*, September 1987, p. 571. Data, except for the People's Republic of China, are from Geert Hofstede's book *Culture's Consequences: International Differences in Work-Related Values* (Beverly Hills: Sage, 1980).

Another good example is provided by China, where in the late 1970s researchers found little high achievement drive. In high achieving societies, work goals such as autonomy, challenge, promotions, and earnings are valued, while the need for affiliation and safety rank farther down the list. Table 5.6 provides standardized scores on work goals for managers from four countries in the Orient. Hong Kong, Taiwan, and Singapore were all major areas of economic activity and the environment encouraged high achievement, while China continued in the late 1970s to remain highly resistant to high achievement ideas. The scores reported in Table 5.6 reinforce this point. Notice that workers in the People's Republic of China had low scores on challenge, promotion, and earnings – all work goals that would be particularly important to high achievers. The Chinese workers had high scores only on autonomy. Conversely, while high achievers would not give high scores to affiliation or safety-related goals such as security, benefits, coworkers who cooperate, or time for nonwork activities, the Chinese workers rated these variables as important. In the following decade, of course, China greatly changed its policies, encouraged entrepreneurship, and had a rapidly growing economy. As a result, it is likely that current data related to the work goals in Table 5.6 would show Chinese worker scores much closer to those of their counterparts in the other countries.

These results help to illustrate why culture is so important to MNEs as they formulate their strategic plans. MNEs prefer to invest in countries and geographic regions that encourage economic activity and achievement drive. In cases like Eastern Europe and China the company would look for those regions where high achievement drive could be most easily cultivated. In China, for example, the southeast provinces and Hong Kong are the fastest-growing economic areas, thanks to new business activity and a flourishing entrepreneurial climate.

Review your answer to Active Learning Case question 4 and make any changes you like. Then compare your answer to the one below.

4. Can pop culture help to encourage achievement motivation in people? How?

Pop culture can help to encourage achievement motivation in two ways. One is through movies and television fare that show a lifestyle that people would like to emulate. A second is by creating a desire in people to copy the famous artists that they see and hear. In both cases individuals would have to work hard to achieve the success, fame, and fortune that others have acquired through their own efforts. To the extent that pop culture convinces people that they, too, can achieve bountiful rewards, the culture serves to build high achievement motivation in people.

Time and the future

A third element of culture that will affect an MNE is society's view of time and how it should be spent. In some European cultures it is important to be on time, while in other cultures tardiness is acceptable behavior. Similarly, in some African cultures time is not a constraint; in fact, lateness is acceptable behavior.[22] As noted earlier in the chapter, the same is true in many Latin cultures of both South America and Europe.

Sometimes a culture's view of time is helpful to MNEs. For example, Japanese managers are known to take a long time to make up their minds to do something. However, once they have decided on a plan of action, implementation takes place over a predetermined period of time. This is in direct contrast to many western cultures where decisions to proceed are often made quickly, but commitment is much slower in coming. So among firms that like rapid implementation, oriental cultures can be ideal.

Indeed, US MNEs have also found that firms in the Far East, especially Japanese companies, are more long range in their planning efforts and do not expect to generate a fast return on their investment. These firms are willing to invest today and to wait five to ten years to make an adequate profit. This makes them particularly attractive to US firms looking for investors. A good example is Walt Disney, which raised almost $1 billion from Japanese investors in the early 1990s. In return, the investors have become limited partners in movies being made by Disney and will share in future profits.[23] The financial arrangement is ideal for both sides. Disney gets interest-free capital that it can use to make films. The investors have future earnings that, if the movies are successful (as are most Disney films), will provide a handsome return on investment.

Cross-cultural training

Multinationals will use information on international cultures to train their people for foreign assignments. Table 5.7 shows the six major types of cross-cultural training that are used to prepare different functional groups for overseas operations. This

Table 5.7   The frequency of training programs among US, European, and Japanese firms

	Job Category											
	CEO			Functional head			Trouble shooter			Operating personnel		
Training programs	Japan	US	Europe	Japan	US	Europe	Japan	US	Europe	Japan	US	Europe
Environmental briefing	52	57	67	54	52	57	44	38	52	31	38	67
Cultural orientation	42	55	14	41	52	14	31	33	19	24	28	24
Culture assimilator	10	21	14	10	17	14	7	10	14	9	14	19
Language training	60	76	52	59	72	57	36	41	52	24	48	76
Sensitivity training	3	3	0	1	3	0	1	3	5	0	3	5
Field experience	6	28	14	6	24	10	4	3	10	1	7	24

Source: Rosalie L. Tung, "Selection and Training Procedures of US, European, and Japanese Multinationals," *California Management Review*, Fall 1982, p. 66. Copyright © 1989 by The Regents of the University of California. Reprinted from the *California Management Review*, vol. 32, no. 1. By permission of The Regents.

table reports the percentage of firms that use one of the six training programs listed. Environmental briefings are designed to provide information on such things as climate, geography, schools, and housing. Cultural orientation programs are geared toward familiarizing the personnel with the cultural institutions and value systems of the host country. Cultural assimilators are programmed learning approaches that are specially designed to acquaint the individuals with some of the basic concepts, attitudes, customs, values, and role perceptions of the other culture. Language training often covers rudimentary speech that will help the individual to say good morning, to order a meal, to ask for the check, to place a telephone call, and so on. Sensitivity training is designed to make people more aware of how their actions affect others. Field experience involves sending the participant to the country of assignment to undergo some of the emotional stress of living and working there.

Research shows that the most useful type of training is language training and that there is good reason for this. Language is extremely valuable in helping overseas personnel to immerse themselves in the culture and to interact more effectively with the local people. It is also an excellent way to learn how and why people in that culture behave as they do.

Another training approach that has gained in popularity in recent years is the **cultural assimilator**, a programmed learning package specially written to acquaint the user with the culture of a particular country or region. The package typically contains a series of vignettes in which the user is asked how he or she would respond to a given situation or is asked to explain the behavior of someone in the story. The person is given three or four alternative responses or answers and asked to choose the correct one. Each choice has an explanation or discussion which relates whether or not the choice was correct and the reason. When the person has completed the program, which typically contains 50 to 100 incidents, the individual has gained a great deal of insight regarding the culture of that society. Another benefit of these assimilators is that they can be used over and over again, so that anyone who is being sent to this particular country can be given cultural assimilator training. Although the cost of developing the program learning package can be expensive, it can pay for itself over time, thanks to repeated use.[24]

SUMMARY

Key points

1. Culture is the acquired knowledge that people use to interpret experience and to generate social behavior. There are two major problems that culture creates for those doing business internationally: understanding the cultures of these other countries and learning how to adapt to these cultures.

2. There are a number of key elements of culture. These elements, working in tandem, can create a complex, multidimensional environment in which outsiders have a great deal of trouble understanding how and why the people act as they do. Some of the major key elements include language, religion, values and attitudes, customs and manners, material culture, aesthetics, and education.

3. While the elements of culture help to explain behavioral differences between people, in recent years researchers have attempted to develop a composite picture of culture by clustering or grouping people based on these differences. One way in which this clustering has been done is through the use of cultural dimensions: power distance, uncertainty avoidance, individualism, and masculinity. Figures 5.1 and 5.2 provide examples of the outcomes. Another way in which clustering has been done is through an analysis of work values and attitudes among countries. Figure 5.3 provides an example.

4. MNEs are particularly interested in the effect of country and geographic cultures on their international operations. In particular, they are concerned with the ways in which work attitudes, achievement motivation, and the society's view of time will impact on productivity and performance of the unit. They are also interested in taking steps to ensure that their enterprise is able to deal effectively with other cultures. Cross-cultural training has proven very effective in doing this, especially language training and the use of cultural assimilators.

Key terms

- culture
- ethnocentrism
- Protestant work ethic
- Confucian work ethic
- Shinto work ethic
- values
- attitude
- customs
- manners
- material culture
- basic economic infrastructure
- social infrastructure
- financial infrastructure
- aesthetics
- power distance
- uncertainty avoidance
- individualism
- collectivism
- masculinity
- femininity
- cultural assimilator

Review and discussion questions

1. In your own words, define *culture*.
2. In what way do ethnocentrism and misconception about other cultures inhibit those doing business internationally?

3. Why is language so critical in understanding international culture? How can this problem be dealt with effectively?

4. In what way is religion a cultural barrier for those doing business internationally? Give an example.

5. What is a value? What is an attitude? In what way are these elements critical to understanding the behaviors of other cultures?

6. What are customs? What are manners? Why would an MNE need to know about international customs and manners?

7. In what way is material culture an important element in understanding international behavior? Cite and explain two examples.

8. Why would an MNE be interested in learning about a country's aesthetics? Give an example.

9. Education is important because it influences so many aspects of culture. What is meant by this statement? Be complete in your answer.

10. In what way do the following cultural dimensions influence behavior: power distance, uncertainty avoidance, individualism, and masculinity? In your answer, be sure to define these four dimensions.

11. Drawing on the information in Figures 5.1 and 5.2, what conclusions can you draw regarding the effect of cultural dimensions on behavior? Cite and discuss two conclusions.

12. Why are attitudinal dimensions useful in understanding international culture? In your answer, integrate a discussion of Figure 5.3.

13. Why are work attitudes of importance to MNEs? Cite and describe two examples.

14. Why would companies interested in doing business overseas be concerned with the achievement motivation of the local personnel?

15. In what way is time a cultural element that is of interest to MNEs?

16. Cross-cultural training is one of the most important ways of helping MNEs to deal with their international culture environments. What specific types of cross-cultural training do firms use? Identify and describe four types.

REAL CASES

MISUNDERSTANDING ASIAN CULTURE

Many people believe that countries such as China, Korea, and Japan are willing to sell products to other nations, but they do not want to buy from other nations. Another misconception is that US products are not properly designed for sale in these countries. These "facts" are incorrect, as illustrated by the following:

● US companies used to be constantly criticized for trying to sell US appliances that were too large to fit into tiny Japanese and Chinese homes. Now you can find Chinese homes where the kitchen door is enlarged so that big, prestige US refrigerators can fit into that room.

● Until the beginning of 1989, the United States could not sell frozen concentrated orange juice in Korea. "The Korean people don't drink it," assured Korean trade officials. But US producers finally negotiated a small opening into this market; Korean officials granted a small quota for the entire year. Sales started in January 1989. By the end of the first month, the entire year's quota had been snapped up by Korean distributors.

Dunkin' Donuts had heard that the Japanese do not eat sugary donuts. Nevertheless, the company decided to give it a try and opened a test outlet in Japan. The firm found that the Japanese do indeed like donuts, but they do not like them big or sugary. So Dunkin' Donuts now bakes smaller, less sugary donuts. Moreover, the company found that the decor in its store was too garish for Japanese tastes. So it made the decor more subtle. The firm also learned that the stools were too high, so they were shortened. Dunkin' Donuts now has a major presence in Japan.

1. What did the observer in the case mean about conventional wisdom being wrong? Explain your answer.
2. How would knowledge of cultural dimensions be useful to a transnational entering the Far East market?
3. What types of training programs would be beneficial to those looking to do business in this market? Be complete in your answer.

Sources: Adapted from Mike Van Horne, "Market-Entry Approaches for the Pacific Rim," *Journal of Business Strategy*, March/April 1990; Therese Eiben, "Exporters Keep on Rolling," *Fortune*, June 14, 1993; Joyce Barnathan et al., "China: The Emerging Economic Powerhouse of the 21st Century," *Business Week*, May 17, 1993.

SARA LEE IN EASTERN EUROPE

Over the last ten years US firms have sought to make inroads in Europe, especially in the eastern sector. For this reason, John Bryan, chairman and chief executive officer of the Sara Lee Corporation, took a trip to Eastern Europe in the early 1990s. Bryan was interested in finding out if his company could establish a business operation there. Along with other executives of the firm, he traveled through Hungary, Poland, and the former Czechoslovakia and talked to both government officials and would-be entrepreneurs.

Doing business in this geographic region might seem to be a fairly simple process for the Chicago-based company that markets its products in over 140 nations. Sara Lee has operations in Germany and France and makes 60 per cent of its household and personal care products revenue in western and central Europe, selling aspirin, coffee, tea, toothpaste, toiletries, hosiery, and underwear, among other products. Yet for all its experience doing business overseas, Bryan found a great many problems facing the company in gaining an eastern European foothold.

In some cases they were too late; the Austrians and Germans had beaten them to the market. In other cases they were more fortunate, but it seemed to be more a matter of luck than skill. In particular, the group found that its knowledge of central European markets, laws, and customs was often rudimentary. For example, while the Sara Lee people signed an agreement with Viking, the largest Hungarian nylon stocking maker, neither group was certain whether the Hungarian government allowed the free import of competitive hosiery into the country. Later, to their delight, the partners learned that hosiery is not on the list of freely importable goods, so the joint venture will be protected from neighboring European competitors.

Sara Lee executives also realized that they really did not know much about the laws, taxes, or business preferences in these countries. The firm is still considering putting together a door-to-door sales organization to sell its cosmetics, but this is a new approach to doing business in Eastern Europe and no one knows if it will be an effective one. Despite these problems, Sara Lee is determined to establish a foothold in this $400 billion market. On the other hand, as John Bryan put it at the end of his trip, "An investment here will be a leap of faith."

1. In what way is culture a barrier for Sara Lee in doing business in Eastern Europe?
2. What preliminary steps should John Bryan have taken before going to Eastern Europe to talk about business deals?
3. Why is investment in Eastern Europe a "leap of faith"? Explain your answer.

Sources: Adapted from Steve Weiner, "On the Road to Eastern Europe," *Forbes*, December 10, 1990, pp. 193–200; Alex Taylor III, "Ford's $6 Billion Baby," *Fortune*, June 28, 1993, pp. 76–81; John Huey, "The World's Best Brand," *Fortune*, May 31, 1993, pp. 44–54; Sara Lee, Annual Report, 1993; *http://www.saralee.com/corporate/corpprofile/index.htm; http://www.sar-alee.com/corporate/faq/index.htm.*

ENDNOTES

1. Pat Joynt and Malcolm Warner, "Introduction: Cross-Cultural Perspectives," in Pat Joynt and Malcolm (eds.), *Managing Across Cultures: Issues and Perspectives* (London: International Thomson Business Press, 1996), p. 3.
2. For additonal insights see Gerry Darlington, "Culture – A Theoretical Review," ibid., pp. 33–55.
3. Rose Knotts, "Cross-Cultural Management: Transformation and Adaptations," *Business Horizons*, January–February 1989, p. 32.
4. Reported in Jane Gibson and Richard M. Hodgetts, *Organizational Communication: A Managerial Perspective*, 2nd ed. (New York: Harper Collins Publishers, 1991), pp. 436–437.
5. John R. Schermerhorn, Jr., "Language Effects in Cross-Cultural Management Research: An Empirical Study and a Word of Caution," *National Academy of Management Proceedings*, 1987, pp. 2–5.
6. Richard M. Hodgetts and Fred Luthans, *International Management*, 4th ed. (Burr Ridge, Ill: Irwin/McGraw 2000), p. 111.
7. Andrew Pollack, "Myths Aside, Japanese Do Look for Bargains," *New York Times*, February 20, 1994, Section E, p. 5.
8. Also, see Cacilie Rohwedder, "Diet Foods Enjoy a U.K. Sales Binge, and the Continents May Join Up Soon," *Wall Street Journal*, January 28, 1994, p. A5.
9. For a contrast see Peter Gumbel and Richard Turner, "Fans Like Euro Disney But Its Parent's Goofs Weigh the Park Down," *Wall Street Journal*, March 10, 1994, pp. A1, A12.
10. Also, see Allessandra Stanley, "Mission to Moscow: Preaching the Gospel of Business," *New York Times*, February 27, 1994, Section F, p. 4.
11. Geert Hofstede, *Culture's Consequences: International Differences in Work-Related Values* (Beverly Hills, Calif.: Sage Publications, 1980).
12. Simcha Ronen and Allen I. Kraut, "Similarities Among Countries Based on Employee Work Values and Attitudes," *Columbia Journal of World Business*, Summer 1977, p. 90.
13. See Brenton R. Schlender, "Japan's White-Collar Blues," *Fortune*, March 21, 1994, pp. 97–104.
14. Ferdinand Protzman, "Rewriting the Contract for Germany's Vaunted Workers," *New York Times*, February 13, 1994, Section F, p. 5.
15. Merry I. White, "Learning and Working in Japan," *Business Horizons*, March–April 1989, p. 47. For more on the work ethic in Japan, see Michael Hirsh, "Families United: The Japanese Work Ethic Is Creating Divided Homes," *Fort Worth Star-Telegram*, January 20, 1991, Section A, p. 15.
16. Linda S. Dillon, "The Occidental Tourist," *Training and Development Journal*, May 1990, p. 76.
17. William Ouchi, *Theory Z: How American Business Can Meet the Japanese Challenge* (Reading, Mass.: Addison-Wesley Publishing, 1981), p. 27.
18. Robert Frank and Thomas M. Burton, "Cross-Border Merger Results in Headaches for a Drug Company," *Wall Street Journal*, February 4, 1997, p. A1.
19. James R. Lincoln, "Employee Work Attitudes and Management Practice in the US and Japan: Evidence from a Large Comparative Survey," *California Management Review*, Fall 1989, pp. 89–106.
20. Itzhak Harpaz, "The Importance of Work Goals: An International Perspective," *Journal of International Business Studies*, vol. 21, no. 1, 1990, pp. 75–93.
21. Reported in Hodgetts and Luthans, op. cit., p. 384.
22. Robert Grosse and Duane Kujawa, *International Business: Theory and Managerial Applications* (Homewood, Ill.: Irwin, 1988), p. 308.
23. Lisa Gubernick, "Mickey Mouse's Sharp Pencil," *Forbes*, January 7, 1991, p. 39.
24. For additional insights into this topic, see J. Stewart Black and Mark Mendenhall, "Cross-Cultural Training Effectiveness: A Review and a Theoretical Framework for Future Research," *Academy of Management Review*, January 1990, pp. 113–136.

ADDITIONAL BIBLIOGRAPHY

Abramson, Neil R., Keating, Robert J. and Lane, Henry W. "Cross-national Cognitive Process Differences: A Comparison of Canadian, American and Japanese Managers," *Management International Review*, vol. 36, no. 2 (1996).

Adler, Nancy J. and Graham, John L. "Cross-Culture Interaction: The International Comparison Fallacy?" *Journal of International Business Studies*, vol. 20, no. 3 (Fall 1989).

Benito, Gabriel R. G. and Gripsrud, Geir. "The Expansion of Foreign Direct Investments: Discrete Rational Location Choices or a Cultural Learning Process?" *Journal of International Business Studies*, vol. 23, no. 3 (Third Quarter 1992).

Black, J. Stewart and Mendenhall, Mark. "Cross-Cultural Training Effectiveness: A Review and a Theoretical Framework for Future Research," *Academy of Management Review*, vol. 15, no. 1 (January 1990).

Cavusgil, S. Tamer and Das, Ajay. "Methodological Issues in Empirical Cross-cultural Research: A Survey of the Management Literature and Framework," *Management International Review*, vol. 37, no. 1 (1997).

Francis, June N. P. "When in Rome? The Effects of Cultural Adaptation on Intercultural Business Negotiations," *Journal of International Business Studies*, vol. 22, no. 3 (Third Quarter 1991).

Gibson, Cristina B. "Do They Do What They Believe They Can? Group Efficacy and Group Effectiveness Across Tasks and Cultures," *The Academy of Management Journal*, vol. 42, no. 2 (April 1999).

Hatch, Mary Jo. "The Dynamics of Organizational Culture," *Academy of Management Review*, vol. 18, no. 4 (October 1993).

Hayes, John and Allinson, Christopher W. "Cultural Differences in the Learning Styles of Managers," *Management International Review*, vol. 28, no. 3 (Third Quarter 1988).

Johnson, Jean L.; Sakano, Tomoaki; and Onzo, Naoto. "Behavioural Relations in Across-Culture Distribution Systems: Influence, Control and Conflict in US–Japanese Marketing Channels," *Journal of International Business Studies*, vol. 21, no. 4 (Fourth Quarter 1990).

Kelley, Lane; Whatley, Arthur; and Worthley, Reginald. "Assessing the Effects of Culture on Managerial Attitudes: A Three-Culture Test," *Journal of International Business Studies*, vol. 18, no. 2 (Summer 1987).

Kogut, Bruce and Singh, Harbir. "The Effect of National Culture on the Choice of Entry Mode," *Journal of International Business Studies*, vol. 19, no. 3 (Fall 1988).

Lane, Henry W. and Beamish, Paul W. "Cross-Culture Cooperative Behaviour in Joint Ventures in LDCs," *Management International Review*, vol. 30 (1990).

Lee, Chol and Green, Robert T. "Cross-Cultural Examination of the Fishbein Behavioural Intentions Mode," *Journal of International Business Studies*, vol. 22, no. 2 (Second Quarter 1991).

Morosini, Piero, Shane, Scott and Singh, Harbir. "National Cultural Distance and Cross-Border Acquisition Performance," *Journal of International Business Studies*, vol. 29, no. 1 (First Quarter 1998).

Morris, Tom and Pavett, Cynthia M. "Management Style and Productivity in Two Cultures," *Journal of International Business Studies*, vol. 23, no. 1 (First Quarter 1992).

Nasif, Ercan G.; Al-Daeaj, Hamad; Ebrahimi, Bahman; and Thibodeaux, Mary S. "Methodological Problems in Cross-Cultural Research: An Updated Review," *Management International Review*, vol. 31, no. 1 (First Quarter 1991).

Parameswaran, Ravi and Yaprak, Attila. "A Cross-National Comparison of Consumer Research Measures," *Journal of International Business Studies*, vol. 18, no. 1 (Spring 1987).

Rosch, Martin and Segler, Kay G. "Communication with Japanese," *Management International Review*, vol. 27, no. 4 (Fourth Quarter 1987).

Schmitt, Bernd H. "Language and Visual Imagery: Issues of Corporate Identity in East Asia," *Columbia Journal of World Business*, vol. 30, no. 4 (Winter 1995).

Selvarajah, Christopher T.; Duignan, Patric; Suppiah, Chandraseagran; Lane, Terry; and Nuttman, Chris. "In Search of the ASEAN Leader: An Exploratory Study of the Dimensions that Relate to Excellence in Leadership," *Management International Review*, vol. 35, no. 1 (1995).

Stening, Bruce W. and Hammer, Mitchell R. "Cultural Baggage and the Adaption of Expatriate American and Japanese Managers," *Management International Review*, vol. 32, no. 1 (First Quarter 1992).

Ueno, Susumu and Sekaran, Uma. "The Influence of Culture on Budget Control Practices in the USA and Japan: An Empirical Study," *Journal of International Business Studies*, vol. 23, no. 4 (Fourth Quarter 1992).

Usunier, Jean-Claude G. "Business Time Perceptions and National Cultures: A Comparative Survey," *Management International Review*, vol. 31, no. 3 (Third Quarter 1991).

Zammuto, Raymond F. and O'Connor, Edward J. "Gaining Advanced Manufacturing Technologies' Benefits: The Roles of Organization Design and Culture," *Academy of Management Review*, vol. 17, no. 4 (October 1992).

CHAPTER 6

International Trade

OBJECTIVES OF THE CHAPTER

An understanding of international trade is critical to the study of international business. The primary objective of this chapter is to examine key economic theories that help to explain why nations trade. In addition, the role and importance of a country's barriers to trade will be studied and discussion will be focused on why most nations use trade barriers despite vigorous international efforts to eliminate them. The specific objectives of this chapter are to:

1. **Define** the term "international trade" and discuss the role of mercantilism in modern international trade.

2. **Contrast** the theory of absolute advantage and the theory of comparative advantage.

3. **Relate** the importance of international product life cycle theory to the study of international economics.

4. **Explain** some of the most commonly used barriers to trade and other economic developments that affect international economics.

5. **Discuss** some of the reasons for the tensions between the theory of free trade and the widespread practice of national barriers to trade.

The decline of the UK market

The UK has experienced a sharp decline in the world market share of many export products (see table below). The 1980s were dominated by the Japanese, and strong exporters like the United States and the UK lost ground as the Japanese expanded. As the data reveal, the UK and the United States, in particular, lost market share in such industries as: automobiles, office and telecom equipment, chemicals, textiles, etc.

In the late 1980s, Korea, Singapore, Taiwan, Thailand, and China were beginning to emerge as the Asian Tigers. For instance, during this period Korea began to expand its automotive industry; and the Chinese market share of office machines and telecom equipment increased from zero to about 1.3 per cent of the market in 1990 and to 2.4 per cent by 1995. Thanks to NAFTA, countries such as Mexico and Canada increased their market share of automotive products and machinery transport equipment, while the UK's share declined. In the process, Japanese firms also lost market share in key industries such as automobiles, computers and telecom equipment.

Today, managers in the UK are finding that imported goods are often of higher quality and lower price than those manufactured domestically. This is not to say that the UK is at a complete disadvantage with its competitors. For instance, the UK's market share of office machines and telecom equipment decreased over the 1990–95 period, but for the period from 1992 to 1996, it continually increased its market share of telecom equipment. This highlights the real situation. It is not that countries are losing market share everywhere, but they need to identify their strengths and specialize in specific products and stages of the production process!

Sources: Adapted from Edmund Faltermayer, "Is 'Made in the USA' Fading Away?" *Fortune*, September 24, 1990, pp. 62–73; Emily Thornton, "Japan's Struggle to Restructure," *Fortune*, June 28, 1993, pp. 84–88. World Trade Organization, *Annual Report*, 1997; *http://www.intracen.org*.

Exports of:	% UK share of the export market			% US share of the export market			% Japanese share of the export market		
	1980	1990	1995	1980	1990	1995	1980	1990	1995
Automotive products	5.8	4.4	4.4	12.7	10.2	11.5	19.8	20.8	17.7
Office machines and telecom equipment	6.4	6.5	6.2	20.2	17.3	16.5	21.1	22.4	17.9
Machinery and transport equipment	7.6	6.1	5.5	17.0	15.9	14.8	14.5	17.7	16.4
Chemicals	8.7	8.0	7.1	14.9	13.3	13.2	4.7	5.3	6.4
Commercial services	10.0	7.9	6.9	16.5	16.3	15.3	5.1	6.3	7.7
Transportation services	6.5	6.6	5.6	15.3	17.0	16.1	9.8	7.9	7.5
Textiles	5.7	4.2	3.4	6.2	5.8	4.9	9.3	5.6	4.7

1. How does the UK finding market niches help to illustrate the theory of comparative advantage?

2. How does a UK manager wanting to buy domestic products illustrate the importance of consumer taste in international trade?

3. In what way could the UK use trade barriers to protect its markets from foreign competitors? Who can be affected by these trade barriers?

INTRODUCTION

International trade is the branch of economics concerned with the exchange of goods and services with foreign countries. Although this is a complex subject, we will focus on two particular areas: international trade theory and barriers to trade.

Some international economic problems cannot be solved in the short run. Consider the US balance of trade deficit. The overall US imbalance is heavily affected by the specific US deficit with Japan. President Clinton has worked hard to change this situation.[1] Pressure on others with whom the United States has a negative trade balance, such as China and Singapore, has been no more fruitful.[2] In practice, the US trade deficit cannot be reduced by political measures but only by long-run economic measures to reduce imports and increase exports. Other nations are also learning this lesson. Simply put, most countries seem to want a favorable trade balance with the others, but this is impossible since a nation with a deficit must be matched by a nation with a surplus.[3]

International trade has become an even more important topic now that so many countries have begun to move from state-run to market-driven economies.[4] Inflation and, in many cases, unemployment are severe problems to these nations. Fortunately, enhanced international trade is one way to address a weak macroeconomy.[5]

International commitment to a free market will bring prosperity to the world economic system. Since the time of Adam Smith in 1790, economists have shown that free trade is efficient and leads to maximum economic welfare. In this chapter we will discuss the economic rationale for free trade and the political impediments to it.

INTERNATIONAL TRADE THEORY

In order to understand the topic of international trade, we must be able to answer the question: Why do nations trade? One of the earliest, and simplest, answers to this question was provided by mercantilism, a theory that was quite popular in the eighteenth century, when gold was the only world currency. **Mercantilism** holds that a government can improve the economic well-being of the country by encouraging exports and stifling imports. The result is a positive balance of trade that leads to wealth (gold) flowing into the country. While most international trade experts believe that mercantilism is a simplistic and erroneous theory, it has had followers.

For example, under President Mitterand in the late 1970s and early 1980s, France sought to revitalize its industrial base by nationalizing key industries and banks and subsidizing exports over imports. By the mid-1980s the French government realized that the strategy was not working and began denationalizing many of its holdings.[6]

A more useful explanation of why nations trade is provided by trade theories which focus on specialization of effort. The theories of absolute and comparative advantage are good examples.

Theory of absolute advantage

The **theory of absolute advantage** holds that by specializing in the production of goods they can produce more efficiently than anyone else, nations can increase their economic well-being. A simple example can illustrate this point. Assume that two nations, North and South, are both able to produce two goods, cloth and grain. Assume further that labor is the only scarce factor of production and thus the only cost of production.

Labor cost (hours) of production for one unit

	Cloth	Grain
North	10	20
South	20	10

Because labor is the only cost of production, lower labor-hours per unit of production means lower production costs, and higher productivity per labor-hour. North has an absolute advantage in the production of cloth since the cost requires only 10 labor-hours, compared to 20 labor-hours in South. Similarly, South has an absolute advantage in the production of grain, which it produces at a cost of 10 labor-hours, compared to 20 labor-hours in North.

Both countries gain by trade. If they specialize and exchange cloth for grain at a relative price of 1:1, each country can employ its resources to produce a greater amount of goods. North can import one unit of grain in exchange for one unit of cloth, thereby "paying," in effect, only 10 labor-hours for one unit of grain. If North had produced the grain itself, it would have used 20 labor-hours per unit, North gains 10 labor-hours from the trade. In the same way South gains from trade when it imports one unit of cloth in exchange for one unit of grain. The effective cost to South for one unit of cloth is only the 10 labor-hours required to make its one unit of grain.

The theory of absolute advantage, as originally formulated, does not predict the exchange ratio between cloth and grain once trade is opened, nor does it resolve the division of the gains from trade between the two countries. The example assumed an international price ratio of 1:1, but this ratio (P_{cloth} to P_{grain}) could lie between 2:1 (the pretrade price ratio in South) and 1:2 (the pretrade price ratio in North). To determine the relative price ratio under trade, we would have to know the total resources of each country (total labor-hours available per year), and the tastes of each country must be known. This would determine the relative gains from trade for each country.

Even this simple model of absolute advantage has several dramatic implications. First, if a country has an absolute advantage in producing a product, there exists a potential for gains from trade. Second, the more a country is able to specialize in the production of the good it produces most efficiently, the greater are its potential gains in national well-being. Third, *within* one country the gains from trade are not evenly distributed by the competitive market. This last implication is illustrated by the following example.

Prior to trade, if grain producers in North worked 20 hours, they would produce one unit of grain that could be exchanged for two units of cloth. After trade, the grain producers who remain can exchange one unit of grain for only one unit of cloth. The remaining grain producers are worse off under trade. Cloth producers in North, however, work 10 hours, produce one unit of cloth, and exchange it for one unit of grain, whereas previously they received only a half unit of grain. They are better off. If grain producers in North switch to cloth production, then 20 hours of labor results in production of two units of cloth, which they can exchange for two units of grain. They are better off under international trade. As long as North does not specialize completely in cloth, there will be gainers (cloth producers and grain producers who switched to cloth) and losers (those who continue as grain producers).

Since the nation as a whole benefits from trade, the gainers could compensate the losers, and there would still be a surplus to be distributed in some way. If such compensation does not take place, however, the losers (continuing grain producers) have an incentive to try to prevent the country from opening itself up to trade. Historically this problem has continued to fuel opposition to a free trade policy that reduces barriers to trade. A good example is Japanese farmers who stand to lose their livelihood if the government opens up Japan to lower-priced agricultural imports.

A more complicated picture of the determinants and effects of trade emerges when one of the trading partners has an absolute advantage in the production of both goods. However, trade under these conditions still brings gains, as David Ricardo first demonstrated in his theory of comparative advantage.

Theory of comparative advantage

The **theory of comparative advantage** holds that nations should produce those goods for which they have the greatest relative advantage. In terms of the previous example of two countries, North and South, and two commodities, cloth and grain, Ricardo's model can be illustrated as follows:

Labor cost (hours) of production for one unit

	Cloth	Grain
North	50	100
South	200	200

In this example North has an absolute advantage in the production of *both* cloth and grain, so it would appear at first sight that trade would be unprofitable, or at least that incentives for exchange no longer exist. Yet trade is still advantageous to both nations, provided the *relative* costs of production differ in the two countries.

Before trade, in North one unit of cloth costs (50/100) hours of grain, so one unit of cloth can be exchanged for one-half unit of grain. In North, the price of cloth is half the price of grain. In South, one unit of cloth costs (200/200) hours of grain or one grain unit. In South, the price of cloth equals the price of grain. If North can import more than a half unit of grain for one unit of cloth, it will gain from trade. Similarly, if South can import one unit of cloth for less than one unit of grain, it will also gain from trade. These relative price ratios set the boundaries for trade. Trade is profitable between price ratios (price of cloth to price of grain) of 0.5 and 1. For example, at an international price ratio of two-thirds, North gains from trade. It can import one unit of grain in return for exporting one and a half units of cloth. Because it costs North only 50 hours of labor to produce the unit of cloth, its effective cost under trade for one unit of imported grain is 75 labor-hours. Under pretrade conditions it costs North 100 labor-hours to produce one unit of grain. Similarly, South gains from trade. It imports one unit of cloth in exchange for two-thirds unit of grain.

Prior to trade, South spent 200 labor-hours to produce the one unit of cloth. Through trade its effective cost for one unit of cloth is 2/3 × 200 or 133 labor-hours – cheaper than the domestic production cost of 200 labor-hours. Assuming free trade between the two nations, North will tend to specialize in the production of cloth and South will tend to specialize in the production of grain.

This example leads to a general principle. There are gains from trade whenever the relative price ratios of two goods differ under international exchange from what they would be under conditions of no trade. Such domestic conditions are often called *autarky*. Free trade is superior to autarky. Trade provides greater economic output and consumption to the trade partners jointly as they specialize in production, exporting the good in which they have a comparative advantage and importing the good in which they have a comparative disadvantage.

The general conclusions of the theory of comparative advantage are the same as those for the theory of absolute advantage. In addition, the theory of comparative advantage demonstrates that countries jointly benefit from trade (under the assumptions of the model) even if one country has an absolute advantage in the production of *both* goods. Total world efficiency and consumption increase under free trade.

As with the theory of absolute advantage discussed previously, Ricardo's theory of comparative advantage does not answer the question of the distribution of gains between the two countries, nor the distribution of gains and losses between grain producers and cloth producers within each country. No country will lose under free trade, but, in theory at least, all the gains could accrue to one country and to only one group within that country.

ACTIVE LEARNING CHECK

Review your answer to Active Learning Case question 1 and make any changes you like. Then compare your answer to the one below.

1. **How does the UK finding market niches help to illustrate the theory of comparative advantage?**

The finding of market niches helps illustrate the theory of comparative advantage because it shows that the UK is picking those areas where it has a relative advantage over the competition and exploiting its strengths in these markets.

Factor endowment theory

In recent years more sophisticated theories have emerged that help to clarify and extend our knowledge of international trade. **Factor endowment theory** holds that countries will produce and export products that use large amounts of production factors that they have in abundance, and they will import products requiring large amounts of production factors that are scarce in their country. This theory is also known as the **Heckscher-Ohlin theory** (after the two economists who first developed it). The theory is useful in extending the concept of comparative advantage by bringing into consideration the endowment and cost of factors of production. The theory also helps to explain why nations with relatively large labor forces, such as China, will

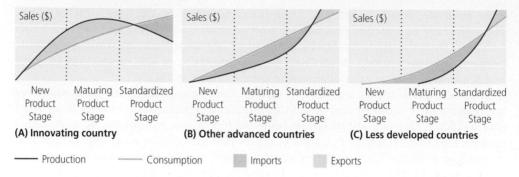

Figure 6.1 The international product life cycle

Source: Raymond Vernon and Louis T. Wells, Jr., *The Manager in the International Economy* (Englewood Cliffs, NJ: Prentice-Hall, 1991), p. 85.

concentrate on producing labor-intensive goods, and countries like the Netherlands, which has relatively more capital than labor, will specialize in capital-intensive goods.

However, there are some weaknesses with the factor endowment theory. One weakness is that some countries have minimum wage laws that result in high prices for relatively abundant labor. As a result, the country may find it less expensive to import certain goods than to produce them internally. Another weakness with the theory is that countries like the United States actually export relatively more labor-intensive goods and import capital-intensive goods, an outcome that appears surprising. This result, discovered by Wassily Leontief, a Nobel prize economist, is known as the **Leontief paradox** and has been explained in terms of the quality of labor input rather than just man-hours of work. The United States produces and exports technology-intensive products that require highly educated labor. These problems with factor endowment theory help us to understand why no single theory can explain the role of economic factors in trade theory.

International product life cycle theory

Another theory which provides insights into international theory is Vernon's **international product life cycle (IPLC) theory**, which concerns the stages of production of a product with new "know-how." Such a product is first produced by the parent firm, then by its foreign subsidiaries, and finally anywhere in the world where costs are the lowest. The theory helps to explain why a product that begins as a nation's export often ends up becoming an import. The theory focuses on market expansion and technological innovation, concepts that are relatively deemphasized in comparative advantage theory. IPLC theory has two important tenets: (1) technology is a critical factor in creating and developing new products and (2) market size and structure are important in determining trade patterns.

Product stages   The IPLC has three stages: new product, maturing product, and standardized product (see Figure 6.1*a*). A new product is one that is innovative or unique in some way. Initially, consumption is in the home country, price is inelastic, profits are high, and the company seeks to sell to those willing to pay a premium price. Cellular telephones are an example.[7] As production increases and outruns local consumption, exporting begins.

As the product enters the mature phase of its life cycle (see Figure 6.1*b*), an increasing percentage of sales is achieved through exporting. At the same time competitors in other advanced countries will be working to develop substitute products so that they can replace the initial good with one of their own. The introduction of these substitutes and the softening of demand for the original product will eventually result in the firm that developed the product now switching its strategy from production to market protection. Attention will also be focused on tapping markets in less developed countries.

As the product enters the standardized product stage (see Figure 6.1*c*), the technology becomes widely diffused and available. Production tends to be shifted to low-cost locations, including less developed countries and offshore locations. The firm will also try to differentiate the product and to prevent the emergence of price competition, where price is the sole determinant of demand.

Personal computers and the IPLC   In recent years a number of products have moved through the IPLC and are now in the standardized product stage. Personal computers (PCs) are a good example, although there is a wide variety of PCs and some versions are in the new product and the maturing product phases. For example, the early version of PCs that reached the market in the 1984 to 1991 period were in the standardized product stage by 1995 and sold primarily on the basis of price. Machines that entered the market in the 1996 to 1998 period were in the maturing stage by 1999. PCs with increased memory capability that were in the new product stage in 1999 quickly moved toward maturity, and by 2000 they were being replaced by even better machines.

The 2001 to 2003 time period is likely to see desktop PCs replaced by laptop and notebook models that are lighter, faster, more sophisticated, and less expensive than their predecessors. In turn these machines will be replaced in the 2004 to 2007 period by notebooks with advanced pentium chips, color monitors, long-term battery capability, and diskettes capable of holding 1 billion bytes. These units are also likely to have telephonic equipment and to serve as a complete communications center from which the international executive can communicate anywhere in the world. These machines will first be manufactured locally and then in foreign markets. Thus PCs will continue to move through an international product life cycle.

The IPLC theory is useful in helping to explain how new technologically innovative products fit into the world trade picture. However, because new innovative products are sometimes rapidly improved, it is important to remember that one or two versions of them may be in the standardized product stage while other versions are in the maturing stage and still others are in the new product phase.

Other important considerations

Many factors beyond those considered in the theories we have looked at greatly influence international trade theory.[8] One is government regulation. Countries often limit or restrict trade with other countries for political reasons. For example, despite the benefits

INTERNATIONAL BUSINESS STRATEGY IN ACTION

Korea's Daewoo enters Europe

The Daewoo group, South Korea's third largest car maker, has launched an ambitious European assault. The firm intends to sell 100,000 cars in Europe, capturing 1 per cent of the car market in each country it enters. In carrying out this strategy, the company is relying on its line of hatchbacks and sedans and targeting the bottom tier of the European auto market which has traditionally been dominated by the likes of Nissan, Fiat, and Ford.

With the strong yen forcing the Japanese to raise prices for their European cars in the early 1990s, Daewoo and its Korean counterparts, Hyundai and Kai, decided to make substantial inroads into the inexpensive car market. So while European car makers were still recovering from the early 1990s recession, the Koreans began exerting strong downward pressures on prices.

In addition, many of Daewoo's cars, unlike imports from Japan and the United States, are not subject to 10 per cent duties in Europe; nor do they face import quotas. The Brussels-based European Automobile Manufacturers Association predicts that 360,000 Korean autos could be imported into the European Union by 2000, up from 131,000 in 1993 – and Daewoo hopes to account for a large percentage of these units.

Daewoo has also bought an assembly plant in Romania with the capacity to produce up to 200,000 vehicles annually. The firm now hopes to take advantage of Romania's status as one of six east bloc countries with preferential trading rights with the EU. In addition, Daewoo plans to export more than half of the plant's production to western Europe. Coupled with a multi-million dollar advertising campaign and foreign direct investment in company-owned service centers throughout the EU, the Korean automaker hopes to shed its image as "the biggest car company you've *never* heard of".

Sources: Charles Siler, "Daewoo Begins Assault on European Markets", *Automotive News*, November 9, 1994, p. 43. Julia Flynn, "Asian Carmakers' European Plan", *Business Week*, November 7, 1994, p. 4. Julia Flynn, "Another Asian Assault Spooks Europe's Carmakers", *Business Week*, October 31, 1994, p. 19. Virginia Marsh, "Daewoo to Build Cars in Romania", *Financial Times*, October 25, 1994, p. 5.

of international trade, the United States has not officially traded with North Korea in over four decades or with Cuba for over three decades. Other important factors include monetary currency valuation and consumer tastes.

Monetary currency valuation When examining why one country trades with another country, we need to consider the **monetary exchange rate**, which is the price of one currency stated in terms of another currency. For example, over 1995–1998 the value of the Japanese yen declined significantly over the value of the US dollar. As a result, many Japanese businesses have found their products becoming more competitive in the US market. Conversely, the dollar's decline against such as the German mark has made US imports more attractive to Europeans with strong currencies. In the next chapter we will discuss exchange rates in more detail.

Consumer tastes International trade is not based solely on price; some people will pay more for a product even though they can buy something similar for less money. This willingness to pay more may be based on prestige, perceived quality, or a host of other physical and psychological reasons. Personal tastes dictate consumer decisions.

ACTIVE LEARNING CHECK

Review your answer to Active Learning Case question 2 and make any changes you like. Then compare you answer to the one below.

2. How does a UK manager wanting to buy domestic products illustrate the importance of consumer taste in international trade?

This example shows that people often buy goods based on personal preference, and such characteristics as low price, high quality, or improved productivity are not the only factors influencing the purchase decision. Of course, this "Buy UK" focus will often come into play only when "all other factors are approximately equal." The manager is unlikely to turn down a German-made product that is 40 per cent cheaper in favor of one that is made domestically. So there are limits to the effect of consumer taste on purchase decisions.

BARRIERS TO TRADE

Why do many countries produce goods and services that could be more cheaply purchased from others? One reason is because of trade barriers which effectively raise the cost of these goods.

Reasons for trade barriers

One of the most common reasons for trade barriers is to encourage local production. Many South American countries rely heavily on such a strategy. Another is to encourage exports and to help the nation build world markets by providing subsidies in the form of tax breaks and low-interest loans to home-based companies. Japan and other southeast Asian countries use this approach, as does the US government,[9] although on a much more limited basis.[10] During the upcoming decade exports will continue to be a major source of international economic activity,[11] and increased attention will be directed toward stimulating such activity.[12] At the same time there are likely to be trade barriers which impede these export efforts. Some of the most common goals of trade barriers are to:

1. Protect local jobs by shielding home country business from foreign competition.
2. Encourage local production to replace imports.
3. Protect infant industries that are just getting started.
4. Reduce reliance on foreign suppliers.
5. Encourage local and foreign direct investment.
6. Reduce balance of payments problems.
7. Promote export activity.
8. Prevent foreign firms from *dumping*, that is, selling goods below cost in order to achieve market share.
9. Promote political objectives such as refusing to trade with countries that practice apartheid or deny civil liberties to their citizens.

Table 6.1   Members of the Organization of Petroleum Exporting Countries (OPEC)

Member country	Quotas (barrels per day)
Algeria	731,000
Indonesia	1,187,000
Iran	3,359,000
Iraq*	736,900
Kuwait	1,836,000
Libya	1,227,000
Nigeria	1,885,000
Qatar	593,000
Saudi Arabia	7,438,000
United Arab Emirates	2,000,000
Venezuela	2,720,000
Total	**23,712,900**

Quotas are for the year starting on April 1999.

*Data for Iraq is for 1995 actual production.

Source: Adapted from *http://www.opec.org/*

Commonly used barriers

There are a variety of barriers that deter the free flow of international goods and services.[13] The following discussion presents six of the most common barriers.

Price-based barriers   Imported goods and services sometimes have a tariff added to their price. Quite often this is based on the value of the goods. For example, some tobacco products coming into the United States carry an ad valorem tariff of over 100 per cent, thus more than doubling their cost to US consumers. Tariffs raise revenues for the government, discourage imports, and make local goods more attractive.

Quantity limits   Quantity limits, often known as **quotas**, restrict the number of units that can be imported or the market share that is permitted. If the quota is set at zero, as in the case of Cuban cigars from Havana, it is called an **embargo**. If the annual quota is set at 1 million units, no more than this number can be imported during one year; once this quota is reached, all additional imports are turned back. In some cases a quota is established in terms of market share. For example, Canada allows foreign banks to hold no more than 16 per cent of Canadian bank deposits, and the European Union limits Japanese auto imports to 10 per cent of the total market.

International price fixing   In some cases a host of international firms will fix prices or quantities sold in an effort to control price. This is known as a **cartel**. A well-known example is OPEC (Organization of Petroleum Exporting Countries), which consists of Saudi Arabia, Kuwait, Iran, Iraq, and Venezuela, among others (see Table 6.1). By controlling the supply of oil it provides, the cartel seeks to control the price and profit. This practice is illegal in the United States and Europe,[14] but the basic idea of allowing competitors to cooperate for the purpose of meeting international competition is being endorsed more frequently in countries such as the United States.[15] For example, US computer firms have now created partnerships for joint research and development efforts.

Nontariff barriers   **Nontariff barriers** are rules, regulations, and bureaucratic red tape that delay or preclude the purchase of foreign goods. Examples include (1) slow processing of import permits, (2) the establishment of quality standards that exclude foreign producers, and (3) a "buy local" policy. These barriers limit imports and protect domestic sales.

Financial limits   There are a number of different financial limits. One of the most common is **exchange controls** that restrict the flow of currency. For example, many Latin American countries will allow exporters to exchange their dollars for local currency, but they place restrictions on access to dollars for purchasing imports. Another common exchange control is the limit of currency that can be taken out of the country; for example, travelers may take up to only $3,000 per person out of the country. A third example is the use of fixed exchange rates that are quite favorable to the country. For example, dollars may be exchanged for local currency on a 1:1 basis, while without exchange controls the rate would be 1:4. These cases are particularly evident where there exists a black market for foreign currency that offers an exchange rate that is much different from the fixed rate.

Foreign investment controls   **Foreign investment controls** are limits on foreign direct investment or the transfer or remittance of funds. These controls can take a number of different forms, including (1) requiring foreign investors to take a minority ownership position (49 per cent or less); (2) limiting profit remittance, for example, to 15 per cent of accumulated capital per year; and (3) prohibiting royalty payments to parent companies, thus stopping the latter from taking out capital.

These barriers can greatly restrict international trade and investment. However, it must be realized that these barriers are created for what governments believe are very important reasons. A close look at one of these, tariffs, helps to make this clearer.

Tariffs

A **tariff** is a tax on goods that are shipped internationally. The most common is the **import tariff**, which is levied on goods shipped into a country. Less common is the **export tariff**, which is levied on goods that are sent out of the country, or a **transit tariff**, which is levied on goods passing through the country. There are a number of bases on which these taxes are levied. A **specific duty** is a tariff based on units such as $1 for each item shipped into the country. So a manufacturer shipping in 1,000 pairs of shoes would pay a specific duty of $1,000. An **ad valorem duty** is a tariff based on a percentage of the value of the item, so a watch valued at $25 and carrying a 10 per cent duty would have a tariff of $2.50. A **compound duty** is a tariff consisting of both a specific and an ad valorem duty. So a suit of clothes valued at

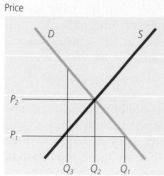

Figure 6.2   Impacts of a tariff

$80 which carries a specific duty of $3 and an ad valorem duty of 5 per cent would have a compound duty of $7.

Governments typically use tariffs to raise revenue and/or to protect local industry. At the same time these taxes decrease demand for the respective product while raising the price to the buyer. This is illustrated in Figure 6.2, which shows what happens when a tariff drives the price of a good from P_1 to P_2 (the world price plus the tariff). As seen in this figure, the quantity demanded declines from Q_1 to Q_2. This price increase allows local producers to sell $Q_3 Q_2$ and thus to take market share away from foreign firms that were exporting $Q_3 Q_1$ into the country. However, as seen in the figure, this is done at the price of charging the consumer more money *and* of reducing the number of buyers who purchase the product. At new price P_2, there are no longer any imports.

There are numerous reasons for using tariffs. One is to protect domestic industries or firms. The US government has used them to prevent foreign companies from selling goods at lower prices in the United States than they sell for back home. US automakers have often accused their overseas rivals of using this tactic. In the case of Japanese car manufacturers, for example, this was a particularly troublesome area when the value of the yen increased sharply in the early 1990s. As a result, argued the US car firms, imported parts and cars had to reflect the increased value of the yen or be subjected to tariffs.[16] Others have made similar arguments. Eastman Kodak, for example, has asked the US Commerce Department to impose steep tariffs on the Fuji Photo Film Company. Kodak's argument is partially based on the rising yen. However, it also reflects a concern with **dumping**, which is the selling of imported goods at a price below cost or below that in the home country. In this case Kodak has argued that Fuji sells color photographic paper for less than 20 cents a square foot in the United States, while charging almost 60 cents a square foot in Japan.[17]

Another reason for using tariffs is to raise government revenue. Import tariffs, for example, are a major source of revenue for less developed countries. A third reason is to reduce foreign expenditures by citizens in order to improve the country's balance of payments.

Tariffs continue to be one of the most commonly used barriers to trade, despite the fact that they often hurt low-income consumers and have limited, if any, impact on upper-income purchasers. In recent years most industrialized countries have tried to reduce or eliminate the use of these trade barriers and to promote more free trade policies.[18] The United States is a good example.

US trade policy

Despite being a highly protectionist nation in its early years, the United States has a policy today that generally strives to lower tariffs and trade barriers through the use of multilateral agreements. Since the protectionist disaster of the depression years, the United States has sought to minimize the use of tariffs. In 1946, 22 countries signed the General Agreement on Tariffs and Trade (GATT). The United States has provided leadership to encourage post-World War II free trade. Today US tariffs average only 3.7 per cent ad valorem to most countries of the world.[19]

The move away from tariffs does not mean US trade policy is completely open.[20] The US government uses a variety of approaches to promote or discourage international trade. For example, to encourage trade, there is the **North American Free Trade Agreement (NAFTA)**, which eliminates most trade restrictions (such as tariffs) between the United States, Canada, and Mexico and extends national treatment to foreign investment, and the **Caribbean Basin Initiative**, which eliminates tariffs on many imports from the Caribbean and Central American regions. Yet the **Trading-with-the-Enemy Act** disallows trade with countries judged to be enemies of the United States, including North Korea and Cuba. Also, the US administration has the authority to prevent sales of goods to foreign governments when they are not deemed to be in the best interests of the United States. These goods can range from computers to chemicals to materials used for making nuclear weapons.[21]

The United States has also used negotiated agreements to limit the type or number of products entering the country. For example, there is a voluntary agreement with Japan that restricts the number of cars imported to the United States to 2.4 million annually. (Also see the box "International Business Strategy in Action: Access to the Japanese Market.") At the same time, the United States encourages exports through legislation such as the **Foreign Sales Corporation Act**, which allows US exporters to establish overseas affiliates and not to pay taxes on the affiliates' income until the earnings are remitted to the parent company. The government also offers **trade adjustment assistance** to US businesses and individuals who are harmed by competition from imports. This aid takes such forms as loans for retooling and job counseling for those seeking alternative employment.

ACTIVE LEARNING CHECK

Review your answer to Active Learning Case question 3 and make any changes you like. Then compare your answer to the one below.

3. In what way could the UK use trade barriers to protect its markets from foreign competitors? Who can be affected by these trade barriers?

There are a number of steps that the UK could take to protect its markets from foreign competitors. Examples include establishing or increasing ad valorem tariffs, placing quantity limits on various imports, and limiting foreign direct investment. Of course, other countries could retaliate and take similar action against UK-produced goods, so the use of these trade barriers must be selective and should not be undertaken unless efforts at negotiated agreements prove fruitless. As a member of the EU, the UK cannot use such trade barriers against fellow member states.

INTERNATIONAL BUSINESS STRATEGY IN ACTION

Access to the Japanese market

One way in which trade barriers are lowered or eliminated is through negotiated agreements. This practice has been particularly important in dealing with the large US trade deficits with Japan. The American government believes that this deficit will be reduced if Japan opens its markets to US goods, and recent negotiations indicate that this is likely to happen increasingly in the future.

Some specific steps that Japan has promised to take include cutting restrictions on large retail stores, altering tax policies so that more land is available for commercial and residential use, making the intricate distribution system more accessible to outsiders, stiffening antitrust penalties, providing import clearance within 24 hours for foreign goods, expanding Japanese government procurement of foreign goods, and curbing the anticompetitive practices of Japanese industrial groups. Japan has also agreed to raise public investment in housing, port facilities, road, and

other programs that will increase the demand for imports. The objective of these measures is to make it as easy for US firms to do business in Japan as it is for Japanese firms to do business in the United States. On the other side of the coin, the Americans are promising to take steps to reduce the trade deficit by pledging to improve education, to bolster saving and investment, and to cut the cost of capital.

For the foreseeable future, at least, both sides are likely to be wary about their dealings and to continue jockeying for position. At the same time, US firms are working to enter the Japanese market and thus to increase their international stake there. However, any reversal of the current trade position is going to take a long time, especially, since the rising value of the yen in the late 1990s has widened the trade deficit to record levels. For the moment, both sides are going to have to be content simply to keep trying to work things out.

Sources: Adapted from Clyde H. Farnsworth, "Japanese Pledge to Lower Barriers to Trade with the United States," *New York Times*, April 6, 1990, pp. A1, D6; Suneel Ratan, "The Big Split," *Fortune*, May 6, 1991, pp. 38–48; Keith Bradsher, "US and Japan Open Talks on New Trade Framework," *New York Times*, June 12, 1993, pp. 17, 24; Charlene Barshefsky, "Report on the United States–Japan Framework for a New Economic Partnership," *Testimony to the House Committee on Foreign Affairs*, July 21, 1993 (*http://www.gwjapan.com/ftp/pub/policy/ustr/1993/cb072193.txt*); Martin Crutsinger, "Big 3 Accuse Japan, South Korea of Unfair Trade," *Detroit Free Press*, September 23, 1997.

NONTARIFF BARRIERS TO TRADE

The economic effects of nontariff barriers (NTBs) to trade are roughly similar to those of tariffs. They are inefficient distortions which reduce potential gains from trade. There is a wide range of NTBs, as seen in Table 6.2.

Nontariff barriers have gained prominence in recent years as they have become more visible and more important. Nations have resorted to them more frequently for protection. For example, the average US tariff rate was reduced from an all-time high of 60 per cent in 1932 to 12 to 15 per cent during the 20 years following World War II to about 5 per cent by 1980. The use of nontariff barriers remained stable until the 1970s, when their use increased. The Tokyo round of the GATT negotiations devoted considerable attention to reducing NTBs. The negotiations listed over 800 NTBs used by member countries.

Some of these NTBs are not imposed by nations to interfere deliberately with trade. Sometimes they arise out of domestic policy and economic management. Examples include tax breaks to reduce regional income disparities or regulations designed to

Table 6.2   Nontariff barriers to trade

Specific limitation	Customs administrative rules	Government participation	Import charges
Quotas (including voluntary)	Valuation systems	Procurement policies	Import deposits
Import licences	Antidumping rules	Export subsidies and incentives	Supplementary duties
Supplementary incentives	Tariff classifications	Countervailing duties	Import credits
Minimum import limits	Documentation needed	Domestic assistance programs	Variable levies
Embargoes	Fees	Trade-diverting	Border levies
Sectoral bilateral agreements	Disparities in quality and testing standards		
Orderly marketing agreements	Packaging, labeling, and marketing standards		

increase local purchasing or employment. These then result in a type of indirect export subsidy. Other NTBs are more blatant devices which restrict imports or foster exports.

Quotas

Quotas are the most important NTBs. A quota restricts imports to a particular level.[22] When a quota is imposed, domestic production generally increases and prices rise. As a result, the government will usually end up losing tariff revenues.

Historically the GATT has prohibited import quotas except on agricultural products, as emergency measures, or when a country has short-run balance of payments problems. Countries have circumvented this regulation most notably for textiles, footwear, and automobiles by negotiating voluntary export restraint agreements which are useful in preventing retaliatory action by the importing country. In general, business would rather be protected by quotas than by tariffs. Under quotas, if future domestic demand is known, businesses can determine their future production levels. Under tariffs, domestic producers must estimate the elasticity of the demand curve for imported products and the future movements in world prices, which is a more difficult challenge.

Buy national restrictions

"Buy national" regulations require national governments to give preference to domestic producers, sometimes to the complete exclusion of foreign firms. In Europe, for example, many of the telephone, telegraph, electricity generation and transmission, airlines, and railroad industries are government-owned and buy from national firms only, thus closing a large market for US exports. On the other hand, the United States has a similarly wide range of inefficient "Buy American" regulations at the national and state levels that discriminate against foreign suppliers.

During the 1970s Tokyo round of the GATT negotiations, a mild code to open up government contracts to foreign suppliers was negotiated. Now governments at least must publicize large procurement contracts to make public the winner's bid price or the basis for selecting the winning bid.

Customs valuation

Also during the GATT Tokyo round, considerable progress was made in the area of customs valuation for the payment of duties. In the United States, there were nine valuation systems prior to the Tokyo round. Value for duty is now generally on the invoice cost. The latitude of customs to reclassify products was also reduced.

Technical barriers

Product and process standards for health, welfare, safety, quality, size, and measurements can create trade barriers by excluding products that do not meet the standards. Testing and certification procedures, such as testing only in the importing country and on-site plant inspections, were (and still are to some extent) cumbersome, time-consuming, and expensive. These costs must be borne by the exporter prior to the foreign sale. National governments have the right and duty to protect their citizens by setting standards to prevent the sale of hazardous products. But such standards can also be used to impede trade. Japan excluded US-made baseball bats from the market because they did not meet the Japanese standard. No product produced outside Japan (even products made by foreign subsidiaries of Japanese MNEs) could bear the certification stamp of the Japanese Industrial Standard (JIS) or the Japanese Agricultural Standard (JAS), and selling in Japan without the JIS or JAS logo was difficult. At one time the new regulations for automobile safety in the United States required that bumpers be above the height practical for imported subcompact cars. The new code on technical barriers to trade requires consultation between trading partners before a standard that impedes trade is put in place. The code also requires that testing and certification procedures treat imports and domestic goods equally and that the importing country accept certification testing conducted in the exporting country.

Antidumping legislation, subsidies, and countervailing duties

The GATT allows importing countries to protect their producers from unfair competition such as "dumping" goods at extremely low prices in an effort to gain market share and to drive out local competition. Importing countries are allowed to impose additional duties on products that have received export subsidies or are "dumped." Before the duties are imposed, however, the country must show that its domestic industry has suffered "material" injury by dumped or subsidized imports. Although products at these artificially low prices provide consumers in the importing country with a "good buy," such competition is thought to be unfair to domestic producers. Domestic producers object to dumping (and also to subsidized imports which can be offset by "countervailing" duties) if the domestic market of the exporting country is closed to them. A good example is the US auto industry, which claims that some Japanese cars are cheaper in the US market than at home, while Japan continues to impede exports of US cars into Japan.

The GATT has developed a code on countervailing duties and antidumping duties that expedited the process of determining whether exports had been dumped or subsidized and whether the domestic industry had been injured. This subject is exceedingly complex. Here are some examples (and answers).

If the EU remits value-added taxes on exports by EU producers, is this a subsidy? (No)

If Canada subsidizes production in a specific sector in one of its depressed regions for domestic purposes, are the exports of a subsidized firm subject to countervailing action? (Yes)

If the British government subsidizes the British steel industry and its losses incurred by selling at home and abroad at prices below full cost, are its exports subject to antidumping or to countervailing duties? (Maybe, sometimes.)

The problem is complex because of the difficulty in determining what material injury is and how it should be measured. This area is likely to be a point of contention for years to come.

Agricultural products

Trade in agricultural products is highly regulated by quotas and fixed and variable tariffs. Domestic producers are often highly subsidized both directly and by artificially high domestic prices. Agricultural exports are often subsidized as well. The EU flatly refused to discuss its Common Agricultural Policy (CAP) at the Tokyo round. The CAP sets variable tariffs on imports to maintain high domestic prices by excluding or impeding imports. Moreover, revenues from these tariffs are used to subsidize exports. The CAP infuriates US agricultural producers since it not only reduces their exports to the large European market, but also it reduces world prices and gives them "unfair" competition in third country markets. The United States is not without guilt in this area, however, since it also subsidizes the export of many agricultural products.

Export restraints

Over the vigorous objections of countries exporting natural resources, the GATT rounds have moved to tighten the conditions under which exports could be restrained. In general, world tariffs increase with the level of processing (e.g., import duties increase as copper is processed from concentrate to blister, to refined copper, to copper wire and bars, to copper pots and pans). This tariff structure makes upgrading of natural resources in the producing country difficult. During the Tokyo round natural resource-producing countries were largely unsuccessful in their attempts to harmonize tariffs on a sectoral basis in order to increase their ability to upgrade prior to export. However, they did argue successfully for their right to restrict exports to induce further domestic processing.

OTHER ECONOMIC DEVELOPMENTS

In addition to the above, there are other economic developments that warrant consideration. These include countertrade, trade in services, and free trade zones.

Countertrade

Countertrade is essentially barter trade in which the exporting firm receives payment in terms of products from the importing country. Countertrade forms a major component of east–west trade (e.g., western pipeline products and technology in exchange for Russian natural gas). It is also important in the aircraft industry (e.g., the purchase of Boeing 747s by British Airways if Boeing uses Rolls Royce engines) and in defense products (e.g., the purchase of US jet fighters by Canada if some of the parts are locally sourced in Canada). By the early 1980s some low- and middle-income countries had also turned to countertrade to try to balance their trade accounts. According to a study by the US International Trade Commission, the 520 companies studied had $28.8 billion (about 5 per cent of that in exports) involving countertrade from 1980 to 1984.[23] It has also been estimated that countertrade accounts for 10 to 20 per cent of total world trade.[24]

Countertrade tends to decrease the efficiency of world trade because it substitutes barter for exchange of goods by the price system. For example, a US exporter of machinery to Indonesia may have to take payment in an "equivalent value" of palm oil or rattan. The exporting firm will then either have to sell these products for which it has no expertise itself or to sell them through a broker or other firm. Some party to the trade – exporter, importer, or consumer – must bear these additional costs. Despite these obvious inefficiencies, countertrade appears likely to continue as an increasingly important factor in the international trade environment of the twenty-first century.

There is, however, one situation in which countertrade may be beneficial. For example, if a US producer of textile machinery exports to China and agrees to take payment in the form of textile products, importers in the United States may perceive a lower risk of variability in product quality and delivery schedules (as a result of US technology and management), and the Chinese may perceive a lower risk of product failure in buying the machinery since the selling firm will not be "paid" unless the machinery performs to specifications.

Trade in services

International trade in services has received relatively little attention from governments or trade economists during trade negotiations. Reliable statistics are seldom collected. However, as high-income countries move toward a service economy, trade in services has grown and become a significant component of the current accounts of many countries.

In 1996 the United States exported goods worth $612 billion and imported goods worth $803 billion, a deficit of $191 billion on merchandise trade. Also in 1996, the United States exported $237 billion and imported $157 billion of services. Its trade surplus in services of $80 billion partly offset its merchandise trade deficit. Finally in 1996, the United States had a surplus of $5 billion in the net income receipts from US FDI abroad. Thus the net deficit on these three accounts was $108 billion. Details of the US services and FDI accounts appear in Table 6.3. (The balance of payments account will be explained in Chapter 7.)

The flow of services internationally is highly regulated. Internationally traded services such as banking, investment income, insurance, media, transportation, advertising, accounting, travel, and technology licensing are subject to a host of national and international regulations for economic, social, cultural, and political reasons. Trade in services largely falls outside the mandate of the GATT. One of the major trade questions for the next decade will be the regulation of trade in services. Will services be brought into the GATT so that reductions in impediments in service flows can be traded for reductions in barriers to the flow of goods? The United States, as the largest

Table 6.3 US balance of current account, 1996

Items	Exports (1) (in billions of US $)	Imports (2) (in billions of US $)	Balance (1)–(2)
Merchandise trade	612	803	−191
Services	237	157	80
Transfers	15	11	4
TPOT:			
Travel	70	49	21
Passenger fares	21	16	5
Other transportation	27	28	−1
Total	118	93	25
FROS:			
Royalties and licence fees	30	7	23
Other private services	103	43	60
US government miscellaneous	5	3	2
Total	138	53	85
FDI Income	206	204	2
Direct investment receipts	99	32	67
Other private receipts	103	100	3
US government receipts	5	71	−66
Total	1,055	1,163	−108

Source: Adapted from US Department of Commerce, *Survey of Current Business*, March 1998.

exporter and importer of services (and the largest net exporter), supports this proposal. Alternatively, a new organization similar to GATT could be founded to facilitate negotiations on barriers to trade in services and to regulate this trade. The United States views this proposal as a poor second-best alternative since it is already relatively open to trade in services and hence has few bargaining chips.

Whatever forum is used, negotiating reductions in barriers to trade in services will be difficult, complex, and lengthy. The barriers are often difficult to list, much less quantify for purposes of negotiation. The issues are often highly charged and not subject to rational analysis. For example, Canada imposes Canadian content requirements on television, radio, and print media to foster a "national cultural identity," to protect its cultural heritage, and to protect the domestic arts, theater, and movie industries. A government that reduced these trade barriers or even agreed to negotiate them would be in trouble with the (protected) Canadian media, as well as with the general public.

Free trade zones

A **free trade zone** is a designated area where importers can defer payment of customs duty while further processing of products takes place (same as a foreign trade zone). Thus the free trade zone serves as an "offshore assembly plant," employing local workers and using local financing for a tax-exempt commercial activity. The economic activity in a free trade zone takes place in a restricted area such as an industrial park since this land is often being supplied at a subsidized rate by a local host government that is interested in the potential employment benefits of the free trade zone.

To be effective, free trade zones must be strategically located either at or near an international port, on major shipping routes, or with easy access to a major airport. Important factors in the location of a free trade zone include the availability of utilities, banking and telecommunications services, and the availability of a commercial infrastructure.

Over 400 free trade zones exist in the world today, often encompassing entire cities (e.g., Hong Kong and Singapore). More than two-thirds are situated in developing countries, and most future growth of these zones is expected to occur there.

The advantages offered by free trade zones are numerous and are mutually beneficial to all the stakeholders. For private firms, free trade zones offer three major attractions. First, the firm pays the customs duty (tariff) only when the goods are ready to market. Second, manufacturing costs are lower in a free trade zone because no taxes are levied. Third, while in the zone, the manufacturer has the opportunity to repackage the goods, grade them, and check for spoilage. Secondary benefits to firms occur in the reduction of insurance premiums (since these are based on duty-free values), the reduction of fines for improperly marked merchandise (since the good can be inspected in a zone prior to customers' scrutiny), and the added protection against theft (resulting from security measures in the bonded warehouses).

On the state and local level, advantages can be realized in terms of commercial services. On a more global level, free trade zones enable domestic importing companies to compete more readily with foreign producers or subsidiaries of MNEs, thereby increasing participation in world trade. Favorable effects are felt on the balance of payments since more economic activity occurs and net capital outflow is reduced. Finally, there is an improved climate for business since a free trade zone reduces bureaucracy with savings to business capital, currently inaccessible because of the delay in paying duties and tariffs. A free trade zone is a step toward free trade and can be an important signal by government to business that the economy is opening up. Opportunity replaces regulation and growth of economic activity should result.

Before the establishment of more free trade zones becomes fully accepted and encouraged, governments must be convinced of their many economic benefits. Free trade zones are a vital necessity if nations are to remain competitive on an international scale. Not only will existing companies benefit from their use, but new industries will be attracted, keeping up the same benefits of world trade.

The **maquiladora industry** along the US–Mexican border is an excellent example of a free trade zone. The low wage rate in Mexico and the North American Free Trade Agreement (NAFTA) of 1993 make the maquiladora region both accessible and important to labor-intensive firms in the United States and Canada. From only 12 maquiladora plants in 1965, approximately 1,700 existed in 1990. Of these, 55 per cent resulted from US investments. The maquiladora industry has been so successful that today only oil earns Mexico more foreign currency.

No Mexican taxes are paid on goods that are processed within the maquiladoras. Foreign companies doing such processing can have the benefits of lower wages and land costs than in the United States as they increase the value added to their products. In return, Mexico attracts foreign direct investment into permanent plants, creates jobs, and collects taxes on any final products sold to the foreign firms, or within Mexico. Even though the United States has several hundred free trade zones of its own, many near seaports or airfields, these lack the low-wage workers of their Mexican counterparts.

Canada does not have free trade zones, but the federal government allows duty drawbacks, which they argue offer many of the advantages of a free trade zone.

Unfortunately, these drawbacks, which are repayments of customs duties, apply retroactively and involve enough paperwork to discourage all but the largest or most dedicated organizations. As such, the NAFTA and the lower-wage labor in Mexico have attracted Canadian firms producing labor-intensive products. Free trade zones exist in many other parts of the world than North America, and the advantages of these zones are enjoyed by businesses worldwide.[25]

SUMMARY

Key points

1. International economics is the branch of economics concerned with the purchase and sale of foreign goods and services. This includes consideration of areas such as international trade, balance of payments, and barriers to trade.

2. A number of international trade theories help to explain why nations trade. These include the theory of absolute advantage, the theory of comparative advantage, the factor endowment theory, the Leontief paradox, and the international product life cycle theory. While no one theory offers a complete explanation of why nations trade, they collectively provide important insights into the area. Other key considerations that offer explanations for why nations trade include monetary currency valuation and consumer tastes.

3. There are a number of different barriers to trade. Some of the most common include price-based barriers, quantity limits, international price fixing, nontariff barriers, financial limits, and foreign investment controls. Like most other countries, the United States uses a variety of trade barriers and negotiated agreements to limit the negative effect of imports and has enacted legislation to encourage exports.

4. Although tariffs are often introduced to maintain local jobs and assist infant industries, they are inefficient. This economic inefficiency results in higher prices of imported goods for the consumers. The redistribution of resources from more efficient industry further adds to the cost of a tariff. Such costs do not occur under free trade.

5. Nontariff barriers (NTBs) provide similar economic inefficiencies to tariffs. Unlike tariffs, however, NTBs are not imposed by nations to interfere deliberately with trade; they arise out of domestic policy. There are several types of NTBs, including quotas, buy national restrictions, technical barriers, and export restraints.

6. Countertrade is a form of barter trade in which the exporting firm receives payments in terms of products produced in the importing country. This type of trade is most pronounced in east–west trade, and although it may be beneficial to the trade partners, it increases the inefficiencies in the world trade system. These economic inefficiencies increase costs and decrease trade volume.

7. Services are an important but somewhat misunderstood component of trade. Despite trade of services in the billions of dollars among high-income countries, the regulation of trade in services has been outside the mandate of GATT. As services increase in importance, future discussion will take place concerning whether an international organization like GATT will carry the mandate to regulate this type of trade.

8. A free trade zone is a designated area where importers can defer payment of customs duty while further processing of products takes place, thus becoming an

offshore assembly plant. The majority of these areas exist in developing countries, and they handle approximately 20 per cent of worldwide trade. Free trade zones are advantageous to all because they provide benefits such as increased employment and lower costs to business.

Key terms

- international trade
- mercantilism
- theory of absolute advantage
- theory of comparative advantage
- factor endowment theory
- Heckscher-Ohlin theory
- Leontief paradox
- international product life cycle (IPLC) theory
- monetary exchange rate
- quotas
- embargo
- cartel
- nontariff barriers
- exchange controls
- foreign investment controls
- tariff

- import tariff
- export tariff
- transit tariff
- specific duty
- ad valorem duty
- compound duty
- dumping
- North American Free Trade Agreement (NAFTA)
- Caribbean Basin Initiative
- Trading-with-the-Enemy Act
- Foreign Sales Corporation Act
- trade adjustment assistance
- countertrade
- free trade zone
- maquiladora industry

Review and discussion questions

1. Why is it difficult to solve international economic problems in the short run?

2. What is the supposed economic benefit of embracing mercantilism as an international trade theory? Are there many disadvantages to the use of this theory?

3. How is the theory of absolute advantage similar to that of comparative advantage? How is it different?

4. In what way does factor endowment theory help to explain why nations trade? How does the Leontief paradox modify this theory?

5. If an innovating country develops a new technologically superior product, how long will it be before the country begins exporting the product? At what point will the country begin importing the product?

6. Of what value is the international product life cycle theory in helping to understand why nations trade?

7. How do each of the following trade barriers work: price-based barriers, quantity limits, international price fixing, nontariff barriers, financial limits, foreign investment controls?

8. What are some of the reasons for trade barriers? Identify and describe five.

9. How does the United States try to encourage exports? Identify and describe two ways.

10. Nontariff barriers have become increasingly predominant in recent years. Describe a nontariff barrier, and list four types, describing how the United States does or could use such a device.

11. How does countertrade work? Is it an efficient economic concept?

12. What is a free trade zone? Is it an efficient economic concept?

REAL CASES

DUMPING ON TRADE COMPLAINTS

One of the biggest problems in international trade is the ability of domestic producers to lobby their home governments to erect barriers to trade. In the past, the textile, apparel, and shoe industries were able to obtain protection from cheaper imports through tariffs, quotas, and special measures. Now multilateral trade agreements under the GATT and WTO (and also regional and bilateral agreements such as NAFTA and the emerging Asian Pacific Economic Cooperation forum) outlaw such blatant instruments of protection. However, these agreements have been replaced by more subtle ones.

Prominent as a new type of protectionist device is the use of "unfair trade laws," especially anti-dumping (AD) and countervailing duty actions (CVD). The economic logic of AD and CVD makes some sense. It is unfair for a foreign producer to "dump" a product in your country below its price in the home country, or below the cost of producing it. Similarly, subsidized foreign products should be offset by a countervailing duty of equivalent effect. The problem, however, lies with the administration of the trade laws, which is subject to political lobbying.

A variety of studies have found that the bureaucrats who administer AD and CVD laws are subject to capture by the home industries, who then use AD and CVD cases as harassment tools against often economically efficient foreign rival producers. For example, Rugman and Anderson (1987) found that the United States administration of AD and CVD was used in a biased manner against Canadian producers, especially in resource-based industries such as softwood lumber, fishing, and agriculture. Thus in the Canadian–US Free Trade Agreement of 1989, and again in NAFTA,

five-person binational panels of trade law experts were set up to review the decision of the US (and Canadian) trade law agencies.

In a subsequent study, Rugman and Anderson (1997) found that these binational panels were able to remand back (i.e. successfully challenge) the decision of the US agencies twice as often in cases involving Canada as in AD and CVD cases involving the rest of the world. In related work it has been found that the EU is just as bad as the United States in that the EU brings in questionable AD measures, especially against Asian countries. Indeed, one of the unresolved problems is how smaller countries can secure access to the protected markets of triad economies such as the United States and the EU. In Japan's case there are similar arguments (including those from its triad rivals) that there are entry barriers in place preventing market access.

1. Why are anti-dumping and countervailing duty measures brought and imposed?

2. What is the impact on a firm from a non-triad country if it faces an AD or CVD case in its major market?

3. What is the solution to the abusive use of AD and CVD measures by triad economies?

Sources:
Anderson, Andrew D. M. *Seeking Common Ground: Canada–US Trade Dispute Settlement Policies in the Nineties* (Boulder, Colo.: Westview Press); Rugman, Alan M. *Multinational Enterprises and Trade Policy* (Cheltenham, England: Edward Elgar, 1996); Rugman, Alan M. and Anderson, Andrew D. M. *Administered Protection in America.* (London and New York: Routledge, 1987); Rugman, Alan M. and Anderson, Andrew D. M., "NAFTA and the Dispute Settlement Mechanisms," *The World Economy* (December, 1997), pp. 935–950; Rugman, Alan M. and Gestrin, Michael, "EC Anti-Dumping Laws as a Barrier to Trade," *European Management Journal*, vol. 9, no. 4 (December 1991), pp. 475–482.

THE UNITED STATES AND APEC

In an attempt to further his free trade agenda, President Clinton spoke to heads of state from 17 nations at the Asia-Pacific Economic Cooperation (APEC) summit in Bogor, Indonesia on November 15, 1994. His goal was a Pacific free trade zone, lower regional trade barriers, a uniform investment code, and copyright protection.

While many APEC countries are encouraging free, open markets by agreeing to lift all trade barriers on manufactured goods by 2020, some nations are hindering President Clinton's agenda. For instance, China has tried to impede his plan by threatening to "block" it until the United States approves China's application to the World Trade Organization (WTO), which was founded on January 1, 1995. However, many rightly predicted that the United States would stand firm on its policy of denying China membership in the WTO until a reform in the economic system was achieved and the Chinese government took measures to stop copyright "theft."

Despite these obstacles, promoting free trade among the APEC countries is vital for the United States. It may help to balance trade among the United States and the Asian countries; there is a trade deficit with Japan of $40–60 billion a year. In addition, the United States has begun running large deficits with China, while at the same time helping to increase Asia's dependency on the United States: 33 per cent of US imports go to Asia and 60 per cent of exports come from there.

All in all, President Clinton sees Asia as a place where the United States could grow tremendously. His APEC talk was a step in this direction.

1. Give three reasons why free trade among the APEC countries will benefit the United States.

2. How could "western markets be devastated by exports from a state-run economy having enormous labor resources" such as China?

3. Describe three reasons why some Asian groups would disapprove of lifting the trade barriers in their respective countries.

Sources: Adapted from Joyce Barnathan and Pete Engardio, "Marching Toward Free Trade in Asia?" *Business Week,* November 14, 1994, pp. 52–54; Eduardo Lachica, "US Urged to Resist China's APEC Offer," *The Asian Wall Street Journal Weekly,* November 7, 1994, pp. 4, 19; Eduardo Lachica, "US Is More Optimistic Than Japan For Free-Trade Pact at APEC Summit," *The Asian Wall Street Journal Weekly,* November 7, 1994, pp. 4, 24; Andrew Pollack, "Asian Nations Wary on Free Trade," November 11, 1994, p. A8; David E. Sanger, "Clinton Asks G.O.P. to Back Free Trade," *The New York Times,* November 11, 1994, p. A8.

ENDNOTES

1. David E. Sanger, "Japan's Big Trade Surplus Is a Minus in US Equation," *New York Times,* February 5, 1993, p. A6.

2. See, for example, Elisabeth Rosenthal, "US Trade Official Says China Market Is Closed Tighter," *New York Times,* September 23, 1998, p. C2.

3. Asra Q. Nomani and Douglas Lavin, "US and Japan Nearing Accord in Trade Dispute," *Wall Street Journal,* March 10, 1994, p. A3.

4. Douglas Harbrecht et al., "Tough Talk," *Business Week,* February 20, 1994, pp. 26–28.

5. See, for example, Dana Weschler Linden, "Dreary Days in the Dismal Science," *Forbes,* January 21, 1991, pp. 68–71.

6. Also, see Steven Greenhouse, "French Shift on State-Owned Sector," *New York Times,* April 8, 1991, p. C2.

7. Andrew Pollack, "America as Trade Micro-Manager," *New York Times,* March 14, 1994, pp. C1–2.

8. For additional insights into trade theory, see Nicolas Schmitt, "New International Trade Theories and Europe 1991: Some Results Relevant for EFTA Countries," *Journal of Common Market Studies,* September 1990, pp. 53–74.

9. Jennifer Lin, "Dusting Off A Weapon," *Miami Herald,* March 4, 1994, Section C, pp. 1, 3.

10. James D. Goodnow and W. Elizabeth Goodnow, "Self-Assessment by State Export Promotion Agencies: A Status Report," *International Marketing Review,* vol. 7, no. 3, 1990, pp. 18–30.

11. Alan Matthews and Dermot McAleese, "LDC Primary Exports to the EC: Prospects Post-1992," *Journal of Common Market Studies,* December 1990, pp. 157–180.

12. See, for example, Donald G. Howard and Daniel Borgia, "Exporting and Firm Size: Do Small Exporters Have Special Needs?" *Journal of Global Marketing*, vol. 4, no. 1, 1990, pp. 79–97; Saeed Samiee and Peter G. P. Walters, "Rectifying Strategic Gaps in Export Management," *Journal of Global Marketing*, vol. 4, no. 1, 1990, pp. 7–37; and Chong S. Lee and Yoo S. Yang, "Impact of Export Market Expansion Strategy on Export Performance," *International Marketing Review*, vol. 7, no. 4, 1990, pp. 41–51.

13. See Richard W. Stevenson, "East Europe Says Barriers to Trade Hurt Its Economies," *New York Times*, January 25, 1993, p. A1, C8.

14. Lucy Walker, "Sir Leon's Cartel Busters Take to the Road Again," *The European*, April 12–14, 1991, p. 25.

15. Edmund Faltermayer, "Is 'Made in the USA' Fading Away?" *Fortune*, September 24, 1990, p. 73.

16. See, for example, Doron P. Levin, "Honda to Hold Base Price on Accord Model," *New York Times*, September 2, 1993, p. C3.

17. Keith Bradsher, "Kodak Is Seeking Big Tariff on Fuji," *New York Times*, September 1, 1993, pp. A1, C2.

18. See, for example, Robert Cohen, "Grumbling over GATT," *New York Times*, July 3, 1993, p. 13.

19. For more on this see Robert Grosse and Duane Kujawa, *International Business: Theory and Managerial Applications* (Homewood, Ill: Irwin 1998), p. 233.

20. See, for example, Chris Adams, "Ailing Steel Industry Launches a Battle Against Imports," *Wall Street Journal*, October 1, 1998, p. B4; and "Steel Vice," *Wall Street Journal*, October 1, 1998, p. A22.

21. As an example, see Clyde H. Farnsworth, "US Slows Computer for Brazil," *International Herald Tribune*, April 13–14, 1991, p. 5.

22. Sometimes these are voluntary quotas, as seen in Andrew Pollack, "Japan Takes a Pre-emptive Step on Auto Exports," *New York Times*, January 9, 1993, pp. 17, 26.

23. Alan M. Rugman (ed.), *International Business in Canada: Strategies for Management* (Prentice-Hall Canada Inc., 1989), p. 69.

24. Dalia Marin, "Tying in International Trade: Evidence on Countertrade," *World Economy*, vol. 13, no. 3, September 1990, p. 445.

25. Anthony DePalma, "Trade Pact is Spurring Mexican Deals in the US," *New York Times*, March 17, 1994, pp. C1, 3.

ADDITIONAL BIBLIOGRAPHY

Anderson, Andrew D. M. *Seeking Common Ground: Canada-US Trade Disputes* (Boulder: Westview, 1995).

Buckley, Peter J. "Government Policy Responses to Strategic Rent Seeking Transnational Corporations," *Transnational Corporations*, vol. 5, no. 2 (August 1996).

Cavusgil, S. Tamer and Sikora, Ed. "How Multinationals Can Counter Gray Market Imports," *Columbia Journal of World Business*, vol. 23, no. 4 (Winter 1988).

Chao, Paul. "Export and Reverse Investment: Strategic Implications for Newly Industrialized Countries," *Journal of International Business Studies*, vol. 20, no. 1 (Spring 1989).

Cho, Kang Rae. "The Role of Product-Specific Factors in Intra-Firm Trade of US Manufacturing Multinational Corporations," *Journal of International Business Studies*, vol. 21, no. 2 (Second Quarter 1990).

Dichtl, Erwin; Koeglmayr, Hans-Georg; and Mueller, Stefan. "International Orientation as a Precondition for Export Success," *Journal of International Business Studies*, vol. 21, no. 1 (First Quarter 1990).

Emmerij, Louis. "Globalization, Regionalization and World Trade," *Columbia Journal of World Business*, vol. 27, no. 2 (Summer 1992).

Eppen, Gray D.; Hanson, Ward A.; and Martin, R. Kipp. "Bundling – New Products, New Markets, Low Risk," *Sloan Management Review*, vol. 32, no. 4 (Summer 1991).

Green, Robert T. and Kohli, Ajay K. "Export Market Identification: The Role of Economic Size and Socio-economic Development," *Management International Review*, vol. 31, no. 1 (First Quarter 1991).

Haigh, Robert, W. "Thinking of Exporting? Export Management Companies Could be the Answer," *Columbia Journal of World Business*, vol. 29, no. 4 (Winter 1994).

Han, C. Min and Terpstra, Vern. "Country-of-Origin Effects for Uni-national and Bi-national Products," *Journal of International Business Studies*, vol. 19, no. 2 (Summer 1988).

Hennart, Jean-François. "Some Empirical Dimensions of Countertrade," *Journal of International Business Studies*, vol. 21, no. 2 (Second Quarter 1990).

Neale, Charles W.; Shipley, David D.; and Dodds, J. Colin. "The Countertrading Experience of British and Canadian Firms," *Management International Review*, vol. 31, no. 1 (First Quarter 1991).

Nollen, Stanley D. "Business Costs and Business Policy for Export Controls," *Journal of International Business Studies*, vol. 18, no. 1 (Spring 1987).

Ostry, Sylvia *The Post-Cold War Trading System* (Chicago: University of Chicago Press, 1997).

Perry, Anne C. "The Evolution of the US International Trade Intermediary in the 1980s: A Dynamic Model," *Journal of International Business Studies*, vol. 21, no. 1 (First Quarter 1990).

Ramstetter, Eric D. "Export Performance and Foreign Affiliate Activity in Japan's Large Machinery Firms," *Transnational Corporations*, vol. 6, no. 3 (December 1997).

Robin, Donald P. and Sawyer, W. Charles "The Ethics of Antidumping Petitions," *Journal of World Business*, vol. 33, no. 3 (Fall 1998).

Robock, Stefan H. "The Export Myopia of US Multinationals: An Overlooked Opportunity for Creating US Manufacturing Jobs," *Columbia Journal of World Business*, vol. 28, no. 2 (Summer 1993).

Ruggiero, Renato, "Foreign Direct Investment and the Multilateral Trading System," *Transnational Corporations*, vol. 5, no. 1 (April 1996).

Rugman, Alan M. *Multinational Enterprises and Trade Policy* (Cheltenham: Elgar, 1996).

Rugman, Alan M. and Anderson, Andrew. *Administered Protection in America* (London: Croom Helm and New York: Methuen, 1987).

Rugman, Alan M. and Anderson, Andrew. "Country-Factor Bias in the Administration of Antidumping and Countervailing Duty Cases," in Michael Trebilcock and Robert York (eds.), *Fair Exchange: Reforming Trade Remedy Laws* (Toronto: C.D. Howe Institute, 1990).

Rugman, Alan M. and Gestrin, Michael. "US Trade Laws as Barriers to Globalization," in Tamir Agmon and Richard Drobnick (eds.), *Small Firms in Global Competition* (New York: Oxford University Press, 1994).

Rugman, Alan M. and Verbeke, Alain. *Global Corporate Strategy and Trade Policy* (London and New York: Routledge, 1990).

Rugman, Alan M. and Verbeke, Alain. "Strategic Trade Policy is Not Good Strategy," *Hitotsubashi Journal of Commerce and Management*, vol. 25, no. 1 (December 1990).

Ryans, Adrian B. "Strategic Market Entry Factors and Market Share Achievement in Japan," *Journal of International Business Studies*, vol. 19, no. 3 (Fall 1988).

Sullivan, Daniel and Bauerschmidt, Alan. "Common Factors Underlying Barriers to Export: A Comparative Study in the European and US Paper Industry," *Management International Review*, vol. 29, no. 2 (Second Quarter 1989).

CHAPTER 7

International Finance

OBJECTIVES OF THE CHAPTER

In one way or another, all businesses are affected by international finance. For example, auto dealers who sell imported Toyotas, Volvos, or Fiats must adjust their prices as the prices they pay for these cars go up or down because of the foreign exchange rate. Similarly, manufacturers who import materials or parts from overseas suppliers are affected by developments such as wage increases paid by suppliers to their own personnel. End users and customers, in the final analysis, are affected because most of these costs are passed on to them.

There are many important areas of international finance with which students of international business should be familiar. This chapter focuses on four areas: balance of payments (BOP), the international monetary system, foreign exchange, and the strategic management of international finance. The specific objectives of this chapter are to:

1. **Describe** the four basic categories that constitute a nation's balance of payments and relate how international transactions are accounted for in this balance.

2. **Relate** the role and functions of the International Monetary Fund.

3. **Explain** why the international debt crisis is going to continue to be a major international finance problem in the new millennium.

4. **Describe** the nature and operations of foreign exchange markets.

5. **Discuss** how exchange rates are determined.

6. **Set forth** international finance strategies that can be used by organizations doing business in the international arena.

ACTIVE LEARNING CASE

Japan's trade surplus with the United States

Since 1980 Japan's global trade surplus has increased dramatically. During the early years of the decade it stood at about $20 billion annually. By 1985 it was up to almost $60 billion annually. The early 1990s saw the annual figure rise to about $110 billion before the surplus began to decline. The latter was mainly due to the appreciation of the yen, the increase in Japanese overseas manufacturing and the Asian crisis of 1998.

Many countries are now running a negative trade balance with Japan. For example, in recent years Southeast Asian nations such as Singapore, South Korea, and Thailand have seen their trade deficits with Japan rise to around $10 billion. The same is true for the European Union. However, the major trade surplus for Japan is with the United States. Americans currently spend around $40 billion a year more on Japanese imports than they receive from exports to Japan. This bilateral annual deficit is not as large as it was in the 1993–94 period when the surplus exceeded $50 billion annually.

From trade data it seems that the United States is selling basic commodities and moderately low technology goods to the Japanese, while it is purchasing state-of-the-art products or sophisticated manufactured goods. The United States feels it must reverse this trend.

Many of Japan's trading partners are also concerned that its exports of goods are continuing to remain much higher than its imports. EU and Pacific Rim countries, as well as the United States, are now putting pressure on Japan to buy more from them. In recent years Americans have been moderately successful in prying open the Japanese market for imports. For example, US cigarette manufacturers now have 16 per cent of the Japanese market and Japan imports almost as much US farm produce as all of Western Europe. In addition, Japan Airlines is the world's largest customer for Boeing's 747s and most of the semiconductor market that is held by foreign firms in Japan is in the hands of American companies. Nevertheless, there is a long way to go before major trading partners such as the United States will find Japan buying as much from America as it sells there.

Sources: Adapted from Lee Smith, "Why Japan's Surplus Is Rising," *Fortune*, December 30, 1991, pp. 95–97; David E. Sanger, "Japan's Big Trade Surplus Is a Minus in US Equation," *New York Times*, February 5, 1993, p. A6; Carla Rapoport, "How Clinton is Shaking Up Trade," *Fortune*, May 31, 1993, pp. 103–108.

1. Why is Japan's trade surplus with the United States of concern to the United States?

2. Some countries believe that those with large trade surpluses should reinvest them in poorer countries in order to help these economies. Is Japan in a position to do this?

3. Did the devaluation of the US dollar during the 1980s help or hinder US competitiveness in Japan?

4. How are US firms located in Japan able to profit from the appreciation of the Japanese yen?

INTRODUCTION

International finance is an area of study concerned with the balance of payments (BOP) and the international monetary system. A development in one of these areas can affect the other. For example, in recent years a growing number of US firms have established research and development (R&D) centers in Japan.[1] This required a foreign direct investment (FDI), as well as the purchase of foreign exchange (yen) for handling domestic expenses. Have these decisions been successful? In the sense that they are designed to help develop the firm's R&D expertise, the companies report that they have indeed been wise decisions. From a financial standpoint, however, they would get mixed reviews because over the past five years the value of the yen has fluctuated against the dollar. If the companies were to build these facilities in late 1999, the dollar cost would be much higher because the yen had strengthened signficantly.

The changing value of the US dollar against some major currencies has also affected the cost of some exports and imports.[2] US exports, in some cases, have become more attractive while imports to the United States have become more expensive.[3] As a result, more foreign firms have been looking into setting up operations in the United States, thus shielding themselves against the risk of exporting into a country with a weakening international currency.[4]

This chapter will examine each of the main areas of international finance. We begin with the balance of payments because this topic sets the stage for a discussion of the international monetary system and foreign exchange.

BALANCE OF PAYMENTS

One way of measuring a country's economic activity is by looking at its balance of payments. The **balance of payments (BOP)** is the record of the value of all trans-actions between a country's residents and the rest of the world. There is a wide variety of accounts that determine the BOP, but for purposes of analysis they can be grouped into three broad categories: current account items, capital account items, and reserves.

BOP is a double-entry system, similar to that used in accounting. Every transac-tion is recorded in terms of both a debit and a credit. Debits record transactions such as the import of a good or service, an increase in assets, or a reduction in liabilities. Credits record the export of a good or service, a decrease in assets, or an increase in liabilities. Using Table 7.1 as a point of reference, the following discussion examines the three broad BOP categories.

Broad BOP categories

The **International Monetary Fund (IMF)**, an agency that seeks to maintain balance of payments stability in the international financial system, has developed a standardized BOP system and form of presentation. Table 7.1 presents an abbreviated version of this system. This presentation form is important because it is so widely used. As we see, the table describes each of the three broad BOP categories.

Current account   The **current account** consists of merchandise trade, services, and unrequited transfers. (See Table 7.1, parts *A* and *B*.)

Merchandise trade is typically the first part of the current account. It receives more attention than any of the other accounts because this is where the imports and exports of goods are reported, and these are often the largest single component of all inter-national transactions.[5] In this account, sales of goods to foreigners (exports) are reported as credits because they are a source of funds or a claim against the purchasing coun-try. Conversely, purchases of goods from overseas (imports) are recorded as debits because they use funds. This payment can be made by either reducing current claims on foreigners or increasing foreign liabilities.

Table 7.1 Balance of payments: IMF presentation

	Debits	Credits
I. Current account		
A. *Goods, services, and income:*		
1. Merchandise	Imports from foreign sources (acquisition of goods).	Exports to foreign destinations (provision of goods).
Trade balance		
2. Shipment and other transportation	Payments to foreigners for freight and insurance on international shipments; for ship repair, stores and supplies; and international passenger fares.	Receipts by residents from foreigners for services provided.
3. Travel	Expenditures by residents (including internal transportation) when traveling in a foreign country.	Receipts by residents for goods and services (including internal transportation) sold to foreign travelers in reporting country.
4. Investment income	Profits of foreign direct investments in reporting country, including reinvested earnings; income paid to foreigners as interest, dividends, etc.	Profits of direct investments by residents in foreign countries, including reinvested earnings; income received by residents from abroad as interest, dividends, etc.
5. Other official	Foreign purchases by government not included elsewhere; personal expenditures of government civilian and military personnel stationed in foreign countries.	Expenditures of foreign governments for goods and services, not included elsewhere; personal expenditures of foreign civilian and military personnel stationed in reporting country.
6. Other private	Payments to foreigners for management fees, royalties, film rentals, construction, etc.	Receipts from foreigners for management fees, royalties, film rentals, construction, etc.
Goods, services, and income balance		
B. *Unrequited transfers:*		
1. Private	Payments in cash and kind by residents to foreigners without a quid pro quo such as charitable gifts and gifts by migrants to their families.	Receipts in cash and kind by residents from foreigners, individuals or governments without a quid pro quo.
2. Official	Transfers by government of reporting country for pensions, reparations, and grants for economic and military aid.	Transfers received by government from foreigners in the form of goods, services, or cash as gifts or grants. Also tax receipts from nonresidents.
Current account balance		
II. Capital account		
C. *Capital, excluding reserves:*		
1. Direct investment	a. Increased investment in foreign enterprises controlled by residents, including reinvestment of earnings. b. Decreases in investment by residents in domestic enterprises controlled by foreigners.	a. Decreased investment in foreign enterprises controlled by residents. b. Increases in investment in domestic enterprises by foreigners.
2. Portfolio investment	a. Increases in investment by residents in foreign securities. b. Decreases in investment by foreigners in domestic securities such as bonds and corporate equities.	a. Decreases in investments by residents in foreign securities. b. Increases in investment by foreigners in domestic securities.

Table 7.1 *(cont'd)*

	Debits	Credits
3. Other long-term, official	a. Loans to foreigners. b. Redemption or purchase from foreigners of government securities.	a. Foreign loan reductions. b. Sales to foreigners of government securities.
4. Other long-term, private	a. Long-term loans to foreigners by resident banks and private parties. b. Loan repayments by residents to foreign banks or private parties.	a. Long-term loans by foreigners to resident banks or private parties. b. Loan repayments by foreigners to residents.
5. Other short-term, official	a. Short-term loans to foreigners by central government. b. Purchase from foreigners of government securities, decrease in liabilities constituting reserves of foreign authorities.	a. Short-term loans to resident central government by foreigners. b. Foreign sales of short-term resident government securities, increases in liabilities constituting reserves of foreign authorities.
6. Other short-term, private	a. Increases in short-term foreign assets held by residents. b. Decreases in domestic assets held by foreigners, such as bank deposits, currencies, debts to banks, and commercial claims.	a. Decreases in short-term foreign assets held by residents. Increase in foreign liabilities of residents. b. Increase in domestic short-term assets held by foreigners or decrease in short-term domestic liabilities to foreigners.

III. Reserves

D. *Reserves:*

	Debits	Credits
1. Monetary gold 2. Special drawing rights (SDRs) 3. IMF reserve position 4. Foreign exchange assets	Increases in holdings of gold, SDRs, foreign convertible currencies by monetary authorities; decreases in liabilities to IMF or increase in IMF assets position.	Decreases in holdings of gold, SDRs, foreign convertible currencies by monetary authorities; increases in liabilities to IMF or decrease in IMF assets position.
E. *Net errors and omissions:*	Net understatement of recorded debts or overstatement of recorded credits.	Net understatement of recorded debts or overstatement of recorded credits.

Balances:
Balances on merchandise trade   *A-1 credits minus A-1 debts*
Balance on goods, services, and income   *A-1 through A-6 credits minus A-1 through A-6 debits*
Balance on current account   *A and B credits minus A and B debits*

Merchandise trade transactions can affect a country's BOP in a number of ways. Assume that Nissan Motor of Japan has sold General Motors in the United States $600,000 worth of engines and these engines will be paid for from GM's account in a Detroit bank. In this case the imports are a debit to the current account (A-1) and a credit to the "other short-term, private" capital account (C-6b). Here is how the entry would be recorded:

		Debit	Credit
A-1	Merchandise imports	$600,000	
C-6b	Increase in domestic short-term assets held by foreigners		$600,000

The result of this purchase is that the United States has transferred currency to foreigners and thus reduced its ability to meet other claims.

Services   The services category includes many payments such as freight and insurance on international shipments (A-2); tourist travel (A-3); profits and income from overseas investment (A-4); personal expenditures by government, civilians, and military personnel overseas (A-5); and payments for management fees, royalties, film rental, and construction services (A-6). Purchases of these services are recorded as debits, while sales of these services are similar to exports and are recorded as credits. For example, extending the earlier example of Nissan and GM, assume that the US automaker must pay $125,000 to Nissan to ship the engines to the United States. The transaction would be recorded this way:

		Debit	Credit
A-2	Shipment	$125,000	
C-6b	Other short-term private capital		$125,000

GM purchased a Japanese shipping service (a debit to the current account) and paid for this by increasing the domestic short-term assets held by foreigners (a credit to the capital account).

Unrequited transfers   **Unrequited transfers** are transactions that do not involve repayment or the performance of any service. Examples include the American Red Cross sending $10 million in food to refugees in Somalia; the United States paying military pensions to residents of the Philippines who served in the US army during World War II; and British workers in Kuwait shipping money home to their families in London. Here is how the American Red Cross transaction would appear in the US BOP:

		Debit	Credit
B-1	Unrequited transfers, private	$10 million	
A-1	Merchandise exports		$10 million

Capital account   **Capital account items** are transactions that involve claims in ownership. Direct investment (C-1) involves managerial participation in a foreign enterprise along with some degree of control. The United States classifies direct investments as those investments that give the investor more than 10 per cent ownership. Portfolio investment (C-2) is investment designed to obtain income or capital gains. For example, if Exxon shipped $20 million of equipment to an overseas subsidiary the entry would be:

		Debit	Credit
C-1	Direct investment	$20 million	
A-1	Exports		$20 million

"Other long-term" capital accounts are differentiated based on whether they are government (C-3) or private (C-4) transactions. These transactions have a maturity of over 1 year and involve either loans or securities. For example, Citibank may have loaned the government of Poland $50 million. "Other short-term" capital accounts are also differentiated based on whether they are governmental (C-5) or private (C-6). Typical short-term government transactions are short-term loans in the securities of other governments. Private transactions often include trade bill acceptances or other short-term claims arising from the financing of trade and movements of money by investors to take advantage of interest differentials among countries.

Reserves Reserves are used for bringing BOP accounts into balance. There are four major types of reserves available to monetary authorities in meeting BOP deficits (D1 through D4 in Table 7.1). These reserves are analogous to the cash or near-cash assets of a private firm. Given that billions of dollars in transactions are reported in BOP statements, it should come as no surprise that the amount of recorded debits are never equal to the amount of credits. This is why there is an entry in the reserve account for net errors and omissions. If a country's reporting system is weak or there is a large number of clandestine transactions, this discrepancy can be quite large.

US balance of payments

The official presentation of the US BOP is somewhat different from the IMF format presented in Table 7.1. Because the United States plays such a dominant role in the world economy, it is important to examine the US system. Table 7.2 presents US international transactions for two recent years.

A number of select entries in Table 7.2 help to highlight the US BOP. Lines 1 and 15 show that exports in 1996 were $108.2 billion less than imports. This was a slight improvement over 1995, but it shows that the United States continues to have trade deficit problems.

To assess the trade situation accurately, however, we need to examine the data in more depth. This information is provided in Table 7.3. The table shows that US exports are strong in areas such as agricultural, industrial supplies and materials, capital goods, and consumer goods. On the other hand, the United States is importing a great deal of industrial supplies and materials, machinery, auto vehicles and parts, and manufactured consumer goods.

In the early 1980s US trade deficits were offset by large amounts of income generated by direct investments abroad. Later in the decade these deficits were offset by massive international borrowing. More recently the situation has improved somewhat, and dollar devaluation has helped to generate stronger demand for US exports, thus partially reducing the annual trade deficit. However, more concerted action will be needed if the United States is to continue on this course. One way is to continue to increase US competitiveness in the international market. Another way is to get other countries to reduce their trade barriers and to make international markets more open.[6]

It is important to realize that when a country suffers a persistent balance of trade deficit, the nation will also suffer from a depreciating currency and will find it difficult to borrow in the international capital market.[7] In this case there are only two choices available. One is to borrow from the International Monetary Fund (IMF) and be willing to accept the restrictions that the IMF puts on the country, which are designed to introduce austerity and force the country back onto the right economic track. The other approach is for the country to change its fiscal policy (tariffs and taxes), resort to exchange and trade controls, or devalue its currency. In order to prevent having to undertake austerity steps, the United States will have to continue working very hard to control its trade deficit.[8] One way of understanding how this can be done is through a knowledge of the International Monetary System, the next topic that we consider.

Table 7.2   US international transactions: 1995–96

Line	(Credits +; debits –)	1995 (in millions of US $)	1996 (in millions of US $)
1	Exports of goods, services, and income	969,189	1,055,233
2	Merchandise, adjusted, excluding military	575,940	612,069
3	Services	210,590	236,764
4	Transfers under US military agency sales contracts	13,405	14,647
5	Travel	61,137	69,908
6	Passenger fares	18,534	20,557
7	Other transportation	28,063	27,216
8	Royalties and license fees	29,953	29,974
9	Other private services	61,724	73,569
10	US government miscellaneous services	775	893
11	Income receipts on US assets abroad	182,659	206,400
12	Direct investment receipts	88,882	98,890
13	Other private receipts	89,064	102,866
14	US government receipts	4,713	4,644
15	Imports of goods, services, and income	1,082,268	1,163,450
16	Merchandise, adjusted, excluding military	749,364	803,239
17	Services	142,230	156,634
18	Transfers under US military agency sales contracts	9,820	10,861
19	Travel	45,855	48,739
20	Passenger fares	14,313	15,776
21	Other transportation	29,205	28,453
22	Royalties and license fees	6,312	7,322
23	Other private services	33,970	42,796
24	US government miscellaneous services	2,755	2,687
25	Income payments of foreign assets in the United States	190,674	203,577
26	Direct investment payments	31,418	32,132
27	Other private payments	97,977	100,103
28	US government payments	61,279	71,342
29	Unilateral transfers	35,075	39,968
33	US assets abroad, net (increase/capital outflow(–))	307,856	352,444
48	Foreign assets in the United States, net (increase/capital inflow (+))	424,462	547,555
64	Balance on goods (lines 2 and 16)	–173,424	–191,170
65	Balance on services (lines 3 and 17)	68,360	80,130
66	Balance on goods and services (lines 64 and 65)	–105,064	–111,040
67	Balance on investment income (lines 11 and 25)	–8,016	2,824
68	Balance on goods, services and income (lines 1 and 15 or lines 66 and 67)	–113,079	–108,216
69	Unilateral transfers, net (line 29)	–35,075	–39,968
70	Balance on current account (lines 1, 15, and 29 or lines 68 and 69)	–148,154	–148,184

Source: US Department of Commerce, Survey of Current Business, May 1997 and March 1998.

Table 7.3   US merchandise trade, 1995 and 1996

	1995 (in millions of US $)	1996 (in millions of US $)
Exports	575,871	612,069
Foods, feeds, and beverages	50,473	55,534
Industrial supplies and materials	146,247	147,652
Capital goods, except automotive	233,046	252,895
Automotive vehicles, engines and parts	61,828	60,021
Consumer goods (nonfood), except automotive	64,425	70,138
Other goods	28,723	33,836
Adjustments	–8,871	–13,006
Imports	749,431	803,239
Foods, feeds, and beverages	33,176	35,710
Industrial supplies and materials	181,849	204,482
Capital goods, except automotive	221,431	229,050
Automotive vehicles, engines and parts	123,795	128,938
Consumer goods (nonfood), except automotive	159,905	171,007
Other goods	23,387	26,102
Adjustments	5,888	7,950

Source: US Department of Commerce, *Survey of Current Business*, May 1997 and March 1998.

ACTIVE LEARNING CHECK

Review your answer to Active Learning Case question 1 and make any changes you like. Then compare your answer to the one below.

1. Why is Japan's trade surplus with the United States of concern to the United States?

There are a number of reasons that this surplus is of concern to the United States. One reason is that it is the largest single component of international transactions and thus greatly affects the overall balance of payments. A second is that continuing deficits in this account must be offset by income generated from direct investment abroad, international borrowing, or dollar devaluation. A close analysis of these reasons helps to explain why the Americans are determined to reduce this surplus sharply and, in the process, to strengthen their own economy.

INTERNATIONAL MONETARY SYSTEM

The **international monetary system** is an institutional arrangement among the central banks of the countries that belong to the International Monetary Fund (IMF). This overall monetary system includes a wide variety of institutions, financial instruments, rules, and procedures within which foreign exchange markets function. The objective of this system is to create an international environment that is conducive to the free flow of goods, services, and capital among nations. This system also strives to create a stable foreign exchange market, to guarantee the convertibility of currencies, and to ensure adequate liquidity. The IMF is one of the primary organizations in this system.

International monetary fund

Near the end of World War II there was an international meeting of the major Allied governments to restructure the international monetary system. The group met at Bretton Woods, New Hampshire, in 1944 and agreed to establish a new monetary order. This meeting helped to create the International Monetary Fund (IMF), a multigovernment organization designed to promote exchange rate stability and to facilitate the flow of international currencies. The Bretton Woods agreement also resulted in the formation of the **International Bank for Reconstruction and Development** (popularly known as the **World Bank**), a multigovernment-owned bank that was created to promote development projects through the use of low interest loans. The 40 initial participating countries set fixed exchange rates under which each established a par value for its currency, based on gold and the US dollar. Participating countries also funded the IMF and agreed to keep the value of their currency within 1 per cent of the official parity or devalue the currency. If it became necessary to devalue a currency by 10 per cent or more, IMF approval was needed. The overall goals of the IMF were to:

1. Facilitate the balanced growth of international trade.
2. Promote exchange stability and orderly exchange arrangements and discourage competitive currency depreciation.
3. Seek the elimination of exchange restrictions that hinder the growth of world trade.
4. Make financial resources available to members, on a temporary basis and with adequate safeguards, to permit them to correct payment imbalances without resorting to measures destructive to national and international prosperity.

The original IMF framework functioned well for about 15 years. However, by the 1960s problems were beginning to develop. One reason was that the United States had been supplying international liquidity through a steady net outflow of dollars for such things as economic aid, private foreign direct investment, and military expenditures. Western European countries were using these dollars to replenish their depleted international reserves. However, as the United States began to run large balance of payments deficits, confidence in the dollar began to decline and countries like France started exchanging dollars for gold. Simply put, the fixed exchange rate system was breaking down and changes were needed. In 1968 the United States suspended the sale of gold except to official parties, and in mid-1971 the United States closed the gold window completely, refusing to exchange gold for dollars.

During the 1970s as the economies of more and more countries strengthened, it became evident that gold and internationally acceptable currencies could not handle the reserve requirements of these nations. In 1970, to help increase international reserves, the IMF created the **special drawing right (SDR)** as a unit of value to replace the dollar as a reserve asset, and today a number of countries peg their currency to the SDR. When first created, the SDR was linked to gold, but since 1974 its value has been based on the daily market exchange rates of a basket of currencies consisting of the US dollar, British pound, French franc, German mark, and Japanese yen (see Table 7.4). Another major development was a 1976 IMF amendment that resulted in

Table 7.4 World exchange rate arrangements, 1997

Pegged to a single currency	Pegged to a currency composite	Cooperative arrangements	Other managed floating	Independently floating
Angola (US$)	Bangladesh	Austria	Algeria	Afghanistan
Antigua and Barbuda (US$)	Botswana	Belgium	Belarus	Albania
Argentina (US$)	Burundi	Denmark	Brazil	Armenia
Bahamas (US$)	Cape Verde	Finland	Cambodia	Australia
Barbados (US$)	Cyprus	France	Chile	Azerbaijan
Belize (US$)	Czech Republic	Germany	China	Bolivia
Benin (French franc)	Fiji	Ireland	Colombia	Bulgaria
Bhutan (Indian rupee)	Iceland	Italy	Costa Rica	Canada
Bosnia and Herzegovina (deutsche mark)	Jamahiriya*	Luxembourg	Croatia	Eritrea
Brunei Darussalam (Singapore dollar)	Jordan	Netherlands	Dominican Republic	Ethiopia
Burkina Faso (French franc)	Kuwait	Portugal	Ecuador	Gambia
Cameroon (French franc)	Latvia*	Spain	Egypt	Ghana
Central African Rep. (French franc)	Libyan Arab*		El Salvador	Guatemala
Chad (French franc)	Malta		Georgia	Guinea
Comoros (French franc)	Morocco		Greece	Guyana
Congo, Rep. Of (French franc)	Myanmar*		Honduras	Haiti
Côte d'Ivoire (French franc)	Nepal		Hungary	India
Djibouti (US$)	Seychelles		Indonesia	Jamaica
Dominica (US$)	Slovak Republic		Iran	Japan
Equatorial Guinea (French franc)	Solomon Islands		Israel	Kenya Republic
Estonia (deutsche mark)	Thailand		Kazakhstan	Korea
Gabon (French franc)	Tonga		Kyrgyz Republic	Lebanon
Grenada (US$)	Vanuatu		Lao P.D.R.	Liberia
Guinea-Bissau (French franc)	Western Samoa		Macedonia, former	Madagascar
Iraq (US$)			Malaysia	Malawi
Kiribati (Australian dollar)			Maldives	Mauritania
Lesotho (South African Rand)			Mauritius	Mexico
Lithuania (US$)			Nicaragua	Moldova
Mali (French franc)			Norway	Mongolia
Marshall Islands (US$)			Pakistan	Mozambique
Micronesia, Federated States of (US$)			Poland	New Zealand
Namibia (South African Rand)			Russian Federation	Papua New Guinea
Niger (French franc)			Singapore	Paraguay
Nigeria (US$)			Slovenia	Peru
Oman (US$)			Sri Lanka	Philippines
Panama (US$)			Sudan	Romania
San Marino (Italian lira)			Suriname	Rwanda
Senegal (French franc)			Tunisia	São Tomé and Principe
St. Kitts and Nevis (US$)			Turkey	Sierra Leone
St. Lucia (US$)			Turkmenistan	Somalia
St. Vincent and the Grenadines (US$)			Ukraine	South Africa

continued overleaf

Table 7.4 (cont'd)

Pegged to a single currency	Pegged to a currency composite	Cooperative arrangements	Other managed floating	Independently floating
Swaziland (South African Rand)			Uruguay	Sweden
Syrian Arab Republic (US$)			Uzbekistan	Switzerland
Togo (French franc)			Venezuela	Tajikistan, Rep.
			Vietnam	Tanzania
				Trinidad and Tobago
				Uganda
				United Kingdom
				United States
				Yemen, Rep. of
				Zaïre
				Zambia
				Zimbabwe

*Pegged to the IMF's Special Drawing Right (SDR) a composite of currencies.

Bahrain, Qatar, Saudi Arabia and the United Arab Emirates have limited flexibility to the US dollar.

Source: Adapted from Francesco Caramazza and Jahangir Aziz, "Fixed or Flexible? Getting the Exchange Rate Right in the 1990s." *IMF Economic Issues,* April 17, 1998 (*http://www.imf.org/external/pubs/ft/issues13/index.htm*).

a managed float system, characterized by flexible exchange rates in which the value of currencies can change. Table 7.4 lists current exchange rate systems.

The managed float system

The managed float system that is used today had its origins in January 1976 when IMF members met in Jamaica and hammered out an agreement. The main elements of the agreement included: (a) floating rates were accepted and IMF members were allowed to enter the foreign exchange market to deal with any unwarranted speculative fluctuations; (b) gold was abandoned as a reserve asset; (c) the amount of contributions made by IMF member countries was increased; and (d) less developed countries were given greater access to these funds.

Major currencies were now allowed to float in relation to each other. As a result, during the 1976–94 time period, the US dollar, in the main, weakened against the other two major world currencies, the German mark and the Japanese yen. However, beginning around 1994 the dollar then began to strengthen, especially against the yen, as the Japanese economy sank into an economic malaise. This type of fluctuation of currency values led some to ask whether a floating exchange rate is a good idea or whether there should be a return to fixed rates. There are arguments to be made on each side.

The case for floating exchange rates has two major parts. First, it is argued that a floating exchange rate gives countries autonomy over their own monetary policy. Under a fixed system, the nation's ability to expand or contract its money supply is limited by the need to maintain exchange rate parity. On the other hand, with a floating exchange rate if a government were faced with unemployment and wanted to increase its money supply to stimulate domestic demand and reduce unemployment, it could do so. Another argument for floating rates is that they would automatically bring about trade balance adjustments. For example, if a nation were importing more than it was exporting and had trouble breaking out of this cycle, the devaluation of its currency in the international market would make its exports cheaper and its imports more expensive. As a result, the exchange rate depreciation would ultimately correct the trade deficit.

On the other side are those who argue for fixed exchange rates. One of their arguments is that these rates force countries to discipline themselves and not expand their money supplies at inflationary rates – something that politicians might do because it was politically expedient. A second argument is that if rates are not allowed to float then speculators cannot buy and sell currencies and cause wild fluctuation in the exchange rates. A third reason is that fixed rates help make business planning easier and reduce the risks associated with exporting, importing, and foreign investment.

Today the argument between fixed and floating rates continues. Each side has its advocates. Certainly it would be impossible to return to the fixed exchange rate system that emerged from the Bretton Woods agreement. However, a different kind of fixed exchange rate system might be more enduring and foster the kind of stability that would facilitate more rapid growth of international trade and investment. For the moment, however, floating exchange rates continue.

The European Monetary System

In the discussion of the European Union in Chapter 4, it was noted that the EU committed itself to establishing a single currency, a commitment that dated back to the Treaty of Maastricht in December 1991. In achieving this single currency goal, the EU's initial objective was to attain convergence between the inflation rates and interest rates of its member states. In particular, the Maastricht Agreement set forth the following convergence criteria: (a) inflation must be no more than 1.5 percentage points above the average of the three lowest inflation rates in Europe; (b) long-term interest rates must be no more than 2 percentage points higher than the average of the three lowest; (c) the exchange rate must have stayed within the narrow band of the EU's exchange rate mechanism for two years without realignment; and (d) the accumulated stock of public debts must not exceed 60 per cent of gross domestic product.[9] The **European Monetary System (EMS)** is a mechanism for attaining this goal. When the EMS was created in 1979 it was given three objectives: (1) to create a zone of monetary stability in Europe by reducing exchange rate volatility and converging national interest rates; (2) to control inflation through the use of monetary discipline; and (3) to coordinate exchange rate policies versus non-EU currencies such as the US dollar and the Japanese yen. Two instruments designed to achieve these objectives are the European currency unit (ecu) and the exchange rate mechanism (ERM).

The "ecu" is a basket of EU currencies that serves as a unit of account for the EMU. The share of each country's currency in the ecu depends on that nation's relative economic weight within the community. For example, 30.1 per cent of the ecu's value was established by the value of the mark in 1989 because that was the estimate of Germany's relative strength and size in the EU economy at that time.

Until 1992 the ERM worked this way: each national currency in the EU was given a "central rate" *vis-à-vis* the ecu. For example, in 1989 one ecu was equal to 2.05853 German marks, 6.90404 French francs, or 0.739615 British pounds. From these

Table 7.5 Exchange rates and the euro

Country	Currency	Dollar rate	Euro rate
Austria	Schilling	0.08	13.91
Belgium	Franc	0.271	40.78
Finland	Mark	0.1842	6.01
France	Franc	0.1666	6.35
Germany	Mark	0.558	1.98
Ireland	Punt	1.4058	0.80
Italy	Lira	0.000566	1,958.0
Luxembourg	Guilder	0.496	2.23
Portugal	Escudo	0.00545	202.70
Spain	Peseta	0.00658	168.20

Source: Reported in the *Wall Street Journal*, May 4, 1998, p. A17.

central rates, it was possible to determine the value of a mark against the Italian lira or a pound against the Spanish peseta. Moreover, this central rate could be changed only by a commonly agreed realignment. Prior to 1992, currencies were not allowed to depart by more than $2^{1}/_{4}$ per cent from their bilateral central rate with other ERM participating currencies. If any of the currencies did reach its outer margin of fluctuation relative to another, the central banks of the two countries were supposed to intervene and keep their currencies within the $2^{1}/_{4}$ per cent band. In particular, the central bank of the country with the stronger currency was supposed to buy the weaker currency and vice versa. In practice, however, the situation was often left in the hands of the country with the weaker currency.

Supporters of the ERM point to the virtues of fixed rate systems that were discussed in the previous section. However, things have not always worked according to plan. For example, in 1992 speculators began selling the British pound and the Italian lira and buying the mark. Despite efforts by the central banks of both Great Britain and Italy, their currency values fell outside the ERM band. As a result, both nations pulled out of the ERM. This resulted in the EU countries changing the fluctuation band for a time from the initial $2^{1}/_{4}$ per cent to 15 per cent, although it is now $2^{1}/_{4}$ per cent again. Since this time there have been speculative pressures that have forced devaluation of the Spanish peseta and the Portuguese escudo. However, the agreement did hold together and in January 1999 most EU countries accepted the euro as their currency of exchange and beginning in 2002 new euro bank notes and coins will reach the general public.

Eleven countries agreed to the exchange rate between their respective currencies and the euro. Table 7.5 provides these data. As a result of this agreement, it is now possible for customers to compare prices between countries because everything can be done in a uniform currency. Beginning almost immediately, a number of auto manufacturers, including Daimler-Benz, announced that they would make the euro their currency of reference. In turn, their suppliers will do the same thus hurrying along the process. Other companies, including Siemens, whose products extend from microchips to power plants, wrote to thousands of companies of its intention to switch its accounting systems from national currencies to euros. As a result, it is likely that within a few more years most of the business done in the EU will be in euros and, perhaps, those nations that have not agreed to the common currency, will adopt it.[10]

The IMF and the World Bank today

Over the last couple of decades the role of the IMF has declined. Floating exchange rates have resulted in a diminished demand for short-term loans, and no major industrialized country has borrowed money from the IMF for over 20 years. Nations such as Great Britain and the United States have financed their deficits by borrowing private money rather than relying on IMF funds. As a result, inspired by the OPEC oil price hikes of 1973 and 1979 and the resulting third world crisis, the IMF has found a new mission for itself.

OPEC price increases of the 1970s resulted in massive flows of funds from major oil-importing countries such as Japan and the United States to oil producing countries that now sought investment opportunities for these monies. Commercial banks quickly stepped in to recycle these funds by borrowing from OPEC and lending to third world governments in Latin America and Africa. These loans were based on optimistic assessments that proved to be highly inaccurate. A number of reasons accounted for the failure of these third world countries to generate strong economic growth including: (a) rising short-term interest rates worldwide which increased the cost of these debts; (b) poor management of the economies; (c) and a slowdown in the growth rate of the industrialized nations, the main markets for third world products.

As a result, there was a massive debt crisis. Commercial banks held over $1 trillion of bad debts and there was no hope of ever being repaid. Even Mexico, long thought to be highly creditworthy, announced that it could no longer service its $80 billion in international debt without an immediate new loan of $3 billion. Brazil and Argentina, among others, also were unable to make their debt repayments. The international monetary system was on the verge of a major crisis.

This is when the IMF stepped in. Working with several western governments including the United States, Mexico's debt was rescheduled, new loans were made, and an IMF-dictated series of macroeconomic policies were accepted by the Mexican government including tight control over the growth of the money supply and major cuts in government spending. The IMF followed a similar approach in helping other countries. However, there was a problem with the IMF solution. It rested on the economy of these countries turning around and generating sufficient growth to repay the rescheduled debt. By the mid-1980s it was apparent that this was not happening and by 1989 it was evident that the mere rescheduling of debt was not a long-run solution to the problem. In April of that year the IMF endorsed a new approach first proposed by Nicholas Brady, US Secretary of the Treasury.

The Brady Plan rested on the belief that debt reduction was a necessary part of the solution and the IMF and World Bank would have to assume roles in financing it. In essence, the plan called for the IMF, the World Bank, and the Japanese government to each contribute $10 billion to the task of debt reduction. In order to obtain these funds, each debtor nation would have to submit to a set of imposed conditions for macroeconomic policy management and debt repayment. The first application of the plan was the Mexican debt reduction of 1989 which cut that country's debt of $107 billion by about $15 billion.

One result of the IMF's involvement in resolving the third world debt crisis has been the blurring of the line between itself and the World Bank. Under the original

Bretton Woods agreement, the IMF was to provide short-term loans and the World Bank was to provide long-term loans. However, the collapse of communism in Eastern Europe and the break up of the Soviet Union have resulted in a flood of applications for IMF membership from these newly democratic nations, including Russia. These nations are seeking long-term funds for economic growth.

At the same time the World Bank has been moving closer to the IMF. During the 1970s the bank found that many of its loan projects for irrigation, energy, transportation, etc. were not producing the kind of long-term economic gains that had been predicted. On close examination, the bank found that many of these projects were being undermined by the broad policy environment of the particular country. It was obvious that loan conditions needed to extend beyond the project to the economy at large. So the World Bank devised a new type of loan. In addition to providing funds to support specific projects, the bank now provides loans for the government to use as it sees fit in return for promises on macroeconomic policy. This, of course, is the same thing that the IMF has done in recent years, lending money to debtor nations in return for promises regarding macroeconomic policy.

Today both the IMF and the World Bank are actively involved in their new commitments in Eastern Europe. However, given that both seem to be doing similar jobs, it is quite possible that the two will eventually be merged.

Economic cooperation

No matter what steps are taken to alter the international monetary system, without cooperation among the major economic powers, nothing substantive will happen. In particular, there will have to be greater coordination in the conduct of national policies by the industrialized nations.[11]

> The underlying issue is the extent to which member countries will make exchange rate stability an important part of national policy rather than a residual of domestically oriented policy actions. The freedom in domestic policy making that the present system permits is both a strength and a weakness of the system. The system allows nations to insulate their domestic price levels from inflation abroad and facilitates the pursuit of sound monetary policies geared more directly to domestic conditions. At the same time, considerable volatility in exchange rates can result when major nations adopt fiscal and monetary policies independently, without serious consideration of the impact of these national policies on the world economy.[12]

It will also be necessary for the developing and industrial countries to resolve their differences regarding the problem of international liquidity. Developing countries, for example, want to see the allocation of SDRs increased on an annual basis with a view to ensuring that their proportion in reserves rises progressively. Industrial countries argue that new SDR allocations could delay needed adjustments that should be made by countries that currently have monetary problems. Each side has arguments in its favor; each has a position it wants to protect.

Finally, it is important to realize that few nations are willing to give up national control over their economic and monetary policies.[13] Yet without some movement in this direction, it is hard to understand how true economic global cooperation will ever be achieved. At present it is virtually impossible for any world monetary organization to rein in the United States, Germany, or Japan, to name but three, and to force cooperative policies on them. So for the near future, at least, economic cooperation is likely to be more of an ideal than a reality.

ACTIVE LEARNING CHECK

Review your answer to Active Learning Case question 2 and make any changes you like. Then compare your answer to the one below.

2. Some countries believe that those with large trade surpluses should reinvest them in poorer countries in order to help these economies. Is Japan in a position to do this?

Japan certainly is in a position to do this. In fact, her trade surplus has reached new heights and the country is now in a better position than many others to help third world nations by investing there and by lending or giving money for humanitarian projects.

FOREIGN EXCHANGE

Foreign exchange is any financial instrument that carries out payment from one currency to another. The most common form of conducting foreign exchange payments between banks is the telephone transfer. Between companies it is the draft. By tourists it is the physical exchange of one currency for another. For example, a tourist from Chicago who is visiting Madrid, Spain, will exchange dollars for pesetas. The **exchange rate** is the amount of one currency that can be obtained for another currency. Table 7.6 provides an example. Notice that on May 1, 1998 a Spanish peseta had a value of around six-tenths of one US cent. So for each dollar the tourist exchanged the individual would receive 152.45 pesetas. This exchange rate would also dictate large exchanges of currency, so that a New York bank that wanted to convert $100,000 into Spanish currency on this day would have received 15,245,000 pesetas ($100,000 × 152.45).

For purposes of international business, there are three important areas of foreign exchange that warrant consideration: (1) foreign exchange markets in the United States, (2) participants in foreign exchange markets, and (3) determination of exchange rates.

Foreign exchange markets in the United States

There are three major ways of conducting foreign exchange in the United States: between banks, through a broker, and through forward transactions. The interbank market for foreign exchange involves transactions between banks. For example, if an importer wants to buy $100,000 of French francs, the most likely route would be for the individual to ask his or her bank to handle the transaction. If the bank does not trade in foreign exchange, it will contact a large bank, Bankers Trust, for example, which does, and this bank will sell the francs out of its holdings or enter the interbank market and buy them from other banks.

The brokers' market consists of a small group of foreign exchange brokerage companies that make markets in foreign currencies. These brokers do not take currency positions. They simply match up buyers and sellers and charge a commission for their services. This is in contrast, for example, to Bankers Trust, which might carry millions of dollars of foreign currencies that it hopes to sell at a profit.

Table 7.6 Exchange rates

Country	Currency per US $		Country	Currency per US $	
	Thursday	Wednesday		Thursday	Wednesday
Argentina (peso)	0.9999	0.9999	Jordan (dinar)	0.7075	0.7075
Australia (dollar)	1.5385	1.5399	Kuwait (dinar)	0.3053	0.3056
Austria (schilling)	12.64	12.638	Lebanon (pound)	1520.25	1520.5
Bahrain (dinar)	0.377	0.377	Malaysia (ringgit)	3.7325	3.745
Belgium (franc)	37.065	37.06	Malta (lira)	0.3915	0.3925
Brazil (real)	1.1436	1.1447	Mexico (peso)		
Britain (pound)	0.5985	0.5989	Floating rate	8.486	8.49
1-month forward	0.5994	0.5998	Netherlands (guilder)	2.0219	2.0218
3-months forward	0.6011	0.6015	New Zealand (dollar)	1.806	1.8073
6-months forward	0.6033	0.6036	Norway (krone)	7.4628	7.4733
Canada (dollar)	1.431	1.4369	Pakistan (rupee)	43.61	43.61
1-month forward	1.4301	1.436	Peru (new sol)	2.8089	2.8129
3-months forward	1.4284	1.4345	Philippines (peso)	40.175	40.054
6-months forward	1.4261	1.4324	Poland (zloty)	3.4055	3.4055
Chile (peso)	452.85	452.65	Portugal (escudo)	184.01	184.06
China (renminbi)	8.2781	8.2782	Russia (ruble)	6.134	6.133
Colombia (peso)	1365.72	1371.35	Saudi Arabia (riyal)	3.7503	3.7504
Czech. Rep. (koruna)			Singapore (dollar)	1.5835	1.589
Commercial rate	32.995	33.149	Slovak Rep. (koruna)	34.546	34.605
Denmark (krone)	6.8475	6.849	South Africa (rand)	5.06	5.0495
Ecuador (sucre)			South Korea (won)	1335.5	1334.5
Floating rate	5010	5010	Spain (peseta)	152.45	152.52
Finland (markka)	5.448	5.449	Sweden (krona)	7.7388	7.7703
France (franc)	6.0195	6.02	Switzerland (franc)	1.5013	1.4978
1-month forward	6.0088	6.0092	1-month forward	1.4959	1.4923
3-months forward	5.9886	5.9888	3-months forward	1.4857	1.4817
6-months forward	5.9605	5.9594	6-months forward	1.4707	1.4668
Germany (mark)	1.7959	1.7955	Taiwan (dollar)	32.97	32.991
1-month forward	1.7928	1.7924	Thailand (baht)	38.605	38.6
3-months forward	1.787	1.7864	Turkey (lira)	249150	249020
6-months forward	1.7785	1.7778	United Arab (dirham)	3.673	3.673
Greece (drachma)	314	316.4	Uruguay (new peso)		
Hong Kong (dollar)	7.7485	7.7425	Financial	10.315	10.315
Hungary (forint)	210.87	211.24	Venezuela (bolivar)	536.63	536.88
India (rupee)	39.725	39.732			
Indonesia (rupiah)	8085	8250			
Ireland (punt)	0.7119	0.7114	SDR*	0.7426	0.743
Israel (shekel)	3.706	3.7033			
Italy (lira)	1772	1774			
Japan (yen)	132.83	132.38			
1-month forward	132.24	131.77			
3-months forward	131.12	130.66			
6-months forward	129.34	128.92			

*Special Drawing Rights (SDR) are based on exchange rates for the US, German, British, French, and Japanese currencies. *Source:* IMF.
Source: Adapted from *Wall Street Journal*, Friday, May 1, 1998.

There are three types of exchange rates that are important to those dealing in foreign exchange: spot, forward, and cross. A **spot rate** is the rate quoted for current foreign currency transactions. For example, if someone were to buy 100 British pounds for immediate delivery, the individual would pay the spot rate. The **forward rate** is the rate quoted for the delivery of foreign currency at a predetermined future date such as 90 days from now. A **cross rate** is an exchange rate that is computed from two other rates. This rate is of interest to dealers or businesses that are doing business in more than two currencies. For example, suppose that a US firm is doing business with companies in both Switzerland and Germany and that the current value of both currencies as expressed in US dollars is: 1.60 DM per dollar and SwF 1.39 per dollar. The cross rate would then be:

$$\frac{\text{SwF } 1.39}{\text{DM } 1.60} = \text{SwF } 0.8688 \text{ per DM}$$

This means that it takes one German mark to equal 0.8688 Swiss francs. The US firm would want to keep track of this relationship because of the impact it can have on the company's cost of goods and profits should the value of either currency increase *vis-à-vis* that of the other nation.

The forward foreign exchange market is particularly important to MNEs because it lets a customer "lock in" an exchange rate and thus protect against the risk of an unfavorable change in the value of the currency that is needed. This exchange market is very important to firms doing business overseas and dealing in foreign currency.

For example, suppose that a large construction firm in Atlanta, Georgia, orders £500,000 of specially made furniture from a British firm in London with payment due in British pounds within 90 days. As we see in Table 7.6, a British pound on this day was selling for $1.6708 ($1.00/0.5985). So to pay the seller £500,000 today, the construction company would have to remit a total of $835,420 (£500,000 × 1.67). If the company waits and pays the bill in 90 days, however, there is an exchange rate risk. If the value of the pound rises *vis-à-vis* the dollar, the final price will be more than $835,420. Of course, the pound might decline in value, and by waiting 90 days the overall cost will be less than this amount. However, on large amounts most firms will lock in their position. The construction company can do this by purchasing £500,000 today with delivery in 90 days. This is done by purchasing a contract in the forward foreign exchange market. Table 7.6 shows that the 90-day rate is $1.6636 ($1.00/0.6011) per pound. This transaction can be handled through a major bank.

For a fee Bankers Trust will sell the company a contract guaranteeing to provide pounds at $1.6636 ($1.00/1.6011) in 90 days. So the company can purchase this contract and know the price it will be paying, which is $1.6636 × 500,000 or $831,808. In addition, there is typically a fee of 1 per cent on the total value of the transaction, or about $8,318. Thus by locking into an exchange rate today, the firm will end up paying a total of about $840,126 ($831,808 + $8,318). Of course, the pound might decline below $1.6636 by the end of 90 days and the company would have been better off not purchasing the futures contract. On the other hand, the firm is more interested in limiting its exchange rate risk than in making a profit by correctly anticipating the exchange rate of the pound.

The box "International Business Strategy in Action: Indonesia and the Asian Crisis" provides an example of how changes in the value of foreign currency can affect MNE performance in international markets.

INTERNATIONAL BUSINESS STRATEGY IN ACTION

Indonesia and the Asian crisis

Indonesia is the fourth most populous country in the world with a population of 200 millions. The nation has also been praised as one of the economic miracles of Asia. By the early 1990s many investors were rushing to take advantage of the country's rapid economic growth. All of this changed in 1997, however, when Indonesia became one of the worst victims of the Asian Flu. In less than one year the rupiah lost 80 per cent of its value, while its stock market plummeted by 60 per cent. And soaring unemployment and inflation led to riots that forced the resignation of President Suharto.

In particular, Suharto was blamed for corruption and a lack of accountability in the country. His poor health, his age, and his unwillingness to prepare for a transition to a more democratic system, in the view of many foreign investors, merely served to aggravate the problem. In addition, the banking system that the government fostered was plagued with bad loans for many unreliable projects. These loans benefited and created wealth for well positioned individuals – in particular, members of the Shuharto family. However, the loans did nothing for the rest of the country.

Some financial observers believe that western speculators were a major reason for the financial troubles in the region. The trend toward deregulation of the world capital markets and the free flow of capital, it was argued, contributed to the currency panic. Additionally, the relatively good health of the nation prior to 1997 made it attractive to foreign investors and lenders. Unfortunately, many of these loans were short term and were in foreign currency. So while the

economy grew the loans presented no problem, but when trouble looked likely the foreign lenders began calling in their loans. When this happened, the value of the rupiah plummeted and the loans payable in foreign currencies created a debt crisis.

It was initially believed that the Asian economic problem would be contained in that geographic region. However, by mid-1998 the crisis was having an effect on the global economy. The cross-border interconnections of global industries and the resulting interdependence spread the problem to other regions. Among other things, the crisis led to decreases in the prices of many commodities such as oil, metals, grain, pulp, and paper.

Industrial nations came to the aid of these Asian governments. The IMF and the Indonesian government agreed to a $40 billion dollar bailout. Initially, the IMF wanted the government to decrease its budget deficit and to maintain stable interest rates. By July 1998, however, the IMF was allowing increases in deficits and lower interest rates. At the same time the government merged its state-run banks and closed other banks under a newly formed Indonesian Bank Restructuring Agency. In an effort to gather capital, the government also lifted restrictions on foreign ownership of banks. This was likely to help ease some of the problems, although there was still a lot of disagreement regarding what else needed to be done. For example, some observers argued that the government needed to continue to deregulate the country's capital markets, while others blamed the economic disaster on this deregulation.

Sources: Anonymous, "Crisis-ridden Indonesia to Overhaul Ailing Banking Sector," *Boston Globe on Line*, January 27, 1998 (*http://www.boston.com/dailynews/*); Canada, Department of Foreign Affairs and International Trade, "Government of Canada to provide Bilateral Support Package to Indonesia," *News Release*, March 31 1998 (*http://dfait-maeci.gc.cal*); Anonymous, "EU to Get Tough with Indonesia as New Crisis Fears Grow," *Nando.net*, March 29, 1998 (*http://www.nand.net/newsrooml*); Richard Gwyn, "Asian Flu Shows No Sign of Letting Up," *Toronto Star*, July 10, 1998; Anonymous, "A Crisis of Dictatorship," *Washington Post*, Sunday 11, 1998; Raffi Anderian, "Everybody Is Going Down," *Sunday Star*, July 12, 1998.

Participants in foreign exchange markets

There are five major groups that are active participants in foreign exchange markets: traders/brokers, speculators, hedgers, arbitrageurs, and governments.

Traders/brokers **Foreign exchange traders** work in commercial banks where they buy and sell foreign currency for their employer. These transactions can be at either the spot rate or the forward rate. This is usually done in response to customer orders, but sometimes the bank will take a position in a currency. Since this can be risky, most banks will keep their exposure to a minimum, focusing primarily on serving clients who need international currency.

Foreign exchange brokers work in brokerage firms where they often deal in both spot rate and forward rate transactions. These individuals typically deal only in foreign exchange transactions, in contrast to banks which provide this service as just one of many.

Speculators In foreign exchange markets a **speculator** is a participant who takes an open position. This means that the individual either has foreign currency on hand (called a "long position") or has promised to deliver foreign currency in the future and does not have it on hand (called a "short position"). If the speculator is long in a currency, the individual is betting that the price will go up. If the speculator is short in a currency, the individual is betting that the price will go down. For example, if a speculator believes that the British pound will increase in value in the near future, the individual will buy pounds and then sell them when the price rises. Conversely, if the speculator believes that the price is going down, the individual will sell pounds today and replace them at a lower price in the future. Of course, if the market price moves in the opposite direction, the speculator can lose a lot of money unless the individual covers the open position and minimizes the loss.

Hedgers **Foreign exchange hedgers** limit their potential losses by locking in guaranteed foreign exchange positions. Many business firms engage in foreign exchange hedging. The Atlanta construction firm, in our earlier example, hedged its position by purchasing British pounds in the futures market in order to guarantee that it would be able to buy at $1.664 a pound. Sellers may fit into any one or more of the categories just discussed above. They may be traders or brokers who are long in British pounds and feel that $1.664 is a good price because the pound will rise. Or they may simply be willing to buy the currency today at market price for a client and make their profit from the commission. Or they may be speculators who believe that the price will sink below $1.664 before they have to deliver the pounds and thus will profit by taking a short position. Or they may be hedgers who have bought the currency at a lower price and want to lock in their profit at $1.664.

Arbitrageurs **Foreign exchange arbitrageurs** are individuals who simultaneously buy and sell currency in two or more foreign markets and profit from the exchange rate differences. Arbitrageurs do not incur much risk because the difference in the prices often guarantees a profit. Here is a simple example: Assume that the British pound is being quoted at £1 = 1.68 in New York and £1 = $1.65 in London. By purchasing 1 million pounds in London and selling them in New York, the arbitrageur makes 3 cents per pound, or $30,000 (1,000,000 × 0.03). Of course, there would be expenses associated with carrying out the transaction, and it might not be possible to purchase 1 million pounds at £1 = $1.65 or to sell them at £1 = $1.68 given the forces of supply and demand. However, the transaction does illustrate the basic idea behind arbitrage.

Governments   Although the currencies of most developed countries are allowed to float on the open market, governments will sometimes intervene as buyers or sellers in order to create or maintain a particular price. For example, many countries of the world hold US dollars, so it would not be in their best interests to see the dollar drop sharply. Such a development would reduce the value of their holdings as well as increase the United States' ability to export to them (since imports would now be cheaper given the increased value of their foreign currencies). So governments would intervene to buy dollars in the marketplace in order to shore up the value of the US currency.

Determination of exchange rates

Exchange rates are determined by the activities of the five groups discussed in the previous section. However, there are economic relationships such as purchasing power parity and interest rate parity, as well as other factors, that influence exchange rates.

Purchasing power parity (PPP)   Purchasing power parity (PPP) theory holds that the exchange rate between two currencies will be determined by the relative purchasing power of these currencies. This idea is best illustrated by considering the price of a similar good in two countries, say the United States and Germany, and then looking at the effects of inflation. If a particular car in the United States costs $22,000 and a similar car in Germany costs 39,510 deutschmarks (DMs), one DM would be worth just over 55 cents (39,510 DM/$22,000 = 1.7959 marks per dollar or 55.68 cents per mark), which is where it was in May 1998 (see Table 7.6). But suppose that inflation in the United States was 5 per cent in the next year and in Germany it was 10 per cent. The cost of the US car would then rise to $23,100 ($22,000 × 1.05), whereas the cost of the German car would rise to 43,461 DM (39,510 DM × 1.10). The DM would then, according to the purchasing power parity theory, decline to just under 60 cents (43,461 DM/$23,100 = 1.8814 marks per dollar, or 53.15 cents per mark).

If the price of all other goods and services in Germany were rising faster than in the United States, we would conclude that purchasing power in the United States was greater than in Germany. Moreover, according to the PPP theory, the value of the DM would decline in order to adjust the country's purchasing power parity. Using the automotive example to represent consumer purchases in general in both countries, the DM would drop to 53.15 cents ($23,100/43,461 DM). Simply stated, inflation affects purchasing power, and in order to reestablish parity, foreign currencies will have to increase or decrease in value to reflect these changes.

It is important to realize that the PPP theory is not perfect. Even today there are currencies that are undervalued or overvalued given their purchasing power parity. However, the theory is useful in helping to explain how exchange rates are determined. Interest rate parity also provides insights into this process.

Interest rates   In order to relate interest rates to exchange rates, we must first relate interest rates to inflation. This is done through the **Fisher effect**, which describes the relationship between inflation and interest rates in two countries. There are three key elements in the Fisher effect: (1) the **nominal rate of interest**, which is the interest rate that is being charged to a borrower, called the "money" rate of interest to distinguish it from the "real" rate; (2) the rate of inflation in the country; and (3) the

real interest rate, which is the difference between the nominal rate and the inflation rate. The Fisher effect holds that as inflation rises, so will the nominal interest rate because lenders will want to protect the real interest rate. So if bankers in both the United States and Germany want to earn a 5 per cent real interest rate and the rate of inflation in Germany is higher than that in the United States, then the nominal rate of interest will also be higher in Germany.

The link between interest rates and exchange rates is explained by the **international Fisher effect (IFE)**, which holds that the interest rate differential is an unbiased predictor of future changes in the spot exchange rate. Again, using the United States and Germany as an example, the IFE holds that if nominal interest rates in Germany are higher than those in the United States, the value of the DM will fall by that interest rate differential in the future. This differential is also important in determining forward exchange rates because this rate would be that which neutralizes the difference in interest rates between the two countries. For example, if interest rates in Germany are higher than those in the United States, the forward exchange rate for the DM would be lower than the dollar by the interest rate differential. So the yield in dollars on a US investment would be equal to the yield in dollars of a DM investment converted at the forward rate. Thus the forward rate would allow investors to trade currencies for future delivery at no exchange risk and no differential in interest income. If such a differential did exist, traders would then take advantage of this situation and earn income until the difference was eliminated.

Other considerations   Other factors also help to determine exchange rates. One is confidence in the currency. Many people hold dollars because they are convinced that it is a safe haven for their money. Even though the United States has run massive trade deficits in recent years, this has not shaken the confidence of many investors. They prefer to have their money in US currency, and this helps to strengthen the demand for US dollars.

Other factors that influence exchange rates are called "technical factors." These consist of such things as the release of national economic statistics, seasonal demands for a currency, the slight strengthening of a currency followed by a prolonged weakness, and the slight weakening of a currency following a sharp run-up in the exchange rate. Although technical factors do not generally result in large exchange rate changes, they do account for some of the movement.

ACTIVE LEARNING CHECK

Review your answer to Active Learning Case question 3 and make any changes you like. Then compare your answer to the one below.

3. Did the devaluation of the US dollar during the 1980s help or hinder US competitiveness in Japan?

Based strictly on the price of the yen, and overlooking trade barriers or other impediments to selling in Japan, US competitiveness increased. This is because it became easier for the Japanese to buy US imports given that it took fewer yen to pay for them. Of course, for those US companies that were operating in Japan and selling goods locally, the devaluation of the dollar had no effect on sales since their goods were priced in yen.

INTERNATIONAL BUSINESS STRATEGY IN ACTION

The European Monetary Union

On January 1, 1999 most of the European Union member states joined a single currency area. This has a single foreign exchange rate, a single currency (the "euro") with its own notes and coinage, and an integrated monetary and fiscal policy. The 11 countries in "Euroland" are: Austria, Belgium, Finland, France, Germany, Ireland, Italy, Luxembourg, the Netherlands, Portugal and Spain. The United Kingdom chose not to join the European Monetary Union (EMU) in 1999, but it may do so in the future.

To qualify for this stage three of the EMU, countries must keep their public sector budget deficits to within 3 per cent of GDP, a guideline set out in the Maastricht Treaty of 1992 which presented a game plan for the single integrated market of the EU. The process of moving towards a single currency itself helped to enhance economic convergence among the participating countries. Interest rates and monetary policy are being harmonized, as well as fiscal policy and budget deficits.

The economic policy result of the single currency is that the foreign exchange rate can no longer be used as a mechanism for economic adjustment by any of the 11 members of Euroland. Instead, they need to make internal adjustments in wage rates and other domestic expenditures when these countries perform at different stages of the business cycle. The problem here is that some countries may have high unemployment as exchange rate devaluation is not allowed.

To manage the new single currency the EU has set up an independent European Central Bank. It has the authority to control the money supply and thereby interest rates. To this extent, monetary policy has ceased to be an instrument of economic policy for any of the 11 members of the EMU. Their political independence to set interest rates, exchange rates, and fiscal policy has been reduced. This is one of the reasons that the British governments of Prime Ministers Thatcher, Major and Blair all found it difficult to join the EMU. Their governments have also been opposed to the EU goal of social union through harmonization of social policy, although Blair's position is fluid.

There are few precedents for a common currency among so many member states that remain politically sovereign. Previous attempts to secure full economic integration with political independence failed, as in the Latin American Currency Union of the nineteenth century and the Scandinavian Currency Area. At a time when Asian countries are engaged in currency devaluation to help restore external and internal economic balance it is doubtful that the EU single currency will survive without a major crisis.

Sources: http://www.eurunion.org/magazine.eurospec.htm; Lionel Barber, "Countdown to the Euro Momentous Meeting Will Choose Charter Members" (http://www.eurunion.org/magazine/current/p08/p08-9804.htm); "Fanfare for the Euro," The Economist, May 2, 1998.

STRATEGIC MANAGEMENT AND INTERNATIONAL FINANCE

International finance is extremely important in strategic planning by organizations that are doing business in the international arena. These firms do not have to be MNEs; they can be operating locally and simply buying or selling merchandise in the international market.

One of the primary areas of strategic consideration is strategies for dealing with currency exchange rate risk. Another is the financing of international operations.

Strategies for managing currency exchange rate risk

Exchange risk is the probability that a company will be unable to adjust prices and costs to offset changes in the exchange rate. There are a number of reasons that businesses need to develop strategies for managing currency exchange rate risk. One is that it often is impossible to pass along exchange rate increases in the form of higher prices. For example, assume that a giant US computer retailer is purchasing notebook computers from a manufacturer in Hong Kong. The cost to the US firm is $500 per unit, the machine retails for $1,000, and all invoices are payable in Hong Kong dollars. As we saw in Table 7.6, a Hong Kong dollar is worth 0.1291 US dollars, so for every machine it purchases the retailer must pay 3,873 ($500/0.1291) Hong Kong dollars.

Now assume that the US dollar is devalued so that Hong Kong currency is now worth $0.15 US dollars. If the manufacturer continues to charge 3,873 Hong Kong dollars, this raises the effective purchase price for the retailer to $580.95 (3,873 × 0.15) per unit and cuts $80.95 off the merchant's profit. The question now becomes: can the company pass this $80.95 increase on to the customer? If not, the company must adjust its strategy.

One step is to negotiate a lower price with the Hong Kong supplier and thus share the effects of the devaluation. A second is to pass along the price increase as much as possible and absorb the rest. A third, and complementary, approach is to take steps to minimize exchange risk. The three most common ways of doing this are exchange risk avoidance, exchange risk adaptation, and currency diversification.

Exchange risk avoidance is the elimination of exchange risk by doing business locally. For the retail firm this means buying notebook computers that are manufactured in the United States. In this way if the dollar is devalued against other currencies, it will not affect the price of labor or materials in the United States. The retailer will continue to pay the same price as before the dollar devaluation.

Exchange risk adaptation is the use of hedging to provide protection against exchange rate fluctuations. One of the most common methods is the purchase of a forward contract, which was explained earlier in the chapter. Another method is to negotiate a fixed dollar price with the other party, such as $500 per unit for a period of 24 months. In this way a change in the exchange rate during this period will not affect unit purchase price.

Currency diversification is the spreading of financial assets across several or more currencies. For example, the computer retailer would be protected, at least initially, against dollar devaluation if it carried enough Hong Kong dollars to pay for purchases through the next 12 months. Only after this time period would the dollar devaluation be felt. Moreover, if the company stopped doing business with the Hong Kong firm before it had spent all of these local dollars, the retailer would profit from the currency diversification since these dollars would have cost 12.91 cents and are now worth 15 cents.

Of these three approaches, exchange risk adaptation is most commonly used. The second most popular strategy is currency diversification, but this tends to be more common among large MNEs that have an ongoing need for these currencies.

Financing of operations

Until now our discussion of financial markets has been limited to foreign exchange and the ways in which businesses try to reduce the risks in this market. However, there is another important area that warrants consideration: foreign capital markets. Not all financing is done in the home country. Quite often companies will seek capital on an international basis and borrow or lend money where the rates are most attractive.[14]

Borrowing and lending   MNEs that are setting up operations in foreign markets will sometimes borrow money from local banks and institutions there. One reason is that local governments usually subsidize such loans through tax breaks, lower interest rates, and other financial considerations that limit the company's loss potential. For example, many states in the United States offer a financial incentive package to companies willing to establish operations in their locale. The states feel that the cost of these packages is more than offset by the jobs and economic strength that the company brings to the community. A second reason for borrowing locally is that MNEs with worldwide operations are able to hedge the risks of holding fluctuating currency by not having all their holdings in one currency. For example, if a company has operations in the United Kingdom, France, Germany, and Japan, as well as in the United States, the exchange rate of the foreign currencies of these countries will fluctuate *vis-à-vis* the US dollar. However, the company is unlikely to suffer as a result because its debt obligations on local loans are due in local currency. So if the French franc doubles in value against the dollar, this has no impact on US or French loans that are still due in local currency. The only risk the company runs is that of holding a large percentage of its liquid assets in the currency of a country whose currency becomes devalued. This will decrease the overall assets of the company, although it is unlikely to affect the firm's ability to operate internationally.

Sometimes an MNE will lend money in the international money market. For example, if Bank of America finds that it can get a higher interest rate in Singapore than in the United States, it may deposit some money there. Similarly, if General Motors finds that there are limitations on the amount of profit that it can transfer out of a country, the company may invest in local financial instruments and thus gain interest on funds that would otherwise sit idle.

Eurocurrencies   One of the international money markets that has become extremely important for large MNEs is the Eurocurrency market. **Eurocurrency** is any currency that is banked outside its country of origin. For example, **Eurodollars** are dollars banked outside the United States. Similarly there are euro-Swiss francs, euro-German marks, euro-French francs, euro-Japanese yen, and euro-British pounds, to name but five other types of Eurocurrency. The major sources of Eurodollars include (1) companies with excess cash, (2) European banks with foreign currency in excess of their current needs, (3) foreign governments or businesspeople who want to hold dollars outside the United States, and (4) reserves of countries such as Japan and some OPEC nations that have large trade surpluses.

The Eurocurrency market is primarily a Eurodollar market. This market is extremely large (in excess of $4 trillion) and is a wholesale market in which transactions are conducted by governments, banks, and major corporations. Deposits are primarily short term and consist of savings and time deposits rather than demand deposits. Loans are typically pegged to a certain percentage above the **London Inter-Bank Offered Rate (LIBOR)**, which is the interest rate banks charge one another on Eurocurrency loans.

There is also an international bond market which is available to both domestic and foreign investors. This market consists of both foreign bonds and Eurobonds. A **foreign bond** is a bond that is sold outside the borrower's country but which is denominated in the currency of the country where it has been issued. For example, a German corporation floating a bond issue in Spanish pesetas in Spain is floating a foreign bond. A **Eurobond** is a financial instrument that is typically underwritten by a syndicate of banks from different countries and is sold in countries other than the one in which its currency is denominated. For example, a Eurobond to raise $50 million for a Swiss company might be underwritten by a syndicate from five different countries, floated in French francs, and sold in Luxembourg, the Netherlands, Spain, and Italy.

The Eurobond market is centered in Europe, but the bonds are sold worldwide. Some of these bonds offer currency options, which allow the buyer to demand repayment in one of several currencies. This can reduce the exchange risk inherent in a single-currency foreign bond. Corporate Eurobonds have become more popular with investors in recent years because many of them offer a convertibility option that allows the holder to convert the bond into common stock. Another reason that the Eurobond market has become a popular source of funds is that the market is relatively unregulated, so there is little red tape associated with floating an issue. Also, the fact that the issue transcends national boundaries allows the underwriters to create offerings that appeal to a wide geographic segment rather than just a specific national market. Increasingly, US firms are offering nondollar Eurobonds in an effort to tap available international money sources.

ACTIVE LEARNING CHECK

Review your answer to Active Learning Case question 4 and make any changes you like. Then compare your answer to the one below.

4. How are US firms located in Japan able to profit from the appreciation of the Japanese yen?

US firms operating in Japan do business in the local currency. So if the value of the yen increases 10 per cent against the dollar, the value of Japanese assets will increase by a similar percentage. For example, if a firm bought land for 10 million yen for a new plant site last year and sold the land today for the same price, it would still have made a 10 per cent profit when valued in dollars since the yen is worth 10 per cent more than when the initial purchase was made. Moreover, company profits in Japan will result in higher earnings for the MNE when it converts these yen into dollars in computing the annual income. For example, if the subsidiary earned a profit of $1 million before the yen increased in value, the profit would now be $1.1 million. So US firms doing business in Japan do indeed profit from a strengthening of the yen.

SUMMARY

Key points

1. The balance of payments (BOP) is the record of the value of all transactions between a country's residents and the rest of the world. There are three broad BOP categories: current account, capital account, and reserves. The current account consists of merchandise trade, services, and unrequited transfers. Capital account items are transactions that involve claims in ownership. Reserves are funds for bringing BOP accounts into balance.

2. The international monetary system is a market among central banks of the countries that belong to the International Monetary Fund (IMF). The IMF's objectives

include the facilitation of balanced growth of international trade, promotion of exchange stability, and the making of financial resources available to the members of the Fund. In recent years the fixed monetary system created by the IMF members in 1944 has been replaced by a managed float system. Currently the IMF faces a number of major problems, including helping third world countries to deal with their international debt crisis and increasing international liquidity.

3. Foreign exchange is any financial instrument that carries out payment from one currency to another. There are three major foreign exchange markets in the United States: interbank, brokers, and forward. The five major groups that are active participants in foreign exchange markets are traders/brokers, speculators, hedgers, arbitrageurs, and governments. Exchange rates are determined by the activities of these five groups. The rates are also influenced by purchasing power parity, interest rates, and technical factors such as national economic statistics and seasonal demands.

4. There are a number of international finance strategies that can be of value to firms doing business overseas. Two of the most important are strategies for managing currency exchange rate risk and strategies for financing international operations.

Key terms

- international finance
- balance of payments (BOP)
- International Monetary Fund (IMF)
- current account
- merchandise trade
- unrequited transfers
- capital account items
- international monetary system
- International Bank for Reconstruction and Development
- World Bank
- special drawing right (SDR)
- European monetary system (EMS)
- foreign exchange
- exchange rate
- spot rate
- forward rate
- cross rate
- foreign exchange traders

- foreign exchange brokers
- speculator
- foreign exchange hedgers
- foreign exchange arbitrageurs
- purchasing power parity (PPP) theory
- Fisher effect
- nominal rate of interest
- real interest rate
- international Fisher effect (IFE)
- exchange risk
- exchange risk avoidance
- exchange risk adaptation
- currency diversification
- Eurocurrency
- Eurodollars
- London Inter-Bank Offered Rate (LIBOR)
- foreign bond
- Eurobond

Review and discussion questions

1. What is meant by the term "balance of payments"?

2. What are the three major accounts in the balance of payments?

3. How would the following transactions be recorded in the IMF balance of payments?
    a. IBM in New York has sold an $8 million mainframe computer to an insurance company in Singapore and has been paid with a check drawn on a Singapore bank.
    b. A private investor in San Francisco has received dividends of $80,000 for stock she holds in a British firm.
    c. The US government has provided $60 million of food and medical supplies for Kurdish refugees in Turkey.
    d. The Walt Disney Company has invested $50 million in a theme park outside Paris, France.

4. What were the original purposes of the International Monetary Fund? How have these purposes changed or been altered?

5. How does the managed float system work? Explain with an illustration.

6. What are two future problems and challenges that will have to be addressed by the international monetary system during the millennium? Describe each.

7. What are the three major foreign exchange markets in the United States? Identify and describe how each works.

8. Who are the most active participants in foreign exchange markets? Identify and describe these groups.

9. How are exchange rates determined? In your answer be sure to include a discussion of the purchasing power parity theory.

10. How can a company manage its currency exchange rate risk? Identify and describe three strategies that can be employed.

11. How can a US firm obtain funds in the international money markets? Include in your answer a discussion of Eurocurrencies and Eurobonds.

REAL CASES

HONG KONG AND SHANGHAI BANK: WORLD NUMBER ONE

What is the world's largest bank? Prior to the merger of Citicorp and Travellers in 1998, it was the Hong Kong and Shanghai Banking Corporation (HSBC). Formed in 1865 by a Scotsman in the then British Colony of Hong Kong, HSBC grew to over 5,000 bank offices in 78 countries by 1997. In the process it became the world's first truly global bank, offering a full range of financial services from retail to corporate banking to insurance and financial management. HSBC built this global business based on its strong Hong Kong base. The bank owns Hong Kong Bank and most of Hang Seng Bank, giving it over 40 per cent of the market in the now Hong Kong Special Administrative Region of China that was created on July 1, 1997.

Perhaps less well known is that HSBC is also the owner of the former Midland Bank chain in Britain, the Marine Midland banks in the United States, and the Hong Kong Bank of Canada. It has also acquired large banks in Latin America including Banco Bamerindus in Brazil and Grupo Financiero Serfin in Mexico. In all these cases HSBC greatly improved the efficiency of the underperforming local banks through better systems and processes.

Today HSBC is now well developed across the triad regions of Asia, Europe and the Americas. Its diversification strategy helped to insulate it from the Asian financial crisis of 1997–98. And its first mover advantage as a truly global bank will prove hard to match by banks in the still regulated markets of North America and Europe. There is constant pressure in banking to reduce costs through greater scale economies and improved information technology, and HSBC is well positioned to continue as an industry leader because of its successful globalization strategy.

▶

In retrospect, the world's largest bank came from one of the world's smallest economies. And it did this despite the regulatory barriers to entry for foreign-owned firms in Europe and North America. As a result the HSBC is an example of a bank using modern management systems and market forces to win out over old fashioned protectionism in a highly regulated worldwide industry.

1. If the HSBC were to do business with the People's Republic of China and have substantial holdings of Chinese yuan (renminbi) on hand, what risk might this pose for the bank?

2. How would a devaluation of the Hong Kong dollar impact on the HSBC?

3. How could the HSBC manage its currency exchange rate risk?

Sources: "An Empire at Risk: HSBC," *The Economist*, September 7, 1996; S. Kahn, "The Future of Global Banks," *Global Finance*, May 1998, p. 28; and W. Green, "Bland – and Proud of It," *Forbes*, July 14, 1997, p. 94.

THE MEXICO PESO CRISIS

In late 1994 Mexico suffered one of the worst financial crises in its history. In less than one month the Mexican peso devaluated from 3.45 to the US dollar to 5.57 to the dollar; by the end of 1995 the peso was trading at about 6.5 to the dollar. This was accompanied by heavy inflation, unemployment, and a severe stock market crash. Some critics claimed that all of this was a result of NAFTA, but this was not so. It was caused by the Mexican government which had liberalized trade and financial flows, but had not allowed the peso to float. Moreover, previous governments had kept the peso overvalued. As a result, in less than one year Mexico's foreign reserves were depleted by 75 per cent and the country's current account deficit was equal to 8 per cent of GDP.

Other factors also contributed to the low real price of the peso. For instance, as a result of the Zapatist armed rebellion in Chiapas, in southern Mexico, both foreign and Mexican investors took tens of millions of dollars out of the country. The difficulties of the new government of Ernesto Zedillo also contributed to the panic.

The peso crisis had far-reaching consequences. Other Latin American countries were affected as investors, fearing a similar crash, withdrew from these economies. Foreign investors from industrial countries, particularly the United States, saw their investments plummet.

One unexpected development of the Mexican peso crisis was the devaluation of the Canadian dollar which was sideswiped by the Latin American currency crisis. Thanks to NAFTA, Canada and Mexico had become linked in the international currency markets. At the same time international investors began showing a preference for the US dollar against both the Mexican peso and the Canadian dollar.

Perhaps the most surprising thing about the peso crisis was how quickly the country bounded back. With the help of a $50 billion loan from the US and other countries, a tough economic reform that saw cuts in government spending, and increases in deregulation and privatization, the Mexican economy began to revive. Hardly a year had passed when investors who were running from the region were quickly lured back by short-term interest rates of up to 40 per cent. Additionally, the stock market crash had led to underpriced shares and investors began buying these issues and driving the prices back up. Today the financial crisis of 1995 in Mexico is a thing of the past. The economy is healthy and investors are back. At the same time, however, there are some critics who believe that the turnaround will be short-lived because the government will not continue making the necessary changes to sustain growth. For the moment, at least, they are in the minority.

1. How does a decrease in the value of the Mexican peso affect foreign direct investment?

2. How is trade affected by the devaluation of the peso?

3. How are customers in Mexico affected by the devaluation of the peso?

Sources: "The Egg on Zedillo's Face," *The Economist*, January 7, 1995; "Pounding the Peso," *The Economist*, November 18, 1995; Richard D. Hylton, "Mexico's Hangover Fades," *Fortune*, February 5, 1996; Alan M. Rugman, "The Northern Peso," *The G7 Report*, vol. 4, no. 1; http://sddt.com/files/librarywire/DN95_12_20_1j.html.

ENDNOTES

1. Susan Moffat, "Picking Japan's Research Brains," *Fortune*, March 25, 1991, pp. 84–96.
2. Jonathan Moore and Moon Ihlwan, "Cheaper Exports? Not So Fast," *Business Week*, February 2, 1998, pp. 48–49.
3. Christopher Farrell et al., "At Last, Good News," *Business Week*, June 3, 1991, pp. 24–25.
4. At the same time, there is investment the other way as seen in Carla Rapoport, "The New US Push into Europe," *Fortune*, January 10, 1994, pp. 73–74.
5. See, for example, Andrew Pollack, "Japan's Trade Surplus Leaps, Putting Pressure on Clinton," *New York Times*, January 23, 1993, pp. 1, 21.
6. Barnaby J. Feder, "Motorola, Long a Proponent of Sanctions Against Japan," *New York Times*, February 15, 1994, p. C2.
7. See, for example, Marcus Brauchli, "China Is Facing Trade Deficit, Raising Fears," *Wall Street Journal*, December 15, 1993, p. A11.
8. Also, see Peter Passell, "Big Trade Deficit with Japan: Some Think It's No Problem," *New York Times*, February 15, 1994, pp. A1, C2.
9. "From Here to EMU," *The Economist*, August 5, 1995, p. 72.
10. Thomas Kamm, "French Labor Unrest, Austerity Budget Renews Doubts About Monetary Union," *Wall Street Journal*, September 21, 1996, p. A21.
11. For some additional insights, see Edmund Faltermayer, "Does Japan Play Fair?" *Fortune*, September 7, 1992, pp. 38–52.
12. Stefan H. Robock and Kenneth Simmonds, *International Business and Multinational Enterprises*, 4th ed. (Homewood, Ill.: Irwin, 1989), p. 108.
13. See, for example, Keith Bradsher, "US Panel Urges Setting Export Target Levels," *New York Times*, February 12, 1993, pp. C1, 7.
14. For more on this topic, see Bruce G. Resnick, "The Globalization of World Financial Markets," *Business Horizons*, November–December 1990, pp. 34–41.

ADDITIONAL BIBLIOGRAPHY

Abdallah, Wagdy M. "How to Motivate and Evaluate Managers with an International Transfer Pricing System," *Management International Review*, vol. 29, no. 1 (First Quarter 1989).

Aggarwal, Raj and Soenen, Luc A. "Managing Persistent Real Changes in Currency Values: The Role of Multinational Operating Strategies," *Columbia Journal of World Business*, vol. 24, no. 3 (Fall 1989).

Al-Eryani, Mohammad F.; Alam, Pervaiz; and Akhter, Syed H. "Transfer Pricing Determinants of US Multinationals," *Journal of International Business Studies*, vol. 21, no. 3 (Third Quarter 1990).

Bhide, Amar. "Bootstrap Finance: The Art of Start-Ups," *Harvard Business Review*, vol. 70, no. 6 (November/December 1992).

Brewer, H. L. "Components of Investment Risk and Return: The Effects on Common Shareholders from Firm Level International Involvement," *Management International Review*, vol. 29, no. 1 (First Quarter 1989).

Carstens, Agustin. "Foreign Exchange and Monetary Policy in Mexico," *Columbia Journal of World Business*, vol. 29, no. 2 (Summer 1994).

Choi, Jongmoo Jay. "Diversification, Exchange Risk, and Corporate International Investment," *Journal of International Business Studies*, vol. 20, no. 1 (Spring 1989).

Daly, Donald J. "Porter's Diamond and Exchange Rates," *Management International Review*, vol. 33, no. 2 (Second Quarter 1993).

Damanpour, Faramarz. "Global Banking: Developments in the Market Structure and Activities of Foreign Banks in the United States," *Columbia Journal of World Business*, vol. 26, no. 3 (Fall 1991).

Finnerty, Joseph E; Owers, James; and Creran, Francis J. "Foreign Exchange Forecasting and Leading Economic Indicators: The US–Canadian Experience," *Management International Review*, vol. 27, no. 2 (Second Quarter 1987).

George, Abraham M. and Schroth, C. William. "Managing Foreign Exchange for Competitive Advantage," *Sloan Management Review*, vol. 32, no. 2 (Winter 1991).

Hale, David D. "Global Finance and the Retreat to Managed Trade," *Harvard Business Review*, vol. 68, no. 1 (January/February 1990).

Hartmann, Mark A. and Khambata, Dara. "Emerging Stock Markets: Investment Strategies of the Future," *Columbia Journal of World Business*, vol. 28, no. 2 (Summer 1993).

Holden, Alfred C. "The Reposition of Ex-Im Bank," *Columbia Journal of World Business*, vol. 31, no. 1 (Spring 1996).

Kanas, Angelos. "Exchange Rate Economic Exposure when Market Share Matters and Hedging Using Currency Options," *Management International Review*, vol. 36, no. 1 (1996).

Khanna, Ashok. "Equity Investment Projects in Emerging Markets," *Columbia Journal of World Business*, vol. 31, no. 2 (Summer 1996).

Kish, Richard J. and Vasconcellos, Geraldo M. "An Empirical Analysis of Factors Affecting Cross-Border Acquisitions: US–Japan," *Management International Review*, vol. 33, no. 3 (Third Quarter 1993).

Kleiman, Gary and Morrissey, Elizabeth R. "African Equity Markets: Testing Latin America's Path," *Columbia Journal of World Business*, vol. 29, no. 2 (Summer 1994).

Kryzanowski, Lawrence and Ursel, Nancy D. "Market Reaction to the Formation of Export Trading Companies by American Banks," *Journal of International Business Studies*, vol. 24, no. 2 (Second Quarter 1993).

Kwok, Chuck C. Y. and Brooks, LeRoy D. "Examining Event Study Methodologies in Foreign Exchange Market," *Journal of International Business Studies*, vol. 21, no. 2 (Second Quarter 1990).

Kwok, Chuck C. Y. and Lubecke, Thomas H. "Composite Foreign Exchange Forecasting to Managers of Multinational Corporations," *Management International Review*, vol. 28, no. 4 (Fourth Quarter 1988).

Kwok, Chuck C. Y. and Lubecke, Thomas H. "Improving the 'Correctness' of Foreign Exchange Forecasts Through Composite Forecasting," *Management International Review*, vol. 30, no. 4 (Fourth Quarter 1990).

Lee, Kwang Chul and Kwok, Chuck C. Y. "Multinational Corporations vs. Domestic Corporations: International Environmental Factors and Determinants of Capital Structure," *Journal of International Business Studies*, vol. 19, no. 2 (Summer 1988).

Luehrman, Timothy A. "The Exchange Rate Exposure of a Global Competitor," *Journal of International Business Studies*, vol. 21, no. 2 (Second Quarter 1990).

Luehrman, Timothy A. "Exchange Rate Changes and the Distribution of Industry Value," *Journal of International Business Studies*, vol. 22, no. 4 (Fourth Quarter 1991).

Luehrman, Timothy A. "Financial Engineering at Merck," *Harvard Business Review*, vol. 72, no. 1 (January/February 1994).

Nichols, Nancy A. "Efficient? Chaotic? What's the New Finance?" *Harvard Business Review*, vol. 71, no. 2 (March/April 1993).

Oxelheim, Lars and Wihlborg, Clas G. "Corporate Strategies in a Turbulent World Economy," *Management International Review*, vol. 31, no. 4 (1991).

Prywes, Menahem. "The Good Work of Financial Crises," *Columbia Journal of World Business*, vol. 27, no. 1 (Spring 1992).

Rada, Juan and Trisoglio, Alex. "Capital Markets and Sustainable Development," *Columbia Journal of World Business*, vol. 27, no. 3, 4 (Fall/Winter 1992).

Strange, Susan. *Mad Money* (Manchester: Manchester University Press, 1998).

Weisman, Lorenzo "The Advent of Private Equity in Latin America," *Columbia Journal of World Business*, vol. 31, no. 1 (Spring 1996).

INTERNATIONAL BUSINESS STRATEGIES

PART ONE: THE WORLD OF INTERNATIONAL BUSINESS

Chapter 1 Introduction	Chapter 2 MNEs	Chapter 3 Triad

PART TWO: THE ENVIRONMENT OF INTERNATIONAL BUSINESS

Chapter 4 Political Environment	Chapter 5 Cultural Environment	Chapter 6 Economic Environment	Chapter 7 Financial Environment

PART THREE: INTERNATIONAL BUSINESS STRATEGIES

Chapter 8 Strategic Planning	Chapter 9 Organizing Strategy	Chapter 10 Production Strategy	Chapter 11 Marketing Strategy

Chapter 12 Human Resource Strategy	Chapter 13 Political Risk/Negotiation	Chapter 14 Financial Strategy

PART FOUR: INTERNATIONAL BUSINESS STRATEGIES IN ACTION
To do Business in International Markets Including:

Chapter 15 Corporate Strategy/National Competitiveness	Chapter 16 EU

Chapter 17 Japan	Chapter 18 North America	Chapter 19 Non-Triad Nations

PART FIVE: INTERNATIONAL BUSINESS HORIZONS

Chapter 20 Future of International Business

CHAPTER 8

Global Strategic Planning

OBJECTIVES OF THE CHAPTER

Multinational enterprises operate in two or more countries. Because of the complexity of this environment, it is particularly important for these MNEs to have well-formulated strategic plans. Large MNEs will conduct a very thorough analysis of their environments and often develop detailed, comprehensive plans for coordinating overall activities. These plans will set forth objectives for all major divisions and units and will provide for systematic follow-up and evaluation. Smaller MNEs will use less sophisticated plans. However, all multinationals that conduct strategic planning will use a three-step process in their plans: formulation, implementation, and control. The objectives of this chapter are to:

1. **Define** the term *"strategic planning"* and discuss the strategic orientations that affect this planning process.

2. **Explain** how strategy is formulated, giving particular emphasis to external and internal environmental assessment.

3. **Describe** how strategy is implemented, with particular attention to location, ownership decisions, and functional area implementation.

4. **Discuss** the ways in which MNEs control and evaluate their strategies.

ACTIVE LEARNING CASE

Mazda: moving into the big leagues

Mazda is the fourth largest auto firm in Japan. Its 6 per cent market share puts it behind Honda (10 per cent) and the two industry giants, Toyota (43 per cent) and Nissan (25 per cent). In fact, Mazda managed 47 per cent growth in 1990. Mazda is on the move – and it is not restricting itself to the Japanese market. The company currently holds 2.5 per cent of the US market but is tailoring a strategy that may make it the number one Japanese automaker in the country.

Mazda's strategy has two parts. First, the company is developing new products for the market. Second, it is building alliances with other automakers. For years Mazda survived with a limited product line, relying most heavily on its midsize 323 sedan, called the "Familia" in Japan. Now the company has rolled out a broader line of products, including the MPV (a minivan), the Carol (a minicar), and the Eunos Roadster (a small convertible). Mazda has introduced a more luxurious 929 sedan in the US market. The company has enhanced its 323 sedan by adding more power and a plusher interior. It has priced the 323 below competitive models. As a result, Mazda is doing very well in Japan, and the company has plans to introduce four to six more cars over the next two years, which should help it to maintain this sales momentum.

At the same time the company is putting together strategic alliances with other automakers. For example, Mazda has a joint venture with Ford which provides it with a wide range of imports, including the Ford Festiva, Probe, and Thunderbird for sale in Japan, and its agreement with Ford and Sanyo allows the company to make car radios in Malaysia. The firm also has arrangements with Fiat (Italy) and Citroën (France) that provide it with additional products to sell. Mazda's goal is to use these imports to help boost market share in Japan. Mazda is also looking for joint ventures in Europe. The firm would like to build a production plant there and is currently talking to several European manufacturers.

The company is also pumping money into the US market to increase the number of dealerships. Commenting on the competitiveness of the US auto market and the difficulty of gaining and keeping market share, the president of Mazda recently noted, "Our asset is our ten-year association with Ford, something our competitors don't have. Cooperation will be the future of our industry, and in this area we are way ahead." Quite clearly Mazda is moving into the big leagues, and the firm intends to get there with a strategy that is built on a wide variety of approaches, including new product development, joint ventures, and strategic alliances. As the Japanese economy continued its slow down in 1998 and the US economy remained strong, Mazda found both its US and market shares increasing. A weakening Japanese yen and effective cost cutting were proving to be successful strategies for the firm.

Sources: Carla Rapoport, "Mazda's Bold New Global Strategy," *Fortune*, December 17, 1990, pp. 109–113; Doron P. Levin, "Mazda Said to Plan Shift in Top Roles," *New York Times*, February 5, 1993, p. C3; Alex Taylor III, "Japan's Automakers: A Controlled Skid?" *Fortune*, May 17, 1993, p. 12; Lisa Schuchman, "Honda, Mazda Post Strong Profits for Six Months Amid Weaker Yen," *Wall Street Journal*, November 13, 1998, p. A17; *http://www.e.mazda.co.jp/Mazda/Brief/no1.html*.

1. Given the competitiveness of the environment, how much opportunity exists for Mazda in the international automobile market?
2. What type of generic strategy does Mazda employ? Defend your answer.
3. What forms of ownership arrangement is Mazda using to gain world market share? Explain.
4. On what basis would a firm like Mazda evaluate performance? Identify and describe two.

INTRODUCTION

Strategic planning is the process of evaluating the enterprise's environment and its internal strengths, next identifying long- and short-range objectives, and then implementing a plan of action for attaining these goals. Multinational enterprises (MNEs) rely heavily on this process because it provides them with both general direction and specific guidance in carrying out their activities. Without a strategic plan, these enterprises would have great difficulty in planning, implementing, and evaluating operations. With strategic planning, however, research shows that many MNEs have been able to increase their profitability.[1] For example, in recent years Ford Motor has been very successful in both gaining market share and generating high profits in Europe. This success is due in large part to the firm's ability to formulate and implement a plan of new car introductions coupled with state-of-the-art engineering and design, improved performance quality, and careful cost control. As a result of this strategic planning, Ford is finding Europe to be one of its most lucrative markets.

STRATEGIC ORIENTATIONS

Before examining the strategic planning process, we must realize that MNEs have strategic predispositions toward doing things in a particular way. This predisposition helps determine the specific decisions the firm will implement. There are four such predispositions: ethnocentric, polycentric, regiocentric, and geocentric. Table 8.1 lists each predisposition and its characteristics.

An MNE with an **ethnocentric predisposition** will rely on the values and interests of the parent company in formulating and implementing the strategic plan. Primary emphasis will be given to profitability and the firm will try to run operations abroad the way they are run at home. This predisposition is used most commonly by firms trying to sell the same product abroad that they sell at home.

An MNE with a **polycentric predisposition** will tailor its strategic plan to meet the needs of a local culture. If the firm is doing business in more than one culture, the overall plan will be adapted to reflect these individual needs. The basic mission of a polycentric MNE is to be accepted by the local culture and to blend into the country. Each subsidiary will decide the objectives it will pursue, based on local needs. Profits will be put back into the country in the form of expansion and growth.

An MNE with a **regiocentric predisposition** will be interested in obtaining both profit and public acceptance (a combination of the ethnocentric and polycentric approaches) and will use a strategy that allows it to address both local and regional needs. The company is less focused on a particular country than on a geographic region. For example, an MNE doing business in the EU will be interested in all the member nations.

An MNE with a **geocentric predisposition** will view operations on a global basis. The largest international corporations often use this approach. They will produce global products with local variations and will staff their offices with the best people they can find, regardless of country of origin. Multinationals, in the true meaning of the word, have a geocentric predisposition. However, it is possible for an MNE to have

Table 8.1 Typical strategic orientations of MNEs

MNE orientation	Ethnocentric	Polycentric	Regiocentric	Geocentric
Company's basic mission	Profitability	Public acceptance (legitimacy)	Both profitability and public acceptance	Both profitability and public acceptance
Type of governance	Top down	Bottom up (each local unit sets objectives)	Mutually negotiated between the region and its subsidiaries	Mutually negotiated at all levels of the organization
Strategy	Global integration	National responsiveness	Regional integration and national responsiveness	Global integration and national responsiveness
Structure	Hierarchical product divisions	Hierarchical area divisions with autonomous national units	Product and regional organization tied together through a matrix structure	A network of organizations (in some cases this includes stockholders and competitors)
Culture	Home country	Host country	Regional	Global
Technology	Mass production	Batch production	Flexible manufacturing	Flexible manufacturing
Marketing strategy	Product development is determined primarily by the needs of the home country customers	Local product development based on local needs	Standardized within the region, but not across regions	Global products with local variations
Profit strategy	Profits are brought back to the home country	Profits are kept in the host country	Profits are redistributed within the region	Redistribution is done on a global basis
Human resource management practices	Overseas operations are managed by people from the home country	Local nationals are used in key management positions	Regional people are developed for key managerial positions anywhere in the region	The best people anywhere in the world are developed for key positions everywhere in the world

Source: Adapted from Balaji S. Chakravarthy and Howard V. Perlmutter, "Strategic Planning for a Global Business," *Columbia Journal of World Business*, Summer 1985, pp. 5–6. Based on some of Perlmutter's earlier work.

a polycentric or regiocentric predisposition if the company is moderately small or limits operations to specific cultures or geographic regions.

The predisposition of an MNE will greatly influence its strategic planning process. For example, some MNEs are more interested in profit and/or growth than they are in developing a comprehensive corporate strategy that exploits their strengths.[2] Some are more interested in large-scale manufacturing that will allow them to compete on a price basis across the country or region, as opposed to developing a high degree of responsiveness to local demand and tailoring a product to these specific market niches.[3] Some prefer to sell in countries where the cultures are similar to their own so that the same basic marketing orientation can be used throughout the regions.[4] These orientations or predispositions will greatly influence the strategy.[5]

STRATEGY FORMULATION

Strategy formulation is the process of evaluating the enterprise's environment and its internal strengths. This typically begins with consideration of the external arena since the MNE will first be interested in opportunities that can be exploited. Then attention will be directed to the internal environment and the resources the organization has available, or can develop, to take advantage of these opportunities.

External environmental assessment

The analysis of the external environment involves two activities: information gathering and information assessment. These steps help to answer two key questions: What is going on in the external environment? How will these developments affect our company?[6]

Information gathering   Information gathering is a critical phase of international strategic planning. Unfortunately, not all firms recognize this early enough. In the case of Harley-Davidson, the large US-based motorcycle manufacturer, it was not until the Japanese began dominating the motorcycle market that Harley realized its problem. A systematic analysis of the competition revealed that the major reason for Japanese success in the US market was the high quality of their products, a result of extremely efficient manufacturing techniques. Today Harley is competitive again. It achieved renewed success because it rethought its basic business, reformulated company strategy, vastly improved product quality, and rededicated itself to the core business: heavy-weight motorcycles.

There are a number of ways that MNEs conduct an environmental scan and then forecast the future. Four of the most common methods include (1) asking experts in the industry to discuss industry trends and to make projections about the future, (2) using historical industry trends to forecast future developments, (3) asking knowledgeable managers to write scenarios describing what they foresee for the industry over the next two to three years, and (4) using computers to simulate the industry environment and to generate likely future developments. Of these, expert opinion is the most commonly used.[7] The Japanese and the South Koreans provide excellent examples. Mitsubishi has over 700 employees in New York City whose primary objective is to gather information on American competitors and markets. Similar strategies are employed by all large Japanese corporations operating in the United States. The same is true for large South Korean trading firms, who require their branch managers to send back information on market developments. These data are then analyzed and used to help formulate future strategies for the firms.

This information helps MNEs to identify competitor strengths and weaknesses and to target areas for attack. This approach is particularly important when a company is delivering a product or service for many market niches around the world that are too small to be individually profitable. In such situations the MNE has to identify a series of different niches and to attempt to market successfully in each of these geographic areas.[8] The information is also critical to those firms that will be coming under attack.

INTERNATIONAL BUSINESS STRATEGY IN ACTION

Arthur Andersen and McKinsey

One rapidly growing type of global organization is the professional service firm that specializes in areas such as consulting, accounting, publishing, law, public relations, advertising, and so on. Today there are strong globalization pressures to link separate country offices of these firms in order to provide a seamless service to multinational clients. Good examples are provided by Arthur Andersen and McKinsey, two major international consulting companies.

Arthur Andersen started in Chicago in 1913 as an accounting firm and by 1998 had grown to 60,000 people in 363 offices in 72 countries. By then the firm's audit and accounting services were matched by its global management and technology consulting group – Andersen Consulting. Today Arthur Andersen has created a "knowledge sharing network" to link its country offices. This consists of a set of online Internet database sites with useful public information, propriety information on clients, projects and industries, and global best practices.

Another major international consulting firm is McKinsey & Company, which started in Chicago in

1926. Today the firm has 76 offices worldwide and generates 60 per cent of its revenue from outside the United States. The company's core strength is its brand name built on the in-house training and management of highly skilled people from the top business schools. Additionally, there is continuous personnel learning through team-based project work.

Both Arthur Andersen and McKinsey, along with the other leading global consulting firms, seek to secure long-term relationships with large MNEs and other global organizations. Their firm-specific advantage is built on their brand name and reputation for quality. They also have links to the best university business schools, whose faculty provide "thought leadership" which the consulting firm then translates into useful advice for clients.

As globalization continues, the demand for high quality and responsive consulting firms will also grow. At the same time each of these firms will have to continue developing and maintaining a differentiated service that gives attention to clients, in-house training, and personnel development.

Sources: Andersen Worldwide 1996 Annual Report; Anonymous, "Arthur Andersen Legal Link-up Confirmed," *Accountancy*, April 1998, vol. 121, no. 1256; Anonymous, "DREF, Arthur Andersen Form Partnership," *Industrial Distribution*, vol. 86, no. 9, September 1997; Anonymous, "Arthur Andersen and Stephen Shortell Form Global Health Care Industry Alliance," *Health Care Strategic Management*, vol. 15, no. 11, November 1997; Anonymous, "Andersen/Garrigues Merger Is Completed," *International Financial Law Review*, vol. 16, no. 3, March 1997; Anonymous, "AW Battle Could Take Years," *Accountancy*, vol. 121, no. 1257, May 1998; C. A. Bartlett (1996), *McKinsey & Company: Managing Knowledge and Learning*, Harvard Business School Case No. 9-396-357; http://www.mckinsey.com; http://www/mckinsey.com/about/feet_on_the_street.html.

Information assessment Having gathered information on the competition and the industry, MNEs will then assess the data.[9] One of the most common approaches is to make an overall assessment based on the five forces that determine industry competitiveness – buyers, suppliers, potential new entrants to the industry, the availability of substitute goods and services, and rivalry among the competitors.[10] Figure 8.1 shows the connections among these forces.[11]

Bargaining power of buyers MNEs will examine the power of their buyers because they will want to predict the likelihood of maintaining these customers. If the firm believes buyers may be moving their business to competitors, the MNE will want to formulate a strategy for countering this move. For example, the company may offer a lower price or increase the amount of service it provides.

Bargaining power of suppliers An MNE will look at the power of the industry's suppliers to see if it can gain a competitive advantage here.[12] For example, if there are a number of suppliers in the industry, the MNE may attempt to play them off

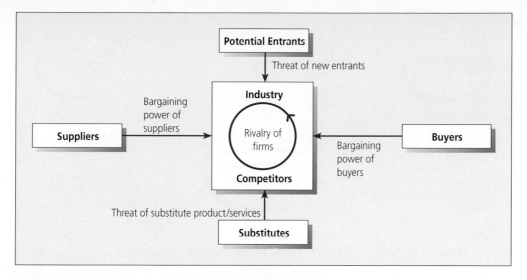

Figure 8.1 The five forces of industry competitiveness

Source: Michael Porter, *Competitive Strategy* (New York: Free Press, 1980), p. 4.

against each other in an effort to get a lower price. Or the company may move to eliminate any threat from the suppliers by acquiring one of them, thus guaranteeing itself a ready source of inputs.

The new entrants   The company will examine the likelihood of new firms entering the industry and will try to determine the impact they might have on the MNE. Two typical ways that international MNEs attempt to reduce the threat of new entrants are by (1) keeping costs low and consumer loyalty high and (2) encouraging the government to limit foreign business activity through regulation such as duties, tariffs, quotas, and other protective measures.

The threat of substitutes   The MNE will look at the availability of substitute goods and services and try to anticipate when such offerings will reach the market. There are a number of steps that the company will take to offset this competitive force, including (1) lowering prices, (2) offering similar products, and (3) increasing services to the customer.

Rivalry   The MNE will examine the rivalry that currently exists between itself and the competition and seek to anticipate future changes in this arrangement.[13] Common strategies for maintaining and/or increasing market strength include (1) offering new goods and services, (2) increasing productivity and thus reducing overall costs, (3) working to differentiate current goods and services from those of the competition, (4) increasing overall quality of goods and services, and (5) targeting specific niches with a well-designed market strategy.

As the MNE examines each of these five forces, it will decide the attractiveness and unattractiveness of each. This will help the company to decide how and where to make strategic changes. Figure 8.2 shows the five forces model applied to the semiconductor industry.

Notice in Figure 8.2 that the suppliers in the semiconductor industry, at the time this analysis was conducted, were not very powerful, so this was an attractive force for the MNE. Buyers did not have many substitute products from which to choose (an attractive development), but there was some backward integration toward

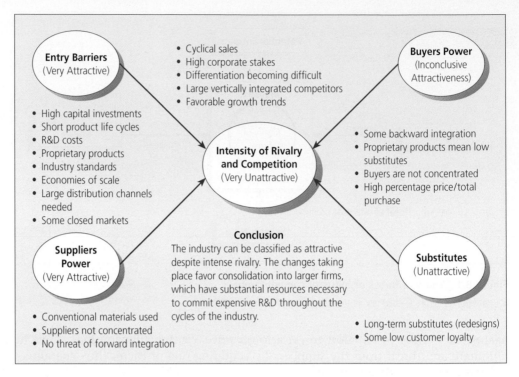

Figure 8.2   The five forces model applied to the semiconductor industry

Source: Scott Beardsley and Kinji Sakagami, *Advanced Micro Devices: Poised for Chip Greatness*, unpublished student paper, Sloan School of Management, MIT, 1988. Reported in Arnoldo C. Hax and Nicolas S. Majluf, *The Strategy Concept and Process: A Pragmatic Approach* (Englewood Cliffs, NJ: Prentice-Hall, 1991), p. 46.

purchasing their own sources of supply (an unattractive development). Overall, the attractiveness of buyer power was regarded as inconclusive. The third force, entry barriers, was quite attractive because of the high costs of getting into the industry and the short product life cycles that existed there. It was very difficult for a company to enter this market. The fourth force, substitutes, was unattractive because new products were being developed continually and customer loyalty was somewhat low. The fifth and final force, industry rivalry, was also unattractive because of the high cost of doing business, the cyclical nature of sales, and the difficulty of differentiating one's products from those of the competition.

On an overall basis, however, the industry was classified as attractive. It also appeared that the industry would see consolidation of smaller firms into larger firms that would have greater resources to commit to research and development.

MNEs operating in the semiconductor industry would use this analysis to help them increase the attractiveness of those forces that currently are not highly attractive. For example, they could work to develop state-of-the-art semiconductors that might be substituted for the competition's products, and they would attempt to maintain a technological advantage so that the substitute force would not become a problem for them. In the process they would likely be better able to increase their power over the buyers since their products would be so high tech that the customers could not do better by purchasing from a competitor. In summary, environmental assessment, such as that provided by an analysis of competitive forces, is used to determine MNE opportunities and threats and to help identify strategies for improving market position and profitability.

ACTIVE LEARNING CHECK

Review your answer to Active Learning Case question 1 and make any changes you like. Then compare your answer to the one below.

1. Given the competitiveness of the environment, how much opportunity exists for Mazda in the international automobile market?

There is a great deal of opportunity in the international auto market for Mazda if it can continue to develop new, attractive products and maintain international alliances with other major players in the industry. Two of the biggest problems faced by auto companies are new product offerings, which provide substitutes and thus weaken the firm's market appeal, and oversupply, which results in the customer gaining advantage over the seller. Mazda's new offerings and strategic alliances should be useful in dealing with these two major problems.

Internal environmental assessment

The internal environmental assessment helps to pinpoint MNE strengths and weaknesses. There are two specific areas that a multinational will examine in this assessment: (1) physical resources and personnel competencies and (2) the way in which value chain analysis can be used to bring these resources together in the most synergistic and profitable manner.

Physical resources and personnel competencies   The physical resources are the assets that the MNE will use to carry out the strategic plan. Many of these are reported on the balance sheet as reflected by the firm's cash, inventory, machinery, and equipment accounts. However, this does not tell the whole story. The location and disposition of these resources is also important. For example, an MNE with manufacturing plants on three continents may be in a much better position to compete worldwide than a competitor whose plants are all located in one geographic area. Location can also affect cost. Until a few years ago it was possible for Japanese steel makers to sell their product in the United States at a lower price than could their US competitors. However, since then the United States has improved its steel-producing technology and built small minimills that are highly efficient. Today, because of the costs of shipping the steel across the Pacific, the Japanese no longer have a cost advantage in the United States.

Another important consideration is the degree of integration that exists within the operating units of the MNE. Large companies, in particular, tend to be divided into **strategic business units (SBUs)**. These are operating units with their own strategic space; they produce and sell goods and services to a market segment and have a well-defined set of competitors.[14] SBUs are sometimes referred to as "businesses within the business." Mitsubishi, the giant Japanese conglomerate, has a host of SBUs that constitute its corporate network. These include steel making, auto production, electronics, and banking. So when a Mitsubishi SBU that manufactures and sells consumer goods is looking for help with financing, it can turn to the banking SBU. If the bank finds that a customer needs a firm to produce a particular electronics product, it can refer the buyer to the electronics SBU.

In fact, many large MNEs own assets that allow them to handle almost everything involved in producing a good or service and delivering it to the customer, known as **vertical integration**. Many large Japanese manufacturing firms, in particular, have moved toward vertical integration by purchasing controlling interests in their suppliers.[15] The objective is to obtain control over the supply and to ensure that the materials or goods are delivered as needed. Many US and European firms have shied away from this strategy because "captured suppliers" are often less cost effective than independents. For example, a number of years ago *Time* magazine owned the forests for producing the paper it needed. However, the company eventually sold this resource because it found that the cost of making the paper was higher than that charged by large paper manufacturers that specialized in this product. So vertical integration may reduce costs in some instances, but it can be an ineffective strategy in other cases.[16] In particular, one of the major problems with vertical integration is defending oneself from competitors who are less vertically integrated and are able to achieve cost efficiencies as a result.

Personnel competencies are the abilities and talents of the people. An MNE will want to examine these because they reflect the company's strengths and weaknesses. For example, if the firm has an outstanding R&D department, it may be able to develop high-quality, state-of-the-art products. However, if the company has no sales arm, it will sell the output to a firm that can handle the marketing and distribution. Conversely, if a company lacks a strong R&D department but has an international sales force, it may allow the competition to bring out new products and to rely on its own R&D people to reverse engineer them, that is, to find out how they are built and to develop technologies that can do the same thing. This strategy has been used by many internationally based personal computer (PC) firms that have taken PC technology and used it to develop similar, but far less expensive, units that are now beginning to dominate the world market.

An understanding of what one does well can help a company to decide whether the best strategy is to lead or to follow close behind and copy the leader. Not every MNE has the personnel competencies to be first in the field, and many are happy to follow because the investment risk is less and the opportunity for profit is often good.

Value chain analysis A complementary approach to internal environment assessment is an examination of the firm's value chain.[17] A **value chain** is the way in which primary and support activities are combined in providing goods and services and in increasing profit margins. Figure 8.3 provides the general schema of a value chain. The primary activities in this chain include (1) inbound logistics such as receiving, storing, materials handling, and warehouse activities; (2) operations in which inputs are put into final product form by performing activities such as machining, assembling, testing, and packaging; (3) outbound logistics which involves distributing the finished product to the customer; (4) marketing and sales which are used to encourage buyers to purchase the product; and (5) service for maintaining and enhancing the value of the product after the sale through activities such as repair, product adjustment, training, and parts supply. The support activities in the value chain consist of: (1) the firm's infrastructure, which is made up of the company's general management, planning, finance, accounting, legal, government affairs, and quality management areas; (2) human resource management, which is made up of the selection, placement, appraisal, promotion, training, and development of the firm's personnel; (3) technology in the form of knowledge, research and development, and procedures that can

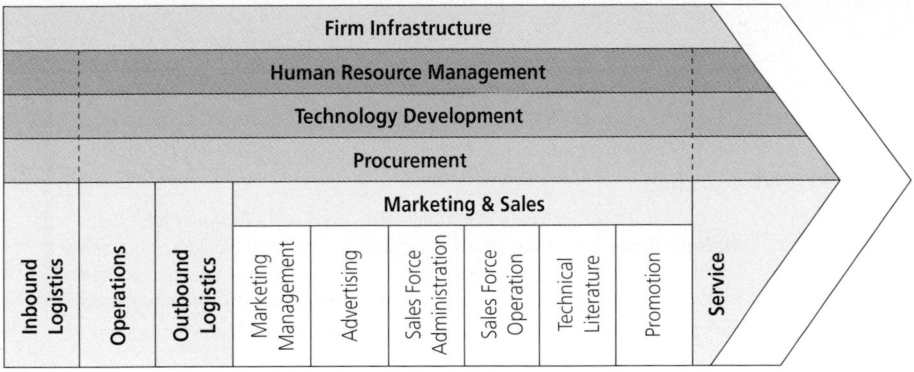

Firm Infrastructure										
Human Resource Management										
Technology Development										
Procurement										
			Marketing & Sales							
Inbound Logistics	Operations	Outbound Logistics	Marketing Management	Advertising	Sales Force Administration	Sales Force Operation	Technical Literature	Promotion		Service

Figure 8.3 A basic value chain

Source: Michael Porter, *Competitive Advantage* (New York: Free Press, 1985), p. 46.

result in improved goods and services; and (4) procurement, which involves the purchasing of raw materials, supplies, and similar goods.

MNEs can use these primary and support activities to increase the value of the goods and services they provide. As such, they form a value chain. An example is provided in Figure 8.4, which helps to explain why IBM has been so effective in the international market. The company combines the primary and support activities so as to increase the value of its products. IBM's alliance with ROLM and MCI and its strengths in software and hardware technologies provide the company with a solid foundation for launching successful strategies in the telecommunications industry.

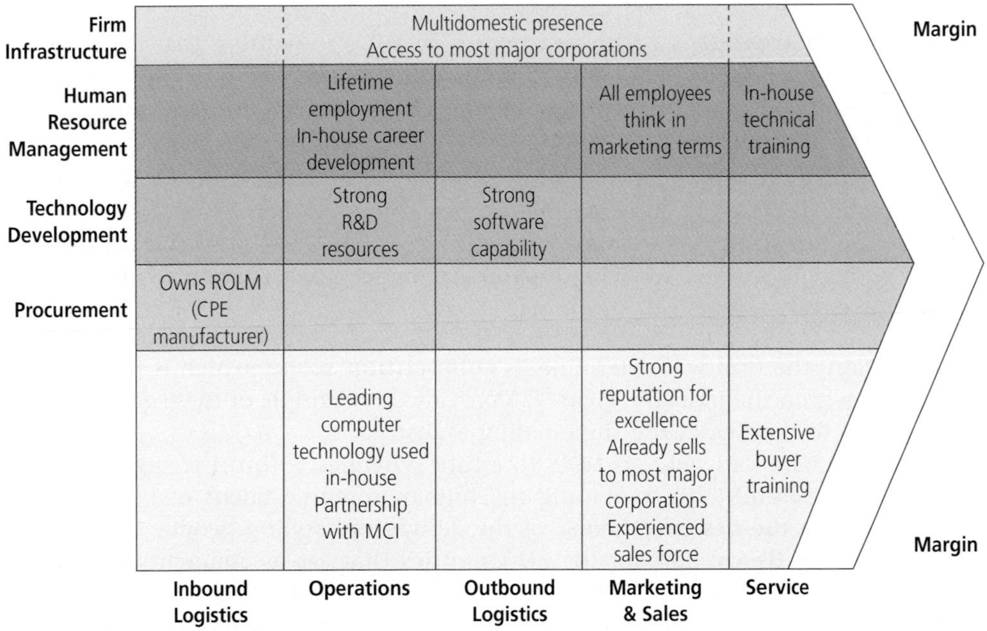

	Inbound Logistics	Operations	Outbound Logistics	Marketing & Sales	Service	
Firm Infrastructure		Multidomestic presence Access to most major corporations				Margin
Human Resource Management		Lifetime employment In-house career development		All employees think in marketing terms	In-house technical training	
Technology Development		Strong R&D resources	Strong software capability			
Procurement	Owns ROLM (CPE manufacturer)					
		Leading computer technology used in-house Partnership with MCI		Strong reputation for excellence Already sells to most major corporations Experienced sales force	Extensive buyer training	Margin

Figure 8.4 The value chain for IBM

Source: Reported in Arnoldo C. Hax and Nicolas S. Majluf, *The Strategy Concept and Process: A Pragmatic Approach* (Englewood Cliffs, NJ: Prentice-Hall, 1991), p. 82.

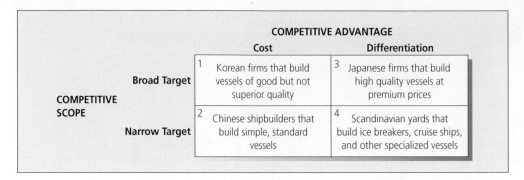

Figure 8.5   Generic strategies in worldwide shipbuilding

Source: Adapted from Michael Porter, *Competitive Advantage* (New York: Free Press, 1985), p. 39.

This idea of a value chain can be applied by any firm. For example, Makita of Japan has become a leading competitor in power tools because it was the first to use new, less expensive materials for making tool parts and to produce in a single plant standardized models that it then sold worldwide.

Analysis of the value chain can also help a company to determine the type of strategy that will be most effective. In all, there are three generic strategies: cost, differentiation, and focus.[18]

1. **Cost strategy** relies on such approaches as aggressive construction of efficient facilities, vigorous pursuit of cost reductions and overhead control, avoidance of marginal customer accounts, and cost minimization in areas like R&D, service, sales, and advertising.

2. **Differentiation strategy** is directed toward creating something that is perceived as being unique. Approaches to differentiation can take many forms, including the creation of design or brand image, improved technology or features, and increased customer service or dealer networks.

3. **Focus strategy** involves concentrating on a particular buyer group and segmenting that niche based on product line or geographic market. While low-cost and differentiation strategies are aimed at achieving objectives industrywide, a focus strategy is built around servicing a particular target market, and each functional policy is developed with this in mind.[19]

In addition, the firm will determine its **competition scope**, which is the breadth of its target within the industry. Figure 8.5 provides an example of these generic strategies applied to the worldwide shipbuilding industry.

The value chain can help an MNE to create synergies within the organization's activities. For example, by combining the human resource talent of its European salespeople with the design expertise of the design and styling people, Ford Motor has been able to design cars for the EU countries that are as competitive as those built by local firms. Similarly, IBM relies heavily on its Swiss R&D facilities to produce technological breakthroughs that can be used in the machines it sells worldwide. By analyzing the ways of combining primary and support activities, MNEs will build a strategy that allows them to use their strengths and to minimize their weaknesses.[20]

ACTIVE LEARNING CHECK

Review your answer to Active Learning Case question 2 and make any changes you like. Then compare your answer to the one below.

2. What type of generic strategy does Mazda employ? Defend your answer.

Mazda uses a focus strategy that is geared toward identifying market niches and meeting the needs of the customers in these target groups. Notice how its different product offerings appeal to different groups. There is the larger, plusher 323, the Carol minicar, and the sporty Eunos Roadster. Each is targeted to a different group based on the company's focus strategy.

Goal setting

The external and internal environmental analyses will provide the MNE with the information needed for setting goals. Some of these goals will be determined during the external analysis, as the company identifies opportunities that it wants to exploit. Others will be finalized after the value chain analysis is complete. In either event one of the outcomes of strategy formulation will be the identification of goals.[21]

There are two basic ways of examining the goals or objectives of international business operations. One is to review them on the basis of operating performance or functional area. Table 8.2 provides an illustration. Some of the major goals will be related to profitability, marketing, production, finance, and human resources. A second way is to examine these goals by geographic area or on an SBU basis. For example, the European group may have a profitability goal of 16 per cent, the North American group's profitability goal may be 17 per cent, and the Pacific Rim group's goal may be 18 per cent. Then there will be accompanying functional goals for marketing,

Table 8.2 Typical goals of an MNE

Profitability	Marketing	Production	Finance	Human resource management
Level of products	Total sales volume	Ratio of foreign to domestic production share	Financing of foreign affiliates – retained earnings or local borrowing	Development of managers with global orientation
Return on assets, investment, equity, sales	Market share – worldwide, region, country	Economies of scale via international production integration	Taxation – minimizing the burden globally	Management development of host country nationals
Annual profit growth	Growth in sales volume			
Annual earnings per share growth	Integration of country markets for marketing efficiency and effectiveness	Quality and cost control	Optimum capital structure	
		Introduction of cost-efficient production methods	Foreign exchange management – minimizing losses from foreign fluctuations	

Source: Adapted from Arvind V. Phatak, *International Dimensions of Management*, 2nd ed. (Boston: PWS Kent Publishing, 1989), p. 72.

production, and finance. If the MNE has SBUs, each strategic business unit in these geographic locales will have its own list of goals.

This approach uses what is called a "cascading effect" because, like a cascade of water rippling down the side of a hill, it reaches the bottom by moving from one level to the next. The MNE will start out by setting a profitability goal for the overall enterprise. Each geographic area or business until will then be assigned a profitability goal which, if attained, will result in the MNE reaching its overall desired profitability. The same approach will be used in other key areas such as marketing, production, and finance. Within each unit, these objectives will then be further subdivided so that every part of the organization understands its objectives and everyone is working toward the same overall goals.

STRATEGY IMPLEMENTATION

Strategy implementation is the process of attaining goals by using the organizational structure to execute the formulated strategy properly. There are many areas of focus in this process. Three of the most important are location, ownership decisions, and functional area implementation. The box "International Business Strategy in Action: Fuji Xerox Saves Xerox" illustrates how these considerations can be used in gaining market entry.[22]

Location

Over the past decade MNEs have greatly expanded their international presence. Some of the areas in which they have begun to set up operations include China, the former Soviet Union, and Eastern Europe.[23]

Location is important for a number of reasons.[24] Local facilities often provide a cost advantage to the producer. This is particularly true when the raw materials, parts, or labor needed to produce the product can be inexpensively obtained close to the facility. Location is also important because residents may prefer locally produced products. For example, many people in the United States like to "buy American." Some locations may be attractive because the local government is encouraging US investment through various means such as low tax rates, free land, subsidized energy and transportation rates, and low-interest loans. Imported goods may be subject to a tariff, quota, or other governmental restriction, making local manufacture more desirable.[25] Finally, the MNE may already be doing so much business in a country that the local government will insist that it set up local operations and begin producing more of its goods internally. This is one of the major reasons that Japanese auto manufacturers have started to establish operations in the United States.

Although the benefits can be great, there can be a number of drawbacks associated with placing operations overseas. An unstable political climate may leave an MNE vulnerable to low profits and bureaucratic red tape. In Russia, for example, the government has encouraged joint ventures, but because of political and economic uncertainty, many businesspeople currently regard Russian investments as highly risky ventures. One western diplomat has noted that "Anyone considering investing in Russia should sit on his wallet. . . . And no one should come who can't afford to lose his entire stake."[26] A second drawback is the possibility of revolution or armed conflict.

Fuji Xerox saves Xerox

Fuji Xerox was created in 1962 as a joint venture between Xerox and Fuji Photo Film. It is regarded as the most successful partnership between US and Japanese firms. The arrangement developed from a sales operation for Xerox products in Japan into a fully integrated organization with its own R&D and manufacturing and by 1990 its $4 billion revenue constituted 25 per cent of Xerox's worldwide revenues. By then Fuji Xerox had a world product mandate to supply the entire Xerox Group with the low-to-mid-range copiers that were the core of its business. Indeed, as the Xerox monopoly on large copiers began to dwindle in the 1970s, it was its Japanese partner, Fuji Xerox, which rode to the rescue with its new and high-quality smaller copiers.

In 1975 Xerox was forced by the US Federal Trade Commission to license its original core copier technology to rivals such as IBM, Kodak, Ricoh, and Canon. If it had not been for Fuji Xerox developing new copier technology, Xerox would have failed. The firm's early monopoly in the world copier business was eroded sharply by intense rivalry from Japanese competitors such as Canon and Ricoh as well as from Kodak and IBM. These rivals produced higher quality, lower priced, more technologically advanced, and more reliable copiers than Xerox.

Fuji Xerox recognized the threat and its managers, acting autonomously, started R&D into new small copiers. The US head office was slow to take on board the technology and products of its Japanese partner. Loss of market share, especially to Canon, however, eventually led to ever closer degrees of cooperation between Xerox and Fuji Xerox. In particular, the high quality standards of Fuji Xerox were spread throughout the Xerox Group, and the total quality management techniques of Fuji Xerox helped Xerox regain market. In this context Xerox was helped by having its partner, Fuji Xerox, based in Japan, the hotbed of TQM and copier innovation in the 1970s and 1980s.

One of the reasons for success in the collaboration between Xerox and Fuji Photo Films was that the latter acted as a silent partner in the 50–50 joint venture and allowed Fuji Xerox to develop its own management cadre, who became skilled in R&D and copier technology, and in the manufacturing and marketing of small copiers. Fuji Xerox also transformed itself from a marketing subsidiary into a full line business, thus ending up being more innovative and responsive to the market than Xerox itself.

Sources: Adapted from Benjamin Gomes-Casseres and Krista McQuade, *Xerox and Fuji Xerox*, Harvard Business School Case 9–391–156; David T. Kearns and David A. Nadler, *Prophets in the Dark: How Xerox Reinvented Itself and Beat Back the Japanese* (New York: Macmillan, 1992); and Benjamin Gomes-Casseres, "Group Versus Group: How Alliance Networks Compete," *Harvard Business Review*, July/August, 1994, pp. 62–74.

In Liberia, for example, the government was recently overthrown and many MNEs found their business operations suffering as a result of lost sales. MNEs with operations in Kuwait lost just about all of their investment in the Gulf War, and MNEs with locales in Saudi Arabia and other mideast countries affected by the Gulf War also withstood losses in the region. In some cases they are finding a way of "hedging their bets," as noted in the following example:

Some . . . opt for locales where the cost of running a small enterprise is significantly lower than that of running a large one. In this way they spread their risk, setting up many small locations throughout the world rather than one or two large ones. Manufacturing firms are a good example. Some production firms feel that the economies of scale associated with a large-scale plant are more than offset by the potential problems that can result should economic or political difficulties develop in the country. These firms' strategy is to spread the risk by opting for a series of small plants spread throughout a wide geographic region.[27]

Ownership

Ownership of international operations has become an important issue in recent years. Many Americans, for example, believe that the increase in foreign-owned businesses in the United States is weakening the economy. People in other countries have similar feelings about US businesses there. In truth, the real issue of ownership is whether or not the company is contributing to the overall economic good of the country where it is doing business. As one researcher noted, ". . . because the US-owned corporation is coming to have no special relationship with Americans, it makes no sense for the United States to entrust our national competitiveness to it. The interests of American-owned corporations may or may not coincide with those of the American people."[28] Countries that want to remain economically strong must be able to attract international investors who will provide jobs that allow their workers to increase their skills and build products that are demanded on the world market. In accomplishing this objective, two approaches are now in vogue: international joint ventures and strategic alliances.

International joint ventures An **international joint venture** is an agreement between two or more partners to own and control an overseas business.[29] There are a number of reasons for the rise in popularity of these ventures. One is government encouragement and legislation, designed to make it attractive for foreign investors to bring in local partners. A second is the need for partners who know the local economy, the culture, and the political system and who can cut through red tape in getting things done. A third is a desire to find partners who have local operations that can create a beneficial synergy with an outside company.[30] For example, an MNE might provide a local partner with technology know-how and an infusion of capital that will allow the local firm to expand operations, increase market share, and begin exporting.[31] The synergy created by the two firms can be profitable to each.[32]

Unfortunately, in many cases international joint ventures have not worked out well.[33] Several studies indicate a failure rate of 30 per cent for ventures in developed countries and 45 to 50 per cent in less developed countries.[34] The major reason has been the desire by MNEs to control the operation, which sometimes has resulted in poor decision making and/or conflicts with the local partners. In general, joint ventures are difficult to manage and are frequently unstable. This is why many MNEs have turned to the use of strategic partnerships.

Strategic partnerships A **strategic partnership** is an agreement between two or more competitive MNEs for the purpose of serving a global market.[35] In contrast to a joint venture where the partners may be from different businesses, strategic partnerships are almost always formed by firms in the same line of business. A good example is the General Motors and Toyota partnership that builds small cars in the United States. Other strategic agreements in the industry have brought together Nissan and Subaru, Volkswagen and Audi, Chrysler and Mitsubishi, and Ford Motor and Mazda. Strategic partnerships are also gaining popularity in other industries. For example,

Motorola and Toshiba have a manufacturing facility in Japan, and they exchange a broad range of microprocessor and memory chip technology. Motorola is strong in the microprocessor area and Toshiba is a leader in chip technology, so the strategic alliance has benefits for both firms.

These alliances help to illustrate the growing popularity of international business ownership agreements. The final determinant will always be whether the arrangement is in the best interests of all involved parties. When it is, a strategic alliance is likely to be formed.[36]

ACTIVE LEARNING CHECK

Review your answer to Active Learning Case question 3 and make any changes you like. Then compare your answer to the one below.

3. What forms of ownership arrangement is Mazda using to gain world market share? Explain.

Mazda is using two major forms of ownership arrangements. One is the joint venture as seen by its relationship with Ford Motor. The other is strategic alliances with Ford and with other auto producers that provide Mazda with a product to sell in the Japanese market.

Functional strategies

Functional strategies are used to coordinate operations and to ensure that the plan is carried out properly. While the specific functions that are key to the success of the MNE will vary, they typically fall into six major areas: marketing, manufacturing, finance, procurement, technology, and human resources. For purposes of analysis, they can be examined in terms of three major considerations: marketing, manufacturing, and finance.

Marketing   The marketing strategy is designed to identify consumer needs and to formulate a plan of action for selling the desired goods and services to these customers.[37] Most marketing strategies are built around what is commonly known as the "four Ps" of marketing: product, price, promotion, and place. The company will identify the products that are in demand in the market niches they are pursuing. It will apprise the manufacturing department of any modifications that will be necessary to meet local needs, and it will determine the price at which the goods can be sold. Then the company's attention will be devoted to promoting the products and to selling them in the local market.

Manufacturing   The manufacturing strategy is designed to dovetail with the marketing plan and to ensure that the right products are built and delivered in time for sale. Manufacturing will also coordinate its strategy with the procurement and technology people, so as to ensure that the desired materials are available and that the products have the necessary state-of-the-art quality. If the MNE is producing goods in more than one country, it will be giving attention to coordinating activities where needed. For example, some firms produce goods in two or more countries and then assemble and sell them in other geographic regions. Japanese auto firms send car parts to the United States for assembly and then sell some of the assembled cars in Japan. Whirlpool builds appliances worldwide with operations in Brazil, Canada, Mexico, the Netherlands, and seven other countries. Such production and assembly operations have to be coordinated carefully.

Finance   Financial strategies used to be formulated and controlled out of the home office. However, in recent years MNEs have learned that this approach can be cumbersome, and, because of fluctuating currency prices, it can be costly. Today overseas units have more control over their finances than before, but they are guided by a carefully constructed budget that is in accord with the overall strategic plan. They are also held to account for financial performance in the form of return on investment, profit, capital budgeting, debt financing, and working capital management. The financial strategy often serves both to lead and lag the other functional strategies. In the lead position, finance limits the amounts of money that can be spent on marketing (new product development, advertising, promotion) and manufacturing (machinery, equipment, quality control) to ensure that the desired return on investment is achieved. In the lag position, the financial strategy is used to evaluate performance and to provide insights regarding how future strategy should be changed.

CONTROL AND EVALUATION

The strategy formulation and implementation processes are a prelude to control and evaluation. The control and evaluation process involves an examination of the MNE's performance for the purpose of determining (1) how well the organization has done and (2) what actions should be taken in light of this performance. This process is tied directly to the overall strategy in that the objectives serve as the basis for comparison and evaluation[38] Figure 8.6 illustrates how this process works.

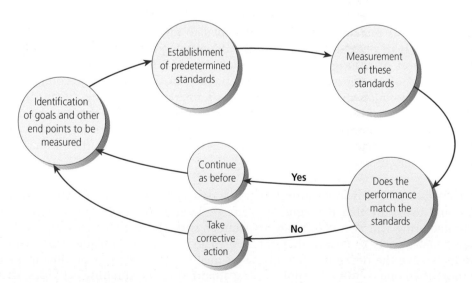

Figure 8.6   The control and evaluation process

If the comparison and evaluation show that the strategic business unit or overseas operation is performing according to expectations, then things will continue as before. The objectives may be altered because of changes in the strategic plan, but otherwise nothing major is likely to be done. On the other hand, if there have been problems, the MNE will want to identify the causes and work to eliminate or minimize them. Similarly, if the unit has performed extremely well and achieved more than forecasted, the management may want to reset the objectives to a higher level because there is obviously greater market demand than was believed initially. In making these decisions, the company will use a variety of measures. Some will be highly quantitative and depend on financial and productivity performance;[39] others will be more qualitative and judgmental in nature. The following discussion examines six of the most common methods of measurement used for control and evaluation purposes.

Common methods of measurement

Specific methods of measurement will vary depending on the nature of the MNE and the goals it has established. However, in most cases **return on investment (ROI)**, which is measured by dividing net income before taxes by total assets, is a major consideration. There are a number of reasons that ROI is so popular as a control and evaluation measure. These include the fact that ROI (1) is a single comprehensive result that is influenced by everything that happens in the business, (2) is a measure of how well the managers in every part of the world are using the investments at their command, and (3) allows a comparison of results among units in the same country as well as on an intercountry basis. Of course, there are shortcomings in using ROI, such as that (1) if one unit is selling goods to another unit, the ROI of the former is being artificially inflated; (2) the ROI in a growing market will be higher than that in markets which are just getting off the ground or which are maturing, so that a comparison of the ROI performance between units can be misleading; and (3) the ROI is a short-term measure of performance, and if it is relied on too heavily, managers will not develop the necessary long-term time horizons. Despite such shortcomings, however, the ROI remains a major measure of performance.

Another measure is sales growth and/or market share. Units will be given sales targets that usually require greater sales this year than last year. If the firm has made an estimate of the total demand, a market share figure will accompany the sales target. The reason for this is twofold: (1) the MNE wants to increase its sales and (2) the firm wants at least to maintain, if not increase, market share. If the market is judged to be declining, sales targets will be lowered but the MNE will still try to maintain market share.

A third performance area is costs. The MNE will want to achieve increased sales and market share at as low a cost as possible. The firm will also want to maintain close control of production costs. So expenses will be monitored carefully. This is particularly important in declining markets, where the company will want to cut costs as sales decline. For example, if an MNE estimates that it has but three years of product life in the market, it is likely that much of the advertising and promotion expenses will be dropped as the company focuses attention on supplying an ever decreasing number of customers. This strategy is often successful because the remaining customers are highly loyal and do not need promotional efforts to convince them to buy the product.

New product development is another area of performance measure. This area is extremely important for firms that rely on new offerings. A good example is Nintendo, the Japanese manufacturer of such well-known video games as Mario Brothers: in order to maintain market share and sales growth, the company must continually introduce new product offerings. MNEs in high-tech areas such as electronic goods and computers also fall into this category. In an environment where product improvement or innovation is critical to success, new product development is a key area for control and evaluation.

MNE/host country relations is another performance area that must be evaluated. Overseas units have to work within the cultural and legal framework of the host country. Many attempt to do this by blending into the community, hiring local managers and employees, adapting their product to the demands of that market, reinvesting part (if not all) of their profits back into the country, and working to improve the economic conditions of the area. As a result, they get on well in the country and there are no problems with the government or other local groups. One thing MNEs know from long experience is that poor host country relations can seriously endanger profits and may result in a loss of invested capital.

Finally, management performance must be considered. In rating this criterion, the MNE will consider two types of measures: quantitative and qualitative. In the quantitative area, in addition to those discussed above, other common considerations include return on invested capital and cash flow. In the qualitative area, in addition to host country relations, consideration will be given to relations with the home office, the leadership qualities of the unit's managers, how well the unit is building a management team, and how well the managers of the unit have implemented the assigned strategy.

These methods of measurement will be used in arriving at an overall assessment of the unit's performance. Based on the results, the MNE will then set new goals and the international strategic planning process will begin anew.

ACTIVE LEARNING CHECK

Review your answer to Active Learning Case question 4 and make any changes you like. Then compare your answer to the one below.

4. On what basis would a firm like Mazda evaluate performance? Identify and describe two.

There are a number of bases that Mazda would use. One is market share, a performance criterion that is extremely important to international auto companies. A second is new product development. Notice how much attention Mazda is giving to this objective in an effort to distinguish itself from the competition and to provide competitive alternatives.

SUMMARY

Key points

1. Strategic planning is the process of determining an organization's basic mission and long-term objectives and then implementing a plan of action for attaining these goals. In carrying out their strategic plan, most MNEs have a specific

predisposition. There are four predispositions: ethnocentric, polycentric, regiocentric, and geocentric, and each was described in the chapter.

2. The international strategic planning process involves three major steps: strategy formulation, strategy implementation, and the control and evaluation of the process. Strategy formulation entails the evaluation of the enterprise's environment and the identification of long-range and short-range objectives. The analysis of the external environment typically involves information gathering and information assessment. In this process consideration is given to the five forces that determine industry competitiveness: buyers, suppliers, new entrants to the industry, the availability of substitute goods and services, and rivalry among the competitors. The analysis of the internal environment involves consideration of the firm's physical resources and personnel competencies and the way in which a value chain analysis can be used to bring these resources together in the most synergistic and profitable manner.

3. Strategy implementation is the process of attaining predetermined goals by properly executing the formulated strategy. Three of the most important areas of consideration are location, ownership decisions, and functional area implementation.

4. The control and evaluation process involves an examination of the MNE's performance for the purpose of determining how well the organization has done and for deciding what action now needs to be taken. Some of the most common measures include return on investment, sales growth, market share, costs, new product development, host country relations, and overall management performance.

Key terms

- strategic planning
- ethnocentric predisposition
- polycentric predisposition
- regiocentric predisposition
- geocentric predisposition
- strategy formulation
- strategic business units (SBUs)
- vertical integration
- value chain
- cost strategy
- differentiation strategy
- focus strategy
- competitive scope
- strategy implementation
- international joint venture
- strategic partnership
- return on investment (ROI)

Review and discussion questions

1. Define the term "strategic planning."

2. In what way will the following basic predispositions affect strategic planning by an MNE: ethnocentric, polycentric, regiocentric, geocentric?

3. How will an MNE carry out an external environmental assessment? Identify and describe the two major steps that are involved in this process.

4. Of what practical value is an understanding of the five forces model presented in Figure 8.1? How would an MNE use this information in the strategic planning process?

5. In conducting an internal environmental assessment, why would an MNE want to identify its physical resources and personnel competencies?

6. What is a value chain? How can this chain be used in an internal environmental assessment?

7. What are the three generic strategies? When would an MNE use each? Use examples to support your answer.

8. What are some typical MNE goals? Identify and briefly describe four major types.

9. One of the most important considerations when implementing a strategy is that of location. What is meant by this statement?

10. When are MNEs likely to use an international joint venture? When would they opt for a strategic partnership? Defend your answer.

11. Functional strategies are used to coordinate operations and to ensure that the plan is carried out properly. What are some of the most common types of functional strategies? Identify and describe three.

12. How do MNEs control and evaluate their operations? Describe the basic process. Then discuss some of the common methods of measurement.

REAL CASES

NINTENDO'S WORLDWIDE STRATEGY

Nintendo is the most successful company in the worldwide home video game market. This success is accounted for by its powerful products and vise-like grip on the distribution channels, where marketers sell Nintendo games exclusively. Nintendo offers more than 200 different games, ranging from baseball to medieval warfare. The best-known game is Mario Brothers, the all-time highest selling series of games (more than 39 million copies) which involves quests through fantasy realms by an Italian plumber who can transform himself into a raccoon. The game is so well known that a poll of US schoolchildren found Mario to be more popular than Mickey Mouse.

Nintendo's strategic approach for capturing and maintaining the market has been well formulated. First, it continually develops new products. This is critical because many customers already have numerous Nintendo games, so the firm must bring new offerings to market. This is done through in-house development and the purchase of games from other developers. When outside developers produce a product, Nintendo pays a royalty on all games that are sold; this arrangement has made more than a few Japanese entrepreneurs very wealthy.

Before bringing a game to market, Nintendo puts it through a rigorous testing procedure to ensure that there are no problems in the program. At the Nintendo research and development center, it is common to find groups of designers testing and refining the products in an effort to ensure quality and customer acceptance.

Once the product is ready for release, Nintendo sends it to retailers throughout the world. These firms have agreements with Nintendo that they will not sell competing lines. This helps Nintendo to maintain strong market channels and thus reduces competition from other game companies. These retail agreements are so critical to success in the industry that competitors such as Atari Games have filed antitrust suits against Nintendo in the United States.

If Nintendo is to continue growing in a market that could well be saturated by the millennium, it must develop products and new market niches. Some of the firm's future plans include (1) games for adults, (2) the development of a new generation game console that will provide more lavish video images, (3) expansion into Europe, (4) the development of nationwide tournaments in which customers can compete from their living rooms using Nintendos and televisions hooked up to telephone lines, and (5) research into areas such as childhood learning, in order to understand better how to develop educational games for young children.

One of the biggest threats that the company faces is the shrinking demand brought on by competitive offerings and a decline of interest in video games. The company is also concerned about losing its exclusivity with distributors. On the other hand, if Nintendo can continue to grow as rapidly as it did during the 1990s, the firm will be one of the largest corporations in the world in the twenty-first century.

1. Using Figure 8.1 as the basis of your analysis, what does the industry look like from Nintendo's point of view?

2. Relying on Figure 8.1, what are the primary strengths of Nintendo? What are the firm's basic weaknesses?

3. How could Nintendo make use of value chain analysis? Give an example.

Sources: Adapted from Susan Moffat, "Can Nintendo Keep Winning?" *Fortune*, November 5, 1990, pp. 131–136; Robert Neff, "What Do Japanese CEOs *Really* Make," *Business Week*, April 26, 1993, pp. 60–61; Richard Brandt, "Video Games: Is All That Gore Really Child's Play?" *Business Week*, June 14, 1993, p. 38 *http://www.nintendo.com.*

BENETTON IN THE FAST LANE

Famous for its shocking advertisements Benetton started in 1955 as a small business. Lucianno Benetton and his family started by selling coloured sweaters door to door in Treviso, Italy. Over time a regional network of family, friends and agents set up a closely monitored set of distinctive retail outlets. Over a 15-year period Benetton built up 300 affiliated but independently owned outlets in Italy and a factory with new methods to dye and condition wool. Benetton was not directly involved in the retail outlets, who received high-quality products at low costs. Part of the manufacturing savings are realized by outsourcing to neighbouring subcontractors.

Today Benetton has kept this loose network of independent production subcontractors and distribution agents but has now built up to a global network of over 7,000 retail stores. Of these, Benetton owns only about 50 flagship stores and the great majority are operated by independent entrepreneurs. Over 80 per cent of production still takes place in Italy and the company is still 72 per cent owned by the Benetton family.

Benetton is one of those successful global companies that was partly successful because its production and design concept was built on a strong home base. It then expanded the marketing end of its business through closely monitored (but not owned) independent stores. These were able to use the Benetton brand name and distinctive colours and were supported by clever international advertising.

Benetton does not advertise its clothes directly. Rather its advertisements are for a "lifestyle." The "United Colors of Benetton" ads are designed for a homogeneous global consumer interested in fast cars and a fast lifestyle. Benetton goes in for cutting-edge advertising that grabs public attention. This creates an image of new-age awareness, as Benetton advertising has featured Formula 1 cars, AIDS, high art and "attitude."

How well this plays out globally is uncertain. For example, in 1988 Benetton had 700 retail stores in the United States but by 1995 it only had 150. Is this because Benetton has too European an image to succeed in middle America? How can an Italian family firm understand the American lifestyle from its European bases?

1. Is Benetton a multinational enterprise?

2. What are the country-specific factors that have helped Benetton be a success?

3. What are Benetton's firm-specific advantages?

Sources: Adapted from: *Benetton SpA: Industrial Fashion (A)*, Harvard Business School Case No. 9-685-614; *Benetton (B)*, Harvard Business School Case No. 9-685-020; INSEAD-CEDEP Case No. 01/97-4520, 1996; David Stillit "Benetton: Italy's Smart Operator," *Corporate Finance*, June 1993; Anonymous, "Benetton's Network," *Ivey Business Quarterly*, 1997.

ENDNOTES

1. M. Welge and M. E. Kenter, "Impact of Planning on Control Effectiveness and Company Performance," *Management International Review*, vol. 28, no. 2, 1988, pp. 9–10.

2. M. A. Hitt, "The Meaning of Organizational Effectiveness: Multiple Domains and Constituencies," *Management International Review*, vol. 28, no. 2, 1988, p. 28.

3. David Lei, John W. Slocum, Jr., and Robert W. Slater, "Global Strategy and Reward Systems: The Key Roles of Management Development and Corporate Culture," *Organizational Dynamics*, August 1990, p. 29.

4. See David Norburn, Sue Birley, Mark Dunn, and Adrian Payne, "A Four National Study of the Relationship Between Marketing Effectiveness, Corporate Culture, Corporate Values, and Market Orientation," *Journal of International Business Studies*, vol. 21, no. 3, 1990, pp. 451–468.

5. For a good example see Keith Bradsher, "Effective Today, Chrysler and Daimler-Benz Are One," *New York Times*, November 12, 1998, p. C4.

6. For some specific applications of these ideas, see Michael M. Robert, "Managing Your Competitor's Strategy," *Journal of Business Strategy*, March/April 1990, pp. 24–28.

7. J. E. Preble, P. A. Rau, and A. Reichel, "The Environmental Scanning Practices of US Multinationals in the Late 1980s," *Management International Review*, vol. 28, no. 4, 1988, p. 10.

8. For more on this, see R. C. Hoffman, "The General Management of Foreign Subsidiaries in the USA: An Exploratory Study," *Management International Review*, vol. 28, no. 2, 1988, pp. 41–55.

9. Stephen D. Moore, "Nova Nordisk Looks to Drug for Relief," *Wall Street Journal*, April 7, 1998, p. A14.

10. See John J. Curran, "China's Investment Boom," *Fortune*, March 7, 1994, pp. 116–124.

11. For more on this, see Michael Porter, *The Competitive Advantage of Nations* (New York: Free Press, 1990), Chapter 2.

12. Andrew Pollack, "Nissan Plans to Buy More American Parts," *New York Times*, March 26, 1994, pp. 17, 26.

13. See, for example, Dean Takahashi, "How the Competition Got Ahead of Intel In Making Cheap Chips," *Wall Street Journal*, February 12, 1998, pp. A1, 11.

14. Arnoldo C. Hax and Nicolas S. Majluf, *The Strategy Concept and Process: A Pragmatic Approach* (Englewood Cliffs, NJ: Prentice-Hall, 1991), p. 416.

15. Also, see Julie Pitta, "Score One for Vertical Integration," *Forbes*, January 18, 1993, pp. 88–90.

16. For an excellent discussion of this topic see Hax and Majluf, op. cit.., Chapter 12.

17. C. K. Prahalad and Kenneth Lieberthal, "The End of Corporate Imperialism," *Harvard Business Review*, July–August 1998, pp. 69–79.

18. For the application of these ideas to the European market, see Susan P. Douglas and Dong Kee Rhee, "Examining Generic Competitive Strategy Types in US and European Markets," *Journal of International Business Studies*, Fall 1989, pp. 437–463.

19. Hax and Majluf, op. cit., p. 83.

20. For another good example, see Seth Lubove, "Make a Better Mousetrap," *Forbes*, February 1, 1993, pp. 56–57.

21. Leslie Kaufman, "Avon's New Face," *Newsweek*, November 16, 1998, pp. 59–60.

22. Also, see W. Chan Kim and Peter Hwang, "Global Strategy and Multinationals' Entry Mode Choice," *Journal of International Business Studies*, First Quarter 1992, pp. 29–53.

23. See, for example, Fred Martin, "Heard the One About the Copy Shop in Budapest?" *New York Times Magazine*, December 16, 1990, pp. 42–48.

24. See Masaaki Kotabe, "Assessing the Shift in Global Market Share of US Multinationals," *International Marketing Review*, vol. 6, no. 5, 1989, pp. 20–35; and Keith L. Alexander, Alan Fine, and Eric Schine, "Mandela's Welcome Mat Starts Drawing Visitors," *Business Week*, October 11, 1993, p. 54.

25. See Paul Magnusson and Laxmi Nakarmi, "Seoul's Crackdown on Imports May Be a Luxury It Can't Afford," *Business Week*, January 21, 1991, p. 46.

26. Paul Hofheinz, "The Soviet Winter of Discontent," *Fortune*, January 28, 1991, p. 85.

27. Richard M. Hodgetts and Fred Luthans, *International Management*, 4th ed. (Burr Ridge, Ill: McGraw/Irwin, 2000), p. 260.

28. Robert B. Reich, "Who Is Us?" *Harvard Business Review*, January–February 1990, p. 59.

29. Audrey Choi, "BMW's Chairman Plans Visit to Honda to Discuss Future of Jointly Held Rover," *Wall Street Journal*, February 18, 1994, p. A7.

30. Gautam Naik, "AT&T, BT Form World-Wide Alliance," *Wall Street Journal*, July 27, 1998, p. A3.

31. Jennifer Cody, "Supermarket Giant Ito-Yokado Plans Venture to Import Goods of Wal-Mart," *New York Times*, March 24, 1994, p. A11.

32. Also, see K. R. Harrigan, "Strategic Alliances and Partner Asymmetries," *Management International Review*, Special Issue, 1988, pp. 53–72.

33. Eleonara Cattaneo, "Managing Joint Ventures in Russia: Can the Problem Be Solved?" *Long Range Planning*, December 1992, pp. 68–72.

34. Stefan H. Robock and Kenneth Simmonds, *International Business and Multinational Enterprises*, 4th ed. (Homewood, Ill.: Irwin, 1989), p. 216.

35. Peter Lorange, Johan Roos, and Peggy Simcic Bronn, "Building Successful Strategic Alliances," *Long Range Planning*, December 1992, pp. 10–17.

36. F. J. Contractor and P. Lorange, "Competition vs. Cooperation: A Benefit/Cost Framework for Choosing Between Fully-Owned Investments and Cooperative Relationships," *Management International Review*, Special Issue, 1988, pp. 5–18.

37. Matt Marshall, "In Brazil, Coke Sells Foam as Well as Fizz," *Wall Street Journal*, July 28, 1997, p. A12.

38. Jeffrey E. Garten, "Opening The Doors For Business In China," *Harvard Business Review*, May–June 1998, pp. 167–175.

39. Sheryl R. Lee, "GE's European Lighting Unit to Report Earnings for '93 in Major Turnaround," *Wall Street Journal*, January 28, 1994, p. A5.

ADDITIONAL BIBLIOGRAPHY

Barkeman, Harry G., Shenkar, Oded, Vermeulen, Freek and Bell, John H. J. "Working Abroad, Working with Others: How Firms Learn to Operate International Joint Ventures," *The Academy of Management Journal*, vol. 40, no. 2 (April 1997).

Bleeke, Joel A. "Strategic Choices for Newly Opened Markets," *Harvard Business Review*, vol. 68, no. 5 (September/October 1990).

Capon, Noel, Christodoulou, Chris, Farley, John U. and Hulbert, James M. "A Comparison of the Strategy and Structure of United States and Australian Corporations," *Journal of International Business Studies*, vol. 18, no. 1 (Spring 1987).

Castrogiovanni, Gary J. "Environmental Munificence: A Theoretical Assessment," *Academy of Management Review*, vol. 16, no. 3 (July 1991).

Cravens, David W., Downey, H. Kirk, and Lauritano, Paul. "Global Competition in the Commercial Aircraft Industry: Positioning for Advantage by the Triad Nations," *Columbia Journal of World Business*, vol. 26, no. 4 (Winter 1992).

Dacin, M. Tina, Hitt, Michael A. and Levitas, Edward. "Selecting Partners for Successful International Alliances: Examination of US and Korean Firms," *Journal of World Business*, vol. 32, no. 1 (Spring 1997).

Deschamps, Jean-Philippe and Nayak, P. Ranganath, "Competing Through Products: Lessons from the Winners," *Columbia Journal of World Business*, vol. 27, no. 2 (Summer 1992).

Douglas, Susan P. and Craig, C. Samuel. "Evolution of Global Marketing Strategy: Scale, Scope and Synergy," *Columbia Journal of World Business*, vol. 24, no. 3 (Fall 1989).

Douglas, Susan P. and Rhee, Dong Kee. "Examining Generic Competitive Strategy Types in US and European Markets," *Journal of International Business Studies*, vol. 20, no. 3 (Fall 1989).

Egelhoff, William G. "Great Strategy or Great Strategy Implementation – Two Ways of Competing in Global Markets," *Sloan Management Review*, vol. 34, no. 2 (Winter 1993).

French, Hilary F. "Clearing the Air: A Global Agenda," *Columbia Journal of World Business*, vol. 25, nos. 1, 2 (Spring/Summer 1990).

Hamel, Gary and Prahalad, C. K. "Strategy as Stretch and Leverage," *Harvard Business Review*, vol. 71, no. 2 (March/April 1993).

Hitt, Michael A., Hoskisson, Robert E. and Kim, Hicheon. "International Diversification: Effects on Innovation and Firm Performance in Product-Diversified Firms," *The Academy of Management Journal*, vol. 40, no. 4 (August 1997).

Huo, Y. Paul and McKinley, William. "Nation as a Context for Strategy: The Effects of National Characteristics on Business-Level Strategies," *Management International Review*, vol. 32, no. 2 (Second Quarter 1992).

Jones, Robert E., Jacobs, Lester W., and van Spijker, Willem. "Strategic Decision Processes in International Firms," *Management International Review*, vol. 32, no. 3 (Third Quarter 1992).

Kanter, Rosabeth Moss. "Collaborative Advantage: The Art of Alliances," *Harvard Business Review* (July–August 1994).

Kim, W. Chan and Mauborgne, Renne A. "Making Global Strategies Work," *Sloan Management Review*, vol. 34, no. 3 (Spring 1993).

Kim, W. Chan and Mauborgne, Renne A. "Effectively Conceiving and Executing Multinationals' Worldwide Strategies," *Journal of International Business Studies*, vol. 24, no. 3 (Third Quarter 1993).

Kotabe, Masaaki and Omura, Glenn S. "Sourcing Strategies of European and Japanese Multinationals: A Comparison," *Journal of International Business Studies*, vol. 20, no. 1 (Spring 1989).

Milliken, Frances J. "Three Types of Perceived Uncertainty About the Environment: State, Effect and Response Uncertainty," *Academy of Management Review*, vol. 12, no. 1 (January 1987).

Mintzberg, Henry. "The Fall and Rise of Strategic Planning," *Harvard Business Review*, vol. 72, no. 1 (January/February 1994).

Normann, Richard and Ramirez, Rafael. "From Value Chain to Value Constellation: Designing Interactive Strategy," *Harvard Business Review*, vol. 71, no. 4 (July/August 1993).

Parkhe, Arvind "Understanding Trust in International Alliances," *Journal of World Business*, vol. 33, no. 3 (Fall 1998).

Porter, Michael E. "The Competitive Advantage of Nations," *Harvard Business Review*, vol. 68, no. 2 (March/April 1990).

Roth, Kendall, Schweiger, David M. and Morrison, Allen J. "Global Strategy Implementation at the Business Unit Level: Operational Capabilities and Administrative Mechanisms," *Journal of International Business Studies*, vol. 24, no. 2 (Second Quarter 1993).

Rugman, Alan M. "Multinationals and Global Competitive Strategy," *International Studies of Management and Organization*, vol. 15, no. 2 (Summer 1985).

Schoemaker, Paul J. H. "How to Link Strategic Vision to Core Capabilities," *Sloan Management Review*, vol. 34, no. 1 (Fall 1992).

Sugiura, Hideo. "How Honda Localizes Its Global Strategy," *Sloan Management Review*, vol. 32, no. 1 (Fall 1990).

Tallman, Stephen and Li, Jiatao. "Effects of International Diversity and Product Diversity on the Performance of Multinational Firms," *The Academy of Management Journal*, vol. 39, no. 1 (February 1996).

Thakur, Manab and Das, T. K. "Managing the Growth-Share Matrix: A Four-Nation Study in Two Industries," *Management International Review*, vol. 31, no. 2 (Second Quarter 1991).

Thomas, Howard, Pollock, Timothy and Gorman, Philip. "Global Strategic Analyses: Frameworks and Approaches," *The Academy of Management Executive*, vol. 13, no. 1 (February 1999).

CHAPTER 9

Organizing Strategy

The primary purpose of an organizing strategy is to help an enterprise implement its strategic plan. There are a number of basic organization structures from which to choose, although most MNEs tailor-make their design and sometimes use a combination of different structures. Another major area of organizing strategy is the organizational processes of decision making, communicating, and controlling. These processes are fundamental to the efficient operation of the structure, and management will need to decide how they should be carried out. This chapter examines the key elements of organizing strategy. The specific objectives of this chapter are to:

1. **Examine** organization structures used by enterprises that are just beginning their international expansion.

2. **Describe** the international division and global structures that are used as firms increase their international presence.

3. **Analyze** the key structural variables that influence international organization designs.

4. **Review** the role of the organizational processes in ensuring that the structure is both effective and efficient.

ACTIVE LEARNING CASE

Organizational designers

The apparel industry in the United States is very competitive, as seen by the strategies of such well-known firms as Sears Roebuck and Ann Taylor. However, this has not stopped some international firms from gaining market entry. A good example is Gruppo GFT, a world-famous Italian apparel company based in Turin, Italy. The firm manufactures designer clothes and competes at the highest end of the apparel business in "ready-to-wear" collections. Among its labels are Giorgio Armani, Emanuel Ungaro, and Valentino. Men's suits and women's outfits sell for as much as $1,200.

Until 1980 GFT was a relatively small, primarily Italian firm. However, global interest in European fashions grew into a multibillion dollar industry in the 1980s. GFT began selling more goods abroad, and by the end of the decade the company had annual sales in excess of $1 billion with approximately 60 per cent coming from markets outside Italy. Sales in the United States during the decade rose from $7 million to $304 million.

Because of this growth, GFT needed to rethink its overall strategy. Since the company's inception, all product development, innovation, and manufacturing had been done in Turin. The goods were then exported throughout the world. So the same Armani jacket could be sold in Milan, Madrid, Montreal, or Miami. By the end of the 1980s, however, it was becoming increasingly clear that clothing designs did not travel well. The suit that was extremely popular in Madrid often did not sell in Montreal. Sizes, fabrics, and colors that suited people in Germany or England were not right in Florida or California. As one senior GFT manager put it, "The company may be global, but the consumer is not." At the same time the firm saw that customers were becoming much more educated and discerning about fashion and that they were beginning to demand higher quality and lower prices.

GFT addressed this changing market place by reorganizing the firm and by getting closer to the customer. The company gave subsidiaries in key markets around the world sufficient autonomy so that they could mold themselves to the particularities of their local region. The United States had long been regarded as an export market for company products. With the reorganization, GFT has become a financial holding company that consists of six autonomous operating divisions. Two are organized on the basis of key global markets: North America (the United States, Canada, and Mexico) and the Far East. The remaining four are organized on the basis of GFT's fabric business and its three main product lines: menswear, womenswear, and sportswear. These four product divisions focus on the European market.

GFT USA is the flagship company of the North American division. This subsidiary is responsible for meeting annual profit objectives, but otherwise the managers are free to run the subsidiary as they see fit. As a result, GFT USA is highly decentralized. The firm consists of six small companies, four based on product lines and one each for manufacturing and distribution operations. This structure allows the US subsidiary to respond quickly to the distinctive features of the US market. In fact, fashion trends often first take place in the United States and then in the rest of the world, so GFT USA has become a type of lab for innovations that are now used by other company subsidiaries worldwide.

This latest organization design is working well for the company and promises to help GFT to maintain its worldwide prominence. Commenting on the ongoing organizational challenges facing the company, one individual noted that the senior-level managers will have to be "organizational designers" who continually invent and reinvent the company according to the ever-changing requirements of the business.

Sources: Adapted from Robert Howard, "The Designer Organization: Italy's GFT Goes Global," *Harvard Business Review*, September–October 1991, pp. 28–44; Sunita Wadekar Bhargava, "Ann Retaylored," *Business Week*, May 17, 1993, pp. 70–72; and Kevin Kelly, "The Big Store May Be on a Big Roll," *Business Week*, August 30, 1993, pp. 82–85.

1. What type of organizational arrangement did Gruppo GFT use for its US operations during the 1980s? What type of structure does it use today?

2. What factor primarily resulted in GFT's choice of this most recent organizational arrangement? Identify and describe this factor.

INTRODUCTION

Once an organization decides to go international, it must begin to implement the decision.[1] Some companies do so by simply shipping their goods to a foreign market and having a third party handle sales activities. If the firm's international market continues to grow, however, the enterprise will need to review this strategy and decide whether to play a more active role in the distribution and sale of its products. As this happens, the company's organizing strategy will change.[2]

Major MNEs such as IBM, General Motors,[3] Mercedes, and Mitsubishi have sophisticated global structures that form the basis of their organizing strategies. Sometimes these firms will also have subsidiaries or affiliates that are integrated into the overall structure. For example, Mitsubishi has 28 core groups that are bound together by cross-ownership and other financial ties, interlocking directorates, long-term business relationships, and social and historical ties. Among these are Mitsubishi Bank, Mitsubishi Heavy Industries, Asahi Glass, Tokyo Marine and Fire Insurance, Nikon Corporation, and Kirin Brewery.[4] The Mitsubishi group obviously needs a carefully designed global structure that allows it to integrate and coordinate the activities of these many businesses. Sometimes this undertaking involves more time and effort than the formulation of the strategic plan.

ORGANIZATIONAL STRUCTURES

Multinational enterprises cannot implement their strategies without an effective structure.[5] The strategy sets forth the plan of action, but the structure is critical in ensuring that the desired goals are met efficiently.[6] There are a number of choices available to an MNE when deciding on an organizational arrangement, and a number of factors will influence this choice. For example, firms that are just getting into the international arena are likely to choose a structure that differs from that of firms with seasoned overseas operations. Conversely, companies that use their structures as worldwide sales organizations will have a different arrangement from those that locally manufacture and sell goods in various international markets. International structures will change in compliance with the strategic plan, and if a structure is proving to be unwieldy or inefficient, it will be scrapped in favor of one that addresses these problems.[7] The following discussion examines some of the most common organizational arrangements used by MNEs.

Early organizational structures

When a company first begins international operations, it is typical for these activities to be extensions of domestic operations. The firm's primary focus continues to

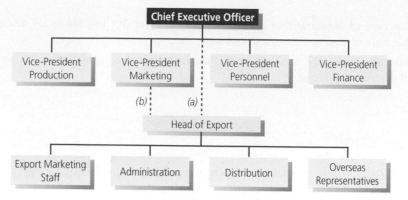

Figure 9.1 **An export department structure**

Figure 9.2 **Use of subsidiaries during the early stages of internationalization**

be the local market, and international involvement is of secondary importance. International transactions are conducted on a case-by-case basis, and there is no attempt to consolidate these operations into a separate department. Under this arrangement international sales are viewed as supplements to the income earned from home country operations.

As international operations increase, however, the MNE will take steps to address this growth structurally. One way is by having the marketing department handle international sales. All overseas operations are coordinated through this department; and if sales warrant it, some of the salespeople will handle international transactions exclusively. In this way the company develops marketing specialists who learn the specific needs and marketing techniques to employ in overseas selling.

An alternative arrangement is to create an export department. This department may report directly to the chief executive officer (CEO) (Figure 9.1, line (*a*)) or be a subdepartment within the marketing area (Figure 9.1, line (*b*)). If the department operates independently of the marketing department (option (*a*)), it is either staffed by in-house marketing people whose primary focus is on the international market or it is operated by an outside export management company that is hired for the purpose of providing the company with an international arm. Whichever approach is taken, it is important to realize that MNEs planning to increase their international presence must ensure that the export department is a full-fledged marketing department and not just a sales organization.

Another possible arrangement is the use of overseas subsidiaries (see Figure 9.2). This is often a result of individual ventures in various geographic locales in which

INTERNATIONAL BUSINESS STRATEGY IN ACTION

Rhône-Poulenc organizes in the United States

Rhône-Poulenc is a French-based chemicals firm that has sought, through mergers and acquisitions, to become a global top ten player. The global chemicals industry is highly competitive. Major producers include US firms such as DuPont and Dow Chemical and European firms such as Hoecht, BASF, Ciba Geigy, and ICI. In 1985 Rhône-Poulenc was the twelfth largest chemical company in the world with 80 per cent of its sales in Europe.

The chemical industry is increasingly structured on a "triad" basis. So in the 1980s Rhône-Poulenc decided to consolidate its successful European base and move into the US market. Between 1986 and 1989 it made 18 acquisitions in the United States, the major acquisitions being of Union Carbide Agrochemical Products in 1986 and Stauffer Basic Chemicals in 1987, and by 1990, as seen in the table opposite, the firm was the seventh largest chemical manufacturer in the world. By this time the company was generating over 20 per cent of its total sales in the US market.

Managing the US operation has not been easy. The takeover of Union Carbide worked well, as its pesticide products were complementary to Rhône-Poulenc's herbicides and fungicides and the corporate cultures were similar. However, the Stauffer acquisition was more difficult because there were overlapping product lines and the US managers at Stauffer had little international experience.

In order to make a go of its diverse US operations, Rhône-Poulenc adapted a highly decentralized organizational structure, consolidating its US business into a strong US country group with headquarters at

Largest chemical manufacturers, 1990

Company	Country	Sales ($ billions)
1. BASF	Germany	31.20
2. Hoechst	Germany	30.02
3. Bayer	Germany	27.86
4. ICI	United Kingdom	24.91
5. DuPont	United States	22.27
6. Dow Chemical	United States	19.77
7. Rhône-Poulenc	France	15.48
8. Ciba-Geigy	Switzerland	15.46
9. Shell	United States	12.70
10. Atochem	France	10.40
11. AZO	Netherlands	10.23
12. Exxon	United States	9.59
13. Monsanto	United States	9.00
14. Solvay	Belgium	8.32
15. Sumitomo Chemicals	Japan	7.87

Source: Compiled from various annual reports of the companies listed.

Princeton, New Jersey. The language of business is English, not the French of the parent firm. As an intermediate step on the path towards true globalization, this US regional headquarters has served Rhône-Poulenc well, helping to create a strong US presence in the face of vigorous rivals with efficient production and effective staffing. In the future a more "transnational" structure for this company is anticipated.

Sources: Rhône-Poulenc (1996) *Annual Report 1995: Rhône-Poulenc*, Courbvoie Cedex, France; Rhône-Poulenc (1997) *Annual Report 1996: Rhône-Poulenc*, Courbvoie Cedex, France; Rhône-Poulenc (1998) "News: Rhône-Poulenc Rorer Announces Measures to Improve Productivity," *Internet: Rhône-Poulenc Home Page*, June 4, 1998, p. 1; H. Banks, "The Road From Serfdom," *Forbes*, October 21, 1996, p. 156; D. Hunter, "Reshaping Rhône-Poulenc," 1995, *Chemical Week*, vol. 156, no. 23, p. 30; D. Owen and D. Green, "Rhône-Poulenc to Focus on Pharmaceuticals Business," *Internet: FT McCarthy*, June 27, 1997, p. 1.

the head of the venture is given a great deal of autonomy and reports directly to the CEO. As long as the subsidiary shows sufficient profit, it is allowed to operate free from home office interference.

As MNEs become more involved in foreign markets, the export department structure or subsidiary arrangement is generally discarded or supplemented because it cannot meet the changing needs of the organization. As a result, the company will

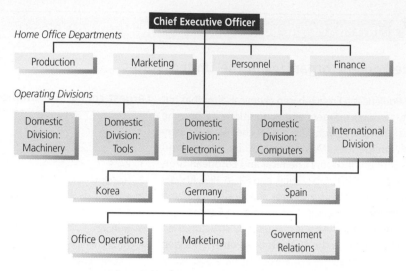

Figure 9.3 An international division structure

now look into joint ventures[8] and foreign direct investment. As this happens the firm is likely to opt for an international division structure.

The international division

The **international division structure** centralizes all the international operations (see Figure 9.3). This arrangement provides a number of advantages. One is that it reduces the CEO's burden of direct operation of overseas subsidiaries and domestic operations.[9] A second benefit of this structure is that it raises the status of overseas operations to that of the domestic divisions. All information, authority, and decision making related to foreign efforts is channeled to this division, so there is one central clearing point for international activities. This structure also helps the MNE to develop a cadre of internationally experienced managers.

But the international division structure also has some significant drawbacks. One is that separating operations into two categories, domestic and international, can create rivalries between the two. A second shortcoming is that this arrangement puts pressure on the home office to think in global terms and to allocate resources on the basis of overall market opportunity. This can be extremely difficult for a management that has been domestically focused and makes the majority of its sales in the home market. Despite these drawbacks, the international division structure remains dominant among US MNEs.

Global organizational structures

As MNEs generate more and more revenues from their overseas operations, their strategies become more global in focus and the structures used to implement these strategies follow suit. European firms are a good example. Because their domestic markets are fairly small, these companies have traditionally had global structures. In all, there are six basic types: (1) global product, (2) global area, (3) global function, (4) mixed, (5) matrix, and (6) transnational network.

Figure 9.4   A global product structure

Global product structure   A **global product structure** is a structural arrangement in which domestic divisions are given worldwide responsibility for product groups. Figure 9.4 provides an example. In this arrangement each product division sells its output throughout the world. As seen in the case of Product Division C, the European group operates in a host of countries. The same would be true for the other four geographic areas noted in the figure. In each case the manager of the product division would have internal functional support for the entire product line. All production, marketing, personnel, and finance activities associated with Product C would be under the control of this individual.

The global product division structure relies on the "profit center" concept. Each product line is expected to generate a predetermined return on investment (ROI), and the performance of each line is measured on this profit basis. Each product line is also operated like an autonomous business, with the product division manager given a great deal of authority regarding how to run the operation. As long as the product line continues to generate the desired ROI, the division is usually allowed to operate unfettered by home management controls. The only major exception is budgetary constraints that are imposed by central management.

There are a number of benefits associated with a global product division structure. If the firm produces a large number of diverse products, the structure allows each major product line to focus on the specific needs of its customers. This would be particularly difficult to achieve if the company were trying to sell all these products out of one centralized marketing department. This approach also helps to develop a cadre of experienced, well-trained managers who understand a particular product line. A third benefit of the product structure is that it helps the company to match its marketing strategy to the specific needs of the customer. For example, in some areas of the world a product may be in the introduction stage, while in other areas it may be in the growth, maturity, or decline stage. These differing life cycles require close technological and marketing coordination between the home market and the foreign market, and this can be best achieved by a product division approach. The product structure also helps the organization to establish and maintain the necessary link between the product development people and the customer. By continually feeding back information from the field to the home office, the product division personnel ensure that new product offerings meet consumer needs.

At the same time there are drawbacks to the product division arrangement. One is the necessity of duplicating facilities and staff personnel within each division. A second is that products that sell well are often given primary attention and those that need special handling or promotion are often sidetracked, even though this may result in the long-run loss of profit. A third is that an effective product division requires managers who are knowledgeable about the worldwide demand for their products. Most managers know the local market but do not know a lot about international markets. So it takes time to develop the necessary managerial staff to run this type of structure. A fourth shortcoming is the difficulty of coordinating the activities of different product divisions. For example, the electronics division may decide to subcontract components to a plant in Germany, while the computer division is subcontracting work to a firm in France. If the two divisions had coordinated their activities, it might have been possible to have all the work done by one company at a lower price. Finally, lack of cooperation among the various product lines can result in lost sales, given that each division may have information that can be of value to the other. However, because of the profit center concept, each product line operates independently and communication and cooperation are downplayed, if not discouraged.

Global area structure   A **global area structure** is one in which primary operational responsibility is delegated to area managers, each of whom is responsible for a specific geographic region. This is a polycentric (host-country-oriented) structure. Figure 9.5 provides an example. Under this arrangement each regional division is responsible for all functions within its area, that is, production, marketing, personnel, and finance. There appears to be some structural similarity between a global area and a global product arrangement; however, they operate in very different ways. With a global product arrangement, each product division is responsible for its output throughout the world. With a global area structure, on the other hand, the individual product lines are subsumed within each of the geographic areas. So the manager in charge of Belgian operations, for example, will be responsible for each of the product lines sold in that region.

A global area structure is commonly used by MNEs that are in mature businesses and have narrow product lines that are not differentiated by geographic area. Food products are a good example:

> In the United States, soft drinks have less sugar than in South America, so the manufacturing process must be slightly different in these two locales. Similarly, in England people prefer bland soups, but in France the preference is for mildly spicy. In Turkey, Italy, Spain, and Portugal people like dark, bitter coffee; Americans prefer a milder, sweeter blend. In northern Europe, Canada, and the United States people prefer less spicy food; in the Middle East and Asia they like more heavily spiced food.[10]

The global area structure provides division managers with the autonomy to make rapid decisions that depend on local tastes and regulations; because of this, the firm can become more "nationally responsive." Also, the company gains a wealth of

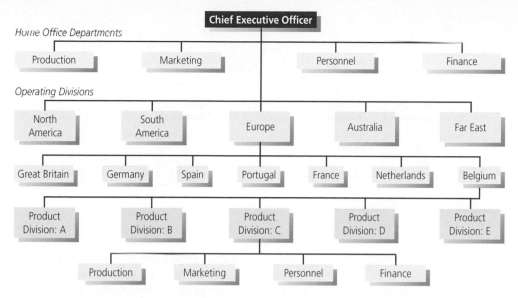

Figure 9.5 A global area structure

experience regarding how to satisfy these local tastes and, in the process, often builds a strong competitive advantage. The global area structure works well where economies of scale in production require a region-sized unit for basic production. For example, by setting up operations in the EU, a US company is able to achieve production cost advantages that would not otherwise be possible. Finally, under this structure the company can eliminate costly transportation associated with importing goods produced overseas.

If a product sells well in the United States, the company is likely to try to market it worldwide without making any modifications for local taste. Under the area structure the opposite viewpoint holds; the product must be adapted to the local tastes. But this means that the usual product emphasis in a company must be subsumed to the company's geographic orientation and the authority of the area managers. Another shortcoming with this organization structure is the expense associated with duplicating facilities. Each division has its own functional areas and is responsible for both production and marketing. Since production efficiency is often based on the amount of output, small plants are usually less efficient than large ones. Companies using a global area division structure also find it difficult to coordinate geographically dispersed divisions into the overall strategic plan. Quite often international cooperation and synergy among divisions end up being sacrificed. Finally, companies that rely heavily on R&D to develop new products often find that these offerings are not readily accepted by the global area divisions. This is because each group is trying to cater to the specific needs of its current market, and new products often require modification to meet the needs of these local customers. Research shows that division managers prefer to sell products that have already been accepted by the market and are reluctant to take on new, untried products. Unfortunately, since most products have fairly short life cycles, this attitude is potentially dangerous to the long-run success of the MNE and the home office must continually fight this "anti-new product" drift.

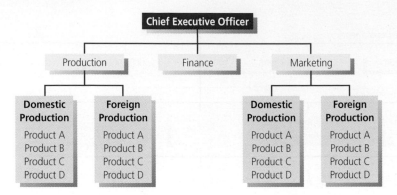

Figure 9.6   A global functional structure

Global functional structure   A **global functional structure** is one that is built around the basic tasks of the organization. For example, in manufacturing firms production, marketing, and finance are the three primary functions that must be carried out for the enterprise to survive. Figure 9.6 shows such an arrangement.

Under this arrangement the head of the production department is responsible for all domestic and international manufacturing. Similarly, the head of marketing is responsible for the sales of all products here and abroad. This structure is most commonly used by MNEs that have a narrow product line that has reached a stable plateau of global coverage and a level of demand that does not face major changes in a competitive attack.

A primary advantage of the global functional structure is that it allows a small group of managers to maintain control over a wide-reaching organization. A second advantage is that there is little duplication of facilities. Finally, the structure allows tight, centralized control.

A disadvantage of this structural arrangement is that it can be difficult to coordinate the production and marketing areas since each operates independently of the other. This can be particularly troublesome if the MNE has multiple product lines. A second disadvantage is that responsibility for profits rests primarily with the CEO because there is little diffusion of operating authority far down the line.

Researchers have found that the global functional arrangement is most common among raw materials extractors with heavy capital investment. It is also used by energy firms. However, this is not a structure that suits many other kinds of businesses.

Mixed structure   A **mixed structure** is a hybrid organization design that combines structural arrangements in a way that best meets the needs of the enterprise. Figure 9.7 provides an illustration. Different businesses with different patterns of global demand, supply, and competition demand different management structures. However, sometimes the mixed structure is a temporary one, and the organization opts for a more common form (global product, area, or functional) after a year or two. In other cases the structure remains in place indefinitely or a new mixed structure replaces the old one. The primary advantage of this organizational arrangement is that it allows the enterprise to create the specific types of design that best meets its needs. On the other hand, the arrangement sometimes is so flexible and different from anything the enterprise has used previously that personnel have trouble operating

Figure 9.7   A mixed structure

Regions Products	Country A	Country B	Country C
Product 1			
Product 2			
Product 3			

Figure 9.8   Geographic matrix structure

efficiently. Problems emerge with communication flows, chains of command, and groups going their own way. In deciding whether or not to use the mixed structure, MNEs must carefully weigh the benefits and drawbacks.

Matrix structure   A **matrix structure** is an organizational arrangement that blends two organizational responsibilities such as functional and product structures or regional and product structures. The functional emphasis provides attention to the activities to be performed, whereas the product emphasis provides attention to the good that is being produced. This structure is characterized by a dual command system that emphasizes both inputs (functions) and outputs (products). This facilitates development of a globally oriented management attitude. Figure 9.8 illustrates a product-region matrix.

There are three types of managers in this geocentric matrix structure: regional managers, product managers, and matrix managers. **Regional managers** are charged with business in their markets. Budgets for these operations include selling any of the products made by the MNE, subject to the decision of each regional manager. These regional managers have a polycentric focus. **Product managers** are responsible for coordinating the efforts of their people in such a way as to ensure the profitability of a particular business or product line. These managers have an ethnocentric attitude. The matrix managers are responsible to *both* regional and product managers – they have two bosses.

The matrix design in Figure 9.9 is more complex than that in Figure 9.8, as it has three dimensions. It illustrates how the matrix organizational arrangement can be used to coordinate and manage wide-reaching international operations. **Resource managers** are charged with providing the people for operations, whereas **business**

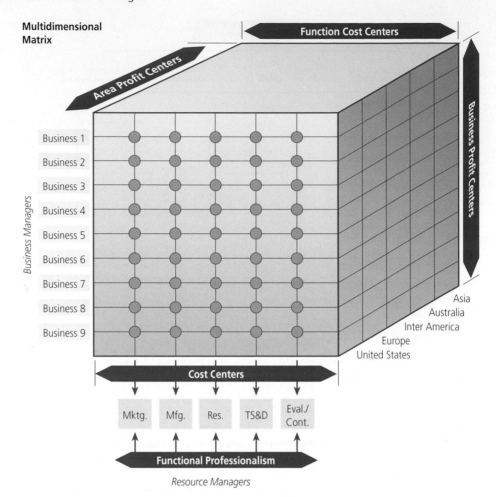

Figure 9.9 A multinational matrix structure

Source: Allan R. Janger, *Matrix Organizations of Complex Businesses* (New York: The Conference Board, 1979), p. 31.

managers are responsible for coordinating the efforts of these people to make profits for the product line. The resource managers are concerned with inputs; the business managers are concerned with outputs. At the bottom of Figure 9.9 there are functional specialists from such areas as marketing, manufacturing, and research. Individuals from each of these areas are assigned to each of the company's nine businesses. In turn these nine profit centers operate in five different areas of the world, including the United States, Europe, and Asia. Each business is run by a business board which (although not shown in the figure) reports to senior-level management.

The matrix design in Figure 9.9 is sometimes referred to as a three-dimensional model because when it is drawn, it has width, height, and depth. Additionally, it is interesting to note that this multidimensional matrix addresses three major areas: function, product, and geography. So the structure is really a combination of some of the designs discussed earlier.

One of the major advantages of the multinational matrix is that it allows management to address more than one primary area of consideration. In Figure 9.9 the company is able to focus on functional, product, and geographic considerations. MNEs that need to balance a product and a global location strategy can benefit from this type of structure.[11]

On the other hand, there are a number of drawbacks to the use of the matrix structure in international operations. One is the complexity of the design and the use of dual command. This can result in confusion regarding what everyone is responsible for doing and to whom one reports on various matters. A second drawback is the large number of meetings and discussions that often result from efforts to coordinate a variety of different groups, each with its own agenda. A third is that it often takes time for managers to learn to operate in a matrix structure, and if the enterprise has rapid turnover, there is always a significant portion of the personnel who do not fully understand how to function effectively in this environment. The box "International Business Strategy in Action: Making Matrix Work" describes how some of these problems can be handled.

The matrix structure is seldom the first choice of MNEs. The design typically evolves gradually, as the organization realizes that other structural designs are not adequate. In recent years, however, some companies have abandoned the matrix structure. Skandia, the Swedish insurance firm, for example, has scrapped its matrix design and moved back to a more classical organizational arrangement.[12] As with mixed structures, the matrix is sometimes a temporary arrangement as the enterprise searches for some hybrid design that will help it to operate more efficiently in the international arena.[13]

Transnational network structure　One of the newest forms of international organizational arrangements to emerge is the **transnational network structure** which is designed to help MNCs take advantage of global economies of scale while also being responsive to local customer demands. This structural design combines elements of functional, product, and geographic designs, while relying on a network arrangement to link the various worldwide subsidiaries. At the center of the transnational network structure are nodes, which are units charged with coordinating product, functional, and geographic information. Different product group units and geographical area units have different structures depending on what is best for their particular operations. A good example of how the transnational network structure works is provided by NV Philips, which has operations in more than 60 countries and produces a diverse product line ranging from light bulbs to defense systems. In all, the company has eight product divisions with a varying number of subsidiaries in each – and the focus of the latter varies considerably. Some specialize in manufacturing, others in sales; some are closely controlled by headquarters, others are highly autonomous.

The basic structural framework of the transnational network consists of three components: dispersed subunits, specialized operations, and interdependent relationships. *Dispersed subunits* are subsidiaries that are located anywhere in the world where they can benefit the organization. Some are designed to take advantage of low factor costs, while others are responsible for providing information on new technologies or consumer trends. *Specialized operations* are activities carried out by subunits that focus on particular product lines, research areas, and marketing areas, and are designed to tap specialized expertise or other resources in the company's worldwide subsidiaries. **Interdependent relationships** are used to share information and resources throughout the dispersed and specialized subunits.

The transnational network structure is difficult to draw in the form of an organization chart because it is complex and continually changing. Figure 9.10, which provides a view of NV Philips' network structure, shows how complex the design can be.

INTERNATIONAL BUSINESS STRATEGY IN ACTION

Making matrix work

Many multinationals use matrix structures in their international operations. Some of these structures work out very well; some do not. The reason for success can often be tied to three important criteria: clarity, continuity, and consistency. If all three are achieved, the matrix tends to work well; if one or more are missing, the structural design is often ineffective.

Clarity refers to how well people understand what they are doing and why they are doing it. If the company's basic objectives are clear, if relationships in the structure are spelled out in direct, simple terms, and the relevance of jobs is enunciated, there is a good chance that clarity will be achieved. A good example is NEC, the giant Japanese MNE that decided to integrate computers and communication and to make this the focus of its business efforts. This message was clearly communicated to the personnel so that everyone in the organization understood what the company wanted to do. On the other hand, competitors like AT&T tried the same strategy but failed to clarify what they were doing. As a result, NEC has been more successful in its pursuit of the computer/communication market.

Continuity means that the company remains committed to the same core objectives and values. This provides a unifying theme and helps to ensure that the personnel are committed. General Electric's Brazilian subsidiary is a good example of how a lack of continuity can hurt. In the 1960s the subsidiary built televisions. During the 1970s it was told to switch to large appliances. Then it was told to focus on housewares. By this time the company's dominant franchise in Brazil's electrical products market had all but dissipated. In contrast, Unilever set up operations in Brazil and, despite volatile changes in the economy, continued to focus its efforts on the electrical products market. Today Unilever has a thriving market in that country.

Consistency relates to how well all parts of the organization are moving in accord with each other. This is often a reflection of how well managers of the various operating divisions are pursuing the same objectives. For example, Philips NV launched an international strategy for its videocassette recording system, the V2000. However, its US subsidiary did not support these efforts because it felt that Matsushita's VHS format and Sony's Beta system were too well established. Because of this, Philips was unable to build the efficiency and credibility it needed to challenge the Japanese dominance of the VCR business.

Matrix structures can be complex organizational arrangements. However, if the MNE is able to achieve clarity, continuity, and consistency, the matrix approach can be very effective.

Sources: Christopher A. Bartlett and Sumantra Ghoshal, "Matrix Management: Not a Structure, a Frame of Mind," *Harvard Business Review*, July–August 1990, pp. 138–145; Courtland L. Bovee et al., *Management* (New York: McGraw-Hill, Inc., 1993), pp. 321–323; and Richard M. Hodgetts and Fred Luthans, *International Management* 4th ed. (Burr Ridge, Ill: Irwin/McGraw 2000), Chapter 7.

ACTIVE LEARNING CHECK

Review your answer to Active Learning Case question 1 and make any changes you like. Then compare your answer to the one below.

1. What type of organizational arrangement did Gruppo GFT use for its US operations during the 1980s? What type of structure does it use today?

Initially the company used an export department structure and then changed it to an international division structure. Today, however, the firm uses a mixed structure similar to that in Figure 9.7. The North American subsidiaries now have a great deal of authority to make decisions that affect local market operations, and Turin management maintains a more passive role although the company's central management does establish financial goals for US operations.

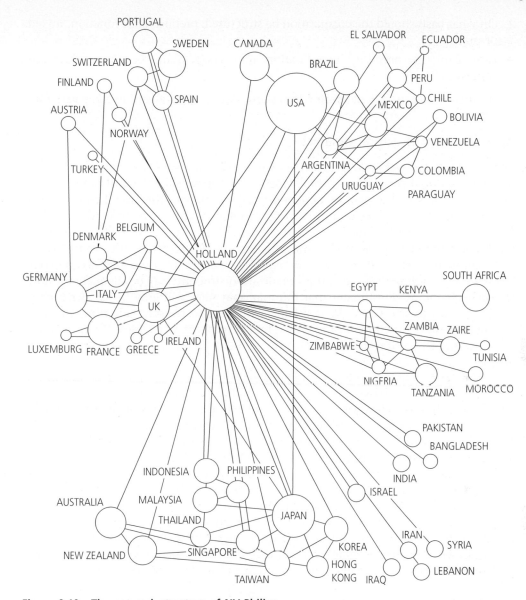

Figure 9.10   The network structure of NV Philips

Source: Sumantra Ghoshal and Christopher A. Bartlett, "The Multinational Corporation as an Interorganizational Network," *Academy of Management Review*, October 1990, p. 605.

STRATEGIC MANAGEMENT AND ORGANIZING STRATEGY

Research has shown that effective organizations follow the adage "from strategy to structure."[14] They begin by formulating a strategy and only then design a structure that will efficiently implement this plan.[15] In determining the best structure, three questions must be answered:

1. Can the company operate efficiently with domestic divisions or are international divisions also necessary?

2. On what basis should the organization be structured: product, area, function, mixed, or matrix?

3. How can the necessary coordination and cooperation be most effectively achieved?

These answers are usually determined through a careful analysis of five key variables.

Analysis of key structural variables

There are five key variables that MNEs examine in choosing from among alternative organizational structures. In some cases one of these variables will outweigh the others and the structure will be designed to accommodate this one. In most cases, however, there are three or four interacting variables that the structure must address.

First, the MNE will evaluate the relative importance of international operations at the present time and project what the situation might be within three to five years. If the company is currently doing 5 per cent of its business overseas and has an export department handling these sales, this organization structure may be adequate for now. However, if the MNE estimates that international sales will grow to 25 per cent of total revenues in five years, the company will want to consider adopting an international division structure or one of the global arrangements. Unless the firm is prepared to make this transition, it may prove difficult to handle the anticipated rapid growth.

Second, the company will take into account its past history and experience in the international arena. If the firm has done very little business abroad, it is likely to choose a simple structure that is easy to understand and control. If the company has been doing business overseas for many years, it will probably have experienced managers who can work well in a more sophisticated structure, and so it may choose a mixed design or a matrix.

A third area of consideration is the company's business and product strategy. If the company offers a small number of products and there is little need to adapt them to local tastes, a global functional structure may be the best choice. On the other hand, if the products must be tailored for local markets, a global product arrangement will probably be more effective. If the company is going to be doing business in a number of diverse geographic areas, a global area structure will likely be used.

A fourth influencing variable is management's philosophy of operating. If the company wants to expand rapidly and is prepared to take risks, the firm will choose a structure that is quite different from that used by an MNE that wants to expand slowly and is conservative in its risk-taking. Similarly, if the home office wants to keep a tight rein on operations, it will not use the same structure as a firm that gives local subsidiaries autonomy and encourages them to make decisions about how to keep the unit competitive at the local level. French and German subsidiaries, for example, tend to be more centralized than US units. There are also differences in the way operations are controlled. For example, Japanese MNEs like to use face-to-face informal controls while US multinationals prefer budgets, financial data, and other formalized tools.

A final key variable is the enterprise's ability to adjust to organizational changes. As MNE world sales increase, there will be continual modifications in the structure. For example, when the company is small, the domestic divisions will dominate. As the international side of operations grows, the managers of the domestic divisions

Table 9.1 Factors that encourage centralization or decentralization of decision making in multinational operations

Encourage centralization of decision making	Encourage decentralization of decision making
Large enterprise	Small enterprise
Large capital investment	Small capital investment
Relative importance of the unit to the MNE	Relative unimportance of the unit to the MNE
Highly competitive environment	Stable environment
Strong volume-to-unit-cost relationship	Weak volume-to-unit-cost relationship
High degree of technology	Moderate to low degree of technology
Low level of product diversification	High level of product diversification
Homogeneous product lines	Heterogeneous product lines
High interdependence between the units	Low interdependence between the units
Few highly competent managers in the host country	Many highly competent managers in the host country
High experience in international business	Low experience in international business
Small geographic distance between home office and subsidiary	Large geographic distance between home office and subsidiary

will have to cede some of their authority and influence. If they are unable or unwilling to do this, the structure will be affected. Similarly, if international executives begin gaining greater authority and there is a need to revamp overseas operations, their willingness to adjust to organizational changes will affect the structure. In some cases MNEs have found that overseas managers, just like their domestic counterparts, build small empires and often are unwilling to give up this power.

The ultimate choice of organization structure rests with top management. However, this group seldom tries to force such a decision on those who will be directly affected. Instead, there is a give-and-take in which the needs of the enterprise and the personnel are considered. The result is a structure that is both efficient and humanistic. In carrying this out, the company will address the organizational processes that take place within the structure.

Organizational processes

The formal structure provides the skeletal framework within which the personnel operate. The structure is designed to answer the question: What is to be done? The organizational processes – decision making, communicating, and controlling – help to make the structure work efficiently. These processes help to answer the question: Who is to do what, and how will they do it? These processes help to put the organization structure into action.

Decision making **Decision making** is the process of choosing from among alternatives. In international operations one of the primary areas of consideration is where the ultimate decision-making authority will rest on important matters. If the home office holds this control, decision making is centralized; if the subsidiary can make many of these important decisions without having to consult the home office, decision making is decentralized. Table 9.1 provides some examples of factors that encourage both these types of decision making.[16]

Research shows that decision making in MNE subsidiaries tends to vary from country to country or culture to culture. For example, among British organizations there is a great deal of decentralized decision making. Many upper-level managers do not understand the technical nature of business operations such as financial budgeting or cost control. So they delegate the authority for these matters to middle-level managers while they focus on strategic matters.

French and German subsidiaries tend to be fairly centralized in their decision-making approaches. French senior executives like to maintain control of operations and tend to delegate less authority than do their English counterparts. German managers are hierarchical in their approach and most important decisions are made at the top.

In Scandinavian countries like Norway, Sweden, and Denmark, operations are highly decentralized both in Scandinavian-based firms and abroad. The Scandinavians place a great deal of emphasis on the quality of work life, and they are more interested in the well-being of the worker than in maximizing profit.

The Japanese use a combination of decentralization and centralization. They make heavy use of a decision-making process called **ringsei**, or decision making by consensus:

> Under this system any changes in procedures and routines, tactics, and even strategies of a firm are originated by those directly concerned with these changes. The final decision is made at the top level after an elaborate examination of the proposal through successively higher levels in the management hierarchy and results in acceptance or rejection of a decision only through consensus at every echelon of the management structure.[17]

At the same time top management maintains a great deal of authority over what will be discussed at lower levels. Thus there is both decentralization and centralization exercised by senior-level management.

US MNEs, surprisingly perhaps, tend to use fairly centralized decision making in managing their overseas operations. This is particularly true in areas such as marketing policies, financial matters, and decisions on production capacity. Moreover, this is the current trend worldwide as MNEs work to increase economies of scale and to attain higher operational efficiency. In fact, it is highly likely that in countries such as Sweden, where the quality of work life has long been a major area of concern, there will be a move toward more centralized decision making in the future. The Swedes are finding that "humanistic manufacturing" is not always profitable, as seen by the results at Volvo's new auto production plant in Uddevalla.[18]

Communication **Communication** is the process of transferring meanings from sender to receiver.[19] However, the way in which this is done often varies from one MNE to another. For example, US MNEs use direct communications with their subsidiaries and overseas units. Directives are spelled out clearly and precisely. However, Japanese MNEs prefer more indirect communications in which things are implied and it is up to the listener to determine what to do. The direct approach works well for Americans, whose culture encourages openness and specific communications. The indirect approach works well for the Japanese, whose culture encourages indirect and implied communications. Ouchi, after conducting a series of interviews with Americans working for a Japanese bank in the United States, found that this problem can be particularly disconcerting because each side is unable to understand the other's approach, as illustrated by the following:

AMERICAN MANAGERS

We have a non-stop running battle with the president. We simply cannot get him to specify a performance target for us. We have all the necessary reports and numbers, but we can't get specific targets from him. He won't tell us how large a dollar increase in loan volume or what percent decrease in operating costs he expects us to achieve over the next month, quarter, or even year. How can we know whether we're performing well without specific targets to shoot for?

JAPANESE BANK PRESIDENT

If only I could get these Americans to understand our philosophy of banking. To understand what the business means to us – how we feel we should deal with our customers and our employees. What our relationship should be to the local communities we serve. How we should deal with our competitors, and what our role should be in the world at large. If they could get that under their skin, then they could figure out for themselves what an appropriate objective would be for any situation, no matter how unusual or new, and I would never have to tell them, never have to give them a target.[20]

These types of culturally based differences can greatly affect the MNE's ability to get things done.

Another communication-based problem is nonverbal messages. In international business these take two major forms: kinesics and proxemics. **Kinesics** deals with the conveying of information through the use of body movement and facial expression. For example, when verbally communicating with someone in the United States, it is good manners to look the other party in the eye. However, in many other cultures, such as Arab and Middle East, this is not done, especially if one is talking to a member of the opposite sex. Such behavior would be considered rude and disrespectful.[21]

Proxemics deals with how people use physical space to convey messages. For example, in the United States, businesspeople typically stand two to three feet away from those with whom they are communicating. However, in the Middle East and in many South American countries, it is common to stand right next to the person. This often makes Americans feel very uncomfortable because this space is generally reserved only for family members and close friends. Business is not conducted at this distance. One group of authors summarized the problem this way:

> Americans often tend to be moving away in interpersonal communication with their Middle Eastern or Latin counterparts, while the latter are trying to physically close the gap. The American cannot understand why the other is standing so close; the latter cannot understand why the American is being so reserved and standing so far away; the result is a breakdown in communication.[22]

Another example of proxemics is office layout and protocol. In the United States, a large office connotes importance, as does a secretary who screens visitors and keeps away those whom the manager does not wish to see. In Japan, most managers do not have large offices, and if they do, they spend little time in them since they are generally out talking to the employees and walking around the workplace. If the manager were to stay in the office all day, it would be viewed as a sign of distrust or anger at the work group. In Europe, many managers do not have walled-in offices. The bosses are out in the same large room as their people; there is no one to screen the brokers from the boss.

Every country has some unique communication patterns or behaviors.[23] These behaviors can be particularly troublesome to outsiders who are working locally and are unfamiliar with local approaches to communication. Figure 9.11 provides an

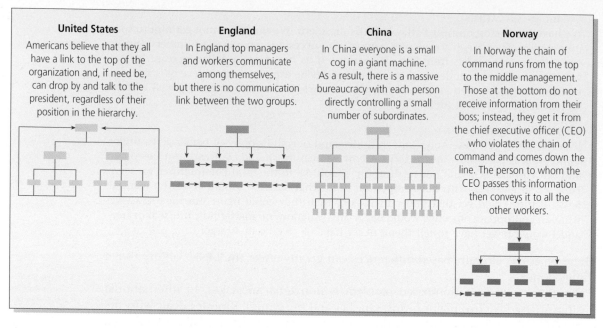

United States

Americans believe that they all have a link to the top of the organization and, if need be, can drop by and talk to the president, regardless of their position in the hierarchy.

England

In England top managers and workers communicate among themselves, but there is no communication link between the two groups.

China

In China everyone is a small cog in a giant machine. As a result, there is a massive bureaucracy with each person directly controlling a small number of subordinates.

Norway

In Norway the chain of command runs from the top to the middle management. Those at the bottom do not receive information from their boss; instead, they get it from the chief executive officer (CEO) who violates the chain of command and comes down the line. The person to whom the CEO passes this information then conveys it to all the other workers.

Figure 9.11   Organizational epigrams

An epigram is a terse, witty statement. The organizational epigrams are designed to poke fun at the way communication flows in international organizations. Each was created by an individual with experience in the respective country. The explanation accompanying the respective epigram explains the logic behind the drawing. These epigrams illustrate that communication flows throughout the world are less efficient than the enterprise would like. They also illustrate that each country has its own unique approach to conveying information.
Source: Adapted from Simcha Ronen, *Comparative and Multinational Management* (New York: John Wiley & Sons, 1986), pp. 318–319.

interesting example in the form of epigrams that have been drawn from organization structures throughout the world.

Controlling   **Controlling** is the process of determining that everything goes according to plan. This process is to reward performance and it consists of three steps: (1) establishing standards, (2) comparing performance against standards, and (3) correcting deviations. Controlling is closely linked to communication since it is virtually impossible to evaluate performance and make changes without communicating information; many of the same organizational problems discussed above also apply here.

One of the major differences between US and Japanese firms is the use of explicit versus implicit control. One of the major differences between US and European firms is that US MNEs tend to rely more heavily on reports and other performance-related data, whereas Europeans make heavy use of behavioral control. US multinationals compare results of a foreign unit with those of other foreign units, as well as with domestic units, in evaluating performance. European MNEs tend to be more flexible and to judge performance on an individual basis rather than simply making a comparative judgment. Other differences include:

1. Control in US MNEs relies on precise planning and budgeting that are suitable for comparison purposes. Control in European MNEs takes into consideration a high level of companywide understanding and agreement regarding what constitutes appropriate behavior and how such behavior supports the goals of the subsidiary and the parent company.

2. US multinationals do not encourage their managers to remain in overseas positions for a long period of time. As a result, these companies use large central staffs and centralized information gathering to carry out evaluations. European multinationals, on the other hand, encourage their managers to remain in overseas positions, and these companies rely heavily on these managers to provide input regarding how well the unit is doing.

3. Managers of US MNEs often report to a counterpart back in headquarters who, in turn, conveys information up the line. European multinationals have a more direct reporting channel so that the head of a foreign subsidiary reports to someone who is closer to the top of the structure.[24]

Another major difference is the way in which personnel are evaluated. In the United States and in Europe, it is common to single out high performers and to reward them. In Japan, however, credit is given to the entire group and not just to one or two individuals. Singling people out for special attention is not regarded as complimentary. Rather, such attention would make an individual feel that he or she was not regarded as a team player, and this would be insulting. Another important difference is the time period for personnel evaluations. Most US and European firms evaluate their people on an annual basis. However, in Japan, the first major evaluation often does not occur until the employee has been with the firm for almost a decade.[25] These controlling differences greatly affect the way the structure is managed. As a result, running an overseas operation the same way it is done at home is often difficult.

ACTIVE LEARNING CHECK

Review your answer to Active Learning Case question 2 and make any changes you like. Then compare your answer to the one below.

2. What factor resulted in GFT's choice of this most recent organizational arrangement? Identify and describe this factor.

The most important factor was the need to give subsidiaries the authority to address local conditions such as changing consumer taste. The company realized that decisions being made in Turin were not adequate in addressing the needs of customers worldwide. This became particularly evident as consumer knowledge about quality and price increased and buyers began to feel that they no longer had to rely on designers in Italy to tell them what they should be wearing. This grassroots development eventually resulted in GFT's changing its structure and giving local managers the authority to make decisions that most directly affected their particular markets.

SUMMARY

Key points

1. When a company first enters the international arena, it is common to find that these efforts are mere extensions of domestic operations. The MNE will typically handle foreign sales directly through its own marketing department, an export

department, or an overseas subsidiary that is the result of a joint venture. As international operations become more important, however, the firm is likely to centralize these operations by adopting an international division structure. This organizational arrangement remains quite popular with many MNEs.

2. As multinationals generate increased revenues from their overseas operations, they are likely to adopt a global organizational structure. There are six basic types: global product, global area, global functional, mixed, matrix, and transnational network. Each type has specific advantages and disadvantages.

3. There are five key variables that MNEs examine in choosing from among alternative organizational structures. These include (a) the relative importance of international operations, (b) past history and experience in the international arena, (c) the company's business and product strategy, (d) management philosophy, and (e) the organization's ability to adjust to organization changes.

4. The formal structure provides the skeletal framework within which the personnel operate. The organization process of decision making, communicating, and controlling make the structure work efficiently. In the decision-making process, one of the key areas of consideration is the amount of centralization or decentralization that will be used by the home office. In communicating, culturally based differences will be of major importance, including nonverbal messages. In controlling, areas of concern include explicit and implicit control and the ways in which personnel will be evaluated.

Key terms

- international division structure
- global product structure
- global area structure
- global functional structure
- mixed structure
- matrix structure
- transnational network structure
- regional managers
- product managers
- resource managers
- business managers
- decision making
- ringsei
- communication
- kinesics
- proxemics
- controlling

Review and discussion questions

1. How does an export department structure function? Who handles the overseas sales?

2. If a company's initial international expansion is conducted through the use of subsidiaries, how closely does it control these subsidiaries? Why?

3. Why do MNEs use an international division structure? Are there any drawbacks to this organizational arrangement?

4. How does a global product structure work? Why would an MNE opt for this arrangement? What are two drawbacks to using this structure?

5. When would an MNE use a global area structure? When would the firm reject this structural arrangement in favor of a different structure?

6. How does a global functional structure work? When would it be a popular approach? When would it be of very little value in organizing international operations?

7. When would a company opt for a mixed structure? Why? Defend your answer.

8. How does a matrix structure work? When would an MNE opt for this organizational arrangement?

9. There are five key variables that MNEs examine in choosing from among alternative organizational structures. What are these five? Identify and briefly describe each.

10. Why are some overseas operations highly decentralized while others are very centralized? What factors influence this arrangement?

11. Why are US international operations more centralized than those in Sweden? Why is the US model becoming more popular among MNEs?

12. In what way is implicit versus explicit communication important in understanding how home office managements coordinate international activities?

13. What type of control techniques do US MNEs prefer? How does this preference differ from that of the Japanese? Compare and contrast the two.

REAL CASES

NORTEL AS A TRANSNATIONAL CORPORATION

Northern Telecom, now called Nortel, has transformed itself from a Canadian-based multinational enterprise in 1977 to a North American-based MNE by 1987 to a transnational corporation by 1997. Between 1985 and 1995, its revenue increased from $4.2 billion to $10.7 billion and total employees from 46,500 to 63,000.

In 1985, over 90 per cent of its sales were within North America. Today Nortel has 92 per cent of its sales outside Canada, and 40 per cent of all sales outside of North America. It has a very large ratio of R&D to sales of over 20 per cent (R&D spending in 1995 was $1.6 billion on revenues of $10.7 billion). Today one in four of Nortel's employees focuses on R&D. Overall, the number of knowledge workers has increased from 42 per cent in 1985 to 66 per cent in 1995, rising to an expected 75 per cent by 1998.

While Nortel competes globally in the telecommunications sector, it is not operating as if borders do not exist. Despite the globalization in the telecom sector, there remains a very high degree of government regulation and a set of regionally-separated national markets. Even with the WTO's International Technology Agreement of 1995,

there is no single world market for telecommunications. Nortel must be flexible enough to respond to differences in national regulations and consumer tastes, so it has adopted a policy of national responsiveness. Other companies which are nationally responsive include Unilever and Asea Brown Boveri (ABB). With a national responsiveness strategy, a firm like Nortel can be "close to the customer" and responsive to the local regulator. Such decentralized firms are called "transnational corporations" (TNCs). Nortel qualifies as a TNC on three grounds.

First, Nortel has decentralized decision-making, to reflect the regional nature of the telecommunications market for products and services. A large degree of autonomy is given to product sector managers and country managers.

Second, Nortel has an internal managerial resource strategy which decentralizes key decision making to some 200 top executives in more than a dozen markets around the world. In 1987, Northern Telecom was run by five to ten people out of head office in Mississauga, Ontario. Today, the 200 top managers making key decisions operate with the large degree of autonomy typical of the TNC.

261

Third, Nortel's decentralized top management structure is held together by heavy use of the Internet for inter-office communication. Nortel has its own internal electronic mail, voice, and data network which is heavily used by senior managers, as well as all other employees. The senior managers are members of the President's Council, which conducts its business through the corporate intranet.

The key managerial challenge for Nortel today is how to organize effective "networks" with allies and strategic partners across the segmented regional markets that characterize the telecommunications sector. Nortel's objective is to be the global resource for digital network solutions and services. By building and integrating both wireline and wireless digital networks on a global basis and purchasing Bay Networks in 1998 Nortel has moved towards achieving this objective.

1. What type of organizational structure does Northern Telecom use?

2. Why does the firm rely so heavily on decentralized decision making?.

3. How does the company control operations? Explain.

Source: Annual Reports of Northern Telecom.

MITSUBISHI'S KEIRETSU

In the United States, Mitsubishi is well known for its automobiles, but not many people realize that the company is Japan's largest keiretsu. The group has annual sales in excess of $110 billion, and there are almost 30 core members who are bound together by cross-ownership and other financial ties (see Table 10.5 for a complete list of this keiretsu). Ten of these firms, along with the percentage of shares of each that are held by other members of the Mitsubishi group, are as follows:

Mitsubishi Aluminum	100%
Mitsubishi Motors	55
Mitsubishi Mining & Cement	37
Asahi Glass	28
Nikon Corporation	27
Mitsubishi Bank	26
Mitsubishi Rayon	25
Tokyo Marine & Fire Insurance	24
Mitsubishi Heavy Industries	20
Kirin Beer	19

Although the companies operate independently of each other, they can call upon each other for help. For example, when Akai Electric had financial problems in the early 1980s, it was rescued by Mitsubishi Bank. When Mitsubishi Heavy Industries' shipbuilding business ran into trouble in the mid-1980s, it was able to find work at other group companies for those personnel who were laid off. The cross-holding structure also comes in handy when warding off takeovers. For example, when Texaco bought Getty Oil in 1984, it was prepared to sell Getty's 50 per cent share of Mitsubishi Oil to Kuwait Petroleum. However, the members of the group got together and outbid the Kuwaitis for Getty's shares. The group has also made important acquisitions and struck major deals in a variety of areas. Mitsubishi companies have participated in the $940 million purchase of the Pebble Beach golf course in California, won a $400 million power plant deal in Virginia, and launched a $150 million futures trading joint venture in Chicago. The group has also set up a plant to build cars in the former Soviet Union. Overall, Mitsubishi has hundreds of interdependent companies and they are building an empire that stretches from Asia to Europe to the United States.

1. How would a company like Kirin Beer be organized for international purposes? Why would it use this particular organizational arrangement?

2. How would Mitsubishi organize a joint venture with Daimler-Benz in Russia? Explain

Sources: http://www.rolf.ru/; http//www.mitsubishi.com/; http://www.hoovers.com/capsules/41773.html; William J. Holstein et al., "Mighty Mitsubishi Is on the Move," *Business Week*, September 24, 1990, pp. 98–107; "Japan's Automakers: A Controlled Skid," *Fortune*, May 17, 1993, p. 12; Emily Thornton, "Japan's Struggle to Restructure," *Fortune*, June 28, 1993, pp. 84–88; *mitsubishi.com/ghp_ japan/financial/financial.html.*

ENDNOTES

1. Joanne Lee-Young, "Starbucks' Expansion in China Is Slated," *Wall Street Journal*, October 5, 1998, p. A27C.
2. For example, many Japanese and American MNEs are now trimming back their work forces in order to increase overall efficiency. See Andrew Pollack, "Think Japan Inc. Is Lean and Mean? Step Into This Office," *New York Times*, March 20, 1994, p. F11; and Brenton R. Schlender, "Japan's White-Collar Blues," *Fortune*, March 21, 1994, pp. 97–104.
3. Brad Mitchener, "GM Takes a Gamble on Eastern Europe," *Wall Street Journal*, June 23, 1997, p. A10.
4. William J. Holstein et al., "Mighty Mitsubishi Is on the Move," *Business Week*, September 24, 1990, p. 99.
5. Robert L. Simison, "New Dana Illustrates Reshaping of Auto Parts Business," *Wall Street Journal*, September 2, 1997, p. B4.
6. See, for example, Stewart Toy et al., "Europe's Shake-out," *Business Week*, September 14, 1992, pp. 44–51.
7. A good example is offered by Peter Siddall, Keith Willey, and Jorge Tavares, "Building a Transnational Organization for BP Oil," *Long Range Planning*, February 1992, pp. 37–45.
8. For some excellent examples, see Charles H. Ferguson, "Computers and the Coming of the US Keiretsu," *Harvard Business Review*, July–August 1990, pp. 55–70; and Benjamin Gomes-Casseres, "Joint Ventures in the Face of Global Competition," *Sloan Management Review*, Spring 1989, pp. 17–26.
9. Richard M. Hodgetts and Fred Luthans, *International Management*, 4th ed (Burr Ridge, Ill: McGraw/Irwin, 2000), p. 303.
10. Ibid., p. 306.
11. Yves L. Doz, Christopher A. Bartlett, and C. K. Prahalad, "Global Competitive Pressures and Host Country Demands," *California Management Review*, Spring 1981, p. 66.
12. Also, see Fred V. Guterl, "Goodbye, Old Matrix," *Business Month*, February 1989, pp. 32–38.
13. For more on this topic, see John S. McClenahen, "Managing More People in the '90s," *Industry Week*, March 20, 1989, pp. 30–36.
14. Alfred D. Chandler, Jr., *Strategy and Structure* (Garden City, New York: Anchor Books, Doubleday & Company, Inc., 1966).
15. Saul Hansell, "Is This The Factory of the Future?" *New York Times*, July 26, 1998, Section 3, pp. 1, 12.
16. Also see Rebecca Blumenstein, "GM Is Building Plants In Developing Nations To Woo New Markets," *Wall Street Journal*, August 4, 1997, pp. A1, 5.
17. Raghu Nath, *Comparative Management: A Regional View* (Cambridge, Mass.: Ballinger Publishing, 1988), p. 125.
18. Steven Prokesch, "Edges Fray on Volvo's Brave New Humanistic World," *New York Times*, July 7, 1991, p. F5.
19. See, for example, Jim Manzi, "Computer Keiretsu: Japanese Idea. US Style," *New York Times*, February 6, 1994, p. F15.
20. For an excellent contrast of American and Japanese communication problems, see William G. Ouchi, *Theory Z* (Reading, Mass.: Addison-Wesley Publishing, 1981), pp. 33–35.
21. Jane Whitney Gibson, Richard M. Hodgetts, and Charles W. Blackwell, "Cultural Variations in Nonverbal Communication," in *Proceedings of the 55th Annual Convention of the Association for Business Communication*, 1990, p. 213.
22. Hodgetts and Luthans, op. cit., p. 212.
23. David E. Sanger, "Tokyo's Tips For New York," *New York Times Magazine*, February 6, 1994, pp. 28–29.
24. William G. Egelhoff, "Patterns of Control in US, UK, and European Multinational Corporations," *Journal of International Business Studies*, Fall 1984, pp. 81–82.
25. Ouchi, op. cit., p. 22.

ADDITIONAL BIBLIOGRAPHY

Bartlett, Christopher A. and Ghoshal, Sumantra. "Managing Across Borders: New Organizational Responses," *Sloan Management Review*, vol. 29, no. 1 (Fall 1987).

Bartlett, Christopher A. and Ghoshal, Sumantra. "Matrix Management: Not a Structure, a Frame of Mind," *Harvard Business Review*, vol. 68, no. 4 (July/August 1990).

Bartlett, Christopher A. and Ghoshal, Sumantra, "What Is a Global Manager?" *Harvard Business Review*, vol. 70, no. 5 (September/October 1992).

Beldona, Sam, Inkpen, Andrew C. and Phatak, Arvind. "Are Japanese Managers More Long-Term Oriented than United States Managers," *Management International Review*, vol. 38, no. 3 (1998).

Doktor, Robert and Lie, John. "A Systems Theoretic Perspective upon International Organizational Behaviour: Some Preliminary Observations and Hypotheses," *Management International Review*, vol. 31 (1991).

Duck, Jeanie Daniel. "Managing Change: The Art of Balancing," *Harvard Business Review*, vol. 71, no. 6 (November/December 1993).

Geringer, J. Michael. "Strategic Determinants of Partner Selection Criteria in International Joint Ventures," *Journal of International Business Studies*, vol. 22, no. 1 (First Quarter 1991).

Ghoshal, Sumantra and Bartlett, Christopher A. "The Multinational Corporation as an Interorganizational Network," *Academy of Management Review*, vol. 15, no. 4 (October 1990).

Gregersen, Hal B., Morrison, Allen J. and Black, J. Stewart. "Developing Leaders for the Global Frontier," *Sloan Management Review*, vol. 40, no. 1 (Fall 1998).

Itaki, Masahiko. "Information-Processing Theory and the Multinational Enterprise," *Journal of International Business Studies*, vol. 22, no. 3 (Third Quarter 1991).

Kogut, Bruce and Zander, Udo. "Knowledge of the Firm and the Evolutionary Theory of the Multinational Corporation," *Journal of International Business Studies*, vol. 24, no. 4 (Fourth Quarter 1993).

Kotova, Tatiana and Zaheer, Srilata. "Organizational Legitimacy Under Conditions of Complexity: The Case of the Multinational Enterprise," *The Academy of Management Review*, vol. 24, no. 1 (October 1999).

Lee, Kwang Chul and Kwok, Chuck C. Y. "Multinational Corporations vs. Domestic Corporations: International Environmental Factors and Determinants of Capital Structure," *Journal of International Business Studies*, vol. 19, no. 2 (Summer 1988).

Maljers, Floris A. "Inside Unilever: The Evolving Transnational Company," *Harvard Business Studies*, vol. 70, no. 5 (September/October 1992).

Martin, Roger. "Changing the Mind of the Corporation," *Harvard Business Review*, vol. 71, no. 6 (November/December 1993).

Martinez, Jon I. and Jarillo, J. Carlos. "The Evolution of Research on Coordinating Mechanisms in Multinational Corporations," *Journal of International Business Studies*, vol. 20, no. 3 (Fall 1989).

McCormick, Janice and Stone, Nan. "From National Champion to Global Competitor: An Interview with Thomson's Alain Gomez," *Harvard Business Review*, vol. 68, no. 3 (May/June 1990).

Mills, D. Quinn. "The Decline and Rise of IBM," *Sloan Management Review*, vol. 37 (Summer 1996).

Parkhe, Arvind. "Interfirm Diversity, Organizational Learning, and Longevity in Global Strategic Alliances," *Journal of International Business Studies*, vol. 22, no. 4 (Fourth Quarter 1991).

Poole, Marshall Scott and Van de Ven, Andrew H. "Using Paradox to Build Management and Organization Theories," *Academy of Management Review*, vol. 14, no. 4 (October 1989).

Prahalad, C. K. and Oosterveld, Jan P. "Transforming Internal Governance," *Sloan Management Review*, vol. 40, no. 3 (Spring 1999).

Rosenzweig, Philip M. and Singh, Jitendra V. "Organizational Environments and the Multinational Enterprise," *Academy of Management Review*, vol. 16, no. 2 (April 1991).

Roth, Kendall. "International Configuration and Coordination Archetypes for Medium-Sized Firms in Global Industries," *Journal of International Business Studies*, vol. 23, no. 3 (Third Quarter 1992).

Rugman, Alan M. and Verbeke, Alain. "A Note on the Transnational Solution and the Transaction Cost Theory of Multinational Strategic Management," *Journal of International Business Studies*, vol. 23, no. 4 (Fall 1992).

Sanyal, Rajib N. "An Empirical Analysis of the Unionization of Foreign Manufacturing Firms in the US," *Journal of International Business Studies*, vol. 21, no. 1 (First Quarter 1990).

Sullivan, Daniel. "Organization in American MNCs: The Perspective of the European Regional Head-quarters," *Management International Review*, vol. 32, no. 3 (Third Quarter 1992).

CHAPTER 10

Production Strategy

OBJECTIVES OF THE CHAPTER

Production strategy is critical to effective international operations. Since most goods and services have very limited lives, MNEs must continually provide new offerings, and this can be accomplished only through a well-formulated production strategy. The purpose of this chapter is to examine how MNEs carry out this process. In doing so, we will focus on the entire range of production strategies from research and development to manufacturing, to shipment, and to the final international destination. We will look at the most current approaches, including speed to market, concurrent engineering, and continuous cost reduction. The specific objectives of this chapter are to:

1. **Examine** the role of research, development, and innovation in production strategy.

2. **Relate** some of the most critical steps in generating goods and services, including global sourcing, costing techniques, quality maintenance, effective materials handling, inventory control, and the proper emphasis on service.

3. **Describe** the nature and importance of international logistics in production strategy.

4. **Review** some of the major production strategies being used by MNEs, including strategic alliances and acquisitions.

The GE production strategy just keeps getting better and better

General Electric is a multibillion dollar, multinational corporation whose products range from 65-cent light bulbs to billion-dollar power plants. In fact, based on revenues, assets, profits, and market value, the firm was recently listed by *Forbes* magazine as number one in the world. One reason for the company's annual revenue of more than $90 billion is its ability to manage a diverse multiproduct-line operation. Much of its success can be attributed to the production-related concepts that it employs worldwide: work-out, process mapping, and best practices.

Work-out is a training program designed to empower employees and to implement their problem-solving ideas. In this process a group of 40 to 100 people, picked by management from all ranks and functional areas, attend a three-day meeting. The first day consists of a manager leading the group in roughing out an agenda related to areas where productivity can be increased. Then the manager leaves and for the next $1\frac{1}{2}$ days the group breaks into teams to tackle the agenda. On the last afternoon the manager returns and one by one the team members make their proposals for improved productivity. The manager can make only three responses: agree, disagree, or ask for more information – in which case the individual must empower a team to get it by an agreed-upon date. These work-out sessions have proved extremely successful. In one case a group of workers convinced management to allow their factory to bid against an outside vendor for the right to build new protective shields for grinding machines. As a result, the GE group completed the job for $16,000 versus $96,000 for the vendor.

The second method, *process mapping*, involves the creation of a flowchart developed to show all steps, no matter how small, that are used in making or doing something. The map is analyzed for ways of eliminating steps and of saving time and money. In one case a work group was able to

reorganize production, cut manufacturing time in half, and reduce inventory by $4 million.

The third method, *best practices*, consists of finding companies that do things better than GE does and then emulating them. In this process GE personnel try to answer the question: What is the secret of this other company's success? Quite often it includes such things as getting products to market faster than anyone else, or treating their suppliers like partners, or having superior inventory management. As a result of best practices, GE is now leaving executives in their jobs for longer periods of time rather than rotating them quickly through new jobs; the best practices process revealed that frequent changes create problems in new product introductions. The company is also learning how to use continuous improvement processes more effectively so that it can bring a new product into the market ahead of the competition and then work on introducing new technologies. In the past the firm would try to perfect all technologies first and then introduce the final version of the product.

These three concepts – work-out, process mapping, and best practices – have become a part of GE's production strategy. The results have been astounding. In the company's appliance division for example, production cycle time has been cut by 50 per cent, product availability has increased by 6 per cent, and inventory costs are down by 20 per cent. The overall cost of these changes has been less than $3 million and the company estimates that it saved more than $300 million within the first year.

Sources: Thomas A. Stewart, "GE Keeps Those Ideas Coming," *Fortune*, August 12, 1991, pp. 40–49; Tim Smart, "What's Wrong with This Profit Picture?" *Business Week*, February 8, 1993, pp. 26–27; Zachary Schiller, "GE's Appliance Park: Rewire, or Pull the Plug," *Business Week*, February 8, 1993, p. 30; "The World Super Fifty," *Forbes*, July 27, 1998, p. 118.

1. How does General Electric use work out to increase speed to market?

2. How could GE use process mapping to reduce cost and to improve quality in a consumer good? In each case, give an example.

3. In what way could best practices help GE to develop more effective international strategies? Explain.

INTRODUCTION

Production management has been responsible for many new goods and services. Examples range from electronic organizers from Sharp to lightweight computers from Dell, to sleekly designed subcompacts from General Motors,[1] to digital video-disk players from Samsung,[2] to five-star hotel operations at the Ritz-Carlton. The nature of production management in the MNE is similar in many respects to that in domestic firms. Both are concerned with the efficient use of labor and capital. Both are also interested in investing in research and development (R&D) and in organizing operations to generate successful new product lines and to increase production and service efficiency.

Like domestic firms, MNEs need to organize their production management so that they can minimize operating costs through the use of logistics and inventory control. A good example is provided by Honda, which has been able to offset the rising value of the yen with cost savings in its factories, thus allowing the firm to hold the price line on many of its new cars.[3] However, pressures from host country governments or interest groups can affect the multinational's decision making in these areas. For example, many resource-based MNEs are criticized by host governments for backward, forward, and horizontal integration. **Backward integration**, which is the ownership of equity assets used earlier in the production cycle, such as an auto firm acquiring a steel company, is criticized for doing little for employment or development in the host nation. **Forward integration**, which is the purchase of assets or facilities that move the company closer to the customer, such as a computer manufacturer that acquires a retail chain that specializes in computer sales, is criticized on the basis that MNEs use this strategy to homogenize consumer tastes to the detriment of national identities. **Horizontal integration**, which is the acquisition of firms in the same line of business, such as a computer chip manufacturer that buys a competitor, is attacked for introducing similar product lines on a worldwide basis and for undercutting the existence of local firms, most of which lack the economies of scale that can be achieved by MNEs.[4]

There are similar challenges in the industrial relations area, where MNEs must take into account different labor practices and wage rates. For example, multinationals are often under pressure from host governments to use local sourcing for their supplies, to hire local workers, to train home country managers and supervisors, and to help improve the production environment in the host nation. These decisions can sometimes result in higher production costs, although most international auto firms, for example, use local suppliers and workers to offset this problem.

The financing of operations is another production-related challenge. The choice between local and international borrowing and the use of internally generated funds to minimize the cost of capital is complicated by foreign exchange risk, international tax laws, and government controls on capital. Additionally, MNEs need to know where they are on their production cost curves in each country, as well as globally, so as to exploit any cost advantages with an appropriate organizational structure. For example, as Toyota's worldwide market share has begun to stabilize, the firm has found that it needs to become increasingly more efficient.[5]

The above examples illustrate some of the common production-related problems facing international firms. However, experienced MNEs have learned how to deal with these challenges. In doing so, they employ a wide gamut of production strategies that address research, development, innovation, global sourcing, costing techniques, and inventory control.[6] The following sections examine each of these production strategies.

RESEARCH, DEVELOPMENT, AND INNOVATION

Production strategies do *not* begin with manufacturing. In the past many MNEs focused most heavily on this aspect of operations, failing to realize that an effective production strategy begins with new product development. This conclusion gains in importance when one considers that many of today's best-selling products and services were unavailable a short time ago. Examples include notebook computers, portable cellular phones, satellite navigation devices, compact disk players, and specialized discount stores that cater to selective product lines such as home-related goods or office supplies. Many other products and services have been greatly improved over the last ten years. Examples include antidepressant medication, automobiles, facsimile machines, hazardous waste treatment services, home delivery food services, medical diagnostic equipment, pacemakers, personal computers, photocopiers, telephones, and televisions. MNEs have come to realize that if they are not developing new goods and services, they must be improving their current offerings. In either case the focus is on research and development (R&D) and innovation.

New product/service development

There are many new products and services, or improvements of old ones, that are introduced every year.[7] Table 10.1 provides a brief list of some of them in which US MNEs excel.

There are also many foreign MNEs that depend heavily on new product and services development. Examples include Toyota, Sony, and Matsushita of Japan; Samsung, Daewoo, and Goldstar of South Korea; British Petroleum, Imperial Chemical Industries, and BAT Industries of Great Britain; Volkswagen, Siemens, and Bayer of Germany; Elf Aquitaine, Renault, and Peugeot of France; Volvo, Electrolux, and L. M. Ericsson of Sweden; and Nestlé, Ciba-Geigy, and Sandoz of Switzerland. Most of these MNEs develop their own goods and services, but some of them rely on others to provide the innovative offerings. A good example is the fairly unknown Kyocera Corporation of Japan. Kyocera manufacturers few products under its own name; most products are produced for other firms. For example, Kyocera manufactured some of the first laptop computers in the world; they were sold at Radio Shack under the Tandy label. The company is also the major manufacturer of VCRs for Hitachi.[8] Similarly, many of Nintendo's video games are developed by outside firms

Table 10.1 America's best offerings: some selected examples

Product/service	Manufacturers
Amusement parks	Walt Disney
Anticholesterol drugs	Merck
Artificial heart valves	St. Jude Medical
Bulldozers	Caterpillar
Car rental	Avis, Hertz
Communication satellites	General Electric, Hughes Aircraft
Fiber optics	Corning
CT scanners	General Electric
Fast food	Burger King, McDonald's, Pizza Hut
Geophysical equipment and services	Halliburton, Western Geophysical
Industrial controls	Honeywell
Large tractors, combines	J. I. Case, Deere
Large aircraft	Boeing
Management consulting	Boston Consulting Group, Booz Allen, McKinsey
Massive parallel supercomputers	Intel, Thinking Machines
Pianos	Steinway & Sons
Power boats	Brunswick, Cigarette, Outboard Marine
Razors	Gillette
Soft drinks	Coca-Cola, PepsiCo
Ultralight utility helicopters	Robinson Helicopter

Source: Adapted from *Fortune*, Special edition, Spring/Summer, 1991, pp. 86–7.

that are paid a royalty on sales. In fact, many small, innovative R&D-oriented firms are springing up across Japan, Europe, and the United States, and these companies are continually providing large corporations with new products.[9]

In other cases companies are forming alliances to produce and market new products jointly, while continuing to produce still others on their own. For example, AT&T and Zenith are now working on digital technology for creating high-definition television,[10] IBM and Siemens have teamed up to develop a new generation of memory chips,[11] and Fujitsu and Siemens are cooperating on the development of a new generation of mainframe computers.[12] The box "International Business Strategy in Action: General Motors Raises Productivity" provides still another example.

Speed to market

One of the major manufacturing challenges facing MNEs is the speed with which they develop and get new products to market.[13] In recent years many firms have found that a "speed to market" strategy can be extremely profitable. Table 10.2 provides some data to support this statement. Notice from the table that a company that enters the market one month ahead of the competition can increase annual gross profit by $150,000 on a product that generates $25 million and $600,000 on a product that generates $100 million. Simply put, by carefully designing the product and getting it out the door, the company can dramatically increase profitability.

INTERNATIONAL BUSINESS STRATEGY IN ACTION

General Motors raises productivity

The automobile business is constantly expanding in the United States with three manufacturers in the forefront: General Motors (GM), Ford, and Chrysler. The latter, in an effort to increase competitiveness, has cut costs in many ways including reducing the time it takes to put a car together and minimizing the number of workers in their factories. These cost-reducing techniques have aided the firms in their expansion into the automobile market. Conversely, GM is having great difficulty with productivity and is falling behind the others in terms of controlling costs.

Although GM has cut its expenses in similar ways to Ford and Chrysler, it is still facing a serious problem competing in this rapidly growing market. A couple of the main problems it faces in its North American operations are that there are too many vacations for the assembly line workers and once a project is ready to go to the production stage there are typically problems with starting the launch. And lengthy product development time and efficiency problems are not helping GM get its cars rolling into dealership lots. These problems are resulting in tough price competition for GM and, with a poor product mix, the firm does not appear to be headed in the right direction. In particular, GM will have to innovate quickly and improve on productivity in order to keep up with the rapidly expanding automobile industry. The firm is just now introducing changes that Ford and Chrysler made years ago and now, with their new innovative methods, Ford and Chrysler can afford to hire more workers to keep their product lines moving. GM will have to get the ball rolling again to survive in this rapidly growing and innovative market.

Sources: John A. Byrne, "Rumble in Buick City," *Business Week*, October 10, 1994, pp. 42–43; Jerry Flint, "Sometimes You're the Windshield, Sometimes You're the Bug," *Forbes*, November 21, 1994, pp. 44–45; Kathleen Kerwin, "Vapor Lock at GM," *Business Week*, November 7, 1994, pp. 28–29; Rebecca Blumenstein, "GM Is Building Plants in Developing Nations to Woo New Markets," *Wall Street Journal*, August 4, 1997, pp. A1, 5.

Table 10.2   The cost of arriving late to market (and still be on budget)

If the company is late to market by:					
6 months	5 months	4 months	3 months	2 months	1 month
Gross potential profit is reduced by:					
–33%	–25%	–18%	–12%	–7%	–3%
If time to market is improved profit will go up by:					
11.9%	9.3%	7.3%	5.7%	4.3%	3.1%
For revenues of $25 million, annual gross profit will increase by:					
$400,000	$350,000	$300,000	$250,000	$200,000	$150,000
For revenues of $100 million, annual gross profit will increase by:					
$1,600,000	$1,400,000	$1,200,000	$1,000,000	$800,000	$600,000

Source: Reported in Joseph T. Vesey, "The New Competitors: They Think in Terms of 'Speed-to-Market'," *Academy of Management Executive*, May 1991, p. 25.

There are a number of steps that MNEs have taken to ensure early delivery of their products. For example, Sun Microsystems has eliminated its New Products Group, which had centralized control for production development, and made the group part of the manufacturing department. Now both groups work together in designing and manufacturing new products. Next, Inc., founded by Steve Jobs of Apple fame, has streamlined the relationship between design and production so that the plant can manufacture a totally new circuit board design in 20 minutes. BMW has combined engineering, development, and production planning in bringing new cars to market in record time.[14]

The strategic emphasis is on increasing speed by developing **time to market accelerators**, which are factors that help to reduce bottlenecks and errors and to ensure product quality and performance. These accelerators will vary from firm to firm, but they all produce the same results. For example, the Ballistic Systems Division of Boeing Aerospace created a multifunctional product development team to speed developmental efforts and was able to cut design analysis from two weeks to 38 minutes and to reduce the average number of engineering changes per drawing from 20 down to one.[15]

In the past many MNEs placed the bulk of their production attention on the manufacturing side of the operation. However, recent research shows that the best way to reduce defective products and to speed delivery is by placing the greatest attention on product design and planning of operations. This is accomplished through what is known as **concurrent engineering**, which involves design, engineering, and manufacturing people working together to create and build the product. Concurrent engineering is useful for two reasons. First, if the product is carefully designed, there are fewer changes needed later on and the good can be swiftly brought to market. (Figure 10.1 provides an illustrative example.) Second, the costs associated with changes increase as the product gets closer to completion; that is, it is almost twice as expensive to correct a problem during production than during product design.

Once a product or service has been planned out, the MNE's attention will turn to production. This strategy is focused very heavily on minimizing costs and increasing quality and productivity.

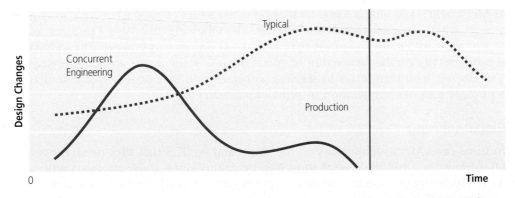

Figure 10.1   Design changes using concurrent engineering versus using a typical approach

Source: Joseph T. Vesey, "The New Competitors: They Think in Terms of 'Speed-to-Market'," *Academy of Management Executives*, May 1991, p. 30.

ACTIVE LEARNING CHECK

Review your answer to Active Learning Case question 1 and make any changes you like. Then compare your answer to the one below.

1. How does General Electric use work-out to increase speed to market?

The primary way that GE uses work-out to increase speed to market is by looking for ways to eliminate production bottlenecks and to streamline operations. The strategy of work-out asks the participants: How can we change the operation so that we can get more done in less time? The workers who are familiar with the operations often have a wealth of information to share, and this is sometimes the first time that anyone has asked them their opinions. They are delighted to offer suggestions and recommendations. As a result, the company can produce more products in less time than ever before.

GENERATION OF GOODS AND SERVICES

Most people think of the production process as one in which physical goods are produced. However, the process can also be used in generating services, and quite often the two are interlinked.[16] For example, General Motors manufactures cars but the company also offers auto maintenance and repair services[17] and Boeing builds aircraft and services them as well. In other cases services are primary. For example, the Hilton Corporation offers hotel accommodations, Hertz and Avis lease cars, and CNN provides international news coverage.

Sometimes goods and/or services are provided directly by the MNE; other times the firm will have an arrangement with outside firms or suppliers (some of them being direct competitors) to assist in this process. For example, some of the Hewlett-Packard and Apple laptops are made by other firms, but these two computer companies have their names put on the units and assume responsibility for marketing the machines. Service organizations follow a similar strategy. Some airlines purchase their in-flight food from companies like Marriott, and some rely on aircraft maintenance firms such as Ryder to service their craft. Many motels subcontract their food service to companies that specialize in this area, including fast-food franchisors such as McDonald's and Burger King. So there is often a mix of product/service strategies at work when generating goods and services. The following discussion examines some of the most important functions that are carried out in this process. The emphasis is most heavily on the production of goods because some of the areas under discussion do not lend themselves to services, although one that does is global sourcing, a primary area of consideration in production strategy.

Global sourcing

In some cases MNEs will produce all the goods and services that they need. However, oftentimes they will use **global sourcing**, by calling upon those suppliers who can more efficiently provide the needed output regardless of where they are geographically located.[18]

There are a number of reasons that global sourcing has become important. The most obvious one is cost. If General Motors (GM) wants to be price competitive in

INTERNATIONAL BUSINESS STRATEGY IN ACTION

Global Sourcing

Most people believe that low cost is the reason that MNEs use global sourcing. While this is one of the benefits, there are many others. One is to strengthen the reliability of the supply network. If the company does not have two or three international sources of supply, it can face serious problems if the sole supplier fails to provide the needed materials or parts.

A second reason for global sourcing is that the MNE may be unable to get the needed materials from domestic sources. For example, most US products that use small motors are fitted with supplies from Asia because few other regions can produce small motors cost effectively.

A third reason is quality. There are certain areas of the world where suppliers offer the highest quality output. For example, Japan is well known for its robotics, German packaging machines are the best, and Italian ceramics are the finest in the world. When MNEs need high-quality inputs, they are likely to source them internationally by purchasing from the highest-quality producer.

A fourth reason is penetration of growth markets. A foothold in a promising new market can often be obtained by sourcing in that market. For example, Toyota sources from the Pacific Rim not just to achieve lower costs, but also to enter markets with restrictive quotas by increasing the local component content of its cars.

A successful global sourcing strategy depends on the implementation of a handful of important guidelines. One is a commitment from top management to continually seek the best sources of supply regardless of the geographic distance. A second is not just to examine the costs involved, but also to weigh the quality of the supply source and the dependability of the supplier. A third is to develop the trust and respect of the supplier, and thus promote an ongoing, long-term relationship. A fourth is to use technologies that improve the ability to communicate with the supplier, to keep the individual apprised of company needs, and to work with the supplier to ensure that there is mutual understanding. A fifth is to be prepared to accept the risk of global sourcing, including the impact of fluctuating foreign currencies and the possibility that political turmoil can result in the loss of a valuable supplier. If the MNE can follow these five guidelines, the company stands an excellent chance of developing an effective global sourcing strategy.

Sources: Mark L. Fagan, "A Guide to Global Sourcing," *Journal of Business Strategy,* March/April 1991, pp. 21–25; Edward W. Davis, "Global Outsourcing: Have US Managers Thrown the Baby Out with the Water?" *Business Horizons,* July–August 1992, pp. 58–65; Alex Taylor III, "VW's Rocky Road Ahead," *Fortune,* August 23, 1993, pp. 64–68; Robert L. Simison, "New Dana Illustrates Reshaping of Auto Parts Business," *Wall Street Journal,* September 2, 1997, p. B4.

the EU (European Union), one strategy is to build and ship cars from Detroit to Europe at a price equal to, or less than, that charged by EU competitors. Since this is not possible, GM uses overseas suppliers and assembly plants to build much of what it sells in Europe. In deciding who will provide these parts and supplies, the company uses global sourcing, as do other MNEs. The box "International Business Strategy in Action: Global Sourcing" outlines some of the other reasons that multinationals use global sourcing and how they go about ensuring that this approach is successful.

It is important to remember that not all global sourcing is provided by outside suppliers. Some MNEs own their own source of supply or hold an equity position in a supplier. This relationship does not guarantee that the supplier will get the MNE's business on every bid. However, if the supplier is unable to match the cost or quality performance of competitive suppliers, the MNE will eventually terminate the relationship. So there is a great deal of pressure on the supplier to develop and maintain

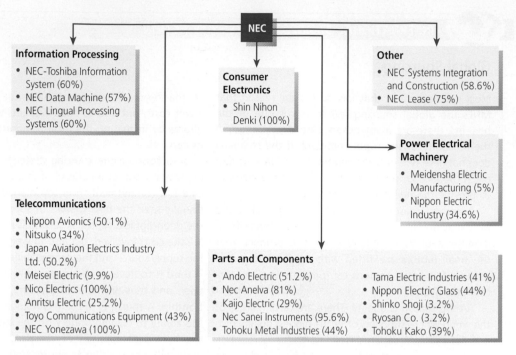

Figure 10.2 NEC's supply group

Note: With percentage of supplier owned by NEC in parentheses.
Source: Reported in Charles H. Ferguson, "Computers and the Coming of the US Keiretsu," *Harvard Business Review,* July–August, 1990, p. 63.

state-of-the-art production facilities. Additionally, since the supplier works closely with the MNE, the company knows how its multinational client likes things done and is able to operate smoothly with the MNE's design and production people.

In recent years some giant MNEs have taken equity positions in a number of different suppliers. Japanese multinationals are an excellent example. These firms often have a network of parts suppliers, subcontractors, and capital equipment suppliers who can be called on. Figure 10.2 provides an illustration for NEC, the giant electronics MNE. A close look at the figure shows that much of the supply needs of NEC can be handled by its network of suppliers.

At the same time these suppliers often provide goods and services to other firms. This helps them to maintain their competitive edge by forcing them to innovate, adapt, and remain cost-effective. If these suppliers are in similar or complementary industries, as in the case of NEC's suppliers, then technological innovations or revolutionary changes in manufacturing processes will be quickly accepted or copied by others. So the close proximity of the suppliers coupled with their business relationships helps to ensure that they attain and hold positions as world-class suppliers, and this advantage carries over to the customers, who gain both innovative ideas and high-quality, low-cost supplies. Commenting on the benefit of these domestically based suppliers, Porter notes:

> Perhaps the most important benefit of home-based suppliers . . . is the *process of innovation and upgrading.* Competitive advantage emerges from close working relationships between world-class suppliers and the industry. Suppliers help firms perceive new methods and opportunities to apply new technology. Firms gain quick access to information, to

new ideas and insights, and to supplier innovations. They have the opportunity to influence suppliers' technical efforts, as well as to serve as test sites for development work. The exchange of R&D and joint problem solving lead to faster and more efficient solutions. Suppliers also tend to be a conduit for transmitting information and innovations from firm to firm. Through this process, the pace of innovation within the entire national industry is accelerated. All these benefits are enhanced if suppliers are located in proximity to firms, shortening the communication lines.[19]

A good example is the leather footwear industry in Italy. Manufacturers regularly interact with leather suppliers, designers, and producers of other leather goods. As a result, leather footwear manufacturers are extremely knowledgeable regarding industry technology, production techniques, fashion trends, and supply sources.

These advantages also help to explain why many US suppliers are going international. By setting up operations near world-class competitors, these suppliers find it easier to monitor developments, to remain alert to changes in technology and production processes, and to maintain state-of-the-art facilities.[20] In fact, when manufacturers expand operations to another country, it is common to find their major suppliers setting up operations nearby in order to continue serving the manufacturer. The other reason is to prevent local competitors from capturing some of this business, which is what often happens when the supplier attempts to compete from the home country.

When MNEs turn to global sourcing, there is typically a hierarchical order of consideration. The company will give first preference to internal sources, such as having subassemblies produced by the manufacturing department or the subsidiary that specializes in this work. However, if a review of outside sources reveals that there is a sufficient cost/quality difference that would justify buying from an external supplier, this is what the company will do. In fact, sometimes an MNE will not attempt to make a particular part or product because it lacks the expertise to do so efficiently. The firm will simply solicit bids from outside suppliers and award the contract based on predetermined specifications (price, quality, delivery time, etc.). Over time the MNE will learn which suppliers are best at providing certain goods and services and will turn to them immediately. When this process is completed, attention will then be focused on the actual manufacture of the goods.

Manufacturing of goods

MNEs face a variety of concerns in manufacturing goods and services. Primary among these are cost,[21] quality, and efficient production systems.[22]

Cost Multinationals seek to control their costs by increasing the efficiency of their production processes. Often this means utilizing new, improved technology such as new machinery and equipment. Although these purchases can be expensive, they may be the best way to increase productivity and to lower costs and thus maintain competitive advantage. A good example is provided by Usinor-Sacilor, the giant state-owned French steel company that is emerging as a formidable player in the global steel market. In recent years Usinor-Sacilor has purchased operations in Germany and the United States, in addition to investing over $16 billion in new blast furnaces and computer-controlled rolling mills. The company now has the second largest steel production facilities in the world and is beginning to put this advantage to use. The firm's US operations are competing vigorously for a share of the auto industry steel market.

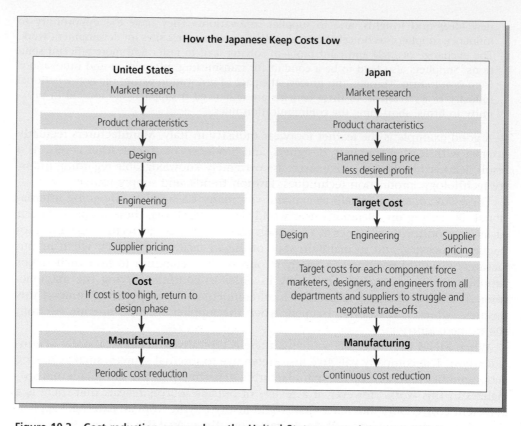

Figure 10.3   Cost reduction approaches: the United States versus Japan

Source: Ford S. Worthy, "Japan's Smart Secret Weapon," *Fortune*, August 12, 1991, p. 73.

In Europe, Usinor-Sacilor has forged important links with Peugeot and Renault and supplies Nissan's British factories with specially crafted anticorrosion sheet steel. The company is also working on developing new technology that will further drive down the cost of steel. For example, the firm's stainless steel division is now working on a strip-casting process that will cool steel in superthick sheets instead of rolled slabs. The potential savings will be in the range of $130 per ton.[23]

A second approach is to tap low-cost labor sources. A good example is the *maquiladora* industry (as discussed in Chapter 6) that has sprung up in Mexico just across the United States border. Hundreds of US plants have been established in this area. Examples include TRW Inc., which has a factory where workers assemble seat belts, and Mattel, which has a plant where workers turn out Barbie-doll houses and Disney teething rings.[24] Labor costs in these facilities are less than 20 per cent of those of similar workers in the United States. Also, because this is a free trade zone, United States duties are levied on the imports only to the extent of the value added in Mexico, so low wage rates in Mexico help to keep down the import duty.

A third approach is the development of new methods used to cut costs.[25] For example, in the United States, it is typical for a firm to calculate selling price after a new product is developed. If the price is judged to be too high, the product is sent back to the drawing board to be reworked or the company accepts smaller profit on the product. In Japan, a new system has been introduced (see Figure 10.3). The

Japanese begin by determining the target cost of the product *before* going into design, engineering, and supplier pricing. The latter groups then work to bring the product in at the desired price. This unique cost-management system is helping Japanese firms to cut costs and to undersell competitors.[26]

A fourth method that is gaining popularity with MNEs is that of costing products not on an individual basis but as part of a portfolio of related goods. Instead of evaluating the expenses of developing one new soft drink, for example, a company will look at the costs and revenues associated with the entire line of beverages. Coca-Cola of Japan provides an example. Every year there are more than 1,000 new soft drinks, fruit drinks, and cold coffees introduced into the Japanese market. Ninety per cent of them fail, but this does not stop Coke from introducing approximately one new product a month. From a cost accounting standpoint, this is not a profitable strategy. However, as one Coke executive in Japan puts it, "We know that some of these . . . products will survive only a month or two, but our competitors have them, so we have to have them."[27]

Quality   For well over a decade quality has been one of the major criteria for business success.[28] As the president of an international consulting firm recently put it, "Products are expected to be nearly perfect."[29] Nowhere is this more clearly reflected than in the auto industry, where the Japanese have garnered a large share of the international market by using what is called **kaizen**, or continuous improvement.[30] A good example is Toyota Motors, which has continually worked to reduce costs and to improve performance.[31] One way in which the company has achieved this goal is partly through large R&D expenditures. Another important factor has been meticulous design, engineering, and production processes that ensure a proper fit of all parts and overall durability of the unit.[32] In recent years US auto manufacturers (particularly Ford) have also been successful in improving their quality and, as a result, have gained market share. European car makers today are also heavily focused on quality, aware that the Japanese are a major threat to their markets.[33]

Another good example is provided by auto suppliers such as Monroe Auto Equipment, which has continually increased its product quality. Monroe is a major supplier of parts in North America, holding 50 per cent of the US market for replacement shocks and 33 per cent of the market for new shocks. The company also does a thriving international business, including Ford, Chrysler, and Nissan in Europe and Toyota in Japan.

Other excellent examples of MNEs that have succeeded because of a strong focus on quality include such lesser-known firms as Stanley Works, the WD-40 Co., and A. T. Cross. Stanley Works manufactures tape measures in Asia and then has the accuracy of samples checked by sophisticated laser computers back in New Britain, Connecticut, before selling them worldwide. Stanley Works has also developed a host of other high-quality products from double-toothed saws that cut on both the upstroke and the downstroke, for the Asian market, to hammers without claws for carpenters in Central Europe who prefer to use pliers to pull out bent nails, to levels shaped like elongated trapezoids, which the French market prefers.

The WD-40 Co. of San Diego manufactures only one product: WD-40, a water-displacing lubricant that fights rust, cleans heel marks from linoleum and walls, and provides a variety of other services around the house. Car mechanics use it to loosen sticky valves and to remove moisture from balky carburetors; handymen apply it to frozen locks and screws. Today the blue-and-yellow spray can be found in stores throughout

Table 10.3   Ford Fiesta production network

United Kingdom
  Dagenham: Final assembly. Body panels, engine, foundry production of casting for all engines
  Enfield: Instruments, fuel and water gauges, plugs
  Treforest: Spark plug insulators
  Leamington: Foundry production of engine components
  Basildon: Radiators, water pump assembly, engine components

Ireland
  Belfast: Carburetors and distributors

Belgium
  Genk: Body panels, road wheels

Germany
  Wulfrath: Transmission parts, engine components
  Cologne: Die-cast transaxie casing, gear engine components.
  Saarlouis: Final assembly. Body panels, fuel tanks, trim production

France
  Bordeaux: Transmissions

Spain
  Valencia: Final assembly. Body panels, engines, trim production

the world, where it enjoys fanatic customer loyalty. WD-40 is a best-seller in Great Britain and is rapidly gaining market share throughout Europe and Asia.[34]

A. T. Cross of Providence, Rhode Island, has been manufacturing mechanical pens and pencils for almost 150 years. The units are assembled by hand and "every one of the company's hourly employees is a quality control expert who is responsible for checking the tolerances of the engraved grooves to within one ten-thousandth of an inch and for detecting nearly microscopic scratches or the slightest clotting of ink on a pen ball."[35] A. T. Cross's product quality is so high that despite a lifetime guarantee, less than 2 per cent are ever returned for repair. Today the company's pens and pencils are one of the most popular US-made gifts in Japan.[36]

Production systems   A **production system** is a group of related activities designed to create value. In the generation of goods and services this system includes location, layout, and materials handling.

Location   Location is important because of its impact on production and distribution costs. Many MNEs have found that governments (national and local) are willing to provide tax breaks or other financial incentives to encourage them to set up operations. Accompanying considerations include the availability and cost of labor, raw materials, water, and energy and the development of the country's transportation and communication systems. As noted earlier, many suppliers set up operations near their major customers. So Ford Motor has built up an integrated production network in Western Europe (see Table 10.3). Ford suppliers are part of this production network in order to maintain their business relationship. Location is also important to service enterprises because they usually require face-to-face contact with their customers. Hotels and airlines are typical examples. Personal service firms such as those of accountants, lawyers, and management consultants also fall into this category.[37]

Layout   Plant layout is important because of its impact on efficiency. For example, most auto producers use an assembly line layout in which the workers remain at their station and as the cars move past them, they perform the necessary functions such as installing radios, air conditioners, interior trim, and so on. In the case of Volvo, the employees work in small teams to build an entire car and the plant is laid out to accommodate this work flow.[38] In other manufacturing settings, however, worldwide competitive firms tend to use U-shaped-cell flow lines because these are more efficient. Schonberger, an internationally known manufacturing expert, has noted that U-shaped production designs enable one person to tend several workstations and to increase the speed with which materials can be delivered and defective parts can be reworked.[39]

In service organizations the layout will vary widely, although it appears to be universal in use. Most hotels, regardless of the country, have the check-in and check-out areas in the same place as such support groups as the bellhops, concierge, and cashier. In fast-food units the food preparation area is situated so that the personnel can quickly serve both in-unit and drive-through customers. In movie houses the concession area is located in the lobby and the projection room at the back of the theater.

Materials handling   **Materials handling** involves the careful planning of when, where, and how much inventory will be available to ensure maximum production efficiency. Part of this is resolved through careful inventory control processes. Part of it is handled when the production layout is determined. For example, General Electric uses **process mapping**, a flowchart that shows every small step that goes into producing a product. As a result, the company is able to study every step in an operation and determine those that are redundant or that can be streamlined. Consequently, the company has been able to reduce work time on some jobs by as much as 50 per cent.[40]

Inventory control

Inventory control has received a great deal of attention in recent years because a well-designed inventory strategy can have dramatic effects on the bottom line.[41] One of the most popular concepts has been **just-in-time inventory** (JIT for short), which is based on delivering parts and supplies just as they are needed. If this concept were carried to the extreme, it would mean that manufacturers would not need to store materials because suppliers would be delivering them just in time for shipment to the factory floor.

JIT is an important concept that has been adopted by MNEs throughout the world. However, the degree of use will vary based on the product and the company's production strategy. For example, the Big Three US automakers use JIT to keep inventory to a minimum. In Japan, firms like Toyota have taken the concept even further and apply it to the way airlines handle reservations: supply is matched directly to demand. Dealers order directly from the factory, which means that customers can get their built-to-order car in seven to ten days.

One of the major problems with JIT is that its success rests heavily on the quality and reliability of the suppliers. In Japan, where MNEs often have an equity position in these companies, suppliers will go out of their way to meet the demands of their partners. However, in the United States and Europe, most suppliers are independent businesses that work under a contract relationship, so that the bonds are often not as strong between the two parties. This helps to explain why Toyota, which buys US-made parts for cars made in the United States, also keeps Japanese-made parts on hand as insurance against defective US materials.[42]

A second problem with JIT is that while many firms find it works well in managing delivery of parts to the assembly line, few have been able to apply the concept to the entire production process. Most firms still manufacture and ship their output to dealers to sell, in contrast to Toyota's approach of matching supply and demand before producing.

One of the most important things to remember about JIT is that it involves strong support from the workers and the suppliers. Everyone must be operating in unison. If the workers are slow, there will be excess inventory on hand; if the supplier is late, the workers will be sitting by idly.

Developing a strong service orientation

As noted earlier, many products have a service element associated with them. Sometimes this element is more important than the product itself. For example, many people will not purchase a car or home appliance unless it can be easily serviced. Service is also important when choosing a bank, insurance agent, lawyer, or doctor. Many of the ideas that we have discussed in this section, including sourcing, cost, and quality are also key factors when shopping for services. In addressing this area, MNEs will do two things: (1) consider whether their strategy needs to be oriented toward a product, a service, or a combination of the two, and (2) determine the ideal degree of service to provide.

Determining the product/service balance   Some outputs lend themselves to a strong production orientation; others require much more attention to service. Figure 10.4 offers an illustration. While the figure is designed more as a point of reference than as a factual source that addresses every firm in the respective industry, it is evident that some MNEs need to have a strong product-dominated focus while others benefit most from a service orientation. A good example is offered by aircraft manufacturers that must be concerned with both ends of the continuum. In Poland, Polskie Linie Lotnicze (LOT) is the country's national airline. The fleet consists of approximately 30 Soviet Tupolev and Ilyushin jets, which need continuous service because of poor production quality and continual breakdowns, ranging from basic electronics to hydraulics. Additionally, the aircraft are gas guzzlers, and when compared to planes manufactured by firms like Boeing, they are extremely inefficient. In order for LOT to service and maintain the airline, it is going to require a great deal of investment. Quite clearly, LOT needs to strike a deal with aircraft manufacturers to provide necessary service.[43]

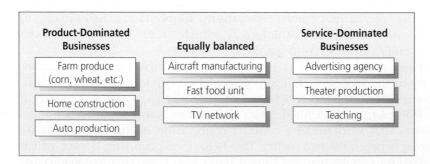

Figure 10.4   Product- and service-dominated businesses

On the other hand, there are manufactured products that require far less service than they used to need. A good example is photocopiers. Manufacturers of these machines have improved the quality of their product so substantially that many units are now sold on the basis of price. Service is no longer a major factor because everyone's product is of such high quality.

Knowing whether to sell on the basis of product or service (or a combination of the two) is critical to the success of many MNEs. A mistake at this point can result in emphasis on the wrong sales factors.

Providing the right amount of service   Once the MNE has determined the proper balance of product and service domination, it will evaluate the specific type of service that is warranted. This is particularly important because many MNEs find that the strategy used in their own country does not work overseas. A good example is the Japanese approach to retail services.[44] The amount of personal service that is provided in Japan would surprise many westerners. For example, auto dealers typically provide pick-up and delivery for repair service customers. They also make new car sales calls to customers' homes. In department stores, it is common to find executives and sales clerks alike line up to bow to the first customers in the store. Japanese banks often help their customers to sell or buy homes, to find distributors for merchandise, and to provide them with tax advice.

While these services help Japanese companies to maintain customer satisfaction, research has found that they are of little value to doing business in other countries. For example, Japanese banks in the United States have discovered that US customers want only a limited amount of quality service; they prefer quantity and efficiency in the form of a variety of different services offered at low prices. As a result, Japanese banks here offer the same types of services as do other US banks. Would they be more successful if they changed this strategy and tried to emulate the approach used back home? Given the nature of the US market, they believe that this would be a mistake. The lesson is clear: When competing in terms of service, one must match the competition but not exceed it unless the customer is willing to pay for this service. In the United States, the banking customer is not willing.[45]

ACTIVE LEARNING CHECK

Review your answer to Active Learning Case question 2 and make any changes you like. Then compare your answer to the one below.

2. How could GE use process mapping to reduce cost and to improve quality in a consumer good? In each case, give an example.

GE can use process mapping to reduce cost by identifying those activities that can be eliminated or combined in the production process. For example, can an individual who is performing one assembly line task take on other tasks and thus reduce the number of people needed for producing the product? Can inventory be ordered and delivered in smaller amounts, thus making greater use of just-in-time? Consideration of these types of questions can help to reduce cost. In improving product quality, the work group can examine how well all parts of the product fit together, examine the durability of the unit, and look for additional ways of testing the product to ensure that it measures up to quality standards.

INTERNATIONAL LOGISTICS

International logistics is the designing and managing of a system to control the flow of materials and products throughout the firm. This includes the inflow of materials, movement through the production process, and flow out to the wholesale/retail firm or final consumer. International logistics is an important area of strategic consideration because these expenses "currently comprise between 10% and 25% of the total landed cost of an international order."[46] The materials management aspect of international logistics has already been discussed. The following discussion examines three other key topics: transportation, packaging, and storage.

Transportation

In examining international logistics, we will focus on the primary modes of transportation: ocean and air. The others – rail, pipeline, and motor carrier – are of importance in some regions (such as the EU), but they are not as commonly used in moving goods from an MNE's plant to their final destination. Moreover, their use is highly dependent on the infrastructure of the country, that is, the extensiveness and quality of the nation's road system and railroad network. In many nontriad countries the infrastructure is poor and the MNE's use of them is greatly limited.

Ocean shipping   International firms can choose from a fairly wide variety of ocean carriers. The three most common carriers are conventional container ships, cargo vessels, and roll-on-roll-off (RORO) vessels. **Container ships** are used to carry standardized containers that can be simply loaded onto the carrier and then unloaded at their destination, without any repackaging of the contents of the containers. **Unconventional cargo vessels** are used for shipping oversized and unusual cargoes. **Roll-on-roll-off (RORO) vessels** are ocean-going ferries that can carry trucks that drive onto built-in ramps and roll off at the point of debarkation. A carrier similar to the RORO is the **lighter aboard ship (LASH) vessel**, which consists of barges that are stored on the ship and lowered at the point of destination. These individual barges can then operate on inland waterways.

   One of the major problems in planning an ocean shipping strategy is the limitations caused by the lack of ports and port services. In developing countries, for example, seaports sometimes lack the equipment necessary to load or unload container cargo, thus limiting the country's ability to export and import. In recent years a number of third world countries have been working to improve their ports so that they can become more active in the international trade arena.

Air shipping   Most countries of the world have airports that can accommodate air freight. The problem with this mode of transportation is its high cost. So although international air freight has grown dramatically over the last 30 years, it still accounts for less than 1 per cent of the total volume of international shipments. This transportation mode is used in trade more commonly among industrialized nations than any others, and it is usually restricted to high-value items which must reach their destination quickly.

   A number of developments have occurred over the past couple of decades that have helped to increase the amount of air shipments. These include more efficient ground facilities, larger aircraft, and better marketing of these services to shippers. In particular, the development by aircraft manufacturers of jumbo cargo jet planes and combination passenger and cargo aircraft has helped immensely.

Choice criteria

In deciding the best transportation mode to use, MNEs tend to focus on four important criteria: time, predictability, cost, and noneconomic factors.

Time   The period between departure and arrival of a carrier can vary significantly between an ocean freighter and an aircraft. So one of the questions the firm will have to answer is: How quickly is delivery needed? A number of factors will influence the answer. One is the perishability of the product. Exotic flowers from South America are flown to the United States because they would not survive a sea voyage. A second factor is how soon the goods are needed to replenish current stocks. Autos from Japan are brought into the United States by ship because the length of the trip will not negatively affect the supply of cars on hand at local dealerships.

In businesses where speed is of the most importance, companies are now coordinating their worldwide supply chains in order to reduce the amount of time needed to get the goods through the production cycle and to the customer. An example of how this is being done has been provided by Victor Fung, CEO of Li & Fung, Hong Kong's largest export trading company and an innovator in the development of supply chain management.

> Say we get an order from a European retailer to produce 10,000 garments. It's not a simple matter of our Korean office sourcing Korean products or our Indonesian office sourcing Indonesian products. For this customer we might decide to buy yarn from a Korean producer but have it woven and dyed in Taiwan. So we pick the yarn and ship it to Taiwan. The Japanese have the best zippers and buttons, but they manufacture them mostly in China. Okay, so we go to YKK, a big Japanese zipper manufacturer, and we order the right zippers from their Chinese plants. Then we determine that, because of quotas and labor conditions, the best place to make the garments is Thailand. So we ship everything there. And because the customer needs quick delivery, we may divide the order across five factories in Thailand. Effectively, we are customizing the value chain to best meet the customer's needs.
>
> Five weeks after we have received the order, 10,000 garments arrive on the shelves in Europe, all looking like they came from one factory, with colors, for example, perfectly matched.[47]

Predictability   Although both air and water transportation are basically reliable, they are subject to the vagaries of nature. Bad weather can close an airport; inadequate seaport facilities can slow the loading and unloading of cargo. Because of the great difference in delivery time between the two modes, the choice of mode is often obvious. If a company needs to have a package delivered tomorrow, it will come by air; if the firm wants to clear merchandise out of the warehouse today but the international customer does not need it for 90 days, it will be sent by water. However, certain carriers are more reliable than others, and the MNE will use its experience in determining which companies to choose for delivery. Reliability is particularly important for air shipments, where the difference of one day could significantly influence the saleability of the product.

Cost   The expense associated with shipping is a major consideration when choosing an international transportation mode. Since air freight is significantly more costly than shipment by water, the cost must be economically justifiable. Typically, an MNE will use air shipments only when time is critical and/or the product has high value. For example, if the company has purchased expensive watches in Zurich for its specialty outlets in New York and San Francisco, the watches will be flown to the retailers. Similarly, if a London-based MNE has bought a US-made supercomputer for the home office and wants it installed immediately, the unit will be flown over from the United States. On the other hand, if the merchandise is bulky or the cost of air freight is a significant portion of the value of the product, it will be sent by water. For example, autos are exported by ship as are bulk commodities and resources such as oil and coal.

Noneconomic factors   Sometimes noneconomic factors influence the choice of transportation mode. For example, in the United States, all government cargo must use national flag carriers when available. So there is seldom a question of how to send these goods. Similarly, other governments own or subsidize their carriers, and there is pressure on MNEs to use these transportation modes when doing business with these countries. Such political considerations must be taken into account when formulating the transportation strategy.

Packaging

Packaging is important in ensuring that the product is shipped in a safe container and that it arrives undamaged. When goods are transported a long distance or to areas with climates that are different from the one where they are manufactured, the container can prevent spoilage or leakage. Chemicals, for example, must be carefully sealed in containers that can withstand impact and will not crack open if tipped over or dropped. Machines, such as personal computers, must have interior packing that prevents damage during transit.

Packaging is also important because of its direct effect on cost. If units must be shipped in odd-shaped containers, fewer of them can be loaded into the hold of the transport than if they are shipped in square or rectangular containers and can be loaded atop and alongside each other. The weight of the packing material is also important, especially when goods are being shipped by air and costs are based on both distance and weight.

Additionally, packaging is important in reducing loading and unloading costs and in minimizing theft and pilferage. In recent years many shippers have begun using **intermodal containers**, which are large metal boxes that fit on trucks, railroad trains, and airplanes and help to reduce handling cost and theft losses by placing the merchandise in an easy-to-move unit that is tightly sealed.

As more goods are shipped internationally, packaging will continue to be a focal point of attention. Such considerations can help an MNE to maximize shipping space and to minimize transportation costs.

Storage   In some cases goods that are shipped internationally have to be stored before being moved to their final destinations. In the United States, public storage is widely available. In other countries, including Japan, warehousing facilities are in short supply. Additionally, the configuration of many warehouses is different from that in the United States. Ceilings are often lower and there is little automation for handling such common chores as loading and unloading packages or stacking containers on top of each other. In these cases the MNE must decide whether to invest in warehouse facilities or to ship goods only when needed, thus eliminating the warehouse function.

As discussed in Chapter 6, in some countries there are **foreign trade zones**, which are areas where foreign goods may be held and processed and then reexported without incurring customs duties (same as a free trade zone). These zones are usually found at major ports of entry (including international air terminals). The effective use of these trade zones can help an MNE: (1) to temporarily store its goods while breaking a large shipment into smaller ones to be shipped to other locales; (2) to combine small shipments into larger ones and then reship them; (3) to process the goods and perform a host of value-added activities before repackaging them for the market; and (4) to give those goods that will remain in the local market a "made in" status so that they can be sold as locally produced products.

An effective storage strategy can be particularly helpful in carrying out the final stages of an MNE's production plan. The strategy can also help to minimize overall product cost, to reduce delivery time, and to increase customer satisfaction.[48]

STRATEGIC MANAGEMENT AND PRODUCTION STRATEGY

MNEs are currently focusing on a number of areas in improving their production strategies. Three that are getting particular attention include: (a) technology and design; (b) continuous improvement of operations; and (c) the use of strategic alliances and acquisitions.

Technology and production design

MNEs are now spending more money on R&D than they have in the past. For example, Ford Motor and Nissan put 4 per cent of their annual net sales into R&D and Toyota, Honda, and General Motors put 5 per cent.[49] These investments help to explain why auto engineering and quality have improved so much over the last decade. However, the problem for many US firms is that much of the emphasis is on new R&D, whereas that of their international competitors is on improved R&D. Research shows that corporate America spends two-thirds of its R&D funds to discover original products, whereas in Japan, two-thirds goes to upgrade manufacturing processes. A telling report on US technology illustrates this (see Table 10.4). Notice in the table that theoretical and advanced applications tend to be near the top, whereas applied products are near the bottom. During the 1990s US MNEs began changing their R&D focus and started developing more improved products.

A second current trend is the use of concurrent engineering, which was discussed earlier in the chapter. Many MNEs are now realizing that a team approach to product development, which combines the talents of research, design, and manufacturing people, as well as customers and clients, results in a more successful good. Ford Motor is an excellent example. Ford put together a group called Team Taurus to develop its Taurus and Sable automobile lines. Team members were drawn from designing, engineering, and production and were brought together with customers. Collectively the group discussed how to build the new cars and replaced the sequential approach to manufacturing autos (first design the cars, then produce them, then market them) with a concurrent approach which involved addressing the design, production, and marketing issues all at the same time. The result of this strategy was a Taurus that captured a significant market niche and helped Ford close the gap between itself and the competition.[50]

Table 10.4 America's technology scorecard

Database systems	A
Genetic engineering and other biotechnologies	A
Jet and rocket propulsion	A
Magnetic information storage	A
Pollution reduction and recycling	A
Software	A
Voice recognition and vision in computers	A
Computers	A–
Design and engineering tools	B+
Portable telecommunications, equipment and systems	B+
Automotive power train	B
Gallium arsenide	B
Information network and communications	B
Joining and fastening technologies	B
Superconductors	B
Electronic controls	B–
Materials processing	B–
Microelectronics	B–
Composites and advanced structural materials	C+
Manufacturing process systems	C+
High-speed and precision machining	C
Printing, copying, and scanning equipment	C
Optoelectronic components	C
Chipmaking equipment and robotics	D
Electronic ceramics and packaging materials	D
Electronic packaging and interconnections	D
Flat panel displays	D
Optical information storage	D

Source: Thomas A. Stewart, "The New American Century: Where We Stand," *Fortune*, Spring/Summer 1991, p. 23.

Coupled with these strategies are innovative human resource development programs that are designed around the concept of **empowerment**, which involves giving employees increased control over their work. This strategy is particularly effective because it creates a feeling of pride and ownership in the job and makes employees feel that they are important assets. The use of empowerment is not limited to the research and design areas; it is important in all phases of production, beginning with the creation of the good. Additionally, if things go smoothly at this early stage of the production cycle, there are likely to be fewer problems later on.

Continuous improvement

Due to the success of Japanese MNEs, *kaizen* (continuous improvement) is being emulated by MNEs worldwide. No matter what the good or service is, every day the company tries to do the job better. Some consultants have referred to this strategy as "rapid inch-up,"[51] and this certainly captures the essence of the concept. US firms, in particular, have benefited from this idea as reflected by the dramatic increases that have been achieved in productivity. For example, during the 1980s US factories accounted for 23 per cent of the gross national product, thanks to productivity increases of 3.9 per cent annually throughout the decade. This was the best performance of US manufacturers since World War II, and the millennium promises even greater increases.[52]

A large number of firms helped to account for these results. One is Xerox, internationally known for its photocopiers. At the beginning of the 1980s the company was losing market share to overseas competitors. However, the firm then began implementing a production strategy for dramatically improving quality and reducing cost. Today Xerox is again the world's leader in copiers.

Another example is AMP of Harrisburg, Pennsylvania. The company produces high-tech, high-volume commodity electrical and electronic components used in products ranging from aircraft to washing machines. Thanks to new molding and drilling techniques, the company has sharply reduced its reliance on foreign suppliers and currently exports ten times more than it imports.[53]

As discussed in an earlier section, JIT is a related concept the MNEs are using to achieve continuous improvement. In the past JIT was used almost exclusively for managing inventory, but now the concept is being employed in still other ways. For example, Toyota's use of JIT helps it to assemble a car in 13 man-hours, as compared with 19 to 22 man-hours for Honda, Nissan, and Ford.

Alliances and acquisitions

Another current strategic production trend is the development of alliances and acquisitions.[54] Many MNEs are finding that they cannot compete effectively without entering into joint ventures or other alliances with MNEs that can complement their production strategy.[55] For example, Compaq is well known for its personal computers, but many of the components in these machines are purchased from outside suppliers or are developed by these firms under an alliance agreement. When Compaq needed a hard disk drive for its first laptops, it financed Conner Peripherals, a Silicon Valley startup with a disk drive already under way, rather than develop the machine in-house. More recently Compaq has ventured into the market for powerful desktop workstations that are used primarily by scientists and engineers. Instead of going head-to-head with market leaders such as Sun Microsystems and Hewlett-Packard, the company assembled a dozen hardware and software firms, including these two computer giants, and put together an alliance aimed at defining a new technical standard for high-speed desktop computing. The objective of the alliance is to develop a standard that will work with any workstation, and thus allow customers the freedom to buy the latest, fastest machine without fear of being tied to any single manufacturer.

Compaq's approach is not unique. The Japanese keiretsu system has been using it for years.[56] In fact, some researchers claim that industry alliances account for more of the success of Japanese firms than does just-in-time or any other manufacturing technique. Working in unison with each other, keiretsu companies have been able to wield a great deal of power. Many of these firms have monthly meetings in which they exchange information and ideas. Table 10.5 provides a brief overview of six of the country's major keiretsu members. Looking closely at the table, we see that it illustrates how valuable cooperation between the members can be. The idea has not been lost on US firms, among others, which are now beginning to put together their own "mini-keiretsus." For example, Eastman Kodak has acquired a number of

Table 10.5 Japan's biggest business groups that regularly attend monthly council meetings

	Mitsubishi	Mitsui	Sumitomo	Fuyo	DKB	Sanwa
Financial services	Mitsubishi Bank Mitsubishi Trust & Banking Meiji Mutual Life Tokio Marine & Fire	Mitsui Taiyo Kobe Bank Mitsui Trust & Banking Mitsui Mutual Life Taisho Marine & Fire	Sumitomo Bank Sumitomo Trust & Banking Sumitomo Life Sumitomo Marine & Fire	Fuji Bank Yasuda Trust & Banking Yasuda Mutual Life Yasuda Fire & Marine	Dai-Ichi Kangyo Bank Asahi Mutual Life Taisei Fire & Marine Fukoku Mutual Life Nissan Fire & Marine Kankaku Securities Orient	Sanwa Bank Toyo Trust & Banking Nippon Life Orix
Computers, electronics & electrical equipment	Mitsubishi Electric	Toshiba	NEC	Oki Electric Industry Yokogawa Electric Hitachi*	Fujitsu Fuji Electric Yaskawa Electric Mfg. Nippon Columbia Hitachi*	Iwatsu Electric Sharp Nitto Denko Kyocera Hitachi*
Cars	Mitsubishi Motors	Toyota Motor*		Nissan Motor	Isuzu Motors	Daihatsu Motor
Trading & retailing	Mitsubishi	Mitsui Mitsukoshi	Sumitomo	Marubeni	C. Itoh Nissho Iwai* Kanematsu Kawasho Seibu Dept. Store	Nissho Iwai* Nichimen Iwatani International Takashimaya
Food & beverages	Kirin Brewery	Nippon Flour Mills		Nisshin Flour Milling Sapporo Breweries Nichirei		Itoham Foods Suntory
Construction	Mitsubishi Construction	Mitsui Construction Sanki Engineering	Sumitomo Construction	Taisei	Shimizu	Toyo Construction Obayashi Sekisui House Zenitaka
Metals	Mitsubishi Steel Mfg. Mitsubishi Materials Mitsubishi Aluminum Mitsubishi Cable Industries	Japan Steel Works Mitsui Mining & Smelting	Sumitomo Metal Industries Sumitomo Metal Mining Sumitomo Electric Industries Sumitomo Light Metal Industries	NKK	Kawasaki Steel Kobe Steel* Japan Metals & Chemicals Nippon Light Metal Furukawa Furukawa Electric	Kobe Steel* Nakayama Steel Works Hitachi Metals Nisshin Steel Hitachi Cable

Real estate	Mitsubishi Estate	Mitsui Real Estate Development	Sumitomo Realty & Development	Tokyo Taternono	Tokyo Dome	
Oil & coal	Mitsubishi Oil			Tonen	Showa Shell Sekiyu	Cosmo Oil
Rubber & glass	Asahi Glass		Nippon Sheet Glass		Yokohama Rubber	Toyo Tire & Rubber
Chemicals	Mitsubishi Kasei Mitsubishi PetroChemic Mitsubishi Gas Chemical Mitsubishi Plastics Mitsubishi Kasei Poly	Mitsui Toatsu Chemicals Mitsui Petrochemical Industries	Sumitomo Chemical Sumitomo Bakelite	Showa Denko Nippon Oil & Fats Kureha Chemical Industries	Kyowa Hakko Kogyo Denki Kagaku Kogyo Nippon Zeon Asahi Denka Kogyo Sankyo Shiseido Lion	Ube Industries Tokuyoma Soda Hitachi Chemical Sekisui Chemical Kansai Paint Tanabe Seiyaku Fujisawa Pharmaceuticals
Fibers & textiles	Mitsubishi Rayon	Toray Industries		Nisshinbo Industries Toho Rayon	Asahi Chemical Industry	Unitika Teijin
Pulp & paper	Mitsubishi Paper Mills	Oji paper		Sanyo-Kokusaku Pulp	Honshu Paper	
Mining & forestry		Mitsui Mining Hokkaido Colliery & Steamship	Sumitomo Forestry Sumitomo Coal Mining			
Industrial equipment	Mitsubishi Heavy Industries Mitsubishi Kakoki	Mitsui Engineering & Shipbuilding	Sumitomo Heavy Industries	Kubota Nippon Seiko	Niigata Engineering Iseki Ebara Kawasaki Heavy Industries Ishikawajima-Harima Heavy Industries	NTN Hitachi Zosen Shin Meiwa Industry
Cameras & optics	Nikon			Canon	Asahi Optical	Hoya
Cement		Onoda Cement	Sumitomo Cement	Nihon Cement	Chichibu Cement	Osaka Cement
Shipping & transportation	Nippon Yusen Mitsubishi Warehouse & Transportation	Mitsui OSK lines Mitsui Warehouse	Sumitomo Warehouse	Shawa line Keihin Electric Express Railway Tobu Railway	Kawasaki Kisen Shibusawa Warehouse Nippon Express*	Navix Line Hankyu Nippon Express*

* Companies affiliated with more than one group.
Source: Adapted from *Fortune,* July 15, 1991, p. 81.

distributors in Japan and has taken small stakes in some 50 suppliers and customers, and IBM is investing venture capital in a host of small European computer-related firms. Motorola has not taken equity positions, but it uses a keiretsu approach by developing extremely close ties with suppliers.

Fujitsu offers another interesting production strategy: acquisition coupled with autonomy. In recent years the company has purchased Amdahl, the giant Silicon Valley manufacturer of IBM-compatible mainframe computers, and International Computers Ltd., Britain's biggest computer company. Fujitsu has also acquired Nokia Data of Finland, the sixth largest computer maker in Europe. Fujitsu realizes that it cannot continue to grow without increasing international sales. At the same time the company knows that growing nationalism is leading many governments to question acquisitions by foreign firms. Additionally, the firm is convinced that Japanese management approaches cannot be universally exported. Companies in other nations have their own way of doing things. So it pays to give overseas acquisitions the autonomy to make most decisions as they see fit. A Fujitsu executive recently put it this way: "Our overseas managers learned to eat T-bone steaks and speak English. But in substantial matters, trying to be worldly isn't enough. A 100% Japanese company simply can't be successful overseas, just as a 100% American or European company can't be in Japan."[57]

ACTIVE LEARNING CHECK

Review your answer to Active Learning Case question 3 and make any changes you like. Then compare your answer to the one below.

3. In what way could best practices help GE to develop more effective international strategies? Explain.

Best practices could help General Electric to develop more effective international strategies by encouraging the firm to identify those MNEs that are most successful and then to discover how they accomplish that feat. Do these firms manage to develop more new products than do their competitors? Or are they best at quickly getting their new goods into the marketplace? Do they produce the highest-quality goods? Or are they are lowest-cost producers? What accounts for their ability to achieve such an excellent performance? By asking and answering these questions, GE can gain insights into how it needs to change its own production processes in order to emulate those MNEs successfully.

SUMMARY

Key points

1. Many of today's goods and services will be replaced during the millennium with faster, more efficient, and cheaper substitutes. For this reason, MNEs need to continually research, develop, and bring new offerings to the marketplace. One way in which this is being done is through the use of time to market accelerators. A good example is concurrent engineering.

2. The generation of goods and services entails a number of specific functions. One function is obtaining materials or supplies. Many MNEs have found that global sourcing is the best strategy because it helps to keep down costs while providing

a number of other benefits, including ensuring an ongoing source of supply and helping the company to penetrate overseas markets.

3. In the production of goods and services, MNEs focus on a number of key factors, including cost, quality, and well-designed production systems. While these three factors are often interrelated, each merits specific attention. Multinationals have also developed very effective inventory control systems that help to minimize carrying costs and to increase productivity. Attention is also focused on gaining the proper balance between production and service domination. Figure 10.4 illustrates this point.

4. International logistics is the designing and managing of a system to control the flow of materials and products throughout the firm. In addition to inventory control, this involves transportation, packaging, and storing.

5. MNEs are currently focusing on a number of areas in improving their production strategies. Three approaches that have been receiving particular attention include (1) technology and design, (2) continuous improvement of operations, and (3) the use of strategic alliances and acquisitions. These approaches are helping multinationals to meet new product and service challenges while keeping costs down and quality up.

Key terms

- backward integration
- forward integration
- horizontal integration
- time to market accelerators
- concurrent engineering
- global sourcing
- kaizen
- production system
- materials handling
- process mapping

- just-in-time (JIT) inventory
- international logistics
- container ships
- unconventional cargo vessels
- roll-on-roll-off (RORO) vessels
- lighter aboard ship (LASH) vessels
- intermodal containers
- foreign trade zones
- empowerment

Review and discussion questions

1. Why are MNEs so interested in new product development? Why do they not simply focus on improving their current offerings?

2. Why is "speed to market" such an important production strategy? Explain.

3. What are "time to market accelerators"? In what way is concurrent engineering one of these accelerators?

4. Why do many MNEs use global sourcing? Why do they not produce all the parts and materials in-house? Be complete in your answer.

5. Why are world-class suppliers often located next to world-class manufacturers? What forms of synergy often exist between the two groups?

6. How do MNEs try to reduce production costs? Identify and describe three steps.

7. In what way is the continuous reduction cost method used by Japanese manufacturers (see Figure 10.3) different from the periodic cost reduction method employed by many US firms? Compare and contrast the two.

8. Some MNEs use a production strategy that involves costing a portfolio of related goods rather than just costing each individually. What is the logic behind this strategy?

9. How does kaizen help to bring about increased quality? Is this approach limited to Japanese firms or are other MNEs using it as well?

10. What types of issues does an MNE confront when it seeks to improve its production system? Identify and describe three.

11. How does JIT help an MNE to control its inventory? Give two examples.

12. Why would an MNE want to determine the degree to which its primary business was product-dominated and service-dominated? Explain.

13. Why are MNEs concerned with international logistics? How does this help the companies to increase their competitiveness?

14. In recent years MNEs have been focusing on a number of areas in improving their production strategies. What are two of these? Identify and describe each.

REAL CASES

ZYTEC: QUALITY FROM A TO Z

Some of the highest-quality multinational firms in the world are small- and medium-sized companies that are best known only by their suppliers and customers. For example, Bamberger Kaliko is famous for bookbinding textiles, but few people outside of Germany have ever heard of the firm. Similarly, Zytec is a manufacturer of power supplies for electronic equipment, but few people outside of Minnesota know of the company's existence. Yet this has not stopped these firms from becoming world leaders. In the case of Zytec, a company with fewer than 600 employees, total quality management concepts are used throughout the company and the firm is now able to boast a defect rate approaching four errors per million parts. This means that Zytec's quality is on a par with the world's best manufacturers, and much of this success is a result of effective production strategies.

One way in which Zytec maintains its quality standards is by purchasing from a small number of carefully selected suppliers. The quality from these suppliers is so high that Zytec does not need to examine or sample the incoming materials. They are accepted at face value, but the company knows that the suppliers are delivering error-free parts. As a result, Zytec saves money by not having to inspect in-coming materials.

Another way the company reduces costs is by purchasing on a hand-to-mouth basis and tying this process to just-in-time inventory. When the production floor needs more materials or parts, the order is sent electronically to the warehouse and delivery is made within an hour. In turn, with a carefully designed production flow system, the average unit moves through production and on to the shipping dock within 90 minutes. This means that material is in process for only a short period of time, thus reducing the company's inventory carrying costs.

A third interesting total quality management concept used by the company is statistical process controls. Although many firms shy away from using these controls because they appear to be too sophisticated, Zytec teaches formal courses to each of its people so that they learn how to keep track of their output, to identify problems, and to formulate solutions. These statistical controls range from fairly simple approaches to keeping track of error rates to more sophisticated techniques for determining when a process is getting out of control. In either event, the workers have been taught how to turn out zero-defect units.

Zytec has been so successful that its customers come from as far away as Japan and include such well-known names as IBM, Eastman Kodak,

Motorola, and Fujitsu. There are many others who would like to be added to this list, but the company limits the number with whom it will deal in order to ensure that it can work closely with these customers and continue to maintain the highest-quality standards. In fact, the firm has done so well that it was awarded one of the national Baldrige awards that are given annually to the handful of US firms that are regarded as having the highest quality.

1. How critical are suppliers to Zytec's success? Explain.

2. In what way does the company employ a just-in-time system? Could the firm maintain its worldwide quality without such a system?

3. One of the bases for Zytec's success is its belief in continuous improvement. How can the firm's statistical process controls help it to achieve this objective? Give an example.

NIKE

One of the rules of international production strategy is: manufacture the highest quality product and the world is likely to beat a path to your door. A number of firms help to illustrate this rule. One is Nike, the sports-shoe producer. The company makes a wide variety of high-quality shoes. The company catalogue lists more than 800 models for use in approximately 25 sports. In 1998 Nike had 33 per cent of the world's market for training-shoes (and 40 per cent in the United States). Its sales were over $9 billion. Its "swoosh" logo is one of the most recognized global symbols. In an effort to keep ahead of the competition, Nike updates each shoe at least every six months. Most of these ideas are generated by Nike's R&D centre in Beaverton, near Portland, Oregon, where physiologists and mechanical engineers study the stresses on an athlete's feet and collaborate with stylists on new shoe ideas. The company takes these technologies and designs and contracts with foreign factories for production.

Nike's high-quality production is matched by superb marketing skills. The world might be making a path to Nike's door, but the company makes sure the world knows where they are. Basketball superstars Michael Jordan, Shaquille O'Neil, football icon Ronaldo, tennis players Pete Sampras and Andre Agassi, and golf tyro Tiger Woods all signed as Nike's celebrity sponsors. The idea is: if you can make the "cool" guys wear your products, then the rest will follow. Large marketing campaigns and event sponsorship all serve to keep the brand name in consumers' minds. But by 1998, Nike was no longer cool and mountains of unsold trainers

built up. There was a big fall in profits and over 1,000 US workers were laid off. In 1998 Nike trainers were being sold at huge discounts in the "grey" market by British supermarkets like Tesco.

Perhaps the only thing Nike doesn't like to be remembered for is the bad publicity around its labour practices in Asia. A report by Ernst & Young, on the health and safety conditions of Vietnamese workers at one of Nike's largest factories found that the air concentrations of some hazardous chemicals exceeded by 177 the legal standards in Vietnam and that 77 per cent of the work force suffered respiratory problems. Allegations of long working hours, bad ventilation, and physical abuse on a mostly young female work force has tarnished Nike's reputation. The company has attempted to clean up its act, and reported that it has taken measures to improve working conditions.

One of the co-founders of Nike, Phil Knight, apologized in May 1998 for the company's labour relations and introduced measures to improve the working conditions of Nike's 350,000 employees in Asia. The company is attempting to exercise greater corporate social responsibility in its global operations. Its new Alpha line of shoes and sportswear reflect a back-to-basics focus on high quality production with less attention to endorsements by superstar athletes.

1. What is the key to Nike's production strategy? Explain.

2. What are the advantages of frequent design changes in Nike's sneakers?

3. Why is it important for Nike to clean up its labour practices in Asia? How would you recommend the company approach the issue?

Sources: Adapted from *http://www.nikebiz.com/*; *http://www.saigon.com/nike/*; Dylan Jones, "No More Mr. Nike Guy," *The Sunday Times Magazine*, August 23, 1998; Steve Greenhouse, "Nike Shoe Plant in Vietnam Is Called Unsafe for Workers," *New York Times*, November 8, 1997; Catherine Arnst, "Now, HP Stands for Hot Products," *Business Week*, June 14, 1993, p. 36. Erik Calonius, "Smart Moves by Quality Champs," *Fortune*, Spring/Summer 1991, pp. 24–28.

ENDNOTES

1. Alex Taylor III, "Why GM Leads the Pack in Europe," *Fortune*, May 13, 1993, pp. 83–87.

2. Laxmi Nakarmi and Patrick Oster, "The Korean Tiger Is Out for Blood," *Business Week*, May 31, 1993, p. 54.

3. Doron P. Levin, "Honda to Hold Base Price on Accord Model," *New York Times*, September 2, 1993, p. C3.

4. Also see Emily Thornton, "Mazda Learns To Like Those Intruders," *Business Week*, September 14, 1998, p. 172.

5. Alex Taylor III, "How Toyota Copes with Hard Times," *Fortune*, January 25, 1993, pp. 78–81.

6. For a good example of these challenges, see Ferdinand Protzman, "Daimler's Quest Collides with Slump," *New York Times*, August 3, 1993, pp. C1, C5.

7. For some interesting insights into this process, see Christopher Power et al., "Flops," *Business Week*, August 16, 1993, pp. 76–82.

8. Gene Bylinsky, "The Hottest High Tech Company in Japan," *Fortune*, January 1, 1990, pp. 82–88.

9. See Joel Kotkin, "Creators of the New Japan," *Inc.*, October 1990, pp. 96–107.

10. Andrew Kupfer, "The US Wins One in High-Tech TV," *Fortune*, April 8, 1991, pp. 60–64.

11. Bill Powell and Joanna Stone, "The Deal of the Decade," *Newsweek*, July 15, 1991, p. 40.

12. Andrew Pollack, "Fujitsu Joins Siemens in Alliance," *New York Times*, June 18, 1993, p. C3.

13. See Don Clark, "Intel to Ship Its Next-Generation Chip in 1995, Boosts Outlay for Production," *Wall Street Journal*, January 28, 1994, p. B5.

14. Also see C. K. Prahalad and Kenneth Lieberthal, "The End of Corporate Imperialism," *Harvard Business Review*, July–August 1998, pp. 69–79.

15. Joseph T. Vesey, "The New Competitors: They Think in Terms of 'Speed-to-Market'," *Academy of Management Executive*, May 1991, p. 26.

16. Saul Hansell, "Is This the Factory of the Future?" *New York Times*, July 26, 1998, Section 3, pp. 1, 12.

17. Rebecca Blumenstein, "GM Is Building Plants in Developing Nations to Woo New Markets," *Wall Street Journal*, August 4, 1997, pp. A1, 5.

18. Larry Holyoke, William Spindle, and Neil Gross, "Doing the Unthinkable," *Business Week*, January 10, 1994, pp. 52–53; and Andrew Pollack, "Nissan Plans to Buy More American Parts," *New York Times*, March 26, 1994, pp. 17, 26.

19. Michael E. Porter, *The Competitive Advantage of Nations* (New York: Free Press, 1990), p. 103.

20. For more on this, see Earl Landesman, "Ultimatum for US Auto Suppliers: Go Global or Go Under," *Journal of European Business*, May/June 1991, pp. 39–45.

21. Laurie Hays, "IBM's Finance Chief, Ax in Hand, Scours Empires for Costs to Cut," *Wall Street Journal*, January 26, 1994, pp. A1, A6.

22. For an interesting development in this area see Kathy Chen, "Would America Buy A Refrigerator Labeled 'Made in Qingdao'?" *Wall Street Journal*, September 17, 1997, pp. A1, 14.

23. Laura Jereski, "A Gallic Threat for American Steel," *Forbes*, November 26, 1990, pp. 144–146.

24. Larry Reibstein et al., "A Mexican Miracle?" *Newsweek*, May 20, 1991, p. 42.

25. Ernest Beck, "Why Foreign Distillers Find It So Hard to Sell Vodka to the Russians," *Wall Street Journal*, January 15, 1998, pp. A1, 8.

26. Ford S. Worthy, "Japan's Smart Secret Weapon," *Fortune*, August 12, 1991, pp. 72–75.

27. Ibid., p. 75.

28. See Louis Kraar, "Korea Goes for Quality," *Fortune*, April 13, 1994, pp. 153–159; and Gale Eisenstodt, "Sullivan's Travels," *Forbes*, March 28, 1994, pp. 75–76.

29. Erick Calonius, "Smart Moves by Quality Champs," *Fortune*, Spring/Summer ed., 1991, p. 24.

30. See, for example, Christopher Palmeri, "A Process That Never Ends," *Forbes*, December 21, 1992, pp. 52–54.

31. Alex Taylor III, "How Toyota Defies Gravity," *Fortune*, December 8, 1997, pp. 100–108.

32. For more on this, see Thomas A. Stewart, "Brace for Japan's Hot New Strategy," *Fortune*, September 21, 1992, pp. 62–74.

33. Richard A. Melcher and Stewart Toy, "On Guard, Europe," *Business Week*, December 14, 1992, pp. 54–55.

34. Louis S. Richman, "What America Makes Best," *Fortune*, Spring/Summer 1991, p. 80.

35. Ibid., p. 81.

36. Michael Shari and Pete Engardio, "The Sweet Sound of Success," *Business Week*, September 8, 1997, p. 56.

37. See Michael E. McGrath and J. Gordon Stewart, "Professional Service Firms in Europe Move Toward Integrated European Practices," *Journal of European Business*, May/June 1991, pp. 26–30.

38. Steven Prokesch, "Edges Fray on Volvo's Brave New Humanistic World," *New York Times*, July 7, 1991, p. F5.

39. Richard J. Schonberger, *Building a Chain of Customers* (New York: Free Press, 1990), pp. 50–51.

40. Thomas A. Stewart, "GE Keeps Those Ideas Coming," *Fortune*, August 12, 1991, p. 48.

41. Lucinda Harper, "Trucks Keep Inventories Rolling Past Warehouses to Production Line," *Wall Street Journal*, February 7, 1994, p. B3.

42. Alex Taylor III, "Why Toyota Keeps Getting Better and Better and Better," *Fortune*, November 19, 1990, p. 79.

43. Peter Fuhrman, "You Think Pan Am's Got Problems?" *Forbes*, June 10, 1991, pp. 82–83.

44. David A. Aaker, "How Will the Japanese Compete in Retail Services?" *California Management Review*, Fall 1990, pp. 54–67.

45. For still other examples of service-related problems in Japan, see Jon Woronoff, *The Japanese Management Mystique: The Reality Behind the Myth* (Chicago: Probus Publishing, 1992), pp. 120–124.

46. Michael R. Czinkota, Pietra Rivoli, and Ilkka A. Ronkainen, *International Business* (Hinsdale, Ill: Dryden Press, 1989), p. 427.

47. Joan Magretta, "Fast, Global, and Entrepreneurial: Supply Chain Management, Hong Kong Style: An Interview with Victor Fung," *Harvard Business Review*, September–October 1998, pp. 105–106.

48. See, for example, Hellene S. Runtagh, "GE Tracks Transportation and Distribution Opportunities in the EC," *Journal of European Business*, September/October 1990, pp. 22–25.

49. Taylor, "Why Toyota Keeps Getting Better and Better," p. 69.

50. Vesey, op. cit.

51. Ibid., p. 66.

52. See Lucinda Harper, "Productivity in US Jumped by 2.7% in 1992," *Wall Street Journal*, February 5, 1992, P. A2.

53. Stewart, op. cit., p. 18.

54. Paul Lawrence and Charalambos Vlachoutsicos, "Joint Ventures in Russia: Put the Locals in Charge," *Harvard Business Review*, January–February 1993, pp. 44–54.

55. Stratford Sherman, "Are Strategic Alliances Working?" *Fortune*, September 21, 1992, pp. 77–78; and Thornton, op. cit.

56. Robert L. Cutts, "Capitalism in Japan: Cartels and Keiretsu, *Harvard Business Review*, July–August 1992, pp. 48–55.

57. Brenton R. Schlender, "How Fujitsu Will Tackle the Giants," *Fortune*, July 1, 1991, p. 79.

ADDITIONAL BIBLIOGRAPHY

Adler, Paul S. and Cole, Robert E. "Designed for Learning: A Tale of Two Auto Plants," *Sloan Management Review*, vol. 34, no. 3 (Spring 1993).

Arnold, Ulli. "Global Sourcing – An Indispensable Element in World-wide Competition," *Management International Review*, vol. 29, no. 4 (Fourth Quarter 1989).

Avishai, Bernard. "A European Platform for Global Competition: An Interview with VW's Carl Hahn," *Harvard Business Review*, vol. 69, no. 3 (July/August 1991).

Beatty, Carol A. "Implementing Advanced Manufacturing Technologies: Rules of the Road," *Sloan Management Review*, vol. 33, no. 4 (Summer 1992).

Blakley, Daniel; Doyle, Barry; and Murray, L. William. "Improving the Effectiveness of Offshore Production Agreements in Dynamic Product Markets," *Management International Review*, vol. 27, no. 3 (Third Quarter 1987).

Cheng, Joseph L. C. and Bolon, Douglas S. "The Management of Multinational R&D: A Neglected Topic in International Business Research," *Journal of International Business Studies*, vol. 24, no. 1 (First Quarter 1993).

Cusumano, Michael A. "Manufacturing Innovation: Lessons from the Japanese Auto Industry," *Sloan Management Review*, vol. 30, no. 1 (Fall 1988).

Deschamps, Jean-Philippe and Nayak, P. Ranganath. "Competing Through Products: Lessons from the Winners," *Columbia Journal of World Business*, vol. 27, no. 2 (Summer 1992).

Douglas, Susan P. and Wind, Yoram. "The Myth of Globalization," *Columbia Journal of World Business*, vol. 22, no. 4 (Winter 1987).

Drucker, Peter F. "The Emerging Theory of Manufacturing," *Harvard Business Review*, vol. 68, no. 3 (May/June 1990).

DuBois, Frank L., Toyne, Brian, and Oliff, Michael D. "International Manufacturing Strategies of US Multinationals: A Conceptual Framework Based on a Four-Industry Study," *Journal of International Business Studies*, vol. 24, no. 2 (Second Quarter 1993).

Flaherty, M. Therese. "Global Sourcing Strategy: R&D, Manufacturing, and Marketing Interfaces," *Journal of International Business Studies*, vol. 24, no. 1 (First Quarter 1993).

Garvin, David A. "Manufacturing Strategic Planning," *California Management Review*, vol. 35, no. 4 (Summer 1993).

Ghoshal, Sumantra and Bartlett, Christopher A. "Creation, Adoption, and Diffusion of Innovations by Subsidiaries of Multinational Corporations," *Journal of International Business Studies*, vol. 19, no. 3 (Fall 1988).

Julian, Scott D. and Keller, Robert T. "Multinational R&D Siting: Corporate Strategies for Success," *Columbia Journal of World Business*, vol. 26, no. 3 (Fall 1991).

Khurana, Anil. "Managing Complex Production Processes," *Sloan Management Review*, vol. 40, no. 2 (Winter 1999).

Kotabe, Masaaki. "The Relationship Between Offshore Sourcing and Innovativeness of US Multinational Firms: An Empirical Investigation," *Journal of International Business Studies*, vol. 21, no. 4 (Fourth Quarter 1990).

Kotabe, Masaaki and Murray, Janet Y. "Linking Product and Process Innovations and Modes of International Sourcing in Global Competition: A Case of Foreign Multinational Firms," *Journal of International Business Studies*, vol. 21, no. 3 (Third Quarter 1990).

Lei, David and Slocum, John W., Jr. "Global Strategy, Competence-Building and Strategic Alliances," *California Management Review*, vol. 35, no. 1 (Fall 1992).

Levy, David L. "Lean Production in an International Supply Chain," *Sloan Management Review*, vol. 38 (Winter 1997).

Madura, Jeff and Rose, Lawrence C. "Are Product Specialization and International Diversification Strategies Compatible?" *Management International Review*, vol. 27, no. 3 (Third Quarter 1987).

McGrath, Michael E. and Hoole, Richard W. "Manufacturing's New Economies of Scale," *Harvard Business Review*, vol. 70, no. 3 (May/June 1992).

Patel, Pari and Pavitt, Keith. "Large Firms in the Production of the World's Technology: An Important Case of 'Non-Globalization'," *Journal of International Business Studies*, vol. 22, no. 1 (First Quarter 1991).

Quinn, James Brian and Hilmer, Frederick G. "Strategic Outsourcing," *Sloan Management Review*, vol. 35 (Summer 1994).

Reddy, Prasada. "New Trends in Globalization of Corporate R&D and Implications for Innovation Capability in Host Countries: A Survey from India," *World Development*, vol. 25, no. 11 (November 1997).

Rehder, Robert R. "Building Cars as if People Mattered: The Japanese Lean System vs. Volvo's Uddevalla System" *Columbia Journal of World Business*, vol. 27, no. 2 (Summer 1992).

Rugman, Alan M. and Bennett, Jocelyn. "Technology Transfer and World Product Mandating," *Columbia Journal of World Business*, vol. 17, no. 4 (Winter 1982).

Serapio, Manuel G., Jr. "Macro-Micro Analyses of Japanese Direct R&D Investments in the US Automotive and Electronics Industries," *Management International Review*, vol. 33, no. 3 (Third Quarter 1993).

Sobek, Durward K., 2d, Ward, Allen C. and Liker, Jeffrey K. "Toyota's Principles of Set-Based Concurrent Engineering," *Sloan Management Review*, vol. 40, no. 2 (Winter 1999).

Swamidass, Paul M. "A Comparison of the Plant Location Strategies of Foreign and Domestic Manufacturers in the US," *Journal of International Business Studies*, vol. 21, no. 2 (Second Quarter 1990).

Swamidass, Paul M. and Kotabe, Masaaki. "Component Sourcing Strategies of Multinationals: An Empirical Study of European and Japanese Multinationals," *Journal of International Business Studies*, vol. 24, no. 1 (First Quarter 1993).

Vandermerwe, Sandra. "Increasing Returns: Competing for Customers in the Global Market," *Journal of World Business*, vol. 32, no. 4 (Winter 1997).

Yip, George S. "Global Strategy . . . In a World of Nations?" *Sloan Management Review*, vol. 31, no. 1 (Fall 1989).

Young, S. Mark. "A Framework for Successful Adoption and Performance of Japanese Manufacturing Practices in the United States," *Academy of Management Review*, vol. 17, no. 4 (October 1992).

CHAPTER 11

Marketing Strategy

OBJECTIVES OF THE CHAPTER

Every multinational has a marketing strategy that is designed to help identify opportunities and to take advantage of them. This plan of action typically involves consideration of four primary areas: the product or service to be sold, the way in which the output will be promoted, the pricing of the good or service, and the distribution strategy to be used in getting the output to the customer. The primary purpose of this chapter is to examine the fundamentals of international marketing strategy. We will look at five major topics: market assessment, product strategy, promotion strategy, price strategy, and place strategy. We will consider such critical marketing areas as product screening, modification of goods and services in order to adapt to local needs, modified product life cycles, advertising, personal selling, and ways in which MNEs tailor-make their distribution systems. The specific objectives of this chapter are to:

1. **Examine** the process used in conducting international market assessment of goods and services.

2. **Study** the criteria that affect an MNE's decision to alter a good or service in order to adapt the offering to local market tastes.

3. **Describe** some of the ways in which MNEs use advertising and personal selling techniques to promote their product in worldwide markets.

4. **Review** some of the major factors that influence international pricing and distribution strategies.

Worldwide marketing by Volkswagen

During the 1960s Volkswagen AG (VW for short) held more market share in the United States than all other auto imports combined, and in the 1970s, despite growing foreign competition, VW sales reached 300,000 units annually. However, the 1980s and early 1990s were not good for the company; annual sales in the US market were down to 150,000 units. In less than ten years market share had dropped from 3 per cent to under 1.5 per cent, and VW had become a minor competitor in the US auto market.

In more recent years, however, Volkswagen has made a stunning comeback in America. Perhaps its biggest success story is the New Beetle which was introduced in March 1998. By the end of the year the company had sold 55,842 units including 7,516 in December. Its Jetta line that year led the list with total sales of 89,311, the third best in the model's 19-year history. The Volkswagen Passat model posted all-time record sales of 39,272 units, an increase of 164 per cent over 1997's mark of 14,868; and another record was set by the Volkswagen Cabrio with sales of 15,230 units, a 59.7 per cent increase over 1997 and the best in the model's 18-year history. In all, Volkswagen sold 219,679 cars in the US market, an increase of 59.3 per cent over 1997 and the best showing since 1981 when it sold 278,513. As a result, the firm's 1998 share of the American car market stood at 3.4 per cent – the highest ever. Of course, part of this success is accounted for by the fact that cars account for only around 53 per cent of new vehicle sales. The other major group is light trucks where Ford, General Motors, and Chrysler hold 80 per cent of the market. Moreover, in the case of Ford and Chrysler, sales of light trucks are significantly greater than those of automobiles. Yet this growth market has not gone unnoticed by Volkswagen which recently introduced its EuroVan into the US. The van is built in Hanover, Germany and comes with a V6 engine and a host of standard equipment and safety features. If this new entry does as well as predicted, it will combine with the New Beetle to sharply increase the firm's US market share.

It is the Beetle that holds the greatest promise. In addition to brisk sales the first year, the auto was selected as the 1999 North American Car of the Year by an independent jury of 48 journalists who cover the auto industry for daily newspapers, magazines, television, radio, and the Internet. The award is a comprehensive evaluation of the year's most outstanding new car based on consumer appeal, quality, and driving characteristics. Each jury member is allowed to allot 25 votes to a small selection of finalist cars. The New Beetle garnered 292 votes, more than double the second place finisher, the Honda Odyssey with 142 votes, and well ahead of the third place car, the Chrysler 300M, with 124 votes. Indeed, Volkswagen is back!

Sources: Bernard Avishai, "A European Platform for Global Competition," *Harvard Business Review*, July–August 1991, pp. 103–113; Richard M. Hodgetts and Fred Luthans, *International Management* 4th ed. (Burr Ridge, Ill: Irwin/McGraw 2000), p. 519. John Templeman and Gail E. Schares, "A Hard U-Turn at VW," *Business Week*, March 15, 1993, p. 47; Audrey Choi, "VW's Lopez Says German Auto Maker Is Moving Quickly to Revitalize Itself," *Wall Street Journal*, March 25, 1994, p. A6; *www.vw.com*.

1. How would Volkswagen use market assessment to evaluate sales potential for its cars in the United States?

2. Does VW need to modify its cars for the US market? Why or why not?

3. Would the nature of VW's products allow the company to use an identical promotional message worldwide or would the company have to develop a country-by-country promotion strategy?

4. How would currency fluctuations affect VW's profit in the US market?

5. What type of distribution system would be most effective for VW in the United States?

INTRODUCTION

International marketing is the process of identifying the goods and services that customers outside the home country want and then providing them at the right price and place.[1] In the international marketplace this process is similar to that carried out at home, but there are some important modifications that are used to adapt marketing efforts to the needs of the specific country or geographic locale.[2] For example, some MNEs are able to use the same strategy abroad as they have at home. This is particularly true in promotions where messages can carry a universal theme. Some writing implement firms advertise their pens and pencils as "the finest writing instruments in the world," a message that transcends national boundaries and can be used anywhere. Many fast-food franchises apply the same ideas because they have found that people everywhere have the same basic reasons for coming to their unit to eat. In most cases, however, it is necessary to tailor-make the strategy so that it appeals directly to the local customer.

These changes fall into five major areas: market assessment, product decisions, promotion strategies, pricing decisions, and place or distribution strategies. The latter four areas – product, promotion, price, and place – are often referred to as the four P's of marketing,[3] and they constitute the heart of international marketing efforts.

INTERNATIONAL MARKET ASSESSMENT

International marketing strategy starts with **international market assessment**, an evaluation of the goods and services that the MNE can sell in the global marketplace.[4] This assessment typically involves a series of analyses aimed at pinpointing specific offerings and geographic targets. The first step in this process is called the initial screening.

Initial screening: basic need and potential

Initial screening is the process of determining the basic need potential of the MNE's goods and services in foreign markets. This screening answers the question: Who might be interested in buying our output?[5] International auto manufacturers will list the EU countries, North America, and Japan as potential buyers. Boeing will target the countries that will be rebuilding their air fleets during the millennium.[6] Kellogg's, General Mills, and Nestlé will be interested in the United States and the EU as well as in developing nations that offer potentially new markets.

One way in which initial screening is carried out is by examining the current import policies of other countries and identifying those goods and services that are now being purchased from abroad. A second way is by determining local production. A third way is by examining the demographic changes that are taking place in the country which will create new, emerging markets. These cursory efforts help the MNE to target potential markets. Following the initial screening, the company will begin to narrow its selection.

Second screening: financial and economic conditions

Secondary screening is used to reduce the list of market prospects by eliminating those that fail to meet financial and economic considerations. Financial considerations include inflation rates, interest rates, expected returns on investment, the buying habits of customers, and the availability of credit. These factors are important in determining whether markets that passed the initial, general screening are also financially feasible.

Economic considerations relate to a variety of market demand influences, including market indicators. **Market indicators** are used for measuring the relative market strengths of various geographic areas. These indicators focus on three important areas: market size, market intensity, and market growth. **Market size** is the relative size of each market as a percentage of the total world market. For example, industrialized countries account for virtually all the market for cellular telephones, and a few nations such as the United States and Japan account for the largest percentage of this total. **Market intensity** is the "richness" of the market or the degree of the purchasing power in one country, compared to others. For example, the United States and Canada are extremely rich markets for automobiles, telephones, and computers, so MNEs selling these products will highlight these two countries. **Market growth** is the annual increase in sales. For example, the market for portable telephones and notebook computers in the United States will continue to grow during the millennium, whereas the market for autos will increase much more slowly. However, given the large purchasing power in the US economy, MNEs selling these products will continue to target the United States. In recent years other economies such as Japan and Great Britain have become increasingly rich in terms of purchasing power, so they too are now target markets for high-tech products.

Quite often these data are analyzed through the use of quantitative techniques. Sometimes these approaches are fairly simple. **Trend analysis**, for example, is the estimation of future demand either by extrapolating the growth over the last three to five years and assuming that this trend will continue or by using some form of average growth rate over the recent past. A similar approach is **estimation by analogy** through which forecasters predict market demand or growth based on information generated in other countries. For example, if the number of refrigerators sold in the United States is 2.5 times the number of new housing starts, a US MNE that is planning to manufacture these products in the EU will estimate demand based on the same formula. A more sophisticated approach is the use of **regression analysis**, a mathematical approach to forecasting which attempts to test the explanatory power of a set of independent variables. In the case of selling refrigerators in the EU, for example, these would include economic growth, per capita income, and the number of births, in addition to other variables including new housing starts. Another sophisticated approach is **cluster analysis**, which is a marketing approach involving the grouping of data on the basis of market area, customer, and so on, based on similar variables. Then a marketing strategy would be formulated for each group. For example, US MNEs providing services in such areas as insurance, legal, financial, and management consulting know that their approaches must often vary from country to country.

Third screening: political and legal forces

The third level of screening involves looking at political and legal forces. One of the primary considerations is entry barriers in the form of import restrictions or limits on local ownership of business operations. Analysis of these barriers often results in identifying loopholes around the various restrictions or data that indicate barriers are far less extensive than initially believed.[7] For example, some MNEs have been able to sidestep legal restrictions by forming joint ventures with local firms. Production restrictions or limitations on profit remittance that restrict operating flexibility must also be considered. The stability of the government is an important factor in starting a successful operation; however, it is often difficult to predict. VW, for example, has been looking for worldwide expansion but is wary about expanding into Russia because of the uncertain political and economic environment. Another consideration is the protection offered for patents, trademarks, and copyrights. In some countries such as China and Taiwan, pirating has been fairly common, resulting in a flooding of markets with counterfeit or look-alike products.

Fourth screening: sociocultural forces

The fourth level of screening typically involves consideration of sociocultural forces such as language, work habits, customs, religion, and values. As noted earlier, culture greatly affects the way people live and MNEs want to examine how well their operations will fit into each particular culture. For example, although Japanese auto manufacturers have set up assembly plants in the United States, operations are not identical to those in Japan because of the work habits and customs of Americans. In the United States, the work pace is less frantic and most people are unwilling to work the typical $5^1/_2$ day week which is so common in Japan. Moreover, US managers are accustomed to going home to their families after work, whereas Japanese managers often go out for dinner and drinks and discuss business until late in the evening. MNEs will examine these sociocultural differences in determining where to locate operations.

Fifth screening: competitive environment

The fifth level of screening is typically focused on competitive forces. If there are three or four locations that are equally attractive, the MNE will often make a final choice based on the degree of competition that exists in each locale. In some cases companies do not want to enter markets where there is strong competition. However, in many cases MNEs will decide to enter a competitive market because they believe that potential benefits far outweigh the drawbacks. By going head-to-head with the competition, the company can force itself to become more efficient and effective and thus improve its own competitiveness. The company can do this by taking market share away from a strong competitor and by putting the opposition on the defense. And the MNE can force the opposition to commit more resources to defending the market under attack and to reduce its ability to retaliate effectively. Of course, these conditions do not always hold true, but they help to illustrate why MNEs will consider entering markets that are dominated by competitors.

Final selection

Before making a final selection, MNEs will usually enhance their information by visiting on-site and talking to trade representatives or local officials. Such field trips are very common and can do a great deal to supplement currently available information. Sometimes these trips take the form of a **trade mission**. This is a visit sponsored by commercial officers in the local US embassy and is designed to bring together executives from US firms that are interested in examining the benefits of doing business in the particular country.

Based on the outcome of the screenings and the supplemental data, an MNE will make a choice regarding the goods and services to offer overseas.[8] The marketing strategy that is employed in this process revolves around what is commonly called the four Ps of marketing: product, promotion, price, and place.

ACTIVE LEARNING CHECK

Review your answer to Active Learning Case question 1 and make any changes you like. Then compare your answer to the one below.

1. How would Volkswagen use market assessment to evaluate sales potential for its cars in the United States?

There are a number of steps that VW would take. One would be to look at the number of cars being imported into the country, as well as the number being built locally, since this would provide important information regarding current product supply. Another would be to find out the number of auto registrations and how fast this number is growing annually because this would be useful in predicting new sales potential. A third would be to examine the trend of new car sales over the last couple of years and to forecast overall industry sales for the next two to three years. A fourth would be to compare the strengths offered by VW cars to those offered by the competition and to make an evaluation of how the company can position its offering for maximum market penetration.

PRODUCT STRATEGIES

Product strategies will vary depending on the specific good and the customers.[9] Some products can be manufactured and sold successfully both in the United States and abroad by using the same strategies. Other products must be modified or adapted and sold according to a specially designed strategy.[10] Figure 11.1 shows a range of possibilities. Products and services located on the left side of the continuum require little modification; those on the right must be modified to fit the market.

Little if any modification required	Moderate amount of modification required	Extensive modification required
Heavy equipment	Automobiles	High-style comsumer goods
Electronic watches	Clothing	Cosmetics
Notebook computers	Appliances	Prepackaged foods
Chemical processes	Pharmaceuticals	Education products
Writing implements	Aircraft	Advertising
Cameras	Athletic running shoes	Packaging
Tennis rackets	Television sets	Restaurant meals
Cigarettes	Beer	Health services
		Cultural products
		Consumer distribution

Figure 11.1   Selected examples of product modification in the international arena

Little or no modification

Industrial goods and technical services are good examples of products that need little or no modification. A bulldozer, a notebook computer, and a photocopying machine serve the same purposes and are used the same way in the United States as they are in France or in China.[11] Alterations would be minor and include such things as adapting the machine to the appropriate electric voltage or changing the language used for instructions and labels on the machine. The same is true for many types of services. For example, international engineering and construction firms find that their product strategies are similar worldwide. People interested in having a dam or a power plant constructed use the same basic concepts and have similar needs throughout the world. In fact, experience is the greatest selling point in convincing clients to hire an MNE in engineering or construction. For example, US firms that had experience in putting out oil well fires in the United States and cleaning up the *Exxon Valdez* oil spill in Alaska found a demand for their services in the aftermath of the Gulf War of 1991. Companies with a strong international brand image have also been able to succeed without a differentiation strategy. For example, Chivas Regal, the world-famous Scotch, is sold in many countries, and the product is identical in each case. Similarly, Schweppes (tonic water) and Perrier are internationally known and these respective products are identical worldwide.

Moderate to high modification

A number of factors will result in an MNE using moderate to high product modification. These include economics, culture, local laws, level of technology, and the product's life cycle.

Economics   There are many examples of how economic considerations affect the decision to modify a product. For example, in the United States chewing gum packages often contain 10 to 20 sticks. But in many other countries weak purchasing power of the customers necessitates packaging the gum with only five sticks. In many countries consumers must carry their goods home from the store, and so smaller packages and containers are preferable to larger, heavier ones.

Economics is also important when the cost of a product is either too high or too low to make it attractive in another country. For example, in economically advanced countries cash registers are electronic; virtually no one uses hand-cranked machines. However, in many countries of the world electronic cash registers are too expensive and sophisticated for most retail stores and small establishments. So MNEs like National Cash Register continue to manufacture the hand-cranked versions. On the other hand, inexpensive calculating machines are widely employed throughout the world and many stores use hand-held calculators to total customer purchases (although in some places calculations may be cross-checked for accuracy with an abacus).

Similarly, in economically advanced countries products are likely to have frills or extras, whereas in less economically advanced countries only the basic model is offered. For example, in the United States, bicycles are used for exercise and recreation and will have a number of special features that make bicycle riding particularly enjoyable. However, in many countries bicycles are a primary source of transportation. So while US bikes are built for comfort and ease of handling, in third world countries they are built for economy and ease of maintenance. As a result, manufacturers will modify the product to fit customer needs.

Culture   In some cases a product must be adapted to different ways people are accustomed to doing things. For example, the French prefer washing machines that load from the top, whereas the British like front-loading units. The Germans prefer high-speed machines that take out most of the moisture in the spin-dry process, whereas the Italians like slower spin speeds because they prefer to hang-dry laundry in the sun. So manufacturers who sell washing machines in the EU must produce a variety of different units.

Food is often an item that must be modified or sold differently. In fast-food franchises like McDonald's, portions of the menu are similar throughout the world and some items are designed to cater specifically to local tastes. For example, coffee in South American units tends to be a much stronger blend than that sold in North America. And in certain parts of Europe and Asia, the food is more highly seasoned in keeping with local tastes. For products that are not modified the marketing focus will be different because of the way the item is used. Schweppes tonic water, for example, typically serves as a mixer in the United States and Britain where drinks like gin and tonic are popular. In some countries, France, for example, Schweppes is drunk without alcohol. Clearly, the marketing approaches would be different in these two situations. The marketing message is also important when selling hard liquors. The products remain the same but many places have social customs that frown upon excessive consumption. In these cases MNEs such as Seagram of Canada have tailored their advertising messages along the lines of moderate drinking and the use of mixers to reduce the alcoholic content per serving.

Culture also influences purchasing decisions made on the basis of style or aesthetics. Cosmetics and other beauty aids are good examples. Perfumes that sell well in Europe often have difficulty gaining market share in the United States because they do not appeal to American women. Similarly, many products that sell well in the United States, such as shampoos and deodorants, have limited market appeal elsewhere. People may not use these products or may have difficulty differentiating the product from local offerings. For example, Gillette has found that it is difficult to develop a distinctive edge in selling toiletries because many people feel that these products are all basically the same.

Convenience and comfort are other culturally driven factors that help to explain the need for product modification. Early Japanese autos in the United States were designed to attack other foreign imports, specifically the VW Beetle. Researchers found that the two biggest complaints with the Beetle were the small amount of room in the back seat and the heater, which took too long to warm up the car. Aware that Americans wanted an economical car with these additional features, Japanese imports offered greater leg room for back seat passengers and a heater that was superior to the VW offering. Within a few years these imports began to erode VW's market share. Foreign manufacturers also identified a group that wanted a large number of convenience and comfort features. The result has been the emergence of luxury Japanese and German cars that now compete extremely well with US models in the upper end of the market.

Other culturally based reasons for product modifications include color and language. In the United States, the color black is worn for mourning, whereas in other countries, white is for mourning and so it is not used for consumer goods. Similarly, most shampoos in the United States are light-colored, whereas in some oriental countries consumers prefer dark-colored shampoo. Language can be an important point of modification because a product may need to carry instructions regarding contents or use procedures. In locations where two or more languages are spoken, such as Canada and Switzerland, this information is provided in all appropriate languages. Language is also important in conveying the right image for the product. Quite often it is difficult to replicate the message because the saying or slogan has no meaning in another language.

Local laws   Local laws can require modification of products in order to meet environmental and safety requirements. For example, US emission-control laws have required Japanese and European car importers to make significant model changes before their autos can be sold in the United States. Food and pharmaceutical regulations require packaging and labeling that are often quite different from those in the home country. For example, in Saudi Arabia the label of any product containing animal fat or meat must clearly state the kind of animal used and the fact that no swine products were used. Brand-name protection can also require product modification. For example, Ford Motor found that in Mexico it had to rename the Ford Falcon because this brand name was registered to another firm. The same happened to Ford in the case of the Mustang in Germany.

Product life cycle   Another reason for modifying a product is to cope with the limited product life cycle (PLC) of the good. Ford Motor, for example, was extremely profitable in Europe during the 1980s, but those earnings disappeared by the early 1990s because Ford did not develop new, competitive products.[12] This is in contrast to Coca-Cola of Japan, which introduces an average of one new soft drink per month and has the competition scurrying to keep up. Another good example is provided by Gillette, which has been particularly effective in combining technology and marketing to bring new products to market before the market share of old offerings begins to decline significantly. The box "International Business Strategy in Action: Gillette Storms the Market" describes the company's latest approach.

One of the most effective strategies has been to shorten the PLC by offering new goods and services before the demand for the old ones has dropped significantly. Figure 11.2 provides a graphic illustration. Note in the figure that there are two types of PLCs. One is the standard PLC which covers an extended time continuum, often four to five years. The other is a short life cycle that lasts much less. Many companies are discovering that by shortening the PLC and offering new product adaptations, they are able to capture and retain large market share. This is typically done by offering a new product and then modifying it and bringing out a new version before the competition can effectively combat the first offering. For example, a company will offer a notebook computer with a 64-megabyte internal memory. Then within six months the company will come out with a 128-megabyte internal memory and a built-in modem. Six months later the firm will offer still another version of the product with additional features. In each case the competition is left scurrying to keep up. As long as the firm can continue this adaptation strategy, it can outmode the old product (and those of competitors as well) and maintain market position. At some point the competition may gain the advantage by offering a product that revolutionizes the field, but as long as a product improvement strategy remains viable, the firm will continue to be the product leader, and this strategy is being implemented by MNEs throughout the world.[13]

INTERNATIONAL BUSINESS STRATEGY IN ACTION

Gillette storms the market

The razor blade market is extremely competitive, and while successful products can provide short-run market domination, new products must be introduced every three to five years. In the case of Gillette, for example, the Trac II blade was brought to market in the United States in October 1971 and managed to garner almost 30 per cent of the market by 1975. After this time market share began to fall off, but in 1978 the company introduced the Atra blade, and for the next eight years Atra's market share climbed to over 20 per cent before starting to fall.

In the late 1990s Gillette introduced its Mach 3 blade, and this offering has done well as it is completely reengineered, with a strip to signal the need to change the cartridge. While most new products cannibalize older systems by getting customers to switch from one product to another, the Mach 3 has helped Gillette to capture new worldwide market share. About 700 million people around the world use Gillette blades. Today the company has 62 plants in 25 countries and it distributes products to 200 countries.

The company's strategy of new product introductions also extends to its acquisitions such as Braun AG, world-famous for its electric shavers and small appliances. Today Braun's coffee-makers, coffee-grinders, hairdryers, curlers, and dental hygiene products are known for their high quality and sophisticated technology. Braun has also introduced a low-priced shaver

that has been a spectacular success. By 1997 Braun's sales hit $1.7 billion with operating earnings of $304 million. Not bad for an acquisition that cost Gillette just $64 million in 1967.

Another successful line is the company's writing instruments division. Gillette has acquired Papermate and the Waterman Pen Company of France, both of which do extremely well in the world market. Today this division covers the entire writing instruments market from inexpensive disposable pens that sell for less than $1 to Watermans that cost in excess of $400. With sales of more than $500 million annually, Gillette is now the world's largest writing instruments company.

Gillette has not been successful in toiletries such as shampoos or deodorants – products that are extremely difficult to differentiate. However, the company is now offering a new line of brand toiletries for men. This is in keeping with Gillette's overall strategy of continuing to offer new products for the international market, both to replace products that are reaching the end of their product life cycle and to generate demand in new consumer markets that are beginning to emerge. In recent years the firm has been ranked as one of the most admired in America, and it has generated an annual average return on investment of 30 per cent. If Gillette continues "business as usual," it should have no trouble meeting future challenges.

Sources: Subrata N. Chakravarty, "We Had to Change the Playing Field," *Forbes,* February 4, 1991, pp. 82–86; "Corporate Regulations," *Fortune,* February 8, 1993, p. 60; Susan E. Kuhn, "How to Get High Returns from Top-Quality Stocks," *Fortune,* March 8, 1993, pp. 27–30; *www.Gillette.com; www.braun.com.*

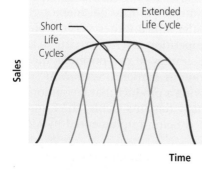

Figure 11.2 Product life cycles: two different approaches

Review your answer to Active Learning Case question 2 and make any changes you like. Then compare your answer to the one below.

2. Does VW need to modify its cars for the US market? Why or why not?

Based on the case data, it appears that VW needs to make some changes in styling and engineering. The company is convinced that Americans will buy cars that offer German engineering and quality, and in the past VW has made the mistake of producing cars that look "too American." Because of this, many people bought cars from Ford, General Motors, and Chrysler because there were no distinctive qualities that VW could use in attracting these buyers. By modifying its cars and giving them European styling and German engineering, VW can lead from strength and exploit its market advantage.

PROMOTION

Promotion is the process of stimulating demand for a company's goods and services.[14] MNEs promote their goods and services through advertising and personal selling. The specific approach that is used, however, will be determined by the nature of the product.

Nature of the product

In promoting a product, a company can use a variety of approaches. The choice will be heavily influenced by whether the firm believes that the same message can be used worldwide or that it needs to be adapted, and whether the product will remain the same or be modified. Here are four variations on this theme:

- *Identical product and identical message.* This approach is used when the MNE intends to sell the same product worldwide and believes that an identical promotional appeal can be used in all markets. A. T. Cross, for example, uses this strategy because writing instruments do not need to be adapted to local markets, so a universal message can be used.

- *Identical product but different message.* This strategy is used when the product satisfies a different need in various markets. For example, in the United States, many car companies tout the luxury and conveniences of their product, but in other countries the same cars are promoted on the basis of their fuel efficiency or ability to meet basic transportation needs.

- *Modified product but same message.* This strategy is used when the market requires a different version of the product but the needs of the consumer are the same. For example, whether clothes dryers load from the top or the side, they provide the same function and meet the same customer needs. Similarly, in many countries the seasoning of foods differs from that of foods sold in the United States. So while the product is changed, the promotion message remains the same because the needs of the buyer are the same.

- *Modified product and modified message.* When the product use and the buying habits of customers are different from those in the MNE's home market, both the product and promotion message will be modified. For example, breakfast cereal companies such as Kellogg's and General Mills are developing new versions of their popular US cereals for sale in the European market. Since many Europeans do not eat cereal for breakfast, however, the promotion campaign is geared toward changing eating habits rather than (as in the United States) getting consumers to switch product loyalty.

Advertising

Advertising is a nonpersonal form of promotion in which a firm attempts to persuade consumers to a particular point of view. In many cases MNEs use the same advertising message worldwide, and since many products fill similar worldwide needs, the company can use a universal message and reduce advertising costs at the same time. However, there are times when the advertising must be adapted to the local market. Two of the most common reasons are that (1) the way in which the product is used is different from that in the home country and (2) the advertising message does not make sense if translated directly. An example of the latter is the Nike commercials that encourage the viewer to "just do it," or Budweiser commercials that ask, "Why ask why?" These make sense to US viewers, but they are too culturally grounded to be used in many other countries. These commercials would leave the viewer confused as to what the advertiser was saying. As a result, advertisers are very careful to tie the message to buyer needs and wants. The box "International Business Strategy in Action: Ikea in International Markets" provides some examples of how this is being done. On the other hand, there are many advertisements that have been only moderately modified or carried in their entirety because they *do* make sense in other cultures. For example, Marlboro's "cowboy image" has universal appeal, and Nike's ads featuring such internationally known stars as Michael Jordan and Tiger Woods transcend national boundaries, especially after the media exposure they have received.

As in the United States, MNEs use a number of media to carry their advertising messages. The three most popular media are television, radio, and newspapers. Some of the major differences between the approach used in the United States and that employed in other countries include government regulation of media advertising and the fact that many stations do not carry advertising, although in recent years this has been changing. In particular, the use of television advertising has been increasing in Europe, whereas in other areas of the world such as South America and the Middle East newspapers remain the major media for promotion efforts. However, there are restrictions regarding what can be presented. Examples include: (1) some countries prohibit **comparative advertising**, in which companies compare their products with those of the competition; (2) some countries do not allow certain products to be advertised because they want to discourage their use (alcoholic beverages and cigarettes, for example) or because they want to protect national industries from MNE competition; and (3) some (such as Islamic) countries censor the use of any messages that are regarded as erotic.

Personal selling

Personal selling is a direct form of promotion used to persuade customers to a particular point of view. Some goods, such as industrial products or goods that require

INTERNATIONAL BUSINESS STRATEGY IN ACTION

Ikea in international markets

In less than 50 years Ikea has grown from a small, private, Swedish furniture retailer to a multinational business with 140 stores in 30 countries and annual sales of more than $6 billion. This internationalization process is all the more remarkable in that Ikea has remained true to the basic philosophy of founder, Ingvar Kamprad, throughout its global expansion. Today Ikea is still a private company.

Initial success can be traced directly to Kamprad, a creative maverick in the furniture business. He redesigned the industry by introducing knock-down kits that customers could take away from the store and assemble themselves. This saved on delivery and changed furniture from its traditional frosty "showroom" mentality to a more "fun" place with children's playpens, nurseries, and cafes in the stores. Ikea also built on the fast growing informal suburban culture by providing abundant parking and by making a trip to the store an entertainment for the family.

This Scandinavian image of relaxed, informal yet efficient service, was extended to Switzerland in 1973, Munich in 1974, to ten more stores across Germany by 1980 and then throughout the rest of Europe, culminating with entry into Britain in 1987. Internationally, Ikea opened in Australia in 1975 and Canada in 1976. Expansion to the United States began in 1985, through the Canadian IKEA operation, into Eastern Europe in the early 1990s, and into Shanghai, China in 1998.

Ikea also brought innovation to the logistics of furniture production by setting up groups of key suppliers to produce components at low cost. These subcontractors, in turn, made money by getting large-volume orders for standardized components from Ikea.

Additionally, the company has kept tight control over product design and quality to maintain its brand name and the distinctive identity of its furniture. And the firm was able to expand rapidly because it did not have to establish expensive manufacturing facilities around Europe, but rather retained centralized control over the subcontractors.

The firm's marketing strategy has been to build on the Swedish home-base stereotype of clean and efficient service. All furniture is well designed, modern, functional, durable, high quality and price competitive. Its image and brand name are well established and have survived numerous imitators. As a result, Ikea has been able to move from its Scandinavian base to being a strong regional player in Europe, and is now competing successfully in the global arena.

In particular, Ikea is a successful multinational business because it has introduced a highly differentiated product into a traditional industry and has now built a globally recognized brand name for high quality, inexpensive, and attractive furniture. It has also combined the generic strategies of differentiation, low cost, and niching and has outsourced both production and delivery components of the value chain.

Sources: Christopher A. Bartlett and Ashish Nanda, *Ingvar Kamprad and IKEA*, Harvard Business School Case 9-390-132; Joseph R. D'Cruz and Alan M. Rugman, "Developing International Competitiveness: The Five Partners Model," *Business Quarterly*, vol. 58, no. 2 (Winter 1993), pp. 60–72; *www.IKEA.com*.

explanation or description, rely heavily on personal selling. Avon, the cosmetics company, relies primarily on personal selling and has been very successful with this approach even in countries where people are unaccustomed to buying cosmetics from a door-to-door salesperson. In Mexico, for example, Avon managed to gain acceptance by first introducing the idea of personal selling through a massive advertising campaign so that housewives became aware that the Avon salesperson was not a common door-to-door vendor but, rather, a professional trained to help clients look beautiful. Personal selling is also widely used in marketing products such as pharmaceuticals and sophisticated electronic equipment. For example, Pfizer and Upjohn use sales-people to call on doctors and other individuals who are in a position to recommend their products, and General Electric and Westinghouse salespeople use the same approach in selling overseas that they use in the United States.

Because many international markets are so large, some MNEs have also turned to telemarketing. This approach has been very successful in the United States, and the overseas subsidiaries of US firms such as IBM, Ford Motor, and Digital Equipment have been using telemarketing to generate new sales. European firms such as Peugeot have also been adopting this approach.

MNEs have also focused attention on recruiting salespeople on an international basis. In some countries this work is not highly regarded, so MNEs have given these people managerial titles that command importance, such as territory or zone man-ager. Recruiting local talent is extremely important since these people are often bet-ter able to sell to local customers. If the product requires special training to sell, MNEs often bring new salespeople to the home office for training, introduce these individuals to those who are manufacturing the products, and create a feeling of teamwork among the field staff and personnel so that the salespeople are energized to go back into the field and sell.

ACTIVE LEARNING CHECK

Review your answer to Active Learning Case question 3 and make any changes you like. Then compare your answer to the one below.

3. Would the nature of VW's products allow the company to use an identical promotional message worldwide or would the company have to develop a country-by-country promotion strategy?

This answer will depend on where VW is selling its product. In less developed countries the message would be geared toward economy and efficiency. In more developed countries the message would focus on styling, handling, engineering, and noneconomic factors as well. So VW would need to develop a series of different messages because there are a wide number of market niches and no one message will appeal to everyone in the same way.

PRICING

The pricing of goods and services in the international marketplace is often influ-enced by factors present in home market pricing. These factors include government controls, market diversity, currency fluctuations, and price escalation forces.

Government controls

Every nation has government regulations that influence pricing practices. In some countries there are minimum and maximum prices that can be charged to customers. Minimum prices can help to protect local companies from more efficient interna-tional competitors because of a floor on prices that can help to ensure profit for national firms. For example, if the minimum price for a particular type of personal computer is $1,000 and local companies can produce and sell the product for $700, they will make $300 a unit. Foreign competitors may be able to produce and sell the product for $500 and make a $500 profit per unit, but the minimum price laws prevent them from driving out local competition. Without this law, overseas competitors might price the unit at $600 and then raise the price dramatically after local competitors went out of business.

Governments also prohibit **dumping**, or the selling of imported goods at a price below cost or below the cost in the home country. The General Agreement on Tariffs and Trade (GATT) specifically prohibits this practice, which is designed to help MNEs drive out the local competition and then establish a monopoly and subsequently increase prices at will. A number of US firms have been influential in getting the US government to bring dumping charges against Japanese competitors.

Market diversity

Consumer tastes and demands vary widely in the international marketplace, and this results in MNEs having to price some of their products differently. For example, companies have found that they can charge more for goods sold overseas because of the demand. For example, in the United States, there is a greater demand for light turkey meat than for dark turkey meat. The latter is typically sold at a lower price and is often purchased by animal food producers. However, the plump dark meat of turkey thighs has a strong market in Europe. As a result, firms like the Shenandoah Valley Poultry Company export thousands of metric tons of dark turkey meat to Europe each year.

A second factor influencing market diversity is the perceived quality of the product. For example, in the United States, German automakers such as Mercedes found that some Americans are willing to pay a premium for German cars. In contrast, the Japanese are not willing to pay a premium for German autos, so Mercedes' pricing structure in Japan is different. More recently Japanese luxury autos have themselves proved to be strong competitors for Mercedes in the US market.

Another factor is the tax laws and attitudes about carrying debt. In the United States, some interest payments are tax deductible, and most people have no aversion to assuming at least some debt. In many other countries interest payments are not tax deductible and people are unaccustomed to carrying debt. In Japan, for example, little use is made of consumer credit. In pricing products, MNEs will adjust the local strategy to accommodate the impact of the tax laws and the consumer's willingness to assume debt.

Currency fluctuations

As noted in Chapter 7, when selling products overseas, MNEs often end up assuming the risks associated with currency fluctuations. This risk is particularly important when multinationals have a return on investment target because this objective can become unattainable if the local currency is devalued. For example, if it costs Mercedes $30,000 to manufacture and ship a particular model to the United States and the company sells the car to its dealer for $40,000, Mercedes is making a 33 per cent profit on the sale ($10,000/$30,000). However, if the dollar decreases in value by 10 per cent against the German mark, then the company's profit percentage will decline and the firm will have only two options: (1) to increase the price of the car to the dealer to make up the loss of dollar value, or (2) to absorb the loss and leave

Table 11.1 The effect of MNE pricing on final consumer costs

| | Price charged by each middleman | | | | |
MNE price	1	2	3	4	5
$10	$12.00	$14.40	$17.28	$20.74	$24.88
$13	$15.60	$18.72	$22.46	$26.96	$32.35

Ultimate effect of a $3 increase in MNE price: $32.35 − $24.88 = $7.47 or 30 per cent

the price the same. In recent years Mercedes has absorbed the loss because price increases resulted in sharply lowered demand for the car and even less overall profit for the company. Of course, if the value of the dollar increased against the mark, Mercedes would have profited accordingly and might have lowered that price in order to generate additional sales. Beginning in the late 1980s US firms found that their products were becoming much more attractive to European buyers, thanks to the devaluation of the dollar and the accompanying increase in purchasing power of buyers on the continent.

Price escalation forces

A problem similar to that discussed above is price escalation forces that drive up the cost of imported goods. In the case of Mercedes, for example, if the cost of the car rose from $30,000 to $33,000, the company would want to pass this along to the dealer. In the case of MNEs that sell through a marketing channel where there is a series of middlemen, the effect of a price escalation can be even greater because everyone in the channel will add a percentage increase. For example, if an MNE exports and sells a consumer good for $10 to a large wholesaler and there are five additional middlemen in the channel, each of whom marks up the good by 20 per cent, as seen in Table 11.1, the final price to the consumer is $24.88. If the MNE's cost rises from $10 to $13, the final price to the consumer will now be $32.35, a 30 per cent increase. So price increases by the MNE can dramatically affect what the customer pays, and as long as the multinational continues to export as opposed to manufacture locally, price will be a key marketing consideration because of its effect on consumer demand. In this example it is likely that customer demand would drop substantially unless there are no effective substitutes for this product.

ACTIVE LEARNING CHECK

Review your answer to Active Learning Case question 4 and make any changes you like. Then compare your answer to the one below.

4. How would currency fluctuations affect VW's profit in the US market?

Currency fluctuations would affect VW's profit in the US market according to the value of the German mark in relation to the dollar. If the value of the mark were to decline, VW's profit per car sold in the United States would rise because these dollars would buy more marks. Conversely, if the value of the mark increased, profit per car would decline because these dollars would buy fewer marks.

PLACE

The importance of international logistics was discussed in Chapter 10. The focus of attention here will be on the distribution differences among countries and conditions with which MNEs must be familiar. **Distribution** is the course that goods take between production and the final consumer. This course often differs on a country-by-country basis, and MNEs will spend a considerable amount of time in examining the different systems that are in place, the criteria to use in choosing distributors and channels, and how distribution segmentation will be employed.[15]

Different distribution systems

It is often difficult to standardize the distribution system and to use the same approach in every country because there are many individual differences to be considered. For example, in some countries such as Finland there is a predominance of general line retailers who carry a wide assortment of merchandise. In contrast, the wholesale and retail structure in Italy is characterized by a wide array of stores, many of which specialize or carry limited lines of merchandise. So in distributing goods in these two countries, MNEs need to employ different strategies.

Consumer spending habits can also negate attempts to standardize distribution. In the United States, many middlemen are geared to handling credit sales, whereas in Japan, most consumer purchases are on a cash basis. In both Germany and the United States, mail order buying has increased dramatically in recent years, whereas in Portugal and Spain, the market is quite small. So the route that the goods take to the consumer will vary.

The location where consumers are used to buying will also influence distribution. In economically developed countries where supermarkets have become commonplace, customers purchase a wide variety of food and other products under one roof. In most countries, however, purchases are made in smaller stores and distribution requires the MNE or the local sales manager to deal with a large number of retailers, each of whom is selling a small amount of merchandise. In recent years some wholesalers and retailers have been expanding their operations to other countries. For example, Wal-Mart, the giant US retailer, has expanded into Mexico and Europe: in 1999 it bought the British Supermarket chain, Asda. However, most middlemen operate exclusively within one country, another factor helping to explain why it is still difficult to standardize distribution on an international basis.

Choosing the best distribution system

MNEs use a number of criteria in creating the most efficient distribution system. One is to get the best possible distributors to carry their products. A key factor in evaluating potential distributors is the financial strength of the wholesaler or retailer because the multinational wants to know that the distributor will be able to survive the long run. MNEs that sell goods that require periodic maintenance and servicing will be interested in businesses that can keep sufficient inventory on hand. This is particularly important when selling products such as autos, computers, and electronic equipment. A second factor is how well connected the distributor is in terms of knowing the right people and of providing assistance in handling governmental red tape.

This is an important consideration for Coca-Cola when choosing overseas distributors. A third factor is the number and types of product lines the distributor carries currently so that the multinational can identify middlemen who are most likely to give its goods a strong marketing push.

In many cases distributors will have competitive products or feel that they do not need to add any new product lines. If the multinational wants to tap into this distribution system, the company will have to formulate an incentive program that is designed to convince the distributor to carry its products. Some of the ways in which this is done include (1) helping to pay for local promotion campaigns of the product, (2) providing generous sales incentives, (3) conducting marketing research to identify customer niches and sales forecasts to help the distributor to decide how much inventory to carry,[16] and (4) ensuring that unsold or outmoded merchandise can be returned for a full refund.

Depending on the nature of the market and the competition, the multinational may give exclusive geographic distribution to one local seller or may arrange to have a number of sellers jointly selling the product. For example, auto manufacturers will often have more than one dealer in a major metropolis but be willing to give exclusive geographic distribution rights to dealers located in rural areas. This is in contrast to food products which can be sold in a wide variety of outlets and where exclusivity is unnecessary. In these cases the multinational will try to get a variety of distributors to carry the product.

ACTIVE LEARNING CHECK

Review your answer to Active Learning Case question 5 and make any changes you like. Then compare your answer to the one below.

5. What type of distribution system would be most effective for VW in the United States?

VW would use the same type of distribution system as that employed by other car manufacturers (i.e., auto dealerships). The big challenge for VW will be to open new dealerships and thus increase market coverage. The market in the United States is fairly well blanketed with auto dealerships, but the company could look for successful dealers who would be willing to carry the VW line as well as their current offerings. Another approach is to build VWs in the United States and thus reduce the distance the product has to be transported along the distribution system. This not only reduces cost but also helps to ensure faster delivery.

STRATEGIC MANAGEMENT AND MARKETING STRATEGY

Marketing strategies play a key role in helping MNEs to formulate an overall plan of action. Many approaches are directly related to the major areas that have been examined in this chapter, including ongoing market assessment, new product development, and the use of effective pricing. Table 11.2 illustrates the worldwide market penetration of several MNEs which we shall discuss in this section.

Table 11.2 International market penetration: location of subsidiaries, holdings and joint ventures

	General Motors (US)	Clarins (French)	Daewoo (Korean)	Mitsubishi Electric (Japanese)	Royal Dutch/Shell Group (Dutch/British)
North America	Canada, Mexico, United States	Canada, Mexico, United States	Canada, Mexico, United States	Canada, Mexico, United States	Canada, Mexico, United States
Western Europe	Austria, Belgium, Denmark, Finland, France, Germany, Greece, Ireland, Italy, Netherlands, Norway, Portugal, Spain, Sweden, Switzerland, Turkey, United Kingdom	Austria, Belgium, Germany, Italy, Netherlands, Northern Ireland, Rep. Of Ireland, Spain, Switzerland, United Kingdom	Austria, Belgium, France, Germany, Greece, Italy, Netherlands, Norway, Spain, Sweden, Switzerland, Turkey, United Kingdom, Vietnam	Ireland, Spain, Belgium, France, Germany, Italy, Sweden, The Netherlands, United Kingdom	Andorra, Austria, Belgium, Denmark, Faroe Islands, Finland, France, Germany, Gibraltar, Greece, Iceland, Ireland, Italy, Luxembourg, Netherlands, Norway, Portugal, Spain, Sweden, Turkey, United Kingdom
Central and Eastern Europe	Croatia, Czech & Slovak, Hungary, Russian Fed., Slovenia, Poland		Belarus, Bulgaria, Croatia, Czech Republic, Hungary, Poland, Romania, Russia, Slovakia, Ukraine	Czech, Ukraine	Albania, Belarus, Bulgaria, Croatia, Czech Rep., Estonia, Hungary, Latvia, Lithuania, Poland, Romania, Russia, Slovakia, Slovenia, Switzerland, Ukraine, Yugoslavia
Asia and Oceania	Australia, Hong Kong	Australia, Hong-Kong	Australia, Azerbaijan, Philippines, Singapore	Australia, Japan	Australia, Azerbaijan, Malaysia, New Caledonia

▶

315

Table 11.2 (cont'd)

General Motors (US)	Clarins (French)	Daewoo (Korean)		Mitsubishi Electric (Japanese)	Royal Dutch/Shell Group (Dutch/British)	
		Asia and Oceania (cont'd)				
Indonesia	Japan	Bangladesh	South Korea	Singapore	Bangladesh	New Zealand
Korea	Malaysia	Brunei	Sri Lanka	China	Brunei	Niue Island
New Zealand	Singapore	Burma	Taiwan	Hong Kong	Cambodia	Pakistan
Singapore	South Korea	Cambodia	Thailand	India	China	Papua New Guinea
Thailand	Taiwan	China	Uzbekistan	Indonesia	Cook Islands	Philippines
China		Hong Kong		Korea	Fiji	Singapore
India		India		Malaysia	French Polynesia	Solomon Islands
Japan		Indonesia		New Zealand	Guam	Sri Lanka
Malaysia		Japan		Philippines	Hong Kong	Taiwan
Taiwan		Kazakhstan		Taiwan	India	Thailand
		Kyrgyzstan		Thailand	Indonesia	Tonga
		Laos		Vietnam	Japan	Turkmenistan
		Malaysia			Kazakhstan	Uzbekistan
		New Zealand			Korea	Vietnam
		Pakistan			Laos	Western Samoa
		South America, Central America and the Caribbean				
Argentina		Argentina		Argentina	Antigua	Guyana
Chile		Brazil		Brazil	Argentina	Haiti
Ecuador		Chile		Colombia	Bahamas	Honduras
Paraguay		Colombia			Barbados	Jamaica
Venezuela		Ecuador			Belize	Neth. Antilles
Brazil		El Salvador			Bermuda	Nicaragua
Colombia		Panama			Bolivia	Panama
Mexico		Peru			Brazil	Paraguay
Uruguay		Puerto Rico			Chile	Peru
		Uruguay			Colombia	Puerto Rico
		Venezuela			Costa Rica	St Kitts
					Cuba	St Lucia
					Dominican Rep.	St Vincent
					Ecuador	Surinam
					El Salvador	Trinidad
					Falklands	Uruguay
					Guatemala	Venezuela
					Grenada	Virgin Islands UK
					Guadeloupe	

Middle East			Africa		
	United Arab Emirates				
Iran	Iran	Iran	Egypt	Angola	Lesotho
Jordan	Kuwait	Jordan	South Africa	Benin	Mali
Kuwait	Saudi Arabia	Oman		Botswana	Mauritius
Saudi Arabia	United Arab Emirates	Saudi-Arabia		Burkina Faso	Morocco
				Cameroon	Mozambique
		Syria		Cape Verde	Namibia
		United Arab Emirates		Chad	Niger
				Congo	Nigeria
				Congo (DR)	Reunion
				Cote d'Ivoire	Rwanda
				Djibouti	Senegal
				Egypt	South Africa
				Eritrea	Sudan
				Ethiopia	Swaziland
				Gabon	Togo
				Gambia	Tunisia
				Ghana	Uganda
				Guinea	Yemen
				Guinea-Bissau	Zimbabwe
				Kenya	

Africa (additional lists):

Egypt	Algeria	
Nigeria	Angola	
South Africa	Cameroon	
Kenya	Egypt	
Tunisia	Eritrea	
	Ethiopia	
	Cote d'Ivoire	
	Kenya	
	Libya	
	Mauritius	
	Morocco	
	Nigeria	
	South Africa	
	Sudan	
	Tunisia	
	Yemen	
	Zimbabwe	

* all data from websites is as available from May 1999.

Sources: Adapted from *http://www.gm.com*; *http://www.shell.com*; *http://www.mitsubishi.com*; *http://www.clarins-financials.com*; *http://www.daewoo.com*.

Ongoing market assessment

One of the major areas that is continuing to receive attention by MNEs is data collection and analysis for the purpose of developing and updating market assessments. In some cases this causes multinationals to change their market approach, while in other cases it supports maintaining a current strategy.

Clarins   The French cosmetics firm Clarins SA is a good example of a firm that is continuing to refine its market strategy based on market assessment data.[17] For over two decades the company has been gathering feedback from customers regarding what they like and do not like about the firm's cosmetics. From these surveys the company has learned that women want makeup that is long-lasting, easy to choose, and easy to apply. This information has been invaluable in helping Clarins to increase market share in an industry where competition is fierce. In fact, the company's growth rate in France has been more than twice the industry average, and Clarins is now achieving similar results in the US market. It is particularly interesting that this growth has been achieved despite the cost of Clarins' products. For example, one of its spray deodorants sells for $10, 50 per cent more than the typical price of similar products available. Another climate-controlled skin treatment which sells for over $30 is a cream that responds to changes in humidity and releases different ingredients under different conditions. Aware of what up-scale customers are willing to buy, Clarins has been very successful in using market assessment information to develop and market high-quality skin-care products. One marketing consultant has referred to Clarins as a "Body Shop for rich people," and certainly this target market has paid off well for the company.

Shell Oil   Shell Oil is an MNE whose market assessment has showed the importance of not making significant changes in product or delivery systems.[18] In recent years Shell has limited its product diversification to "tightly linked and synergistic energy and chemical businesses."[19] The company has learned that it is most profitable when staying close to what it knows best. Today Shell works to balance its upstream (exploration and production) and downstream (refining and marketing) and related chemical (industrial, agricultural, and petrochemical) businesses. The company is also developing a strong network of service stations around the world and has learned that its ability to assess situations and to react quickly is an important element in its marketing strategy.

Another approach that Shell uses in improving its assessment skills is to have local operating companies simulate supply disruptions such as dealing with a cutoff of oil from Kuwait. By evaluating these situations, the company was able to bring in alternative, preapproved crudes from other sources after Iraq invaded Kuwait in 1990 and oil from both countries was cut off.

New product development

Another marketing area that is a critical part of many MNEs' strategic management plan is that of new product development. The introduction of new products is helping these firms to maintain market share and to position them for future growth.

General Motors   For much of the 1980s Ford Motor was the leading US automaker in Europe. However, by the early 1990s General Motors had taken over this position, thanks to new product development and expansion.[20] At present GM is building Opel engines in Hungary with a local partner and exporting these products to plants in Western Europe where they will be swapped for Opels to be sold in Hungary. GM plans a similar move in the Czech Republic.[21] Meanwhile, in the eastern part of Germany the company has started a joint venture with AWE, an auto firm that produces clunky little Wartburg cars. GM is also moving to increase its marketing outlets in Germany by signing up new dealers. The company believes that this approach to developing and distributing new products will help it to capture 25 per cent of the eastern German market and put it in second place behind Volkswagen and well ahead of the archrival Ford.[22]

Subaru   Subaru is another example of an auto firm that is turning to new product development for market growth.[23] During the early 1980s the company did extremely well by living up to its advertising slogan: "Inexpensive. And built to stay that way." However, by the latter part of the decade the value of the yen had soared against the dollar, the cost of a Subaru rose sharply, and market share in the United States dropped. Now in the millennium Subaru is attempting a comeback through new product development. The company has introduced a new sports coupe with a powerful six-cylinder engine and is offering more options on its four-wheel-drive vehicles. Market share is now beginning to turn around and the company believes that if it can keep bringing new models into the marketplace, this trend should continue.[24]

IBM   Another example of new product development strategies is offered by IBM, which holds over three-quarters of the world market for top-of-the-line disk drives that are used in mainframe computers. The company recently designated this market as one of its top priorities for the millennium. One reason for this decision is the high profit margins commanded by these disk drives. These margins can run as high as 60 per cent of the selling price. In an effort to stay ahead of the competition, IBM is now introducing higher capacity versions of mainframe disk drives and intends to accelerate the product cycle. This will make it more difficult for competitors to offer lower-priced models because by the time these models are ready for market IBM will be introducing another disk drive. Some industry analysts are predicting the advent of inexpensive disk arrays that will greatly reduce the profitability of the lucrative high end of the disk drive business. However, IBM believes that the complexity of these new drives, which integrate microelectronic controllers and software, will be sufficient to protect margins. The company is also doing well with its new personal computer offerings[25] as well as other telecommunications products.[26]

Effective pricing

Some MNEs use a high-price strategy and skim the cream off the top of the market. Other MNEs employ a low-price strategy designed to penetrate and capture a larger share of the middle and lower parts of the market.[27] Depending on the nature of the market, both strategies can be successful.

Bang & Olufsen   Bang & Olufsen is a Danish electronics company that manufactures stereo components, televisions, and video equipment.[28] The firm aims at the upper-end of the market and sells to style-conscious consumers who are unlikely to flinch at paying $4,500 for a three-piece stereo console, $4,400 for a 26-inch color television with matching video recorder, or $3,500 for a portable compact disc player with a remote control unit. One of the primary reasons customers buy from Bang & Olufsen is that the products are well engineered and designed. Televisions, for example, are sleek, thin, and modern-looking. Stereo consoles are trim, polished, and futuristic in design. While many customers prefer to buy less stylish-looking products at one-third the price, Bang & Olufsen continues to have a steady stream of consumers who are willing to pay top dollar. Because of this, the company's worldwide sales now top the $300 million mark.

Cifra, Inc.   Cifra, Inc. of Mexico is the country's biggest retailer.[29] The company sells a wide variety of products, from powdered milk and canned chili to Korean television sets and videocassette recorders. The firm also owns 35 hypermarkets (very large supermarkets), 33 grocery stores, and a chain of 74 restaurants. Collectively, the company earns almost $200 million annually. One of Cifra's biggest selling points is low prices. Many of its electronic products sell at discounts of up to 50 per cent below prices of other retailers. How has the company managed to be so successful? One way is by copying successful discount retailers in the United States. Today the company pushes what is called a "bodega concept": fast-moving, nonperishable goods that are sold in bulk in poor neighborhoods. By keeping gross margins in the range of 10 to 12 per cent and net profits at 3 to 5 per cent, the bodegas are able to average over $1 million per store each month. These sales are more than twice those of similar K-Mart and Wal-Mart stores in the United States.

SUMMARY

Key points

1. Marketing strategy begins with international market assessment, an evaluation of the goods and services the MNE can sell in the global marketplace. There are a number of steps in this process, including an initial screening that is designed to determine the basic need potential of the company's goods and services, followed by additional screenings that culminate in a final selection of those outputs that the company will market internationally.

2. Product strategies will vary depending on the specific good and the customer. Some products need little or no modification, while others require extensive changes. Some of the factors that influence the amount of modification include economics, culture, local laws, and the product life cycle.

3. There are a number of ways in which MNEs promote their products, although the final decision is often influenced by the nature of the product. The two major approaches used in promotion are advertising and personal selling. Many multinationals try to use the same message worldwide because it is easier and more economical. However, this is not always possible because some messages either have no meaning in other languages or the message lacks the impact of that in other

markets. Similarly, while personal selling is used in some markets, in other markets the customer is unaccustomed to this promotion approach and nonpersonal approaches must be used or the customer must be educated to accept this new form.

4. Pricing in international markets is influenced by a number of factors. Some of these include government controls, market diversity, currency fluctuations, and price escalation forces.

5. Place strategy involves consideration of distribution, or the course that goods will take between production and the final consumer. This course often differs on a country-by-country basis, and MNEs will spend a considerable amount of time in examining the different systems that are in place, the criteria to use in choosing distributors and channels, and how distribution segmentation can be accomplished.

6. There is a variety of marketing strategies that are being used by MNEs when formulating their strategic plans. Three of the most important strategies are ongoing market assessment, new product development, and effective pricing.

Key terms

- international marketing
- international market assessment
- initial screening
- market indicators
- market size
- market intensity
- market growth
- trend analysis
- estimation by analogy
- regression analysis
- cluster analysis
- trade mission
- promotion
- advertising
- comparative advertising
- personal selling
- dumping
- distribution

Review and discussion questions

1. How does initial screening help an MNE to evaluate those goods and services that might be sold in the international market? What are some ways in which this screening is carried out?

2. After an MNE has completed an initial screening of its goods and services, what other steps will it take in further refining the choice of those products to sell internationally? Briefly describe the remainder of the process.

3. Why can some goods and services be sold internationally without having to undergo much, if any, modification? Explain.

4. What factors influence the need for moderate to high modification of goods and services that have sold well in the home country and will now be marketed overseas? Identify and describe three of the most influential factors.

5. When will an MNE use the same promotion strategy overseas that it uses at home? When will the company modify the approach?

6. Many MNEs find that their advertising messages can be used in overseas markets without much, if any, modification. Why is this so?

7. Why do MNEs sometimes have to modify their personal selling strategies when marketing their goods in international markets?

8. What kinds of factors influence the pricing of goods and services in the international marketplace? Identify and describe three.

9. Why do many MNEs find that they cannot use the same distribution strategy overseas that they employed at home?

10. In choosing the best distribution system, what types of criteria do MNEs use? Identify and discuss three.

11. In what ways are multinationals using the following concepts to help them gain greater international market share: ongoing market assessment, new product development, and effective pricing? In each case, offer an example.

REAL CASES

CITIBANK IN LATIN AMERICA

The banking industry faces many barriers to globalization. Overcoming cultural barriers, different regulations, and financial systems make establishing a truly global bank very difficult. No one has done it as well as Citibank who is to banking what Coca-Cola is to the beverage industry. By 1999 this US-based bank had a presence in 100 countries around the globe. About 67 per cent of its revenue is generated outside of North America.

Citibank enters a developing country with its own marketing strategy. Initially it caters to the global customer (usually a large organization) by providing short-term loans, cash management, and foreign exchange services. As the market slowly develops new products are introduced for broader consumer groups and to keep pace with the growth of the local economy.

Latin America has long been part of Citibank's global plan. In 1970 Citibank entered Brazil and since then it has established 166 branches in 19 Latin American countries. Its corporate business in Latin America is larger than in Europe and Japan put together. By 1997 it had over seven million personal accounts in Latin America.

A significant portion of Citibank's income comes from credit cards. Citibank realized early that the US domestic market would be saturated. Fees have almost been eliminated while rates plummet.

Fortunately, the Latin American market has barely been exploited as under 10 per cent of the adult population has a credit card. Citibank is well positioned in these markets and can look to be the bank of choice by millions who already trust its name. Once the credit card market becomes saturated the bank plans to move its Latin American consumers into mortgages, personal loans, pension funds, and other financial products.

1. How can a foreign organization, such as Citibank, make an initial assessment of a host country market (such as Brazil) in deciding how to do business there? What is involved in this process?

2. What steps can Citibank take in conducting additional screening of the Latin American market before entry? Briefly identify and describe each step and discuss how relevant it is/is not to Citibank.

3. Based on the case facts, which of the four Ps of marketing would be relevant for Citibank's entry to Latin America?

Sources: Kerry A. Dolan, "Give 'em Rope," *Forbes*, December 14, 1998, p. 218; Dolly Setton, "The King of Plastic," *Forbes*, December 15, 1997, pp. 172–173; "Citibank. Trading Down," *The Economist*, January 24, 1998, pp. 73–74; *www.citibank.com*; Citicorp, *Citicorp Annual Report, 1997*.

A BATTLE OVER BREAKFAST

In the United States, General Mills and Kellogg are major competitors who collectively account for over half of the breakfast cereal market. The two are also major competitors in Europe, thanks to the formation of a joint venture between General Mills and Nestlé, which is now attacking the 50 per cent share that Kellogg holds in this market. The venture is called Cereal Partners Worldwide (CPW), and, among other things, the group has managed to convince many retailers on the continent to stock its products alongside those of Kellogg. As a result, General Mills' Honey Nut Cheerios and Golden Grahams, which have wide appeal in the United States, are now showing up in Spain, Portugal, and France. In the latter, 90 per cent of the big chain stores have agreed to carry these brands.

This latest move is costing Kellogg some of its European market share, but the company is determined to fight back. Kellogg is retaliating by offering products similar to those of General Mills. For example, there is now Kellogg's Honey Nut Loops, which is very similar to General Mills' Honey Nut Cheerios, and Golden Crackles, which bear a striking resemblance to General Mills' Golden Grahams. However, it is going to take more than look-alike products to stave off the CPW attack.

Nestlé is an important part of the Cereal Partners venture, thanks to its wide food line. In particular, Nestlé has had a large amount of experience in dealing with European retailers, and so it knows how to position and pitch products so that retailers agree to stock them. Nestlé also has excess production capacity that can be converted for making General Mills' cereals. Meanwhile General Mills is helping Nestlé to reformulate cereals that it introduced in Europe and which were unsuccessful. By 1999, General Mills was trying to buy out Nestlé's 50 per cent of the CPW joint venture, which produced its first profit in 1998.

In addition, CPW is now in the process of buying out some competitors so that they have been able to gain market share without a fight. CPW is also expanding into Asia, Africa, and Latin America. CPW is now active in 70 countries and has revenue of over $1 billion a year. The result is that Kellogg appears to be in a marketing fight in Europe that may well spill over to other continents. As a result, it does appear that things are going to get hotter before simmering down in this battle over breakfast.

1. How would Cereal Partners Worldwide have gone about assessing the European market? What steps would it have taken before going forward with new product introductions?

2. In what way is product strategy a critical element in the competition between Kellogg and CPW? Explain.

3. Are both groups, Kellogg and CPW, likely to use the same marketing strategies in Asia? Africa? Latin America? Why or why not?

Sources: Christopher Knowlton, "Europe Cooks Up a Cereal Brawl," *Fortune*, June 3, 1991, pp. 175–179; Graham Button, "Atwater's Triumph," *Forbes*, April 26, 1993, p. 12; Riva Atlas, "Food, Drink, and Tobacco," *Forbes*, January 3, 1994, p. 152; Ernest Beck and Rekha Balu, "Europe Is Deaf to Snap! Crackle! Pop!" *Wall Street Journal*, June 22, 1998, pp. B1–2; David Leonhardt, "Cereal-Box Killers are on the Loose," *Business Week*, October 12, 1998, pp. 73–74; Amy Barett, "Campbell's Wet Noodles," *Business Week*, January 25, 1999, p. 48; Linda Grant, "Where Did the Snap, Crackle & Pop Go? *Fortune*, August 4, 1997, pp. 223–226; *www.nestle.com*; *http://www.scisoc.org/aacc/*.

ENDNOTES

1. See, for example, Carla Rapoport, "The New US Push Into Europe," *Fortune*, January 10, 1994, pp. 73–74.

2. Susan P. Douglas and C. Samuel Craig, "Evolution of Global Marketing Strategy: Scale, Scope, and Synergy," *Columbia Journal of World Business*, Fall 1989, pp. 47–59.

3. Fred Luthans and Richard M. Hodgetts, *Business*, 2nd ed. (Hinsdale, Ill.: Dryden Press, 1993), pp. 378–382.

4. See James Sterngold, "The Awakening Chinese Consumer," *New York Times*, October 11, 1992, Section 3, pp. 1, 6.

5. A good example is provided in Andrew Pollack, "A Translating Phone for Overseas Calls," *New York Times*, January 28, 1993, p. C3.

6. For more on this development, see Agis Salpukas, "Germans Join Boeing in Jet Study," *New York Times*, January 6, 1993, p. C5; and Richard W. Stevenson, "A First Step Toward an 800-Seat Jet," *New York Times*, January 28, 1993, p. C3.

7. See, for example, Joseph A. McKinney, "Degree of Access to the Japanese Market: 1979 to 1986," *Columbia Journal of World Business*, Summer 1989, pp. 53–59.

8. See, for example, James B. Treece et al. "New Worlds to Conquer," *Business Week*, February 28, 1994, pp. 50–52.

9. See Cacilie Rohwedder, "Diet Foods Enjoy a UK Sales Binge, and the Continent May Join Up Soon," *Wall Street Journal*, January 28, 1994, p. A5.

10. John Templeman and James B. Treece, "BMW's Comeback," *Business Week*, February 14, 1994, pp. 42–44.

11. Also see Daniel McGinn and Adam Rogers, "Operation Supercar," *Newsweek*, November 23, 1998, pp. 48–53.

12. Richard A. Melcher and John Templeman, "Ford of Europe Is Going in for Emergency Repairs," *Business Week*, June 17, 1991, p. 48.

13. For another look at growth and market share considerations, see Manab Thakur and T. K. Das, "Managing the Growth-Share Matrix: A Four-National Study in Two Industries," *Management International Review*, vol. 31, no. 2, 1991, pp. 139–159.

14. Luthans and Hodgetts, op. cit., p. 381.

15. Joan Magretta, "Fast, Global, and Entrepreneurial Supply Chain Management, Hong Kong Style," *Harvard Business Review*, September–October 1998, pp. 103–114.

16. See, for example, Robert T. Green and Ajay K. Kohli, "Export Market Identification: The Role of Economic Size and Socioeconomic Development," *Management International Review*, vol. 31, no. 1, 1991, pp. 37–50.

17. John Marcom, Jr., "Forget the Sizzle, Sell the Steak," *Forbes*, August 5, 1991, pp. 86–87.

18. Christopher Knowlton, "Shell Gets Rich by Beating Risk," *Fortune*, August 26, 1991, pp. 79–82.

19. Ibid., p. 82.

20. Also see Keith Naughton et al. "The Global Six," *Business Week*, January 25, 1999, pp. 68–70, 72.

21. Peter Fuhrman, "A Tale of Two Strategies," *Forbes*, August 6, 1990, p. 42.

22. For more on some of General Motors' international expansion see Jonathan Friedland and Joseph B. White, "GM Is Leading an Investment Boom in Mexico," *Wall Street Journal*, December 24, 1998, pp. A5–6; Lisa Schuchman and Joseph B. White, "Global Consolidations in Autos Heat Up," *Wall Street Journal*, December 21, 1998, p. A2; and Seth Faison, "GM Opens Buick Plant in Shanghai," *New York Times*, December 18, 1998, pp. C1, 19.

23. James B. Treece and Karen Lowry Miller, "Subaru Pulls into the Image Shop," *Business Week*, August 19, 1991, pp. 86–87.

24. Also see Larry Armstrong, "Revving Up Japan's Also Rans," *Business Week*, December 14, 1998, pp. 135–136.

25. Catherine Arnst, "The Tiny Shall Inherit the Market," *Business Week*, June 28, 1993, pp. 50–51.

26. Bart Ziegler, "A Giant Stirs: IBM Is Ready to Do Battle. Should Anyone Worry?" *Wall Street Journal*, March 20, 1995, p. R20.

27. See, for example, Jennifer Cody, "Supermarket Giant Ito-Yokado Plans Venture to Import Goods of Wal-Mart," *Wall Street Journal*, January 27, 1994, p. C3.

28. Peter Fuhrman, ."A Beautiful Face Is Not Enough," *Forbes*, May 13, 1991, pp. 105–106.

29. Joel Millman, "The Merchant of Mexico," *Forbes*, August 5, 1991, pp. 80–81.

ADDITIONAL BIBLIOGRAPHY

Andersson, Ulf; Johanson, Jan and Vahine, Jan-Erik. "Organic Acquisitions in the Internationalization Process," *Management International Review*, vol. 37 (1997/2).

Bonaccorsi, Andrea. "On the Relationship Between Firm Size and Export Intensity," *Journal of International Business Studies*, vol. 23, no. 4 (Fourth Quarter 1992).

Calantone, Roger J. and di Benedetto, C. Anthony. "Defensive Marketing in Globally Competitive Industrial Markets," *Columbia Journal of World Business*, vol. 23, no. 3 (Fall 1988).

Cavusgil, S. Tamer; Zou, Shaoming; and Naidu, G. M. "Product and Promotion Adaptation in Export Ventures: An Empirical Investigation," *Journal of International Business Studies*, vol. 24, no. 3 (Third Quarter 1993).

Cordell, Victor V. "Effects of Consumer Preferences for Foreign Sourced Products," *Journal of International Business Studies*, vol. 23, no. 2 (Second Quarter 1992).

Craig, C. Samuel and Douglas, Susan P. "Developing Strategies for Global Markets: An Evolutionary Perspective," *Columbia Journal of World Business*, vol. 31, no. 1 (Spring 1996).

Craig, C. Samuel and Douglas, Susan P. "Responding to the Challenges of Global Markets: Change, Complexity, Competition and Conscience," *Columbia Journal of World Business*, vol. 31, no. 4 (Winter 1996).

Cravens, David W.; Downey, H. Kirk; and Lauritano, Paul. "Global Competition in the Commercial Aircraft Industry: Positioning for Advantage by the Triad Nations," *Columbia Journal of World Business*, vol. 26, no. 4 (Winter 1992).

Dominguez, Luis V. and Sequeira, Carlos G. "Determinants of LDC Exporters' Performance: A Cross-National Study," *Journal of International Business Studies*, vol. 24, no. 1 (First Quarter 1993).

Douglas, Susan P. and Craig, C. Samuel. "Evolution of Global Marketing Strategy: Scale, Scope and Synergy," *Columbia Journal of World Business*, vol. 24, no. 3 (Fall 1989).

Erramilli, M. Krishna and Rao, C. P. "Choice of Foreign Market Entry Modes by Service Firms: Role of Market Knowledge," *Management International Review*, vol. 30, no. 2 (Second Quarter 1990).

Evan, William M. and Olk, Paul. "R&D Consortia: A New US Organizational Form," *Sloan Management Review*, vol. 31, no. 3 (Spring 1990).

Hoang, Peter B. "A Causal Study of Relationships Between Firms Characteristics, International Marketing Strategies, and Export Performance," *Management International Review*, vol. 38 (1998/1).

Kale, Sudhir H. and Barnes, John W. "Understanding the Domain of Cross-National Buyer-Seller Interactions," *Journal of International Business Studies*, vol. 23, no. 1 (First Quarter 1992).

Kashani, Kamran. "Beware the Pitfalls of Global Marketing," *Harvard Business Review*, vol. 67, no. 5 (September/October 1989).

Kaynak, Erdener. "A Cross Regional Comparison of Export Performance of Firms in Two Canadian Regions," *Management International Review*, vol. 32, no. 2 (Second Quarter 1992).

Kotabe, Masaaki and Czinkota, Michael R. "State Government Promotion of Manufacturing Exports: A Gap Analysis," *Journal of International Business Studies*, vol. 23, no. 4 (Fourth Quarter 1992).

Kotabe, Masaaki and Okoroafo, Sam C. "A Comparative Study of European and Japanese Multinational Firms' Marketing Strategies and Performance in the United States," *Management International Review*, vol. 30, no. 4 (Fourth Quarter 1990).

Kramer, Hugh E. "International Marketing: Methodological Excellence in Practice and Theory," *Management International Review*, vol. 29, no. 2 (Second Quarter 1989).

Lim, Jeen-Su; Sharkey, Thomas W.; and Kim, Ken I. "Determinants of International Marketing Strategy," *Management International Review*, vol. 33, no. 2 (Second Quarter 1993).

Liouville, Jacques. "Under What Conditions Can Exports Exert a Positive Influence on Profitability?" *Management International Review*, vol. 32, no. 1 (First Quarter 1992).

Melin, Leif. "Internationalization as a Strategy Process," *Strategic Management Journal*, vol. 24, no. 3 (Third Quarter 1993).

Mitchell, Will; Shaver, J. Myles; and Yeung, Bernard. "Performance Following Changes of International Presence in Domestic and Transition Industries," *Journal of International Business Studies*, vol. 24, no. 4 (Fourth Quarter 1993).

Norburn, David; Birley, Sue; Dunn, Mark; and Payne, Adrian. "A Four Nation Study of the Relationship Between Marketing Effectiveness, Corporate Culture, Corporate Values, and Market Orientation," *Journal of International Business Studies*, vol. 21, no. 3 (Third Quarter 1990).

Rugman, Alan M. and Verbeke, Alain. "Trade Policy and Global Corporate Strategy," *Journal of Global Marketing*, vol. 2, no. 3 (Spring 1989).

Ryans, Adrian B. "Strategic Market Entry Factors and Market Share Achievement in Japan," *Journal of International Business Studies*, vol. 19, no. 3 (Fall 1988).

Seringhaus, F. H. Rolf. "Comparative Marketing Behaviour of Canadian and Austrian High-Tech Exporters," *Management International Review*, vol. 33, no. 3 (Third Quarter 1993).

Walters, Peter G. P. "Patterns of Formal Planning and Performance in US Exporting Firms," *Management International Review*, vol. 33, no. 1 (First Quarter 1993).

Walters, Peter G. P. and Zhu, Mingxia. "International Marketing in Chinese Enterprises: Some Evidence from the PRC," *Management International Review*, vol. 35, no. 3 (1995).

Yan, Rick. "To Reach China's Consumers, Adapt to Guo Qing," *Harvard Business Review* (September–October 1994).

Yavas, Ugur; Verhage, Bronislaw J.; and Green, Robert T. "Global Consumer Segmentation Versus Local Market Orientation: Empirical Findings," *Management International Review*, vol. 32, no. 3 (Third Quarter 1992).

CHAPTER 12

Human Resource Management Strategy

OBJECTIVES OF THE CHAPTER

Human resource management strategy provides an MNE with the opportunity to truly outdistance the competition. For example, if IBM develops a laser printer that is smaller, lighter, and less expensive than competitive models, other firms in the industry will attempt to reverse engineer this product to see how they can develop their own version of the printer. However, when a multinational has personnel who are carefully selected, well trained, and properly compensated, the organization has a pool of talent that the competition may be unable to beat. For this reason, human resource management is a critical element of international management strategy. This chapter considers the ways in which multinationals prepare their people to take on the challenge of international business. We focus specifically on such critical areas as selection, training, managerial development, compensation, and labor relations. The specific objectives of this chapter are to:

1. **Define** the term "international human resource management" and discuss human resource strategies in overseas operations.

2. **Describe** the screening and selecting criteria often used in choosing people for overseas assignments.

3. **Relate** some of the most common types of training and development that are offered to personnel who are going overseas.

4. **Discuss** the common elements of an international compensation package.

5. **Explain** some of the typical labor relations practices used in the international arena.

6. **Describe** some of the human resource management strategies that are currently receiving a great deal of attention from MNEs.

Coca-Cola thinks international

Coca-Cola has been operating internationally for most of its 100-year history. Today the company has operations in 160 countries and employs over 400,000 people. The firm's human resource management (HRM) strategy helps to explain a great deal of its success. In one recent year Coca-Cola transferred more than 300 professional and managerial staff from one country to another under its leadership development program, and the number of international transferees is increasing annually. One senior-level HRM manager explained the company's strategy by noting:

> We recently concluded that our talent base needs to be multilingual and multicultural. . . . To use a sports analogy, you want to be sure that you have a lot of capable and competent *bench strength*, ready to assume broader responsibilities as they present themselves.

In preparing for the future, Coca-Cola includes a human resource recruitment forecast in its annual and long-term business strategies. The firm also has selection standards on which management can focus when recruiting and hiring. For example, the company likes applicants who are fluent in more than one language because they can be transferred to other geographic areas where their fluency will help them to be part of Coke's operation. This multilingual, multicultural emphasis starts at the top; of the 21 members of the board, only four are Americans.

The firm also has a recruitment program that helps it to identify candidates at the college level. Rather than just seeking students abroad, Coca-Cola looks for foreign students who are studying in the United States at domestic universities. The students are recruited stateside and then provided with a year's training before they go back to their home country. Coca-Cola also has an internship program for foreign students who are interested in working for the company during school break, either in the United States or back home. These interns are put into groups and assigned a project that requires them to make a presentation to the operations personnel on their project. This presentation must include a discussion of what worked and what did not work. Each individual intern is then evaluated and management decides the person's future potential with the company.

Coca-Cola believes that these approaches are extremely useful in helping the firm to find talent on a global basis. Not only is the company able to develop internal sources, but its intern program provides a large number of additional individuals who would otherwise end up with other companies. Coca-Cola earns a greater portion of its income and profit overseas than it does in the United States. The company's human resource management strategy helps to explain how Coke is able to achieve this feat.

Sources: Jennifer J. Laabs, "The Global Talent Search," *Personnel Journal*, August 1991, pp. 40–41; Richard M. Hodgetts and Fred Luthans, "US Multinationals' Expatriate Compensation Strategies," *Compensation & Benefits Review*, January–February 1993, p. 60; John Huey, "The World's Best Brand," *Fortune*, May 31, 1993, pp. 44–54; Roger Lowenstein, "Sipping the Fizz in Coca-Cola's Profit," *Wall Street Journal*, May 1, 1997, p. C1; Nikhil Deogun, "A Coke and a Perm? Soda Giant is Pushing Into Unusual Locales," *Wall Street Journal*, May 8, 1997, pp. A1, 8; www.cocacola.com.

1. **Does Coca-Cola have an international perspective regarding the role of human resource management?**

2. **On what basis does Coca-Cola choose people for international assignments? Identify and describe two.**

3. **What type of training does the firm provide to its interns? Of what value is this training?**

4. **How useful is it for Coca-Cola managers to be fluent in more than one language? Why?**

INTRODUCTION

International human resource management (IHRM) is the process of selecting, train- ing, developing, and compensating personnel in overseas positions. This chapter will examine each of these activities. Before doing so, however, it is important to under- stand the general nature of this overall process, which begins with selecting and hiring.

There are three basic sources of personnel talent that MNEs can tap for positions.[1] One is **home country nationals**, who reside abroad but are citizens of the parent country of the multinational. These individuals are typically called **expatriates**. An example is a US manager assigned to head an R&D department in Tokyo for IBM Japan. A second is **host country nationals**, who are local people hired by the MNE. An example is a British manager working for Ford Motor in London. The last is **third country nationals**, who are citizens of countries other than the one in which the MNE is headquartered or the one in which they are assigned to work by the multi- national. An example is a French manager working for Sony in the United States.

Staffing patterns may vary depending on the length of time that the MNE has been operating. Many MNEs will initially rely on home country managers to staff their overseas units, gradually putting more host country nationals into management positions as the firm gains experience. Another approach is to use home country nationals in less developed countries and employ host country nationals in more developed regions. This pattern has been found fairly prevalent among US and European MNEs.[2] A third pattern is to put a home country manager in charge of a new operation, but once the unit is up and running, turn it over to a host country manager. Figure 12.1 provides an illustration of the types of managers, by nationality

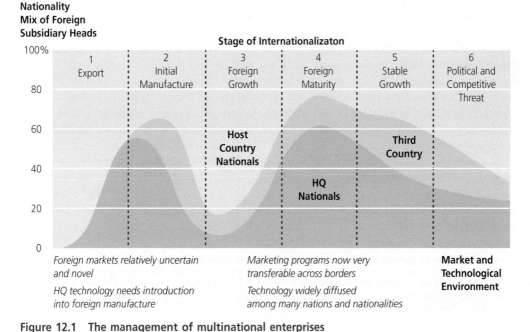

Figure 12.1 The management of multinational enterprises

Source: Lawrence G. Franko, "Who Manages Multinational Enterprises?" *Columbia Journal of World Business,* Summer 1973, p. 33.

INTERNATIONAL BUSINESS STRATEGY IN ACTION

German management gets tough

During the 1970s and 1980s German manufacturing workers made substantial gains at the bargaining table. However, these successes are now coming back to haunt both them and their unions. By 1998 average hourly manufacturing wages in Germany were at the $32 level, compared to $18 in Italy and $14 in the United Kingdom. German automotive workers are paid in the range of $40 compared to $25 for US workers. Volkswagen is prevented from laying off some 30,000 excess German workers by tough unions and labour laws. Job security and high wages are not the only labor disadvantages for German firms who receive shorter labor hour weeks, six weeks paid vacations and a very generous sick leave plan that promotes absenteeism. As a result, German products were having trouble finding international markets. In response, employers began looking for ways of turning things around.

In particular, companies began demanding wage concessions and started working to eliminate jobs. IBM's German subsidiary, which had almost 25,000 employees, divided itself into five companies, leaving only the 6,000 workers in the production unit working under a union contract. The remainder of the employees were not covered by the collective agreement, allowing the company to increase their work week to 40 hours. Other companies began implementing similar strategies, convinced that labor leaders would make concessions in order to ensure the long-run survival of the business. In particular, managers pointed to the fact that international competition was threatening German jobs, and unless productivity could be increased, there was a good chance that more and more local firms would go out of business. This strategy, and a decrease in the exchange rate, has led to real wage decreases and a restructuring of the labor market over the last few years.

There are a growing number of companies that are now winning concessions from their unions. One is CED Informationstechnik GmbH, a small firm that assembles personal computers. The company's union contract allows it to cut back the work force when orders are weak. And since CED focuses on delivery of computers within 24 hours of receiving an order, it has no need to build inventory. So the work force size is tied directly to the amount of orders on hand, thus allowing CED to operate with a basic crew of only 200 people. In turn, another group of approximately 40 workers has contracts guaranteeing them at least 1,000 hours of work annually, so these people can count on approximately 20 hours a week on average – although this is all tied to work orders. The remaining 300 employees at CED work as needed and can find after a month or two of large orders that things dry up and they have no work for the next couple of months. It is a chance they have to take.

A 12 per cent unemployment rate and the relocation of operations outside of Germany by both domestic and foreign companies has increased pressure on unions to accept less favorable contracts. While all of this is a big change from the days when the unions used to dictate terms, it is one that is accepted by both the workers and the CED's worker council. This attitude is reflective of a growing number of unions. For example, the IG Chemie chemical workers union recently signed a milestone agreement that conditionally allows troubled employers to cut wages in return for job security. The contract, which covers approximately 1,700 companies, is designed to trade wages and other financial benefits for job employment. In turn, the new-founded flexibility offers the promise of making German industry more competitive than it has been in a long time!

Sources: John Templeman, "Crunch Time for Germany's Unions," *Business Week*, June 7, 1993, p. 47; Greg Steinmetz, "Under Pressure, Germany's Unions Bend," *Wall Street Journal*, July 29, 1997, p. A10; Dagmar Aalund, "Germany's Jobless Rate Worsens, Inspiring Worry Over a Showdown," *Wall Street Journal*, December 9, 1998, p. A17; Howard Banks, "German Industry Is Fleeing Germany. Why?" *Forbes*, May 5, 1997; Michael Calabrese, "Should Europe Adopt the American Economic Model?" *IntellectualCapital.com*, August 6, 1998; David Fairlamb et. al., "Europe's Big Chance," *Business Week*, September 27, 1999, pp. 62–64.

mix, required over the stages of internationalization. When MNEs are exporting into a foreign market, host country nationals will handle everything. As the firm begins initial manufacture in that country, the use of expatriate managers and third country nationals begins to increase. As the company moves through the ensuing stages of internationalization, the nationality mix of the managers in the overseas unit continues to change to meet the changing demands of the environment.

In some cases staffing decisions are handled uniformly. For example, most Japanese MNEs rely on home country managers to staff senior-level positions. Similarly, some European MNEs assign home country managers to overseas units for their entire career. US MNEs typically view overseas assignments as temporary, and so it is more common to find many of these expatriates working under the supervision of host country managers.

The size of the compensation package also plays an important role in personnel selection and placement. As the cost of sending people overseas has increased, there has been a trend toward using host country or third country nationals who know the local language and customs. For example, in recent years many US multinationals have hired English or Scottish managers for the top positions at subsidiaries in former British colonies such as Jamaica, India, the West Indies, and Kenya.[3]

The above factors influence IHRM strategies and help MNEs to integrate an international perspective into their human resource policies and practices.[4] The box "International Business Strategy in Action: German Management Gets Tough" explains why this is so.

ACTIVE LEARNING CHECK

Review your answer to Active Learning Case question 1 and make any changes you like. Then compare your answer to the one below.

1. Does Coca-Cola have an international perspective regarding the role of human resource management?

The company certainly does have an international perspective regarding the human resource management role. Coca-Cola is interested in recruiting people from anywhere in the world, training and developing them, and then sending them to assignments throughout the globe. The company does not confine itself to recruiting, training, developing, or promoting people from any one particular region or country. Both Americans and non-Americans have equal opportunities in the firm, further reinforcing this international perspective.

SELECTION AND REPATRIATION

Two of the major human resource management challenges facing MNEs are those of selecting qualified people for overseas assignments and, in the case of home country nationals, then effectively repatriating them into the work force upon their return. Each presents a significant challenge.

International screening criteria and selection procedures

International screening criteria are those factors that are used to identify individuals regarded as most suitable for overseas assignment. Some MNEs use an extensive list; others rely on only a handful of factors. There are a number of screening criteria that are commonly used in determining whom to send overseas. These criteria focus on both individual and family considerations.

Adaptability   One screening criterion is an individual's ability to adapt to cultural change.[5] Research shows that many managers are initially pleased to learn that they are being sent overseas. However, within a few months many of these expatriates begin to suffer from culture shock brought on by the large number of changes to which they are subjected.[6] This often results in a decline in job satisfaction. However, as the managers continue their overseas assignment, satisfaction goes back up. Torbiorn, for example, reports that by the end of the first year most managers are through the cultural change phase and are beginning to adjust to their new conditions. For those who stay overseas two or more years, Torbiorn has found that satisfaction reaches new heights and continues rising.[7] Researchers have also found that men tend to adjust slightly faster than women, and people over the age of 35 have somewhat higher levels of satisfaction after the first year.

In determining how well an individual will adapt to cultural change, MNEs examine a number of characteristics, including (1) work experiences with cultures other than one's own, (2) previous overseas travel, (3) knowledge of foreign languages (fluency is not generally necessary), (4) the ability to solve problems within different frameworks and from different perspectives, and (5) overall sensitivity to the environment.[8]

Self-reliance   Managers who are posted to overseas assignments must be self-reliant and independent because they often have to make on-the-spot decisions without consulting the home office. In determining self-reliance, MNEs will evaluate the amount of field experience an individual has had, as well as special project and task force experience, since such assignments often require and nurture self-reliance. Consideration is also given to hobbies or avocations that require a high degree of personal independence.

Age, experience, and education   MNEs often find that young managers are eager for international assignments and want to learn more about other cultures. On the other hand, older managers have more experience and maturity to bring to the assignment. In order to balance the strengths of the two groups, many firms send both young and seasoned personnel to the same overseas post so that each can learn from the other.

Some MNEs believe that a college degree, preferably a graduate degree, is important for international managers. However, there is no universal agreement on this point. Multinationals that sell highly technical products tend to prefer people with science degrees. Other MNEs feel that a good education helps to develop logical thinking, creative ideas, and a broad perspective of the world, so these firms prefer individuals with a liberal arts education. However, the best overall combination seems to be an undergraduate degree coupled with an MBA from a recognized business school.[9]

Health and family status   Expatriates must have good physical and emotional health. Those with physical problems that will limit their activities are screened from consideration. So are those who are judged less likely to withstand the culture shock.

Multinationals also take into account the person's family situation. An unhappy family life will negatively affect employee productivity. One survey of US multinationals found that the primary reason for expatriate failure was the inability of the manager's spouse to adjust to a different physical or cultural environment. For this reason, some firms interview both the spouse *and* the manager before deciding whether to approve the assignment.[10]

Motivation and leadership   Another selection criterion is the individual's desire to work abroad and the person's potential commitment to the new job. Many people who are unhappy with their position at home will consider an overseas assignment, but this is not sufficient motivation. Motivational factors include a desire for adventure, a pioneering spirit, a desire to increase one's chances for promotion, and the opportunity to improve one's economic status.[11]

Additionally, one group of researchers recently examined the factors associated with employee willingness to work overseas and concluded that:

1. Unmarried employees are more willing than any other group to accept expat assignments.
2. Married couples without children at home or those with non-teenage children are probably the most willing to move.
3. Prior international experience appears associated with willingness to work as an expatriate.
4. Individuals most committed to their professional careers and to their employing organizations are prone to be more willing to work as expatriates.
5. Careers and attitudes of spouses will likely have a significant impact on employee willingness to move overseas.

Employee and spouse perceptions of organizational support for expatriates are also critical to employee willingness to work overseas.[12]

Applicants are also evaluated on the basis of their leadership potential since most expatriates will end up supervising others. While this is a difficult factor to assess, there are a number of characteristics that are commonly sought when making this evaluation, including maturity, emotional stability, the ability to communicate well, independence, initiative, and creativity. These characteristics are good indications of leadership potential.[13]

Selection procedures   The most common selection procedure is the interview. However, some companies also use tests to help in making the final choice for overseas assignments.

One international management expert has reported that extensive interviews of candidates and their spouses by senior executives still ultimately provides the best method of selection.[14] Other researchers agree. For example, 52 per cent of the US MNEs that Tung surveyed conducted interviews with both the manager and the spouse, while 47 per cent conducted interviews with the candidate alone. In the case of technically oriented positions, these percentages were 40 and 59 per cent. Other MNEs follow a similar pattern. Based on her research, Tung has concluded that multinationals are becoming increasingly cognizant of the importance of interviewing in effective performance abroad.[15]

Some MNEs also use tests to help predict those most likely to do well in international assignments. However, this approach has not gained a great deal of support because it is expensive and many MNEs feel that tests do not improve the selection process. As a result, the candidate's domestic record and evaluations from superiors and peers, along with the interview, tend to be relied on most heavily.

Repatriation of expatriates

For US expatriates an overseas assignment is usually two to three years, although some companies are now encouraging their people to consider making the international arena a lifetime career choice. Sometimes this process is a difficult one. **Repatriation** is the process of returning home at the end of an overseas assignment. One reason is the change in the standard of living. While overseas many expatriates have generous living allowances and benefits that they cannot match back home. An accompanying problem is the change in cultural lifestyle. For example, a person who is transferred from a cosmopolitan city such as Vienna to a small town in middle America will find it necessary to make major adjustments, ranging from social activities to the pace of life in general. Additionally, it is common to find that those who sold their house before leaving and have been overseas from three to five years are stunned by the high price of a replacement home. Not only have they lost a great deal of equity by selling, but they must come up with a substantial downpayment and much larger monthly mortgage payments.

Reasons for repatriation   Managers are repatriated for a number of reasons. The most common one is that the predetermined time assignment is completed. Another is the desire to have their children educated in the home country. The expatriate may be unhappy overseas, and the company may feel there is more to be gained by bringing the person back than in trying to persuade the individual to stay on. Finally, as in any position, if the manager has performed poorly, the MNE may decide to put someone else in the position.

Readjusting   Although many expatriates look forward to returning, some find it difficult to adjust. A number of reasons can be cited. One is that the home office job lacks the high degree of authority and responsibility that expatriates had in their overseas job. Another is that they feel the company does not value international experience and the time spent overseas seems to have been wasted in terms of career progress.[16] Some companies do not have plans for handling returning managers. If these individuals are assigned jobs at random, they can find their career progress jeopardized.

Recent research shows that the longer people remain overseas, the more problems they are likely to have being reabsorbed into the operations back home. In addition to the factors considered above, several factors make repatriation after longer periods difficult. These include (1) they may no longer be well known among people at headquarters, (2) their old job may have been eliminated or drastically changed, or (3) technological advances at headquarters may have rendered their existing skills and knowledge obsolete.[17]

In many cases it takes from 6 to 12 months before a returning manager is operating at full effectiveness. Adler reports that many expatriates have moderate to low effectiveness for the first 60 to 90 days, but the increase in effectiveness continues month after month as the person readjusts to life back home.

Adjustment strategies   In recent years MNEs have begun to address adjustment problems faced by returning expatriates. Some organizations have now developed transition **strategies** that are designed to help smooth the move from foreign to domestic assignments.

One of these strategies is the **repatriation agreement** which spells out how long the person will be posted overseas and sets forth the type of job that will be given to the person upon returning. The agreement typically does not spell out a particular position or salary, but it does promise a job that is at least equal in authority and compensation to the one the person held overseas. This agreement relieves a great deal of the anxiety that expatriates encounter because it assures them that the MNE is not going to forget them while they are gone and that there will be a place for them when they return.

A second strategy is to rent or maintain the expatriate's home during the overseas tour. Both Union Carbide and the Aluminum Company of America have such arrangements. These plans help to reduce the financial burden that managers face when they learn that their monthly mortgage will now be hundreds of dollars higher than when they left for a three-year tour.

A third strategy is to assign a senior executive as a sponsor for each manager who is posted abroad. In this way there is someone looking after each expatriate and ensuring that his or her performance, compensation, and career path are on track. When the person is scheduled to return home, the sponsor will begin working internally to ensure that there is a suitable position for the expatriate. Companies such as IBM and Union Carbide use this form of the mentoring process, and it is proving to be very effective.

A fourth strategy is to maintain ongoing communications with expatriate managers, thereby ensuring that they are aware of what is happening in the home office. In addition, if the individuals are scheduled to be home on leave for any extended period of time, the company will work them into projects at headquarters. In this way the expatriates are able to maintain their visibility at headquarters and to increase the likelihood that they are viewed as regular members of the management staff rather than as outsiders.

These expatriate strategies help MNEs to maintain a proactive approach in dealing with expatriate concerns, and they are becoming more widespread. For example, Tung reports that the best-managed US, European, Japanese, and Australian firms she studied had (1) mentor programs consisting of one-on-one pairing of an expatriate with a member of the home office senior management staff, (2) a separate organization unit with primary responsibility for the specific needs of expatriates, and/or (3) maintenance of constant contacts between the home office and the expatriate.[18]

ACTIVE LEARNING CHECK

Review your answer to Active Learning Case question 2 and make any changes you like. Then compare your answer to the one below.

2. On what basis does Coca-Cola choose people for international assignments? Identify and describe two.

One of the bases on which the company chooses people is the ability to speak at least two languages fluently. A second is familiarity with at least two cultures. Both are viewed as critical for success in international assignments.

TRAINING AND DEVELOPMENT

Training is the process of altering employee behavior and attitudes in a way that increases the probability of goal attainment. **Managerial development** is the process by which managers obtain the necessary skills, experiences, and attitudes that they need to become or remain successful leaders. Training programs are designed to provide individuals who are going overseas with information and experience related to local customs, cultures, and work habits and thus help these managers to interact and work more effectively with the local work force.[19] Development is typically used to help managers improve their leadership skills, keep up to date on the latest management developments, increase their overall effectiveness, and maintain high job satisfaction.[20]

Types of training

MNEs use a number of types of training and development programs.[21] These can be grouped into two general categories: standardized and tailor-made.

Standardized training programs are generic and can be used with managers anywhere in the world. Examples include programs for improving quantitative analysis or technical skills that can be used universally. Research reveals that many behaviorally oriented concepts can also be handled with a standardized program (although follow-on programs must be tailor-made to meet the specific needs of the country). Examples include programs designed to acquaint the participants with the fundamentals of how to communicate, motivate, or lead people.

Tailor-made training programs are designed to meet the specific needs of the participants and typically include a large amount of culturally based input. These programs are more commonly developed by large MNEs and by multinationals that need a working knowledge of the local country's beliefs, norms, attitudes, and work values. Quite often the input for these programs is provided by managers who currently are working in the country (or have recently worked there) and by local managers and personnel who are citizens of that country. In most cases this training is provided to expatriates before they leave for their assignment, but in some cases it is provided on-site.

Research shows that the following six types of programs are most popular:

1. Environmental briefings used to provide information about such things as geography, climate, housing, and schools.
2. Cultural orientation designed to familiarize the individual with cultural institutions and value systems of the host country.
3. Cultural assimilators using programmed learning approaches designed to provide the participants with intercultural encounters.
4. Language training.
5. Sensitivity training designed to develop attitudinal flexibility.
6. Field experience, which sends the participant to the country of assignment to undergo some of the emotional stress of living and working with people from a different culture.[22]

Typically, MNEs will use a combination of the above programs, tailoring the package to fit their specific needs. A good example is provided by Underwriters Laboratories Inc., which uses a two-day, in-house program to provide training to those personnel who will be dealing extensively with Japanese clients in the United States. The program is designed around a series of minilectures that cover a wide range of topics from how to handle introductions to the proper way to exchange gifts. The program employs a variety of training techniques, including lectures, case studies, role playing, language practice, and a short test on cultural terminology. The two-day training wraps up with a 90-minute question-and-answer period during which participants are given the opportunity to gain additional insights into how to develop effective client relationships.

Some firms extend their training focus to include families. In addition to providing language training, firms such as General Electric Medical Systems Group (GEMS), a Milwaukee-based firm that has expatriates in France, Japan, and Singapore, will match up the family that is going overseas with another family that has been assigned to this country or geographic region. The latter will then share many of the problems that it faced during the overseas assignment and relate some of the ways that these situations were resolved. It is also common to find MNEs offering cultural training to all members of the family, not just to the executive. This helps to create a support group that will work together to deal with problems that arise during the overseas assignment.

ACTIVE LEARNING CHECK

Review your answer to Active Learning Case question 3 and make any changes you like. Then compare your answer to the one below.

3. What type of training does the firm provide to its interns? Of what value is this training?

The company puts interns into groups and assigns projects that require them to investigate or study certain areas of operations. The interns are then evaluated on the outcome. This training is useful in helping the firm to identify those individuals who offer the most promise for the company.

COMPENSATION

In recent years compensation has become a primary area of international human resource management (IHRM) attention.[23] On the one hand, multinationals want to hire the most competent people. On the other hand, they want to control costs and to increase profits. Sometimes these two objectives are not compatible; it can be expensive to relocate an executive overseas. A close look at the breakdown of international compensation packages helps to make this clear.

Common elements in an international compensation package

A typical international compensation package includes base salary, benefits, and allowances. Additionally, most packages address the issue of tax protection and/or tax equalization. The following examines these four elements.

Base salary Base salary is the amount of cash compensation that an individual receives in the home country. This salary is typically the benchmark against which bonuses and benefits are calculated. Survey research reveals that the salaries of expatriates are tied to their home country, so a German manager working for a US MNE and assigned to Spain will have a base salary tied to the salary structure in Germany.[24] This salary is usually paid in either home currency, local currency, or a combination of the two.

In recent years base salary has become an issue when foreign firms have merged or acquired companies in other countries where salaries are significantly higher. For example, when Chrysler and Daimler-Benz merged, the Chairman and CEO of Chrysler had a salary of $1.6 million in contrast to his Daimler-Benz counterpart who was earning $1.1 million.[25] Moreover, a recent comparison of the base salaries of chief executive officers of industrial companies with annual revenues of $250 to $500 million found the following:

United States	$490,000
Brazil	$480,000
United Kingdom	$430,000
Hong Kong	$390,000
France	$360,000
Mexico	$340,000
Japan	$320,000
Germany	$300,000
South Korea	$120,000[26]

So, indeed, base salary can present problems in the international arena.

Benefits Benefits often make up a large portion of the compensation package. Additionally, there are a number of difficult issues which typically must be resolved. These include how to handle medical coverage, what to do about social security, and how to handle the retirement package. Some of the specific issues that receive a great deal of attention include:

1. Whether or not to maintain expatriates in home country programs, particularly if the company does not receive a tax deduction for it.
2. Whether companies have the option of enrolling expatriates in host country benefit programs and/or making up any difference in coverage.
3. Whether host country legislation regarding termination affects benefit entitlements.
4. Whether expatriates should receive home country or host country social security benefits.
5. Whether benefits should be maintained on a home country or host country basis, who is responsible for the cost, whether other benefits should be used to offset any shortfall in coverage, and whether home country benefit programs should be exported to local nationals in foreign countries.[27]

Most US MNEs include their expatriate managers in the company's benefit program and the cost is no more than it would be back home. In those cases where a foreign government also requires contribution to a social security program, the company picks up this expense for the employee. Fortunately, in recent years a number of international agreements have been signed that eliminate requirements for dual coverage.

MNEs also provide vacation and special leave to expatriates. This often includes company-paid air fare back home for the manager and family on an annual basis, as well as emergency leave and expense payments in case of death or illness in the family.

Allowances Allowances are another major portion of some expatriate compensation packages. One of the most common is the **cost-of-living allowance**, which is a payment to compensate for differences in expenditures between the home country and the foreign location. This allowance is designed to provide the employee with the same standard of living that he or she enjoyed in the home country. This allowance can cover a wide variety of areas, including relocation, housing, education, and hardship.

Relocation expenses usually include moving, shipping, and storage charges associated with personal goods that the expatriate is taking overseas. Related expenses can include perquisites such as cars and club memberships, which are commonly provided to senior-level managers.

Housing allowances cover a wide gamut. Some firms will provide the manager with a residence while overseas and pay all expenses associated with running the house. Other firms will give the individual a predetermined amount of money each month and the manager can make the housing choice personally. Some MNEs will also help the individual to sell his or her house back home or to rent it until the manager returns. Expenses associated with these activities are usually paid by the company. Other MNEs such as General Motors encourage their people to retain ownership of their home by paying all rental management fees and reimbursing the employee for up to six months' rent if the house remains unoccupied.

Education allowances for the expatriate's children are an integral part of most compensation packages. These expenses cover such things as tuition, enrollment fees, books, supplies, transportation, room, board, and school uniforms. In some cases attendance at post-secondary schools is also provided.

A **hardship allowance** is a special payment made to individuals who are posted to areas which are regarded as less desirable. For example, individuals posted to Eastern Europe, China, and some Middle East countries typically receive a hardship premium as an inducement to accept the assignment. These payments can be in the form of a lump sum ($10,000 to $25,000) or a percentage (15 to 50) of the individual's base compensation.

Taxation MNEs also provide tax protection and/or tax equalization for expatriates. For example, a US manager who is sent abroad can end up with two tax bills: one for income earned overseas and the other for US taxes on these monies. Section 911 of the US Internal Revenue System code permits a deduction of up to $70,000 on foreign earned income. For some executives, however, there still might be some US taxes due. In handling these situations, most MNEs have a tax equalization program under which they withhold an amount equal to the home country tax obligation of the manager and then pay all taxes in the host country. Another approach is that of tax protection; the employee pays up to the amount of taxes equal to those he or she would pay based on compensation in the home country. In this case the individual is entitled to any difference if total taxes are less in the foreign country than in the home country. Other MNE tax considerations involve state and local tax payments and tax return preparation.[28]

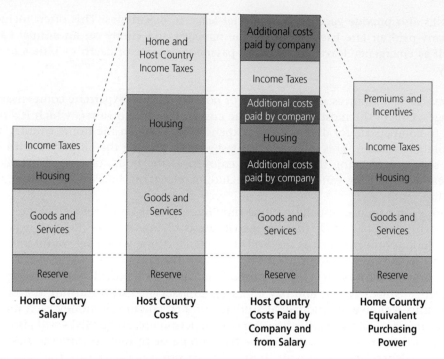

Figure 12.2   Cost of expatriate managers

Source: C. Reynolds, "Compensation of Overseas Personnel," in *Handbook of Human Resource Administration*, 2nd ed., edited by J. J. Famularo (New York: McGraw-Hill, Inc., 1986), p. 51.

The most common approach is for the MNE to determine the base salary and other extras (bonuses, etc.) that the manager would make if he or she were living in the home country. The taxes on this income are then computed and compared to the total due on the expatriate's income. Any taxes over and above that that would have been due in the home country are then paid by the multinational.

Current compensation trends

In terms of compensation, the MNE's objective is to ensure that the expatriate does not have to pay any additional expenses as a result of living abroad. Figure 12.2 illustrates this idea. The income taxes, housing, goods and services, and reserve that the person has in the home country are protected so that the individual's out-of-pocket expenses remain the same. As we see from the figure, the overall package can be substantial. This is why currently there is a trend toward not sending expatriates to overseas positions unless there is a need for their specific services. In fact, the costs have become so prohibitive that firms like Dow Jones & Company, owner of the *Wall Street Journal*, have now radically revised their formula for paying allowances for housing, goods, and services.[29]

Another trend is the creation of special incentive systems designed to keep expatriates motivated. In the process, a growing number of MNEs are now dropping bonuses or premiums for overseas assignments and replacing them with lump-sum premiums. This approach has a number of benefits. One is that expatriates realize that they will be given this payment just once – when they move to the international locale.

Table 12.1 Employer incentive practices around the world

Respondents paying for moves within continents				
	Asia	Europe	North America	Total
	%	%	%	%
Type of premium				
Ongoing	62	46	29	42
Lump sum	21	20	25	23
None	16	27	42	32
Respondents paying for moves between continents				
	Asia	Europe	North America	Total
	%	%	%	%
Type of premium				
Ongoing	63	54	39	49
Lump sum	24	18	30	26
None	13	21	27	22

Source: Geoffrey W. Latta, "Expatriate Incentives: Beyond Tradition," *HR Focus*, March 1998, p. S4.

So the payment tends to retain its value as an incentive. A second is that the costs to the company are less because there is only one payment and no future financial commitment.

The specific incentive program that is used will vary. Researchers have found that some of the factors that influence the type and amount of incentive include whether the person is moving within or between continents and where the person is being stationed. Table 12.1 provides some of the latest survey information related to these incentive practices.

Finally, it is important to realize that many companies are beginning to phase out incentive premiums. Instead, they are focusing on creating a cadre of expats who are motivated by nonfinancial incentives.

> More companies are starting to take an entirely different approach, paying *no* premiums to expatriates regardless of where they send them. According to this philosophy, an assignment itself is its own reward. It's an opportunity for an employee to achieve personal and career growth. In some organizations, succession planning for senior-level positions requires international experience. Others view expatriate assignments as a step toward achieving globalization. Companies that subscribe to the philosophy of paying no premiums only consider cost-of-living issues, not motivational rewards, when designing pay packages.[30]

LABOR RELATIONS

One of the major challenges facing MNEs is that of orienting their strategy to meet the varying demands of organized labor around the world (see Table 12.2). National differences in economic, political, and legal systems create a variety of labor relations systems, and the strategy that is effective in one country or region can be of little value in another country.[31]

Table 12.2 Labor unions worldwide, 1995

Country	Union membership
Argentina	38.70%
Australia	35.20%
Austria	41.20%
Brazil	43.50%
Canada	37.40%
Cuba	70.20%
Denmark	80.10%
Egypt	38.80%
Finland	79.30%
France	9.10%
Germany	28.90%
Greece	24.30%
Hungary	60.00%
Iceland	83.30%
Indonesia	3.40%
Israel	23.00%
Italy	44.10%
Japan	24.00%
Korea, Rep. of	12.70%
Malaysia	13.40%
Malta	65.10%
Mexico*	42.80%
Netherlands	25.60%
New Zealand	24.30%
Philippines	38.20%
Poland	33.80%
Portugal	25.60%
South Africa	40.90%
Spain	18.60%
Sweden	91.10%
Switzerland	22.50%
Thailand	4.20%
United Kingdom	32.90%
United States	14.20%
Venezuela	17.10%

* Mexico data is for 1991.

Source: International Labor Organization, *World Labour Report*, November 1997.

In managing labor relations, most MNEs use a combination of centralization and decentralization with some decisions being made at headquarters and others being handled by managers on-site.[32] Researchers have found that US MNEs tend to exercise more centralized control in contrast to European MNEs such as the British. A number of factors have been cited to explain this development, including: (1) US companies tend to rely heavily on formal management controls and a close reporting system is needed to support this process, (2) European companies tend to deal with labor unions at an industry level compared to US MNEs that deal at the company level, and (3) for many US firms the domestic market represents the bulk of their sales (a situation that is not true for many European MNEs) and the overseas market is managed as an extension of domestic operations.[33]

Labor relations practices

Labor relations practices vary widely. In some countries the economy is strong and unions are able to make major demands; in other countries the economy is weak and the union's ability to bargain is diminished. Similarly, some countries have strong promanagement governments while others are heavily union-oriented. A third factor is the willingness of unions to strike or walk out as opposed to continuing to talk with management in the hopes of resolving differences. Germany and Japan provide some interesting contrasts.

Germany   Labor unions have been traditionally strong in Germany. Although a minority of the labor force is organized, unions set the pay scale for about 90 per cent of the country's workers with wages determined by job classifications.[34] Union membership is voluntary, but there is only one union in each major industry. This union will negotiate a contract with the employers' federation for the industry, and the contract will cover all major issues, including wages and terms of employment. If there is a disagreement over the interpretation or enforcement of the contract, the impasse is typically resolved between the company and the worker with the participation of a union representative or work council. If this procedure is unsuccessful, the matter can then be referred to a German labor court for final settlement.

Despite their power, unions have a much more cooperative relationship with management than do their counterparts in the United States. One reason is that workers serve on the board of directors and can ensure that the rank-and-file are treated fairly.

If there is a strike, it tends to occur after the contract has run out and a new one has yet to be ratified by the workers. As in the United States, several agreements may be in force in a particular company, and these agreements do not have the same termination dates. So one group of workers may be striking or working without a contract while another is working under contract. On occasion, and in violation of law, there may be strikes in the middle of a contract period, but this is rare and in many cases the union and management typically have a good working relationship. However, whether this will continue in the future is difficult to say, as explained previously in the box "International Business Strategy in Action: German Management Gets Tough."

Japan   In Japan, union–management relationships are extremely cooperative. Social custom dictates nonconfrontational behavior. So although labor agreements are often general and vague, disputes regarding interpretations tend to be settled in an amicable manner. Sometimes it is necessary to bring in third-party mediators or arbitrators, but there are no prolonged, acrimonious disputes that end up in a plant being closed down because the two sides cannot work together. Typically, a strike is used merely to embarrass the management and seldom lasts longer than one week. While it is possible to resort to legal action in resolving strikes, this is typically frowned upon by both labor and management and both sides try to stay away from using this means of bringing about solutions to their problems.[35]

Japanese unions are most active during the spring and at the end of the year, the two periods during which bonuses are negotiated. However, these activities do not usually end up in a union–management conflict. If there is a strike, it is more likely when a Japanese union is negotiating with management during industry-wide negotiations. Even here, the objective is to show that the workers are supportive of the union and not to indicate a grievance or complaint with management. In overall terms, Japanese workers tend to subordinate their interests and identities to those of the group. This cultural value helps to account for a great deal of the harmony that exists between unions and management.[36]

Industrial democracy

Unlike the United States, many countries have **industrial democracy**, which is the legally mandated right of employees to participate in significant management decisions. This authority extends into areas such as wages, bonuses, profit sharing, work rules, dismissals, and plant expansions and closings. Industrial democracy can take a number of different forms.

Forms of industrial democracy   At present there are a number of forms of industrial democracy. In some countries one form may be more prevalent than others, and it is common to find some of these forms existing simultaneously. The following describes three of the most popular forms.

Codetermination   **Codetermination** is a legal system that requires workers and their managers to discuss major strategic decisions before companies implement them. Codetermination has brought about worker participation on boards of directors and is quite popular in Europe where in Austria, Denmark, Holland, and Sweden there is legally mandated codetermination. In many cases the workers hold one-third of the seats on the board, although it is 50 per cent in private German companies with 2,000 or more employees. On the negative side, some researchers report that many workers are unimpressed with codetermination and feel that it does not provide sufficient worker input to major decisions.

Work councils   **Work councils** are groups that consist of both worker and manager representatives and are charged with dealing with matters such as improving company performance, working conditions, and job security. In some firms these councils are worker- or union-run, whereas in other companies a management representative chairs the group. These councils are a result of either national legislation or collective bargaining at the company–union level, and they exist throughout Europe. However, the power of these councils varies. In Germany, the Netherlands, and Italy, work councils are more powerful than they are in England, France, and Scandinavia.

Shop floor participation   Shop floor participation takes many forms, including job enrichment programs, quality circles, and various other versions of participative management. These approaches provide the workers with an opportunity to make their voices heard and to play a role in identifying problems and resolving them. Shop floor participation is widely used in Scandinavian countries and has spread to other European nations and to the United States over the last two decades.

Industrial democracy in action

Industrial democracy can be found in different forms throughout the United States, Europe, and Asia. The following discussion examines three examples.

Germany Industrial democracy and codetermination are both very strong in Germany, especially in the steel and auto industries. Private firms with 2,000 or more employees (in the steel industry it is 1,000 employees) must have supervisory boards (similar to a board of directors in the United States) composed of workers as well as managers. There must also be a management board which is responsible for daily operations, and company employees elect members to this board.

Researchers have found that codeterminism works well in Germany. Some critics have argued that there are too many people involved in the decision-making process, and this slows things down, thus resulting in inefficiencies. However, Scholl reports that a study he conducted of both managers and work councils found no such problems.[37] In fact, the millennium is likely to see even greater efforts toward codeterminism in the unified Germany.

Denmark Industrial democracy in Denmark gives workers the right to participate in management on both a direct and an indirect basis. The direct form maintains that employees are members of semiautonomous work groups that provide ideas on how to enhance productivity and quality and schedule work. In indirect form there are shop stewards on the floor who represent the workers, fellow workers on the board of directors, and cooperation committees that consist of both management and worker representatives. Industrial democracy works exceptionally well in Denmark, where researchers have found that cooperation committees contribute substantially to openness, coordination of effort, and a feeling of importance on the part of workers.[38]

Japan Japan's use of industrial democracy concepts is not tied to political philosophy as is the case in Europe; rather, it is oriented more to Japanese culture and the belief in group harmony. Moreover, Japanese industrial democracy is not as extensive as that in the west. Japanese workers are encouraged to identify and help to solve job-related problems associated with quality and the flow of work. Management in turn is particularly receptive to worker ideas that will produce bottom-line results. This process is carried out in a paternalistic setting in which the company looks after the employees and the latter respond appropriately.

Unions play virtually no role in promoting industrial democracy or participative management because they are weak and, in many cases, only ceremonial. One group of researchers put it this way:

> In truth, most workers think of themselves as company employees who are simply associated with the union. Moreover, it is not uncommon to find a union strike in a company with two or three work shifts and no loss of work output. This is because when the strikers are done picketing or marching, they then go to work and the group coming out of the factory takes up the strike activity. In a factory with three shifts, a line employee will work a full shift, picket for a while, go home to eat and sleep, and then return to the factory for her or his shift.[39]

As a result, Japanese MNEs face the greatest challenge from industrial democracy because they are least accustomed to using the idea. On the other hand, as Japanese firms continue to expand into Europe and the United States, it is likely that there will be a growing use of authority-sharing concepts such as codetermination, work councils, and other approaches that are becoming so common in western firms.

STRATEGIC MANAGEMENT AND IHRM STRATEGIES

There are a number of human resource management (HRM) strategies currently receiving attention from MNEs.[40] While there are too many to address here, three that warrant consideration are language training, cultural adaptation, and competitive compensation.

Language training

English is the primary language of international business. However, training in the host country language can be particularly useful because it allows managers to interact more effectively with their local colleagues and workers and to communicate more directly with suppliers and customers. Another advantage of language training is that it allows the manager to monitor the competition more effectively. For example, in recent years a growing number of US MNEs have set up operations in Japan. Included in this group are DuPont, Eastman Kodak, Hewlett-Packard, IBM, Procter & Gamble, and Rockwell International. Many of these MNE expatriate managers and R&D personnel have been given language training, and it has paid off handsomely. For example, Rockwell International recently entered into negotiations with a Japanese firm regarding royalties on a patent it holds on advanced semiconductor processing technology. The Japanese company said that it had no intention of using Rockwell's patent. However, the company negotiators were able to show the Japanese an article from a Japanese newspaper in which their company had boasted about using the new technology. As a result, Rockwell now receives royalties on the use of this technology by the Japanese company.[41] In fact, thanks to language training, Rockwell has been able to discover a host of patent infringements on the same technology by other Japanese firms.

Language training is also useful in recruiting local talent and developing good relations with local organizations. IBM Japan, for example, hires 30 per cent of its research scientists from Japanese universities or companies. Other US firms follow a similar pattern, offering large salaries ($150,000 and up) to attract senior Japanese scientists who can help to create new high-tech products. Language training also comes in handy in developing and sustaining relationships with universities and governmental agencies. In fact, Dow Chemical has created a team for just this purpose.

Another benefit of language training is for monitoring competition. MNEs often locate near their major competitors because new developments by these firms are most likely to be reported in local newspapers and in other sources. It is frequently possible to learn more about what a competitor is doing through local news media than one could ever find out if the investigation were conducted from MNE headquarters. Many foreign MNEs have personnel who are fluent in English, peruse the *Wall Street Journal*, *New York Times*, and US industry publications on a daily basis, and then compile a thick folder on the strategies of their US competitors.

Language training is also useful in helping to learn about the culture of the country and in interacting socially with the people. Recent research reports that most US expatriate managers give low importance to the value of a second language. In contrast, executives from South America, Europe, and Japan place a high priority on speaking more than one language. One research study concluded by noting that "these results provide a poignant indication of national differences that promise to influence profoundly the success of US corporations."[42] Fortunately, universities in the United States are now stepping in to help out. For example, the Massachusetts Institute of Technology, as well as other institutions of higher learning, now offers courses in how to read technical Japanese and understand the Japanese research culture; this educational focus is likely to expand to other countries during the millennium. For the moment, however, language training continues to be a weak link in the development of an effective IHRM strategy for many MNEs.

ACTIVE LEARNING CHECK

Review your answer to Active Learning Case question 4 and make any changes you like. Then compare your answer to the one below.

4. How useful is it for Coca-Cola managers to be fluent in more than one language? Why?

Coca-Cola's managers must be fluent in other languages because the company feels that this allows the individuals to operate effectively in at least two different cultures. This permits the company to transfer managers from one geographic region to another and to know that the manager will be able to become acculturated within a minimum time period. Moreover, since there are common languages in many regions of the world, a manager who is fluent, for example, in English and Spanish could be transferred to countries throughout North America, South America, Europe, Africa, and Australia. Thus bilingualism provides the company with a cadre of managers who can literally span the globe.

Cultural adaptation

Closely tied to language training is the need for managers to understand the culture of the country to which they are assigned. The importance of culture was discussed in Chapter 5, where it was noted that there are major differences between cultural clusters. In preparing managers for overseas positions, MNEs are now using three basic approaches. The simplest and least expensive approach is to design a program that provides cultural orientation by familiarizing the individual with the cultural institutions and value systems of the country. This is often done through a formal training program and/or meetings with company personnel who have just returned from a posting in that country. The second is to provide the individual with language training and, if time and money permit, allow the person to visit the country. Some MNEs tie this approach to the manager's assignment by setting aside the first couple of weeks on-site for orientation and acculturation. A third approach that is fairly expensive but has received high marks for its value is the use of cultural assimilators.

Cultural assimilators   A **cultural assimilator** is a programmed learning technique that is designed to expose members of one culture to some of the basic concepts, attitudes, role perceptions, customs, and values of another culture. Cultural assimilators

Table 12.3 A cultural assimilator situation

Sharon Hatfield, a school teacher in Athens, was amazed at the questions that were asked of her by Greeks whom she considered to be only casual acquaintances. When she entered or left her apartment, people would ask her where she was going or where she had been. If she stopped to talk, she was asked questions like, "How much do you make a month?" She thought the Greeks were very rude.

Page X-2

Why did the Greeks ask Sharon such "personal" questions?

1. The casual acquaintances were acting like friends do in Greece, although Sharon did not realize it.

Go to page X-3

2. The Greeks asked Sharon the questions in order to determine whether she belonged to the Greek Orthodox Church.

Go to page X-4

3. The Greeks were unhappy about the way in which she lived and they were trying to get Sharon to change her habits.

Go to page X-5

4. In Greece such questions are perfectly proper when asked of women, but improper when asked of men.

Go to page X-6

You selected 1: The casual acquaintances were acting like friends do in Greece, although Sharon did not realize it.

Correct. It is not improper for in-group members to ask these questions of one another. Furthermore, these questions reflect the fact that friendships (even "casual" ones) tend to be more intimate in Greece than in America. As a result, friends are generally free to ask questions which would seem too personal in America.

Go to page X-1

Page X-4

You selected 2: The Greeks asked Sharon the questions in order to determine whether she belonged to the Greek Orthodox Church.

No. This is not why the Greeks asked Sharon such questions. Remember, whether or not some information is "personal" depends on the culture. In this case the Greeks did not consider these questions too "personal." Why? Try again.

Go to page X-1

You selected 3: The Greeks were unhappy about the way in which she lived and they were trying to get Sharon to change her habits.

No. There was no information given to lead you to believe that the Greeks were unhappy with Sharon's way of living. The episode states that the Greeks were acquaintances of Sharon.

Go to page X-1

You selected 4: In Greece such questions are perfectly proper when asked of women, but improper when asked of men.

No. Such questions are indeed proper under certain situations. However, sex has nothing to do with it. When are these questions proper? Try to apply what you have learned about proper behavior between friends in Greece. Was Sharon regarded as a friend by these Greeks?

Go to page X-1

Source: Adapted from Fred E. Fiedler, Terence Mitchell, and Harry C. Triandis, "The Culture Assimilator: An Approach to Cross-Cultural Training," *Journal of Applied Psychology*, April 1971, pp. 97–98.

are developed for pairs of cultures such as familiarizing managers from the United States with the culture in Germany. Of course, an assimilator can be developed for expatriates who are assigned to any culture in the world, and the approach almost always takes the same format: The person being trained is asked to read a short episode of a cultural encounter and then to choose an interpretation of what has happened and why. If the person's response is correct, the individual goes on to the next episode. If not, the person is asked to reread the episode and then to make another choice. Table 12.3 provides an illustration.

Cultural assimilators use critical incidents as the basis for the training. These incidents are typically ones in which (1) the expatriate will be interacting with a host nation, (2) the situation may be misinterpreted or mishandled if the individual is not properly trained, and (3) the event is relevant to the expatriate's task or mission requirements.[43] The incidents are provided by expatriates who have served in this particular country, as well as by members of the host nation. Once the incidents are written, they are tested on people who have had experience in this country in order to ensure that the responses are realistic and that one choice is indeed preferable to the others. Typically, 150 to 200 incidents will be developed and then the list will be pruned to 75 to 100 incidents, which are eventually included in the assimilator booklet.

Assimilators can be expensive to create. The typical cost for developing one is approximately $50,000. However, for MNEs that are continually sending people to a particular overseas location, the cost can be spread over many trainees and the assimilator can remain intact for a number of years. A $50,000 assimilator that is used with 500 people over a five-year period will cost the company only $100 per person, and the cost of revising the program is often quite small, so over the long run cultural assimilators can be very cost-effective.

Competitive compensation

MNEs are also beginning to evaluate more carefully the cost of sending people overseas as well as to review the expense of maintaining executive talent in the international arena. The first of these concerns focuses on all expatriates. The second addresses top-level managers only.

Compensation costs vary widely because goods and services in some countries of the world are sharply higher (or lower) than in others. For example, food, clothes, and entertainment in the United States is fairly inexpensive when compared to Japan, Germany, or Great Britain (see Table 12.4 on p. 352). In particular, the cost-of-living allowance for managers in Europe and Japan adds significantly to the MNE's overhead. For this reason, major MNEs from General Motors to IBM to TRW are looking for ways of recruiting and developing local talent to staff operations and thus reducing their reliance on expatriates.

The other major area of compensation that is receiving increased attention is that of hiring and retaining top management talent. Research shows that the cost of hiring senior-level managers is extremely high, and in most cases these individuals received a substantial salary raise when they moved into their new position. Moreover, as the demand for talented executives increases, the salaries of international managers will continue to rise. This is one reason that many MNEs are now hiring people for specific locations and leaving these individuals in place for extended periods of time. This strategy is less costly than continually moving managers from one geographic location to another.

INTERNATIONAL BUSINESS STRATEGY IN ACTION

Two approaches to management training

(a) Gillette

MNEs are finding it extremely expensive to staff overseas operations with expatriate managers. However, many of these companies also believe that expatriates are the most effective managers because they understand how the company works and are loyal to the home office. Gillette, the giant US MNE, has found a way around this dilemma. The company has set up an International Graduate Trainee Program to groom local foreign talent in developing nations. The program works this way: (1) overseas Gillette subsidiaries hire top business students from local prestigious universities, (2) these individuals are then trained for six months at Gillette's office in their home country, and (3) the trainees are then brought to the company's Boston headquarters for an 18-month program in which they learn about basic disciplines such as marketing, finance, manufacturing, and personnel. Each trainee is then paired with an executive/mentor who is responsible for overseeing the individual's training and education in Gillette's operations.

During the time that the individual is in training in the United States he or she receives $1,000 (after taxes) per month, furnished accommodations, medical coverage, vacations, and a $2\frac{1}{2}$ week bonus. If the trainee is successful, the individual is then offered an entry-level position at the division in his or her home country. Gillette finds that 80 per cent of those who begin the training complete it and are offered jobs.

The overall cost of providing this training, including air fare and visa-processing expenses, runs the company between $20,000 and $25,000 per person, and the individual is then prepared to assume an international management position. In contrast, Gillette estimates that it costs between $100,000 and $250,000 to hire an expatriate manager for these same positions. Commenting on this, one human resource management executive noted, "Instead of starting the recruitment process four or five years ago, many companies take the short way out by parachuting in the high-priced expatriate today." This can amount to a huge compensation bill, given that Gillette has 8,200 employees in 48 countries. However, thanks to its International Graduate Trainee Program, the firm is able to train and place local foreign talent at a fraction of what it costs other MNEs.

Sources: Jennifer J. Laabs, "The Global Talent Search," *Personnel Journal*, August 1991, pp. 38–39; Richard M. Hodgetts and Fred Luthans, "US Multinationals' Expatriate Compensation Strategies," *Compensation & Benefits Review*, January–February 1993, pp. 60–61; and Richard M. Hodgetts and Fred Luthans, "US Multinationals' Compensation Strategies for Local Management: Cross-Cultural Implications," *Compensation & Benefits Review*, March–April 1993, pp. 42–48.

(b) P&O cruise ships

Few people know that the "Princess" cruise ships, which were the "love boats" of TV fame, are owned by a British company, P&O. This is a $10 billion transportation and service business that is one of Britain's most international companies.

The Peninsular and Orient Steam Navigation Company, known as P&O, was the sea transportation backbone of the old British Empire. In the nineteenth century it won British government contracts to deliver mail (post) to the Spanish peninsula and (via Africa and the Indian subcontinent) to Australia and the Far East. In the past P&O's ships have been commandeered by the British government in wartime to serve as transport vessels. As recently as the Falklands War of 1982 its large flagship, *Canberra*, played a central role in the British war effort.

Today P&O is using this familiar brand name as a base for its British Commonwealth cruise ships, for cross-Channel ferries, container ships, and for pan-European trucking. In North America, it operates the Princess cruise ships separately. These cruise ships include *Sun Princess*, *Dawn Princess*, *Grand Princess* and the new giant, *Ocean Princess*. With an older population of North America "baby boomers", the growth of cruises has been striking. Occupancy on P&O is usually at 100 per cent of capacity. P&O is the leading cruise tour operator along the North American West Coast to Alaska. Cruises are sold through 28,000 travel agents. The British and European cruise market has been served by *Canberra* (until its withdrawal in 1997 after 36 years service), *Oriana* and *Arcadia* (formerly *Star Princess*).

P&O containers ranked in 1996 as the seventh largest carrier in the world. It then merged with Nedlloyd Lines to form P&O Nedlloyd which is in the world's top three. This is a truly global operation with routes across all the world's oceans, moving the goods of the triad. These container ships are linked up with P&O European Trucks, which is the largest integrated distribution and transport source in Europe. P&O Ferries (which merged with Stena Line in 1996) is the largest operation between Britain and the continent of Europe and they continue to do well despite the opening of the cross-Channel Eurotunnel in 1995. P&O also owns and manages the Earl's Court Olympia exhibition halls in London. It has a joint venture in this exhibition service business in Shanghai, China. It also runs Bovis Homes, a leading British house builder, and the Bovis Construction Group.

P&O has an interesting strategic challenge of integrating diverse business, from trucks to boat shows. In particular it needs to link its very capital-intensive cargo ships, which require good information technology and operational efficiency, with its cruise ships which are in the leisure and entertainment business. The molding of an engineering and technical culture with the marketing, sales, and service activities of the cruise ships is an interesting managerial challenge. P&O has tackled this by extensive programmes of management training. For example, it has developed a series of senior management programmes at Templeton College, Oxford University over the last ten years. These have both improved business efficiency and also moved managers into new areas of customer service, such as environmental and regulatory issues. As a result, P&O is a successful and growing business with a global mindset in its managers.

Sources: Annual Reports of P&O.

During the millennium human resource management strategy will become an increasingly important part of the overall MNE strategic plan. Rising compensation costs are one of the major reasons for this trend. The box "International Business Strategy in Action: Two Approaches to Management Training" details how using a cleverly designed IHRM approach can address the compensation issue.

Specially-designed HRM programs

Another emerging trend is specially-designed IIRM programs. In recent years a growing number of MNEs have begun to realize that HRM practices have to be tailor-made. This has been clearly illustrated by Sparrow and Budhwar, who compared data from 13 different countries on the basis of HRM factors. Five of these factors included the following:

1. Structural empowerment which is characterized by flat organization designs, wide spans of control, the use of flexible cross-functional teams, and the rewarding of individuals for productivity gains.

2. Accelerated resource development which is characterized by the early identification of high potential employees, the establishment of both multiple and parallel career paths, the rewarding of personnel for enhancing their skills and knowledge, and the offering of continuous training and development education.

Table 12.4   Cost of living in select cities (New York = 100)

Location	Cost
Tokyo	148
Hong Kong	120
London	112
Moscow	110
Tel Aviv	103
Beijing	102
New York	100
Singapore	100
Taipei	98
Buenos Aires	95
Sao Paulo	94
Athens	85
Lisbon	78
Santiago	75
Caracas	75
Bogota	74
Mexico City	74
Istanbul	72
Seoul	70
Warsaw	68
Johannesburg	62
Kuala Lumpur	61
Prague	61
Bangkok	55
Manila	53
Budapest	52
Delhi	51
Jakarta	49

Source: Adapted from Economist Intelligence Unit, 1998.

3. Employee welfare emphasis which is characterized by firms offering personal family assistance, encouraging and regarding external volunteer activities, and promoting
   a culture that emphasizes equality in the work place.

4. An efficiency emphasis in which employees are encouraged to monitor their own
   work and to continually improve their performance.

5. Long-termism which stresses long-term results such as innovation and creativity
   rather than just weekly and monthly short-term productivity.[44]

When Sparrow and Budhwar used these HRM approaches on a comparative country-
by-country basis, they found that there were worldwide differences in human resource
management practices. Table 12.5 shows the comparative results, after each of the
13 countries was categorized as being either high or low on the respective factors.

Table 12.5   Human resource management practices in select countries

	Structural empowerment		Accelerated resource development		Employee welfare emphasis		Efficiency emphasis		Long-termism	
	High	Low	High	Low	High	Low	High	Low	High	Low
United States	X			X	X		X			X
Canada	X			X	X			X		X
United Kingdom	X			X		X		X		X
Italy		X		X		X		X		X
Japan		X		X	X		X		X	
India		X		X	X			X	X	
Australia	X		X			X	X		X	
Brazil	X		X		X			X	X	
Mexico	X		X		X			X		X
Argentina		X	X		X			X		X
Germany		X	X			X		X	X	
Korea		X	X			X	X		X	
France		X	X			X	X			X

Source: Adapted from Paul R. Sparrow and Pawan S. Budhwar, "Competition and Change: Mapping the Indiana HRM Recipe Against World-Wide Patterns," *Journal of World Business*, vol. 32, no. 3, 1997, p. 233.

These findings reveal that countries are unique in their approach to human resources management. What works well in the United States may have limited value in France. In fact, a close analysis of Table 12.5 shows that none of the 13 countries had the same profile; each was different. This was even true in the case of Anglo nations such as the United States, Canada, Australia, and the United Kingdom where differences in employee welfare emphasis, accelerated resource development, long efficiency orientation, and long-termism resulted in unique HRM profiles for each. Similarly, Japan and Korea differed on two of the factors, as did Germany and France; and India, which many people might feel would be more similar to an Anglo culture than to an Asian one, differed on two of the factors with both the United States and the United Kingdom, with three of the factors with Canada, and on all four factors with Australia.

These findings point to the fact that MNEs in the millennium will have to increasingly focus on HRM programs designed to meet the needs of local personnel. A good example is provided in Eastern Europe where international managers are discovering that in order to effectively recruit college graduates their firms must provide training programs that give these new employees opportunities to work with a variety of tasks and to help them specialize in their particular fields of interest. At the same time the MNEs are discovering that these recruits are looking for companies that offer a good social working environment. A recent survey of over 1,000 business and engineering students from Poland, the Czech Republic, and Hungary found that almost two-thirds of the respondents said that they wanted their boss to be receptive to their ideas; 37 per cent were looking for managers who had strong industry experience; and 34 per cent wanted a boss who was a good rational decision maker. These findings indicate that multinational human resource management is now becoming much more of a two-way street: both employees and managers need to continually adjust to emerging demands.[45]

SUMMARY

Key points

1. International human resource management (IHRM) is the process of selecting, training, developing, and compensating personnel in overseas positions. IHRM strategies involve consideration of staffing, selecting, training, compensating, and labor relations in the international environment.

2. There are a number of screening criteria that are used in choosing people for international assignments. These include adaptability, self-reliance, age, experience, education, health, family status, motivation, and leadership. The most common selection procedure is the interview, although some firms also use testing. In recent years MNEs have also begun formulating repatriation strategies for integrating returning managers back into the work place at home.

3. Training and development programs are another key part of IHRM strategies. There are a wide variety of these programs, ranging from environmental briefings to language training.

4. There are a number of common parts in a typical international compensation package, including base salary, benefits, allowances, and tax protection and/or equalization. In essence, the package's objective is to ensure that the expatriate does not have to pay any additional expenses as a result of living abroad.

5. Labor relations practices vary widely in the international arena. For example, union–management relations and industrial democracy approaches are different throughout Europe, and these differ dramatically from those in Japan.

6. There are a number of human resource management strategies that currently are receiving a great deal of attention from MNEs. Three of these are language training, cultural adaptation, and competitive compensation.

Key terms

- international human resource management (IHRM)
- home country nationals
- expatriates
- host country nationals
- third country nationals
- international screening criteria
- repatriation
- transition strategies
- repatriation agreement
- training

- managerial development
- standardized training programs
- tailor-made training programs
- base salary
- cost-of-living allowance
- hardship allowance
- industrial democracy
- codetermination
- work councils
- cultural assimilator

Review and discussion questions

1. Many US MNEs are accused of not sufficiently focusing their efforts on internationalization. How can these MNEs develop an international perspective among their managers? Offer three suggestions.

2. What are some of the most common screening criteria for individuals being chosen for international assignments? Identify and discuss four of them.

3. Why do MNEs tend to prefer interviews to testing when selecting people for international assignments?

4. In what way is repatriation proving to be a major problem for MNEs? How can they deal with this issue? Offer two substantive recommendations.

5. What are some of the most common forms of training and development offered to people going international or already operating there? Identify and describe three of them.

6. What are the most important parts of an international compensation package? Identify and describe three of them.

7. Why do some compensation packages have a hardship allowance?

8. In terms of compensation, why do many MNEs prefer to use a local manager rather than to bring in an expatriate?

9. What are some of the primary differences in labor relations practices between Germany and Japan? Identify and discuss two of them.

10. How does industrial democracy work? Compare and contrast its use in Denmark, Germany, and Japan.

11. How are MNEs attempting to improve the language training that is given to their personnel being posted overseas?

12. How would an MNE use a cultural assimilator to prepare people for overseas assignments?

13. What are some of the latest trends in competitive compensation in the international arena? Identify and describe two of them.

REAL CASES

A CROSS-CULTURAL PROGRAM

There are many challenges in preparing people to do business overseas. One of the ways that US MNEs prepare their people to do business in Japan is by providing them with cross-cultural training that focuses on some of the "dos and don'ts" of how to behave when communicating with customers and clients. One of the most interesting approaches is called "Client Relations in Japan," a two-day, in-house training program at Underwriters, Inc. The program is designed for professional members of the staff who travel to Japan to work with clients on projects and for staff members who deal extensively with Japanese clients at the company's offices in the United States.

The program is designed around a series of mini-lectures that cover 50 topics, ranging from a historical perspective of Japan to styles of written, verbal, and nonverbal communication, to business etiquette. The overall purpose of the training is to clarify differences in cultural norms and thus to increase trainee effectiveness in working with Japanese clients.

During the first day of the program participants learn typical greetings and other useful phrases. They are also instructed in proper protocol for business introductions, including how to present a business card, proper words of introduction, and traditional Japanese bowing. Later in the program participants learn about nonverbal communication and their effects on interpersonal relations. Each trainee receives a copy of the Japanese alphabet and English language equivalents, and they must translate several words and phrases. As a result, they begin to see Japanese script as having a recognizable form, rather than being mere scrawlings. Trainees also learn how to plan sentences, to be courteous and patient and not to interrupt, and to pronounce Japanese names correctly. The final part of the course examines Japanese decision making, the business reasons behind after-hours dining and drinking, and the function and etiquette of gift giving. The program then concludes with a 90-minute question-and-answer period. Commenting on the program, one individual noted, "It is hard enough trying to understand and interact with people in the same culture. It is even more difficult to avoid misunderstanding people whose culture and ways of communicating are very different. The more intricate the problem, the finer the tools and skills needed to solve it."

1. Is "Client Relations in Japan" an example of a standardized or tailor-made training program? Explain.

2. In what way does this program illustrate the importance of language and communication training in preparing people for overseas assignments?

3. Does this program use a cultural assimilator? Explain your answer.

Sources: Robert Cyr, "Client Relations in Japan," *Training and Development Journal*, September 1990, pp. 83–85; Richard M. Hodgetts and Fred Luthans, "US Multinationals' Compensation Strategies for Local Management: Cross-Cultural Implications," *Compensation & Benefits Review*, March–April 1993, pp. 42–48; and Richard M. Hodgetts and Fred Luthans, *International Management*, 4th ed. (Homewood, Ill.: Irwin/McGraw, 2000), pp. 447–449.

A FOREIGN ASSIGNMENT

While in the past most MNE executives used to be demoted after returning from working abroad, international experience in today's world is crucial to climbing the corporate ladder. A case in point is Mark Weyna of GE Medical Systems, who moved to Paris to be the quality assurance program manager for X-ray equipment manufactured at GE's newly acquired plant in France.

"Accepting that posting was the best career decision I ever made," says Weyna. This is because working abroad gave him a higher level of responsibility and greater independence. In a business world that is so obviously becoming increasingly globalized, his international performance was regarded highly by his superiors. So much so that at the end of his "tour of duty" he was rewarded with yet another promotion to manage a team of 17 engineers who design CT scan equipment. In addition, he is still in contract with his fellow engineers in France and Asia.

In the past, overseas assignments were usually quite basic, consisting of opening a new office or training foreign workers. At the same time, 20 per cent of workers sent abroad were asked to return home early because of poor performance. Only 11 per cent received promotions after completing a $3\frac{1}{2}$ year assignment, while 77 per cent were demoted.

The case today is the polar opposite. According to Nan Sheppard, manager of global human resources at GE Medical Systems, "Someone who doesn't have a global outlook and a willingness to tackle an overseas posting isn't going to continue to be promoted, period." With international sales becoming an increasing portion of the MNE's annual gross, employers are looking for managers who can handle strategic planning for the region and motivate foreign workers at the same time.

1. What are some ways GE Medical Systems might prepare its employees for their international assignments?

2. Why is international experience so much more important today than it was just a decade ago?

3. How might Mark Weyna be of special help in future international projects taken on by GE Medical Systems?

Source: Kerry Hannon, "The Fast Track Now Leads Overseas: Global Companies Now Want Top Managers Who've Been Around," *US News & World Report*, October 31, 1994, pp. 94–98.

ENDNOTES

1. Brian O'Reilly, "Your New Global Work Force," *Fortune*, December 14, 1992, pp. 52–66.

2. Rosalie L. Tung, "Selection and Training Procedures of US, European, and Japanese Multinationals," *California Management Review*, Fall 1982, p. 59.

3. Richard M. Hodgetts and Fred Luthans, *International Management* 4th ed. (Homewood, Ill.: Irwin/McGraw, 2000), p. 430.

4. Ellen Brandt, "Global HR," *Personnel Journal*, March 1991, pp. 38–44; and Stephanie Overman, "Shaping the Global Workplace," *Personnel Administrator*, October 1989, pp. 41–44.

5. Rosalie L. Tung and Edwin L. Miller, "Managing in the Twenty-first Century: The Need for Global Orientation," *Management International Review*, vol. 30, no. 1, 1990, pp. 5–18.

6. Indrei Ratiu, "Thinking Internationally: A Comparison of How International Executives Learn," *International Studies of Management & Organization*, Spring–Summer 1983, pp. 139–150.

7. Ingemar Torbiorn, *Living Abroad* (New York: John Wiley & Sons, 1982), p. 98.

8. Hodgetts and Luthans, op. cit., p. 434

9. Jean E. Heller, "Criteria for Selecting an International Manager," *Personnel*, May–June 1980, p. 48.

10. Jeffrey L. Blue and Ulric Haynes, Jr., "Preparing for the Overseas Assignment," *Business Horizons*, June 1977, p. 62.

11. Torbiorn, op. cit., pp. 156–161.

12. Patricia C. Borstorff, Stanley G. Harris, Hubert S. Field, and William F. Giles, "Who'll Go? A Review Of Factors Associated with Employee Willingness to Work Overseas," *Human Resource Planning*, vol. 20, no. 3, 1997, p. 38.

13. See also Agis Salpukas, "From Brooklyn, Around the World, To Mobil's Top Job," *New York Times*, February 6, 1994, p. F8.

14. Heller, op. cit., p. 53.

15. Tung, "Selection and Training Procedures of US, European, and Japanese Multinationals," p. 64.

16. Gary R. Oddou and Mark E. Mendenhall, "Succession Planning for the 21st Century: How Well Are We Grooming Our Future Business Leaders?" *Business Horizons*, January–February 1991, pp. 26–34.

17. Rosalie L. Tung, "Career Issues in International Assignments," *Academy of Management Executive*, August 1988, p. 242.

18. Ibid., p. 243.

19. See, for example, J. Bernard Keys and Robert M. Fulmer, *Executive Development and Organizational Learnings for Global Business* (New York: International Business Press, 1998), pp. 1–9.

20. Stephen H. Rhinesmith, John N. Williamson, David M. Ehlen, and Denise S. Maxwell, "Developing Leaders for the Global Enterprise," *Training and Development Journal*, April 1989, pp. 25–34; Patricia A. Galagan, "Executive Development in a Changing World," *Training and Development Journal*, June 1990, pp. 23–35; and Madelyn R. Callahan, "Preparing the New Global Manager," *Training and Development Journal*, March 1989, pp. 29–32.

21. See Steven H. Rhinesmith, "An Agenda for Globalization," *Training and Development Journal*, February 1991, pp. 22–29; Benton Randolph, "When Going Global Isn't Enough," *Training*, August 1990, pp. 47–51; and Ronald Henkoff, "Companies That Train Best," *Fortune*, March 22, 1993, pp. 62–75.

22. Tung, "Selection and Training Procedures of US, European, and Japanese Multinationals," p. 65.

23. See Lin P. Crandall and Mark I. Phelps, "Pay for a Global Work Force," *Personnel Journal*, February 1991, pp. 28–33.

24. Peter J. Dowling and Randall S. Schuler, *International Dimensions of Human Resource Management* (Boston: PWS-Kent Publishing, 1990), p. 121.

25. Greg Steinmetz and Gregory L. White, "Chrysler Pay Draws Fire Overseas," *Wall Street Journal*, May 26, 1998, p. B1.

26. Adam Bryant, "American Pay Rattles Foreign Partners," *New York Times*, January 17, 1999, Section 4, p. 1.

27. Dowling and Schuler, op. cit., p. 125.

28. Ibid., p. 123.

29. Alex S. Jones, "Dow Jones Plans to Tighten Foreign Policy for Workers," *New York Times*, September 9, 1991, p. C6.

30. Geofferey W. Latta, "Expatriate Incentives: Beyond Tradition," *HR Focus*, March 1998, p. S4.

31. A good example is workplace discrimination, which is a major issue in the US but not in many other countries. See Susan Antilla, "Workplace Discrimination? Don't Try It Around Here," *New York Times*, February 13, 1994, p. F7.

32. See, for example, Laurie Hays, "IBM's Finance Chief, Ax in Hand, Scours Empires for Costs to Cut," *Wall Street Journal*, January 26, 1994, pp. A1, A6.

33. C. K. Prahalad and Y. L. Doz, *The Multinational Mission: Balancing Logical Demands and Global Vision* (New York: Free Press, 1987).

34. Ferdinand Protzman, "Rewriting the Contract for Germany's Vaunted Workers," *New York Times*, February 13, 1994, p. F5.

35. Keith Atkinson, "State of the Unions," *Personnel Administrator*, September 1986, p. 58.

36. For additional insights into Japanese labor management practices, see Karen Lowry Miller and Larry Armstrong, "How Honda Hammered Out Its New

Accord," *Business Week*, December 21, 1992, p. 86; and David E. Sanger, "Layoffs and Factory Closings: Shaking the Japanese Psyche," *New York Times*, March 3, 1993, pp. A1, C16.

37. Wolfgang Scholl, "Codetermination and the Ability of Firms to Act in the Federal Republic of Germany," *International Studies of Management & Organization*, Summer 1987, pp. 27–37.

38. Reinhard Lund, "Industrial Democracy in Denmark," *International Studies of Management & Organization*, Summer 1987, pp. 27–37.

39. Hodgetts and Luthans, op. cit., p. 504.

40. For specific examples of HRM practices throughout the world, see Michael J. Marquardt and Dean W. Engel, *Global Human Resource Development* (Englewood Cliffs, NJ: Prentice-Hall, 1993).

41. Susan Moffat, "Picking Japan's Research Brains," *Fortune*, March 25, 1991, p. 94.

42. Reported in "Report: Shortage of Executives Will Hurt US," *Omaha World Herald*, June 25, 1989, p. 1-G.

43. Fred E. Fiedler, Terence Mitchell, and Harry C. Triandis, "The Culture Assimilator: An Approach to Cross-Cultural Training," *Journal of Applied Psychology*, April 1971, p. 95.

44. Paul R. Sparrow and Pawan S. Budhwar, "Competition and Change: Mapping the Indian HRM Recipe Against World-Wide Patterns," *Journal of World Business*, 1997, vol. 32, no. 3, p. 231.

45. Bodil Jones, "What Future European Recruits Want," *Management Review*, January 1998, p. 6.

ADDITIONAL BIBLIOGRAPHY

Abramson, Neil R., Lane, Henry W., Nagai, Hirohisa, and Takagi, Haruo. "A Comparison of Canadian and Japanese Cognitive Styles: Implications for Management Interaction," *Journal of International Business Studies*, vol. 24, no. 3 (Third Quarter 1993).

Adler, Nancy J. and Bartholomew, Susan. "Academic and Professional Communities of Discourse: Generating Knowledge on Transnational Human Resource Management," *Journal of International Business Studies*, vol. 23, no. 3 (Third Quarter 1992).

Banai, Moshe and Reisel, William D. "Expatriate Managers' Loyalty to the MNC: Myth or Reality? An Exploratory Study," *Journal of International Business Studies*, vol. 24, no. 2 (Second Quarter 1993).

Black, J. Stewart and Gregersen, Hal B. "The Other Half of the Picture: Antecedents of Spouse Cross-Cultural Adjustment," *Journal of International Business Studies*, vol. 22, no. 3 (Third Quarter 1991).

Black, J. Stewart and Mendenhall, Mark. "Cross-Cultural Training Effectiveness: A Review and a Theoretical Framework for Future Research," *Academy of Management Review*, vol. 15, no. 1 (January 1990).

Boyacigiller, Nakiye. "The Role of Expatriates in the Management of Interdependence, Complexity and Risk in Multinational Corporations," *Journal of International Business Studies*, vol. 21, no. 3 (Third Quarter 1990).

Camuffo, Arnaldo and Costa, Giovanni. "Strategic Human Resource Management – Italian Style," *Sloan Management Review*, vol. 34, no. 2 (Winter 1993).

De Cieri, Helen and Dowling, Peter J. "Strategic International Human Resource Management: An Asia-Pacific Perspective," *Management International Review*, vol. 37 (1997/1).

Doyle, Frank P. "People-Power: The Global Human Resource Challenge for the '90s," *Columbia Journal of World Business*, vol. 25, nos. 1, 2 (Spring/Summer 1990).

Ebrahimpour, Maling and Cullen, John B. "Quality Management in Japanese and American Firms Operating in the United States: A Comparative Study of Styles and Motivational Beliefs," *Management International Review*, vol. 33 (First Quarter 1993).

Erden, Deniz. "Impact of Multinational Companies on Host Countries: Executive Training Programs," *Management International Review*, vol. 28, no. 3 (Third Quarter 1988).

Feldman, Daniel C. and Thomas, David C. "Career Management Issues Facing Expatriates," *Journal of International Business Studies*, vol. 23, no. 2 (Second Quarter 1992).

Geringer, J. Michael and Frayne, Colette A. "Human Resource Management and International Joint Venture Control: A Parent Company Perspective," *Management International Review*, vol. 30 (1990).

Haigh, Robert W. "Building a Strategic Alliance – The Hermosillo Experience as a Ford-Mazda Proving Ground," *Columbia Journal of World Business*, vol. 27, no. 1 (Spring 1992).

Harvey, Michael G. "Repatriation of Corporate Executives: An Empirical Study," *Journal of International Business Studies*, vol. 20, no. 1 (Spring 1989).

Harvey, Michael. "Empirical Evidence of Recurring International Compensation Problems," *Journal of International Business Studies*, vol. 24, no. 4 (Fourth Quarter 1993).

Harvey, Michael. "The Selection of Managers for Foreign Assignments: A Planning Perspective," *Columbia Journal of World Business*, vol. 31, no. 4 (Winter 1996).

Hempel, Paul S. "Designing Multinational Benefit Programs: The Role of National Culture," *Journal of World Business*, vol. 33, no. 3 (Fall 1998).

Marsick, Victoria J. and Cederholm, Lars. "Developing Leadership in International Managers – An Urgent Challenge!" *Columbia Journal of World Business*, vol. 23, no. 4 (Winter 1988).

McElrath, Roger. "Environmental Issues and the Strategies of the International Trade Union Movement," *Columbia Journal of World Business*, vol. 23, no. 3 (Fall 1988).

Milliman, John, Von Glinow, Mary Ann, and Nathan, Maria. "Organizational Life Cycles and Strategic International Human Resource Management in Multinational Companies: Implications for Congruence Theory," *Academy of Management Review*, vol. 16, no. 2 (April 1991).

Norburn, David. "Corporate Leaders in Britain and America: A Cross-National Analysis," *Journal of International Business Studies*, vol. 18, no. 3 (Fall 1987).

Roth, Kendall and O'Donnell, Sharon. "Foreign Subsidiary Compensation Strategy: An Agency Theory Perspective," *The Academy of Management Journal*, vol. 39, no. 3 (June, 1996).

Sanyal, Rajib N. "An Empirical Analysis of the Unionization of Foreign Manufacturing Firms in the US," *Journal of International Business Studies*, vol. 21, no. 1 (First Quarter 1990).

Schuler, Randall S. and Rogovsky, Nikolai. "Understanding Compensation Practice Variations Across Firms: The Impact of National Culture," *Journal of International Business Studies*, vol. 29, no. 1 (First Quarter 1998).

Sergeant, Andrew and Frenkel, Stephen. "Managing People in China: Perceptions of Expatriate Managers," *Journal of World Business*, vol. 33, no. 1 (Spring 1998).

Shenkar, Oded and Zeira, Yoram. "Human Resources Management in International Joint Ventures: Directions for Research," *Academy of Management Review*, vol. 12, no. 3 (July 1987).

Stark, Andrew. "What's the Matter with Business Ethics?" *Harvard Business Review*, vol. 71, no. 3 (May/June 1993).

Sullivan, Jeremiah J. and Peterson, Richard B. "A Test of Theories Underlying the Japanese Lifetime Employment System," *Journal of International Business Studies*, vol. 22, no. 1 (First Quarter 1991).

Taylor, Sully, Beechler, Schon, and Napier, Nancy. "Toward an Integrative Model of Strategic International Human Resource Management," *The Academy of Management Review*, vol. 21, no. 4 (October 1996).

Townsend, Anthony M., Scott, K. Dow, and Markham, Steven E. "An Examination of Country and Culture-Based Differences in Compensation Practices," *Journal of International Business Studies*, vol. 21, no. 3 (Fourth Quarter 1990).

Tung, Rosalie L. and Miller, Edwin L. "Managing in the Twenty First Century: The Need for Global Orientation," *Management International Review*, vol. 30, no. 1 (First Quarter 1990).

Tung, Rosalie L. "American Expatriates Abroad: From Neophytes to Cosmopolitans," *Journal of World Business*, vol. 33, no. 2 (Summer 1998).

Vanderbroeck, Paul. "Long-Term Human Resource Development in Multinational Organizations," *Sloan Management Review*, vol. 34, no. 1 (Fall 1992).

CHAPTER 13

Political Risk and Negotiation Strategies

OBJECTIVES OF THE CHAPTER

Political change often has a tremendous impact on the business climate. Yet it is frequently difficult to predict. For example, who could have guessed that during the late 1980s the former Soviet Union would begin to move toward a market economy[1] or that in the early 1990s the Soviet Union would break up completely? These developments were greeted enthusiastically by western businesspeople, who now see the newly independent republics as countries with great economic potential. At the same time many western business executives are reluctant to invest heavily in these countries because of the uncertainty of how far the market-based economic reforms will go. Even when political changes appear to move in a direction that is favorable to market forces, there are political risks. This chapter examines political risk, how multinational enterprises (MNEs) forecast this risk, and how they use negotiating tactics to minimize their political risk. The objectives of this chapter are to:

1. **Examine** the nature of political risk.

2. **Discuss** some of the most common ways that multinationals go about managing their political risk.

3. **Review** typical negotiation strategies and tactics used in "hammering out" agreements.

4. **Present** some of the strategies used by MNEs to protect their overseas investments.

Singapore Airlines

Singapore Airlines (Singapore for short) is one of the most successful airlines in the industry. While companies like Eastern Airlines, Pan American, and TWA have been closing their doors or taking big financial losses, Singapore has been profitable. In 1990, for example, the company netted over $500 million.

One of the main reasons for this success is its high-quality service. For example, Singapore has added telephones and extra legroom so that customers will be comfortable during their international flights. And the airline is now installing seats in business class that have four additional inches of pitch, thus providing travelers a more restful position during a long flight. The company is also considering putting small television sets in the back of seats.

Company policy requires that flight attendants learn everyone's name, even of those passengers who are flying in the coach section. Additionally, Singapore is working to develop an information system that will tell flight attendants what drink a certain frequent traveler prefers. Also, the airline will not let any flight attendant serve for more than 15 years, thus ensuring that the group consists of young people who convey a bright, cheerful appearance and who can keep up with the rigorous demands of the job. Singapore backs up this strategy by requiring that most employees take annual training, thus making sure that the highest levels of service are maintained both in the air and on the ground.

Singapore is now expanding its routes to cover the Atlantic, as well as more of Asia. For example, it has instituted coverage from New York to Singapore. The airline had been operating out of Los Angeles, San Francisco, and Honolulu, but this was its first venture to the east coast of the United States. The Singapore flight stops in Frankfurt, which is already one of its European hubs; however, the passengers do not have to change planes. This was the first direct air service from New York to east Asia via the Atlantic and the initial prices were quite high. However, Singapore filed with the requisite governmental agencies to lower these fares. For this to happen, the other carriers that fly this transatlantic leg would have to accept the new rates, something that they would be reluctant to do because it would dilute their own revenue. Additionally, international fares are set by governments that usually act to support the best interests of their own carriers. Yet Singapore does not seem concerned. The airline has over $1 billion in cash, more than enough resources to continue operating while it works to gain government approvals that will help to expand its international market. In addition, Singapore has now created strategic alliances with a host of different airlines including Lufthansa, Ansett Australia, Scandinavian Airlines, and South African Airways, and is looking to pursue this strategy with other international carriers.

Sources: Adapted from Agis Salpukas, "For Singapore Air, a New Direction," *New York Times*, July 11, 1991, pp. C1, C6; Patricia Sellers, "Companies That Serve You Best," *Fortune*, May 31, 1993, p. 75; Kenneth Labich, "Air Wars Over Asia," *Fortune*, March 4, 1994, pp. 93–98, *http://www.singaporeair.com*.

1. Briefly describe one macro political risk and one micro political risk that Singapore Airlines faces.

2. In what way would doing business in the United States pose a political risk for Singapore Airlines? How would doing business in a country like China pose such a risk?

3. What strengths would Singapore Airlines have if it were negotiating for the rights to operate out of Heathrow airport in London? What needs would such an arrangement fill for the United Kingdom? What needs would it fill for Singapore?

4. Why would the management of Singapore Airlines need to understand cultural differences in negotiating behavior? Would this need be greater than that of a brewer in Amsterdam who wants to negotiate the acquisition of a winery in Madrid? Why?

INTRODUCTION

Political risk is the probability that political forces will negatively affect an MNE's profit or impede the attainment of other critical business objectives. The study of political risk addresses changes in the environment that are difficult to anticipate. Common examples include the election of a government that is committed to nationalization of major industries or one that insists on reducing foreign participation in business ventures.

Most people believe that political risk is confined to third world countries or to those with unstable governments. However, the policies of some past EU governments, such as France, toward limiting Japanese investment illustrate that political risk is also an issue for firms doing business in highly industrialized nations. Another example is the previous restrictions of foreign investment in the energy and communications industries in Canada. US regulations that restrict foreign investment in the banking and commercial airline industries reflect political risk as well.[2]

In addition, there are cultural barriers that can increase political risk. For example, many MNEs feel that it is difficult to crack the Japanese market because the value system of the country discourages purchasing from foreign producers, and the government supports this system. There are also political agreements that can create risks for foreign firms such as the European Airbus consortium that is now cutting into the world dominance of US aircraft manufacturers.[3]

These examples indicate the pervasiveness of political risk. Given the large number of international markets in which US firms operate (see Table 13.1), political risk is going to remain an area of concern for US MNEs.[4] In dealing with this issue, effective negotiating can help to reduce and contain problem areas. This linkage will be explained later in the chapter.

Table 13.1   The Top 10 US export markets

Market	1997 annual sales (in millions of US $)
Canada	168.2
Japan	121.7
Mexico	85.9
China	62.6
Germany	43.1
United Kingdom	32.7
Taiwan	32.6
South Korea	23.2
France	20.6
Singapore	20.1

Source: US Census Bureau, 1998.

THE NATURE OF POLITICAL RISK

Political risk includes both macro- and microfactors. MNEs often begin by examining the macrofactors and then determining how the microfactors further influence the risk.

Macro political risk

A **macro political risk** is one that affects all foreign enterprises in the same general way. **Expropriation**, the governmental seizure of private businesses coupled with little, if any, compensation to the owners, is an example of a macro political risk. Communist governments in Eastern Europe and China expropriated private firms following World War II. Fidel Castro did the same in Cuba from 1958 to 1959. In more recent years governments in Angola, Chile, Ethiopia, Peru, and Zambia have expropriated private enterprises. In all these cases both large and small businesses felt the impact of the political decision.

Macro political risk can also be the result of political boycotts.[5] Since 1955 a number of Arab countries have boycotted firms with branches in Israel or companies that have allowed the use of their trade name there. Macro political risk can also come about because of **indigenization laws**, which require that nationals hold a majority interest in all enterprises.

In recent years the macro political risk in many nations has changed.[6] For example, eastern European countries, such as Poland, Hungary, and the Czech Republic, now welcome and encourage private investments,[7] as does Russia.[8] These developments have reduced macro political risk and may well encourage foreign investments.[9] However, there is still micro political risk to be considered.

Micro political risk

A **micro political risk** is one that affects selected sectors of the economy or specific foreign businesses. These risks are typically a result of government action in the form of industry regulation, taxes on specific types of business activity, and local content laws.[10] Canada's 1981 decision (now rescinded) to reduce foreign ownership in its petroleum industry from 75 to under 50 per cent is an example. Peru's decision to nationalize its copper mines is another good example. The US decision to tax textile imports is a third.

A number of factors help to determine the degree of micro political risk. One is the dominance of foreign firms. For example, in recent years the US government has insisted that Japanese automakers establish manufacturing facilities in the United States. When the Japanese auto firms were small, they did not attract much attention. Now that they are a large part of the US market, there is more interest in regulating them. Similarly, Nintendo, which holds a dominant share of the video game market in the United States, has become the target of antitrust lawsuits.

A second factor is the ease with which the MNE's operations can be managed. If a government can run a factory just as efficiently as the foreign owner, the operation may be nationalized. However, if special skills or training are required, the risk of takeover is smaller. Likewise, if the operation needs a continual inflow of new technology from the home office in order to maintain competitive efficiency, the risk is lower because the MNE will halt technology inflow if the operation is seized. On the other hand, if the necessary technology can easily be acquired elsewhere, the risk is much higher.

Retaliation is another source of micro political risk. If the MNE is not in a position to strike back, the micro political risk increases. For example, when Iran under the Ayatollah Khomeini took over US firms in that country, Iranian assets in the United States were frozen as part of a retaliatory legal action. If the multinational is large or highly influential, the backlash can be severe. Some third world countries have seized banks and found to their dismay that the international financial community has refused to do any more business with them.

A fourth factor is the changing priorities of the country. As the countries of the former Soviet Union work to reform their economies, the political risk in industries such as high-tech, petroleum, and manufacturing are likely to lessen because the governments are trying to encourage investment in these areas.

Finally, competing political philosophies affect micro political risk. The Russian Commonwealth consists of a host of groups with different political beliefs. Most of them have renounced communism, some want to modify the principles of that ideology, and some still want to adhere to the basic beliefs with which they have grown up. As a result, many MNEs believe that there will be different rules applied to different industries in different geographic locales, depending on which political group has the most influence over their operations.

ACTIVE LEARNING CHECK

Review your answer to Active Learning Case question 1 and make any changes you like. Then compare your answer to the one below.

1. Briefly describe one macro political risk and one micro political risk that Singapore Airlines faces.

One macro political risk is that some of the countries in which Singapore does business will require all foreign operations to have local partners. One micro political risk is that the airline industry in some countries will prevail on their government to protect them from competition by not letting Singapore lower its rates to match their own.

Sources of political risk

There are a number of sources of political risk. Table 13.2 presents some important sources and their effects.

The major risk is a change in the political philosophy of those who are running the country. This can be a result of one government being ousted by another, as when Castro replaced Batista in Cuba, or a change in government actions such as when the Chinese government suddenly squelched the student movement in Tiananmen Square and imprisoned its leaders. These actions send a clear message to businesses that are operating or considering doing business there. Conversely, a change in government philosophy toward encouraging foreign investments can have an impact. For example, when Michael Manley was prime minister of Jamaica in the 1970s, the country moved toward socialism and US investment dried up. Manley's subsequent

Table 13.2 Political risk: sources, agents, and effects

Sources of political risk	Groups that can generate political risk	Effects of political risk
Political philosophies that are changing or are in competition with each other	Current government and its various departments and agencies	Expropriation of assets (with or without compensation)
Changing economic conditions	Opposition groups in the government that are not in power but have political clout	Indigenization laws
Social unrest	Organized interest groups such as teachers, students, workers, retired persons, etc.	Restriction of operating freedom concerning, e.g., hiring policies and product manufacturing
Armed conflict or terrorism		
Rising nationalism	Terrorist or anarchist groups operating in the country	Cancellation or revision of contracts
Impending or recent political independence	International organizations such as the World Bank or the United Nations	Damage to property and/or personnel from terrorism, riots, etc.
Vested interests of local business groups	Foreign governments that have entered into international alliances with the country or that are supporting opposition to the government	Loss of financial freedom such as the ability to repatriate profits
Competing religious groups		Increased taxes and other financial penalties
Newly created international alliances		

defeat at the polls was a result of strong local interests and a populace that became convinced that without outside investors and US tourism, the economy would never turn around. In the late 1980s Manley was returned to power and moved much closer to the center of the political continuum than before.

Sometimes, however, pressure is applied for a "get tough" approach. After the Muammar Qaddafi regime assumed control in Libya in the late 1960s, that country began taking steps to revise its agreements with the international oil companies. One reason was to show the populace that the government was strong. Another was to undermine the position of the oil firms by blaming them for corrupting the previous government with bribes.

So a variety of motivations help to explain political risk. The MNE's challenge is to identify these motivations and then to decide how to manage them.

FORECASTING AND MANAGING POLITICAL RISK

MNEs use a number of strategies in managing political risk. A typical approach is to first forecast the specific risks and then determine how to reduce or eliminate those risks that are considered unacceptable.

Forecasting political risk

Some MNEs use an informal approach to assessing risk, whereas others employ formal systematic procedures. Some MNEs will create an *ad hoc* group to deal with these issues, whereas others will have a standing committee that is charged with this responsibility. In each case, however, those making the assessment will focus on two areas: (1) the political system in which the company will be doing business and (2) the goods to be produced and the operations to be carried out. Based on this evaluation, the MNE will determine its risk vulnerability.

Examining the political system   An MNE needs to understand the host country's political system because politics greatly influences the economy and political risk.[11] This linkage helps to explain why many MNEs are interested in doing business in the countries of the former Soviet Union but remain cautious about making any major investments there. The MNEs are concerned that another change in the political climate would result in massive financial losses. Similar reasoning can be used in explaining MNE hesitation about investing in China and other countries where the government still exercises totalitarian control.

MNEs will also cast a critical eye on governments that seem to give home country companies a decided advantage over foreign firms. MNEs have become more involved in lobbying both home and host governments, and over the last decade trade negotiations between many countries have started to deal with investment and trade issues of direct relevance to MNEs.[12] The US free trade agreements with Canada and Mexico are examples,[13] as are the US initiatives with Japan (see the box "International Business Strategy in Action: US–Japan Relations").[14]

Other forms of governmental action have also proved useful. For example, the US role in the Gulf War of 1991 increased its influence in that region and helped to ensure the sale of US goods and services in Kuwait and Saudi Arabia.[15] Another example is the pressures that industrialized nations have put on countries like the Russian Commonwealth and China, in which economic assistance is tied to political and economic reform.[16]

MNEs will evaluate the impact of these changes. They will also examine the political clout that host country firms have with their own government. In the United States, for example, lobbyists and special interest groups in areas such as steel, textiles, and semiconductors have been particularly effective in securing protection from imports.[17]

ACTIVE LEARNING CHECK

Review your answer to Active Learning Case question 2 and make any changes you like. Then compare your answer to the one below.

2. **In what way would doing business in the United States pose a political risk for Singapore Airlines? How would doing business in a country like China pose such a risk?**

The primary political risk that Singapore faces in the United States is that the government would not want the airline to take too much business away from US international carriers, especially because many US carriers are in poor financial straits. However, there are minimum risks for the airline in the United States. Doing business in China, however, is a different story. Here the airline might find that the government makes much greater demands such as allowing local residents to pay for their tickets in Chinese currency, insisting that the airline fly certain internal routes even if there is limited traffic on those routes, and staffing most of its China-based facilities with local personnel. Additionally, there is the risk associated with the stability of the Chinese political system. So political risk would be of much greater concern to Singapore Airlines if it wanted to open up routes in China than if it wanted to secure landing sites in the United States.

INTERNATIONAL BUSINESS STRATEGY IN ACTION

US–Japan relations

One of the major international issues for the next decade is going to be the economic relationship between the United States and Japan. Over the last decade there have been some major disagreements between the two nations, with each side feeling that the other is asking for too much and giving too little. Worse yet, each seems to be running out of patience with the other.

The Americans, in particular, believe they continually come out on the short end of many negotiations. For example, it took the US government seven years to get Japan to buy US supercomputers. By that time Japanese companies had learned how to make the machines themselves and held 95 per cent of the giant public sector market in Japan. In another case the two countries agreed to expand US access to the Japanese semiconductor chip market in return for suspending some import duties that had been imposed on Japanese products when the US share of the Japanese computer market had failed to meet an earlier agreement of 20 per cent. By 1996, foreign companies held over 30 per cent of the Japanese semiconductor market. The US continued to push to open markets while the Japanese argued that there was no more need for government intervention. A final settlement was reached that ended government intervention but created an independent institution to monitor the semiconductor market.

The automotive sector is another source of conflict as 60 per cent of the bilateral trade deficit is attributed to this industry. In 1995 the US government threatened to impose a 100 per cent tax on imports of 13 luxury cars unless an agreement was reached to decrease Japan's trade surplus. An agreement was reached but by 1997 the American Automobile Manufacturers Association was urging the Clinton administration to impose trade sanctions on Japanese luxury cars for failing to meet the requirements of the 1995 agreement.

Meanwhile the Japanese point out that the increase in the trade deficit in the late 1990s is a result of the weakening of the yen and that they are now producing more goods in US-based factories. Additionally, many major US firms, including Coca-Cola, Motorola, and Procter & Gamble, are doing extremely well in Japan. Others have formed successful joint ventures, such as Fuji Xerox.

Another important factor that is likely to affect future negotiations is the rapid worldwide expansion of Japanese MNEs. As the US market accounts for a declining percentage of overall Japanese sales, will the US's ability to influence Japan's trade policies also decline? Many people fail to realize that while Japan buys more from other countries than it did ten years ago, the United States is not getting a large percentage of this increased trade. The biggest gains in this market share have been garnered by neighboring Asian countries that sell inexpensive consumer goods in Japan and the European nations that have been able to tap the new Japanese appetite for French wines, Italian suits, and Mercedes-Benz autos.

On the positive side, the United States and Japan stand to gain from trade with each other. As long as this is true, then each will continue to pressure the other to change laws and trade policies and thus to make it easier to do business in that country. As a result, the millennium will see an ongoing process of working things out between the two economic superpowers.

Sources: Adapted from David E. Sanger, "Japan Sets Tough Rules on Business," *New York Times*, June 11, 1991, pp. C1–C2; David E. Sanger, "A New Japan: Whose Plan?" *New York Times*, July 9, 1993, pp. A1–A4; Andrew Pollack, "Japan Seems to Ease Stand on Setting Trade Targets," *New York Times*, September 11, 1993, pp. 17, 26; Martin Crutsinger, "US Automakers Blast Japan and South Korea on Trade Accords," *detnews.com*, September 23, 1997; *http://www.nttls.co.jp/fpc/e/shiryo/jb/j20.htl*; *http://www.fas.org/man/crs/97-004.htm*.

Evaluating products and operations Products and operations also face political risk. One example is government restrictions on local ownership. If the government requires joint ventures or local participation in operations, the MNE must determine the degree of risk associated with doing business under these conditions. Some firms have never agreed to joint ventures, whereas others have tried to minimize this risk by limiting local control of operations.

A related risk is that the joint partner will steal product knowledge or technology. A good example is publishing ventures in China. US firms no longer enter into such ventures because they have learned that copyrights are not legally enforceable in China; there is no way of preventing Chinese partners from publishing translated works as their own. Technology theft is another example. If local laws do not protect patent infringement, a joint venture participant may simply steal the other's technology without any fear of retaliation.[18]

A third example is government policy regarding the purchase of foreign-made goods. If the government buys only locally produced goods and encourages a "buy local" policy, the political risk increases accordingly.

Product and operation risk can also grow out of a government's approach to pricing practices, monopolies, and collusion among competitors. In the United States, there are antitrust laws that encourage competition. In many other countries, however, collusion and the formation of cartels are legal. In recent years the US government has brought pressure on countries like Japan to prohibit price fixing and other practices that reduce the ability of US MNEs to crack this market. One result has been the recent publication of new trade laws that promise to make the market more accessible to outsiders. Some specific changes that have been introduced are: (1) companies are forbidden from enforcing "suggested retail prices," thus opening the way for discount stores; (2) firms cannot join together to boycott firms trying to enter a market; (3) dominant companies are not allowed to use their influence to force clients to shun competitive goods; and (4) the Japanese Fair Trade Commission can order a company to sell its stock holdings in another firm, if such action is deemed necessary to eliminate violation of the Antimonopoly Act.[19]

Quantifying risk vulnerability

After an MNE examines the political system and the risks inherent in going international, the company will try to express this risk in explicit terms. Table 13.3 provides an illustration of select criteria that can be used in this procedure. This process allows the firm to then compare the political risk of doing business in one country with that of doing business in another nation. For example, it is possible to compare the political risks associated with starting a joint venture in the former USSR versus Poland, Chile versus Venezuela, or France versus Germany. Or the company can develop a list of countries with political risk scores, ranging from the highest to the lowest and can decide which scores fit within their "range of acceptance."

The factors that are quantified in Table 13.3 are not all-inclusive, but they do illustrate the types of criteria that are considered when assessing political risk. As seen in the table, some criteria have wider minimum and maximum ranges than others because the risk varies more widely. However, the important result is the overall score for a particular country. If this score is too high, the MNE will drop it from further consideration unless there are ways of reducing the risks associated with some of the criteria. For example, it may be impossible to influence the first criterion in Table 13.3

Table 13.3 An illustration of select criteria for evaluating political risk

Major area	Criteria	Scores	
		Minimum	Maximum
Political economic environment	1 Stability of the political system	3	14
	2 Imminent internal conflicts	0	14
	3 External threats to stability	0	12
	4 Degree of control of the economic system	5	9
	5 Reliability of the country as a trading partner	4	12
	6 Constitutional guarantees	2	12
	7 Effectiveness of public administration	3	12
	8 Labor relations and social peace	3	15
Domestic economic conditions	9 Size of the population	4	8
	10 Per capital income	2	10
	11 Economic growth over the last 5 years	2	7
	12 Potential growth over the next 3 years	3	10
	13 Inflation over the past 2 years	2	10
	14 Accessibility of the domestic capital market to outsiders	3	7
	15 Availability of high-quality local labor force	2	8
	16 Possibility of employing foreign nationals	2	8
	17 Availability of energy resources	2	14
	18 Legal requirements regarding environmental pollution	4	8
	19 Infrastructure, including transportation and communication systems	2	14
External economic relations	20 Import restrictions	2	10
	21 Export restrictions	2	10
	22 Restrictions on foreign investments	3	9
	23 Freedom to set up or engage in partnerships	3	9
	24 Legal protection for brands and products	3	9
	25 Restrictions on monetary transfers	2	8
	26 Revaluation of the currency during the last 5 years	2	7
	27 Balance of payments situation	2	9
	28 Drain on foreign funds through oil and energy imports	3	14
	29 International financial standing	3	8
	30 Restriction on the exchange of local money into foreign currencies	2	8

Source: Adapted from E. Dichtl and H. G. Koeglmayr, "Country Risk Ratings," *Management International Review*, vol. 26, no. 4, 1986, p. 6.

(stability of the political system), but it may be possible to strike a deal with the local union (number 8 in the table) and thus improve the chances of good labor relations. It may also be possible to negotiate an improvement in restrictions on imports, exports, and monetary transfers (numbers 20, 21, and 25 in the table). As a result, the political risk score might be reduced to an acceptable level.

If a country is highly interested in having an MNE set up operations there, the government may offer special concessions that will reduce the political risks for this company but not for others. This is particularly valuable because it provides the firm with a competitive advantage. On the other hand, if negotiations with the country end up reducing political risk for all global firms doing business there, the MNE will want to consider the impact of this action on its competitive stance and profitability. This is where effective negotiating strategies enter the picture.

NEGOTIATION STRATEGIES

There are two key steps in developing effective negotiating strategies. First, the MNE will evaluate its own position and that of the other group(s) in order to determine how the interests of both can fit together. For example, Apple examined Sony's manufacturing ability and competitive challenge before deciding to have Sony build the low-end models of the Apple Powerbook computer. Second, the company will examine the behavioral characteristics of the other parties in order to understand their style of negotiating. For example, when negotiating with the Japanese media for the rights to provide Olympic game coverage in Japan, Olympic committee negotiators have continually found that these media executives always begin the process with very low bids. So the Olympic negotiators always start with very high offers.

Evaluation of positions

Sometimes an MNE will enter negotiations with a host country in order to secure a variety of guarantees such as low taxes, the right to repatriate profits, and a promise regarding freedom of operations. At other times these negotiations will be directed toward a potential partner, such as working out the terms of a joint venture. Still other times the MNE will negotiate with a host of parties: country officials, potential partners, and the like. In all these cases the first step is to evaluate the strengths and needs of all parties.

Strengths   The strengths of the parties are those assets or benefits that each brings to the bargaining table. In the case of an MNE examples include technology, products, services, managerial expertise, and capital. For example, when General Motors sets up a new operation in Mexico, the company invests capital, uses modern technology to build the autos, and employs managerial expertise in getting the operation off and running. When the Hilton Corporation builds a new hotel in Germany, it invests capital, employs managerial expertise, and offers a variety of world-class hospitality services to the guests. MNEs also hire local personnel, stimulate the economy, and in industries such as manufacturing, textiles, and mining help to generate exports for the country.

The bargaining strengths of the country will include such factors as large consumer markets, economic and political stability, sources of capital, tax breaks, and an appropriate labor force. The United States, for example, offers all these strengths to MNEs. As a result, the bargaining position of foreign MNEs *vis-à-vis* the US government is diminished. This is in comparison with the situation faced by companies looking to set up operations in third world countries where the latter have a weak bargaining position because of their small consumer market, political instability, and/or financial strength.

The bargaining strengths of parties will depend on their specific contributions. For example, in many cases a local partner knows the market and has conducted business there for years. This makes the partner valuable to the MNE. Other contributions of local partners can include capital, a well-trained work force, factories or retail outlets for moving the goods to the customer, and government contractors who can help to eliminate red tape.

Other parties to the transaction can include stockholders or other interest groups that monitor the company's operations. During the 1980s many MNEs stopped doing business in South Africa because of pressure from these investor groups. Companies involved in manufacturing war material, producing chemicals, and building nuclear energy plants have also come under investor and social pressure. MNEs may also encounter complaints from partners in other joint ventures who feel that this latest investment will negatively affect their current venture.

Needs   The needs of the parties in the negotiation will also influence the agreement. An MNE may want to set up operations in Belgium in order to secure entry into the EU, to sidestep import tariffs, and to be able to compete in one of the world's largest and fastest growing consumer markets. The company may also have an annual 15 per cent sales growth target and be unable to achieve this goal without entering the EU. So the firm's need to expand is quite strong.

The host country may have a need for the type of technology or product that the company is planning to produce. If the MNE sets up operations here, the country may also find that the firm is prepared to invest capital and to hire and train local personnel. Additionally, as a result of these operations, exports may increase and the general economy will benefit. On the other hand, if the MNE has nothing special to offer, the host country may be willing to give few, if any, incentives.

The needs of other groups will also influence the negotiation. For example, if the stakeholders want to see vigorous expansion into the European market, they may be willing to have the company make large initial concessions because of the strong future growth potential offered in the market. If the MNE is going to be working in the host country with local partners or purchasing from local suppliers, there is pressure on that country to let in the company.

ACTIVE LEARNING CHECK

Review your answer to Active Learning Case question 3 and make any changes you like. Then compare your answer to the one below.

3. **What strengths would Singapore Airlines have if it were negotiating for the rights to operate out of Heathrow airport in London? What needs would such an arrangement fill for the United Kingdom? What needs would it fill for Singapore?**

Some of the strengths that Singapore Airlines would bring to the negotiating table include employment opportunities for local personnel, potential capital investment in local facilities, and the providing of first-class air service to the Orient. Some of the needs it would fill for the United Kingdom include an increase in tourists and other visitors to the country, the opening up of more direct routes to the Orient for business travelers, and the generation of income. Some of the needs the arrangement would fill for Singapore include increased revenues, a greater international presence, and the opportunity to develop new routes.

Behavioral characteristics of the participants

Next, the MNE will examine the negotiating behaviors of the parties. What can be expected in terms of offers, counteroffers, ploys, and other stratagems? These answers will help the MNE to minimize surprises.

Table 13.4 Negotiating styles of North American and South American negotiators

North American negotiators	South American negotiators
Place a low value on emotional sensitivity	Place a high value on emotional sensitivity
Prefer to use a straightforward, impersonal approach	Tend to use emotional and passionate appeals rather than logic *per se*
Try not to be influenced by special interests, which are viewed as unethical pressures	Are often influenced by special interests, which are not only expected but condoned as well
Use teamwork between members of the group in arriving at a final negotiating position	Receive a final negotiation position from an individual who is high up in the organization
Make decisions on a cost-benefit basis, even if this means looking foolish	Place strong value on face saving and preserving honor and dignity, even at the cost of profit
Put great importance on to the use of documentation as a means of proving facts	Tend to be impatient with documentation and view it as an obstacle to understanding the "big picture"
Rely heavily on methodical, organized decision making	Use impulsive, spontaneous decision making
Try to avoid personal involvement and conflict of interest situations	Believe that personalism is critical to effective negotiating
Are highly driven by a profit motive	Are highly driven by what is good for people with profit being given secondary consideration

Source: Adapted from Richard M. Hodgetts and Fred Luthans, *International Management*, 4th ed. (Burr Ridge Ill.: Irwin/McGraw, 2000), pp. 286–288.

Cultural differences   Although the objective of the negotiation process may be universal (strike as good a deal as possible), the way in which the process is carried out will be greatly influenced by the cultural values and norms of the participants. Commenting on the difference between Arab and US negotiators, one group of researchers noted:

> . . . Arabs . . . in contrast to the logical approach of . . . Americans, tend to use an emotional appeal in their negotiation style. They analyze things subjectively and treat deadlines as only general guidelines for wrapping up negotiations. They tend to open negotiations with an extreme initial position. However, the Arabs believe strongly in making concessions, they do so throughout the bargaining process, and they almost always reciprocate an opponent's concessions. They also seek to build a long-term relationship with their bargaining partners. For these reasons, Americans typically find it easier to negotiate with Arabs than with representatives from many other regions of the world.[20]

There are also differences in negotiating styles. Table 13.4 provides some examples. It illustrates that in many cases North American and South American negotiators use very different approaches.

One of the major differences is the amount of authority that the negotiator has to approve an agreement. In some societies, such as the United States and Great Britain, negotiators are given authority to make deals or at least to express agreement on the basic arrangement that is being negotiated. This approach works well when doing business with many Western firms, as well as with Chinese negotiators (see the box "International Business Strategy in Action: Doing business in China"). However, it is often of limited value when dealing with people from other cultures. In fact, the other parties may not have the authority to give the go-ahead on anything. For example, Japanese and Russian negotiators are often lower-level personnel who are not authorized to approve agreements. This can be frustrating to Americans who feel that

INTERNATIONAL BUSINESS STRATEGY IN ACTION

Doing business in China

China promises to be a major market for MNEs during the millennium. However, doing business in this country can present major problems since many international managers have had, at best, limited experience in dealing with Chinese managers. What are some steps that can help to ensure success? One China expert recently noted the following:

1. Doing business in China requires a long-term commitment. Firms that are hoping for fast profit will be disappointed. It may take five to ten years, in some cases, before a company will begin to earn a return on its investment.

2. Personal connections are important. Companies that want to be successful have to meet the right people and persuade them to help the business. If this happens, the MNE will find that a great deal of red tape can be eliminated.

3. While many firms like to set up joint ventures, companies that establish direct operations that tap China's pool of inexpensive labor often do much better because they have control over their own operations and are helping the government to keep the work force employed.

4. The Chinese like to deal with negotiators who have authority to make decisions. They respect people with authority and are disappointed if the negotiators have to contact the home office continually regarding how to proceed.

5. On the other hand, negotiators have to understand that the Chinese are not rapid decision makers. Determination and patience are important because the Chinese are thorough and methodical in their evaluation of a project or proposal.

6. Written contracts tend to be shorter than those in the West because the Chinese do not believe that everything must be written down. Friendship and trust between the parties is used to resolve any disputes. As a result, written agreements are similar to what in the West are known as "memos of general understanding." However, these agreements do contain the obligations and duties of each party and stipulations regarding how any differences will be resolved, so they are not as open-ended as one might think.

Sources: Adapted from L. S. Tai, "Doing Business in the People's Republic of China: Some Keys to Success," *Management International Review*, vol. 28, no. 1, 1988, pp. 5–9; Amy Borrus, "The Best Way to Change China Is from the Inside," *Business Week*, May 17, 1993, p. 69; Philip R. Harris and Robert T. Moran, *Managing Cultural Differences*, 4th ed. (Houston: Gulf Publishing, 1996), pp. 252–257; Fons Trompenaars and Charles Hampden Turner, *Riding the Waves of Culture: Understanding Diversity in Global Business*, 2nd ed. (New York: McGraw-Hill, 1998); Jeanne M. Brett, Debra L. Shapiro, and Anne L. Lytle, "Breaking the Bonds of Reciprocity in Negotiations," *Academy of Management Journal*, August 1998, pp. 410–424; Elisabeth Rosenthal, "US Trade Official Says China Market Is Closed Tighter," *New York Times*, September 23, 1998, p. C2.

they are wasting their time. The lack of face-to-face interaction with those who will be making the final decision can be unsettling. On the other hand, many foreign negotiators use this ploy because they have learned that it often leads to greater concessions from US businesspeople, who become anxious to sign a deal and thus are more flexible on terms.

Another cultural difference in negotiating style is the objective of the negotiators. US businesspeople tend to be very practical and to focus on short-term results. Negotiators from the Far East tend to move more slowly, like to get to know the other party, and have a more long-run focus.

Social custom plays an important part in negotiations between people of different cultural backgrounds. Many Americans and other western businesspeople are not accustomed to giving gifts to those with whom they are doing business. However, in some parts of the world it is common to exchange presents to create an initial bond of friendship, and a failure to do so is considered to be bad manners.

A fourth factor is language. When negotiators do not speak the same language and must use interpreters, there are more chances for a misinterpretation or misunderstanding to occur. This problem also exists in written communications. Schermerhorn, for example, has found that when documents are translated from one language to another and then translated back to check for accuracy, there are interpretation problems.[21] The original translation appears to convey the desired information, but when another person is called in to translate the document back into the original language, some parts of it are different from that intended initially.

A related cultural problem is the use of written documents. In some countries a written document is used as a basis for establishing what is to be done. As a result, the document is detailed and factual. In other countries a written document is viewed as the basis for a general agreement and the parties then negotiate the implementation as they go along. US MNEs prefer a more detailed document because they feel that everything should be spelled out in writing. Chinese and other Far East negotiators often view this as a sign of distrust and believe a more open-ended agreement should be used.

ACTIVE LEARNING CHECK

Review your answer to Active Learning Case question 4 and make any changes you like. Then compare your answer to the one below.

4. Why would the management of Singapore Airlines need to understand cultural differences in negotiating behavior? Would this need be greater than that of a brewer in Amsterdam who wants to negotiate the acquisition of a winery in Madrid? Why?

The management of Singapore Airlines would need to understand cultural differences in negotiating behavior because they do business with people in a wide variety of cultures. The airline has routes in the Far East, the United States, and Europe and so is continually negotiating with individuals who use a wide variety of different negotiating tactics and styles. The airline's need to understand these differences is greater than that of the brewer in Amsterdam because the negotiation for the acquisition of the winery will not be continually repeated. It is basically a "one-shot deal." Moreover, while managing the winery will require that the brewer continually negotiate with people from a different culture, this is only one culture. Singapore continually negotiates with people from a variety of diverse cultures.

NEGOTIATING AN AGREEMENT

When negotiating an agreement, three areas are of major importance: acceptance zones, renegotiation, and general negotiating behaviors. To the extent that MNE negotiators are knowledgable regarding these areas, their efforts will be successful.

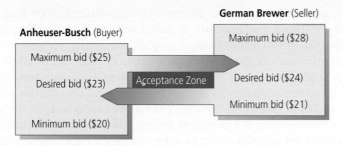

Figure 13.1   Zones of acceptance in the negotiating process (in millions of US $)

Acceptance zones   Each party to a negotiation will have an acceptance zone or an area within which it is willing to negotiate. For example, if Anheuser-Busch, the giant US brewer, wants to buy a brewery in Düsseldorf, Germany, the US MNE will determine three prices: the highest price it is willing to pay, the price it would like to pay, and the offer at which it will begin the bargaining. For purposes of illustration, assume that Anheuser-Busch (AB) is willing to pay up to $25 million for the company but hopes to make the acquisition for $23 million and intends to start the negotiation at $20 million.

Will AB be successful? This depends on the acceptance zone of the Düsseldorf brewer. If the company will not sell for less than $27.5 million, there will be no deal because the buyer's maximum offer is less than the seller's minimum acceptance. However, assume that the German firm will not sell for less than $21 million, would like to get $24 million, and intends to start the negotiation at $28 million. In this case the two sides should be able to strike a deal since they have overlapping zones of acceptance, as illustrated in Figure 13.1.

Notice from Figure 13.1 that when the acceptance zones of the two parties overlap, there is common ground for negotiating. Additionally, keep in mind that if the zones do not overlap, negotiations will not always end in a stalemate. After listening to each other the parties may agree to change their respective bids and offers, adjust the acceptance zones, and end up with common negotiating ground.

In the case of Figure 13.1 the two parties would eventually negotiate within a range of $21 million (the least amount the seller will take) and $25 million (the most the buyer will pay). It is not possible to say what the final price will be because this will depend on how willing each side is to concede ground to the other. However, whatever the final price, the seller is going to get at least the desired minimum and the buyer will not pay more than the established maximum.

Renegotiation   In the above example the negotiation process focused on one issue: acquisition of a brewery. When the purchase price is agreed upon, the process comes to an end. However, many MNE's negotiations with an individual or group will be repeated in the future. For example, Ford Motor may negotiate with a parts supplier in Brussels and sign a two-year contract. During the ensuing 24 months, the two parties may negotiate changes in the agreement, and at the end of this time the parties may renegotiate the overall agreement and settle on a new two-year contract. So in negotiating the MNE must remember that if the other side feels that it gave up more than it should have, then it will expect reciprocity in the future.

It is also important to remember that initial negotiations often lead to one party gaining the upper hand. For example, if Brazil wants Cummins Engine to set up a plant in Brasilia, the country may make a very enticing offer. However, at some point in time the country may begin to bring pressure on Cummins to allow local owner-ship in the operation or to invest more money in plant and equipment and to expand the facilities. If Cummins wants to remain in Brazil, the two parties will then begin renegotiating their agreement. In this case Cummins may accede to the government's request in turn for allowing the company to repatriate more of its profits back to the United States or to set up operations in other locales around the country.

Negotiating behaviors and tactics   During the negotiations it is common to find a wide variety of behaviors and tactics employed. For example, in some countries a great deal of time is spent building interpersonal relationships and getting to know the other parties to the negotiations. This approach is not widely used by US nego-tiators. But, as Adler points out, this can be an important activity.

> Effective negotiators must view luncheon, dinner, reception, ceremony, and tour invita-tions as times for interpersonal relationship building, and therefore as key to the negotiat-ing process. When US negotiators, often frustrated by the seemingly endless formalities, ceremonies, and "small talk," ask how long they must wait before beginning to "do busi-ness," the answer is simple: wait until your opponents bring up business (and they will). Realize that the work of conducting a successful negotiation has already begun, even if business has yet to be mentioned.[22]

Another common behavior or tactic is to learn the time limits of the other party. For example, if the German brewer learns that AB would like to buy a brewery within the next 90 days, the seller can use this information to gain an advantage. By delay-ing the negotiation until the end of this time period, the German company can then dig in its heels and ask for a price that is on the high side of AB's acceptance zone.

Another tactic is the use of reciprocity. Arab and US negotiators tend to recipro-cate by trading favors. If one side gives way on an issue, the other side will respond by giving way on something else. However, researchers have found that this is not always the case. Brazilians, for example, are likely to make initial concessions but then dig in and hold their ground. If the negotiator knows the likelihood of reciprocity, he or she is in a better bargaining position.

Still another tactic is the use of extreme offers or requests such as asking $60 mil-lion for a company that is worth half that amount or, conversely, offering $10 mil-lion for the firm. Researchers have found that Chinese, Arab, and Russian negotiators often use extreme behaviors, in contrast to US and Swedish negotiators whose ini-tial position is fairly close to the one they are seeking.[23] However, US negotiators have been known to use extreme positions. When Peter Ueberroth managed the Olympic games in the United States in 1984, he turned a profit of over $100 million by using extreme position bargaining, among other ways. For example, when the Japanese offered $6 million for the right to televise the games in Japan, Ueberroth countered by ask-ing for $90 million. The two sides eventually agreed on $18.5 million, which was far higher than the $10 million the Olympic Committee hoped to get.[24]

Other common bargaining tactics include promises, threats, rewards, commitments, and the use of self-disclosure. Table 13.5 provides illustrations of some of these nego-tiating behaviors by Japanese, US, and Brazilian negotiators. The table shows that each group has a series of behaviors that make it different from the other two. For

Table 13.5 Twelve examples of the differences in verbal behaviors among Japanese, US, and Brazilian negotiators

Behavior (description)	Number of times behavior was used in a 30-minute negotiating session by members of each group		
	Japanese	US	Brazilian
1 Making promises	7	8	3
2 Making threats	4	4	2
3 Making recommendations	7	4	5
4 Giving warnings	2	1	1
5 Offering rewards	1	2	2
6 Making commitments	15	13	8
7 Asking questions	20	20	22
8 Giving commands	8	6	14
9 Revealing personal information about oneself	34	36	39
10 Making a first offer	61.5	57.3	75.2
11 Granting initial concessions	6.5	7.1	9.4
12 Using the word "no"	5.7	9.0	83.4

Source: Adapted from John L. Graham, "The Influence of Culture on the Process of Business Negotiations: An Exploratory Study," *Journal of International Business Studies*, Spring 1985, p. 88.

example, the Japanese like to make recommendations, the Americans make wide use of promises, and the Brazilians rely heavily on self-disclosure.[25]

Another important negotiating area is nonverbal behaviors. These are characterized by such actions as silent periods, during which the negotiator says nothing, and facial gazing, during which the person stares at the other individual. Researchers have found that the Japanese and the Americans are more likely to use silence, whereas the Brazilians are more likely to use facial gazing.

These behaviors and tactics are often used in international negotiations. Effective negotiators learn how to use them and how to counteract their use by the opposition. Some examples are provided in the next section.

STRATEGIC MANAGEMENT AND POLITICAL RISK

MNEs take many steps to ensure that their strategies do not go awry because of unexpected developments. Two of the most beneficial steps are the use of integrative and protective/defensive techniques and the strategic use of joint ventures and partnerships[26]. The following section examines both.

Use of integrative and protective/defensive techniques

There are a variety of strategems that MNEs employ in reducing risk. Some are collectively known as **integrative techniques**, which are designed to help the MNE become a part of the host country's infrastructure.[27] The objective of an integrative technique is to help the company blend into the environment and to become less noticeable as a "foreign" firm. One of the simplest ways is to use a name that is not identified with an overseas company and, if an acquisition is made, keep the old name in place. For example, Bridgestone is a Japanese tire company, but no one would know this based on the name of the company. Additionally, Bridgestone owns Firestone Tire & Rubber, but few Americans are aware of this fact. Similarly, Hoechst of Germany owns the Celanese Company, and this too is not known by most people. Nor do many people realize that almost 25 per cent of the banks in California are Japanese owned; their names provide no clues to their real owners. This tactic deflects public attention and concern that US assets are being swallowed up by overseas investors.

Another common integrative technique is to develop good relations with the host government and other political groups and to produce as much of the product as possible locally. In turn the MNE will hire and promote local personnel and use them to run a large portion of the operations. This strategy endears the company to the government, and if any action is taken against foreign firms, these firms are likely to be spared.

A good example of an MNE that uses integrative techniques is IBM, which has consistently attempted to immerse itself into the host country's environment and to serve as a major export arm. As a result, the giant computer firm has been very successful in dealing with foreign governments and extracting major concessions from them. For example, IBM does not take on local partners, and host countries have always agreed to this demand.

Protective/defensive techniques **Protective and defensive techniques** are strategies that are designed to discourage a host country from interfering in operations. In contrast to integrative techniques, protective and defensive measures are aimed at fostering *nonintegration* of the MNE into the local environment. A good example is conducting research and development (R&D) at other geographic locales and importing this knowledge as needed. Should the government suddenly decide to seize the firm's facilities, the company's R&D base would not be threatened.

Another protective and defensive technique is to limit the role of the local personnel to those operations that are not vital to the running of the facility. So if the government decides to take over the operation, the host country personnel will not be able to handle things efficiently. Those with the requisite knowledge and training are overseas personnel who are sent on-site by the multinational.

A third technique is to raise as much capital as possible from the host country and local banks. When this happens, the government is reluctant to interfere in operations because this may threaten its own investment and that of the home country banks. In a manner of speaking, this strategy coopts the government and brings it onto the MNE's team. Any strike against the multinational is a blow against the host country.

A fourth technique is to diversify production among a number of countries. In this way, if the MNE's facilities are seized by the government, only one area of production is disrupted. The company can then reallocate production and get back on stream in short order.

Combination strategies MNEs often use a combination of integration and protective/defensive techniques to reduce and manage their political risk. Figure 13.2 provides an example of how companies can do this. In the case of the low-technology manufacturing firm (#1 in Figure 13.2), the only way to employ a protective/defensive strategy is to raise capital locally. As a result, this firm will work to integrate itself into the country and to act very much like a local firm.

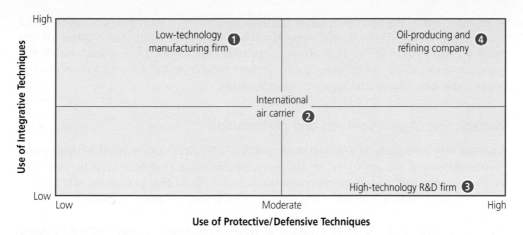

Figure 13.2 Select examples of the use of integrative and protective/defensive techniques

An international air carrier (#2 in Figure 13.2) will use an integrative strategy by setting up local operations and by hiring people to staff the facilities, to maintain the planes, and to handle arrivals and departures. The airline will also help to generate money for the country by bringing in tourists and businesspeople. At the same time the company will seldom have more than a small percentage of its planes in this locale on any one day. Additionally, the pilots will often come from other countries and be highly skilled individuals, and the top management team will be operating out of headquarters in the home country. So while the air carrier will take some steps to accommodate the country, it will also be well positioned should the country decide to seize its aircraft or to increase taxes or airport fees. Moreover, aside from facilities at the airport, the company will usually have no other fixed assets except for the planes. Therefore any crackdown on the airline might result in retaliatory action by other airlines, which would refuse to fly into the country. Such action could seriously hamper the country's economic growth. Consequently, a strategy that provides for the intermediate use of both integrative and protective/defensive techniques often works extremely well.

A high-technology R&D firm (#3 in Figure 13.2) will not put much emphasis on integrative techniques because it does not want to become integrated into the local economy. The firm may be situated where it is because the company finds that it is easier to recruit top talent to live in that region. Or other competitors may be headquartered there, and the company finds that it's easier to keep tabs on these firms by situating nearby. So while the company may hire local people to staff basic operations, the R&D and other sophisticated functions will all be handled by personnel from other countries who live locally. If the firm should hire local people for some of these R&D positions, the company will work to keep them loyal to the firm and not to the country. Thus if there is an attempt to seize the firm's R&D facilities, the loss will be minimized.

In the case of an oil-producing and refining company (#4 in Figure 13.2), the firm is likely to make strong use of both integrative and protective/defensive techniques. The company will need to get on well with the government since it is tapping the country's natural resources. There is likely to be a great deal of hiring of local personnel for routine jobs. The firm will also work hard to generate as much revenue as possible since the government is unlikely to interfere with the operations of a revenue-producing firm. At the same time the MNE will maintain control of the more sophisticated jobs so that these cannot be carried out by anyone else. If the company were to be taken over, local workers would be unlikely to know how to operate the machinery and equipment efficiently.

Strategic use of joint ventures and partnerships

Another way in which MNEs deal with political risk is by using joint ventures and partnerships that are approved by the government since that will help to build the local economy and/or to support current businesses.[28] This helps to explain why Eastern Europe is becoming a hotbed of investment and entrepreneurial activity.[29]

Two major examples   A good example is IBM's European strategy, which is being used to help the firm maintain dominance on the continent.[30] Another example is General Electric's joint ownership of Tungsram of Hungary.[31]

IBM Europe   In recent years IBM has been teaming up with European firms and using these alliances and joint ventures to help maintain market share. Many European governments that are concerned over the fact that their own computer firms are being bought up by the Japanese[32] are looking favorably on IBM's efforts to cement ties with the remaining firms. IBM teamed up with Siemens of Germany to develop high-capacity 64-megabit memory chips, and the two are now working on other projects. IBM is also stepping up production so that it can sell microchips, finished subsystems, disk drives, and telecommunications equipment to companies like Siemens and Groupe Bull, and the firm is not stopping here:

> In an effort to forge new links, IBM has become a major source of venture capital for independent suppliers of software and services. . . . Recently IBM Europe has plowed more than $100 million into nearly 200 joint ventures and partnerships, from a German software maker to a Danish supplier of network services.[33]

General Electric   General Electric (GE) and Tungsram, the giant Hungarian light bulb manufacturer, have joined forces in an agreement in which GE paid $150 million for 50.1 per cent of the company and then eventually bought full ownership. Prior to the agreement GE held only 2 per cent of the Western European light bulb market. After the purchase this jumped to 9 per cent.

GE is introducing more modern technology into the plant while studying some of the technological breakthroughs that the R&D people at Tungsram have already achieved, including their work on tungsten filaments. These breakthroughs help to explain why GE wanted Tungsram; despite having to operate under a communist regime that took away most of its profits, the firm had managed to produce some excellent products and to make some important technological discoveries.[34]

GE believes that with Tungsram in its corner, it can increase its European market share during the millennium and perhaps replace Philips as the major firm on the continent. Given the manner in which it has approached the project, the Hungarian government is solidly behind GE's efforts and political risk has been minimized.

Minimizing failure of cooperative efforts   While joint ventures and joint ownership are important ways of dealing with political risk, MNEs are also aware of the problems that can result if there is a falling out between the partners.[35] This can be

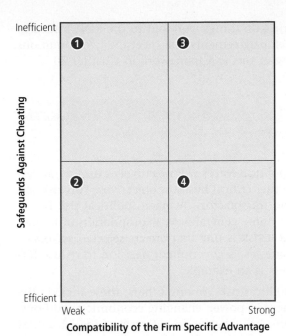

Figure 13.3 Ensuring the success of a joint venture or an ownership agreement

particularly troublesome if the local government were to support the home company's actions. For this reason, MNEs often make use of two strategic factors when deciding on a joint venture or joint ownership arrangement: (1) compatibility of firm specific advantages and (2) safeguards against unethical behavior.[36]

Firm specific advantages **Firm specific advantages** (FSAs for short) are the strengths or benefits specific to the firm that each partner brings to a joint venture or ownership arrangement. For example, IBM can offer venture capital to small firms in Europe while they can provide IBM with product technology. GE can offer capital, technology, and management expertise to Tungsram and the latter can provide a reputation for quality-produced goods, a factory, and a labor force. If the FSAs of the parties complement each other, the arrangement can be profitable for both. However, there is one other key consideration. What will happen if one party to the agreement takes advantage of the other, for example by stealing technology, breaking the deal, and going its own way? If this is done by the local partner, the MNE must hope that the local government will provide the necessary protection and return of its assets, patents, and so on.

Many MNEs believe that if there is a breakdown between the two partners to a joint venture agreement, the local company will come out ahead, so they take steps to prevent such an occurrence by protecting themselves from the start. For example, if the local partner steals the technology and begins producing the product under a different name or trademark, the MNE will have plans to retaliate by finding another local partner with whom to do business and possibly to drive the initial partner from the market. If the local partner takes venture capital funds and spends them on R&D activities that have no relationship to the venture, the MNE will refuse to commit more money to the project. In each of these cases the MNE is able to retaliate effectively. Aware of this, the partner is unlikely to undertake unethical behavior.

Figure 13.3 provides an illustration of how the compatibility of FSAs and the safeguards against cheating can result in a successful or an unsuccessful venture or ownership agreement. Only in quadrant 4 do things work out to the MNE's advantage. For this reason, it will work to develop agreements that meet the two conditions in this quadrant.[37] We make further use of this FSA framework in Chapter 20.

SUMMARY

Key points

1. Political risk is the probability that political forces will negatively affect an MNE's profit or impede the attainment of other critical business objectives. This risk can be examined in terms of macro- and microfactors. A macro political risk is one that affects foreign enterprises in the same general way. Expropriation of foreign firms is an example. A micro political risk is one that affects selected sectors of the economy or specific foreign businesses. A government decision to reduce foreign ownership in the airline business is an example.

2. There are a number of sources of political risk. Among others, these include the political philosophy of the government in power, changing economic conditions, rising nationalism, social unrest, terrorism, the vested interests of local business groups, and newly created international alliances.

3. MNEs use a number of approaches in managing political risk. One is to forecast this risk by examining the political system and by evaluating the overall risk. Another approach is to examine the impact of this risk on company products and operations. Based on the results, the company will then determine the risk vulnerability. In some cases, as seen in Table 13.3, this vulnerability is quantified.

4. There are three key steps in developing effective negotiating strategies. First, the MNE will evaluate its own position and that of the other parties to the negotiation. Second, the firm will examine the behavioral characteristics of the other parties in order to better understand their style of negotiation. Third, the MNE will use this information to hammer out an agreement that is acceptable to both sides. In carrying out the latter step, the MNE will give particular attention to identifying the acceptance zone of the other party and to using behaviors and negotiating tactics that will result in both sides feeling that they are getting what they want.

5. MNEs tend to use a combination of integrative and protective/defensive techniques in minimizing political risk. They also rely on the strategic use of joint ventures and partnerships and carefully analyze each situation before entering into the agreement.

Key terms

- political risk
- macro political risk
- expropriation
- indigenization laws
- micro political risk
- acceptance zone
- integrative techniques
- protective and defensive techniques
- firm specific advantages

Review and discussion questions

1. What is meant by the term "political risk"? Is there political risk in every country of the world? Explain.

2. How does macro political risk differ from micro political risk? Compare and contrast the two.

3. What are some factors that help to determine the degree of micro political risk? Identify and describe three of them.

4. Drawing on the information in Table 13.2, what are three major sources of political risk? What is the likely effect of each source?

5. When predicting political risk, why will an MNE be interested in examining the political system of the country?

6. When an MNE evaluates the political risk associated with its products and operations, what areas will it investigate? Identify and discuss three of them.

7. How can an MNE quantify its political risk vulnerability? Use Table 13.3 as a point of reference.

8. If Citicorp is thinking about opening startup operations in a country in Eastern Europe, how would the firm evaluate its own strengths and needs when preparing for the negotiations?

9. Why will an MNE be interested in the behavioral characteristics of the participants to a negotiation? How can such information help to improve its negotiating position?

10. In a negotiation, why would an MNE be interested in the acceptance zone of the other party?

11. What are some bargaining tactics that are used in international negotiating? Identify and describe three of them.

12. How do MNEs use integrative techniques in order to reduce their political risk? Describe an example.

13. How do MNEs use protective/defensive techniques in order to reduce their political risk? Describe an example.

14. How could an MNE ensure the success of a joint venture or ownership agreement through consideration of firm specific advantages and safeguards against cheating? Give an example.

REAL CASES

INVESTING IN RUSSIA

Since the end of the Cold War in 1989, Russia has been making overtures towards a free market economy. During the early 1990s annual economic growth rates among developed countries such as the United States, Germany, and Japan dropped from an average of 5 per cent down to 2 per cent. At the same time Eastern European and the Russian economies fell much more sharply, with annual growth rates tumbling from 4 per cent in 1988 to –10 in 1991! Clearly, the Russian economy was in big trouble.

Investment from the West was seen as a way to improve the economy. However, significant changes needed to take place to reduce political risk in Russia. Initially, five steps were recommended by outside experts: (1) change the relationship between the national government and the republics in order to set up a federal political system in which central powers are limited; (2) eliminate or slash most state subsidies, including defense spending, and create a uniform sales tax and personal and corporate income tax system; (3) establish a commercial banking system, boost interest rates, and create an independent bank that will halt current inflationary practices; (4) break up state monopolies and industrial cartels; and (5) free the price of most goods immediately and gradually add to this list those changes that must be phased in more slowly: energy, public transportation, housing, and basic consumer goods such as milk, bread, and meat.

By the mid-1990s things looked good; the republics had become more autonomous from the central government and new private banks had begun to emerge. Most importantly, by 1997, the private sector accounted for more than half of Russia's output. Some 18,000 industrial firms had been privatized and over 1 million new businesses were created. The old Russia, its ideology and institutions, had ceased to exist.

Yet the late 1990s proved to be a wake-up call to foreign investors in Russia. The Asian crisis left many feeling Russia could be next and it would have been had the IMF and the World Bank not been ready to bail the country out. The Russian government had pegged the ruble to the US dollar and used interest rates to defend the exchange rate. This led to skyrocketing interest rates that reached over 50 per cent in peak periods. When the government allowed the ruble to float, investors lost on the devaluation what they had earned on interest rates.

What brought this about? While Russia's steps towards liberalization have been significant, the country is only mid-way to becoming a truly democratic free market. The new private banks are not real banks. They offer no real credit system. They lack credibility, which makes Russians more likely to hold currency or send their savings to foreign banks than to deposit them in these new banks. A large bureaucratic web still exists and a small corrupt mafia is proving difficult to police. Ongoing political crises continue to threaten the stability of the Yeltsin government.

1. What political risks do MNEs face in Russia? Identify and describe three of them.

2. What strengths would a consumer goods manufacturing firm bring to the country? What Russian needs would it help to meet?

3. How could this manufacturer employ integrative or protective/defensive techniques in the country? Identify and describe one approach that could be used for each.

Sources: Adapted from Leonard Silk, Rose Brady et al., "Can Gorbachev Pound Missiles into Plowshares?" *Business Week*, July 29, 1991, pp. 42–43; Steven Erlanger, "To Russia, with Good Ol' American Know-How," *New York Times*, June 13, 1993, p. F5; Rob Norton and Kerry L. Hubert, "The Good News About Russia," *Fortune*, April 14, 1997, p. 32; Steve H. Hanke, "Is the Ruble Next?" *Forbes*, March 9, 1998, p. 64; Danie Yergin and Thane Gustafson, "Don't Write Off Russia – Yet," *Fortune*, September 28, 1998, pp. 99–102; Domingo F. Cavallo, "The Immensity of Russia's Problems," *Forbes*, August 24, 1998, p. 263; Steve H. Hanke, "Capitalism Without Banks," *Forbes*, September 7, 1998, pp. 150–151; "Russia's Economic Quagmire," *The Economist*, April 24, 1999, pp. 69–70.

FREEPORT MCMORAN IN INDONESIA

The 1998 financial crisis and revolution in Indonesia has brought the country under great attention. As the world's fourth most populous nation, rich in both manpower and natural resources, it is eager to take its place in the community of nations. However, much of the attention that it has been getting focuses on the government's authoritarian tradition, especially on human rights issues.

Despite the highly negative views on Indonesia, Freeport McMoRan, a US-based mining company, has invested heavily in Indonesia since the mid-1970s, a time during which there was even greater political risk. In the mid-1990s they invested in a $30 million-a-year search for more major copper and gold deposits across Irian Jaya, Indonesia's largest, and least developed island. They struck it big: combined reserves are worth more than $30 billion. In 1991, Freeport McMoRan signed a mining contract with the government that will secure its place for at least the next 50 years: a 30-year deal with options for two one-year extensions. The company also won a 2.5 million hectare land concession in 1989. After the change in President in 1998 these contracts were reviewed.

Freeport McMoRan's chairman James Moffett remains confident in Irian Jaya's future. Freeport and an Indonesian real estate company is building a $500 million city close to the current settlement near the mining site. Once it has finished with this expansion programme, Freeport McMoRan will have increased its investment in Indonesia by over $2.5 billion in a ten-year span.

Freeport's aggressive management style seems to ignore the political risk that has often been associated with foreign direct investment in Indonesia. The company's commitment, however, seems to confirm its choice of the country as one of the major players in the economy of the Pacific basin.

1. Based on the information in the case, how can Freeport McMoRan use defensive techniques with regard to its 50-year contract with Indonesia? Explain.

2. What strengths did Freeport McMoRan bring to a country like Indonesia? What needs would such industry fill for Indonesia?

3. In the early 1990s, Indonesia abolished its indigenization law. How much of a reduction in political risk does the move have for a company like Freeport McMoRan?

Sources: Adapted from John McBeth, "Treasure Island," *Far Eastern Economic Review*, March 10, 1994, pp. 48–53; "Indonesia's Embarrassment," *The New York Times*, November 17, 1994, p. 25.

ENDNOTES

1. Serge Schmemann, "Gorbachev Offers Party a Charter That Drops Icons," *New York Times*, July 26, 1991, pp. A1, A5.
2. Also, see Douglas Harbrecht et al., "Tough Talk," *Business Week*, February 28, 1994, pp. 26–28.
3. Also, see Richard W. Stevenson, "Europeans Join to Build a Fast Plane," *New York Times*, April 8, 1994, pp. C1–C2.
4. For a discussion of United States exports, see James Beeler, "Exports: Ship 'Em Out," *Fortune*, Special ed., Spring/Summer 1991, p. 58.
5. Barnaby J. Feder, "Honeywell's Route Back to South Africa Market," *New York Times*, January 31, 1994, pp. C1, C4.
6. Keith Bradsher, "Push by US to Cut Tariffs Is Reported," *New York Times*, January 8, 1993, pp. C1, C10.
7. However, these countries are also concerned with *quid pro quo*, as seen in Richard W. Stevenson, "East Europe Says Barriers to Trade Hurt Its Economies," *New York Times*, January 25, 1993, pp. A1, C8.
8. See Zbigniew Brzezinski, "Help the New Russian Revolution," *New York Times*, July 14, 1991, p. F13.
9. Also, see Thomas L. Freedman, "Bentsen Seeks Freer Asian Markets," *New York Times*, January 19, 1994, pp. C1–C2.
10. Richard M. Hodgetts and Fred Luthans, *International Management*, 4th ed. (Burr Ridge, Ill: McGraw/Hill,

2000), pp. 277–278, and Jonathon Sapsford, "Japanese Firms Brace for First Laws on Consumer Rights and Insurers Gain," *Wall Street Journal*, March 8, 1994, p. A13.

11. Douglas Jehl, "Clinton Drops 19-Year Ban on US Trade with Vietnam: Cites Hanoi's Help on MIA's," *New York Times*, February 4, 1994, pp. A1, A6.

12. As an example, see Keith Bradsher, "New US–Japan Chip Pact Approved," *New York Times*, June 5, 1991, p. C11.

13. Clyde H. Farnsworth, "Trade Focus Has Changed," *New York Times*, May 28, 1991, pp. C1, C9.

14. Also, see David E. Sanger, "Japan Looking for Ways to Avert US Trade War," *New York Times*, February 18, 1994, pp. C1, C4.

15. Also, see Louis Uchitelle, "Gulf Victory May Raise US Influence in OPEC," *New York Times*, March 5, 1991, pp. C1, C8.

16. R. W. Apple, Jr., "Leaders Express Support for Gorbachev," *New York Times*, July 17, 1991, pp. A1, A6; and Andrew Rosenthal, "Bush Renewing Trade Privileges for China, but Adds Missile Curbs," *New York Times*, March 28, 1991, pp. A1, A4.

17. See, for example, David B. Yoffie, "How an Industry Builds Political Advantage," *Harvard Business Review*, May–June 1988, pp. 82–89. Also, see Alan M. Rugman and Alain Verbeke, *Global Corporate Strategy and Trade Policy* (London and New York: Routledge, 1990), and Pat Choate, *Agents of Influence* (New York: Knopf, 1990).

18. For more on this, see Lee T. Brown, Alan M. Rugman, and Alain Verbeke, "Japanese Joint Ventures with Western Multinationals: Synthesising the Economic and Cultural Explanations of Failure," *Asia Pacific Journal of Management*, vol. 6, no. 2, 1990, pp. 225–242.

19. David E. Sanger, "Japan Sets Tough Rules on Business," *New York Times*, July 15, 1991, pp. C1–C2.

20. Hodgetts and Luthans, op. cit., p. 287.

21. John R. Schermerhorn, Jr., "Language Effects in Cross-Cultural Management Research: An Empirical Study and a World of Caution," *National Academy of Management Proceedings*, 1987, pp. 102–105.

22. Nancy J. Adler, *International Dimensions of Organizational Behavior*, 2nd ed. (Boston: PWS-Kent Publishing, 1991), p. 197.

23. Hodgetts and Luthans, op. cit., pp. 287–288.

24. Ibid., p. 290–291.

25. For additional insights into negotiating, see Brian Mark Hawrysh and Judith Lynne Zaichkowsky, "Cultural Approaches to Negotiations: Understand-ing the Japanese," *International Marketing Review*, vol. 7, no. 2, 1990, pp. 28–42.

26. For a detailed discussion of protective/defensive techniques see Ann Gregory, 'Political Risk Manage-ment', pp. 310–329 in Alan M. Rugman (Ed.) International Business in Canada (Toronto: Prentice-Hall Canada, 1989).

27. For a good example of how Japan does this, see Andrew Pollack, "Japan Takes a Pre-emptive Step on Auto Exports," *New York Times*, January 9, 1993, pp. 17, 26; and Richard W. Stevenson, "Japanese Cars Get British Accents," *New York Times*, February 25, 1992, pp. C1, C14.

28. Stephen O. Spinks and Robert C. Stanley, "Joint Ventures Under EC Antitrust and Merger Control Rules: Concentrative or Cooperative," *Journal of European Business*, March/April 1991, pp. 29–34; and Edmund L. Andrews, "Sprint Forms Joint Venture with Alcatel," *New York Times*, February 4, 1993, p. C3.

29. Paul Hofheinz, "New Light in Eastern Europe?" *Fortune*, July 29, 1991, pp. 145–152.

30. Carol J. Loomis, "Can John Akers Save IBM?" *Fortune*, July 15, 1991, pp. 40–56; Douglas Harbrecht, Neil Gross, and Peter Burrows, "Suppose They Have a Trade War and Nobody Came," *Business Week*, March 29, 1993, p. 30; and Gary McWilliams and Neil Gross, "DEC: New Chip, New Partner, New Ball Game?" *Business Week*, March 29, 1993. p. 31.

31. Gail E. Schares, Zachary Schiller, and Patrick Oster, "GE Gropes for the On-Switch in Hungary," *Business Week*, April 26, 1993, pp. 102–103.

32. Jonathan B. Levine and Gail E. Schares, "IBM Europe Starts Swinging Back," *Business Week*, May 6, 1991, p. 52.

33. Ibid., p. 53.

34. See Steven Greenhouse, "Running on Fast-Forward in Budapest," *New York Times*, December 16, 1990, Section 3, pp. 1, 8.

35. Jordan D. Lewis, "How to Build Successful Strategic Alliances," *Journal of European Business*, November/December 1990, pp. 18–29; and Tom Lewis and Mark Turley, "Strategic Partnering in Eastern Europe," *International Executive*, January–February 1991, pp. 5–9.

36. See Brown et al. (endnote 18).

37. For additional insights, see Peter J. Pettibone, "Negotiating a Business Venture in the Soviet Union," *Journal of Business Strategy*, January/February 1991, pp. 18–23; Keith A. Rosten, "Soviet–US Joint Ventures: Pioneers on a New Frontier," *California Management Review*, Winter 1991, pp. 88–108.

ADDITIONAL BIBLIOGRAPHY

Averyt, William F. "Canadian and Japanese Foreign Investment Screening," *Columbia Journal of World Business*, vol. 21, no. 4 (Winter 1986).

Benedick, Richard E. "Behind the Diplomatic Curtain: Inner Workings of the New Global Negotiations," *Columbia Journal of World Business*, vol. 27, no. 3, 4 (Fall/Winter 1992).

Brett, Jeanne M. and Okumura, Tetsushi. "Inter- and Intracultural Negotiations: US and Japanese Negotiators," *The Academy of Management Journal*, vol. 41, no. 5 (December 1998).

Brewer, Thomas L. "Government Policies, Market Imperfections, and Foreign Direct Investment," *Journal of International Business Studies*, vol. 24, no. 1 (First Quarter 1993).

Brewer, Thomas L. "An Issue-Area Approach to the Analysis of MNE–Government Relations," *Journal of International Business Studies*, vol. 23, no. 2 (Second Quarter 1992).

Chase, Carmen D.; Kuhle, James L.; and Walther, Carl H. "The Relevance of Political Risk in Direct Foreign Investment," *Management International Review*, vol. 28, no. 3 (Third Quarter 1988).

Cosset, Jean-Claude and Roy, Jean. "The Determinants of Country Risk Ratings," *Journal of International Business Studies*, vol. 22, no. 1 (First Quarter 1991).

Eiteman, David K. "Political Risk and International Marketing," *Columbia Journal of World Business*, vol. 23, no. 4 (Winter 1988).

Gavin, Joseph G. III. "Environmental Protection and the GATT: A Business View," *Columbia Journal of World Business*, vol. 27, no. 3, 4 (Fall/Winter 1992).

Geringer, J. Michael. "Strategic Determinants of Partner Selection Criteria in International Joint Ventures," *Journal of International Business Studies*, vol. 22, no. 1 (First Quarter 1991).

Geringer, J. Michael and Hebert, Louis. "Measuring Performance of International Joint Ventures," *Journal of International Business Studies*, vol. 22, no. 2 (Second Quarter 1991).

Gomes-Casseres, Benjamin. "Joint Ventures in the Face of Global Competition," *Sloan Management Review*, vol. 30, no. 3 (Spring 1989).

Grosse, Robert. "Restrictive Business Practices in International Service Industries: Examples from Latin America," *Transnational Corporations*, vol. 6, no. 2 (August 1997).

Hillman, Amy and Keim, Gerald. "International Variation in the Business-Government Interface: Institutional and Organizational Considerations," *The Academy of Management Review*, vol. 20, no. 1 (January 1995).

Inkpen, Andrew C. and Beamish, Paul W. "Knowledge, Bargaining Power, and the Instability of International Joint Ventures," *The Academy of Management Review*, vol. 22, no. 1 (January 1997).

Kogut, Bruce. "A Study of the Life Cycle of Joint Ventures," *Management International Review*, vol. 28 (1988).

Lee, Suk Hun. "Relative Importance of Political Instability and Economic Variables on Perceived Country Creditworthiness," *Journal of International Business Studies*, vol. 24, no. 4 (Fourth Quarter 1993).

Li, Jiatao and Guisinger, Stephen. "Comparative Business Failures of Foreign-Controlled Firms in the United States," *Journal of International Business Studies*, vol. 22, no. 2 (Second Quarter 1991).

Lin, Xiaohua and Germain, Richard. "Sustaining Satisfactory Joint Venture Relationships: The Role of Conflict Resolution Strategy," *Journal of International Business Studies*, vol. 29, no. 1 (First Quarter 1998).

Luo, Yadong. "Joint Venture Success in China: How Should We Select a Good Partner," *Journal of World Business*, vol. 33, no. 2 (Summer 1998).

Makhija, Mona Verma. "Government Intervention in the Venezuelan Petroleum Industry: An Empirical Investigation of Political Risk," *Journal of International Business Studies*, vol. 24, no. 3 (Third Quarter 1993).

Miller, Kent D. "Industry and Country Effects on Managers' Perceptions of Environmental Uncertainties," *Journal of International Business Studies*, vol. 24, no. 4 (Fourth Quarter 1993).

Nigh, Douglas and Smith, Karen D. "The New US Joint Venture in the USSR: Assessment and Management of Political Risk," *Columbia Journal of World Business*, vol. 24, no. 2 (Summer 1989).

Ofori-Dankwa, Joseph. "Murray and Reshef Revisited: Toward a Typology/Theory of Paradigms of National Trade Union Movements," *Academy of Management Review*, vol. 18, no. 2 (April 1993).

Rajan, Mahesh N. and Graham, John L. "Nobody's Grandfather Was a Merchant: Understanding the Soviet Commercial Negotiation Process and Style," *California Management Review*, vol. 33, no. 3 (Spring 1991).

Rice, Gillian and Mahmoud, Essam. "A Managerial Procedure for Political Risk Forecasting," *Management International Review*, vol. 26, no. 4 (Fourth Quarter 1986).

Rolfe, Robert J.; Ricks, David A.; Pointer, Martha M.; and McCarthy, Mark. "Determinants of FDI Incentive Preferences of MNEs," *Journal of International Business Studies*, vol. 24, no. 2 (Second Quarter 1993).

Rugman, Alan M. and Verbeke, Alain. "Mintzberg's Intended and Emergent Corporate Strategies and Trade Policy," *Canadian Journal of Administrative Sciences*, vol. 8, no. 3 (September 1991).

Sebenius, James K. "Negotiating Cross-Border Acquisitions," *Sloan Management Review*, vol. 39 (Winter 1998).

Shan, Weijian. "Environmental Risks and Joint Venture Sharing Arrangements," *Journal of International Business Studies*, vol. 22, no. 4 (Fourth Quarter 1991).

Sherr, Alan B. "Joint Ventures in the USSR: Soviet and Western Interests with Considerations for Negotiations," *Columbia Journal of World Business*, vol. 23, no. 2 (Summer 1988).

Singer, S. Fred. "Sustainable Development vs. Global Environment: Resolving the Conflict," *Columbia Journal of World Business*, vol. 27, no. 3 (Fall/Winter 1992).

Stewart, Sally and Keown, Charles F. "Talking with the Dragon: Negotiating in the People's Republic of China," *Columbia Journal of World Business*, vol. 24, no. 3 (Fall 1989).

Tai, L. S. "Doing Business in the People's Republic of China: Some Keys to Success," *Management International Review*, vol. 28, no. 1 (1988).

Tallman, Stephen B. "Home Country Political Risk and Foreign Direct Investment in the United States," *Journal of International Business Studies*, vol. 19, no. 2 (Summer 1988).

CHAPTER 14

International Financial Management

OBJECTIVES OF THE CHAPTER

International business operations can be extremely complex. One reason is that the impact of financial decisions or developments in one locale can affect the operations or performance of subsidiaries in other locales, as well as in the MNE at large. For example, a Japanese subsidiary in the United States may have a sales goal of 300 million yen based on an exchange rate of 110 yen to the dollar. However, if the yen's value declines to 125 per dollar, the subsidiary is faced with a number of financial decisions, including whether to raise or lower prices, whether to increase or decrease the amount of inventory being imported from Japan, and whether to speed up or slow down the collection of receivables from US vendors. In this chapter we will focus on some of the major financial strategies and techniques that are used to manage international operations and to protect the MNE against wide fluctuations in local currencies. The objectives of this chapter are to:

1. **Compare** and **contrast** how polycentric, ethnocentric, and geocentric solutions are used in determining the financial planning and controlling authority that is given to subsidiaries.

2. **Study** some of the most common techniques that are used in managing global cash flows, including funds positioning and multilateral netting.

3. **Examine** foreign exchange risk strategies that are used to protect the multinational against financial losses.

4. **Explain** how capital expenditure analysis and capital budgeting are carried out.

5. **Provide** examples of international financial strategies currently being used by multinationals.

ACTIVE LEARNING CASE

British Airway's expansion plans

By the end of the 1980s there were only three dominant airlines in the United States: American, Delta, and United. The others were either smaller carriers or were facing big financial problems. However, in mid-1992 British Airways (BA) announced that it was entering into an arrangement with USAir to form a giant transatlantic alliance. If the BA plan comes to fruition, it will mean that passengers on both sides of the Atlantic will be able to travel throughout Europe and the United States by relying on just one carrier: BA/USAir. One of the major stumbling blocks, however, will be the US government.

The Big Three are asking the US government to block this arrangement because it will give too much of the US market to a foreign company. However, some people in Washington, DC, feel that this merger could save thousands of US jobs and thus are supporting it. Many others believe that this is an ideal way of forcing the EU to open up its skies to US carriers.

If the merger goes through, the two combined carriers will indeed be a major force in the industry. Their combined 1991 revenues were in excess of $15 billion; they carried almost 80 million passengers that year and had a combined fleet of over 470 aircraft. However, the merger would not occur immediately. There is to be a five-year period during which the two carriers intend to integrate the core aspects of their businesses. During this time they will coordinate ticket pricing, catering, advertising, and the network of flights and connections. At the end of this period, if all goes according to plan, a passenger will be able to fly from Indianapolis to London with USAir handling the domestic leg and BA flying the international portion.

BA is prepared to spend heavily to buy into USAir. The company's initial plans called for investing $750 million for a 44 per cent equity stake and a 21 per cent voting stake, and there would be more investment later. However, there was flexibility in the deal in that either company could back out within the five-year period. Many industry

observers did not think that this was likely, given that BA was continuing to build a worldwide network and USAir could play a key role in this strategy. In fact, the two carriers had been expanding their focus. USAir was trying to buy some of the assets of TWA, the bankrupt US carrier, and BA had purchased a German regional airline and had taken a one-third stake in a Moscow-based joint venture, Air Russia.

After the proposed merger was announced, management at both companies began focusing on integrating overall operations. They looked at how to pare costs by combining purchasing, maintenance, and operations. They also proposed uniformity of service throughout the system. Eventually uniforms, food, and cabin interiors would be the same. If the carriers implement this proposed plan successfully, the BA/USAir system would be the largest and most profitable one in the world. However, a great deal of this success would depend on how well they could carry out the financial end of their strategy and get government approval.

In late 1992 these plans were all thrown into disarray. The US and British governments could not work out an agreement that was satisfactory to both sides, and BA announced that it was not going forward with the plan. Then in early 1993 the firm decided to take a different approach. BA announced plans to invest $300 million for a 20 per cent stake of USAir as part of a newly proposed deal. Once again, the US government announced that it would look into the proposal and hear arguments from both sides.

Sources: Adapted from Paula Dwyer et al., "Air Raid: British Air's Bold Global Push," *Business Week*, August 24, 1992, pp. 54–61; Agis Salpukas, "The Big Foreign Push to Buy into US Airlines," *New York Times*, October 11, 1992, p. F11; Edmund L. Andrews, "US Is Said to Oppose USAir Deal," *New York Times*, December 21, 1992, pp. C1, C5; Richard W. Stevenson, "British Air Drops Plans to Purchase Big Stakes in USAir," *New York Times*, December 23, 1992, pp. A1, C2; Jeanne B. Pinder, "British Airways Buys 20% Stake in USAir in a New Linkup Move," *New York Times*, January 22, 1993, pp. A1, C3; Agis Salpukas, "After Era of Failing Airlines, New Carriers Begin to Grow," *New York Times*, May 19, 1993, pp. A1, C5; and Adam Bryant, "British Air Halts Move Into USAir," *New York Times*, March 8, 1994, pp. C1, C4.

1. Is the BA/USAir alliance going to use a polycentric, ethnocentric, or geocentric solution to handling operations?

2. If the two carriers complete their merger and the US dollar then weakens against the British pound, how will this affect the financial statements of the company?

3. If BA believed that the British pound was going to appreciate in relation to the German mark, how could the company use a lead and lag strategy to its advantage?

4. How great is the political risk that BA faces in the United States? Explain.

5. How is the BA/USAir arrangement designed to reduce financial risk and to control costs? Give two examples.

INTRODUCTION

International financial management encompasses a number of key areas. These include the management of global cash flows, foreign exchange risk management, and capital expenditure analysis and capital budgeting. Decisions in each of these areas can significantly impact the others. For example, if the exchange rate of the Mexican peso sharply declines against the dollar, the multinational may decide to transfer more dollars to its Mexican subsidiary so that the unit can continue paying for imports from the United States. At the same time the MNE may decide not to allow the subsidiary to renovate the administrative offices because the unit's profitability (in dollars) is going to be below expectations. The manager of the Mexican unit cannot be blamed for the declining peso, but this development has resulted in the parent company making decisions that affect local operations.

The objective of international financial management strategies is to provide assistance to all geographic operations and to limit financial losses through the use of carefully formulated cash flow guidelines, the timely execution of foreign exchange risk management strategies, prudent capital expenditures, and careful capital budgeting. The responsibility for these activities is spread throughout the organization, and some of these decisions are made on a day-to-day basis, whereas others are determined only periodically. Additionally, some of these decisions are made by the parent company, whereas others fall within the purview of the subsidiary. In an effort to ensure that each group understands its limits of financial authority, it is common to find financial management planning beginning with a determination of parent–subsidiary relationships.

DETERMINING PARENT-SUBSIDIARY RELATIONSHIPS

Because finance is such an important area of operations, it is critically important that parent companies firmly establish the relationships that will exist regarding financial planning and control authority. On the one hand, each branch or subsidiary should be responsible for its own planning and control system. On the other hand, there must be some central control in order to coordinate overall operations and to ensure both efficiency and profitability. In addressing this challenge, MNEs tend to opt for one of three solutions: polycentric, ethnocentric, or geocentric.

Polycentric solution

A **polycentric solution** is to treat the MNE as a holding company and to decentralize decision making to the subsidiary levels. In this arrangement financial statements are prepared according to generally accepted accounting principles in both the overseas subsidiary's and the parent's home country, and the subsidiary's performance is evaluated against that of similar domestic and foreign concerns.

The advantages of the polycentric approach are those commonly obtained with decentralization. Decisions are made on the spot by those most informed about market conditions, and international subsidiaries tend to be more flexible, motivated, efficient, and competitive. On the other hand, this solution reduces the authority of the home office, and senior corporate management often dislike this dilution of their authority. Additionally, an MNE may find that a polycentric approach results in competition between different international subsidiaries and lowers overall profits for the company.

Ethnocentric solution

The **ethnocentric solution** is to treat all foreign operations as if they were extensions of domestic operations. In this case each unit is integrated into the planning and control system of the parent company.

The advantage of this system is that management is able to coordinate overall operations carefully. This usually results in centralization of the finance function so that cash not needed for day-to-day operations can be invested in marketable securities or transferred to other subsidiaries or branches that need working capital. The primary drawback of this solution is that it can cause problems for the individual subsidiary, which may feel that it needs more cash than is left on hand or that it is hindered in its efforts to expand because the parent company is siphoning off necessary resources.

Geocentric solution

The **geocentric solution** is to handle financial planning and controlling decisions on a global basis. These decisions are typically influenced by two factors. One is the nature and location of the subsidiary. For example, British investment in North America has predominantly been via holding companies, the polycentric approach, since the quality of local management largely rewards decentralization. Conversely, investment in developing countries has typically been centralized, with the parent company maintaining close control of financial expenditures. A second influencing factor is the gains that can be achieved by coordinating all units in a carefully synchronized way. When an MNE's overseas units face a myriad of tax rates, financial systems, and competitive environments, it is often more efficient to centralize most of the financial control decisions because this is the best way to ensure that profit and efficiency are maximized. For example, if there are two subsidiaries which are equally able to sell a particular product to a major customer, with centralized financial planning the parent company could ensure that the sale would be made by the unit located in the country with the lowest corporate income-tax rate. Additional examples of the ways in which financial operations could be directed by using a geocentric solution are seen in the management of global cash flows.

ACTIVE LEARNING CHECK

Review your answer to Active Learning Case question 1 and make any changes you like. Then compare your answer to the one below.

1. Is the BA/USAir alliance going to use a polycentric, ethnocentric, or geocentric solution to handling operations?

The alliance is going to use a geocentric solution to handling operations. This is clear from the way in which the two air carriers are beginning to merge their operations so that they are both working in harmony. However, there are also some signs that ethnocentric solutions are occasionally used, as reflected by the fact that BA seems to be making most of the decisions and that the merger is going to be more influenced by the British carrier than by USAir.

MANAGING GLOBAL CASH FLOWS

One of the key areas of international financial management is the careful handling of global cash flows. There are a number of ways in which this is done. Three of the most important ones include the prudent use of internal funds flows, the use of funds positioning, and the use of multilateral netting. The following sections examine each of these three.

Internal funds flows

When an MNE wants to expand operations or fund activities, one of the simplest ways of obtaining the needed monies is by getting them from internal sources such as **working capital**, which is the difference between current assets and current liabilities. For example, if General Motors' German subsidiary wants to hire more employees, it may be able to pay for this payroll increase out of the funds it generates from ongoing operations. Another way of raising money internally is by borrowing from a local bank or from the parent company. For example, an MNE's Chilean subsidiary will get a loan from the parent company or the German subsidiary and then repay the money with interest out of operations. A third way is by having the parent company increase its equity capital investment in the subsidiary. In turn the subsidiary could pay the parent dividends on the investment. These examples are illustrated in Figure 14.1 and help to show that there are many ways for multinational firms to generate internal cash for operations.

Which method is most likely to be used? The answer will depend on a number of factors, including government regulations regarding intercompany lending. For example, when tax rates are high for a profitable subsidiary, it is common to find those units willing to lend money at low rates of interest to other subsidiaries in the MNE that need funds to expand into growth markets. The logic behind this strategy is quite simple: the highly profitable unit does not need to charge a high interest rate because much of this interest will be taxed away by the government. Conversely, the subsidiary that is borrowing the money needs low interest rates so as to conserve its cash for expansion purposes. By shifting the money around in this fashion, the

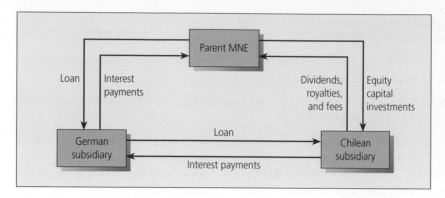

Figure 14.1 Common example of internal sources and flows of funds

MNE is able to support expansion efforts, to minimize taxes, and to increase the sales potential of the subsidiaries. In an effort to prevent multinationals from taking advantage of such tax loopholes, in recent years some governments have changed their tax laws and established a minimum rate that can be charged on these intercompany loans.

Another area of concern is government limits on a parent company's ability to charge subsidiaries a licensing or royalty fee for the use of technology or to assess a management fee that covers the subsidiary's fair share of corporate overhead. When there are no government restrictions in these areas, the MNE has greater freedom in drawing funds from subsidiary operations, thus providing the parent with a pool of money that can be used for other worldwide operations. The ways in which this is done are commonly referred to as funds positioning techniques.

Funds positioning techniques

Funds positioning techniques are strategies that are used to move monies from one multinational operation to another. While there are a variety of approaches, three of the most common are transfer pricing, tax havens, and fronting loans.

Transfer pricing   A **transfer price** is an internal price that is set by a company in intrafirm trade such as the price at which the Chilean subsidiary will purchase electric motors from the German subsidiary. An initial conclusion would be that the German firm will sell the motors at the same price as it would to any outside purchaser. A second conclusion is that the Chilean subsidiary will receive a discount because it is an intrafirm transaction and the parent will not allow its subsidiaries to profit at the expense of each other. However, both of these conclusions are incorrect when a transfer pricing strategy is employed. The final price will be determined by local regulations and will be set at a level that allows the MNE to achieve certain desired goals such as to increase profit, to reduce costs, and/or to move money among the subsidiaries.

A good example is provided by a multinational that has a subsidiary located in Country A, which has a low corporate income tax and is selling goods to a subsidiary located in Country B, which has a high corporate income tax. If the transfer price is

Table 14.1 **Shifting profits by transfer pricing**

	"Arm's length" price		Transfer price	
	Country A	Country B	Country A	Country B
Sales	$10,000 exports	$12,000	$12,000 exports	$12,000
Costs of sales	8,000	→ 10,000	8,000	→ 12,000
Profit	2,000	2,000	4,000	Nil
Tax rate	800	1,000	1,600	Nil
(A: 40%, B: 50%)				
Net profit	1,200	1,000	2,400	Nil

set carefully, it is possible to reallocate taxable income away from the highly taxed subsidiary to the subsidiary with the low tax rate. Table 14.1 provides an example by contrasting arm's length pricing with transfer pricing. An **arm's length price** is the price a buyer will pay for merchandise in a market under conditions of perfect competition. As seen in the table, it cost the subsidiary in Country A $8,000 for the goods it is selling to the subsidiary in Country B. Under an arm's length price the seller is adding $2,000 for profit and selling the goods for $10,000. In turn the second subsidiary is selling these goods for $12,000. Thus both subsidiaries are making a profit of $2,000. As also seen in the table, the tax rate in Country A is 40 per cent, whereas in Country B it is 50 per cent. So the first subsidiary will have a net profit of $1,200, whereas the second subsidiary will net $1,000.

Under a transfer price arrangement, however, the objective is to maximize profits in the low tax rate country and to minimize them in the high tax rate country. In this case, as seen in Table 14.1, the first subsidiary sells the goods for $12,000, and after paying 40 per cent tax on the $4,000 profit, it ends up with a net profit of $2,400. The second subsidiary sells the goods for $12,000 and makes no profit. However, thanks to the transfer pricing strategy, the multinational's overall profit is greater than it was with arm's length pricing ($2,400 versus $2,200).

One of the obvious benefits of transfer pricing is that it allows the multinational to reduce taxes. A second benefit is that the strategy lets the firm concentrate cash in specific locales such as with the first subsidiary. One of the problems with transfer pricing is that the financial statements do not accurately reflect subsidiary performance because the profit margins are manipulated. A second problem is that the strategy does not encourage efficient performance by the seller, whose primary objective is to unload merchandise on the other subsidiary at a profit as high as can be justified.

In recent years countries have been rewriting their tax codes to prevent arbitrary transfer pricing. In the United States, for example, the Internal Revenue Service (IRS) now asks multinationals to apply for an advanced determination ruling (ADR) before establishing a transfer pricing policy. After the firm submits the ADR request, the IRS will determine whether or not the policy is appropriate. The objective of the tax agency is to ensure that MNEs charge their overseas subsidiaries the same price for components and products as they charge independent third parties, thus effectively eliminating price manipulation for tax purposes.[1]

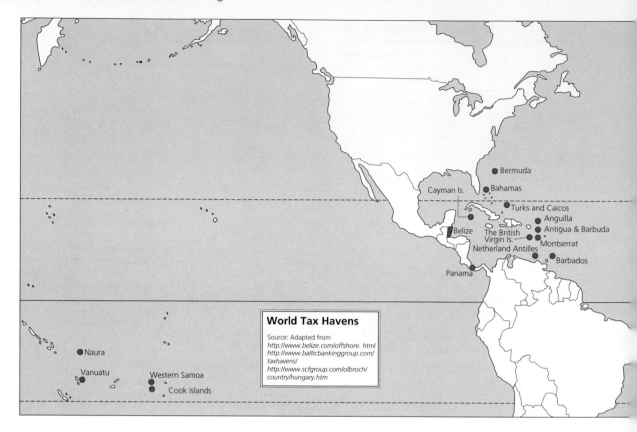

World Tax Havens

Source: Adapted from
http://www.belize.com/offshore. html
http://www.balticbankinggroup.com/
taxhavens/
http://www.scfgroup.com/olbroch/
country/hungary.htm

Table 14.2   Transfer pricing through tax havens

	Country A subsidiary	Country B subsidiary (tax haven)	Country C subsidiary
Sales	$8,000 exports	$12,000 exports	$12,000
Costs of sales	8,000	8,000	12,000
Profit	—	—	—
Tax rate	—	—	—
(A: 40%, B: 0%, C: 50%)			
Net profit	0	4,000	0

Tax havens   A second funds positioning technique is the use of **tax havens**, which are low tax countries that are hospitable to business (see accompanying map). This strategy is typically used in conjunction with transfer pricing and involves a subsidiary selling its output at a very low cost to a subsidiary in a tax haven which in turn sells the merchandise at a very high price to a third subsidiary. Table 14.2 provides an example, which is similar to that in Table 14.1, except that the sales are now routed through a subsidiary located in a tax haven, Country B, where no tax is paid at all.

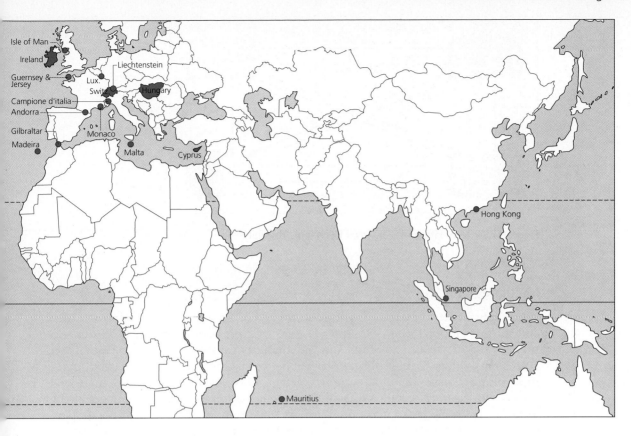

The result of the example in the table is a net profit of $4,000. This is greater than that illustrated in Table 14.1, where a simple case of transfer pricing was employed.

Fronting loans A **fronting loan** is a funds positioning strategy that involves having a third party manage the loan. For example, if a US multinational decided to set up operations in China, the MNE might be concerned with the political risk that accompanies such a decision. Is it possible that the government might expropriate the subsidiary's assets, including all the cash on hand? In an effort to protect their investments, the parent company could deposit funds with a major international bank that has strong ties to China and is on good terms with the government. In turn the subsidiary would apply for a loan with this bank and the multinational company's deposit would be given to the subsidiary in the form of a loan. It is highly unlikely that the Chinese government would expropriate the subsidiary and endanger the loan or its relationship with the international bank. Thus the MNE has successfully positioned its funds.

Funds positioning strategies are important in moving money around a multinational, as well as in helping the MNE to cope with political and legal roadblocks that stand in the way of such action. However, these strategies are always complemented by an internally operated netting process that controls the flow of funds and ensures that bills are paid promptly. This process is often collectively referred to as multilateral netting.

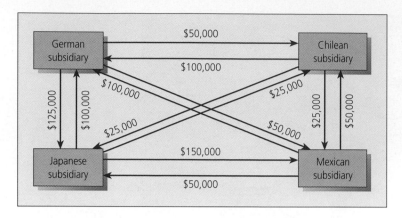

Figure 14.2   Multilateral dollar flows between subsidiaries

Multilateral netting

When subsidiaries do business with each other, each may owe money to the others and in turn be owed money by them. Figure 14.2 provides an example of four subsidiaries that have both amounts due and amounts payable from each of the others. Over time, of course, these obligations will be resolved by the individual subsidiaries. In an effort to make the process more efficient, however, many multinationals have now set up clearing accounts in a certain location and assigned the manager at this location the authority to make the transfers that are necessary to pay intracompany subsidiary obligations. This process of **multilateral netting**, which involves a determination of the net amount of money owed to subsidiaries through multilateral transactions, begins with a computation of the amounts owed to each. Table 14.3, which has been constructed based on the information in Figure 14.2, shows these net positions. Based on this information, those that owe money are required to transfer it to a centralized clearing account (see Figure 14.3), whereas those that are owed money are paid from this central account.

The clearing account manager is responsible for seeing that this process occurs quickly and correctly. Typically, this individual will receive monthly transaction information from all the subsidiaries and will use these data to determine the net position of each unit. The manager will then see that the necessary transfers are made. These transfers usually take place in the currency of the payer, so the German subsidiary will pay its obligation in DMs, whereas the Mexican subsidiary will pay in pesos. The process will be handled by the clearing account manager's staff.

Table 14.3   Net cash positions of subsidiaries

Subsidiary	Total receivables	Total payables	Net positions
German	$300,000	$225,000	$75,000
Chilean	125,000	150,000	−25,000
Japanese	200,000	275,000	−75,000
Mexican	225,000	200,000	25,000

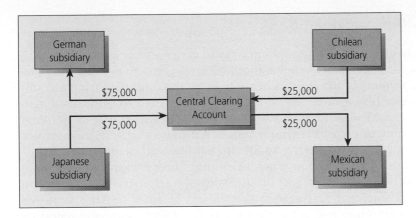

Figure 14.3 Centralized netting process in action

There are a number of reasons that multilateral netting has become popular. One advantage is that it helps the parent company to ensure that financial interactions between the units are quickly brought to completion. If bills are allowed to be outstanding for months at a time, it can result in the other units not wanting to do business with slow-paying subsidiaries. Netting helps to reduce the likelihood of such problems. A second advantage is that those units which are owed money have faster access to their funds. A third advantage is that the parent company knows which subsidiaries are amassing large amounts of cash and can tap these sources if necessary to support activities in other locales. A fourth advantage is that the cost of converting foreign exchange is minimized because the central clearing account manager can convert large amounts at the same time.

There are also some problems associated with multilateral netting. One is that many governments place controls on these operations by allowing them only for trade transactions. So the MNE's ability to use netting for moving funds can be limited. A second problem is that in other cases governments have required that payment for imports be delayed until these goods clear customs, thus slowing down the netting process by as much as 60 to 90 days. A third is that of getting local subsidiary managers to cooperate and keep the central clearing account manager fully apprised of all transactions affecting this process. Sometimes there is a reluctance to cooperate on the part of those managers whose cash outflows are substantially larger than their inflows. Under a netting process they can no longer delay payments for three or four months while working to reverse the flow and to pay their bills out of current earnings.

Multilateral netting can help an MNE to ensure that intersubsidiary accounts are balanced, and the process is extremely useful in assisting the parent company in managing global cash flows. However, there is an inherent problem in this process that requires special attention and which netting cannot resolve: foreign exchange risk as typified by the fluctuating value of international currencies. This risk is particularly important when MNEs do business with buyers who are paying in weak currencies. In dealing with this dilemma, MNEs often formulate a foreign exchange risk management strategy.

FOREIGN EXCHANGE RISK MANAGEMENT

There are a number of ways that multinationals try to manage their foreign exchange risk. For example, if the company believes that Mexico is going to devalue the peso, it will reduce the amount of those pesos being held by the central clearing account by using them to pay bills. Conversely, if the peso is forecasted to gain in strength against the dollar, the MNE will hold on to those pesos but will reduce its holdings of dollars. This is only one simple example, but it illustrates that foreign exchange risk strategies are important to effective multinational financial management.

A number of areas merit attention when examining foreign exchange risk management. One is inflation and its impact on the value of foreign exchange. A second is the types of exposure that exchange rates create. A third is hedging strategies that can be used to minimize risk. A fourth is the types of forecasting and reporting systems that must be developed in order to plan and control company response. The following sections examine each of these four areas.

Inflation

Every nation faces varying degrees of annual inflation. On the positive side, inflation can make financial liabilities attractive. For example, if General Electric (GE) were to buy an office building in Monterrey, Mexico, for 3 million pesos and the bill is due in three annual installments, inflation can influence the overall value of the deal. Among other things, if inflation were to run at 10 per cent annually, the building would be worth a great deal more than 3 million pesos at the end of this three-year period. So inflation encourages buyers to purchase now while prices are lower. On the other hand, inflation affects interest rates (see the international Fisher effect discussed in Chapter 7) by driving up the cost of loans. Inflation also affects the value of local currency in the international marketplace. So there is a downside to inflation. (See the box "International Business Strategy in Action: Buying a Big Mac.")

When MNEs do business in a country that is facing rapid inflation, there are a number of financial strategies that they often use. These include (1) rapid depreciation of fixed equipment so as to recover the value of these assets as quickly as possible; (2) slower payment of outstanding accounts to sellers who are taking payment in local currency – since the value of this currency is declining and the longer payment is postponed, the better it is for the subsidiary; (3) greater emphasis on collecting current receivables since this currency is losing value each month; (4) holding minimum amounts of local currency while transferring the rest of these funds into more stable or appreciating currencies; and (5) looking for other sources of capital since local borrowers are going to be increasing the interest rate in order to protect their real return on investment. Multinationals will also consider raising their prices so as to protect their profitability in the face of inflation.

Addressing exchange rate fluctuations

Multinationals will also want to reduce their exposure to exchange rate fluctuations. The most common forms of exposure are translation, transaction, and economic.

Translation exposure **Translation** is the process of restating foreign financial statements in the currency of the parent company. For example, PepsiCo will translate

INTERNATIONAL BUSINESS STRATEGY IN ACTION

Buying a Big Mac

One of the most interesting ways of determining whether a subsidiary's value is affected by inflation is to compare the value of the local currency and that in the home country. For example, as the Swiss franc strengthens against the dollar, US multinationals with operations in Switzerland will benefit from the profits generated from a greatly enhanced dollar value of that unit.

Another interesting way of gauging these values is to examine the purchasing power parity (PPP) of the overseas currency and the US dollar by comparing the cost of food in the two countries. Some international analysts also point out that this is a good way of determining whether a currency is undervalued or overvalued. For example, if a Big Mac costs $2.43 in the United States and 294 yen in Japan, the official exchange rate should be 121 yen to the dollar (294/2.43), assuming that the Big Mac is an accurate form of PPP comparison. If the official exchange is less than 121 to the dollar, then the dollar is undervalued. Conversely, if the exchange rate is more than 121 to the dollar, the US currency is overvalued. This same logic

can be applied throughout the world, thus obtaining some insights into how closely the purchasing power of the dollar comes to the actual exchange rate. The table below provides some recent information on this subject.

As seen from the table, the dollar is undervalued in many countries, including most of the euro area. From the viewpoint of global macroeconomic stability the United States would want these countries to revalue their currency, although this would negatively affect the ability of US firms to sell abroad. On the other hand, East Asia's currencies are undervalued against the dollar mainly as a result of the Asian crises. This makes East Asian products cheaper in the international markets. Additionally, there are a number of reasons that PPP prices are higher or lower than expected, including local taxes, transportation costs, property costs, and, as in the case of Germany and Japan, typically high retail markups. However, the Big Mac example does provide some interesting insights regarding the purchasing power of the local currency.

The Hamburger Standard

| Country | Big Mac prices | | Implied PPP* of the dollar | Actual $ exchange rate 30/03/99 | Under (–)/over (+) valuation against the dollar, % |
	in local currency	in dollars			
United States[†]	$2.43	2.43	–	–	–
Argentina	Peso 2.50	2.50	1.03	1.00	+3
Australia	A$ 2.65	1.66	1.09	1.59	–32
Brazil	Real 2.95	1.71	1.21	1.73	–30
Britain	Pound 1.90	3.07	1.28[‡]	1.61[‡]	+26
Canada	C$ 2.99	1.98	1.23	1.51	–19
Chile	Peso 1.25	2.60	518	484	+7
China	Yuan 9.90	1.20	4.07	8.28	–51
Denmark	DKr 24.75	3.58	10.19	6.91	+47
Euro area	Euro 2.52	2.71	0.97[§]	1.08[§]	+11
France	FFr 8.50	2.87	7.20	6.10	+18
Germany	DM 4.95	2.72	2.04	1.82	+12

▶

(cont'd)

Country	Big Mac prices		Implied PPP* of the dollar	Actual $ exchange rate 30/03/99	Under (−)/over (+) valuation against the dollar, %
	in local currency	in dollars			
United States†	$2.43	2.43	–	–	–
Italy	Lire 4,500	2.50	1,852	1,799	+3
Netherlands	Fl 5.45	2.66	2.24	2.05	+10
Spain	Pta 375	2.43	154	155	0
Hong Kong	HK$ 10.2	1.32	4.20	7.75	−46
Hungary	Forint 299	1.26	123	237	−48
Indonesia	Rupiah 14,500	1.66	5,967	8,725	−32
Israel	Shekel 13.9	3.44	5.72	4.04	+42
Japan	Yen 294	2.44	121	120	0
Malaysia	M$ 4.52	1.19	1.86	3.80	−51
Mexico	Peso 19.9	2.09	8.19	9.54	−14
New Zealand	NZ $ 3.40	1.82	1.40	1.87	−25
Poland	Zloty 5.50	1.38	2.26	3.98	−43
Russia	Ruble 33.5	1.35	13.79	24.7	−44
Singapore	S$ 3.20	1.85	1.32	1.73	−24
South Africa	Rand 8.60	1.38	3.54	6.22	−43
South Korea	Won 3,000	2.46	1,235	1,218	+1
Sweden	SKr 24.0	2.88	9.88	8.32	+19
Switzerland	SFr 5.90	3.97	2.43	1.48	+64
Taiwan	NT$ 70.0	2.11	28.8	33.2	−13
Thailand	Baht 52.0	1.38	21.4	37.6	−43

* Purchasing-power parity: local price divided by price in United States.

† Average of New York, Chicago, San Francisco and Atlanta.

‡ Dollars per pound.

§ Dollars per euro.

Source: McDonald's. Adapted from *The Economist*, April 3, 1999.

Source: Adapted from "Big MacCurrencies," *The Economist*, April 18, 1992, p. 81; "Big MacCurrencies," *The Economist*, April 17, 1993, p. 79; "Big MacCurrencies" *The Economist*, April 11, 1998; Kevin Kelly, Neil Gross, and James B. Treece, "Besting Japan," *Business Week*, June 7, 1993, pp. 26–28; "Currency Markets," *New York Times*, December 28, 1993; "The Big Mac Index Goes East," *The Economist*, May 26, 1998; "Big MacCurrencies," *The Economist*, April 3, 1999, p. 90; "Ten Years of the Big Mac Index," *The Economist* (only on the web: http://www.economist.com/editorial/freeforall/focus/bigmac_webonly.html).

the balance sheets and income statements of its subsidiaries into dollars. In this way management and the stockholders can see how each unit is doing. The company will also combine the major financial statements of subsidiaries into composite statements for the parent firm through a process known as **consolidation**. The procedures that US firms follow in this process are found in Financial Accounting Standards Board (FASB) Statement No. 52, which deals with foreign currency translation. Statement

52 requires that sales be recorded at the spot exchange rate that is in effect on the date of the transaction. Receivables and payables are recorded at subsequent balance sheet dates at the spot exchange rate on those dates. Any foreign exchange gains and losses that arise from these transactions are then reflected directly on the income statement.

Translation exposure is the foreign exchange risk that a firm faces when translating foreign currency financial statements into the reporting currency of the parent company. A good example of this exposure for a US MNE is when the currency of a local country weakens in relation to the dollar. For example, if the Chilean peso declined by 10 per cent against the dollar, the value of the Chilean subsidiary's peso account at the local bank would also decline when translated into dollars in the consolidation process. If the company had the equivalent of $100,000 (US) on deposit, this account would now be worth $90,000 in translation and consolidation. Of course, this decline would not affect the number of pesos on deposit, and the local purchasing power of these pesos, at least in the short run, would remain the same. However, the decline would negatively affect the subsidiary's ability to purchase imports from countries with strong currencies since it would now take more pesos than before to buy these goods.

Transaction exposure **Transaction exposure** is the risk that a firm faces when paying bills or collecting receivables in the face of changing exchange rates. For example, if a US retailer were to purchase 10,000 shirts from a Mexican manufacturer for $90,000 and agree to pay the bill in 90 days in pesos (assuming a current exchange rate of 10 pesos to the dollar), the transaction exposure would be the risk that the peso would strengthen against the dollar. If the US firm were to pay the bill immediately, it would remit 900,000 pesos to the manufacturer. If it waits until the end of 90 days and the exchange rate is now 8.9 pesos to the dollar, the company would still pay 900,000 pesos but the cost in dollars is $101,235.90 (900,000/8.9), higher than it was initially. On the other hand, if a US manufacturer had sold goods to a Mexican firm and payment was due in pesos, the increasing value of the peso would result in a gain to the US company. For example, if the multinational had sold household appliances valued at 7 million pesos, the original sale would have generated $700,000 (7,000,000/10), but by the time the Mexican firm remitted the pesos, the company would have received $786,516.85 (7,000,000/8.9) for an additional gain of $86,516.85. So in international sales and purchases there is transaction exposure on the part of both the buyer and the seller.

Economic exposure **Economic exposure** is the foreign exchange risk involved in pricing products, sourcing parts, or locating investments in order to develop a competitive position. Economic exposure covers a wide gamut of risk. In the case of pricing products, when the currency of a foreign buyer changes in relation to that of the seller, the latter will have to decide how to deal with the accompanying risk. For example, if the Japanese yen strengthens against the dollar, should a US firm that is selling to a Japanese supplier lower its price? If all sales are in yen, the US firm will gain more dollars by leaving the price alone. On the other hand, if the US company lowers the price, may that stimulate more demand from the buyer? Conversely, if the yen weakens against the dollar, should the US seller hold the price line or raise it to ensure dollar sales and profit margins? The fluctuating yen/dollar relationship creates a risk for the US firm.

A related decision deals with subsidiary assets. If the value of the local currency strengthens, the sale of inventory will generate larger dollar profits. However, would it be wiser to lower price, to take less profit per item, but to generate more demand? Similarly, would it be wise now to sell fixed assets such as buildings or factories and then to lease them back from the purchaser? Some US firms in Tokyo found that by the early 1990s the land and buildings that they had bought years before were now worth hundreds of times their original purchase price. Believing that the local real estate market was as high as it was going to go and feeling that it would be more advisable to sell the properties and rent them back, these firms sold their office buildings and made tremendous profits. The ensuing decline of Tokyo real estate prices showed that these firms had made very wise decisions.[2]

Another example of economic exposure is the risk that companies take when selling to a country with a weakening currency. In this case many MNEs have sought to increase their own production efficiency, lower their costs, and continue to generate acceptable profit.[3] Firms such as Honda, Nissan, and BMW have complemented this strategy by setting up operations in the United States, their largest international market.[4] In the process the firms have reduced their economic exposure.

As seen here, there are a variety of ways that MNEs deal with exchange rate changes. Another way, used particularly by multinationals that conduct a large amount of business in the international arena, is hedging strategies.

ACTIVE LEARNING CHECK

Review your answer to Active Learning Case question 2 and make any changes you like. Then compare your answer to the one below.

2. If the two carriers complete their merger and the US dollar then weakens against the British pound, how will this affect the financial statements of the company?

This will depend on whether the two carriers continue to issue separate financial statements. If they do, USAir's financials will be affected only by the amount of sterling that it has on hand. Otherwise there will be no effect, since changes in the pound do not affect the cost to USAir of doing business in the United States. In the case of BA the accounts payable that are due in dollars will negatively affect the airline's financials. If the two carriers combine their statements into one, the overall effect will be a result of how these transactions net out. This would be determined based on the rules in FASB Statement No. 52.

Hedging strategies

A **hedge** is a form of protection against an adverse movement of an exchange rate. If a multinational would suffer a large financial loss if the dollar were to weaken against the yen, the company would likely hedge its position to ensure that if the dollar did weaken, the firm would not suffer a major loss. A hedge, therefore, is a form of insurance that helps to minimize the risk of loss. The following sections examine some of the most common forms of hedging.

Operating financial strategies   Operating financial strategies are designed to minimize the effect of changing exchange rates on the local unit's profitability. In an economy suffering from severe inflation and whose currency is expected to depreciate, for example, local subsidiaries will limit credit sales and will try to collect their receivables as quickly as possible because prices are constantly rising and eroding the purchasing power of these funds. Conversely, these companies will delay paying obligations that are denominated in local currency because it is cheaper to do so, but they will promptly pay all bills that are denominated in strong currencies. At the same time subsidiaries will consider buying fixed assets that are likely to benefit from inflation.

Closely linked to the above discussion is the use of lead and lag strategies, which are used to protect cash flows. A **lead strategy** calls for collecting foreign currency receivables before they are due if the currency is expected to strengthen and paying foreign currency payables before they are due if the currency is expected to strengthen. The logic behind a lead strategy is obvious: the company wants to obtain a currency before its value increases and to pay promptly bills due in a currency that is going to strengthen. A **lag strategy** calls for a company to delay receiving foreign currency payments if the currency is expected to strengthen and to delay paying foreign currency payables when this currency is expected to weaken. The logic is the reverse of that used with a lead strategy.

Inventory decisions will be based on the subsidiary manager's reading of the situation. If inflation is rapidly driving up prices, the subsidiary will minimize the amount being carried while profiting from the price increases. If inventory is being imported, the manager will try to stock up on these goods before the local currency weakens. If local currency is strengthening, however, the manager will spread out the purchases so that the goods being bought can be purchased with a stronger currency. Some multinationals supplement these inventory and selling strategies by following this rule: make purchases in a weak currency and sales in a strong currency.

Debt strategies will also be handled on a contingency basis. Although some firms prefer to borrow as much as possible from local sources and to minimize their reliance on other sources, this strategy has shortcomings. For example, during inflationary periods the cost of local borrowing will be very high. Similarly, the use of weak local currency limits the firm's ability to purchase from countries with strong currencies. Because a number of factors need to be carefully weighed, most MNEs make these decisions on a case-by-case basis.

Forward exchange contracts   A **forward exchange contract** is a legally binding agreement between a firm and a bank that calls for the delivery of foreign currency at a specific exchange rate on a predetermined future date. The purpose of such a contract is to minimize the risk associated with foreign exchange fluctuations. A case example would be a US supplier that sells equipment to a Japanese firm for 50 million yen with payment due in 90 days. If the spot exchange rate is 104 yen to the dollar, the value of the contract is $480,769.23 (50,000,000/104). However, what will the exchange rate be in 90 days? If the US firm does not want to take a chance that the yen will strengthen, it will purchase a forward contract from the bank for, say, 106 yen to the dollar. So the supplier is willing to take a guaranteed $471,698.11 (50,000,000/106) in 90 days in exchange for the 50 million yen that the Japanese are paying. In the interim, if the value of the yen were to weaken and go above 106 yen per dollar, the company will have saved money. If the price remains at 104 yen per dollar, the company gives up $9,701.12 ($480,769.23 minus $471,698.11) for the guarantee. Of course, if the yen were to strengthen to 100 per dollar by the end of the 90 days, the forward exchange contract would have cost the firm a total of $28,301.89 ($500,000 minus $471,698.11) and the company would have been better off accepting the risk. On the positive side, forward exchange contracts provide safety against the decline of the buyer's currency. On the negative side, these contracts can sometimes prove costly.

Currency options   A **currency option** is an instrument that gives the purchaser the right to buy or sell a specific amount of foreign currency at a predetermined rate within a specified time period. Currency options are more flexible than forward exchange contracts because the buyer does not have to exercise the option. Using the above example, the seller wants to protect the value of the 50 million Japanese yen. This could be done by purchasing an option to deliver 50 million yen for dollars at a predetermined exchange rate of, say, 104 yen per dollar in 90 days. The company would have to pay an option cost (assume it is $25,000) for this right, but then the currency's value would be protected. No matter what happens to the exchange rate between the dollar and the yen, the company can turn the 50 million yen over to the person who sold the option and the individual must give the firm $480,769.23 (50,000,000/104). Of course, the company will exercise this option *only* if the value of the yen in 90 days is less than this amount. If the yen were to increase in value to 102 per dollar, the currency would be worth $490,196.07 (50,000,000/102) and the firm would not exercise its option. On the other hand, if the yen declined in value to 106 per dollar, the 50 million yen would be worth only $471,698.11 (50,000,000/106) and the firm *would* exercise its option. Regardless of what happens to the yen per dollar exchange rate, however, the company must deduct $25,000 from its revenues because this is the price for the option. Many firms feel that this is a reasonable price to pay in order to ensure that they will not suffer the ill effects of a rapidly declining yen.

Developing forecasting and reporting systems

The management of foreign exchange risk can be both complex and cumbersome. A multinational with 20 subsidiaries can present a formidable challenge to the parent company because so many foreign exchange risk decisions need to be made and monitored. However, there are a number of steps that MNEs typically take in creating the necessary system for managing these decisions. They may:

1. Decide the types and degrees of economic exposure that the company is willing to accept.
2. Develop the necessary expertise (in-house personnel and/or outside economists or consultants) for monitoring exchange rates and for forecasting those rates that are applicable to the identified exposures.
3. Construct a reporting system that allows the firm to identify exposed accounts, to measure this exposure, and to feed back information on what the firm is doing and the status of these decisions.
4. Include all MNE units in this reporting system so that each better understands the risks it is assuming and is aware of the actions that must be taken to deal with these risks.

5. Keep senior-level management fully apprised of what is going on in each area of responsibility so that every regional or divisional manager is able periodically to revise the exposure risk and to make those strategy changes that will help more effectively to manage the process.

As firms begin to implement these five steps, they are better able to deal with the management of foreign exchange risk. Another financial area that receives considerable attention is capital expenditure analysis and capital budgeting.

ACTIVE LEARNING CHECK

Review your answer to Active Learning Case question 3 and make any changes you like. Then compare your answer to the one below.

3. If BA believed that the British pound was going to appreciate in relation to the German mark, how could the company use a lead and lag strategy to its advantage?

If BA believed that the pound was going to get stronger against the mark, and if it were owed marks, the firm would try to collect them immediately before their value declined. At the same time BA would delay payment of those obligations that were fixed in marks, for it would be getting more marks per pound after the appreciation, thus making it easier to pay those bills. The firm would lead collections and lag payables.

CAPITAL EXPENDITURE ANALYSIS AND CAPITAL BUDGETING

Capital expenditures are major projects in which the costs are to be allocated over a number of years. Examples include major acquisitions, the building of new plants, and the refurbishing of existing equipment. Because the firm has to live with the results of these decisions for a long period of time, mathematical techniques of analysis are often used, including discounted cash flow techniques such as net present value (NPV) and internal rate of return. Traditional methods such as payback period and accounting rate of return are also employed, either as a first-cut approximation technique or to provide additional information. In fact, the basic techniques that are appropriate to domestic analysis are often applied to capital expenditure analysis in multinationals as well as to foreign projects in general.

In contrast to domestic projects, however, one basic question must be answered: who should conduct the analysis, the parent or the foreign subsidiary? Typically, the initial analysis is done at the subsidiary or branch level and then passed up to the head office for modification and/or approval. For example, two subsidiaries may both want to build a new tire plant and sell to the same market. Without coordination, they would compete against each other and the expected profits would not materialize. So the parent corporation will make a decision that benefits the entire organization. In this latter role the parent may have to turn down a positive NPV project from one subsidiary in favor of a higher NPV project from another subsidiary. The same process applies in reverse to plant closures; the shutdown will be at the plant with the largest negative NPV. Similarly, factories or holdings that do not generate sufficient profit may be sold.[5]

Use of net present value

The parent company will review expenditure proposals because it has the necessary overall information to make these decisions. Moreover, such expenditure decisions will often be different from those of the subsidiary because the latter may use faulty valuation techniques or fail to address adequately the impact of political risk. In explaining why these differences occur, we must first review the basic NPV criterion. This criterion separates the financing and operating parts of the problem by discounting operating cash flows by a weighted average cost of capital that embodies the financing decision. The NPV equation is

$$NPV = \sum_{t=0}^{T} \frac{I_t + C_t}{(1 + K_A)^t} \qquad \text{(Eq. 14.1)}$$

where

$$K_A = k_e \frac{S}{V} + k_d(1 - t_x)\frac{D}{V} \qquad \text{(Eq. 14.2)}$$

The definitions of the terms are:

I_t = investment cash outlays in year t
C_t = cash inflows in year t
T = terminal date or end of project
K_A = weighted average cost of capital
k_e = cost of equity capital
k_d = cost of debt financing
t_x = tax rate
D/V, S/V = debt and equity ratios, respectively
NPV = incremental net present value for the project

In examining what determines the NPV, we must realize that disagreement between parent and subsidiary can arise because of the discount rate K_A, investment cost, and annual cash flows. Political risk can also affect all values. For example, the risk of foreign currency controls can cause some of the future cash flows to be largely ignored by the parent. From the parent's perspective, if funds can no longer be remitted, their value is substantially reduced since they are not available for dividend payments or for reinvestment elsewhere. Conversely, once foreign exchange controls are in place, the parent will often treat blocked funds as being less valuable. From the parent's perspective, the cost of future investments in the country, financed by these blocked funds, is reduced. In both cases the subsidiary is not directly concerned with the problem of foreign exchange controls, and it will discount all cash flows that are incremental from its own perspective.

Similarly, political risk may cause the parent to increase the discount rate or required return to reflect that risk. However, if the subsidiary does not agree with that perception, it will not increase the discount rate, so its calculation of the present value of the cash inflows and NPV will be higher. Moreover, if foreign exchange controls are enforced, the local capital markets can be isolated from the international capital market. From the subsidiary's perspective, the result may be lower local real interest rates, which make local investment opportunities seem attractive. However, the parent, looking at global opportunities, may decide that it will make more sense to draw capital out of the country for reinvestment elsewhere.

Another reason that parent and local NPVs may differ is faulty application of the NPV framework. The most common errors are in incorrectly choosing t_x and K_A. The tax rate t_x is relevant in two places, the incremental tax that results from the incremental profits and the incremental tax shield that results from debt financing. Here, the errors usually come from a failure to determine the incremental tax rate. From the subsidiary's perspective the tax rate is the extra tax that it pays locally. However, the parent must also consider any incremental tax that it will pay once dividends are remitted.

In determining the discount rate K_A, several problems emerge. First, it is common that discount rates differ by several percentage points. The reason is obvious: inflation differs across different countries, and thus the inflationary premium built into the discount rate will differ. What the firm can never do is to use a discount rate from one country to evaluate cash flows denominated in another currency. The correct procedure is to calculate the real discount rate and then to "gross it up" for the inflationary expectations of the relevant country.

Additionally, debt ratios differ across subsidiaries, and the weights in Equation 14.2 may alter the cost of capital. This will inevitably occur if the multinational maximizes the use of debt financing in a country with subsidized borrowing rates. However, the debt ratio of that country is then not appropriate for determining the cost of capital since the excess debt can be carried only because that subsidiary is part of a multinational. Similarly, it is a mistake to use the local real cost of debt to determine the cost of capital. In both these examples, if the MNE uses local debt norms and local debt costs, it is negating the advantage of being a multinational. That advantage is the ability to raise debt internally where it is the cheapest. As a result, in a country with a high debt cost the firm may have very little debt, whereas in a country with subsidized interest costs it may have a large amount of debt. In both cases there is no effect on the overall cost of funds to the multinational. Hence local debt norms and interest costs will be ignored unless local regulations restrict the use of debt funds to projects within that country. In this instance, if the firm accepts a local project, it can also raise more subsidized foreign debt. If the money cannot be removed from the country by transfer pricing or whatever, then its cost is relevant in Equation 14.2.

In general, the financing options open to a multinational are greater than those of a domestic firm. The Eurobond market and foreign bond markets give the multinational the ability to raise funds where the cost is the cheapest. Moreover, the extensive national network of the MNEs enables them to take advantage of local incentive programs. These include regional investment incentives, tax holidays for new investments, export insurance, and loan guarantees. The result is a lower overall cost. However, in the analysis of any particular project the discount rate should reflect only the subsidized rates that would not be available unless the project was undertaken. The latter application errors are frequently made and can serve to drive a wedge between the parent and the subsidiary, often resulting in considerable acrimony between the respective staffs.[6]

Institutional features

Thus far the focus has been on the technical question of how to evaluate capital expenditures. However, there are two institutional factors that warrant attention: government subsidies and controls and political risk insurance.

Government subsidies and controls   Government intervention can affect the profitability of a project or its financing. For example, in considering foreign investments, countries such as Australia and Canada have **foreign investment review agencies**, which review these investments to ensure that they benefit the local economy. As a result, foreign investment is often contingent on factors such as local employment quotas, local sourcing of components, the transfer of technology, and a degree of local ownership. This intervention can obviously complicate capital expenditure analysis. Frequently the result is to forecast specific, quantitative outcomes. For example, if technology is locally licensed, what is the possible impact of its being leaked to different countries? If the MNE has to train local middle management and to sell shares locally, how does this affect the probability of forcible divestiture at some future date? In many cases the result of local content regulations is to expropriate all the advantages possessed by the multinational. One of the particular problems here is local ownership requirements. The parent's viewpoint is dominant on the assumption that the objective of the firm is to maximize its market value, which is owned by shareholders in the home country. However, once joint ventures and significant minority shareholdings are traded locally, this solution breaks down. The problem now becomes whose market value should be maximized. The result is that while minority ownership reduces the political risk of expropriation, it restricts the multinational's freedom of action. It is, therefore, not surprising that where political risk is lowered, minority shareholders get bought out. For example, Ford acquired its British minority shareholdings in 1961, and Shell bought out its minority US shareholdings in 1984.

However, government regulation is not all bad. Outside North America the interventionist approach of most governments creates unique opportunities for the MNE. For example, most countries provide concessionary financing that is contingent on the use of certain local resources. The **British Export Credits Guarantee Department** has some of the lowest cost money for export financing as long as the borrower uses British equipment. By structuring an investment to use British equipment, a multinational might be able to borrow $10 million at 3 per cent interest instead of at a market rate of, say, 9 per cent. In effect, this subsidized loan represents a gift by the British taxpayers. This value has to be factored into the analysis. The inclusion of subsidies also occurs in domestic capital expenditure analysis, for example with the proliferation of small business financing programs. However, in an international project, rather than being unusual, it is rare *not* to determine the value or cost of a particular government program. Recently government regulation of MNEs has been falling, leading to more cross-listings on the world stock exchange.

Political risk insurance   Political risk insurance is available in most countries for exports and foreign direct investment. In the United States, the **Overseas Private Investment Corporation (OPIC)** was established in January 1971 to provide insurance for US foreign investment against blocked funds, expropriation and war, and revolution and insurrection. The terms of political risk insurance are similar across different countries. Usually there is approval by the host government of the investment, some type of bilateral agreement on foreign investment, and coverage limited to some multiple of the initial investment for up to 20 years For specific types of risk this coverage can be insured separately. In the United States, it is estimated that about 70 per cent of foreign investment in less developed countries is insured through OPIC.

Political risk insurance creates another option that is available for analysis. In effect, the company has to decide the incremental value of this insurance. This is typically done by considering how the MNE can restructure the foreign investment, such as by fronting loans or long-term contracts at high transfer prices as alternatives to political risk insurance. The ultimate decision will reflect the optimum structuring of the proposal under analysis.

ACTIVE LEARNING CHECK

Review your answer to Active Learning Case question 4 and make any changes you like. Then compare your answer to the one below.

4. How great is the political risk that BA faces in the United States? Explain.

The company certainly faces some risk in that there is growing pressure not to allow the merger. On the other hand, if this opposition is based on gaining a *quid pro quo* arrangement in which US carriers are given broader access to the European market, then the risk is quite small. The concern that is being evinced is merely a smokescreen by the US airlines for gaining a better bargaining position.

STRATEGIC INTERNATIONAL FINANCE

There are a number of ways that MNEs apply the international financial concepts that have been discussed in this chapter. One way is by employing a geocentric approach that helps to coordinate subsidiary operations and ensures that there is a uniform, harmonious strategy.[7] This approach is particularly evident in the way that some multinationals are now closing local operations in favor of overseas production and are using joint ventures and other partnership arrangements to reduce their financial risk.[8] Another approach is the manner in which financial management analysis is used in choosing sites for overseas operations. This is particularly true for foreign firms with strong currencies.

Establishing overseas operations

Because the United States is a major market for many international firms, foreign MNEs have been particularly concerned about the value of the US dollar. For example, when Ford Motor acquired Volvo's automotive business, the Swedish firm insisted on receiving the purchase price in krona.[9] This concern has also resulted in foreign firms setting up operations in the US in order to offset the competitive impact associated with having a currency that is very strong *vis-à-vis* the American dollar. For example, BMW built an auto production facility in South Carolina because it found it was 20 per cent less costly to produce cars here than to bring them in from Germany.[10] Other companies have made acquisitions in the US market in order to protect their overall profitability. For example, BASF has acquired a Mobil plastic unit for $330 million; Benckiser purchased Coty, the fragrance maker, from Pfizer for $440 million; Siemens spent $1.2 billion to purchase ROLM, a manufacturer of telecommunications equipment, from IBM, and Daimler-Benz bought Chrysler for almost $40 billion.[11]

At the same time US firms are continuing to move abroad, especially since many Asian currencies are at a low ebb and purchase prices have fallen. General Motors, for example, is now producing light trucks in China, has 16 ventures there related to producing auto components, and has opened a Buick plant in Shanghai. As of the end of 1998 the company was assembling close to 500,000 cars annually, most of which were small sedans or subcompacts.[12] At the same time Atlantic Richfield and Phillips China have invested in ventures for drilling for methane gas, IBM is expanding its investment there in the computer business, Telluride International Energy is building a power plant, and Lucent Technologies has earmarked millions of dollars to expand its Internet backbone in the country.[13]

European and US firms are not alone in their efforts to establish overseas operations. Pacific-based MNEs are also realizing the benefits of going local, and this group is not limited to automakers. South Korean firms such as Daewoo, Goldstar, and Samsung are now using direct investment and joint ventures to help open markets in Europe and the United States. High labor costs, runaway interest rates, and low-cost competition are battering these firms at home, and local content laws have been holding down market acceptance abroad. In an effort to circumvent these problems, Daewoo Electronics is now building a $150 million integrated color television plant in France. These units will be designed in France and most of the components will be European-made. Goldstar is using alliances to widen its market share, as seen by its collaboration with Gepi of Germany and Iberna of Italy to produce refrigerators for the European market. Goldstar designs the units in its Ireland facility, Gepi supplies the components, and Iberna assembles the finished products. Samsung has purchased Werk für Fernsehelektronik, a former East German picture tube maker, and is spending $120 million to upgrade the plant, which will be capable of turning out 1.2 million television sets annually. The company is also negotiating to buy an even larger German television maker, RFT, and has moved its Portuguese and Spanish color plants to England and its videocassette recorder plant from England to Spain in order to lower operational costs, to improve quality, and to increase employment.[14]

Reducing financial risk

Although some of the above strategies are useful in reducing risk, there are other tactics that are also particularly useful, including mergers, acquisitions,[15] joint ventures for new, high-risk projects, partnering with established MNEs in order to gain international market share, and cutting operating costs through new plant design.[16]

Alliances   In recent years an increasing number of MNEs have been joining together to share the costs of high-tech projects. This sharing involves not only research and development expenses, but also the costs of manufacturing and selling the finished products. The box "International Business Strategy in Action: Lufthansa and Boeing" describes a recent example.

A similar example is provided by Microsoft which has entered into an alliance with Sony to link personal computers and consumer electronics devices, thus moving closer together on technology standards for digital television and other consumer products. The two firms have endorsed a technology that can connect videocassette recorders, camcorders, personal computers, and other devices.[17] Another example is GM and Isuzu which are now extending their alliance in advanced vehicle technologies such as electric vehicles and fuel cells.[18] A third example is Kita Kyushu Coca-Cola Bottling

INTERNATIONAL BUSINESS STRATEGY IN ACTION

Lufthansa and Boeing

MNEs can often be exposed to high levels of risk that arise from exchange rate fluctuations. A classic case emerged when Lufthansa (the Germany airline) signed a contract to purchase aircraft from Boeing (US) for the amount of $3 billion. At that time the US dollar was steadily appreciating against the deutschmark. Managers at Lufthansa realized that if the US dollar continued to appreciate, the value of the purchase could skyrocket in their own currency. However, some analysts believed that the US dollar was bound to decrease, which would gradually reduce the total payments due to Boeing.

Lufthansa decided to hedge its exchange risk using a forward contract on $1.5 billion. If the US dollar continued to appreciate, the total price of the purchase would increase but the company would only be faced with the increase accruing from the $1.5 billion it did not hedge. If, on the other hand, the US dollar

depreciated, the company would gain on the 1.5 billion it let fluctuate but lose on the other half. The result was that when the dollar began to depreciate the company was worse off than had it not hedged at all. This of course was impossible to forecast prior to the events unfolding.

Lufthansa had other alternatives to protect itself from risk. It could have opted to use options that would have given it the choice of taking a forward contract, but not forced it to. The main reason why options are not used often by companies is because they are more expensive than forward contracts. This occurs since the options transfer the risk to the financial institution that issues them. Finally, Lufthansa and Boeing could have come up with a risk-sharing agreement. If the exchange rate fluctuated outside a specified range, both companies would have shared the difference.

Sources: Adapted from *http://www.lufthansa-usa.com*; "A Survey of Corporate Risk Management: Too Hot to Handle?" *The Economist*, February 10, 1996, p. 70; "Lost in a Maze of Hedges," *The Economist*, October 3, 1992, p. 84.

and Sanyo Coca-Cola Bottling, two major bottlers in southwest Japan which have agreed to merge their operations and thus combine a somewhat fragmented distribution system into a smoother, seamless approach that should boost profitability.[19]

Cost-cutting Another key financial strategy is cutting costs[20] and investing in new plant and equipment,[21] resulting in higher productivity and lower expenses. Still another strategy is the renegotiation of labor contract agreements in high-cost areas of the world.

Investment in new plant and equipment will be critical to the success of MNEs during the millennium. This is particularly true in Japan, where many auto manufacturers are finding it increasingly difficult to hire new people. Worse yet, the turnover rate in some factories runs as high as 50 per cent annually. In explaining the reason for this turnover, many workers refer to the three K's: kiken (dangerous), kitsui (difficult), and kitanai (dirty). Young people, in particular, prefer the slower-paced world of office work where people wear suits and ties, take leisurely lunch hours, and are not exhausted at the end of a long day.

In an effort to deal with this problem, Nissan Motor has built a new factory that promises to be far less stressful on the workers than anything yet. Company officials refer to it as a "dream factory" and claim that it is designed to reduce many of the pitfalls of past manufacturing plants. The latter, for example, are characterized by the traditional conveyor belt from which cars are suspended. When the car reaches the workers, the employees scramble to install parts and to complete their tasks as quickly as possible. This typically involves squatting on the floor, stretching across the seat or the hood, ducking under the car, or reaching across the top of the vehicle to install or tighten something. If the workers are unable to keep up with the line, the conveyer belt must be stopped until they finish because all cars advance in lockstep. In contrast, Nissan's new plant has done away with the conveyer belt. All cars are now placed on motor-driven dollies. These dollies can be raised or lowered so that the workers do not have to stretch or squat. Additionally, even if it takes longer than usual to complete a particular task, this creates no problem for the factory. The workers can simply scoot the dolly up to the next station as soon as they are finished.

Another difference between the Nissan plant and more conventional ones is that the work area is brightly lit with natural sunlight filtering in through skylights, compared to the poorly lit work environments in other plants. Additionally, the factory is air-conditioned and the temperature is kept at 77°F (degrees Fahrenheit), in contrast to other auto plants where there is no air-conditioning. Another welcome feature is the use of robots to perform the dirtiest and most difficult jobs, painting and welding. And to reduce worker exhaustion, a large percentage of the actual assembly is carried out by robots. A huge robot arm, for example, grabs seats from an overhead rack and swings them into the car with a flick of its mechanical wrist. Then a small robot arm bolts the seat to the floor. Nissan contends that this new plant will not only cut down on worker absenteeism and turnover, but that the factory will be 30 per cent more efficient than those of the competition.[22]

Other Japanese manufacturers are also heavily focused on cost-cutting. For example, Honda and Toyota operations in the United States have been simultaneously reducing costs while increasing quality. The result is that car prices for many of their models have remained the same or dropped slightly in recent years, while the number of features have increased. This "more value for your money" concept has been influential in helping both automakers to increase their US market share and profitability.[23] Ford has been following a similar approach through a vigorous outsourcing program and by seeking to cut $1 billion from its costs, thus boosting its return on investment from the North American market and, hopefully, helping drive up stock price as well.[24] Simply put, cost-cutting is now a critical part of many financial investment strategies.

ACTIVE LEARNING CHECK

Review your answer to Active Learning Case question 5 and make any changes you like. Then compare your answer to the one below.

5. How is the BA/USAir arrangement designed to reduce financial risk and to control costs? Give two examples.

The arrangement is set up to consolidate operations and to eliminate overlap, duplication, and waste. One way in which this is being done is by combining overall purchasing, maintenance, and operations. A second approach is by standardizing the way service is delivered throughout the system. Both of these approaches should result in reduction of financial risk and better control of costs.

SUMMARY

Key points

1. International financial management encompasses a number of critical areas, including the management of global cash flows, foreign exchange risk management, capital expenditure analysis, and capital budgeting. In carrying out these financial activities, MNEs can use three approaches or solutions: polycentric, ethnocentric, or geocentric.

2. There are three main areas of consideration in managing global cash flows. One is the movement of cash so that each subsidiary has the working capital needed to conduct operations. A second area is the use of funds positioning techniques that can help to reduce taxes and to deal with political and legal roadblocks that impede cash flows. A third is multilateral netting which ensures that transactions between the subsidiaries are paid in a timely manner.

3. Foreign exchange risk management encompasses a variety of financial strategies that are designed to limit the multinational's exposure to exchange rate fluctuations. In particular, the MNE will want to reduce translation, transaction, and economic exposure. One of the most common ways of doing this is through hedging. Examples include lead and lag strategies, the purchase of forward exchange contracts, and the use of currency options.

4. A third major strategic financial issue is capital expenditure analysis. This entails computation and deliberation of such matters as the weighted cost of capital and the degree of political risk that is being assumed. Some of the methods of dealing with these issues were discussed with attention given to the fact that the final decision on capital expenditures is often affected by subjective considerations as well as by objective evaluations.

5. At present MNEs are taking a number of important international financial steps. Some of the primary ones include establishing overseas operations, creating joint ventures, and cutting operating costs.

Key terms

- polycentric solution
- ethnocentric solution
- geocentric solution
- working capital
- funds positioning techniques
- transfer price
- arm's length price
- tax havens
- fronting loan
- multilateral netting
- translation
- consolidation
- translation exposure
- transaction exposure
- economic exposure
- hedge
- lead strategy
- lag strategy
- forward exchange contract
- currency option
- capital expenditures
- foreign investment review agencies
- British Export Credits Guarantee Department
- Overseas Private Investment Corporation (OPIC)

Review and discussion questions

1. In determining parent–subsidiary relationships, how does a polycentric solution differ from an ethnocentric or geocentric solution? Compare and contrast all three.

2. What is meant by the term "working capital," and what are two of the most common ways that parent companies can provide this capital to their subsidiaries? What are two ways in which the parent can obtain funds from the subsidiaries?

3. How can an MNE shift profits through the use of transfer pricing? Provide an example.

4. Of what value is multilateral netting in helping MNEs to manage cash flows? Give an example.

5. If a foreign country is facing high inflation, what are three financial strategies that the local multinational unit might employ? Identify and describe each.

6. Why are MNEs interested in translation and consolidation of financial statements? Of what practical value is this activity to the company?

7. Under what conditions will an MNE face translation exposure? What financial strategy might the organization use to minimize this exposure?

8. When might an MNE face transaction exposure? What is a financial strategy that the firm could use to minimize this risk?

9. What is meant by the term "economic exposure"? What is a financial strategy that an MNE could use to minimize this risk?

10. When would a multinational use a lead strategy to hedge a risk? When would a multinational use a lag strategy for this purpose? In each case, give an example.

11. When might an MNE use a forward exchange contract? Why might the firm decide to forgo this strategy in lieu of purchasing a currency option?

12. What role does net present value (NPV) play in the review of capital expenditure proposals? Give an example.

13. How can political risk affect the computation of NPV? Will the risk result in the MNE wanting a higher or a lower NPV? Explain.

14. Why do parent and local subsidiaries sometimes differ in their calculation of NPV for a particular project or expenditure? How can this difference be resolved?

15. How does the availability of political risk insurance change the structure of the capital expenditure analysis process? Give an example.

REAL CASES

METAL LEVE (BRAZIL)

Some foreign firms believe that Brazil will be a good investment during the next decade. At the same time, a number of Brazilian MNEs are expanding into triad markets like the United States. A good example of the latter is Sao Paulo-based Metal Leve, now a member of the Mahle group of Germany. Metal Leve is a world leader in producing parts for diesel-engine pistons, bearings, and machine tools. Established in 1950 to supply the growing but protected Brazilian automotive industry, the company managed to become a world player.

Metal Leve's success has been the direct result of a protectionist industrial policy of the Brazilian government. By far the largest country in Latin

America, Brazil could extract concessions from foreign producers. Thus, GM, Ford, and Volkswagen all set up productions plants in Brazil but had to conform to a domestic content law. The content law helped Metal Leve and other local automotive suppliers to start up but it also served to shelter them from the competitive world market. In spite of this, Metal Leve aimed to be a world technology leader. By 1965 it had won approval from the FAA (Federal Aviation Administration) to supply parts to the US aviation market. So it started to develop and research new products according to the specific needs of its new international customers.

Metal Leve made its first investment in the United States in 1988, plunking down $14 million for a research and testing lab in Ann Arbor, Michigan, and a piston plant in Orangebourg, South Carolina. Since then, the company has brought a plant in Greensburg, Indiana, to produce bearings and another plant in Sumter, South Carolina, to make pistons. Metal Leve even found that its foreign (US-based) operations helped it to upgrade at home and provide just-in-time delivery to customers.

Unfortunately, the years of protection and shelter led to inefficiencies in domestic auto parts production in Brazil. Metal Leve could foresee that domestic protectionism would not last forever and that it lacked the ability to compete internation-ally. Thus it began to form joint ventures with German manufacturers to gain technological know-how. When the Brazilian doors were finally opened in the 1990s and its automotive firms began to source their parts from competitive producers around the world, Metal Leve found its domestic market share plummeting. The company needed large investments that its owners could not provide and so it was sold to the Mahle group, in 1996.

1. Is the MNE described above using a polycentric, ethnocentric, or geocentric approach in implementing its expansion strategies? Defend your answer.

2. In what way would a foreign MNE doing business in the United States face a foreign exchange exposure problem? Provide an example.

3. How would the firm in this case use net present value to help it make decisions regarding expansion into new markets or joint ventures with other firms? Give an example.

Sources: Adapted from Joel Millman, "The Brazilians are coming," *Forbes*, June 22, 1992, pp. 78–79; Jonathan B. Levine, "Europe Blows a Fuse," *Business Week*, July 6, 1992, pp. 45, 48; Joel Millman, "The Sick Man of Latin America," *Forbes*, September 13, 1993, pp. 114–128; *http://www.metalleve.com.br/ml_i.ap*; "Brazilian Takeovers: the Buying and Selling of Brazil Inc.," *The Economist*, November 9, 1996, pp. 115–118; "Buy, Buy, Buy," *The Economist*, December 6, 1997, p. 17.

NATIONAL CASH REGISTER

Originally named the National Cash Register Company, NCR was founded in 1884 by John H. Patterson to sell mechanical cash registers. From its inception, NCR was a clear example of a company ready to take on new technological developments. In 1906 the firm added an electric motor to its cash register. In the 1950s it developed magnetic ink character recognition, which allowed documents, such as checks, to be read electronically. During the same period NCR, in a joint venture with General Motors, created the first fully transistorized mainframe computer. The 1960s brought the first NCR bank teller machines. These machines allowed immediate customer account updating from bank branches, severely simplifying banking. By the 1980s the company produced a second generation of self-serve machines. These units allowed cash withdrawals as well as the purchase of airline tickets. "Drive-Thru" ATMs (automated teller machines) and the introduction of pentium PCs for retail and financial applications are a few examples of how the company contributed to the development of new technology in the 1990s.

Nor did NCR lose any time in becoming a multinational. By 1886 the firm began selling abroad and soon had operations in 121 countries. Today, 51 per cent of NCR's revenue is generated in international markets including such principal locations as Germany, France, Australia, Spain, Italy, Canada, and Switzerland. In Great Britain over 80 per cent of all ATM terminals are NCR's. Furthermore, the company has distribution networks that span the world.

NCR has followed a variety of strategies including the effective use of partnerships. In fact, a recent partnership with APACS from the UK is helping NCR strengthen its already dominant position in the ATM market. This deal will provide customers a myriad of services through a single card built with a microchip (smartcard) replacing the magnetic strip of today's bankcards.

Another approach is the use of distribution partnerships that allow regionally oriented firms to market NCR products. For instance, I. E. Mittwoch & Sons is the sole NCR distributor in Israel, while Hardwood International Corporation functions as a worldwide indirect sales channel for specialized NCR products.

Meanwhile customers serve a dual purpose for the firm. Many of them are multinationals themselves and the application of NCR's products to worldwide operations of companies such as Hallmark, Wal-Mart and K-Mart contribute to the company's internationalization.

In order to tie the different parts of its global operations, NCR also has developed worldwide customer support networks that are co-administered with its business partners. In 1997 the company announced it would realign global operations within the business units to implement global process efficiency. This new organizational setup is expected to give more operational freedom to the different business units, decreasing infrastructure and allowing for better communication between the parts.

1. Why are NCR's operations in developing countries important? How are they different than their principal markets in developed countries?

2. Why would NCR choose to maintain distribution partnerships rather than internalize and distribute directly?

3. How can customers who are multinationals help market NCR products in other countries?

Sources: Adapted from *http://www3.ncr.com*; Connie Guglielmo, "Here Come The Super-ATMs," *Fortune*, October 14, 1996; NCR, "APACS and NCR Lighten Wallets to Make Britain a Smartcard Leader," *Press Release*, July 9, 1998; *http://www3.ncr.com/press_release/pr070998a.html*; *http://www.hardwood-intl.com/*.

ENDNOTES

1. Edward Neumann, "MNCs Start Taking IRS Surveillance of Transfer Pricing More Seriously," *Business International Money Report* (New York: Business International Corporation, May 7, 1990), p. 167.

2. Also, see Neil Weinberg, "Rent Shokku," *Forbes*, June 7, 1993, p. 108.

3. Doron P. Levin, "Honda to Hold Base Price on Accord Model," *New York Times*, September 2, 1993, p. C3.

4. For more on Honda, see Alex Taylor III, "How Toyota Copes with Hard Times," *Fortune*, January 25, 1993, pp. 78–81.

5. See John Rossant, "Privatize the Beast," *Business Week*, May 24, 1993, p. 54.

6. For more detailed discussion of the strategic aspects of the capital budgeting decision and the manner in which decisions can be centralized or decentralized, see Alan M. Rugman and Alain Verbeke, "Strategic Capital Budgeting Decisions and the Theory of Internalization," *Managerial Finance*, vol. 16, no. 2, 1990, pp. 17–24.

7. See William C. Symonds et al., "High-Tech Star," *Business Week*, July 27, 1992, pp. 54–58.

8. See Brian Coleman and Thomas R. King, "Euro Disney Rescue Package Wins Approval," *Wall Street Journal*, March 15, 1994, p. A3.

9. "Ford to Pay $6.47 Billion in Volvo Deal," *Wall Street Journal*, January 29, 1999, Section A, pp. 3, 6.

10. Also, see John Templeman and James B. Treece, "BMW's Comeback," *Business Week*, February 14, 1994, pp. 42–44.

11. Keith Bradsher, "Industry's Giants Are Carving Up the World Market," *New York Times*, May 8, 1998, pp. C1, 4; and Robyn Meredith, "A Joining of Opposites Could Help Customers," *New York Times*, May 8, 1998, p. C4.

12. Seth Faison, "GM Opens Buick Plant in Shanghai," *New York Times*, December 18, 1998, pp. C1, 19.

13. "Opening the Door a Crack," *New York Times*, June 30, 1998, p. A10.
14. Laxmi Nakarmi and Igor Reichlin, "Daewoo, Samsung, and Goldstar: Made in Europe?" *Business Week*, August 24, 1992, p. 43.
15. Rita Koselka, "A Tight Ship," *Forbes*, July 20, 1992, pp. 141–142, 144.
16. Craig Torres, "TRW Plans Mexican Venture to Start a Credit Operation in Guadalajara," *Wall Street Journal*, January 7, 1994, p. A5.
17. Don Clark and David Bank, "Microsoft, Sony to Cooperate On PCs, Devices," *Wall Street Journal*, April 8, 1998, p. B6.
18. Lisa Shuchman and Joseph B. White, "Global Consolidations in Autos Heat Up," *Wall Street Journal*, December 21, 1998, p. A2.
19. Nikhil Deogun, "Coca-Cola to Put Together the Merger of Two Bottlers in Japan to Lift Sales," *Wall Street Journal*, January 14, 1999, p A4.
20. See, for example, John Templeman, Stewart Toy, and Paula Dwyer, "How Many Parts Makers Can Stomach the Lopez Diet?" *Business Week*, June 28, 1993, pp. 45–46.
21. See Richard W. Stevenson, "Lopez Plan for Factory Is Studied," *New York Times*, June 15, 1993, pp. C1, C19.
22. Andrew Pollack, "Assembly-Line Amenities for Japan's Auto Workers," *New York Times*, July 20, 1992, pp. A1, C5.
23. Valerie Reitman, "Honda Sees Performance and Profits from New Accord," *Wall Street Journal*, August 27, 1997, p. B4.
24. Fara Warner and Joseph B. White, "Ford Plans to Reduce Costs by Another $1 Billion," *Wall Street Journal*, January 8, 1999, p. A3.

ADDITIONAL BIBLIOGRAPHY

Adler, Michael and Dumas, Bernard. "Exposure to Currency Risk: Definition and Management," *Financial Management* (Summer 1984).

Ahadiat, Nasrollah. "Geographic Segment Disclosure and the Predictive Ability of the Earnings Data," *Journal of International Business Studies*, vol. 24, no. 2 (Second Quarter 1993).

Albach, Horst. "Financial Planning in the Firm," *Management International Review*, vol. 32 (First Quarter 1992).

Batten, Jonathan; Mellor, Robert; and Wan, Victor. "Foreign Exchange Risk Management Practices and Products Used by Australian Firms," *Journal of International Business Studies*, vol. 24, no. 3 (Third Quarter 1993).

Booth, Laurence D. "Hedging and Foreign Exchange Exposure," *Management International Review*, vol. 22, no. 1 (1982).

Choi, Frederick D. S. "Accounting and Control for Multinational Activities: Perspective on the 1990's," *Management International Review*, vol. 31 (1991).

Damanpour, Faramarz. "Global Banking: Developments in the Market Structure and Activities of Foreign Banks in the United States," *Columbia Journal of World Business*, vol. 26, no. 3 (Fall 1991).

Doupnik, Timothy S. and Salter, Stephen B. "An Empirical Test of a Judgemental International Classification of Financial Reporting Practices," *Journal of International Business Studies*, vol. 24, no. 1 (First Quarter 1993).

Dufey, Gunter and Giddy, Ian H. "Innovation in the International Financial Markets," *Journal of International Business Studies* (Fall 1981).

Eiteman, David K. and Stonehill, Arthur I. *Multinational Business Finance*, 5th ed. (Reading, Mass.: Addison-Wesley, 1989).

Fatemi, Ali M. "Shareholder Benefits from International Corporate Diversification," *Journal of Finance* (December 1984).

Folks, William R. and Aggarwal, Raj. *International Dimensions of Financial Management* (Boston: PWS-Kent, 1987).

Forester, Stephen R. and Karolyi, G. Andrew. "International Listings of Stocks: The Case of Canada and the US," *Journal of International Business Studies*, vol. 24, no. 4 (Fourth Quarter 1993).

George, Abraham M. and Schroth, C. William. "Managing Foreign Exchange for Competitive Advantage," *Sloan Management Review*, vol. 32, no. 2 (Winter 1991).

Hekman, Christine. "A Financial Model of Foreign Exchange Exposure," *Journal of International Business Studies* (Summer 1985).

Holland, John. "Capital Budgeting for International Business: A Framework for Analysis," in *The International Finance Reader*, edited by Robert Kolb (Miami: Kolb Publishing, 1990).

International Monetary Fund. *Exchange Arrangements and Exchange Restrictions Annual Report 1989* (Washington, DC: IMF, 1989).

Jacque, Laurent L. "Management of Foreign Exchange Risk: A Review Article," *Journal of International Business Studies* (Spring/Summer 1981).

Jesswein, Kurt R., Kwok, Chuck C. Y. and Folks, William R., Jr. "Corporate Use of Innovative Foreign Exchange Risk Management Products," *Columbia Journal of World Business*, vol. 30, no. 3 (Fall 1995).

Khambata, Dara M. *The Practice of Multinational Banking* (New York: Quorum Books, 1986).

Khoury, Sarkis J. *Recent Developments in International Banking and Finance*. (New York: North-Holland, 1990).

Kwok, Chuck C. Y. and Brooks, LeRoy D. "Examining Event Study Methodologies in Foreign Exchange Markets," *Journal of International Business Studies*, vol. 21, no. 2 (Second Quarter 1990).

Lee, Kwang Chul and Kwok, Chuck C. Y. "Multinational Corporations vs. Domestic Corporations: International Environmental Factors and Determinants of Capital Structure," *Journal of International Business Studies*, vol. 19, no. 2 (Summer 1988).

Lessard, Donald R. *International Financial Management*, 2nd ed. (New York: John Wiley & Sons, 1985).

Lubecke, Thomas H., Markland, Robert E., Kwok, Chuck C. Y. and Donohue, Joan M. "Forecasting Foreign Exchange Rates Using Objective Composite Models," *Management International Review*, vol. 35, no. 2 (1995).

Luehrman, Timothy A. "The Exchange Rate Exposure of a Global Competitor," *Journal of International Business Studies*, vol. 21, no. 2 (Second Quarter 1990).

Mokkelbost, Per B. "Financing the New Europe with Participating Debt," *Management International Review*, vol. 31, no. 1 (First Quarter 1991).

Parkhe, Arvind. "International Portfolio Analysis: A New Model," *Management International Review*, vol. 31, no. 4 (1991).

Rugman, Alan M. *International Diversification and the Multinational Enterprise* (Lexington, Mass.: D.C. Heath, 1979).

Rugman, Alan M. "Implications of the Theory of Internalization for Corporate International Finance," *California Management Review*, vol. 23, no. 2 (Winter 1980).

Rugman, Alan M. "International Diversification and Multinational Banking," in Sarkin J. Khoury and Alo Gosh (eds.) *Recent Developments in International Banking and Finance* (Lexington, Mass.: D.C. Heath, 1987).

Rugman, Alan M. and Anderson, Andrew. "Globalization of Banking Services: Canada's Strategies in the Triad," in Yair Aharoni (ed.) *Coalitions and Competition: The Globalization of Professional Business Services* (London: Routledge, 1993).

Rugman, Alan M. and Eden, Lorraine. *Multinationals and Transfer Pricing* (London: Croom Helm and New York: St. Martin's Press, 1985).

Shapiro, Alan C. *Multinational Financial Management*, 3rd ed. (Boston: Allyn & Bacon, 1989).

Stanley, Marjorie T. "Capital Structure and Cost of Capital for the Multinational Firm," *Journal of International Business Studies*, vol. 21, no. 2 (Spring/Summer 1981).

Tsetsekos, George P. and Gombola, Michael J. "Foreign and Domestic Divestments: Evidence on Valuation Effects of Plant Closings," *Journal of International Business Studies*, vol. 23, no. 2 (Second Quarter 1992).

INTERNATIONAL BUSINESS STRATEGIES IN ACTION

PART ONE: THE WORLD OF INTERNATIONAL BUSINESS

Chapter 1 Introduction	Chapter 2 MNEs	Chapter 3 Triad

PART TWO: THE ENVIRONMENT OF INTERNATIONAL BUSINESS

Chapter 4 Political Environment	Chapter 5 Cultural Environment	Chapter 6 Economic Environment	Chapter 7 Financial Environment

PART THREE: INTERNATIONAL BUSINESS STRATEGIES

Chapter 8 Strategic Planning	Chapter 9 Organizing Strategy	Chapter 10 Production Strategy	Chapter 11 Marketing Strategy
Chapter 12 Human Resource Strategy	Chapter 13 Political Risk/Negotiation		Chapter 14 Financial Strategy

PART FOUR: INTERNATIONAL BUSINESS STRATEGIES IN ACTION
To do Business in International Markets Including:

Chapter 15 Corporate Strategy/National Competitiveness	Chapter 16 EU

Chapter 17 Japan	Chapter 18 North America	Chapter 19 Non-Triad Nations

PART FIVE: INTERNATIONAL BUSINESS HORIZONS

Chapter 20 Future of International Business

CHAPTER 15

Corporate Strategy and National Competitiveness

OBJECTIVES OF THE CHAPTER

The primary objective of this chapter is to provide an overall framework for understanding how both nations and MNEs must fashion their strategies to achieve international competitiveness. In doing so, we give particular consideration to Canada and Mexico. The objectives of this chapter are to:

1. **Examine** the determinants and external variables in Porter's "diamond" model of national competitiveness and critique and evaluate this model.

2. **Present** a "double diamond" model that illustrates how firms in nontriad countries such as Canada are using their diamond to design corporate strategies for the North American market.

3. **Discuss** the benefits and effects of a free trade agreement and a North American Free Trade Agreement on both Mexico and Canada.

4. **Describe** how Mexico is using a double diamond model to tap into the North American market.

5. **Define** the terms "globalization" and "national responsiveness" and relate the importance of these two concepts to MNE strategies throughout the world.

Worldwide operations and local strategies of ABB

Asea Brown Boveri (ABB) is headquartered in Zurich, Switzerland, and is one of Europe's major industrial firms. Since the merger in 1987 that created the company, ABB has been acquiring or taking minority positions in a wide number of firms throughout the world. In recent years it has purchased Westinghouse's transmission and distribution operations and Combustion Engineering, the manufacturer of power-generation and process-automation equipment. The conglomerate, which currently employs 200,000 people worldwide, has annual revenues in excess of $20 billion. Sixty per cent of its revenues come from Europe, 25 per cent from North America, and 15 per cent from Asia.

The company operates on both local and global terms. On the one hand, the firm attempts to maintain deep local roots wherever it operates so that it can modify both products and operations to that market. For example, managers are trained to adapt to cultural differences and to learn how to communicate effectively with local customers. At the same time ABB works to be global and to produce products that can be sold anywhere in the world because the technology and quality give them a worldwide appeal.

A good example of a business that demonstrates ABB advantages is transportation. The company generates $2 billion a year in revenues from such products as subway cars, locomotives, suburban trains, trolleys, and the electrical and signaling systems that support these products. This is possible for four reasons: (1) the company's research and development makes it a technology leader in locomotives and power electronics, enabling the firm to develop and build high-speed trains and rail networks throughout the world; (2) the company's operations are structured to take advantage of economies of scale and thus keep prices competitive; (3) the company adapts to local

environments and works closely with customers so that it is viewed as a national, not a foreign, company; and (4) the company works closely with companies in other countries that are favored by their own government but need assistance in financing and producing locomotive equipment for that market. As a result, ABB is able to capitalize on its technological and manufacturing expertise and to develop competitive advantages in both triad and nontriad markets.

In some cases ABB has gone as far as taking an ownership position in companies that are located in emerging economic markets. For example, the firm purchased 76 per cent of Zamech, Poland's leading manufacturer of steam turbines, transmission gears, marine equipment, and metal castings. ABB has bought into two other Polish firms that make a wide range of generating equipment and electric drives. ABB is now in the process of reorganizing these firms into profit centers, transferring its own expertise to local operations, and developing worldwide quality standards and controls for production. If all goes according to plan, ABB will soon have a thriving Polish operation that will be helping to rebuild Eastern Europe.

The company works hard to be a good "citizen" of each country in which it operates, while also maintaining its supranational status. As a result, ABB is proving that it is possible to have worldwide operations and local strategies that work harmoniously.

Sources: Adapted from William Taylor, "The Logic of Global Business: An Interview with ABB's Percy Barnevik," *Harvard Business Review*, March–April 1991, pp. 91–105; Carla Rapoport, "A Tough Swede Invades the US," *Fortune*, June 29, 1992, pp. 76–79; Carol Kennedy, "ABB: Model Merger for the New Europe," *Long Range Planning*, 1992, vol. 25, no. 5, pp. 10–17; Edward L. Andrews, "ABB Will Cut 10,000 Jobs and Switch Focus to Asia," *New York Times*, October 22, 1997, p. C2.

1. In what way does ABB's strategy incorporate Porter's four country-specific determinants and two external variables?

2. Why did ABB buy Zamech? How can the company link Zamech to its overall strategic plan?

3. How does ABB address the issues of globalization and national responsiveness? In each case, cite an example.

INTRODUCTION

Some multinational firms rely on their home market to generate the research, development, design, or manufacturing that is needed to sell their goods in international markets. More and more, however, MNEs are finding that they must focus on the markets where they are doing business and on strategies for tapping the resources of these markets and gaining sales entry. In short, multinationals can no longer rely exclusively on the competitive advantage that they hold at home to provide them with a sustainable advantage overseas.

In addition, many small countries realize that they must rely on export strategies to ensure the growth of their economies. Those that have been most successful with this strategy have managed to tap into markets within triad countries. Good examples are Canada and Mexico; both have found the United States to be a lucrative market for exports and imports. As a result, many successful business firms in these two countries have integrated themselves into the US economy, and in the process have created what some international economists call a North American market. In the future many more MNEs are going to be following this pattern of linking into the economies of triad members.

The basic strategy that these MNEs are following can be tied directly to the Porter model that was presented in Chapter 1, although some significant modifications of this model are in order. We will first examine Porter's ideas in more detail and then show how these ideas are serving as the basis for developing firm strategies and international competitiveness in Canada and Mexico.

PORTER'S DIAMOND

In Chapter 1 we identified four determinants of national competitive advantage, as set forth by Porter (see Figure 1.1). We noted that these factors can be critical in helping a country to build and maintain competitive advantage. We will now return to Porter's "diamond" framework in more depth, see how his findings apply specifically to triad countries, and then determine how these ideas can be modified and applied to nations that are not triad members.

Determinants and external variables

Porter's "diamond" model is based on four country-specific determinants and two external variables. The determinants include:

1. *Factor conditions.* These include (1) the quantity, skills, and cost of the personnel; (2) the abundance, quality, accessibility, and cost of the nation's physical resources such as land, water, mineral deposits, timber, hydroelectric power sources, and fishing grounds; (3) the nation's stock of knowledge resources, including scientific, technical, and market knowledge that affect the quantity and quality of goods and services; (4) the amount and cost of capital resources that are available to finance industry; and (5) the type, quality, and user cost of the infrastructure, including the nation's transportation system, communications system, health-care system, and other factors that directly affect the quality of life in the country.

2. *Demand conditions.* These include (1) the composition of demand in the home market as reflected by the various market niches that exist, and buyer sophistication and how well the needs of buyers in the home market precede those of buyers in other markets; (2) the size and growth rate of the home demand; and (3) the ways through which domestic demand is internationalized and pulls a nation's products and services abroad.

3. *Related and supporting industries.* These include (1) the presence of internationally competitive supplier industries that create advantages in downstream industries through efficient, early, or rapid access to cost-effective inputs and (2) internationally competitive related industries that can coordinate and share activities in the value chain when competing or those that involve complementary products.

4. *Firm strategy, structure, and rivalry.* These include (1) the ways in which firms are managed and choose to compete, (2) the goals that companies seek to attain as well as the motivations of their employees and managers, and (3) the amount of domestic rivalry and the creation and persistence of competitive advantage in the respective industry.

The four determinants of national advantage shape the competitive environment of industries. However, two other variables, chance and government, also play important roles:

1. *The role of chance.* Chance events can nullify the advantages of some competitors and bring about a shift in overall competitive position because of developments such as (1) new inventions, (2) political decisions by foreign governments, (3) wars, (4) significant shifts in world financial markets or exchange rates, (5) discontinuities in input costs such as oil shocks, (6) surges in world or regional demand, and (7) major technological breakthroughs.

2. *The role of government.* Government can influence all four of the major determinants through actions such as (1) subsidies, (2) education policies, (3) the regulation or deregulation of capital markets, (4) the establishment of local product standards and regulations, (5) the purchase of goods and services, (6) tax laws, and (7) antitrust regulation.[1]

Figure 15.1 provides an illustration of the complete system of these determinants and external variables. Each of the four determinants affects the others and all in turn are affected by the role of chance and government.

Critique and evaluation of the model

In applying this model to international business strategy, we must first critique and evaluate Porter's paradigm and supporting arguments. First, the Porter model was constructed based on statistical analysis of aggregate data on export shares for ten countries: Denmark, Italy, Japan, Singapore, South Korea, Sweden, Switzerland, the United Kingdom, the United States, and West Germany. In addition, historical case studies were provided for four industries: the German printing press industry, the US patient-monitoring-equipment industry, the Italian ceramic tile industry, and the Japanese robotics industry. In each case the country is either a member of the triad or an industrialized nation. Since most countries of the world do not have the same economic strength or affluence as those studied by Porter, it is highly unlikely that his model can be applied to them without modification.

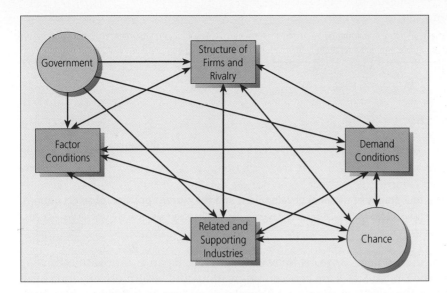

Figure 15.1 Porter's single diamond framework

Source: Adapted from Michael E. Porter, *The Competitive Advantage of Nations* (New York: Free Press, 1990), p. 72.

Second, the government is of critical importance in influencing a home nation's competitive advantage. For example, it can use tariffs as a direct entry barrier to penalize foreign firms, and it can employ subsidies as an indirect vehicle for penalizing foreign-based firms. Government actions such as these, however well intentioned, can backfire and end up creating a "sheltered" domestic industry that is unable to compete in the worldwide market.[2]

Third, although chance is a critical influencing factor in international business strategy, it is extremely difficult to predict and guard against. For example, until the day Saddam Hussein invaded Kuwait in 1991, the US government was predicting that there would be no invasion. In a similar vein, technological breakthroughs in computers and consumer electronics have resulted in rapid changes that, in many cases, were not predicted by market leaders.

Fourth, in the study of international business Porter's model must be applied in terms of company-specific considerations and not in terms of national advantages. As Porter so well notes in his book, "Firms, not nations, compete in international markets."[3]

Fifth, in support of his model, Porter delineates four distinct stages of national competitive development: factor-driven, investment-driven, innovation-driven, and wealth-driven (see Figure 15.2). In the factor-driven stage successful industries draw their advantage almost solely from the basic factors of production such as natural resources and the nation's large, inexpensive labor pool. Although successful internationally, the industries compete primarily on price. In the investment-driven stage companies invest in modern, efficient facilities and technology and work to improve these investments through modification and alteration. In the innovation-driven stage firms work to create new technology and methods through innovation within the firm and with assistance from suppliers and firms in related industries. In the wealth-driven stage firms begin to lose their competitive advantage, rivalry ebbs, and there is a decline in motivation to invest. As seen in Figure 15.2, Porter believes that Singapore

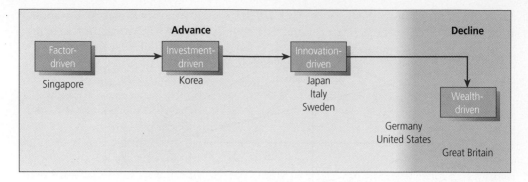

Figure 15.2   The four stages of national development and the current position of select nations
Source: Adapted from Michael E. Porter, *The Competitive Advantage of Nations* (New York: Free Press, 1990), pp. 563, 566.

is in the factor-driven stage, Korea is investment-driven, Japan is innovation-driven, Germany and the United States are between innovation- and wealth-driven, and Great Britain is wealth-driven. Since the stage of development greatly influences the country's competitive response, the placement of countries in Figure 15.2 is critical. So too is the logic that countries move from one stage to another, rather than spanning two or more of these stages because there are likely to be industries or companies in all major economies that are operating at each of these stages.

Sixth, Porter contends that only outward FDI is valuable in creating competitive advantage, and inbound foreign investment is never the solution to a nation's competitive problems. Moreover, foreign subsidiaries are not sources of competitive advantage and "widespread foreign investment usually indicates that the process of competitive upgrading in an economy is *not entirely healthy* because domestic firms in many industries lack the capabilities to defend their market positions against foreign firms."[4] These statements are questionable and have already been rejected in this text. For example, Canadian-based scholars such as Safarian,[5] Rugman,[6] and Crookell[7] have all demonstrated that research and development undertaken by foreign-owned firms is not significantly different from that of Canadian-owned companies. Additionally, Rugman has found that the 20 largest US subsidiaries in Canada export virtually as much as they import (the rate of exports to sales is 25 per cent, whereas that of imports to sales is 26 per cent).[8]

Seventh, as seen in Figure 15.2, reliance on natural resources (the factor-driven stage) is viewed by Porter as insufficient to create worldwide competitive stature.[9] However, Canada, for one, has developed a number of successful megafirms which have turned the country's comparative advantage in natural resources into proprietary firm-specific advantages in resource processing and further refining, and these are sources of sustainable advantage.[10] Moreover, case studies of the country's successful multinationals such as Alcan, Noranda, and Nova help to illustrate the methods by which value added has been introduced by the managers of these resource-based companies.[11]

Eighth, the Porter model does not adequately address the role of MNEs. Researchers such as Dunning[12] have suggested including multinational activity as a third outside variable (in addition to chance and government). Certainly there is good reason to question whether MNE activity is covered in the "firm strategy, structure, and rivalry" determinant, and some researchers have raised the question regarding how the same rivalry determinant can both include multinationality for global industries and yet exclude it for multidomestic industries. As Dunning notes, "there is ample evidence to suggest that MNEs are influenced in their competitiveness by the configuration of the diamond in other than their home countries, and that this in turn may impinge upon the competitiveness of home countries."[13] For example, Nestlé earns 95 per cent of its sales outside Switzerland. Thus the Swiss diamond of competitive advantage is less relevant than that of the countries in which Nestlé operates. This is true not only for MNEs in Switzerland but for 95 per cent of the world's MNEs as well. For example, virtually all of Canada's large multinationals rely on sales in the United States and other triad markets. Indeed, it could be argued that the US diamond is more relevant for Canada's industrial multinationals than Canada's own diamond; over 70 per cent of Canadian MNE sales take place in the United States. Other nations with MNEs based on small home diamonds include Australia, New Zealand, Finland, and most, if not all, Asian and Latin American countries as well as a large number of other small countries. Even small nations in the EU, such as Denmark, have been able to overcome the problem of a small domestic market by gaining access to one of the triad markets. So in applying Porter's framework to international business at large, one conclusion is irrefutable: *different diamonds need to be constructed and analyzed for different countries.*

ACTIVE LEARNING CHECK

Review your answer to Active Learning Case question 1 and make any changes you like. Then compare your answer to the one below.

1. In what way does ABB's strategy incorporate Porter's four country-specific determinants and two external variables?

The strategy incorporates Porter's country-specific determinants as part of a well-formulated global strategy that is designed to tap the strengths of various markets. For example, the company draws on the factor conditions and demand conditions in Europe to support its transportation business. The company also draws on supporting industries to help sustain its worldwide competitive advantage in that industry. At the same time the company's strategy, structure, and rivalry are designed to help it compete at the local level. The strategy incorporates the external variable of government by considering relations between countries as a lubricant for worldwide economic integration. The strategy addresses the variable of chance by operating globally and thus reducing the likelihood that a war or a regional recession will have a major negative effect on operations. The firm's heavy focus on core technologies and research and development also helps to minimize this chance variable.

OTHER "DIAMOND" MODELS: TWO CASE EXAMPLES

Researchers have recently begun using the Porter diamond as a basis for analyzing the international competitiveness of smaller countries. This approach builds on Porter's theme of corporate strategy and process as a source of competitive advantage for a nation.

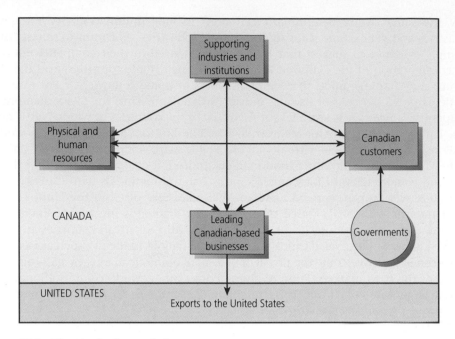

Figure 15.3   The single diamond view

Source: Adapted from Alan M. Rugman and Joseph R. D'Cruz, *Fast Forward: Improving Canada's International Competitiveness* (Toronto: Kodak Canada, 1991), p. 35.

Canada and the double diamond

Figure 15.3 illustrates how Porter's single diamond would look if it were applied to Canada's case.[14]

Two themes have recurred consistently in Canadian industrial policy: export promotion for natural resource industries and import substitution in the domestic arena. The Canadian market has always been seen as too small to support the development of economies of scale that are required in modern industry. Hence it has been the practice in Canada to provide the base for developing large-scale resource businesses that are designed to exploit the natural resources found in the country. Export strategies have placed emphasis on commodity products that have been developed in isolation from major customers. In the past these strategies had been encouraged by US government policies that removed or eliminated tariffs on imports of commodities that are not produced extensively in the United States. The Canadian government's role had been to help leading Canadian-based businesses by establishing relatively low taxes on resource extraction and by subsidizing the costs of capital through grants, low-interest loans, and loan guarantees.

With respect to import substitution, the Canadian goal had been to use tariff and nontariff measures to provide a protected environment for development of secondary industry. Under this arrangement the country's approach to business was largely focused inwardly; it relied solely on the extent and quality of national resources as the base for the creation of wealth.

By the mid-1960s, however, it became clear that a more international focus was needed. The 1967 Canada–United States Auto Pact demonstrated that significant economic benefits would result from the elimination of tariffs on trade between the

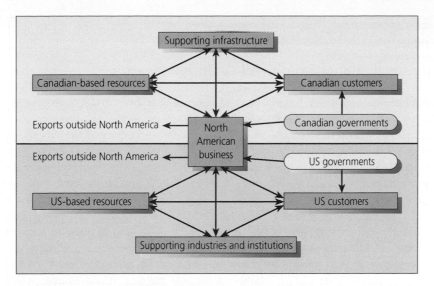

Figure 15.4 Canadian–US double diamond

Source: Adapted from Alan M. Rugman and Joseph R. D'Cruz, "The 'Double Diamond' Model of International Competitiveness: the Canadian Experience," *Management International Review*, vol. 33, Special Issue no. 2, 1993, p. 32.

two countries in autos and parts. This agreement eventually became the model for the United States–Canada Free Trade Agreement.[15] In the process Canadian plants gained economies of scale by producing for the North American market as a whole rather than for the Canadian market alone. For corporate strategy, the result of North American economic integration has been the development of a Canada-United States "double diamond." This double diamond shows that the two countries are integrated for strategy purposes into a single market (see Figure 15.4).

Under this new arrangement Canadian businesses are now in direct competition with firms operating in a diamond of their own in the United States.[16] In order to survive this rivalry with leading US firms, Canadian-based businesses have to develop competitive capabilities of a high order.[17] They can no longer rely on their country's home diamond and natural resource base. Innovation and cost competitiveness are equally important, and this requires strategies that are designed to access the US diamond. Now Canadian managers need a "double diamond perspective" for their strategic decisions. The double diamond is, of course, relevant for other small, open economies like Finland and Sweden. (The box "International Business Strategy in Action: Nokia and Ericsson: Small Phones from Small Countries" provides an example).

The Free Trade Agreement has also created a series of unique pressures on the Canadian subsidiaries of US multinationals. Many of these subsidiaries were created for the purpose of overcoming Canadian tariff barriers that were designed to encourage development of local operations. These businesses are now unnecessary, and many of them are currently in direct competition with their US-based parent. If they cannot compete successfully, future business will go south of the border.[18]

Meanwhile, major Canadian firms are working to develop competitive positions in the United States as well as worldwide.[19] A good example is Northern Telecom, the country's leading manufacturer of telephone equipment. The firm has now established a significant manufacturing and product development presence in the

INTERNATIONAL BUSINESS STRATEGY IN ACTION

Nokia and Ericsson: small phones from small countries

The largest producer of mobile phones is Nokia, based in one of the world's smallest countries, Finland. Nokia is the leader in Europe and second to Motorola in the United States, the leader in analog technology.

Nokia was founded in 1865 and was a major manufacturer of paper products before it transformed itself into a high-technology producer of electronics products, especially cellular phones, starting in the 1970s. By 1997, Nokia was the largest company in Finland with sales of nearly US $10 billion. It had sales in 130 countries and employed 36,000 production people in 45 countries.

From the beginning Nokia has pursued foreign sales. This internationalization strategy was necessary because Finland only has 3 million people and today only 5 per cent of its sales are in its home base. So Nokia became the mobile phone leader in Scandinavia, despite competition from Ericsson of Sweden. Next it became the leader in Britain and then the rest of Europe and formed strategic alliances with US distributors such as Radio Shack and US telecom companies like AT&T. The firm has also developed special phones for Chinese and Japanese users.

Nokia spends a large amount on R&D and it is attempting to provide mobile phones which enable "global roaming" by being usable across different telecom systems worldwide. This requires that it work closely with different political regimes in order to try and develop an industry standard. In this venture it works with its great rival, Ericsson. They are attempting to establish GSM as the standard for mobile phones across Europe, and as one of the global standards. The next generation of mobile phones may build on a system like GSM.

L. M. Ericsson has over 100,000 employees and sales of US $20 billion in the 130 countries in which it operates. In 1997, Ericsson was the world's largest producer of digital mobile phones. Only 6 per cent of its sales occur in Sweden, with nearly 40 per cent of its sales in Europe, 27 per cent in Asia and 16 per cent in North America. Unlike Nokia, which started as a paper and rubber producer, Ericsson has always been in telecommunications, starting in 1876 as a telephone manufacturer. It has always been innovative and, today, one-fifth of all employees work in R&D. In other areas of business it developed telephone switches in which it competes with firms such as Canada's Nortel and France's Alcatel. Ericsson was well positioned to benefit from the telecom deregulation of the 1980s and 1990s. This has created new demand, especially for new equipment like mobile phones where there were few local monopoly producers.

Ericsson has formed alliances with Compaq, Intel, Hewlett Packard, and Texas Instruments. These firms act as key suppliers of components and products that Ericsson uses for voice and data transmission. The relative weakness Ericsson has, compared to Nokia and Motorola, is its brand name. The firm has strong production technology but needs to improve on its marketing side.

Firms like Ericsson and Nokia will benefit from the alliance between AT&T and British Telecom, and between Sprint, France Telecom and Deutsche Telekom. These big alliances help set standardized services to which mobile phone producers can respond efficiently. In the future mobile phones will become even smaller, but the two producers from small countries, Nokia of Finland and Ericsson of Sweden, will become even bigger.

Sources: Annual Reports; Richard Hylton, Nick Moore, and Roger Honour, "Making Money in the Tech Market," *Fortune*, May 13, 1996; Erick Schonfeld, "Hold the Phone: Motorola Is Going Nowhere Fast," *Fortune*, March 30, 1998.

United States from which it sources a large part of its product line. The company has two major operating centers: one in Canada outside Toronto and the other near Washington, DC. Vigorous rivalry between operations in both countries has helped Northern to develop global competitiveness, as recently demonstrated by its success in winning a large contract with Japan's Nippon Telephone and Telegraph.[20]

Another example is provided by Bombardier Inc. Beginning as a Canadian manufacturer of snow-going equipment, the company has now grown into a multinational firm with interests in aviation, transportation, and financial services. In the aviation/aerospace business, Bombardier has major operations in Canada and the United States, among other locations, and manufactures corporate jets, small airliners, amphibious planes, weapons systems, and space systems. The company's transportation operations has locations throughout North America and Europe and makes passenger trains, mass transit railcars, and engines. Its recreational products division, located primarily in North America, manufactures snowmobiles, boats, all-terrain vehicles, and small electric cars. The firm's business/financial service operations, which is also heavily based in Canada and the United States, provides business and consumer financial assistance.[21]

Other major Canadian firms are following suit, operating from a North American perspective in order to lay the groundwork for becoming globally competitive.[22] This involves viewing the United States and Canada as home-based markets and integrating the use of both "diamonds" for development and implementation of strategy. In particular, this requires:

1. Developing innovative new products and services that simultaneously meet the needs of the US and Canadian customer, recognizing that close relationships with demanding US customers should set the pace and style of product development;

2. Drawing on the support industries and infrastructure of both the US and Canadian diamonds, realizing that the US diamond is more likely to possess deeper and more efficient markets for such industries; and

3. Making free and full use of the physical and human resources in both countries.[23]

Strategic clusters in the double diamond   The primary advantage of using the double diamond is that it forces business and government leaders to think about management strategy and public policy in a more productive way. Rather than viewing the domestic diamond as the unit of analysis, it encourages managers from smaller countries always to be outward looking. Doing well in a double diamond is the first step toward global success.

Once a country has recognized the benefit of the double-diamond perspective, it should first identify successful and potentially viable clusters of industries within its borders and then examine their linkages and performance across the double diamond. A **strategic cluster** is a network of businesses and supporting activities located in a specific region, where the flagship firms compete globally and the supporting activities are home-based, although some of them can be foreign-owned. In addition, some of the critical business inputs and skills may come from outside the country with their relevance and usefulness being determined by the membership of the strategic cluster. A successful strategic cluster will have one or more large MNEs at its center. Whether these are home- or foreign-owned is irrelevant so long as they are globally competitive. These MNEs are flagship firms on which the strategic cluster depends. Ideally, they operate on a global basis and plan their competitive strategies within the framework of global competition. A vital component of the cluster is companies with related and supporting activities, including both private and public sector organizations. In addition, there are think tanks, research groups, and educational institutions. Some parts of this network can even be based outside the country, but the linkages across the border and the leadership role of the nation's flagships result in world-class competitive multinationals.[24]

Currently there are several strategic clusters in Canada. One is the auto assembly and auto parts industry in southwestern Ontario, led by the big three US auto multinationals with their related and affiliated suppliers and distributors. There are linkages to various high-tech firms and research groups; these linkages span the border, as does the auto assembly industry itself. Other strategic clusters are based in banking and financial services in Toronto, the advanced manufacturing and telecommunications strategic cluster in Toronto, the forest products industries in western and eastern Canada, the energy clusters in Alberta, and the fisheries in Atlantic Canada. Some of these clusters are led by flagship Canadian-owned multinationals such as Northern Telecom, Nova, or Bombardier; others are led by, or include, foreign-owned firms such as IBM Canada and DuPont Canada.[25]

Many Canadian-based clusters are resource-based. The challenge for managers in these clusters is to continue to add value and to eliminate the commodity nature of Canada's resource industries. One way to do this is by developing a global marketing strategy that builds on the Canadian–US double diamond instead of remaining as the extractor or harvester of resources. To implement such a global strategy requires a large investment in people who will bring strong marketing skills and develop a global intelligence network to identify the different tastes and preferences of customers. This network provides a role for smaller knowledge-intensive marketing research and consulting firms to participate in the resource-based cluster. There is also the potential for collaborative ventures.

A 1998 World Economic Forum Report ranks the country as the fifth most competitive in the world with Singapore, Hong Kong, the United States, and the United Kingdom ahead of it.[26] The big problem Canada now faces is that of raising its productivity levels. According to the Organization for Economic Cooperation and Development, since 1990 this level has increased less than half as fast as that of the United States.[27]

Further research is required to investigate Canadian-based strategic clusters and their competitive advantages, compared to rival clusters within North America and also around the world. This will require two types of work. First, the intrafirm competition of clusters within North America needs new data which do not ignore the nature of foreign ownership and whether US and Canadian foreign direct investment (FDI) by sector is inbound or outbound. Instead, direct investment in North America must be regarded as "domestic" and be contrasted with "external" direct investment from Japan[28] and the EU.[29] Similarly, trade flows between Canada and the United States must be thought of as intrafirm when they occur between components of a cluster or even between and among clusters.

This approach is so radical that many existing concepts must be rethought. For example, the level and extent of subsidies available to clusters located in the United States (for example, in the Great Lakes states) must be related to those paid by provinces in Canada (such as Ontario). Yet there is little or no published work on state or provincial subsidies; even the work on federal subsidies in either country is extremely thin.

Finally, the real sources of Canadian competitive advantage are to be discovered not only by statistical analysis, but also by interviews of managers and officials, that is by fieldwork in the strategic clusters. Such "hands-on" research is exceptionally time-consuming and expensive. However, to make the task feasible, a number of important strategic clusters can be selected for analysis, self-audits should be made, conferences should be held, and so on. The future success of these efforts will depend heavily on leadership by Canadian business leaders and government officials.

Table 15.1 Stocks of FDI by Canada, the United States, and Mexico, 1987–96 (in millions of US $)

Year	Canada's FDI in: United States	Canada's FDI in: Mexico	US FDI in: Canada	US FDI in: Mexico	Mexico's FDI in: Canada	Mexico's FDI in: United States
1988	39,602	165	62,656	5,712	25.2	218
1989	44,495	202	63,948	8,264	10.1	350
1990	51,544	212	69,508	10,313	–	575
1991	55,353	176	70,711	12,501	–	747
1992	53,418	375	68,690	13,730	49.7	1,289
1993	52,565	413	69,922	15,221	120.4	1,244
1994	56,236	783	78,018	16,169	130.4	2,069
1995	62,975	823	85,441	15,980	144.0	1,850
1996	68,971	–	91,301	19,900	–	1,436
1997	72,140	–	99,859	25,395	–	1,723

Source: Organization of Economic Cooperation and Development, *International Direct Investment Statistics Yearbook, 1998* (Paris: OECD Publications, 1998).

Mexico and the double diamond

We can also adapt the Porter diamond to analyze firm strategies and international competitiveness in Mexico. The basic concepts in this framework are the same as those discussed in the Canadian diamond.

Linking to the US diamond Mexico's linkage to the US diamond is somewhat different from Canada's. One reason is the fact that there are few home-based MNEs that have the capital to invest in the United States or Canada.[30] (Review Chapter 3 for information on how and why FDI is used by MNEs.) In fact, as seen in Table 15.1, during the 1990s Mexico's FDI in the United States increased by only one and a half billion and it remained negligible in Canada. In contrast, by 1997 Canada had just under one billion invested in Mexico and the United States had over $25 billion there.[31] More importantly, US FDI in Canada reached nearly $100 billion and Canada's FDI in the United States was $72 billion. Thus Mexico's strategy with its North American neighbors relies more heavily on trade than on FDI for outward market access, while using inward FDI to help promote internal development.

As seen in Figure 15.5, Mexico and the United States conduct over $166 billion of trade every year and Canada and Mexico do over $3 billion of business. Additionally, Mexico is the third largest trading partner of the United States, and while the country has a negative trade balance with the world, it runs a positive balance with the United States. In fact, in recent years the latter has accounted for over 70 per cent of Mexico's exports *and* imports. The next most important trading partner is Japan, with a mere 6.1 per cent of Mexico's exports and 4.8 per cent of its imports. So Mexico is closely linked with the US economy, and its economic growth will depend heavily on participation in this North American market.[32] Figure 15.6 illustrates this idea with the US–Mexican double diamond.

Mexico is linking itself to the US diamond in a number of ways.[33] One is by serving as a customer for outside goods. For example, Caterpillar is the main supplier of

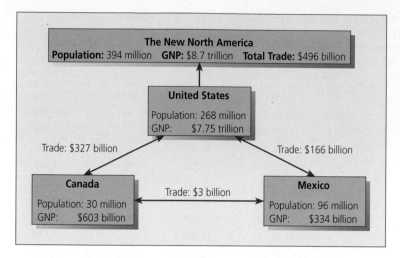

Figure 15.5 The shape of North America

Source: United Nations, *Monthly Bulletin of Statistics* (New York: UN, February 1999); World Bank, *World Development Report 1998/99*; International Monetary Fund, *Direction of Trade Statistics Quarterly*, March 1999.

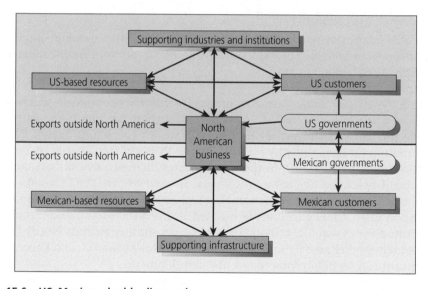

Figure 15.6 US–Mexican double diamond

Source: Richard M. Hodgetts, "Porter's Diamond Framework in a Mexican Context," *Management International Review*, vol. 33, Special Issue no. 2, 1993, p. 48.

heavy equipment for roadbuilding in Mexico; General Electric exports to Mexico over $100 million of goods annually, including locomotives, power-generation equipment, and diagnostic imaging equipment; and Kodak exports over $125 million annually of cameras, film, and other products.[34]

At the same time Mexican businesses are working to expand their links in the US market. Between 1994 and 1998 exports to the US market increased from $60 billion to almost $100 billion. Much of this output is in the form of manufactured goods, in particular automobiles. In fact, auto production in Mexico accounts for employment of over 350,000 workers and generates close to 1 million vehicles, most of which are targeted for the US market.[35] General Motors, for example, has invested about $1 billion in the last five years in setting up local operations and is becoming one of the major producers of cars in Mexico.[36] At the same time US firms are also investing in a wide array of nonautomotive projects.[37] IBM, for example, now produces magnetic readers for computer hard-disk drives in Guadalajara and air ships them to California on a daily basis. Asian firms are no longer able to compete effectively in this market. The same is true in textiles, where Mexican firms are now proving dominant.

> In 1996 Mexico overtook China as the largest supplier of textiles and garments to the US. Now, US mills are rushing to invest. In Altamira on the Gulf of Mexico, for example, Guilford Mills Inc., based in Greensboro, NC, is building a $100 million knitting, dyeing, and finishing plant. In Puebla, several Mexican families set up a venture, Skytex, that is turning out two million yards of polyester fabric per month. Half of it goes the to US. "This plant was conceived for NAFTA," says Deputy Sales Director Alberto Serur: "I can ship to the border in 18 hours, while the Asians take 21 days."[38]

Maquiladoras In 1965 the Mexican government established the maquiladora industry to attract foreign manufacturing operations. Imported products for the maquiladoras' production are exempt from Mexican duties as long as they are used for exports. In recent years certain items such as transportation equipment and computers, not directly involved in production, have also been made exempt from duties. Additionally, maquiladoras are no longer restricted to the border zone, and some have been permitted to settle inland and to sell finished products on the domestic market.

Today the maquiladora industry is one of the country's largest source of hard currency earnings from exports, after oil. In 1965 there were 12 maquiladora plants and by 1990 this number had increased to 1,700.[39] These businesses, which are principally US-owned, are widely considered to have established a basis for more intensified economic cooperation anticipated under an FTA (free trade agreement).[40] At the same time the growth of these companies is creating friction because many Americans feel that the low-wage rates in Mexico are causing firms to transfer work there and to lay off employees back home. The Real Case: "Mexico and the Maquiladoras" examines this development.

What will the future hold regarding Mexico and North America? The most likely developments will be continued investment by US and Canadian firms and the establishment of worldwide competition there. By the year 2000 Mexico is likely to be manufacturing and shipping many more products back north as well as exporting to more countries than they are doing today. In contrast to Canada, which is trying to create and nurture Canadian-owned MNEs that will compete worldwide, Mexico will build these businesses internally with financial and technological investments, primarily from its North American neighbors.[41]

The double diamond examples of Canada and Mexico help to explain how MNEs can use Porter's ideas to formulate strategies. However, these firms also need to address the issue of national responsiveness, the focus of the discussion in the next section.

ACTIVE LEARNING CHECK

Review your answer to Active Learning Case question 2 and make any changes you like. Then compare your answer to the one below.

2. Why did ABB buy Zamech? How can the company link Zamech to its overall strategic plan?

ABB bought Zamech for a number of reasons. The company provides a springboard to the Eastern European market, which is likely to grow dramatically during the coming decade. ABB links Zamech to its overall strategic plan by using the same approach that US firms are employing with Mexico. The company has purchased an equity position and is helping to set up a manufacturing operation that can provide goods for the local market as well as for other markets in both Eastern and Western Europe.

GLOBALIZATION AND CORPORATE STRATEGY

A major trend that has affected the thinking of corporate MNE strategists over the last ten years is that of balancing a concern for globalization with national responsiveness. **Globalization** is the production and distribution of products and services of a homogeneous type and quality on a worldwide basis. To a large extent MNEs have homogenized tastes and helped to spread international consumerism. For example, throughout North America, the wealthier nations of Europe, and Japan, there has been a growing acceptance of standardized consumer electronic goods, automobiles, computers, calculators, and similar products. However, the goal of efficient economic performance through a universal globalization strategy has left MNEs open to the charge that they are overlooking the need to address national concerns. **National responsiveness** is the ability of MNEs to understand different consumer tastes in segmented regional markets and to respond to different national standards and regulations that are imposed by autonomous governments and agencies. Throughout this decade multinationals will continually have to deal with the twin goals of globalization and national responsiveness.

Globalization versus national responsiveness

Conceptually, the twin issues of globalization and national responsiveness can be analyzed through the use of Figure 15.7, which has been adapted from Bartlett[42] and Bartlett and Ghoshal.[43] Transnational MNEs need to reconcile these twin issues.

The vertical axis measures the need for globalization, frequently called "economic integration." Movement up the axis results in a greater degree of economic integration. Globalization generates economies of scale as a firm moves into worldwide markets, selling a single product or service. These economies are captured as a result of centralizing specific activities in the value-added chain. They also occur by reaping the benefits of increased coordination and control of geographically dispersed activities.

The horizontal axis measures the need for corporations to be nationally responsive. Companies must address local tastes and government regulations. This may result in a geographical dispersion of activities or a decentralization of coordination and control for individual firms. On the basis of the two axes in Figure 15.7, four situa-

INTERNATIONAL BUSINESS STRATEGY IN ACTION

Tate & Lyle as a transnational

The dominant firm in the sugar industry is Tate & Lyle Plc, a British MNE founded in 1921. Its early success was based upon processing sugar from plantations in the Caribbean. It is the major sugar provider to Europe, is also present in North America, and now finds its fastest growing market in Asia, especially China, and in developing third world economies.

Tate and Lyle's firm-specific advantages are based on its brand name and reputation for quality and also on economies of scale in its very large sugar refinery plants. Since sugar producers (such as beet farmers in the United States) are highly protected, Tate & Lyle needs to be nationally responsive to local regulations as well as highly globalized, i.e., it has to operate as a "transnational" firm. It has therefore developed a decentralized "regional" organizational structure to help develop responsiveness to local market demands and regulations.

The demand for sugar in wealthy western economies is slowing down due to health concerns and the arrival of sugar substitutes in the form of artifical sweeteners and starches. This has encouraged Tate & Lyle to broaden its market to Asia and the emerging economies of Eastern Europe, as well as to diversify into associated product areas, such as sweeteners, where it markets sucralose. In the 1980s it made numerous acquisitions in the United States, such as Staley (now Western Sugar). As a result it now has 20 per cent of the North American sugar market. Indeed, Tate & Lyle is now so multinational that only 16 per cent of its total sales come from its British home base; 36 per cent are from the United States; 23 per cent from the rest of Europe and 24 per cent from the rest of the world. Truly a transnational firm.

Sources: Tate & Lyle Annual Reports 1995, 1996, 1997; *http://www.hoovers.com/capsules/42402.html*, "Hoover's Company Capsule – Tate & Lyle PLC."

tions can be distinguished. Quadrants 1 and 4 are the simplest cases. In quadrant 1 the need for globalization is high and the need for awareness of sovereignty is low. This focus on economies of scale leads to competitive strategies that are based on price competition. In this environment mergers and acquisitions often occur. The opposite situation is represented by quadrant 4, where the need for national responsiveness is high but the globalization concern is low. In this case niche companies adapt products to satisfy the high demands of sovereignty and to ignore economies of scale since globalization is not very important. Quadrants 2 and 3 reflect opposite situations. Quadrant 2 incorporates those cases where the need for both globalization and national responsiveness is low. Both the potential to obtain economies of scale

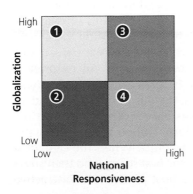

Figure 15.7   Globalization and national responsiveness

Source: Adapted from C. A. Bartlett, "Building and Managing the Transnational: the New Organizational Challenge," in M. E. Porter (ed.), *Competition in Global Industries* (Boston: Harvard Business School Press, 1986); and C. A. Bartlett and S. Ghoshal, *Managing Across Borders: The Transnational Solution*, 2nd ed. (Boston: Harvard Business School Press, 1998).

and the benefits of being sensitive to sovereignty are of little value. Typical strategies in quadrant 2 are characterized by increased international standardization of products and services. This can lead to lower needs for centralized quality control and centralized strategic decision making, while simultaneously eliminating requirements to adapt activities to individual countries.

In quadrant 3 the needs for globalization and national responsiveness are both high. There is a strong need for integration in production, along with higher requirements for regional adaptations in marketing. Quadrant 3 is the most challenging quadrant and one in which many successful "transnational" MNEs operate. Using this framework, we can analyze the impact of various exogenous policy shocks and trends on different industries, firms, banks, and other private sector institutions.

Balancing the trade-offs

MNEs in every industry apply the ideas in Figure 15.7, but they do so in a variety of ways. The following are select examples from three different industries: entertainment, personal computers, and automobiles.

Entertainment One of the most successful entertainment firms in the world is the Walt Disney Company. Its Euro Disney operation in France is a good example of how globalization and national responsiveness are balanced. The park offers many of the same features (globalization) found in Disney's Orlando (Florida), Anaheim (California), and Tokyo operations, including amusement rides and cartoon characters such as Mickey Mouse, Goofy, and Donald Duck. The company is now expanding the European facilities along the lines of its MGM studios near Orlando.[44] This globalization focus which stresses uniformity among the geographically scattered parks is supplemented by national responsiveness that is designed to appeal to European visitors. English and French are the official languages of the park, and there are multilingual guides who are conversant in Dutch, German, Spanish, and Italian. A second example of national responsiveness is found in the international emphasis that the company has given to its Disney characters: Pinocchio is Italian, Cinderella is French, Peter Pan is British. At its movie theater in the park Disney shows a European history film offering (in the United States the film is a travelogue of America).

Another example of globalization/national responsiveness is offered by Sega Enterprises, best known for its Sonic the Hedgehog video game character. Sega is now taking its computer simulation technology and beginning to develop small theme parks that will provide the same thrills as a roller coaster or a trip through space. This is being done through the use of simulators like those used to train airline pilots. By building a series of different amusement simulators, Sega intends to offer a wide array of "rides" without having to bear the expense of physically building these facilities. The idea is captured in the term "virtual reality," which means that participants experience the effects of a situation without literally being there.[45] An example is provided by "Scramble Training," a Sega simulator that is part video and part movie. This interactive game allows eight players to enter a small space capsule and to take their position as pilot trainees. The captain appears on a screen in front of the simulator and gives orders to the players, who in turn launch the capsule and swerve through space, firing missiles and competing for points. When the captain is wounded, the controls are turned over to the player with the best score, who then steers the capsule in for a landing. Sega intends to develop a host of different interactive simulators that will allow it to compete with amusement parks such as Disney. (In fact, Sega's concept is often referred to as "Disney in a Box.") The simulators are uniform in design and construction, thus allowing the company to employ a globalization emphasis. However, the types of games will vary from country to country (national responsiveness) depending on the entertainment interests of the local populace. For example, Sega has found that Americans are very sports-oriented, so there is likely to be an opportunity for players to participate in a world series simulation. In Europe, this game would have little attraction, but many players there would like to participate in the World Cup soccer finals. Thus the company can modify its product characteristics to meet the needs of the customer.[46]

Personal computers   Most personal computer (PC) makers compete on the bases of technology and price. They offer state-of-the-art machines and try to hold down their costs by outsourcing components and by improving assembly efficiency. This strategy is particularly important in markets such as Japan, where less than 25 per cent of the population owns PCs and local demands, such as a need to write in *kanji*, have discouraged foreign competition.

In recent years, however, US firms have been making major headway in this market, thanks to their ability to exploit both globalization and national responsiveness.[47] For example, Compaq and Dell have entered this market with low-priced units that were the same as those sold elsewhere (globalization) but offered sharply lower prices (national responsiveness). As a result, both firms have been able to garner market share. IBM has employed a similar strategy in addition to addressing the desire of local customers to write in *kanji*. The company has now perfected a bilingual version of Microsoft's DOS, the standard operating system that controls approximately 80 per cent of PCs in the world. IBM's version allows these machines to prepare or search documents with Japanese characters, the western alphabet, or both. Apple is also having very good success in Japan, thanks to its willingness to adapt to local needs. For example, the company has a Japanese management team that has helped to surmount local barriers to "buying foreign." The company has also cultivated a strong network of dealers and worked to develop an image as an innovator, both of which are of critical importance in the Japanese market. As a result of this careful balance of globalization and national responsiveness, Apple and IBM alone now account for almost 15 per cent of the Japanese PC market.

Other US firms are also using a carefully formulated globalization/national responsiveness strategy to gain market share. For example, Microsoft, designer of Windows, one of the most popular PC software programs of all time, has written a special version for the Japanese market. Until 1993 only 440,000 copies of the program had been sold, but when the company unveiled its new version of Windows, over 65,000 copies were sold in two days. Summing up the current situation, one observer has noted, "For now, American PC vendors feel the wind at their backs. Not only is the software finally available to help them attack the Japanese market with a coherent strategy, but, in addition, the strengthening yen lets them further undercut the prices of their Japanese counterparts."[48]

Automobiles   Every car manufacturer uses globalization by producing autos that can be made and marketed around the world. In a few cases, the Volkswagen Beetle being the best example, a car will not need to be modified for the local market.[49] In most cases, however, a globalization strategy is complemented by national responsiveness in the form of design, engineering, and manufacturing changes. Ford Motor's Mondeo provides a good example. This car has been developed for the world market and has uniform worldwide engineering standards with almost every specification expressed in the metric system. The company also has created uniform standards for raw materials, design, procurement, and manufacture of individual parts. Identical production tools are used at both European and US locations so that economies of scale can be maximized. At the same time, Ford has taken national responsiveness into consideration. European buyers prefer manual transmissions, while US buyers like automatic drive. Europeans demand cars that handle well, while this is not a priority issue with US customers. On the other hand, Americans want air-conditioned cars, while many European buyers do not. The overall cost of developing the Mondeo was $6 billion. However, initial sales in Europe were brisk and the company believes that it can maintain this momentum in the US market. Ford also believes that it can create additional car models from the Mondeo program and thus can develop a series of new offerings. If this is true, the globalization and national responsiveness strategies used for the Mondeo will help to smooth the way for future auto sales and help the company to recoup this enormous investment.[50]

Honda offers another example of globalization and national responsiveness strategies. The firm now builds a variety of different car sizes from one production platform by bending and stretching the autos to fit the demands of the market. As a result, Honda is able to build cars in the US that are longer and roomier, while offering smaller, more compact models of the same car in Japan. The company is now using this same approach to build sports utility vehicles for the world market.[51]

General Motors (GM) offers another example of globalization and national responsiveness strategies. Like Ford, GM often develops cars for the European market and then introduces them into the United States. As a result, the cars are frequently identical in styling and design but have different features to accommodate local tastes. Corsa, a new subcompact offering in Europe, has more features and fewer parts than competitive models.[52] For example, hooks have replaced nut-and-bolt fasteners, making it easier to assemble the car, and the exhaust system, which was initially designed to include 16 separate pieces, now comes as a single part. These design changes make it easier and less expensive to build the car. When the auto is made in the US market, it will be possible to build and assemble each unit quickly because the process will have been perfected in Europe. This globalization focus is complemented by national responsiveness. The Corsa has mechanical seat belt tensioners which tighten the belts around the driver and front-seat passenger in a collision. This feature helps the car to appeal to the safety concerns of local buyers. At the time that the auto was introduced in Europe, these features were not available on any US car, but they will be. This globalization/national responsiveness strategy is also used by GM within Europe, where conditions are both simpler and more complex than in the United States. On the simpler side, GM's European subsidiary turns out only six basic models of a single line of cars. On the complex side, the subsidiary markets these autos in more than 25 different countries, and in each case customer tastes vary widely. As a result, globalization and national responsiveness both remain key areas of concern.[53]

Competitiveness in the triad

From the viewpoint of MNEs, one of the most important business decisions regards the tradeoff between globalization and national responsiveness. Successful MNEs know that they can no longer afford to ignore the latter and to concentrate solely on globalization.

In the United States The United States experiences considerable decentralization in economic decision making. It is a country in which subnational units (states and provinces) continue to increase in importance. This issue should not be confused with pluralism. A variety of political opinions and parties is a strength of democracy. The problem arises when the institutional structure of the nation and its businesses cannot operate in an efficient manner, relative to global competitors.

The US Constitution was designed to allow Congress to be a broker for regional and special interests. On occasions the Congress works with the Executive branch, and a coordinated economic and even social policy can be both formulated and implemented. Examples of social reform and government economic activity in the Kennedy–Johnson years can be contrasted with a return to more market-based principles and a somewhat reduced role for government in the Reagan years.

However, in many areas affecting the private sector today the overwhelming characteristic of doing business in the United States is the responsiveness of governments to special interest groups and lobbies. The more decentralized the level of government is the more responsive will be the regulatory activity to the lobbyist. On occasions, businesses themselves can be lobbyists, but there are many other groups, such as environmentalists and social activists, who seem to be growing in power. Examples of conflicts in business lobbying occur in the areas of administration of US trade remedy laws and in the current US debate about the possible regulation of inward foreign direct investment (FDI).

It has been demonstrated by Rugman and Anderson,[54] as well as by others, that the current administration of US countervailing duty (CVD) and antidumping (AD) laws is highly responsive to domestic producer interests and biased against foreign firms (see Tables 15.2 and 15.3). It has been found that US corporations use CVD and AD as a competitive strategy to erect entry barriers against rival firms.[55] Thus even when the US government was pursuing negotiations for free trade with Canada, individual US corporations were still using the CVD and AD laws to help restrict Canadian imports. This is a clear example of the US national interest being offset by selective producer interests. Examples have occurred in the softwood lumber, pork, fish, steel and related industries – there were over 50 CVD and AD cases against Canada in the 1980s. More of the same is in store in the future, although Canadian concerns about the administration of CVD and AD laws have been somewhat answered by the establishment of binational panels under the terms of the FTA.

Another area of concern is inward FDI, which some congressional leaders now wish to restrict, and some Americans seem concerned with the growing amount of Japanese FDI. Some members of Congress have urged more screening of such FDI, and there is a strong "Japan-bashing" stance in US trade policy. Yet at the same time state officials have been actively seeking Japanese FDI because they want the jobs and the tax base. This potential clash between Washington "beltway" thinking (anti-Japanese) and state-level activity (pro-Japanese) parallels Canada's experience with the regulation of FDI.

The United States seems destined in the next ten years to repeat many of the mistakes made in Canada over the last 30 years. In 1974 the Trudeau government introduced the Foreign Investment Review Agency (FIRA), which was designed to screen FDI on economic criteria to assess if there was a net benefit to Canada. Over the 1974

Table 15.2 World countervailing duty actions, July 1980 to June 1995

Country/area	Actions	Percentage of world	Definitive duties	Percentage of world
United States	360	56.4	148	79.6
Chile	153	24.0	6	3.2
Australia	69	10.8	15	8.1
Canada	22	3.4	12	6.5
Brazil	11	1.7	1	0.5
New Zealand	7	1.1	–	0.0
European Union (EU)	6	0.9	3	1.6
Peru	4	0.6	–	0.0
Austria	2	0.3	1	0.5
Argentina	2	0.3	–	0.0
Japan	1	0.2	–	0.0
Mexico	1	0.2	–	0.0
Total	638	100.0	186	100.0

Source: Adapted from GATT, *Basic Instruments and Selected Documents* (*BISD*), supplements 27–41.

Table 15.3 World antidumping actions, July 1980 to June 1995*

Country/area	Actions	Percentage of world	Definitive duties	Percentage of world
United States	608	28	366	37
Australia	549	25	193	20
Canada	362	17	190	19
European Union (EU)	377	17	140	14
Finland	15	1	2	0
New Zealand	41	2	15	2
Mexico	81	4	40	4
Poland	24	1	–	–
Brazil	30	1	9	1
Sweden	8	0	–	–
Austria	8	0	–	–
Korea	12	1	5	1
South Africa	9	0	1	0
Argentina	6	0	6	1
India	14	1	–	–
Peru	4	0	–	–
Japan	3	0	–	–
Chile	2	0	3	0
Turkey	2	0	11	1
Singapore	2	0	–	–
Colombia	1	0	2	0
Thailand	–	–	1	0
Total	2,158	100	984	100

*Data for July 1993 to June 1994 was not available.
Source: Adapted from GATT, *Basic Instruments and Selected Documents* (*BISD*), supplements 27–41.

to 1985 period FIRA responded to Ottawa's political winds, at times rejecting as much as 30 per cent of applications but at other times (especially 1982 to 1985) approving virtually everything.[56] The administrators at FIRA and the responsible ministers made political decisions just as the US International Trade Commission and the US Commerce Department do today in US trade law cases.

In 1985 FIRA was abolished and a new agency, Investment Canada, was created with the mandate to attract FDI rather than scare it away.[57] This change in thinking about FDI came with a change in government. In 1984 the Progressive Conservative government was elected with a mandate of job creation. Throughout the lifetime of FIRA most provinces, especially those in Atlantic Canada, wanted FDI for jobs and taxes. The clash between the provinces that favored FDI and the central Canadian economic nationalists led to the federal government giving up many of its powers to regulate FDI by buying into the agenda of the provinces, especially their overwhelming priority about jobs. Perhaps this is some evidence of the triumph of decentralized economic power. But a paradox emerges. In Canada, the economic nationalists, who have used central government power, are in retreat, while it appears that in the United States economic nationalism is just beginning to take off. If Japan-bashing continues, then the US proponents of restrictions on FDI will have the same unhappy experience with the FIRA as did Canada. Private sector US corporate strategists will, therefore, need to respond to a large dose of economic nationalism and its associated protectionist inefficiencies.

In Eastern Europe Another example of the use of sovereignty and the destruction of centralized economic power and values was the 1989 revolution in central Europe and the collapse of the Soviet Union in 1991. The rejection of totalitarian communist regimes by the people of countries such as Romania, Belarus, and Russia will have many implications for business. The key point is that these countries are currently very poor, with inefficient economic and financial systems. The economic development of these nations will probably be through FDI rather than through joint ventures. Popular wisdom to the contrary, joint ventures between poor nations and wealthy corporations do not work. The preferable mode of international business is FDI since western firms can then control their proprietary advantages and not risk dissipation through joint ventures.[58] In the literature on joint ventures in developing countries it has been found that there exists a great deal of instability and joint venture failure.[59] Multinationals prefer FDI and countries such as India and Mexico, which once greatly restricted FDI, experienced inefficient economic development and eventually had to lift such regulations. This experience is relevant for Eastern Europe.

Doing business in Eastern Europe for the next five to ten years will be dominated by the need for economic efficiency. The globalization concept will overwhelm concerns about adapting products for sovereignty. It is in the EU nations that national responsiveness will be important for corporations. In the wealthy triad powers, adapting to sovereignty matters; in the third world and in Eastern Europe, economic efficiency is what matters.

In Japan A key explanation for the success of Japanese MNEs is that they benefit from a highly centralized home market economy. This has permitted Japan to use levers of industrial policy and strategic trade policy that could not be implemented successfully in the other areas of the triad.

Centralized government policy is critical to implementing effective corporate strategy.[60] The Japanese cultural, religious, social, and political system is much more centralized in nature than other triad blocs. This has enabled Japanese MNEs to follow globalization strategies. So, for example, after the two OPEC oil crises of the 1970s Japanese industry was rapidly transformed out of shipbuilding, heavy engineering, and other energy-intensive manufacturing and into computer-based manufacturing, consumer electronics, and high value-added services, including banking and financial services. The government and the MNEs worked together to implement a new industrial strategy in an effective and efficient manner.

Such radical restructuring through industrial policy is unlikely to work in North America and Europe because of the decentralized nature of economic power. Attempts by the United States or Canada to implement a new industrial policy are unlikely to be successful. Whatever government incentives and subsidies are made available will be appropriated by industries seeking shelter from competitors in the triad. The decentralized nature of the economic system will be used by companies to erect entry barriers against foreign competitors. This has already occurred in the United States with companies seeking protection from competitors through the use of CVD and AD laws. US steel, forest products, fish, and semiconductor industries, among others, have been using short-term legal remedies instead of investing in the development of sustainable, proprietary, firm-specific advantages.

What are the implications for corporate strategy of these asymmetrical developments in the triad? Japanese MNEs will continue to pursue a globalization strategy, but these MNEs may face difficulties when they need to operate in the decentralized environments of North America and Europe since marketing-type skills will become more important than production skills. Over the last decade MNEs from Europe and North America have often abused the nature of their home country decentralized systems, and sovereignty has hindered efficient corporate development. However, MNEs from North America and Europe have a potential competitive advantage over Japanese MNEs if they can learn from their past mistakes. Awareness of sovereignty can make the former companies better equipped in the future to be more nationally responsive than their Japanese counterparts. Indeed, Japanese MNEs may become locked into a "globalization only" strategy, just as the world begins to demand much more corporate responsiveness to sovereignty.

ACTIVE LEARNING CHECK

Review your answer to Active Learning Case question 3 and make any changes you like. Then compare your answer to the one below.

3. How does ABB address the issues of globalization and national responsiveness? In each case, cite an example.

ABB addresses the issue of globalization by producing state-of-the-art products for worldwide markets. For example, the same high-speed trains that can carry passengers and goods through the Alps can be used for transporting people and goods across the plains of the United States or the steppes of Russia. It may be necessary to make modifications to address local geographic and climactic conditions, of course, but the basic technology and manufacturing techniques are similar. At the same time ABB addresses national responsiveness by trying to be a local firm that is interested in the needs of that market. As a result, the company balances globalization and sovereignty – a feat that is not accomplished very well by most MNEs.

SUMMARY

Key points

1. Porter's diamond model is based on four country-specific determinants and two external variables (chance and government). This model is extremely useful in examining strategies among triad and other economically developed countries. However, when applying the model to smaller, open, trading economies, a modification of the model is in order.

2. Canada's economic success will depend on its ability to view itself as part of the North American market and to integrate itself into this overall market. This requires the use of a "double diamond" model for corporate strategy. This is resulting in Canadian firms developing competitive capabilities that allow them to compete successfully with US firms in the United States. This is being done by (a) developing innovative products and services that simultaneously meet the needs of the US and Canadian customer, (b) drawing on the support industries and infrastructure of both the US and Canadian diamonds, and (c) making free and full use of the physical and human resources in both countries.

3. Mexico's economic success also depends on its ability to integrate itself into the North American market. However, this strategy is different from that of the Canadians because Mexico does not have the FDI to invest in the US market. Much of its linkage is a result of low labor costs that allow the country to produce inexpensive goods and to export them into the United States. Part of the country's future economic success will be determined by the North American Free Trade Agreement worked out with the United States and Canada in 1993.

4. A major trend that has affected the thinking of corporate MNE strategists over the last ten years is that of balancing a concern for globalization with that of national responsiveness. Many MNEs have focused on globalization without giving sufficient attention to the sovereignty issue. However, during the millennium there will have to be a reversal of this trend and MNEs will become much more interested in national responsiveness if they hope to succeed in overseas markets.

Key terms

- strategic cluster
- globalization
- national responsiveness

Review and discussion questions

1. The Porter diamond is based on four country-specific determinants and two external variables. What does this statement mean? Put it in your own words.

2. Porter notes that "Firms, not individual nations, compete in international markets." How does this statement help to explain some of the major challenges facing MNEs?

3. Using Figure 15.2 as your point of reference, how does the current national development of the United States differ from that of Korea? How does Great Britain's differ from that of Singapore?

4. Why does the Porter diamond need to be modified in explaining the international competitiveness of countries such as Canada and Mexico?

5. How does the double diamond, as illustrated in Figure 15.3, help to explain international competitiveness in Canada?

6. How can Canadian firms view the United States and Canada as home-based markets and integrate the use of both diamonds for development and implementation of strategy? Be complete in your answer.

7. Of what value are strategic clusters in the double diamond? Explain.

8. How does the double diamond in Figure 15.6 help to explain Mexico's international business strategy? Explain.

9. How important are the maquiladoras to the growth of the Mexican economy? In what way do these businesses link Mexico with the Canada–United States double diamond?

10. In what way are globalization and national responsiveness important to MNE strategies?

11. In the entertainment industry, which is more important, globalization or national responsiveness?

12. Based on current developments in the PC market in Japan, which is more important for US MNEs, globalization or national responsiveness? Why?

13. Which is more important for US automakers doing business in Europe, globalization or national responsiveness? Why?

REAL CASES

MEXICO AND THE MAQUILADORAS

During the 1990s an increasing number of US firms have moved business to Mexico's export processing zones, the maquiladoras. These are tax-free production and assembly centres within Mexico where foreign investors can use local labor and export the finalized product without paying customs duties. They are mainly located along the US–Mexican border. For example, when Stanley Cohen realized that his Los Angeles pipe fixture business was losing ground to foreign rivals, he knew that he had only three options: close up shop, move offshore, or take the operation to Mexico. He opted for the latter where workers are paid lower wages than in Los Angeles. As a result, Cohen now has a small headquarters in San Diego, major manufacturing operations in Mexico, and sales in California. This arrangement is not unique. East-man Kodak, Ford, General Motors, IGM, Hewlett-Packard, and Wang Computers among others, all have production operations in Mexico's border region but sales in the United States.

US firms are not the only ones looking to benefit from low wages and closeness to the US market. Volkswagen has shifted its entire North American production to Puebla, east of Mexico City. The company is manufacturing cars there for the central US market. At the same time Asian firms have positioned themselves to take advantage of the maquiladoras as an assembly platform in North America. In Tiajuana, Sanyo turns out one million fridges a year while investments by South Korean and Japanese electronics manufacturers have made the area the television capital of the world. Samsung has just invested $600 million in a plant that will employ 5,000 workers.

Wages are one of the primary reasons for companies moving business to Mexico. In 1998 an entry-level assembly worker at GM earned $10.25 an hour in the United States and $1 an hour in Mexico. A second reason attracting business to Mexico is the labor supply. Mexico's population is increasing faster than that of most other countries, and this is likely to continue well into the new century. A third reason is that when the United States and Canada started the North American Free Trade Agreement (NAFTA) with Mexico in 1994, many of the maquiladoras were transformed from simple border "screwdriver" plants to more modern regional companies that can buy and sell on both sides of the border.

Sony's latest plant, which employs 1,000 workers, now includes a design department. Clean-room technology and the latest equipment from multinationals are transforming the basic structure of the old maquiladoras. One of the main reasons is that, thanks to NAFTA's country-of-origin clauses, it is expected that by the year 2001 producing in Mexico will be cheaper than importing from Asia. From here, the next step will be to produce goods deep in Mexico and to ship them hundreds of miles to the border, as in the case of Kodak, which makes camera parts in Monterrey, and IBM, which makes computers in Guadalajara.

Today there are over 4,000 maquiladoras in the north of Mexico employing over one million Mexicans and supporting industries that employ a similar amount of workers on the north side of the border. Both sides of the border are highly interconnected. For instance, 15,000 people commute to Juarez, Mexico, from El Paso, Texas and 40 per cent of the retail sales in El Paso are to Mexicans coming the other way. The cities have working groups on everything, from infrastructure to sport leagues.

1. What factor conditions make Mexico an attractive market? Explain.

2. How would NAFTA help the US economy? The Mexican economy?

3. In what way are the US and Mexican "diamonds" inter-linked? Explain.

Sources: Louis S. Rickman, "How NAFTA Will Help America," *Fortune*, April 19, 1993, pp. 95–102; Geri Smith and Douglas Harbrecht, "The Moment of 'Truth' for Mexico," *Business Week*, June 28, 1993, pp. 44–45; "A Survey of Mexico," *The Economist*, October 28, 1995, pp. SS.3–16. "One River, One Country," *The Economist*, September 13, 1997, pp. 55–56; "Deep in the Heart of NAFTA," *The Economist*, February 28, 1998, pp. 55–56; "Mexico's New Frontier. Tiajuana Brass," *The Economist*, February 8, 1997, p. 68; Jose Aguayo, "Saint Benedict and the Labor Unions," *Forbes*, February 9, 1998, p. 64.

S. C. FANG BROTHERS

Many large US retail stores buy goods that are produced abroad. Good examples include Sears and Wal-Mart. However, very few people know the names of the manufacturers, despite the fact that some of these firms are extremely large. For example, not many people have ever heard of S. C. Fang Brothers, but a large number of them have worn products produced by this company. The Fangs are one of the families that dominate the textile industry in Asia, and for the last decade they have supplied T-shirts to the Gap and blouses to Calvin Klein, to name but two of their customers. The family began the business after it fled from mainland China in 1949. The Fangs had ordered hundreds of the newest, most technologically advanced cotton spindles to be shipped to Hong Kong. They then escaped from China to Hong Kong and started their business.

At first the company moved into cotton spinning and did very well. However, by the mid-1960s competitors turned to yarn and textiles, and the company changed strategy. It moved into apparel, producing sweaters on a private-label basis for stores in the United Kingdom. Soon the Fangs were major players in the apparel trade, including a large market in the United States, but this did not last long. Labor costs in Hong Kong began to escalate and the US government started imposing restrictions on the quantities of cheap sweaters that could be brought in from Hong Kong. It was time for another change in strategy.

The Fangs spread manufacturing operations across nine countries. By the mid-1990s they made T-shirts in the Philippines and Panama, trousers in Thailand, sweaters in Malaysia, and knit garments in South Carolina. They have also opened retail stores, the best known being the Episode Stores chain. A large percentage of the clothing sold in these stores is made by the Fangs in their worldwide factories. One of their most popular

▶

offerings has been what is called "bridge clothing," which is less expensive than designer outfits but which is still of high quality. This move upmarket has made Fang Brothers more responsive to foreign customers, compared to their early days of exporting alone from Hong Kong.

When the island of Hong Kong reverted from British to Chinese control in 1997, many business people there left as they were worried about the possible adverse economic consequences of integrating a capitalist society into a communist one. The Fang family decided to keep Hong Kong as its home and headquarters. However, if conditions under the Chinese had required them to move, it would not have been too difficult because the company is now situated worldwide. As their factories and revenues are now diversified globally the business is no longer dependent on Hong Kong as its home base.

1. What factor conditions are most important to this company? How has the firm managed to maintain access to these factors?

2. How have the Fang brothers managed to link their operations into triad markets? Describe two examples.

3. How does the company deal with the issue of national responsiveness? Give two examples.

Sources: Adapted from Phyllis Berman and Jean Sherman Chatzky, "Closer to the Consumer," *Forbes*, January 20, 1992, pp. 56–57; Bill Saporito, "David Glass Won't Crack Under Fire," *Fortune*, February 8, 1993, pp. 75–80; and Kevin Kelly, "The Big Store May Be on a Big Roll," *Business Week*, August 30, 1993, pp. 82–85.

ENDNOTES

1. For a detailed discussion of these variables and determinants, see Michael E. Porter, *The Competitive Advantage of Nations* (New York: Free Press, 1990), pp. 69–130.

2. Alan M. Rugman and Alain Verbeke, *Global Corporate Strategy and Trade Policy* (London and New York: Routledge, 1990).

3. Michael E. Porter, *The Competitive Advantage of Nations* (New York: Free Press, 1990), p. 33.

4. Ibid., p. 671.

5. A. E. Safarian, *Foreign Ownership of Canadian Industry* (Toronto: McGraw-Hill, Inc., 1968).

6. Alan M. Rugman, *Multinationals in Canada: Theory, Performance and Economic Impact* (Boston: Martinus Nijhoff, 1980).

7. Harold Crookell, *Canadian-American Trade and Investment Under the Free Trade Agreement* (Westport, Conn.: Quorum Books, 1990).

8. Alan M. Rugman, *Multinationals and Canada-United States Free Trade* (Columbia, SC: University of South Carolina Press, 1990).

9. See Alan M. Rugman, "Strategies for National Competitiveness," *Long Range Planning*, 1987, vol. 20, no. 3, pp. 92–97.

10. Alan M. Rugman and John McIlveen, *Megafirms: Strategies for Canada's Multinationals* (Toronto: Methuen/Nelson, 1985).

11. Ibid.

12. John H. Dunning, "Dunning on Porter." Paper presented at the Annual Meeting of the Academy of International Business, Toronto, October 1990, and published in John H. Dunning, *The Globalization of Business* (London and New York: Routledge, 1993); and John H. Dunning, "Internationalizing Porter's Diamond," *Management International Review* 33, Special Issue 2, 1993, pp. 7–16.

13. Ibid., 1990, p. 11.

14. Alan M. Rugman and Joseph R. D'Cruz, *Fast Forward: Improving Canada's International Competitiveness* (Toronto: Kodak Canada, 1991); and Alan M. Rugman and Joseph R. D'Cruz, "The 'Double Diamond' Model of International Competitiveness: The Canadian Experience." *Management International Review* 33, Special Issue 2, 1993, pp. 17–40.

15. For another view of the FTA, see John N. Turner, "There Is More to Trade Than Trade: An Analysis of the US/Canada Trade Agreement 1988," *California Management Review*, Winter 1991, pp. 109–119.

16. Alan M. Rugman, "The Free Trade Agreement and the Global Economy," *Business Quarterly*, Summer 1988, pp. 13–20.

17. Alan M. Rugman and Alain Verbeke, "Strategic Responses to Free Trade," *Hitotsubashi Journal of Commerce and Management*, December 1988, pp. 69–79; and Alan M. Rugman and Alain Verbeke, "Foreign Subsidiaries and Multinational Strategic Management: An Extension and Correction of Porter's Single Diamond Framework," *Management*

International Review, vol. 33, Special Issue 2, 1993, pp. 71–84.

18. See, for example, Joseph R. D'Cruz and James Fleck, *Yankee Canadians in the Global Economy* (London, Ontario: National Centre for Management Research and Development, 1987); and Alan M. Rugman and Joseph D'Cruz, *New Visions for Canadian Business: Strategies for Competing in the Global Economy* (Toronto: Kodak Canada, 1990).

19. See Andrew Solocha, Mark D. Soskin, and Mark J. Kasoff, "Determinants of Foreign Direct Investment: A Case of Canadian Direct Investment in the United States," *Management International Review*, Fall 1990, pp. 371–386.

20. Also, see "The Spreading Maple Leaf," *Economist*, January 15, 1994, p. 68.

21. Anthony De Palma, "The Transportation Giant Up North," *New York Times*, December 26, 1998, pp. C1, 3.

22. See, for example, Tamsin Carlisle, "Calgary Becomes Outpost on High-Tech Frontier," *Wall Street Journal*, March 24, 1998, p. A19.

23. Also, see Alan M. Rugman and Alain Verbeke, "Multinational Corporate Strategy and the Canada–US Free Trade Agreement," *Management International Review*, Summer 1990, pp. 253–266; and Alan M. Rugman and Alain Verbeke, "How to Operationalize Porter's Diamond of International Competitiveness," *The International Executive*, vol. 35, no. 4, July/August, 1993, pp. 283–299.

24. For more details of this business network approach, see Joseph R. D'Cruz and Alan M. Rugman, *New Compacts of Canadian Competitiveness* (Toronto: Kodak Canada, 1992); Joseph R. D'Cruz and Alan M. Rugman, "Business Networks for International Competitiveness," *Business Quarterly*, vol. 56, no. 4, Spring 1992, pp. 101–107; and Joseph R. D'Cruz and Alan M. Rugman, "Developing International Competitiveness: The Five Partners Model," *Business Quarterly*, vol. 58, no. 2, Winter 1993, pp. 60–72.

25. Ibid., pp. 29–36.

26. World Economic Forum, 1998.

27. Christopher J. Chipello and Roger Ricklefs, "How Productivity Clouds Canada's Competitiveness, Living Standards," *Wall Street Journal*, February 9, 1999, p. A19.

28. Alan M. Rugman, *Japanese Direct Investment in Canada* (Ottawa: Canada-Japan Trade Council, 1990).

29. See Alan M. Rugman and F. Bill Mohri, "Trade and Investment Among Canada and the Triad," Working paper, University of Toronto, July 1991; and Alan M. Rugman (ed.), *Foreign Investment and NAFTA* (Columbia, SC: University of South Carolina Press, 1994).

30. Alan M. Rugman and Alain Verbeke, "Foreign Direct Investment in North America: Current Patterns and Future Relationships in Canada, the United States, and Mexico," Ontario Centre for International Business, Research program working paper, no. 57, November 1991, p. 4, published in Khosrow Fatemi and Dominick Salvatore (eds.), *North American Free Trade Agreement* (London: Pergamon Press, 1994).

31. In contrast, Japanese FDI between 1986 and 1991 dropped from $225 million to $150 million. See Stephen Baker and Karen Lowry Miller, "Why Japan Inc. Is Steering Clear of Mexico," *Business Week*, December 2, 1991, pp. 50–52.

32. Also, see Anthony DePalma, "Mexico Slips Into Recession," *New York Times*, March 16, 1994, pp. C1, C5.

33. Bob Ortega, "Some Mexicans Charge North in NAFTA's Wake," *Wall Street Journal*, February 22, 1994, pp. B1, B5; and Craig Torres, "TRW Plans Mexican Venture to Start a Credit Operation in Guadalajara," *Wall Street Journal*, January 7, 1994, p. A5.

34. Sandra Masur, "The North American Free Trade Agreement: Why It's in the Interest of US Business," *Columbia Journal of World Business*, Summer 1991, pp. 99–103.

35. "Why Mexico Scares the UAW," *Business Week*, August 3, 1998, p. 37.

36. Jonathan Friedland and Joseph B. White, "GM Is Heading An Investment Boom in Mexico," *Wall Street Journal*, December 24, 1998, pp. A5, 6.

37. Joel Millman, "High-Tech Jobs Transfer to Mexico with Surprising Speed," *Wall Street Journal*, April 9, 1999, p. A18.

38. Geri Smith and Elisabeth Malkin, "Mexican Makeover," *Business Week*, December 21, 1998, p. 52.

39. Rugman and Verbeke, "Foreign Direct Investment in North America," op. cit., p. 12.

40. United States International Trade Commission, *The Likely Impact on the United States of a Free Trade Agreement with Mexico*, op. cit., pp. 1–5.

41. Also, see *Lloyd Economic Report* (Guadalajara, Mexico), March 1994.

42. Christopher A. Bartlett, "Building and Managing the Transnational: The New Organizational Challenge," in M. E. Porter (ed.), *Competition in Global Industries* (Boston: Harvard Business School Press, 1986), pp. 367–401.

43. Christopher A. Bartlett and Sumantra Ghoshal, *Managing Across Borders: The Transnational Solution* (Boston: Harvard Business School Press, 1989).

44. "Disney's Euro Problem," *Miami Herald*, July 9, 1993, p. C3.

45. Andrew Pollack, "Sega Takes Aim at Disney's World," *New York Times*, Section 3, July 4, 1993, pp. 1, 6.

46. For more on Sega see Irene M. Kunii, "Sega: 'We're Going to Blow Them Out of the Water'," *Business Week*, December 7, 1998, p. 108.

47. Brenton R. Schlender, "US PCs Invade Japan," *Fortune*, July 12, 1993, pp. 68–73.

48. Ibid., p. 73.

49. Gabriella Stern, "VW's US Comeback Rides On Restyled Beetle," *Wall Street Journal*, May 6, 1997, pp. B1–2.

50. Alex Taylor III, "Ford's $6 Billion Baby," *Fortune*, June 28, 1993, pp. 76–81.

51. Keith Naughton et al., "Can Honda Build a World Car?" *Business Week*, September 8, 1997, pp. 100–108.

52. Alex Taylor III, "Why GM Leads the Pack in Europe," *Fortune*, May 17, 1993, pp. 83–87.

53. Ibid., p. 84.

54. Alan M. Rugman and Andrew Anderson, *Administered Protection in America* (London and New York: Routledge, 1987).

55. Rugman and Verbeke, *Global Corporate Strategy and Trade Policy*, op. cit.

56. Alan M. Rugman, *Multinationals in Canada: Theory, Performance and Economic Impact* (Boston: Martinus Nijhoff, 1980).

57. Alan M. Rugman and Leonard Waverman, "Foreign Ownership and Corporate Strategy," in Leonard Waverman (ed.), *Corporate Globalization Through Mergers and Acquisitions* (Calgary: University of Calgary Press, 1991), pp. 59–87.

58. Alan M. Rugman, *Inside the Multinationals: The Economics of Internal Markets* (London: Croom Helm, and New York: Columbia University Press, 1981).

59. Paul W. Beamish, *Multinational Joint Ventures in Developing Countries* (London and New York: Routledge, 1989).

60. Alan M. Rugman and Alain Verbeke, *Global Corporate Strategy and Trade Policy*, op. cit.

ADDITIONAL BIBLIOGRAPHY

Akers, John F. "Ethics and Competitiveness – Putting First Things First," *Sloan Management Review*, vol. 30, no. 2 (Winter 1989).

Bartlett, Christopher and Ghoshal, Sumantra. *Managing Across Borders: The Transnational Solution* (Boston: Harvard Business Press, 1989, 1998).

Bartlett, Christopher and Ghoshal, Sumantra. *Transnational Management* (Boston: Irwin, 1992).

Boyd, Gavin (ed.) *The Struggle for World Markets: Competition and Cooperation Between NAFTA and the EU* (Cheltenham: Elgar, 1998).

Choate, Pat. "Political Advantage: Japan's Campaign for America," *Harvard Business Review*, vol. 68, no. 5 (September/October 1990).

Dickson, Peter R. and Czinkota, Michael R. "How the United States Can Be Number One Again: Resurrecting the Industrial Policy Debate," *Columbia Journal of World Business*, vol. 31, no. 3 (Fall 1996).

Dunning, John H. "Internationalizing Porter's Diamond," *Management International Review*, vol. 33, no. 2 (Second Quarter 1993).

Dunning, John H. "The Geographical Sources of Competitiveness of Firms: Some Results of a New Survey," *Transnational Corporations*, vol. 5, no. 3 (December 1996).

Kline, John M. "Trade Competitiveness and Corporate Nationality," *Columbia Journal of World Business*, vol. 24, no. 3 (Fall 1989).

Kotler, Philip. *The Marketing of Nations* (New York: The Free Press, 1997).

Kuttner, Robert. "How 'National Security' Hurts National Competitiveness," *Harvard Business Review*, vol. 69, no. 1 (January/February 1991).

Leong, Siew Meng and Tan, Chin Tiong. "Managing Across Borders: An Empirical Test of the Bartlett and Ghoshal (1989) Organizational Typology," *Journal of International Business Studies*, vol. 24, no. 3 (Third Quarter 1993).

Lodge, George C.; Decker, Hans W.; Tonelson, Alan; Brown, John Seely; Pennington, Hilary; Hale, David; Raduchel, William J.; Shapiro, Robert J.; Gilder, George; and Branscomb, Lewis M. "How Real Is America's Decline?" *Harvard Business Review*, vol. 70, no. 5 (September/October 1992).

Martinez, Jon I. and Jarillo, J. Carlos. "Coordination Demands of International Strategies," *Journal of International Business Studies*, vol. 22, no. 3 (Third Quarter 1991).

Merrills, Roy. "How Northern Telecom Competes on Time," *Harvard Business Review*, vol. 4 (July/August 1989).

Narula, Rajneesh. "Technology, International Business and Porter's 'Diamond': Synthesizing a Dynamic Competitive Development Model," *Management International Review*, vol. 33, no. 2 (Second Quarter 1993).

Ostry, Sylvia. "Government & Corporations in a Shrinking World: Trade & Innovation Policies in the United States, Europe & Japan," *Columbia Journal of World Business*, vol. 25, nos. 1, 2 (Spring/Summer 1990).

Porter, Michael E. "The Competitive Advantage of Nations," *Harvard Business Review*, vol. 68, no. 2 (March/April 1990).

Porter, Michael E. *On Competition* (Boston: Harvard Business School Press, 1998).

Radosevich, Raymond and Kassicieh, Suleiman. "Strategic Challenges and Proposed Responses to Competitiveness Through Public-Sector Technology," *California Management Review*, vol. 35, no. 4 (Summer 1993).

Roth, Kendall. "International Configuration and Co-ordination Archetypes for Medium-Sized Firms in Global Industries," *Journal of International Business Studies*, vol. 23, no. 3 (Third Quarter 1992).

Roth, Kendall and Morrison, Allen J. "An Empirical Analysis of the Integration-Responsiveness Framework in Global Industries," *Journal of International Business Studies*, vol. 21, no. 4 (Fourth Quarter 1990).

Ruhli, Edwin and Schuppisser, Stefan. "Switzerland and Its Industry in International Competition," *Columbia Journal of World Business*, vol. 29, no. 4 (Winter 1994).

Rugman, Alan M. "Diamond in the Rough," *Business Quarterly*, vol. 55, no. 3 (Winter 1991).

Rugman, Alan M. "Porter Takes the Wrong Turn," *Business Quarterly*, vol. 56, no. 3 (Winter 1992).

Rugman, Alan M. and D'Cruz, Joseph. "The Double Diamond Model of International Competitiveness: The Canadian Experience," *Management International Review*, vol. 33, no. 2 (1993).

Rugman, Alan M. and Verbeke, Alain. *Research in Global Strategic Management: Vol. 4: Beyond the Three Generics* (Greenwich, Conn.: JAI Press, 1993).

Rugman, Alan M. and Verbeke, Alain. "Foreign Subsidiaries and Multinational Strategic Management: An Extension and Correction of Porter's Single Diamond Framework," *Management International Review*, vol. 33, no. 2 (1993).

Rugman, Alan M. and Verbeke, Alain. "How to Operationalize Porter's Diamond of Competitive Advantage," *The International Executive*, vol. 35, no. 4 (July–August 1993).

Rugman, Alan M. and Waverman, Leonard. "Foreign Ownership and Corporate Strategy," in Leonard Waverman (ed.) *Corporate Globalization Through Mergers and Acquisitions* (Calgary: University of Calgary Press, 1991).

Scott, Bruce R. "Competitiveness: Self-Help for a Worsening Problem," *Harvard Business Review*, vol. 67, no. 4 (July/August 1989).

Smitka, Michael. "Are US Auto Exports the Growth Industry of the 1990s?" *Sloan Management Review*, vol. 35, no. 1 (Fall 1993).

CHAPTER 16

Doing Business in
the European Union

▼

OBJECTIVES OF THE CHAPTER

The European Union (EU) is one of the fastest growing markets in the world. It has been estimated that during the 1990s there was more market potential here than in either the United States or Japan. As a result, many MNEs are now doing business in the EU or are targeting the area in their expansion plans. This chapter examines the EU environment and reviews some of the major strategy considerations that must be addressed by companies doing business in this economic bloc. The objectives of this chapter are to:

1. **Describe** the emerging single European market and the competitive status of the EU in relation to other triad members.

2. **Discuss** how firms carry out an overall strategic analysis of the EU market in terms of competitive intelligence and evaluation of location.

3. **Relate** some of the major strategy issues that must be considered when doing business in the EU, including exporting, strategic alliances and acquisitions, manufacturing considerations, marketing approaches, and management considerations.

Everything is up in the air

One of the EU's primary goals is the elimination of economic barriers between member countries. However, this is proving to be something of a stumbling block in the airline industry where the nature and scope of the competition is causing headaches for regulatory agencies on both sides of the Atlantic. In particular, these agencies are concerned about a small number of airlines being able to dominate the industry and drive out the others.

When deregulation came about in the EU airline industry, it was obvious to many that there would be something of a shakeout. The chief executive of Italy's Alitalia estimated that of the two dozen major EU carriers at that time, most would be driven out or have to merge or enter into alliances with others. This is exactly what had happened in the US market when it deregulated. Major carriers such as American, Delta, and United began to garner market share and both smaller and weaker carriers soon found themselves unable to compete. A good example was Eastern Airlines, one of the largest but also least cost efficient, that was eventually driven from the market, along with a host of smaller carriers.

In an effort to protect themselves, EU airlines began buying competitors and talking with international carriers about tying together their routes with marketing agreements. One of the most prominent arrangements has been that of British Airways and American Airlines. The two entered into their agreement in 1996 and quickly found it under scrutiny by the EU Competition Commissioner, Karel Van Miert. The carriers argued that the commissioner had no standing in the matter because their agreement involved only flights between the United States and the United Kingdom. However, before it was all over the EU regulators forced the two airlines to agree to a number of conditions. Among others, these included giving rival airlines as many as 267 weekly takeoff and landing slots at London's Heathrow and Gatwick airports, equivalent to about 19 daily round trips, with 220 coming from coveted Heathrow. The two airlines also had to curtail for six months their flight frequencies between London and Dallas, Miami, and Chicago.

British Airways and American were not alone. The Commission also curtailed the operations of carriers in other alliances such as the Star Alliance which included United Airlines, Lufthansa, Thai Airlines, Scandinavian Airline Systems, Air Canada, Varig, South African Airways, Singapore, ANA, Air New Zealand, and Ansett Australia. For example, the Commission made United give up as many as 108 weekly slots at Frankfurt and Copenhagen airports and reduce flight frequencies for six months on the Frankfurt–Chicago and Frankfurt–Washington routes.

The primary reason for the Commission's action was to prevent any of the alliances from dominating its markets. In the case of the British Airways and American Airlines arrangement, for example, Mr Van Miert estimated that the alliance would control 60 per cent of the United States–United Kingdom traffic and 70 per cent of the business between New York and London, routes that are extremely profitable. The Commission is also concerned about the possibility of any airline dominating business on the continent.

At the same time, as these airlines fulfill their obligation to the Commission, there is growing pressure to lower airline prices and thus gain market share. A good example is British Airway's no-frills carrier, called Go, which began operations with introductory round-trip fares of $163 from London to Rome, Milan, and Copenhagen. This price was 50 per cent lower than most regular fares and opened up the question of how competitive the EU airline industry will become domestically – and whether the Commission will again step in and try to regulate things. For the moment, it seems that everything is up in the air.

▶

Sources: Adapted from Stewart Toy, Mark Maremont, and John Rossant, "The Carnival is Over," *Business Week*, December 9, 1991, pp. 50–54; "A Business Guide to the New Europe," *New York Times*, January 2, 1993, p. 13; Richard M. Hodgetts and Fred Luthans, *International Management*, 4th ed. (Burr Ridge, Ill.: Irwin/McGraw, 2000), Chapter 1; Adam Bryant, "Objections to British Air–American Tie Seen," *New York Times*, June 4, 1997, pp. C1–2; Stanley Reed, "Is British Air Flying into a Storm?" *Business Week*, June 30, 1997, pp. 52–53; Charles Goldsmith, "British Air's New No-Frills Carrier, Go, to Battle Its Discount Rivals," *Wall Street Journal*, May 22, 1998, p. B2; Charles Goldsmith, "AMR–British Air Linkup Just Keeps Circling, Circling," *Wall Street Journal*, Monday 15, 1998, p. B4; Charles Goldsmith and Julie Wolf, "EU Clears AMR/British Airways Alliance," *Wall Street Journal*, July 9, 1998, p. A3.

1. What barriers have to be surmounted before the airline industry in EU countries becomes part of a single European market? Identify and describe one of them.

2. What types of competitive intelligence would US airlines want to gather in order to operate more effectively in the EU? Identify and describe two of them.

3. In what way will globalization and sovereignty be important issues to US airlines doing business in the EU?

4. In what way will both pricing and positioning be important for US airlines doing business in the EU?

THE EU ENVIRONMENT

The EU currently consists of 15 countries that are closely linked both economically and politically, eleven of whom have agreed to use the euro as their basic currency. Doing business in this bloc offers great opportunities, and many MNEs are interested in tapping this giant potential (see Table 16.1). Before examining the current EU environment, we need to realize that in the early years of the millennium this market will expand to incorporate other countries. This expanded EU will create a "greater Europe," comprising a trading area of some 450 million people in 25 countries (see accompanying map). At the same time, many Eastern European countries are seeking associate status with the EU or have trade agreements with the bloc. So the EU is already emerging as a strong rival triad power to that of the United States and Japan. In the future an expanded European economic market may well become the largest of the triad powers.

Emergence of a Single European Market

The origins of the EU go back to the formation of the European Economic Community (EEC) in the late 1950s, at which time there were six founding members: France, West Germany, Italy, Belgium, the Netherlands, and Luxembourg. By the late 1990s, the EU had grown to include Austria, Finland, Great Britain, Ireland, Denmark, Greece, Spain, Sweden, and Portugal. Over the last 40 years rapid economic growth has led to a high degree of political and social integration.

The objectives of the EU are:

1. Elimination of customs duties among member states.

2. Elimination of obstacles to the free flow of import and/or export of goods and services among member states.

3. Establishment of common customs duties and unified industrial/commercial policies regarding countries outside the community.

Table 16.1 Economic profile of the big three (in US dollars)

	United States	Japan	Euro 11
The economy			
Gross domestic product	$8 trillion	$5.3 trillion	$6.5 trillion
Industrial output trend	+1.5%	−2.0%	+3.2%
Private consumption trend	+4.7%	−1.8%	+2.4%
Government consumption trend	+1.1%	+0.5%	+1.3%
Gross fixed-investment trend	+8.9%	−7.2%	+4.4%
International reserves, excluding gold	$59 billion	$220 billion	$324 billion
Work force			
Labor-force participation (1997)	77.6%	78.0%	68.8%
Employment growth trend	+2.2%	−0.7%	+1.1%
Compensation per employee trend	+4.0%	−0.6%	+1.7%
Unit labor costs trend	+2.6%	+2.0%	+0.2%
Trade			
Current-account balance (% of GDP)	−2.7%	+3.0%	+1.8%
Export of goods/services trend	+0.5%	−2.1%	+6.3%
Import of goods/services trend	+10.9%	−7.9%	+8.0%
Public sector			
Public spending (% of GDP)	37.0%	36.0%	49.6%
Government debt (% of GDP)	63.1%	99.7%	75.2%
Consumers			
New car sales (estimate)	15.5 million	5.9 million	11.2 million
Household disposable income trend	+3.1%	−0.4%	+3.6%
Household savings ratio	−0.7%	15.4%	11.3%
Stock market			
Stock market capitalization	$12.5 trillion	$2.47 trillion	$4.18 trillion
Value of initial public offerings	$33.8 billion	$21.4 billion	$21.1 billion
1998 market performance	+16% (Dow Jones Industrial Average)	−9.28% (Nikkei 225)	+29.8% (DJ Euro Stoxx)
Bond market			
Total market size	$11.051 trillion	$5.325 trillion	$6.909 trillion
Short-term bond yields (2 year)	4.6%	0.7%	3.1%
Long-term bond yields (10 year)	4.7%	2.0%	3.9%

Sources: Adapted from *Wall Street Journal*, January 4, 1999, p. A6; OECD estimates for 1998; New York Stock, Nasdaq, and Amex report, 1998; Ward's Automotive Reports; J. P. Morgan; Deutsche Bank Eurostat; the International Monetary Fund; Moody's Investor Service; the Bond Market Association; and the *World Almanac*, 1999.

The European Union (EU)

⬤ EU member

[Year joined]

Sources: *The World Factbook*, 1993-94;
The Europa World Year Book, 1993

Finland [1995]

Sweden [1995]

Ireland [1973]

Denmark [1973]

United Kingdom [1973]

Netherlands [1967]

Belgium [1967]

Germany [1967]

Luxembourg [1967]

France [1967]

Austria [1995]

Portugal [1986]

Italy [1967]

Spain [1986]

Greece [1981]

4. Free movement of persons and capital within the bloc.

5. Acceptance of common agricultural policies, transport policies, technical standards, health and safety regulations, and educational degrees.

6. Common measures for consumer protection.

7. Common laws to maintain competition throughout the community and to fight monopolies or illegal cartels.

8. Regional funds to encourage the economic development of certain countries/regions.

9. Greater monetary and fiscal coordination among member states and certain common monetary/fiscal policies.[1]

In December 1985 EU leaders adopted a White Paper which contained 279 proposals aimed at achieving a single unified European market by December 31, 1992. Less than two years later the **Single European Act (SEA)** was enacted.[2] One of the most important parts of the SEA was the **EU Council of Ministers**, one of the four major institutions of the EU. It consists of one minister from each of the member states and is responsible for making major policy decisions for the Common Market. The Council could now pass most proposals with a majority vote, in contrast to the unanimous vote that was needed previously. This opened the door for much faster progress toward political, as well as economic, integration among member countries. The EU is now committed to a single European currency, a social charter, complete harmonization of social and economic policies, a common defense policy, and related measures that increase the power of the EU bureaucracy in Brussels.

Will the EU eventually bring about a **single European market (SEM)** in which the above stated goals are achieved? This will depend on the extent of progress in the area of free movement of goods, changes in financial and banking services, and the practice of government procurement.

Free movement of goods   There have been no customs duties between most EU members since March 1, 1986. However, free movement of goods has been hampered by a host of nontariff barriers that are designed to help local industries by obstructing the import of goods. These barriers have included technical standards, administrative barriers, and fragmented local markets.

In the case of technical standards, for example, goods can be shipped to another EU country but they might not be sold if they fail to conform to technical, safety, or other standards and regulations of the importing country. Today these individual standards are being phased out and replaced with common EU standards.

Administrative barriers include such things as refusal to admit food products that contain additives or substitutes that are judged detrimental to the consumer's health. These barriers are also being phased out.

Fragmented local markets have been created by exploiting language differences between countries and by setting artificially high prices for goods. With the growth of discount stores, mail order houses, and cross-border buying deals, these differentials are also being gradually eliminated.

Changes in financial and banking services   Since July 1990, with the exception of a few EU countries, there has been free capital movement among members. This has resulted in the emergence of more Europe-wide financial service corporations. So, for example, an English building association can now sell mortgage loans in Rome through the mail and a French company can sell life insurance to Belgians through a branch in Frankfurt. There will also be a unified equity market and stock brokers will be able to operate freely in every city in the EU. The combined capitalization of the entire EU is over $2 trillion. The combined equity market will create tremendous opportunities, making it easier for companies to raise money by selling stock and giving investors greater access to security issues throughout the EU. There will also be greater uniformity in retail financial areas such as banking services and credit cards. Commenting on the future of the financial services industry in the EU, one group of researchers has predicted that:

> As financial intermediaries consolidate in type and number at a European level, operationally inefficient and uninnovative banks and securities houses that are financially viable only under protected circumstances will find themselves restructured in some form or another. The cross-shareholdings and strategic alliances under which these players are now taking refuge may end up in outright mergers and acquisitions, as financially healthier intermediaries with new value-propositions to the end-clients become bolder in the

pan-European arena. And the buyers of their financial products will certainly gain from being served by more innovative and efficient intermediaries who will now be faced with competitive pressures at a European, rather than national, level . . .[3]

The EU has also created a single currency, the euro,[4] which some believe will challenge the US dollar's dominance of international trade and finance.[5] This development allows retailers, for example, to price their products in both the local currency as well as in euros.[6] Thus buyers will be able to use comparative shopping in seeking the lowest prices.[7] This will be particularly helpful when the euro finally replaces local currencies, which will happen early in the millennium.[8] In the process, this development may well help generate new opportunities for both EU businesses as well as for foreign MNEs doing business in the EU.[9]

Practice of government procurement   EU government procurements account for close to 10 per cent of the gross domestic product (GDP) of their respective nations. In the past it has been common to find governments awarding contracts to national firms. However, with the emergence of the SEM, this is going to diminish. The result will be greater efficiency, lower cost, and an economically stronger Common Market. On the other hand, it is important to realize that in implementing this strategy, many companies are likely to find themselves losing business to competitors in other EU countries who can provide higher quality and service and lower cost. This development will also probably be somewhat slow in coming because of the possible negative impact of the economic growth of individual countries and the desire to favor national firms when awarding government contracts.

ACTIVE LEARNING CHECK

Review your answer to Active Learning Case question 1 and make any changes you like. Then compare your answer to the one below.

1. **What barriers have to be surmounted before the airline industry in EU countries becomes part of a single European market? Identify and describe one of them.**

One of the major barriers that will have to be overcome is that of political opposition. Some politicians and nationalists feel that too much is lost by allowing total deregulation, and as long as there is this opposition, the full integration of the EU will not happen. A good example is government control of the pricing structure. This barrier reduces free trade and movement of goods and services among members.

The competitive status of the EU

The eventual emergence of an integrated EU will help greater Europe to compete more effectively with the other triad members.[10] However, several EU countries currently are at a competitive disadvantage in some areas.

Productivity   High wages, salaries, and fringe benefits put EU firms at a disadvantage in competing with their US and Japanese counterparts. Labor laws in all EU countries make it extremely difficult to fire employees once they have been employed for a year. US companies have much greater freedom and flexibility in hiring and firing their workers on short notice. This means that employees must remain productive to retain their jobs and that companies can adjust more readily to changes in demand for their product or service. Japanese firms tend to treat their workers as a fixed cost and so find the practice of firing to be unnecessary; employees are grateful to their employers and are willing to work hard to upgrade their skills and to increase the economic performance of their companies. European firms are working to increase their productivity and to match that of their major triad competitors.

Investment spending   Investment spending in EU countries has traditionally lagged behind. Part of this can be explained by rapid increases in wages and benefits during the 1980s which were not offset by increases in productivity. As a result, EU firms found themselves without the capital to invest and had to resort to borrowing. Demands for loans resulted in higher interest rates, which also put a strain on investors. By the late 1980s EU government spending had risen to approximately 50 per cent of GDP (in contrast to about 30 per cent for the United States and Japan). Because of this, taxes were raised, thus limiting funds and forcing interest rates to go even higher. More recently EU economies have been doing much better, although they continue to perform below the US level in terms of both annual increases and overall productivity.

Education   Another area where EU countries have failed to maintain a competitive edge is education. While all three triad groups spend approximately 5 per cent of GNP on education, the approaches are different. In Europe, most vocational training is provided at the high school level, whereas in the United States and Japan, it is done later. In addition, in the United States, a higher percentage of the population attends college than in Europe or Japan. The European university curriculum is more theoretical than in either the United States or Japan. European educational institutions are also more rigid and less able to adapt to the changing needs of business. There is less interaction between European educational institutions and industry than in the United States and Japan. As a result, many European students receive training that is inappropriate for the employment needs of European business and industry. This, in part, explains the extremely high unemployment rates in the age group under 25 in many regions of Europe.

The major challenge for European countries will be to modify their education systems and to make them more flexible, more practical, and better able to adapt to the changing demands of industry.

Overall evaluation   In overall terms, the EU has traditionally lagged behind its triad competitors. As Table 16.2 shows, in 1989 eleven EU countries ranked in the top 20 most competitive nations in the world. By 1998 only eight of the group were on this list. The world is becoming a more competitive place, and some EU countries are finding it hard to keep up.

What changes are likely to occur in the millennium? One is an increase in acquisition and mergers among EU firms and between them and companies from outside the bloc. A second change is the emergence of new technologies that will be developed in EU laboratories. A third is additional free trade agreements and other economic arrangements among European countries that are designed to make the EU a stronger, more competitive market.

Table 16.2   The world's most competitive nations, 1989 and 1999

Rank	1989	1999
1	Japan	USA
2	Switzerland	Singapore
3	United States	Finland
4	Canada	Luxembourg
5	Germany	Netherlands
6	Finland	Switzerland
7	Netherlands	Hong Kong
8	Sweden	Denmark
9	Norway	Germany
10	Australia	Canada
11	United Kingdom	Ireland
12	Denmark	Australia
13	France	Norway
14	Belgium/Luxembourg	Sweden
15	Austria	United Kingdom
16	Ireland	Japan
17	New Zealand	Iceland
18	Spain	Taiwan
19	Italy	Austria
20	Turkey	New Zealand
21	Portugal	France
22	Greece	Belgium

Sources: Adapted from IMD and World Economic Forum, *The World Competitiveness Report 1989,* and IMD, The World Competitiveness Report, April 13, 1999; *http://www.imd.ch/wcy/ factors/overall.html.*

CONDUCTING A STRATEGIC ANALYSIS

As we have seen, the EU is likely to be a very competitive market in the future.[11] In preparing to do business in the EU, foreign MNEs must first conduct an overall strategic analysis.[12] This analysis should focus on the competitive nature of the industry that is being targeted. Assuming that the enterprise intends to set up operations by FDI or alternative investments rather than merely export to the market, the analysis must also evaluate location. The following section examines both of these activities.

Using competitive intelligence

Competition in the EU has increased over the last five years. Some of the specific strategies that have been employed include careful market segmentation, increased research and development, and the use of mergers, acquisitions, and alliances to help build market share and to improve competitive strength. By the late 1990s, for example, US car makers such as Ford Motor and General Motors were well positioned to compete successfully in the EU;[13] IBM was reorganizing and seeking to capitalize

INTERNATIONAL BUSINESS STRATEGY IN ACTION

Toys "R" Us in Europe

Many multinationals like to set up operations in Europe, particularly in the largest economy, Germany. Despite its economic downturn in the 1990s, this country has a very strong economy and it greatly influences what happens in the rest of the EU. However, breaking down technical and cultural barriers in Germany can be a major chore. Toys "R" Us offers an excellent case example.

When the company decided to enter the German market, it was greeted by a partial boycott and a public relations blitz that condemned the concept of a self-service toy supermarket as being alien and wrong. Even though the managing director of Toys "R" Us was a German, strong objections were directed against a US retailer wanting large-area sales space in Germany. The company soon learned that legal and cultural barriers can be effectively used to block foreign competition. When Toys "R" Us applied for a construction permit in Cologne, the city fathers asked the local chamber of commerce and retailers' association how they felt about the application. The latter replied that a toy store belongs in the center of the city, not on the edge of town. Yet this is exactly where Toys "R" Us needed to be located so that it could build a sprawling store and a parking lot that was the size of a football field. In addition, the German Toy Manufacturers Association questioned why a toy store would sell so many non-toy items.

The managing director for Toys "R" Us refused to allow these early setbacks to thwart his efforts. He continued making the rounds of trade shows, negotiating for store sites, and presenting the company's plans to local officials; eventually he wore down the resistance. Even the competition began to realize that successful large toy stores could spark a boom in the toy market. This is exactly what happened. By the 1990s the toy industry in Germany was increasing at an annual rate of 10 per cent. In addition, competitors began copying some of the approaches used by Toys "R" Us, such as piling shelves at the back of the store with baby food and diapers. They now realize that parents who come in to get diapers or baby food seldom leave without buying a toy for the child.

By 1995 Toys "R" Us had 59 stores in Germany and it held the largest share of the toy market in Germany. It had another 149 outlets in Europe, including 61 in the United Kingdom, 44 in France and 29 in Spain. By 1997 Toys "R" Us held 30 per cent of its assets outside the United States, but the overall return on foreign assets was so poor that it closed 50 of its 448 foreign stores in 1998. The German experience has taught the management that despite cultural, legal, and technical barriers, a retail company can succeed in Europe if it is patient, maintains a strong consumer-oriented marketing focus, and is nationally responsive.

Sources: Adapted from Ferdinand Protzman, "Greetings from Fortress Europe," *New York Times*, August 18, 1991, Section 3, pp. 1, 6; John Templeman et al., "Germany Fights Back," *Business Week*, May 31, 1993, pp. 48–51; *www.toysrus.com*; Paul Klebnikov, "Trouble in Toyland," *Forbes*, June 1, 1998, pp. 56–60; Michael Gestrin, Rory Knight and Alan M. Rugman, *The Templeton Global Performance Index* (Templeton College, University of Oxford, 1998).

on its strong European holdings; and companies such as Coca-Cola, Colgate, Gillette, and Procter & Gamble were making plans to build market share. Competitor intelligence has been an essential part of these developments. This approach employs two complementary paths: external information gathering and internal infrastructural analysis.

External information gathering   The information that is critical for competitor analysis is typically located in a variety of sources.[14] For example, in Great Britain, Denmark, and Ireland, centralized government-controlled company registration offices provide financial information on registered firms. Other useful sources of competitive information include the Department of Trade & Industry, trade associations, business information services, and regional and local publications. In France, a great deal of registration information is commonly found in local courthouses. This is also the case in Germany and Italy, where companies must register with the local civil courts in the region where they are headquartered. In these countries chambers of commerce are also excellent sources of information since these organizations work much more closely with business firms than do their counterparts in the United States. Central databases created by the EU Commission can be used to keep abreast of changes in national legislation, thus helping companies to remain aware of new laws and regulations. An understanding of the legal, technical, and cultural barriers often used to keep foreign competition at bay can be particularly important in an environmental analysis. The box "International Business Strategy in Action: Toys 'R' Us in Europe" illustrates this point.

Internal infrastructural analysis   The second step that MNEs take is an analysis of how to manage their infrastructure. Prescott and Gibbons have described four types of infrastructures that can be used to compete effectively: coordinated, market coordination, resource point sharing, and autonomous.[15] The choice of infrastructure is determined by the similarity of national markets among the MNE's businesses and the extent of resource sharing across businesses.

The **coordinated infrastructure** is used when there is a high degree of similarity among national markets and business units share resources in an effort to help each other increase overall sales. Computer firms often use this approach. A **market coordination infrastructure** is used by firms that compete in similar national markets but do little resource sharing among their businesses. This approach is employed by companies that set up each operation as a separate, independent business. Small firms that are geographically dispersed sometimes use this approach. A **resource sharing infrastructure** is used by firms that compete in dissimilar national markets but share resources such as R&D efforts and manufacturing information. Auto manufacturers use this approach. An **autonomous infrastructure** is used by MNEs that compete in dissimilar national markets and do not share resources. Highly diversified MNEs use this approach.

ACTIVE LEARNING CHECK

Review your answer to Active Learning Case question 2 and make any changes you like. Then compare your answer to the one below.

2. **What types of competitive intelligence would US airlines want to gather in order to operate more effectively in the EU? Identify and describe two of them.**

One type of competitive intelligence would be looking at rate schedules so that the airlines know what the competition is charging. A second would be gathering information related to the political forces that influence airline deregulation. This would help to pinpoint the speed and direction that deregulation is likely to take and to identify which markets are likely to open up the fastest for foreign competitors.

Table 16.3 Comparison of investment incentives in selected EU countries based on an actual project evaluation

	Spain		Italy		France		United Kingdom	
	Application area	Level	Application area	Level	Application area	Level	Application area	Level
Grants								
Employment subsidies								
Tax breaks								
Soft loans								

Application area — Available in whole country

Available in parts of the country only

Level — Slightly attractive

Attractive

Very attractive

Source: Adapted from Maria Brindlmayer, "Comparing EC Investment Incentives and Getting the Best Deal," *Journal of European Business*, November/December, 1990, p. 38.

Evaluating locations

Many companies are finding that they need to expand globally if they are to remain competitive. Auto suppliers are a good example. By the beginning of the 1990s North American auto suppliers had seen their world market share decline from 32 down to 28 per cent, whereas Western Europe's world market share rose from 30 to 39 per cent. An international survey reveals that US auto suppliers believe that Europe now promises the greatest potential for them because it is the largest single market in the world, has an industry structure that is similar to that in the United States, and offers a source of low-cost manufacturing.[16] As a result, firms like General Motors and Ford Motor are expanding their European presence through greater foreign direct investment and strategic alliances. Companies in a host of other industries, from computers to consumer goods, are following suit, and many are finding that regions and municipalities are prepared to provide investment incentives to encourage this activity.

Regional incentives   Investment incentives take a number of forms, including grants, low-interest loans, reduced land prices, and training support for personnel. Table 16.3, which was constructed for the purpose of evaluating a specific project, provides a general comparison of investment incentives in several major EU countries. It shows that incentives vary from country to country. Some of these incentives are available only for several years, whereas others remain in effect for a much longer time.

Typically, incentives will be higher when (1) the region is economically depressed, (2) many jobs are being created, (3) the company is making a large investment, and/or (4) the investment is likely to attract other investors. Before agreeing to any contract,

Table 16.4   Comparison of location factors: one example

Source: Adapted from Maria Brindlmayer, "Comparing EC Investment Incentives and Getting the Best Deal," *Journal of European Business*, November/December, 1990, p. 38.

however, it is important that the deal be "locked in" and that any repayment of subsidies be made clear up front.

Other evaluation criteria   While subsidies can be important incentives, most MNEs doing business in the EU consider them as just one element in the evaluation process. Some of the other conditions and costs are described in Table 16.4. They include operational costs such as labor, utilities, transportation, and distance from major markets. A recent survey conducted among 1,000 European companies that were not seeking financial assistance revealed that the most important location factors, in order of importance, were (1) access to customers, (2) quality of labor, (3) expansion prospects, (4) level of wage costs, (5) attractive environment, (6) access to suppliers, (7) non-financial regional assistance, (8) absence of restrictions for expansion, (9) infrastructure, (10) level of rents, and (11) public transportation.[17] Another factor that is often mentioned is the ease with which a company that is not doing well can withdraw. This includes laying off workers and selling facilities, and other factors involved in exiting a market. Gathering location data and the negotiating terms can take a considerable amount of time, but the results often justify the investment.

STRATEGY ISSUES

Many issues have been addressed in this book. We now focus on those strategies that need to be considered when doing business in the EU. These issues include (1) an overall strategic analysis, (2) the feasibility of exporting, (3) the value of strategic acquisitions and alliances, (4) marketing considerations, (5) manufacturing approaches, and (6) management considerations. The following section briefly examines each issue.

Overall strategic analysis for the EU

In formulating a strategy for doing business in the EU, we should look at both the process of globalization through economic integration and the need for a firm to be nationally responsive.[18] This is done on the matrix in Figure 16.1. The horizontal axis represents sovereignty, the need for a firm to be nationally responsive. It is a political axis and takes into account both consumer tastes and government regulations. The vertical axis represents globalization through economic integration. This includes the need to develop economies of scale, to use a value-added strategy, and to reap the benefits of increased coordination and control of geographically dispersed activities.

Quadrants 1 and 4 in Figure 16.1 present relatively simple strategy situations. Quadrant 1 requires a strategy in which the MNE does not need to be concerned with national responsiveness. The company is in a market driven by high globalization and its strategy must be on achieving price competitiveness. Firms operating in this quadrant are often centralized in structure and thus can use mergers and acquisitions to benefit from high economic integration. Companies selling micro-computers frequently operate in quadrant 1.

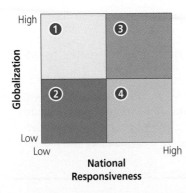

Figure 16.1 Business strategies for the EU

Source: Alan M. Rugman and Alain Verbeke, "Europe 1992 and Competitive Strategies for North American Firms," *Business Horizons*, November/December 1991, p. 77.

In quadrant 4 globalization is less important than sovereignty, so the MNE must focus on adapting products to satisfy the specific demands of each country. In this case globalization is minimized in favor of a decentralized strategy of national responsiveness that is designed to appeal to select niches and target groups. Companies selling food products and designer clothes use this approach.

In quadrant 2 there is low globalization and low sovereignty. The potential of obtaining economies of scale and benefits of regional responsiveness are both small. MNEs operating in this quadrant are vulnerable to triad competitors. In this quadrant there is no advantage in centralized quality control or economies of scale and no ability to adapt activities to individual countries. MNEs selling inexpensive toys that are undifferentiated fall into this quadrant.

MNEs in quadrant 3 use a strategy of high globalization and high sovereignty that is characterized by strong price competitiveness and select target positioning. This is the most challenging quadrant to implement as the firm's organization structure is complex, but it is the one in which many successful globally adaptive multinationals operate. Auto firms fall into this quadrant.

A close look at events in the EU reveals that Brussels' administrators designed a strategy to help European firms move into quadrant 1. This plan is designed to create a natural barrier to entry for outside firms and to help ensure the success of local competitors. A survey of the top management of Europe's 300 largest corporations has confirmed this tendency toward integration. The survey found that European managers anticipate increased integration due to such developments as strategic partnerships, mergers, and takeovers as well as increasing economies of scale.[19] As a result, the managers expect the development of more efficient modern industries. The survey also found that European managers were confident that economic integration was a viable strategy for them, but that it would be detrimental to non-European MNEs. Only 9 per cent of the managers believed that US firms would gain ground in Europe, while 42 per cent said that US firms would lose competitive strength.

Exporting firms operate in quadrant 4. As outsiders in the EU, US firms will find it increasingly difficult to export to Europe and to compete on economies of scale in the face of integration by rival firms in the EU. Not only will costs be higher for exporters, but locally based competitors will have more access to competitive information. As a result, during the millennium many exporting firms will be switching to FDI from exporting in order to meet the new nature of competition in Europe.

ACTIVE LEARNING CHECK

Review your answer to Active Learning Case question 3 and make any changes you like. Then compare your answer to the one below.

3. In what way will globalization and sovereignty be important issues to US airlines doing business in the EU?

Globalization is important because it helps to point out the value of mergers, acquisitions, and price competitiveness. Sovereignty is important because it points out the need to develop market niche strategies that are designed to appeal to select target groups. A knowledge of the degree to which globalization and sovereignty are demanded by the market can be critical in fashioning a highly competitive strategy.

Exporting

Those firms that continue to export to the EU will have to address a number of legal/financial matters. The following sections examine some of the most important issues.

Customs duties and taxes   Goods manufactured outside the EU are subject to customs duties at the point of entry. These duties are determined by an EU-wide tariff system that establishes common rates regardless of entry point. Most duties are based on the value of the good ad valorem, and this value depends on the stage of assembly or completion of the end product.

Excise taxes are levied on certain types of goods such as alcohol, tobacco, and gasoline. These rates are determined by each member state, although the Community is now working on establishing uniform excise duties throughout the bloc.

Product standards   Products exported to the EU must meet standards and technical regulations. Many of these are common throughout the bloc, but when they are not, the product must meet the standards of the country to which it is exported. In many cases products produced in outside countries must be modified in order to gain EU entry.

Conducting export operations   In recent years many US exporters of both goods and services have consolidated their operations with those of European companies, thus helping them to surmount EU barriers. For example, US accounting firms typically operate through local partnerships. Other examples are management consulting firms that have international operations that help them to address the needs of local clients and law firms with overseas offices.

Those MNEs that do choose to export to the EU must carefully select their agents and distributors. Five steps are critical to this process:

1. Examine the legal and business considerations involved in appointing foreign intermediaries and establish criteria that reflect the particular geographic market.
2. Assemble a list of potential candidates by using the various directories and by consulting with other sources of information.
3. Qualify such candidates by applying certain criteria and by conducting a preliminary interview.
4. Visit the proposed intermediary to obtain additional information about its resources and facilities, to get a proper feeling for the intermediary's compatibility with the organization and to check the objectives of the agent or distributor.
5. After selecting an agent or distributor (a) negotiate an agreement that is fair and mutually beneficial, (b) comply in good faith with the terms of the agreement, (c) continue communication between the parties, and (d) make occasional adjustments in the relationship in response to changing circumstances.[20]

Many small and intermediate size MNEs will continue to export to the EU because it is too expensive for them to use any other route. Large MNEs, on the other hand, are turning more and more to strategic acquisitions and alliances.

Strategic acquisitions and alliances

Two of the most popular ways of gaining a foothold in the EU are through strategic acquisitions or alliances. (See the box "International Business Strategy in Action:

INTERNATIONAL BUSINESS STRATEGY IN ACTION

Kingfisher as a European retailer

In a recent study of the profitability of foreign assets a British retailer, Kingfisher, came top of the pack. Its average return on foreign assets was 32 per cent for 1996 and 1997, well above the average of 4.78 per cent for the world's top 500 multinational enterprises. What's more, in that period, Kingfisher only had 9 per cent of its total assets in foreign markets, but by 1999 had increased this to 40 per cent.

Kingfisher is a company that is leveraging its foreign assets to promote growth. Its first successful acquisition was of French electrical retailer Darty, followed in 1998 by a merger with French do-it-yourself retailer Castorama. Kingfisher also has other operations across Europe: in Belgium, the Netherlands, and Germany. It has moved into Asia with the acquisition of an electrical retail chain in Singapore in 1998, and is also in Taiwan.

Kingfisher was only formed in 1989, and consists of the British Woolworths Stores, Comet (electrical products), Superdrug and B&Q (home improvement stores). In 1998 total sales revenues for Kingfisher were £6.4 billion (about US$10 billion). There were 2,500 stores in 13 countries, principally in Britain and France. These retail brand stores operate in chains across Britain. The CEO, Sir Geoffrey Mulcahy, has led the growth drive. He tried to consolidate Kingfisher's leading position in Britain by merging with the large supermarket chain Asda. In 1999, Asda was the third largest British supermarket chain behind Sainsbury and Tesco. However, Wal-Mart has now bought Asda.

Sir Geoffrey Mulcahy also has provided leadership in the foreign expansion through patience and strategic initiative. The merger with Castorama took five years to negotiate, as did the earlier one with Darty. The French managers and workers keep their jobs as "retail is detail" and local knowledge is vital. While its foreign businesses operate autonomously, there are logistical savings and scale economies in purchasing that arise for the Kingfisher group as a whole. Sir Geoffrey has positioned Kingfisher to ride the wave of growth through profitable international expansion.

Another popular way of doing business in the EU is through the use of strategic alliances. Experts agree that four of the most important steps include:

1. Pick a compatible partner and take the time to get to know and trust this company.

2. Choose a partner with complementary products or markets, rather than one who competes directly.

3. Be patient and do not rush into a deal or expect immediate results.

4. Learn about the partner's technology and management but try not to give away your own core secrets.

In some alliances one partner has taken advantage of the other by stealing technology or forcing the partner into a position where it had to sell out to the other. However, this will not happen if both sides make substantive contributions to the undertaking and each realizes that it needs the other. Moreover, even when alliances have not worked out, companies have found it in their best interest to continue looking for other partners for other deals.

Sources: Michael V. Gestrin, Rory F. Knight, and Alan M. Rugman, *The Templeton Global Performance Index* (Templeton College, University of Oxford, 1998); Kingfisher, *Annual Report and Accounts,* 1997, 1998; Corporate Profile: Kingfisher; *The Times,* London, February 1, 1999, p. 44; *Financial Times,* May 18, 1988, December 12, 1989; Bernard M. Wolf, "The Role of Strategic Alliances in the European Automotive Industry," in Alan M. Rugman and Alain Verbeke (eds.), *Research in Global Management,* vol. III (Greenwich, Conn: JAI Press, 1992), pp. 143–163.

Kingfisher as a European retailer.") A *Harvard Business Research* study analyzed 49 strategic alliances and concluded that the chances of success are improved if the parties keep five guidelines in mind: (1) acquisitions work better than alliances when developing core businesses, (2) alliances are effective when firms want to gain entry into new geographic markets or businesses that are tangential to the core business,

(3) alliances between strong and weak companies typically do not work well, (4) alliances that last are characterized by an ability to move beyond the initially established expectations and objectives, and (5) alliances are more likely to be successful when both sides hold an equal amount of financial ownership. In addition, more than three-quarters of the alliances that were studied ended with one of the parties acquiring full control.[21]

Making strategic alliances work It is more common to find MNEs using strategic alliances than using acquisitions, and there are several important steps in making these arrangements work. One is that each partner must complement the other.[22] If one company is strong in research and development (R&D) and the other's strengths are in manufacturing and marketing, the alliance may be ideal. On the other hand, if both are strong in R&D and weak in manufacturing and marketing, there is no synergy and the two may end up trying to steal secrets from each other and competing rather than cooperating. Second, the goals of the two groups must be carefully spelled out. Once the partners have agreed upon the primary criteria such as new product development, increased market share, and return on investment, they can then decide how to commit their resources. These goals provide a basis for overall direction.

The key people from each firm must get to know each other. Building working relationships across the two firms is essential for resolving problems and issues that come up. Communication, networking, and interpersonal relationships are extremely useful in ensuring that the spirit of the alliance is kept alive.

Each group must understand how the other works so that differences can be accommodated. If one partner is responsible for making certain parts and for providing them to the other, there must be a clear understanding regarding such matters as product quality and delivery time. If the partner receiving products prefers to accumulate inventory to prevent stockout problems, the other must develop a manufacturing plan that addresses this need.

The parties must hold frequent meetings and develop a trust. The successful alliance between General Electric and Snecma was a result of mutual respect and dependence. The two companies cooperated fully in developing, manufacturing, and marketing commercial jet engines. As a result, today the joint venture makes the best-selling commercial jet engine in the world.

Marketing considerations

As the EU becomes a true economic union, internal barriers to entry and mobility barriers within the bloc will disappear. This will create both challenges and opportunities. In particular, competition is likely to increase as it becomes easier for competitors to invade each other's territories. As a result, marketing strategies in the millennium will have to reflect concern for both pricing and positioning.

Pricing The European Commission has estimated that the price of goods and services throughout the EU will decline. Five specific developments will make this work: (1) decreasing costs of doing business, now that internal barriers and restrictions have been removed, (2) the opening up of public procurement contracts to broader competition, (3) foreign investment that will increase production capacity, (4) more rigorous enforcement of competition policy, and (5) general intensified competition brought about by economic reforms.[23]

Price will become an even more important marketing factor to the extent that EU customers develop similar tastes and are willing to accept globally standardized products. As this happens, MNEs will be able to sell the same product throughout the bloc without having to make modifications for local tastes. Unfortunately, while some goods can be marketed with this strategy, many will require careful positioning for select target groups.

Positioning   Some global products such as Coca-Cola, Pepsi, and Marlboro cigarettes have universal appeal, but these are more the exception than the rule. For example, in the United Kingdom, the Renault is viewed as a good economy car, but in Spain, it is perceived as a luxury automobile. Similarly, in Great Britain and Holland, toothpaste is viewed as a hygiene product and sells much better than in Spain and Greece, where it is marketed as a cosmetic.[24]

As a result, the marketing motto, "plan globally, act locally," will continue to be a useful dictum. A good example is provided by the EU cellular communications market, which offers tremendous opportunities but is also extremely competitive because there are so many submarkets throughout the community. For example, in the mobile communications market there is dramatic untapped market potential throughout the economic community. Market researchers have found that a great deal of similarity between the US and European markets exists in terms of cellular phone demand among businesspeople. However, the challenge is one of positioning the company to take advantage of this untapped market. There are also a host of potential problems, including that (1) economic downturns tend to hit this industry harder than most, (2) the cost of using the service is high, (3) the influx of strong competition is likely, (4) constant media publicity highlights poor voice quality and service of cellular products, and (5) announcements of new products cause many potential buyers to adopt a wait-and-see attitude. As a result, it is likely that the mobile communications market will end up being divided among a host of major competitors, each of which positions itself for a particular local or regional target group.

Direct marketing   Another strategy that is likely to receive a great deal of attention is direct marketing. Most EU firms tailor their products to narrow markets and direct mail is only now gaining attention. Unlike the United States where businesses have been using telemarketing and other nontraditional channels for well over a decade, this is a new approach for European consumers, and there are a number of challenges that MNEs will have to surmount if they hope to direct market their product, such as: (1) consumers speak different languages, so a universal message or strategy will not work throughout the bloc, (2) inclusion of direct-response telephone numbers in television spots is forbidden by the privacy laws of some member states such as Germany, (3) information about potential clients is fragmented and not easily obtainable, and (4) the infrastructure for direct marketing is weak because credit cards, toll-free numbers, and computer bases are still in their infancy in Europe.[25] Nevertheless, direct marketing is likely to play a major role in MNE efforts to create a pan-European marketing strategy.

ACTIVE LEARNING CHECK

Review your answer to Active Learning Case question 4 and make any changes you like. Then compare your answer to the one below.

4. In what way will both pricing and positioning be important for US airlines doing business in the EU?

Pricing will be important because as the airline industry becomes less regulated, price competition will increase and those with lower fares will take business away from those with higher fares. Positioning will be important because the airlines cannot compete strictly on price. They also will want to identify and appeal to specific market niches, such as the business market where air fares are more price inelastic and there is a greater opportunity to make profit. So airline competitors will be using a mix of pricing and positioning strategies to attack the market.

Manufacturing considerations

As individual country regulations are eliminated and EU members continue to standardize rules and regulations, it will be possible to produce uniform goods for the entire market. This will not come about immediately because of the time needed to change such things as electric systems so that toasters, television sets, and other home appliances can all be manufactured with the same type of plugs. However, MNEs will eventually be able to produce many products with standard parts that work in all EU countries. At the same time manufacturers will continue producing goods that appeal to local market tastes. For example, appliance makers now manufacture self-cleaning ovens for the French because of their tradition of high-temperature cooking. However, they typically leave out this option for the German market where food is generally cooked at lower temperatures. Some major manufacturing considerations that warrant attention by those doing business in the EU include reducing costs, building factory networks, and entering into R&D alliances.

Reducing costs   One manufacturing benefit of producing for a market with 350 million consumers is the ability to reduce cost per unit through the use of standardized components and large production runs. Under this arrangement the cost of the components is kept to a minimum and the large production runs allow the company to spread fixed costs over more units. This means cost per item can be sharply reduced. Moreover, economies of scale can be achieved even when production has to be tailored to local conditions. This is accomplished through the use of **delayed differentiation**, in which all products are manufactured in the same way for all countries of regions until as late in the assembly process as possible. In these final stages differentiation is then used to introduce particular features or special components.

MNEs are also using outsourcing and just-in-time inventory systems to reduce the cost of carrying parts and supplies. By tailoring deliveries and shipments to the production schedule, factories are able to minimize their investment in materials and work-in-process. This system is also used by large retailers such as Marks & Spencer of the United Kingdom, which employs its electronic network system to keep track of inventory at each store in England, as well as on the continent, and to replenish

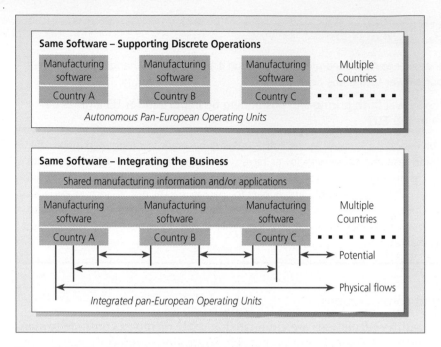

Figure 16.2 Pan-European manufacturing systems

Source: Adapted from Nigel Dunham and Robin Morgan, "The Search for a Truly Pan-European Manufacturing System," *Journal of European Business*, September/October 1991, p. 44.

its outlets as needed. By carefully controlling inventory in its 600 European stores, the firm has added millions of pounds annually to the bottom line.[26]

Another way in which costs are being controlled is by redesigning production processes, thus scrapping old, inefficient techniques in favor of more streamlined methods. This includes careful study of competitive firms in order to identify and copy their successful approaches to cost control. It also entails the elimination of red tape and the use of well-trained, highly motivated work teams.

Factory networks   MNEs in Europe are now beginning to create sophisticated networks of factories that both produce components and finished goods and provide distribution and after-sales services. For example, the Philips television factory in Brugges, Belgium, uses tubes that are supplied from a factory in Germany, transistors that come from France, plastics that are produced in Italy, and electronic components that come from another factory in Belgium.

These factory networks are also integrated with computer software packages that can operate in multiple European countries without the need for modification. Figure 16.2 provides an illustration. The software packages allow companies to make supply, production, and distribution decisions while at the same time satisfy the requirements of the different legal entities in the countries where they operate. Some specific functions that they help companies to perform include forecasting, logistics planning, inventory planning, production planning, and central updating of bills of materials. The software provides each factory manager with the specific information needed and does so in that individual's own language. As a result, MNEs are able to coordinate multiple activities and thus to develop an effective pan-European manufacturing system.

Research and development alliances   Another emerging manufacturing strategy is participation in cooperative R&D programs. In the EU this is taking two complementary paths. First, many companies are teaming up to share R&D expenses. Siemens and Philips have used this approach to develop computer chips and IBM has a number of agreements with European firms for developing advanced computer technology.

Second, many firms are trying to get some of these costs funded by participating in European cooperative R&D programs. The EU is providing European industry with funding for research in such areas as information technology, biotechnology, and energy. The objective of the program is to stimulate cross-border cooperation and to make Europe more productive and competitive in the world market. One of the best-known programs is the **European Research Cooperation Agency** (Eureka, for short), which was launched in 1985 and which emphasizes projects in the fields of energy, medicine, biotechnology, communications, information technology, transport, new materials, robotics, production automation, lasers, and the environment.[27] This program has helped to develop a European standard for high-definition television and has funded semiconductor research. To date more than 2,000 organizations have participated in Eureka-related projects. Those firms that are interested in participating in these cooperative programs typically do so by carrying out six steps:

1. Find out if the company is eligible for EU-funded programs.
2. Carefully study the EU rules regarding rights of ownership and dissemination of results.
3. Carefully choose the best location for a European research and development center.
4. Determine those competitors and major customers who are already participating in the program.
5. Gather recommendations from the firm's EU and local management.
6. Put together the company's application for funding.[28]

Management considerations

As more firms enter the EU, there is growing concern regarding their ability to manage Europeans effectively. Many firms enter the market with preconceived ideas about how to interact with their European partners or employees. Some, for example, believe that management styles that were effective in their country will also work well in Europe. However, as the Japanese have discovered in the United States, effective management approaches must be tailor-made to meet the needs of the local situation. The primary focus must be on adjusting to cultural differences.

Adjusting to cultural differences   There are a number of differences between US and European workers. For example, Europeans are more accustomed to participating in decision making. They have a long history of worker participation programs and of holding seats on the board of directors.

Another difference is employee motivation. Researchers have found that quality of work life is extremely important in Scandinavian countries, whereas opportunities for individual achievement are of particular importance in the United Kingdom. French

Table 16.5   EU antidumping cases by sector, 1980–90

SITC code	Description	Number of AD investigations	Number of AD reviews	Total number of AD cases
0–1	Food, live animals, beverages, tobacco	5	0	5
2	Crude materials, inedible, except fuels	38	17	55
3	Mineral fuels, lubricants, etc.	0	0	0
4	Animal and vegetable oils, fats, waxes	0	0	0
5	Chemicals and related products, n.e.s.	161	63	224
6.5	Textile yarn, fabrics, etc.	9	0	9
6.7	Iron and steel	49	18	67
6.8	Nonferrous metals	18	5	23
7	Machinery and transport equipment	67	24	91
8.4	Apparel and clothing	0	0	0
6 and 8*	Other manufactured goods	74	43	117
	All products listed	**421**	**170**	**591**

* This category includes subsections of sections 6 and 8. From section 6 these include 6.1 (manufactures of leather), 6.2 (rubber), 6.3 (cork and wood), 6.4 (paper and paperboard), 6.6 (nonmetallic minerals), and 6.9 (manufactures of metals). From section 8, subsections 8.1 (prefabricated buildings), 8.2 (furniture), 8.3 (travel goods), 8.5 (footwear), 8.7 (scientific instruments), 8.8 (photographic equipment), and 8.9 (miscellaneous manufactured goods) are included.
Sources: Commission of the European Communities, First through Ninth Annual Reports of the Commission on the Community's Anti-Dumping and Anti-Subsidy Activities (1982–1991).

workers are interested in individual achievement but place strong emphasis on security. German workers place high value on both advancement and earnings.[29] Clearly, no universal list of motivators can be applied throughout the EU. These facts illustrate the importance of MNEs having a global perspective as well as having managers who are focused on the country-specific needs of the area where they are working.

Barriers to EU market access

Throughout the book we have explored the need for access to triad markets. Unfortunately, while the EU has become the world's largest market, some EU-based MNEs have sought to restrict access to this area. Although the overall trend during the postwar period has been toward an increasingly liberalized trade environment, international managers must know how to deal with, or at least anticipate, the use of administrative barriers in foreign markets.

The two most common trade law entry barriers are countervailing duty laws (CVD) and antidumping laws (AD). (These were discussed earlier in Chapters 6 and 15.) While the United States uses CVD as an entry barrier (it had 90 per cent of the world's CVD cases in the 1980s), the EU uses AD as an entry barrier. Both **countervailing duties (CVD)** and **antidumping duties** (AD) are import tariffs which are intended to protect domestic producers from harmful dumping and subsidization by foreign governments. However, it has been demonstrated in several studies that these laws have been "captured" and used by weak firms seeking shelter from strong competition by rival MNEs in the triad.[30]

Table 16.5 shows both the high number of AD cases that were launched and the tendency toward sectoral concentration in the use of AD by EU firms during the

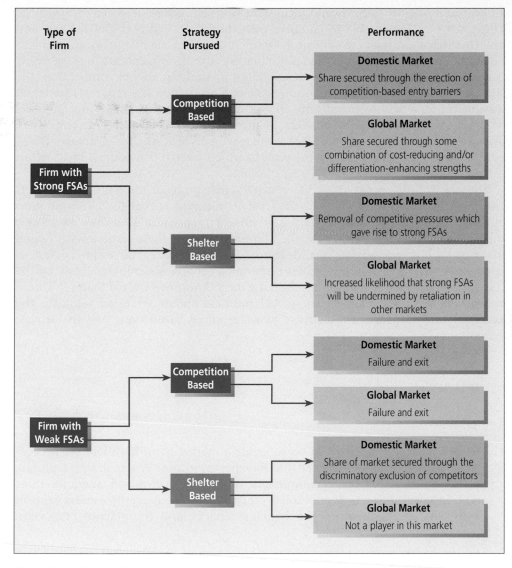

Figure 16.3 Competition and shelter-based strategies

period of 1980 to 1990. Many AD cases were brought in the chemical, machinery and transport, iron and steel, and other "mature" sectors which have weak firm specific advantages.

The use of these trade law instruments to provide shelter is by no means unique to the EU, as the earlier discussion of AD and CVD in Chapter 15 showed.[31] However, from Table 16.5 it is clear that non-EU firms in the chemical, machinery and transport equipment, and iron and steel sectors should probably anticipate some resistance if they plan to begin exporting to the EU market with a view to competing with domestic producers.

Figure 16.3 shows the rationale for the use of AD and CVD laws by particular firms. As with all free-market economies, the EU economy has, at any given point in time, a significant number of firms in difficulty due to the pressure of global competition. These firms are barely able to compete with their more efficient global rivals and find themselves on the verge of exit from the industry. If the main reason for this is international competition, and domestic administrative instruments are in place which would allow such a firm to continue operating by limiting foreign competition, the company is likely to use these instruments. Such a situation is a rare instance when it is logical for a firm to spend time and money on an activity that is not productive from a competitiveness standpoint. By using AD or CVD laws, the uncompetitive firm is able to remain in operation not by improving its firm specific advantages (FSAs) but, rather, by artificially raising the price at which foreign competitors must sell in the domestic market.

The abusive use of AD and CVD is a particular problem for nontriad members and for MNEs from other parts of the triad. The reason is that the administration of these trade laws is discretionary and subject to political pressures. Moreover, there is now strong evidence that the administration of these trade laws is biased in favor of domestic plaintiffs and against foreign firms.[32] The technical test of "material injury" due to the subsidies or dumped exports is routinely abused by the responsible administrative agencies in both the EU and the United States.[33] This is an extremely serious problem for global business and it serves to reinforce the existence of the triad at the expense of a liberalized world trade and investment system.

SUMMARY

Key points

1. The overall objective of the EU is to create a market in which there are no economic barriers to trade between the member countries. When this is achieved, the EU will be the largest economic bloc in the world. However, there are three areas, in particular, where additional progress must be made: free movement of goods, changes in financial and banking services, and the practice of government procurement.

2. The current competitive status of the EU lags that of the United States and Japan in a number of areas, including productivity, investment spending, and education. Greater economic strides will be needed if the EU is to compete effectively with its triad counterparts.

3. In preparing to do business in the EU, MNEs should focus on the competitive nature of the industry that is targeted and on evaluation of location. Competitive intelligence gathering involves external information gathering and internal infrastructural analysis. Location evaluation entails consideration of such factors as regional incentives, operating costs, and distance from major markets.

4. There are many aspects of strategy that need to be considered when doing business in the EU. These include (1) an overall analysis of the environment, (2) the feasibility of exporting, (3) the value of strategic alliances and acquisitions, (4) marketing considerations, (5) manufacturing approaches, and (6) management considerations. Managers need to weigh the choices of globalization and/or national responsiveness very carefully.

5. The EU has a large internal market. Firms located in the EU can use a new type of nontariff barrier to entry to keep out rival firms, namely trade remedy legislation such as countervailing duty laws (CVD) and antidumping (AD) laws. Recent research has found that the use of both CVD and AD is a "shelter" strategy that is designed to protect uncompetitive domestic firms. However, the more successful EU firms concentrate on the development of sustainable firm-specific advantages rather than on the use of CVD and AD laws.

Key terms

- Single European Act (SEA)
- EU Council of Ministers
- single European market (SEM)
- coordinated infrastructure
- market coordination infrastructure
- resource sharing infrastructure
- autonomous infrastructure
- delayed differentiation
- European Research Cooperation Agency
- countervailing duties (CVD)
- antidumping duties (AD)

Review and discussion questions

1. What are the ultimate objectives of the EU? Identify and describe them.

2. Will the EU bring about a single European market? What type of changes will have to take place in order for this to happen? Identify and describe three of them.

3. What is the competitive status of the EU in terms of labor productivity and investment spending? Based on your answer, what is your overall evaluation of this status?

4. How can firms doing business in the EU use competitive intelligence? Identify and describe two major steps that can be used in this process.

5. What types of regional incentives do countries offer MNEs willing to set up operations in their locales? Identify and describe two of them.

6. In addition to regional incentives, what other evaluation criteria should MNEs employ when deciding where in the EU to establish operations? Identify and describe three of them.

7. In formulating a strategy for doing business in the EU, there are two primary areas of initial consideration: national responsiveness and economic integration. What does this statement mean? Be sure to include a discussion of Figure 16.1 in your answer.

8. What do companies that want to export to the EU need to know about doing business there? Discuss five facts or strategies that would be of value to them.

9. In gaining a foothold in the EU, when is it most effective to opt for an acquisition over an alliance? When is a strategic alliance a better choice? In each case, provide an example.

10. Why will marketing strategies in the EU have to reflect a concern for pricing? A concern for positioning? Give an example of when each would be the most important consideration.

11. What is the likely future of direct marketing in the EU? Defend your answer.

12. What are three major manufacturing considerations for companies doing business in the EU? Identify and describe each.

13. How important is it for EU managers to have a global perspective? Be complete in your answer.

14. How can trade laws be used by EU firms to keep out global competitors?

15. What evidence is there that EU firms use antidumping laws?

EVALUATING THE COMPETITION

How prepared are EU firms to compete with MNEs coming from abroad? The jury is still out, but one thing is certain: many European firms will have to trim down and get a lot more productive if they hope to survive over the long run. In recent years Rover, the UK/German manufacturer, and Peugeot of France have both retreated from the US market. Meanwhile, back in Europe, Rolls Royce lost a $700 million jet engine order to its archrival, General Electric. Philips, the giant Dutch electronics firm, has sold its home appliance business to Whirlpool and its computer systems division to Digital Equipment.

On the other hand, many EU businesses are doing quite well. There are now more EU firms on *Fortune*'s Global 500 list than there are any others except those of the US Moreover, if non-EU European countries were included, this group would top the list. Of course, bigger does not always mean better, but it can provide two competitive advantages: financial strength and economies of scale. Overall, however, the EU presents a mixed picture with some industries doing rather poorly while others excel. The automotive, electronics, and chemical/pharmaceutical industries provide interesting contrasts. Table 16.6 provides data on the industrial composition of the world's largest 500 MNEs, showing the 154 EU MNEs and their triad competitors across 45 industry groups.

Table 16.6   World's largest 500 MNEs by industry and country, 1997

Industry	Number of MNEs	United States	Canada	Japan	EU	Others
Aerospace	8	6			2	
Airlines	9	4		1	4	
Banks: commercial and savings	68	11	4	11	33	9
Beverages	5	4	1			
Building materials, glass	2			1	1	
Chemicals	16	4		2	9	1
Computer services and software	2	2				
Computers, office equipment	9	6		3		
Diversified financials	4	4				
Electronics, electrical equipment	25	6	1	9	6	3
Electric semiconductors	2	2				
Energy	6	2	1		2	1
Engineering, construction	10	1		7	2	
Entertainment	5	4				1
Food	13	8		1	3	1
Food and drug stores	28	9	1	3	11	4
Forest and paper products	6	4		1	1	
General merchandisers	13	7		3	3	
Health care	3	3				
Hotels, casinos, resorts	2	1		1		
Industrial and farm equipment	8	2		2	4	
Insurance: life and health (mutual)	17	4		11	1	1

Table 16.6 **(cont'd)**

Industry	Number of MNEs	United States	Canada	Japan	EU	Others
Insurance: life and health (stock)	19	4		2	10	3
Insurance: property, casualty (mutual)	2	2				
Insurance: property, casualty (stock)	16	6		2	6	2
Mail, package, and freight delivery	8	3		2	3	
Metal products	3	1		1	1	
Metals	13	1		6	5	1
Mining, crude-oil production	3				1	2
Motor vehicles and parts	25	5		9	9	2
Petroleum refining	31	12		5	7	7
Pharmaceuticals	10	6			2	2
Publishing, printing	4		2	2		
Railroads	7	2		3	2	
Rubber and plastic products	3	1		1	1	
Scientific, photo, control equipment	3	2		1		
Securities	3	3				
Soaps, cosmetics	3	2			1	
Specialist retailers	9	6			3	
Telecommunications	22	9		2	8	3
Tobacco	3	1		1	1	
Trading	19			11	3	5
Utilities, gas, and electric	16	5		5	5	1
Wholesalers	9	7			2	
Miscellaneous	8	3		3	2	
Total	500	175	10	112	154	49

Source: Adapted from *Fortune*, "The Fortune Global 500 Ranked Within Industries," *Fortune*, August 4, 1998.

As of the late 1990s, European auto firms were running a trade surplus with the rest of the world. This was accounted for largely because of restrictions on Japanese imports and because Ford Motor and General Motors built cars in Europe rather than importing them. On the other hand, research from the Massachusetts Institute of Technology shows that European auto firms require more hours to build a car than do their US or Japanese competitors. As EU auto quotas are phased out, many observers believe that European auto firms will lose significant market share. On the other hand, when it comes to heavy trucks, European firms do extremely well. This is true not only in the EU but also in the United States where Daimler-Benz, Volvo, and Renault collectively hold almost 50 per cent of the market.

In electronics the EU runs a large trade deficit. The major European computer firms have all lost market share to US competitors such as IBM, Compaq, Digital, and Apple. However, EU electronic giants do excel at telecommunications and medical equipment, European household appliances get high ratings for their design features, and EU light bulb manufacturers such as Philips and Siemens are world leaders.

In chemicals and pharmaceuticals European industries lead the way. Europe is the home to six of the ten largest chemical companies in the world, and many of these firms have expanded into specialty chemicals where margins are larger and safer. EU firms are also strong in pharmaceuticals where their heavy spending on R&D has helped them to expand internationally and to remain extremely competitive.

Summing up the situation in the EU as of the late 1990s, European firms have been doing well in some industries, but overall they have major problems in competing with the United States and Japan. They also need to focus on raising both productivity and quality standards through the use of teamwork, just-in-time inventory delivery, statistical quality control, and other integrated techniques of lean manufacturing.

1. What EU industries appear to be the most competitive worldwide? Explain.

2. If the EU were to eliminate all barriers and to allow in foreign exports, would European firms be able to compete successfully against foreign competition? Why or why not?

3. Based on your evaluation of the information in this case, what types of goods and services would US firms be able to sell most easily in the EU? Where would these firms have the most difficulty? Explain your answer.

Sources: Joan Warner, Pete Engardio, and Thane Peterson, "The Atlantic Century?" *Business Week*, February 8, 1999, pp. 64–67; Thane Peterson, et al., "Europe Rising," *Business Week*, February 8, 1999, pp. 68–69.

US TELEPHONE COMPANIES GO TO EUROPE

AT&T and the seven regional phone companies in the United States, popularly known as the "Baby Bells," are well known for their reliable equipment for high-quality service. Now they are taking their expertise to Europe and gaining international market share. Currently most of the major US deals in the EU consist of strategic alliances with local companies. Here are four examples:

● Ameritech has interests in Europe totaling over $6 billion. It purchased WLW, a European provider of business information, which allowed it to take over operations in ten European countries. In Denmark, this "Baby Bell" owns 34.7 per cent of Tele Danmark, which provides all kinds of telecommunication services in Denmark. In Norway it holds a 19.7 per cent stake of NetCom which services Norway's cellular market. The company also has joint ventures with Deutsche Telekom to provide local phone lines, cellular, long distance, and cable TV in Hungary. It has joined a six-way partnership with Tele Danmark, and Singapore Telecom, among others, to provide telecommunication services to Belgium.

● Bell Atlantic and US West are part of a joint venture that has been awarded a contract to work with the state telephone company in the Czech Republic and in Slovakia to build and operate cellular and data networks and to modernize the basic telephone network.

● MCI WorldCom provides an integrated telecommunication network linking major cities throughout the continent, such as Paris, London, Brussels, Frankfurt, Amsterdam, and Stockholm, and it is expecting to triple the size of its pan-European network by the end of 1999.

● Bell South has a 22.5 per cent share of the E-plus consortium in Germany which today services 98 per cent of Germany's population. In Denmark the company has a 46.5 per cent equity share in a joint venture with Sonofon to provide digital cellular services to 500,000 Danes.

AT&T is also playing a big role in the EU market. In 1998 it decided to merge its international operations with British Telecom into a $11 billion enterprise. The company currently has 3,000 international employees, up from 100 in 1984. It has joint ventures or alliances in 44 countries around the world. AT&T also makes a great deal of money on its long-distance service between the United States and Europe. Four of the ten countries that have the most long-distance traffic with the United States are Britain, Germany, France, and Italy. Over 50 per cent of these long-distance calls travel on AT&T equipment.

EU firms are well aware of their US competitors and are now striking back. In many cases they are forming alliances with US companies and/or other European firms. In 1999 Telecom Italy was holding talks with Deutsche Telekom over a possible merger. France Telecom, Deutsche Telekom and Sprint formed Global One, a joint venture to provide voice and data telecommunications. Global One employs 3,800 people in more than 65 countries. While US telecommunications companies are finding the EU to be an attractive market, there is growing local competition that may severely limit the market opportunities for AT&T and the Baby Bells.

1. Why are strategic alliances often very useful in helping US telecommunications firms to establish a beachhead in the EU?

2. How much competition are US telecommunications firms likely to encounter in the EU? Explain.

3. Which marketing strategy would be of more value to the firms in this industry, price or positioning? Explain your answer.

Source: Adapted from Andrew Kupfer, "Ma Bell and Seven Babies Go Global," *Fortune*, November 4, 1991, pp. 118–28; Mark Lewyn, "There's Less and Less Static on These Lines," *Business Week*, January 8, 1990, p. 101; Gary Slutsker, "The Tortoise and the Hare," *Forbes*, February 1, 1993, pp. 66–81; *http://www.ameritech.com/*; *http://www.bellatlantic.com/*; *http://www.wcom.com/*; *http://www.att.com*; *http://www.sprint.com*; "European Telecoms in a Tangle," *The Economist*, April 24, 1999, pp. 83–7.

ENDNOTES

1. Spyros G. Makridakis and Michelle Bainbridge, "Evolution of the Single Market," in Spyros G. Makridakis (ed.), *Single Market Europe: Opportunities and Challenges for Business* (San Francisco: Josey Bass, 1991), p. 9.

2. Also see Trevor Merriden, "How 'Single' is the Single Market?" *Management Review*, March 1998, pp. 27–31.

3. Gabriel Hawawini and Eric J. Rajendra, "Integrating and Legislating Rapid Changes in the Financial Services Industry," in Makridakis (ed.), op. cit., pp. 323–324.

4. Edmund L. Andrews, "11 Countries Tie Europe Together In One Currency," *New York Times*, January 1, 1999, pp. A1, 8.

5. Thomas Kamm, "Emergence of Euro Embodies Challenge and Hope for Europe," *Wall Street Journal*, January 4, 1999, pp. A1, 4.

6. Tatiana S. Boncompagni, "Europe's Retailers Prepare to Switch To The Euro, Seeking to Gain Customers," *Wall Street Journal*, November 9, 1998, p. B13A.

7. Edmund L. Andrews, "Sticker Shocks in Euro Land," *New York Times*, December 27, 1998, Section 3, pp. 1, 6.

8. Thane Peterson, "The Euro," *Business Week*, April 27, 1998, pp. 90–94.

9. Michael Hickins, "US Business Blinks at the Euro," *Management Review*, April 1998, pp. 33–37.

10. Herbert A. Henzler, "The New Era of Euro-capitalism," *Harvard Business Review*, July–August 1992, pp. 57–68.

11. Douglas Lavin, "France, Germany Must Cut More Jobs to Improve Efficiency, Report Suggests," *Wall Street Journal*, March 14, 1997, p. B3A.

12. Jonathan B. Levine, "Grabbing the Controls in Mid-Tailspin," *Business Week*, January 17, 1994, pp. 45–46.

13. Rebecca Blumenstein, "Cadillac Has Designs on Europe's Luxury-Car Buyers," *Wall Street Journal*, September 9, 1997, pp. B1, 14.

14. Virginia O'Brien, "Competitor Intelligence in the European Community," *Journal of European Business*, September/October 1990, pp. 17–21.

15. John E. Prescott and Patrick T. Gibbons, "Europe '92 Provides New Impetus for Competitive Intelligence," *Journal of Business Strategy*, November/December 1991, pp. 20–26.

16. Earl Landesman, "Ultimatum for US Auto Suppliers: Go Global or Go Under," *Journal of European Business*, May/June 1991, pp. 39–45.

17. Ibid., pp. 40–41.

18. Alan M. Rugman and Alain Verbeke, "Europe 1992

and Competitive Strategies for North American Firms," *Business Horizons*, November/December 1991, pp. 76–81.

19. Ibid., p. 78.

20. Thomas F. Clasen, "An Exporter's Guide to Selecting Foreign Sales Agents and Distributors," *Journal of European Management*, November/December 1991, pp. 28–32.

21. Joel Bleeke and David Ernst, "The Way to Win in Cross-Border Alliances," *Harvard Business Review*, November–December 1991, pp. 127–128.

22. See, for example, Bill Vlasic et al., "The First Global Car Colossus," *Business Week*, May 18, 1998, pp. 40–43.

23. Gianluigi Guido, "Implementing a Pan European Marketing Strategy," *Long Range Planning*, October 1991, p. 27.

24. Ibid., p. 30.

25. Ibid, pp. 31–32.

26. Heather Ogilvie, "Electronic Ties That Bind: Marks & Spencer's Pan-European JIT Inventory System," *Journal of European Business*, September/October 1991, pp. 48–50.

27. Jean-Claude Goldenstein and Sandra Thompson, "Participating in European Cooperative R&D Programs," *Journal of European Business*, September/October 1991, p. 51.

28. Ibid., p. 52.

29. For more on this, see Richard M. Hodgetts and Fred Luthans, *International Management*, 4th ed. (Homewood, Ill.: Irwin/McGraw, 2000), Chapter 13.

30. The theory of shelter has been developed in Alan M. Rugman and Alain Verbeke, *Global Competitive Strategy and Trade Policy* (London: Routledge, 1990). A study on the use of EC trade law measures as a shelter strategy is by Alan M. Rugman and Michael Gestrin, "EC Anti-Dumping Laws as a Barrier to Trade," *European Management Journal*, vol. 9, no. 4, December 1991, pp. 475–482. Related data and analysis of EC trade law cases are reported in Patrick A. Messerlin, "Anti-Dumping Regulations or Procartel Law?: The EC Chemical Case," *The World Economy*, vol. 13, no. 4, December 1990, pp. 465–492.

31. For an application of the concept of shelter by the use of US trade laws, see Alan M. Rugman and Michael Gestrin, "US Trade Laws as Barriers to Globalization," *The World Economy*, vol. 14, no. 3, December 1991, pp. 335–352. For earlier data and studies of US trade law cases used as a barrier to entry against rival Canadian firms, see Alan M. Rugman and Andrew D. M. Anderson, *Administered Protection in America* (London and New York: Routledge, 1987).

32. For an excellent discussion of triad power and the use of trade laws as barriers to entry, see Sylvia Ostry, *Governments and Corporations in a Shrinking World* (New York and London: Council on Foreign Relations Press, 1990).

33. For evidence of the abuse of US trade law procedures, see Richard Boltuck and Robert Litan (eds.), *Down in the Dumps: Administration of the Unfair Trade Laws* (Washington, DC: The Brookings Institute, 1991). For recent legal and economic research on this issue, see Michael J. Trebilcock and Robert C. York (eds.), *Fair Exchange: Reforming Trade Remedy Laws* (Toronto: C. D. Howe Institute and McGraw-Hill Ryerson, 1990).

ADDITIONAL BIBLIOGRAPHY

Czinkota, Michael. "The EC '92 and Eastern Europe: Effects of Integration vs. Disintegration." *Columbia Journal of World Business*, vol. 26, no. 1 (Spring 1991).

Deschamps, Jean Claude. "The European Community, International Trade, and World Unity," *California Management Review*, vol. 35, no. 2 (Winter 1993).

Douglas, Susan P. and Rhee, Dong Kee. "Examining Generic Competitive Strategy Types in US and European Markets," *Journal of International Business Studies*, vol. 20, no. 3 (Fall 1989).

Dowling, Michael and Leidner, Alfred. "Technical Standards and 1992: Opportunity or Entry Barrier in the New Europe? *Columbia Journal of World Business*, vol. 25, no. 3 (Fall 1990).

Greer, Thomas V. "Product Liability in the European Economic Community: The New Situation," *Journal of International Business Studies*, vol. 20, no. 2 (Summer 1989).

Henzler, Herbert A. "The New Era of Eurocapitalism," *Harvard Business Review*, vol. 70, no. 3 (July/August 1992).

Kaikati, Jack G. "Europe 1992 – Mind Your Strategic P's and Q's," *Sloan Management Review*, vol. 31, no. 1 (Fall 1989).

Kidd, John B. and Teramoto, Yoshiya. "The Learning Organization: The Case of the Japanese RHQs in Europe," *Management International Review*, vol. 35 (1995/2).

Miller, Alan N. "British Privatization: Evaluating the Results," *Columbia Journal of World Business*, vol. 30, no. 4 (Winter 1995).

Millington, Andrew I. and Bayliss, Brian T. "The Process of Internationalisation: UK Companies in the EC," *Management International Review*, vol. 30, no. 2 (Second Quarter 1990).

Millington, Andrew I. and Bayliss, Brian T. "Non-Tariff Barriers and UK Investment in the European Community," *Journal of International Business Studies*, vol. 22, no. 4 (Fourth Quarter 1991).

Millington, Andrew and Bayliss, Brian T. "The Strategy of Internationalization and the Success of UK Transnational Manufacturing Operations in the European Union," *Management International Review*, vol. 37, no. 3 (1997).

Nitsch, Detlev; Beamish, Paul and Makino, Shige. "Entry Mode and Performance of Japanese FDI in Western Europe," *Management International Review*, vol. 36, no. 1 (1996).

Papanastassiou, Marina and Pearce, Robert. "Technology Sourcing and the Strategic Roles of Manufacturing Subsidiaries in the UK: Local Competence and Global Competitiveness," *Management International Review*, vol. 37, no. 1 (1997).

Quelch, John A. and Buzzell, Robert D. "Marketing Moves Through EC Crossroads," *Sloan Management Review*, vol. 31, no. 1 (Fall 1989).

Rehder, Robert R. and Thompson, Judith Kenner. "Nissan UK: The Japanese Transplant Beachhead in Europe," *Columbia Journal of World Business*, vol. 29, no. 3 (Fall 1994).

Rugman, Alan M.; Theil, Rita; and Verbeke, Alain. "Entry Barriers and Bank Strategies for the Europe 1992 Financial Directives," *European Management Journal*, vol. 10, no. 3 (September 1992).

Rugman, Alan M.; Verbeke, Alain; and Campbell, Alexandria. "Strategic Change in the European Flexible Manufacturing Industry," *European Management Review*, vol. 8, no. 3 (September 1990).

Rugman, Alan M. and Verbeke, Alain. "Environmental Change and Global Competitive Strategy in Europe," in *Research in Global Strategic Management: Volume 2: Global Competition and the European Community* (Greenwich, Conn.: JAI Press, 1991).

Rugman, Alan M. and Verbeke, Alain. *Research in Global Strategic Management: Volume 2: Global Competition and the European Community* (Green-wich, Conn.: JAI Press, 1991).

Rugman, Alan M. and Verbeke, Alain. "Competitive Strategies for Non-European Firms," in B. Burgenmeier and J. L. Mucchielli (eds.), *Multinationals and Europe 1992: Strategies for the Future* (London and New York: Routledge, 1991).

Rugman, Alan M. and Verbeke, Alain. "Europe 1992 and Competitive Strategies for North American Firms," *Business Horizons*, vol. 34, no. 6 (November/December 1991).

Taggart, James H. "An Evaluation of the Integration-Responsiveness Framework: MNC Manufacturing Subsidiaries in the UK," *Management International Review*, vol. 37, no. 4 (1997).

Welfens, Paul J. J. "Foreign Investment in the East European Transition," *Management International Review*, vol. 32, no. 3 (Third Quarter 1992).

CHAPTER 17

Doing Business in Japan

OBJECTIVES OF THE CHAPTER

Japan is one of the world's leading economic powers. Each year the EU and the United States buy billions of dollars of cars, computers, and electronic goods that are made in Japan. Many other nations also rely heavily on Japanese industry to provide them with a wide array of products. At the same time, Japan is becoming a major market for multinational enterprises (MNEs), which see a growing demand for goods and services accompanying the country's dramatic economic prosperity. These MNEs have also come to realize that in order to be a world-class competitor, they need to do business in Japan. The specific objectives of this chapter are to:

1. **Examine** the nature of the Japanese economy and present some of the most important factors that need to be considered when doing business there.

2. **Describe** some of the major characteristics of the Japanese economic system that are critical to doing business in that country.

3. **Relate** six basic steps taken by firms that have successfully entered the Japanese market.

4. **Compare** and **contrast** the benefits and drawbacks associated with start-up strategies, including exporting, licensing agreements, joint ventures, acquisitions, and Japanese subsidiaries.

5. **Discuss** how to manage on-site operations, with particular attention to recruitment, location, organization, and financing.

ACTIVE LEARNING CASE

Figuring out how to do business in Japan

Doing business in Japan presents many challenges to foreign MNEs. One of the biggest is how to carve out a market in a country where keiretsus and other cartel-like arrangements are so common. At first, many MNEs entering Japan find it difficult to compete effectively. Major keiretsu or cartels are billion-dollar firms with business ties that turn them into huge, vertically integrated companies. Some of these cartels own or have business dealings with a host of other companies that ensure that the keiretsu can manufacture and sell its products without ever relying on a firm outside this circle of firms. There are even distribution cartels in Japan that are so encompassing that they can control the flow of products, accessories, services, and prices from the factory floor all the way to the consumer. A good example is Matsushita.

Matsushita manufactures Panasonic, National, Technics, and Quasar products. The firm also controls a chain of approximately 25,000 national retail stores throughout the country, which collectively generate more than 50 per cent of the company's domestic sales. These stores sell a wide variety of products, from batteries to refrigerators. Most importantly, they agree to sell at manufacturers' recommended prices. In turn Matsushita ensures the survival of these stores by giving them a 25 per cent retail margin on sales. This margin is a result of fixed retail prices, manufacturing rebates, advertising subsidies, and protected sales territories from other Matsushita dealers. Other Japanese firms have similar arrangements. Examples include Toshiba, Hitachi, Mitsubishi, Sanyo, and Sony, which, along with Matsushita, collectively control approximately 70,000 small retail stores (about 7.5 per cent of those in the entire country).

Despite such a major obstacle, foreign MNEs are learning that there are a number of useful strategies that can help them to break into the Japanese market. In the case of suppliers, for example, it is important to be patient and to continue to bid for business. At first, many keiretsus turn down foreign companies because they want to stay within their cartel-like arrangement. However, these keiretsus are also interested in pushing out their major competitors, and a foreign supplier with high-quality products will often find that one of the major keiretsus will break with tradition and make a deal. Additionally, many small keiretsus are trying to get off the ground and to gain market share. These too are interested in developing relations with high-quality suppliers. Moreover, because the best local suppliers are usually already tied to keiretsus, foreign sources are often very attractive to these fledgling cartels.

A second strategy is to link forces with established Japanese firms in the form of joint ventures. For example, T. Row Price Associates recently entered into a joint venture with Daiwa Securities and the Sumitomo Bank. The venture will focus on mutual-fund management. And the Swiss Bank Corporation has now formed a host of new joint ventures with the Long-Term Credit Bank of Japan Limited. While there are drawbacks to these ventures, two of the major advantages are sharing the risk and achieving rapid market access.

A third strategy is to team up with Japanese firms to help develop or manufacture new products. One recent example is Motorola and Texas Instruments (TI), which have an arrangement with Sony. TI provides signal processors for Sony compact disc players and Motorola manufactures the chips that go into Sony camcorders. Another example is AT&T's Bell Laboratories and AT&T's Microelectronics, which have a working relationship with NEC. Bell is helping NEC to design products and Microelectronics is making and supplying the chips for these units.

A fourth, and more recent, strategy is acquisition and merger. GE Capital, for example, has bought the leasing businesses of the Japan Leasing Corporation, purchased NC Card Sendai, specialists in financing for installment sales and consumer credit, and set up a merger with a

▶

Japanese firm to expand a ship container leasing business.

There are a number of reasons that MNEs want to do business in Japan. One is the growing market. A second is that Japan is a major economic force in the Pacific and this power is likely to grow over the ensuing decades. By maintaining a presence in Japan worldwide competitors are in the best position to monitor these strategies and to respond with countermeasures. For these multinationals, doing business in Japan is critical to the growth of their enterprises. So it is critical for them to learn how to do business here.

Sources: Adapted from Robert L. Cutts, "Capitalism in Japan: Cartels and Keiretsu," *Harvard Business Review*, July–August 1992, pp. 48–55; Emily Thornton, "Will Japan Rule a New Trade Bloc?" *Fortune*, October 5, 1992, pp. 131–132; Andrew Pollack, "Apple to Work with Toshiba on 'Multimedia' Products," *New York Times*, June 24, 1992, pp. C1, C5; Bill Powell, "Here's a PC for Peanuts," *Newsweek*, January 25, 1993, p. 63; Kathy Rebello, Russell Mitchell, and Evan I. Schwartz, "Apple's Future," *Business Week*, July 5, 1993, pp. 22–28; Bill Spindle, "GE Capital Seeks Out Niches in Japan," *Wall Street Journal*, January 5, 1999, p. A17; Jonathan Sapsford, "GE Capital to Buy $7 Billion in Japanese Assets," *Wall Street Journal*, January 25, 1999, pp. A13, 15; and Jonathan Sapsford, "US Financial Firms Delve Deeper Into Japan," *Wall Street Journal*, January 26, 1999, pp. A13, 15.

1. Why do MNEs need to understand the role of keiretsus in the Japanese economy?

2. How can foreign MNEs use keiretsus to their own advantage? Give an example.

3. Why are joint ventures so popular among foreign MNEs? Cite two reasons.

4. Why is Japan likely to remain a target market for international MNEs? Cite two reasons.

PROFILE OF JAPAN

Japan consists of four main islands (Hokkaido, Honshu, Shikoku, and Kyushu) and a number of smaller islands (see accompanying map). The country is approximately the size of California, and over the last two decades it has become a major industrial power. Today the Japanese yen is one of the strongest currencies in the world as the nation's massive international trade has helped it to maintain vigorous, sustained economic growth.[1]

Political and legal system

The branches of the Japanese government are very similar to those in the United States: legislative, executive, and judicial. Legislative power is vested in the Diet, which consists of a popularly elected House of Representatives and House of Councillors. There are five major political parties. The strongest of these is the Liberal-Democratic party, which is conservative and generally supported by the two most powerful groups in the country: business and agriculture.

Executive power rests with the Cabinet, which is organized and headed by the prime minister, who is elected by the Diet.[2] In addition to the office of the prime minister, there are 21 ministerial divisions and subdivisions in the executive branch.

The judicial power is vested in the Supreme Court. In addition, there are eight high courts and a host of district courts throughout the country.

Japan is divided into 47 prefectures, somewhat similar to US states. Each local political subdivision, including cities, towns, and villages, has its own executive power and operates within the scope of the national law.

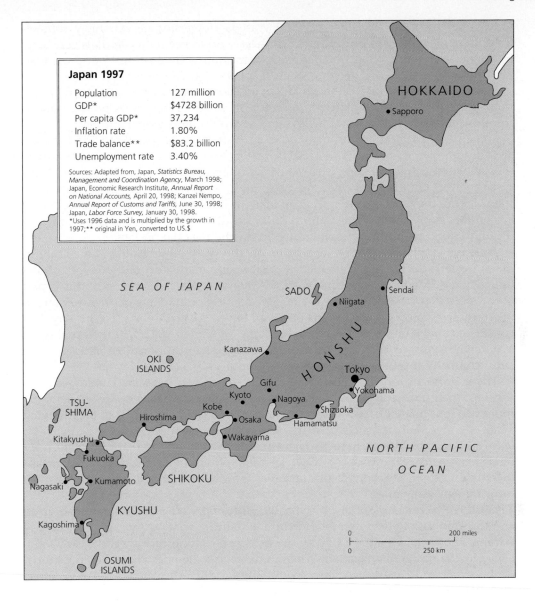

Japan 1997

Population	127 million
GDP*	$4728 billion
Per capita GDP*	37,234
Inflation rate	1.80%
Trade balance**	$83.2 billion
Unemployment rate	3.40%

Sources: Adapted from, Japan, *Statistics Bureau, Management and Coordination Agency*, March 1998; Japan, Economic Research Institute, *Annual Report on National Accounts*, April 20, 1998; Kanzei Nempo, *Annual Report of Customs and Tariffs*, June 30, 1998; Japan, *Labor Force Survey*, January 30, 1998. *Uses 1996 data and is multiplied by the growth in 1997;** original in Yen, converted to US.$

Population and social patterns

There are approximately 127 million people in Japan. But because much of the country is mountainous and unsuitable for living, the population is densely concentrated. Approximately 20 per cent of the people live in or around Tokyo.

The standard dialect of Japanese is understood throughout the country, even though there are some local differences. English is the most frequently taught foreign language, and in business circles visitors can generally communicate in English, although involved negotiations typically require an interpreter.

Education is mandatory in Japan until the age of 14. Primary school lasts six years and junior high school, three years. Further education is optional and usually consists of three years of high school and four years of college. Admission to first-tier public universities such as Tokyo University and Kyoto University and private universities such as Keio University and Waseda University are extremely competitive. Students hoping to gain entrance to these schools begin preparations very early in their school years, often working many extra hours. Graduation from these first-tier universities is often a stepping stone to a good job and career.

Living standards are high, although houses and apartments are typically much smaller than those in the United States. In addition to salaries, employees receive various social insurance benefits, paid holidays and vacations, and retirement pay.

Some social patterns are distinctly different from those in the West.[3] The Japanese are a group-oriented people. This social behavior carries over to business relationships as well, where school ties and friendships are often major factors. The Japanese also place a strong emphasis on harmony, orderliness, and respect for others.[4] Because of these values, the Japanese often seem ambiguous or noncommittal in situations such as contract negotiations. These efforts to avoid direct confrontation are frequently misunderstood by businesspeople sitting across the negotiation table.[5]

Japanese employees place a high value on the work ethic. Unlike the culture in many western countries, job attendance is viewed as mandatory and everyone shows up every day. Managers are required to stay late and work on weekends; this is part of the job and is well accepted by the rest of society. Commenting on the work schedule of these employees, two experts on Japan have explained that, "To this day, it is considered shameful for a husband to be home before ten o'clock in the evening on a workday. Even weekends are spent in the office or on work-related outings – golf trips, company meetings, and travel with customers."[6]

There is also a strong bond between workers and their companies. Employees identify with their firms and are often unwilling to leave even when they are offered more money to join foreign firms.[7] In fact, there is often a stigma attached to making such a career move. This is reflected in the way that the Japanese describe people who leave to work for foreign firms. A Japanese who leaves his company to work for a foreign company is known as a **gairojin**, stemming from the word **gaijin**, which means literally "outsider." Because of this attitude, local recruiting is a major problem for most foreign companies.[8]

Japan is a hierarchical society. Social ranking determines the amount of respect given and the amount of effort that is made in maintaining relationships, in greeting and bowing, and even in framing everyday speech. Social relationships are also greatly influenced by the power of obligation. When someone is a member of a group, the individual is expected to assume certain responsibilities to the other members. For example, many senior managers will spend three or four weekends a year attending the weddings of their employees. In addition, there are business-related responsibilities such as giving gifts to key employees, suppliers, and customers, exchanging critical information with clients, and participating in joint venture arrangements with partners. The burden of such social/business obligations helps to explain why many Japanese shy away from making new social relationships. The accompanying responsibilities are simply too time demanding. It also helps to explain why doing business in Japan often takes much longer than in one's own country. Japanese managers already have so many things to do that they are frequently in no hurry to enter into new relationships.

Business and the economy

Japan has a gross domestic product (GDP) of approximately $3 trillion and one of the largest per capita incomes in world. However, in recent years Japan has also faced

Table 17.1 Japan's changing economic status in recent years

	1990	1998	Change
Business and the economy			
Unemployment rate	2%	4.4%	+2.4 points
Current account surplus	14.902 trillion yen (1998)	11.44 trillion yen (1997)	−23%
Auto production	13.5 million	11 million (1997)	−19%
VCR production	28.2 million (1989)	9.6 million (1997)	−66%
Cost of a square meter of land in Tokyo's Ginza district	38.5 million yen (1991)	10.3 million yen	−73%
Corporate entertainment spending	6.208 trillion yen (1992)	5.409 trillion yen (1996)	−13%
Department store sales (per 100 square meters)	156.01 million yen (1991)	121.6 million yen (1997)	−24%
Society			
Golf club membership cost (at the upscale Koganei Golf Club)	440 million yen (1989)	61 million yen	−86%
Price of a condominium in Tokyo	61.23 million yen	43.74 million yen (1997)	−29%
Cost of a top-of-the-line personal computer	1.2 million yen (1993)	680,000 yen	−43%
Number of bars and restaurants	77,544 (1988)	73,502 (1996)	−5%
Number of nightclubs	1,042	784 (1996)	−25%
Rolls Royce sales	518 cars	51 cars (1997)	−90%
Shipment of cut-rate beer	3,368 kiloliters (1994)	417,780 kiloliters (1997)	+4,893%

Sources: Adapted from David P. Hamilton, "So, How Far Has Japan Fallen? Take a Look at These Numbers," *Wall Street Journal*, July 2, 1998, p. A19; Yumiko Ono and Jacob M. Schlesinger, "Sign of Changed Times: Japan's Jobless Rate Rises to the US Level," *Wall Street Journal*, December 28, 1998, pp. A1, 8.

a prolonged economic slowdown. In particular, the nation's banks were awash in red ink[9] with bad debts in excess of $1 trillion![10] At the same time, the jobless rate increased,[11] firms such as Mitsubishi Motors announced that it was planning layoffs and plant closings,[12] and GDP was declining.[13] Table 17.1 provides some additional contrasting data that show how far the Japanese economy had slid between the mid and late 1990s. At the same time, the economy has a great deal of underlying strength. A number of factors account for this. One is the role of governmental agencies and ministries in promoting economic growth.

Ministry of international trade and industry The **Ministry of International Trade and Industry (MITI)** serves as the coordinating body of the country's powerful commercial machinery. It is MITI's job to identify and rank national commercial pursuits and business opportunities and to guide the distribution of national resources to meet these goals. MITI encourages Japanese companies to pursue targeted opportunities such as developing advanced computer technology, high-tech industrial and agricultural machinery, optical electronics, and world-class auto manufacturing. Firms that are willing to enter these industries are provided with government subsidies and market protection.

When MITI identifies an area where it would like to expand business efforts, it is able to gain support for three reasons: (1) *financial incentives* – as noted earlier, these are made available to companies that are prepared to commit resources; (2) *personal relationship* – most MITI ministers have attended the major universities, and so they have school ties to the captains of industry; and (3) *location* – MITI offices and those of most corporate and financial giants are located in the same area of Tokyo, and so it is common to find the two groups interacting and sharing ideas.

Today MITI coordinates a wide variety of programs spread among regional governments in each prefecture, university, and industry. Primary consideration is now being given to ABCD industries: automation, biotechnology, computers, and data processing. Certain regions of the country have their own market niche, such as Hokkaido for marine technology, Kumamoto for applied machinery, and Okayama for biotechnology. Companies doing business in Japan must be aware of the impact of MITI and its efforts to coordinate and direct business efforts.

Keiretsus Before World War II the Japanese economy was dominated by ten large family-led business giants, which included Mitsui, Mitsubishi, Sumitomo, and Yasuda. After the war the Americans broke up these conglomerates. They have since reappeared in the form of **keiretsus**, which are massive, vertically integrated corporations. There are three main types of keiretsus: banks or financial firms, manufacturing companies, and industrial companies, which are usually led by a trading company.

Six of the 25 biggest commercial and savings banks in the world are Japanese-owned (see Table 17.2). Manufacturing keiretsus include Toyota, Nippon Steel, and Matsushita, well-known for a wide variety of products from cars to consumer goods. Trading companies such as Mitsui and Mitsubishi do billions of dollars in imports and exports, and this trading volume accounts for almost 25 per cent of Japan's GDP.

Keiretsus are so powerful that they often provide all of their own financing and operating needs from internal sources. Foreign MNEs competing in Japan need to evaluate the power of these firms, in terms of both competitiveness and the opportunity for strategic alliances and joint ventures.[14] They also need to evaluate the possibilities and benefits of working with small and medium-size suppliers that are now beginning to gain ground in their battle with these keiretsus.

ACTIVE LEARNING CHECK

Review your answer to Active Learning Case question 1 and make any changes you like. Then compare your answer to the one below.

1. Why do MNEs need to understand the role of keiretsus in the Japanese economy?

MNEs need to understand the role of keiretsus so that they realize some of the difficulties inherent in breaking into the Japanese market. These cartel-like arrangements involve hundreds of companies that are tied together through business relations (and sometimes social relations) and those that are not associated with one of these groups are often at a distinct disadvantage.

Table 17.2 The world's 25 largest commercial and savings companies, 1997

Rank	Bank	Country	Revenues (in millions of US $)
1	Crédit Suisse	Switzerland	48,242
2	Deutsche Bank	Germany	40,792
3	HSBC Holdings	Britain	37,474
4	Bank of Tokyo-Mitsubishi	Japan	34,750
5	Citicorp	United States	34,697
6	Crédit Agricole	France	34,015
7	Chase Manhattan	United States	38,381
8	ABN Amro Holdings	Netherlands	28,946
9	GAN	France	29,937
10	Société Générale	France	29,725
11	Industrial Bank of Japan	Japan	26,918
12	Banque Nationale de Paris	France	24,344
13	Bankamerica Corporation	United States	23,585
14	Fuji Bank	Japan	22,912
15	Sanwa Bank	Japan	22,805
16	Crédit Lyonnais	France	22,420
17	Lloyd's TSB Group	Britain	22,313
18	Westdeutsche Landesbank	Germany	21,859
19	Nations Bank Corporation	United States	21,734
20	Dresdner Bank	Germany	22,534
21	Sakura Bank	Japan	22,292
22	National Westminster Bank	Britain	22,155
23	Barclays Bank	Britain	21,129
24	Sumitomo Bank	Japan	21,008
25	Bank of China	China	20,927

Source: Adapted from "The Fortune Global 500 Ranked Within Industries," *Fortune*, August 3, 1998, pp. F15–16.

Barriers to business   Although Japan has removed many of its import quotas and duties, major nontariff barriers still prevent foreign firms from gaining a market foothold. For example, the **Large Retail Store Law** limits the size of retail stores and requires that local competitors approve the opening of any facility that is more than 500 square meters. While there are ways of minimizing the effects of this law, most large international retailers are effectively limited in their efforts to capture significant market share in Japan.

A second barrier is the informal job-bidding system that goes on behind closed doors. This system eliminates foreign competition and ensures maximum profits for the local participants, who are the only ones allowed to bid. An accompanying problem is a common Japanese practice of below-cost bidding such as offering to provide computer hardware for a low price on a project where costs are as high as $1 million. Then, after securing the contract, the Japanese business will make up the loss by selling the software at astronomical prices. These practices have excluded many

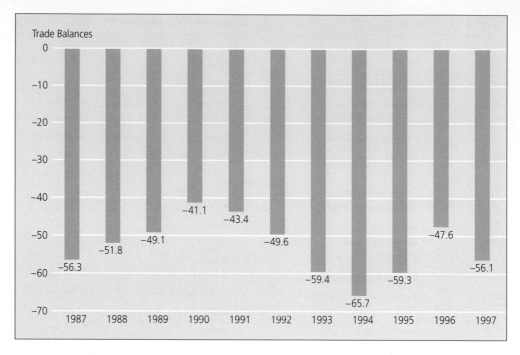

Figure 17.1   The US trade balances with Japan (in billions of US $)

Source: Data are from Citibank, *DRI Basic Economics*, label FZTBJP.

international computer firms from the Japanese market (although IBM Japan is an obvious exception). The Japanese government is now beginning to crack down on these practices, but for the time being, at least, nontariff barriers remain major problems for foreign MNEs.

Trade imbalances   The key business-related issue that dominates the economic scene is the friction over trade imbalances between Japan and the rest of the world. As seen in Figure 17.1 the United States continues to run major trade deficits with Japan. What makes this particularly disconcerting to the United States is the fact that its overall annual deficit with other countries has been declining while the deficit with Japan remains quite large. The United States is not alone. Japan is now running large surpluses with the rest of the world as well. As a result, more and more countries are putting pressure on Japan to open up its markets. If this does not happen, new trade barriers will probably be instituted in the United States, where Japanese auto firms could be badly hurt, and in Europe, where the EU is demanding trade reciprocity as a condition for opening up its bloc market. Because of these reciprocity demands, MNEs who want to do business in Japan see the potential for new business opening up in the next few years.

US impatience with Japanese trading practices is nothing new; for many years people have considered Japanese trade practices to be unfair. Japan was even kept out of GATT until 1955, eight years after the Agreement was signed. At that time the main lobbyist for Japan's membership was the United States. Whereas many European nations were fearful of Japan joining GATT, the United States, as the dominant player in world trade, saw no threat.

Now that Japan is a trading powerhouse, appeals for protectionism are often heard in the United States in some quarters,[15] but many economists do not agree with these sentiments. They believe that the popularity of Japanese products shows the ability of the Japanese to deliver what the US customer demands and that the US industry has not been responsive enough to these consumers. These economists maintain that the key to reducing the trade deficit with Japan lies not in protectionism but, rather, in US companies working harder to meet customer needs.[16] At the same time deregulation of industries such as the financial markets has resulted in an influx of Wall Street firms that are now finding growing opportunities in Japan.[17]

ACHIEVING SUCCESS IN JAPAN: SEVEN BASIC STEPS

Despite the challenges, many US firms have been successful in the Japanese market. Amway, Exxon, Hewlett-Packard, IBM, Intel, McDonald's, Merck, Pfizer, and Xerox all do millions of dollars of business in Japan every year.[18] In fact, more than 50,000 US products are sold in Japan and MITI estimates that there are over 1,000 US firms in the country, operating through subsidiaries or joint ventures. Annual sales by US firms are in the neighborhood of $100 billion. How has this been possible? Researchers have found that foreign MNEs that are most successful in Japan tend to follow seven basic steps.[19]

First: Research the Japanese market

The initial step that successful firms undertake is to research the market. As discussed in Chapter 15, this includes a preliminary analysis of potential customers, the nature of the industry, likely competitors, and firms with whom strategic alliances can be created. It also includes initial estimates of the startup capital and human resources that will be needed. Next comes a detailed plan regarding how to establish a presence in the market and how to differentiate the company's goods and services from those currently offered.

A number of successful firms have supplemented this approach with cultural training. This training typically covers Japanese history, customs, culture, and business practices. Additionally, for those who will be directly involved in on-site operations, rudimentary conversational Japanese is often included. Applied Materials Japan does this through an orientation program that includes (1) specially chosen reading on Japan, (2) talks by Japanese executives who are in the United States on assignment, and (3) weekly visits by groups of four to five managers and engineers from Japan's semiconductor companies. Through this process each executive is immersed in Japanese culture, customer demands, manufacturing technology, quality principles, geography, and everyday language skills.

When the orientation program is complete, Applied Materials sends its top people to Japan for further acculturation and to learn firsthand how things are done there. This also helped the managers to get a better understanding of the market and to formulate ideas for local operations. The box "International Business Strategy in Action: Some Useful Guidelines for Effective Interaction" provides additional details about cultural factors that make a difference when doing business in Japan.

INTERNATIONAL BUSINESS STRATEGY IN ACTION

Some useful guidelines for effective interaction

Foreigners doing business in Japan need to have a good understanding of social etiquette, including how to conduct oneself during business meetings. Six useful guidelines include the following:

1. One should always have business cards available and exchange them with everyone with whom business is being conducted. This exchange should always take place face-to-face, never across a table. The card should be printed in English on one side and Japanese on the other. After the exchange a handshake is proper.

2. In Japanese meetings guests are always seated on the side of the table that is opposite the door, with the most important person placed in the middle of the group. Japanese guests, who should be motioned to the proper side of the table, will arrange the seating order correctly since they understand how it is done.

3. When doing business with major or potential customers, it is acceptable to give a gift. Something from the foreign company's local area and unavailable in Japan is appropriate. Additionally, a list should be kept of the gifts and the people to whom they are given to ensure that individuals of obviously different

organizational rank do not receive the same present. In general, these gifts are given by the host at the end of the visit and by guests at the beginning or end of the visit.

4. When meeting with potential Japanese partners, it is a serious mistake to mention competitors or the names of firms with whom one's company is negotiating. Nor should any comments be made about social or political conditions in Japan. It is always best to focus on the positive: the work ethic of the Japanese people, the high level of service in the country, and the high quality of Japanese-manufactured products.

5. When meeting with a potential partner, it is useful to mention things that one has learned about the firm's operations. This shows an interest in the company and helps to create a favorable initial impression.

6. In preparing for meetings, it is useful to send the drafts of contracts, business plans, and meeting agendas ahead of schedule. In this way the other party can review and thoroughly understand the material prior to the meeting.

Sources: Adapted from James C. Morgan and J. Jeffrey Morgan, *Cracking the Japanese Market* (New York: Free Press, 1991), pp. 274–278; Peter D. Miller, "Getting Ready for Japan: What *Not* to Do," *Journal of Business Strategy*, January/February 1991, pp. 32–35; Emily Thornton, "To Sell in Japan, Just Keep Trying," *Fortune*, January 25, 1993; pp. 103–104; Brenton R. Schlender, "US PCs Invade Japan," *Fortune*, July 12, 1993, pp. 68–73; *Doing Business in Japan* (JETRO, 1999).

Second: Put the customer first

In the Japanese market customer service is used as a strategic weapon to best the competition. Every firm tries to outdo its competitors in pleasing the buyer, and this results in outstanding service. For example, when a customer buys a new car in Japan, the auto dealer delivers it to the buyer. If there is a problem with the car and servicing is required, the dealer will have the auto brought in and will provide a replacement while the car is being fixed.

Service is so important that many Japanese customers will not buy from a company that they feel is unable to provide support for what it sells. This extends from consumer goods to industrial parts that are purchased by manufacturing firms.

The emphasis on service also provides companies with a competitive edge when doing business elsewhere in the world. This is why many firms want to do business in Japan; it helps them to improve their customer service focus and so to compete more effectively in the international arena.

Third: Maintain control of operations

Successful MNEs have found that it pays to operate as close to the customer as possible in Japan. This means eliminating third-party agents. So while exporting, licensing, and distributorships are often employed to help firms break into the Japanese market, the most successful foreign companies limit their use. Rather, they opt for joint ventures or direct operating subsidiaries with their own Japanese management and local sales, marketing, manufacturing, and development capability. Other reasons for using the most direct channel possible include (1) the firm is better able to develop an image as a Japanese company and thus to increase the opportunity for more local business, (2) profits are increased by eliminating middlemen, and (3) local Japanese firms that are unable or unwilling to spend more money to protect their domestic market share lose out to these foreign competitors.

US firms that have followed this approach include Kodak Japan. The company has constructed a large research and development center in Yokohama, consolidated all Japanese operations at this location, increased its investment and advertising expenditures, and is now a major market force in Japan. Kodak claims that this approach has kept its competitors at bay. Having to compete in a highly dynamic market has helped the firm to increase efficiency and effectiveness.

IBM Japan is another good example. The firm started operations in Japan in 1925 and now has over 25,000 employees, several major factories, a world-class semiconductor fabrication center, sales offices throughout the country, and central research laboratories nationwide. Today IBM Japan is one of the largest foreign MNEs in the country, although most Japanese regard the company as a local firm because it has done such a good job of immersing itself in the economy and the culture.

Fourth: Offer the right products

Successful foreign-owned MNEs realize that many products sold elsewhere in the world must be reengineered and specially tailored for the Japanese market. For example, Kentucky Fried Chicken (KFC) Japan customized its product from the very start. Units are positioned as upscale, trendy stores rather than fast-food outlets. The Japanese menu includes fried fish and smoked chicken, cole slaw has a reduced sugar content, and french fries are substituted for mashed potatoes. These adaptations for the Japanese market have made KFC Japan extremely successful. In contrast, Upjohn and Pharmacia has always worked closely with Japanese hospitals and pharmacies in order to obtain feedback on product requirements, to gain acceptance for new products through the regulatory process, and to research new chemicals and processes. Today their Japanese subsidiary is highly profitable.

In other cases adjustment has been a response to poor performance. When Swatch, the Swiss maker of inexpensive, colorful watches entered Japan, its sales were dismal. The Japanese had not been accustomed to wearing watches as a fashion accessory. The company had to develop custom Japanese-designed Swatches and to educate the young people about using them. For example, soon after the Fuji-Xerox partnership introduced Xerox copiers in Japan, the firm realized that the machines did not meet market needs. The copiers had been designed with US secretaries in mind; Japanese secretaries generally had to stand on a box in order to reach the print button. The machines were then redesigned for the local market.

Fifth: Attack and counterattack

MNEs doing business in Japan have learned that no product is immune from attack for more than six months. For example, soon after McDonald's entered the market, a host of competitive hamburger chains began springing up. As a result, McDonald's Japan had to modify its menu continually, introduce aggressive advertising, and use discounting campaigns. In this way the firm has been able to maintain market leadership.

Procter & Gamble (P&G) faced a similar situation. For the first few years after it introduced disposable diapers the company held most of the market. By the mid-1980s, however, competitors had beaten the company's market share down to 5 per cent by offering new, improved products. Since then P&G has introduced product changes at a much faster rate than in the United States and has managed to garner 25 per cent of the Japanese market.

In the case of Fuji-Xerox, by the late 1970s the partnership realized that competition was increasing rapidly. So it began intensely investigating the market and investing heavily in R&D. This was followed by renewed manufacturing emphasis on quality control, vigorous reduction of inventory and production costs, and the introduction of a variety of new office products, including high-speed, low-end copiers. By the mid-1980s Fuji-Xerox had stopped IBM from making inroads into the copier market and was taking market share away from both Canon and Ricoh. Today the company is regarded as the strongest in that industry in Japan.

Sixth: Stay the course

One of the most important challenges that successful firms have to meet is "staying the course" when market share is small and the competition is strong. This has been particularly true in the case of small firms looking to gain an initial foothold. Allen-Edmonds, a small high-quality footwear manufacturer from Wisconsin, found that it had to persevere in the market and to keep plugging away despite the strong competition. Today Japan is a major market for its products. In other cases a partnership arrangement has proved helpful. For example, Sun Microsystems has partnership agreements with Fujitsu, Toshiba, and Fuji-Xerox that provide it with access to technology and markets; IBM has partnership agreements with Ricoh and Nippon Steel for selling and servicing IBM equipment in Japan. In still other cases firms have found that a piggyback arrangement can be ideal. For example, Blue Diamond Almond Growers of California has an agreement with Coca-Cola Bottling in Japan whereby the latter uses its distribution channels to sell almonds, and General Foods (GF) has teamed up with Ajinomoto, a Japanese food processing company, which adapts GF products for the Japanese market.

Seventh: Use Japan as a jumping off point

Many successful MNEs establish Japanese operations because they believe that this provides them with the experience and competitive edge that can be used worldwide.[20]

For example, TI was one of the only surviving US manufacturers of dynamic random access memories (DRAMs), the largest single segment of the semiconductor market. One reason that it had been able to achieve this feat was due to what TI had learned about manufacturing from its Japanese subsidiary and promoted throughout the rest of the company. By bringing in Japanese consultants to teach its workers how to achieve total quality management and by introducing an employee suggestion system, TI was able to improve productivity and empower the workers to control production. The results were astounding. Within five years from the time it started, TI had driven its defect rate from more than 5,000 parts per million (ppm) to fewer than 20 ppm. In the process the company won the Deming Quality award, the first non-Japanese firm to win this prize.

ACTIVE LEARNING CHECK

Review your answer to Active Learning Case question 2 and make any changes you like. Then compare your answer to the one below.

2. How can foreign MNEs use keiretsus to their own advantage? Give an example.

Foreign MNEs can use keiretsus in two ways. One is by teaming up with a keiretsu in a form of joint venture arrangement, thus gaining access to the keiretsu's manufacturing and marketing prowess. A second is by pitting two or more keiretsus against each other in an effort to make a deal with the MNE, thus gaining the best possible business terms.

CHOOSING A STARTUP STRATEGY

Many companies that want to do business in Japan cannot afford to keep control of operations. The following sections examine some of the most common alternative startup strategies.

Exporting

The Japanese government is now taking numerous steps to encourage exporters. Import tariffs have been eliminated on a wide number of products in areas such as agricultural machinery, base metals, chemicals, combustion engines, furniture, glass, home appliances, pharmaceutical products, precious metals, satellites, and sporting goods. The fact that Japan is the largest export market outside of North America for US goods helps to explain why exporting will continue to be a viable strategy for many firms.

MITI has also unveiled a policy of encouraging imports to Japan by offering tax incentives for manufactured imports, making public funds available to finance these goods, increasing the budget for import promotion programs, and focusing on additional steps toward tariff reduction and elimination.

JETRO The government has also created the Japan External Trade Organization (JETRO), which is a nonprofit, government-supported organization dedicated to the promotion of mutually beneficial trade between Japan and other nations. The organization's headquarters are in Tokyo, but it has a worldwide staff of over 1,200 people and a network of offices throughout Japan and 57 other countries. Each of these offices is a comprehensive information center on business and economic relations between the host country and Japan.

JETRO provides a number of services to exporters. These include (1) general information on the Japanese market in the form of economic data such as consumption trends, trading conditions, and distribution channels, (2) information on market trends for various products such as clothing, food, household products, and sporting goods, (3) trade fairs that are held in Japan and designed to help overseas businesses to find trading partners and investigate sales channels, and (4) information databases that are available to potential exporters.

Figures 17.2 and 17.3 illustrate the Trade Opportunity Service (TOPS), which is a closed-access database system for matching potential business partners. The purpose of a TOPS application is to gather information on companies that are interested in doing business in Japan and on the types of products that they are offering. Companies registered with TOPS are formally matched with Japanese importers, and the latter are expected to contact these firms to discuss the possibilities of doing business.

The goal of these efforts is to form distribution agreements between US exporters and Japanese importers. In many cases the importers are large specialty trading companies that buy and sell thousands of products through various divisions in each industrial sector and have their own networks of group companies and sub-distributors for a nearly unlimited variety of products.

Before agreeing to any such arrangement, these companies need to understand the advantages and disadvantages of this approach. On the positive side, a distributor arrangement (1) provides instant market access, (2) minimizes the startup costs and risk of doing business in Japan, (3) ensures that a company which has credibility with the customer is selling the product, and (4) offers a fast, reliable source of cash flow. On the negative side, the distributor (1) may be unfamiliar with the company's specific product or technology, (2) may have a large number of products to sell and devote limited time to this one, (3) may have limited access to the specific customers who are most likely to purchase this product, and (4) will not provide the opportunity for the foreign firm to deal face-to-face with the customer.

Licensing agreements

A **licensing agreement** is an arrangement whereby one firm gives another firm the right to use certain assets such as trademarks, patents, or copyrights in exchange for the payment of a fee. This approach has been extremely common in Japan.

Overall, there are two basic advantages to licensing. First, it can help a company to establish a market and to set operating standards for new technologies and products. Second, it is a method of earning short-term fees with the promise of longer-term profits. Sun Microsystems (Sun), for example, has licensed its microprocessor technology to Toshiba and to other leading computer manufacturers in Japan in order to promote its Sparc/Unix technology as a standard for the entire computer industry. By sharing the basic aspects of the technology with these firms, Sun has been able to expand its own opportunities by preventing the adoption of standards that would have deterred sales growth.

APPLICATION FOR JETRO TOPS   **(C)**   **(I)**
COMPANY INFORMATION

OFFICE	NO.

Date _____ 199 _____

- Please type all information within the bold frame.
- Handwritten application not accepted.
- Application not accompanied by catalog, photo, etc. not accepted.

	Office	Country	Year	Company	Ext.
C					0 0 0

1. Company	
2. President	
3. Address (Head Office)	
	(Country)
4. Telephone	5. Facsimile
6. Telex	7. Cable address
8. Type of business	1. Manufacturing 2. Trading 3. Wholesaling 4. Retailing 5. Transportation 6. Construction 7. Mining 8. Others
9. Line of products	
10. Year of establishment 1	11. Paid-up capital ( ) mil.
12. Annual sales ( ) mil.	13. Number of employees
14. Main bank	1. Bank, Branch 2. Bank, Branch
15. Products to be listed for export to Japan	1. 2. 3. 4.

NOTES:
- Products already handled by a distributor in Japan not included.
- Give a general name for item 15.
- Information on items 11, 12, 13, and 14 is for JETRO use only.

備　考	マッチング	人　力	チェック	コーティング	受　付	カタログ
	／	／	／	／	／	

Figure 17.2 Example of an application form for JETRO TOPS: company information

Source: From JETRO import promotion programs.

APPLICATION FOR JETRO TOPS   (D)
COMPANY INFORMATION

- Please type all information within the bold frame.
- Handwritten application not accepted.
- Application not accompanied by catalog, photo, etc. not accepted.

Company

D	Office	Country	Year	Company	Ext.

1. Brand/Specific Product Name, if any		HS Product Code
2. Product to be listed for Export		
3. Product Use		
4. Product Features, Specifications, Materials		
5. Major Current Export Market	1. 2. 3.	
6. Minimum Export Quantity	←One alphanumeric character per space	
7. Export Manager (Name)		
Section		
Contact Address		
	(Country)	

Telephone		Facsimile	
Telex		Cable address	

8. Membership in Industrial, Commercial Association	1.
	2.

NOTES:
- Give a general product name for item 2.
- Describe the basic use or purpose of the product in detail for item 3.
- Provide any information which may help the product to be better understood for item 4.

備　考	マッチング	人　力	チェック	コーティング	受　付	カタログ
	／	／	／	／	／	

Figure 17.3   Example of an application form for JETRO TOPS: company information

Source: From JETRO import promotion programs.

There are four disadvantages to licensing: (1) competitors are given new technology, processes, or information without having to spend any money on R&D, (2) the licensor typically has no local presence but, rather, relies exclusively on the licensee, (3) there is no chance for complementary opportunities of any kind such as identifying local demand for goods that could be produced by spinning off this technology, and (4) competitive obsolescence is virtually guaranteed as the licensee seeks methods of improving the technology and striking out on its own. Southland Corporation, which licensed its 7-Eleven chain stores to Ito-Yokado in Japan, is a good example. The firm agreed to royalty payments of approximately $200 million annually in exchange for allowing Ito-Yokado to earn billions of dollars in revenues.

In deciding on a licensing agreement, the participating firms must weigh the advantages and disadvantages carefully. Restrictive Japanese laws that made licensing and technology sharing mandatory have now been relaxed. However, their inability to prevent licensees from copying and improving MNE technology has led many multinationals to be more cautious in the case of licensing agreements.

Joint ventures

Joint ventures are another popular method of tapping into the Japanese market. In recent years many Japanese firms have recognized the need to diversify operations and to offer additional goods and services, thus expanding their base of operations. Often a joint venture has provided this opportunity. Some benefits associated with joint ventures include (1) reduction of risk of failure by sharing the burden with a partner, (2) rapid market access and the opportunity for quick profits, and (3) an increase in company and product acceptance brought about by having a local firm serve as the direct interface with the customer. Some primary drawbacks to joint ventures include (1) domination of the local market by the partner, thus effectively insulating the foreign firm from direct contact with the customer, (2) creation of business outlets by the local partner which are in direct competition with the joint venture, and (3) inability to work well with the foreign partner, resulting in either a sellout to the latter or a cessation of the arrangement.

One of the most important steps in creating a joint venture is to research the partner and to learn about its resources and abilities to contribute to the arrangement. Particular attention needs to be focused on the partner's

1. Distribution channels and large customer associations
2. Recognized technical leadership in the field
3. Support and service capabilities
4. Geographic coverage
5. Market image and reputation
6. Complementary/competitive product fit
7. Industrial ranking – first-, second-, or third-tier
8. Willingness to accept a nonexclusive arrangement
9. Industrial or banking group associations
10. Long-term synergies.[21]

Many US firms have found that large, nationally respected Japanese firms offer the most advantages because they best meet the above criteria. However, sometimes the size of the other party also puts it in a position to dominate the relationship and eventually to squeeze out its smaller partner. This is one reason for choosing smaller partners with whom a true $^{50}/_{50}$ relationship can be created. The profits and market growth are not likely to be as great, but the long-range relationship can be more stable and lasting.

It is also important to realize the significance of being an active partner. Foreign MNEs that do not make an equal contribution to the business and play an active role in the operation of the enterprise often lose out to their local partner. For example, when the financial or operating contribution by the foreign partner is less than 50 per cent, the other side frequently takes over more and more control of the venture. Eventually the more active partner will either attempt to buy out the other or to terminate the agreement because it no longer needs the partner.

The most successful joint ventures have been those in which each side views the partnership as a long-run commitment and is determined to succeed as a team. There are a number of important steps that must be carried out in accomplishing this objective, including (1) each must be prepared to accept responsibility for the success of the venture, (2) each must be sensitive and hospitable to the other in day-to-day dealings, (3) the two sides must meet informally so that each gets to know the other on a personal level and to create a deep sense of trust between them, (4) personnel at all levels of the organization must interact and work together, and (5) victories and successes should be celebrated together.

ACTIVE LEARNING CHECK

Review your answer to Active Learning Case question 3 and make any changes you like. Then compare your answer to the one below.

3. Why are joint ventures so popular among foreign MNEs? Cite two reasons.

Joint ventures are popular because they give a company an opportunity for immediate market access and the opportunity for rapid profits. There is also a reduction of the risk of failure since both sides jointly share that risk.

Acquisitions

In the United States, acquisitions are often used as a means of creating synergy and adding value to a company. In recent years acquisitions have become a very attractive way of entering the Japanese market. This is quite different from the situation in the early 1990s when high stock prices and the increasing value of the yen made it prohibitive for foreign buyers to purchase Japanese firms. As a result, in recent years the Travelers Group has purchased 25 per cent of Nikko Securities, Japan's third largest brokerage firm, and foreign investors now have substantial ownership in Japanese firms.[22] For example, 45 per cent of Sony is now held by foreigners, as is 42 per cent of Rohm, 39 per cent of Canon, and 36 per cent of Fuji.[23]

Firms that do acquire Japanese companies must learn how to manage the work force. The personnel have been so long accustomed to working for the previous management that new managers have many barriers to overcome. Bridging the cultural gap and differences in management philosophies after acquiring a Japanese company is often too great a challenge.[24] As a result, acquisitions remain one of the least used approaches for getting into the Japanese market.

Creating a local subsidiary

One of the most popular approaches to doing business in Japan is the wholly owned or majority-owned Japanese subsidiary. In addition to those already mentioned in this chapter, US firms with Japanese subsidiaries include Alcoa, American Express, Amway, Apple Computer, Dow Chemical, Ford Motor, Hewlett-Packard, Philip Morris, Revlon, Tandy, and Warner-Lambert.

Some advantages of a subsidiary include (1) the achieving of closeness to the customer and thus improving market responsiveness and the ability to assess future opportunities, (2) the creation of a unified strategy and objectives on a worldwide basis, and (3) the attainment of world-class performance. Some drawbacks of the approach include (1) heavy fixed expenses and startup costs, (2) the need to generate sales from the ground up, (3) the difficulty of finding a reliable minority partner, (4) the challenge of hiring local personnel, and (5) the problems associated with managing local operations.

While the pros and cons of this strategy must be carefully weighed, the reasons that the subsidiary approach has proven popular with many US firms include the opportunity for future growth and the ability to develop world-class approaches that can be used globally. The following section examines the steps that must be met by those firms opting for this approach.

MANAGING ON-SITE OPERATIONS

Managing on-site operations requires attention to a number of important areas. Primary among these are recruiting, choosing site facilities, organizing the business, and financing operations.

Recruiting

One of the first, and certainly the most difficult, tasks for subsidiaries managing on-site operations in Japan is that of recruiting personnel. Unlike the United States where top managers are often recruited from other firms, in Japan it is difficult to get executives to change companies. As we have seen, Japanese workers are closely aligned with their employers and take pride in their identity as company employees. One of the most effective strategies is first to recruit a top manager and other members of the management team. They in turn will work to attract other managerial and key personnel. Commenting on the challenge of recruiting these people, two Japanese experts have noted:

> Hiring a good manager is not easy; it is an intricate and slow-moving process. It often takes six months to a year (or more) after initial agreement with an individual before he or she actually comes on board. Hiring managers from large Japanese companies, especially when they are your customers, is a sensitive situation, far more so than in America. . . . The hiring dance typically begins with one of your company's top executives meeting with the candidate's employer and even his family to request permission to negotiate with the individual and to provide assurance of his future position, security, and opportunities. From there, several meetings must take place over a long period of time.[25]

One of the prime sources of recruiting is college graduates. Every year recruiters from industry work feverishly to attract these individuals. The problem for foreign firms is that most graduates of the first-tier universities such as Tokyo University, Kyoto University, and Waseda University prefer to work for Japanese companies. In order to recruit effectively in Japan, the foreign firm needs to gain acceptance in the academic community. College professors play the role of mentor to many students, and these professors must be won over if a company is to be successful in generating interest among the students. This process can take many years. The box "International Business Strategy in Action: Going Head to Head" provides some examples of how foreign firms are trying to increase their recruiting effectiveness.

Many firms are now supplementing their managerial and college recruiting strategies with compensation packages that are designed to attract working women. Included in these packages are day-care centers for young children, one-year leave policies for new parents, higher wages, and shorter working hours. US firms have been doing so well in this area that Japanese companies have now begun to respond. Saison, which runs department stores and supermarkets, offers low-cost day-care services and meals for the children of employees. Toyota Motor has a one-year parental leave program, and Nissan Motor offers its people a five-year program. With the growing labor shortage in Japan and the fact that by the early 1990s Japanese women were making less than were 60 per cent of their male counterparts, such competitive measures were predictable. The future will see even more vigorous recruiting competition between Japanese and locally based foreign subsidiaries.

Choosing location and organization

Two of the major operating decisions that must be made are where the firm will be located and how local operations will be organized. Because of the importance of location, this decision is typically made first.

Making a location decision   The cost of doing business in Japan can be prohibitive, especially if the firm wants a location in Tokyo. Land here is costly, construction rates are high, and rents are steep. Rental costs in Tokyo in recent years have been more than double those of many other locations.[26] As a result, many companies now bypass Tokyo (except, perhaps, for a small office that is used more for public relations than for operations) in favor of sites that are closer to the customers and/or labor supply. Manufacturing firms, for example, can now be found in cities like Nagoya, Osaka, Hiroshima, and Kumamoto, and there are new centers of commerce continually springing up throughout the country. In making a final location choice, it is advantageous to talk to the local government and to determine how the company's needs match those of the area. Some prefectures offer small and rural settings, while others have major centers of commerce. These governments are all interested in attracting business and industry and provide a variety of forms of assistance.

Organizing for operations   There are a number of differences between the way that the Japanese manage their operations and the way that this is done in most other countries. One is the relationship that exists between managers and employees. Managers are extremely paternalistic and concerned about the well-being of their people. In turn the employees are loyal, dedicated, and hard working. Firms like IBM Japan have succeeded, in part, because the philosophy of the parent company contains many of

INTERNATIONAL BUSINESS STRATEGY IN ACTION

Going head to head

Not long ago US firms doing business in Japan had little hope of recruiting students from the best universities. Foreign employers were regarded as unstable, unfamiliar, and unprestigious. Today this is changing as western companies have learned how to recruit more effectively and are giving the major Japanese firms strong competition.

Foreign companies typically pay 10 per cent more than their Japanese counterparts. However, what is even more appealing are the other parts of the compensation package, including shorter working hours, more flexibility, and merit-based promotions. These features are typically not offered by major Japanese firms. As a result, a recent poll found that a surprising 7.7 per cent of the graduates of leading universities now list foreign firms as their first employment choice. Moreover, the more western firms succeed in landing top Japanese talent, the better are their chances of breaking into the local market because without Japanese employees a foreign subsidiary has little hope of success.

Recent statistics show that some foreign MNEs are doing very well indeed. For example, Digital Equipment opened shop in Japan in 1970 and hired its first new graduate in 1980. In 1990 the firm hired 295 new graduates and another 400 in 1991.

One of the primary areas of recruiting focus by western firms is female graduates. Japanese women are more willing than men to work for foreign firms, are less afraid of using English, and see a broader scope of responsibility and advancement in this career choice. With the national work force shrinking, however, Japanese firms are also beginning to recruit female graduates more vigorously.

US firms are employing innovative recruiting tactics to gain attention. Citicorp, for example, invites students to spend a week in Tokyo playing a foreign-exchange simulation game. The winners get a free trip to the company's New York trading room. Smaller companies such as WordPerfect Japan have set up their headquarters in a trendy location in central Tokyo where people are eager to work.

These approaches are beginning to pay off for US firms. The only drawback is that there are 143 jobs currently available for every 100 applicants, and this is resulting in counterattacking strategies by Japanese firms who cannot afford to let the graduates get away. Tactics of Japanese firms include inviting job applicants to Hawaii to hear the firm's sales pitch, so the cost of recruiting is beginning to escalate sharply. Nevertheless, those US firms that have decided to keep operations in Japan appear willing to match the competition via even more innovative tactics. As a result, in the future college recruiting in Japan is likely to be fought on a head-to-head basis.

Sources: Adapted from Robert Neff, "When in Japan, Recruit as the Japanese Do – Aggressively," *Business Week*, June 24, 1991, p. 58; James C. Morgan and J. Jeffrey Morgan, *Cracking the Japanese Market* (New York: Free Press, 1991), pp. 393–406; and Philip R. Harris and Robert T. Moran, *Managing Cultural Differences* (Houston: Gulf Publishing, 1991), pp. 471–478.

the same values that are present in Japanese firms. MNEs setting up operations in Japan must use a similar, highly protective leadership approach. Otherwise it is extremely difficult to recruit and retain personnel.

A second important guideline is that of delegating operating authority to the subsidiary. There are two reasons for this. First, home office personnel typically do not know how to interact effectively with Japanese clients and customers. Unless the top staff at headquarters have received extensive cultural training and on-site experience, it is often best to defer local decisions to the subsidiary managers. Second, the subsidiary must gain and maintain credibility in the local market, and this will not happen if customers or clients deal directly with headquarters staff. When headquarters remains in the most visible position, the Japanese conclude that top management view the subsidiary as weak and ineffective. Customers, clients, and competitors must all see a united front in which the subsidiary is the representative of the company and all important matters, at least publicly, are referred to the local organization.

In order to ensure that the subsidiary is not relegated to a minor place in the organizational hierarchy, many MNEs have the head of the unit report directly to the chief executive officer of the multinational. It is also common to find the subsidiary manager actively participating in all worldwide corporate strategy meetings, thus ensuring that Japanese operations are strategically integrated into the overall plan. This organizational arrangement is also a sign of commitment and helps to build trust and cooperation between the subsidiary and the headquarters staff.

Another operating objective is to immerse the company in the local market so that it is seen as inherently Japanese. When this is accomplished, the firm is regarded as having high-quality production, reliable service, and genuine concern for the personnel. Applied Materials, Avon, IBM, TI, and Xerox, among others, are examples of companies that have achieved this objective. When this happens, many barriers that face foreign subsidiaries from recruiting to winning sales contracts begin to fall.

A supplemental approach is the development of formal communication links between the two groups. These interactions typically range from daily phone calls to teleconferences to on-site visits. Executives from the home office will often spend a large amount of their time each year in Japan and subsidiary managers will come to headquarters to discuss operations and strategy. Some firms supplement these meetings with on-site assignments so that personnel from each group work in the other's locale. This helps each to understand the other and is useful in creating long-run harmony.

Financing operations

There are two major areas of financial consideration when doing business in Japan. The first is establishing a banking relationship to handle day-to-day and short-term financial demands. The other is deciding how to finance long-term operations.

Banking relationships Banking in Japan is based on personal relationships. Of course, it is possible to walk into a Japanese bank, deposit funds, and start paying bills and handling other financial obligations that are associated with running the subsidiary. However, the most effective approach is to use a facilitator to introduce the company to a bank. Many people can perform this function: businesspeople, other bankers, and government officials. Major MNEs often accomplish this through their dealings with a Japanese bank elsewhere in the world. For example, a company in San Francisco that is doing business with a Japanese-owned bank in the city will call on its banker to help establish a relationship with a bank in Japan. If the San Francisco bank is directly affiliated with a bank there, this is quite easy. Otherwise the banker will contact a counterpart in Japan and provide a history and working relationship of the company. In turn the Japanese bank will help the foreign subsidiary to handle its financial needs and, if additional services are needed that are outside the scope of the bank, will provide the necessary introductions to other parties. This can be particularly important when the subsidiary is setting up operations in areas where the main bank does not have offices or if the subsidiary wants to apply for assistance or funding from organizations such as the Japan Development Bank.

The **Japan Development Bank (JDB)** is a government-owned institution whose primary objective is to promote industrial development nationwide. Monies for the

JDB are provided by the Ministry of Finance and can be spent in a variety of ways such as funding foreign research and development projects, providing assistance to companies setting up new factories, and lending money to firms that are helping to promote exports. In Japan, there are not as many sources of capital as there are in the United States, but once a company is in the mainstream of financing opportunities, the supplies of capital are usually quite plentiful. These extend from commercial banks to local banks to insurance companies to pension funds.

Raising capital Most MNEs finance their initial foray into the Japanese market with funds from abroad. However, once the operation is established, the company can consider raising long-term capital in the local market. A number of US firms that have gone international in recent years have been quite successful in floating local stock issues to cover the costs of their Japanese operations. For example, Avon Products raised over $240 million with its Japanese issue, $92 million for Shaklee, $90 million for Levi Strauss, and $42 million for Baskin Robbins. During the millennium an increasing number of foreign MNEs will use the local equity markets to help them finance the costs of doing business in Japan.

JAPAN AS A TRIAD POWER

It is important to remember that Japan is a triad power. The country has experienced the fastest and longest period of sustained economic growth in world history over the last 40 years. Although the rate of growth began to slow in 1992 to 1993, Japan's momentum will keep it going into the twenty-first century. Indeed, this century may be the Pacific century, with other Asian nations following the Japanese model of rapid growth and development.

Japan's role as a triad power is confirmed by the data in Table 17.3. This table brings together information presented earlier in this book on Japan's share of the triad's trade, FDI, and proportion of global firms.

Table 17.3 Japan's role in the triad

	Exports				FDI				500 largest MNEs***			
Triad powers	1987 (in billions of US $)	% of world total	1996 (in billions of US $)	% of world total	1985* (in billions of US $	% of world total	1996** (in billions of US $)	% of world total	1989* no.	% of world total	1996 no.	% of world total
Japan	243	10.0	411.2	8	44.0	6.4	330	10.4	111	22.2	126	25.2
United States	264	10.9	622.9	12	251.0	36.4	794	25.0	167	33.4	162	32.4
European Community****	915	37.8	2,041.6	39	286.0	41.4	1,405	44.2	127	25.4	155	31.0

* Data for 1987 are not available.

** Estimates.

*** 1990 is the year the Global 500 list was introduced in *Fortune*. Also, prior to 1995 the Global 500 included only industrial corporations. In 1995 it combined service and industrial corporations.

**** The European Community refers to the the EU prior to 1995. Data for EU does not include Finland, Austria and Sweden prior to 1995, the year these countries joined the union.

Source: IMF, *Direction of Trade Statistics Yearbook, 1996*; UN, *World Investment Report, 1996*; Fortune, *The Fortune 500*, 1990, 1995, and 1997.

Table 17.4 Direction of Japan's trade

Country/region	Exports to				Imports from			
	1987		1996		1987		1996	
	(millions of US $)	% of total	(millions of US $)	% of total	(millions of US $)	% of total	(millions of US $)	% of total
United States	85,017	36.8	113,174	27.5	31,957	21.2	79,115	22.7
Canada	5,661	2.4	5,124	1.2	6,109	4.0	10,120	2.9
European Union	38,305	16.6	63,136	15.4	17,862	11.8	49,571	14.2
Other Asia	62,564	27.0	181,491	44.2	47,220	31.3	131,695	37.7
All others	39,785	17.2	47,976	11.7	47,885	31.7	78,792	22.6
Total	231,332	100.0	410,901	100.0	151,033	100.0	349,293	100.0

Note: European Union in 1986 refers to the European Economic Community.
Source: Adapted from IMF, Direction of Trade Statistics Yearbook, 1997, 1991.

Table 17.4 reports changes in the direction of Japan's trade over the last ten years. This trade has become even more focused on the United States, the rest of Asia, and the EU. While the value of Japanese exports to the United States increased 33 per cent, from $85,017 million to $113,174 million, during this period the value of Japanese exports to the rest of Asia increased by 190 per cent, and to the EU by 65 per cent during the same period.

In terms of shares of total Japanese trade, Table 17.4 also shows the changing distribution of Japan's exports and imports. This has reflected the growing importance of the triad. There is a much greater emphasis on the EU's, the United States', and Japan's immediate neighbors at the expense of "all others," whose share of the total dropped from 17.2 to 11.7 per cent for exports and from 31.7 per cent to 22.6 per cent for imports.

Table 17.5 provides a closer look at Japan's trade relationship with its Asian neighbors. All the newly industrialized economies (NIEs) have negative balance-of-payment positions with Japan, the overall value of Japanese exports to these four countries being 171 per cent higher than its imports in 1995. It is only when Japan's trading relationship with the poorer, primary resource-producing economies of ASEAN is considered that the trade balance evens out. In fact, once the NIEs were excluded, Japan's imports from the rest of Asia ($82,729 million) just exceeds its exports ($81,712 million). This highlights how Japan's competitiveness and success in penetrating markets with its exports has been concentrated in manufacturing, and the extent to which an economic powerhouse like Japan can run large trade surpluses with its competitors but still be dependent on and run trade deficits with other countries.

Table 17.6 reports data on Japan's foreign direct investment (FDI) and the rapid expansion of Japanese FDI stocks abroad. This table shows the distribution of these stocks in different countries and regions of the world (Japanese accounting practices differ considerably from those in the United States, and, as such, the figures reported in Table 17.6 are not directly comparable with the US Department of Commerce data used elsewhere in this book). Briefly, the US share of FDI stocks in 1996 is by far the highest, at 59.8 per cent, followed by Europe at 28 per cent and the rest of Asia at 15 per cent. The total value of Japanese FDI stocks, as reported by the Japanese Ministry

Table 17.5   Japan's trade with East Asia

Country/region	Exports to				Imports from			
	1986		1995		1986		1995	
	(millions of US $)	% of total	(millions of US $)	% of total	(millions of US $)	% of total	(millions of US $)	% of total
NIEs	30,285	57.2	111,699	57.8	12,609	34.9	41,241	33.3
Hong Kong	7,215	13.6	27,780	14.4	1,080	3.0	2,736	2.2
South Korea	10,557	20.0	31,929	16.5	5,334	14.8	17,330	14.0
Singapore	4,611	8.7	23,006	11.9	1,475	4.1	6,846	5.5
Taiwan	7,902	14.9	28,984	15.0	4,720	13.1	14,329	11.6
ASEAN*	7,829	14.8	54,643	28.3	15,394	42.7	41,427	33.4
Indonesia	2,682	5.1	9,969	5.2	7,386	20.5	14,199	11.5
Malaysia	1,723	3.3	16,802	8.7	3,986	11.0	10,545	8.5
Philippines	1,098	2.1	7,100	3.7	1,235	3.4	3,495	2.8
Thailand	2,045	3.9	19,719	10.2	1,401	3.9	10,130	8.2
Brunei	91	0.2	131	0.1	1,302	3.6	1,342	1.1
Vietnam	190	0.4	922	0.5	84	0.2	1,716	1.4
PR of China	9,936	18.8	21,934	11.3	5,727	15.9	35,922	29.0
Other Asia	4,864	9.2	5,135	2.7	2,351	6.5	5,380	4.3
Asia total**	52,914	100.0	193,411	100.0	36,081	100.0	123,970	100.0

* ASEAN excludes Singapore which is a member but is included in NIEs.

** Numbers might not add up due to rounding.

Source: Adapted from IMF, Direction of Trade Statistics Yearbook, 1996, 1991.

of Finance, is around $325 billion. These data help to illustrate why Japan is an economic superpower and why many non-triad nations want to establish linkages with this country.

ACTIVE LEARNING CHECK

Review your answer to Active Learning Case question 4 and make any changes you like. Then compare your answer to the one below.

4. Why is Japan likely to remain a target market for international MNEs? Cite two reasons.

Japan is likely to remain a target market for international MNEs because of its large growing economy and affluent consumer base. A second reason is the value of monitoring Japanese world-class competitors by having local operations that compete head-to-head, thus helping the MNE to maintain a strong, competitive posture.

Table 17.6   Japan's foreign direct investment: position at year-end, 1996

Country/region	1996 investment position (in millions of US $)	% of total
United States	194,429	59.8
Canada	8,261	2.5
North America	202,690	62.3
Europe	91,123	28.0
Asia	76,219	23.4
Indonesia	16,981	5.2
Hong Kong	13,881	4.3
Singapore	9,535	2.9
Thailand	7,184	2.2
South Korea	5,268	1.6
Malaysia	6,357	2.0
China, People's Republic	8,729	2.7
Taiwan	3,997	1.2
Philippines	2,817	0.9
Others	93,574	28.8
World total	325,398	100.0

Note: Figures are based on Japanese data which are not strictly comparable to US Department of Commerce data on FDI.
Source: OECD, *International Direct Investment Statistics Yearbook, 1997.*

SUMMARY

Key points

1. The branches of the Japanese government are similar to those of the United States: legislative, executive, and judicial. Legislative power is vested in the Diet, a bicameral body. Executive power rests with the Cabinet. Judicial power is vested in the Supreme Court.

2. There are approximately 127 million Japanese. There is mandatory education at the lower levels, and general living standards are good.

3. Social patterns are distinctly different from those in the West. Japan is a group-oriented society. Strong emphasis is given to harmony, orderliness, and the respect of others. Social ranking and the power of obligation are both extremely important.

4. Japan has one of the highest per capita incomes in the world. The government plays a key role in keeping the economy strong. MITI and the keiretsus are important in this process.

5. Firms setting up operations in Japan have to be aware of the nontariff barriers, including retail store limitations and the informal bidding system. Another business-related issue that dominates the economic scene is the growing friction over trade imbalances between Japan and the rest of the world.

6. Many US firms have been successful in cracking the Japanese market. Six of the basic steps they have followed include researching the market, putting the customer first, maintaining control of operations, offering the right products, attacking and counterattacking, and using Japan as a jumping off point.

7. In choosing a startup strategy, companies have a number of options available. These include exporting, licensing agreements, joint ventures, acquisitions, and the creation of Japanese subsidiaries.

8. Managing on-site operations requires attention to a number of important areas. Primary among these are recruiting, choosing site facilities, organizing the business, and financing operations.

Key terms

- Diet
- gairojin
- gaijin
- Ministry of International Trade and Industry (MITI)
- keiretsus
- Large Retail Store Law
- Japan External Trade Organization (JETRO)
- licensing agreement
- Japan Development Bank (JDB)

Review and discussion questions

1. How important to the Japanese is harmony and the respect of others? What implications does this have for MNEs doing business here?

2. How does the power of obligation influence Japanese business practices? Give an example.

3. What role does MITI play in Japan? Explain.

4. What are some nontrade barriers to doing business in Japan? Identify and describe three of them.

5. How can MNEs doing business in Japan do the following: research the market, put the customer first, maintain control of operations? In each case, give an example.

6. How can MNEs doing business in Japan do the following: offer the right products, attack, counterattack, and use Japan as a jumping off point? In each case, give an example.

7. What are some of the steps that should be taken by companies interested in exporting to Japan? Identify and describe three of them.

8. How does a licensing agreement differ from a joint venture? Compare and contrast the two and discuss three advantages associated with each.

9. Why is an acquisition strategy for entering the Japanese market often a poor one?

10. When choosing a startup strategy, why do many successful MNEs create a Japanese subsidiary? What are some of the primary advantages of this approach?

11. Why is it difficult to recruit graduating college students in Japan? How can MNEs overcome these problems?

12. What are three useful guidelines that MNEs should follow when organizing operations in Japan? Discuss each.

13. How can the Japan Development Bank be of value to MNEs operating in Japan?

14. How can MNEs in Japan raise long-term capital locally? Explain.

REAL CASES

A JOINT EFFORT

Apple Computer, well known for its wide range of personal computers (PCs), in the mid-1990s expanded its offerings into the area of notebook computers. A joint venture with Sony promised to make Apple a major force in the growing market niche for lighter, smaller, more powerful machines.

One of the offerings of the Apple–Sony arrangement was a notebook size Macintosh computer called the "PowerBook 100." The unit weighed 5 pounds, had 2 megabytes of memory and a 20-megabyte hard drive, and sold for less than $2,500.

Some people criticized Apple's joint venture because they felt it gave Sony expertise in an area that it previously lacked, while there was little gain for Apple. Actually, Sony brought to the venture a great deal of experience in areas that could be of value to Apple, including the manufacture of floppy-disk drives, monitors, and power supplies. At the same time the project provided Sony an opportunity to learn more about the PC business, one of the few high-tech consumer markets where the company had no products. Additionally, the two companies had similar cultures, including a desire to build new products and to define new markets.

When Apple approached Sony with the idea for a notebook computer, the company outlined the dimensions and specifications on a half-page document. Sony liked what it saw, canceled some projects that were on the drawing board, and assigned a group of engineers to design the notebook unit. Within 14 months the project was complete and the product received very high marks from the computer market.

In fact, things went so well that Sony engineers began planning future additions to the PowerBook family. In addition, Sony invested in General Magic, an Apple-backed startup project aimed at making hybrid computer-consumer electronic products, such as electronic books that display text and images stored on disks and personal communicators that combine the features of cellular phones, electronic organizers, and fax machines. There were even rumours that the two planned on teaming up to take on Nintendo, the giant video game manufacturer. Regardless of the direction the joint venture took, Apple was going to be using similar arrangements in the future because the benefits far outweigh the drawbacks.

1. What were the benefits to Apple Computer of joint venturing with Sony? Identify and describe two of them.

2. What were the drawbacks of this approach for Apple Computer? Identify and describe the two of them.

3. Overall, was Apple making a wise decision? Defend your answer.

Sources: Adapted from John Markoff, "Is the Electronic Book Closer Than You Think?" *New York Times*, December 29, 1991, p. E5; Brenton R. Schlender, "Apple's Japanese Ally," *Fortune*, November 4, 1991, pp. 151–152; and Kathy Rebello, Russell Mitchell, and Evan I. Schwartz, "Apple's Future," *Business Week*, July 5, 1993, pp. 22–28.

THE ASIAN FINANCIAL CRISIS

With the Asian financial crisis of 1997–98, most of the Asian Tigers took a big blow. These countries had enjoyed phenomenal growth over the last decades and were models for industrial growth. But, in 1997, the Asian stock markets lost about $400 billion dollars in value. Malaysia, Indonesia, and Thailand were hit hardest and saw their currencies devalued by 33 per cent, 53 per cent and 58 per cent respectively. In Indonesia, 500,000 jobs were lost in the construction business alone and similar unemployment burdened Malaysia and Thailand. Meanwhile, banks and corporations could not borrow money. Asia's banks had close to $200 billion of bad debts, without including Japan and China. The irony was that the financial system that had allowed these countries to grow, was also one of the main reasons for the crisis. Some banks had been lending not on the basis of profitability but due to political ties and they expected the government to bail out any poorly performing companies.

Japan is the second largest economy in the world, and it is the economic center of the Asia Pacific region. Most Asian countries depend on it for trade and investment and 44 per cent of Japan's exports go to Asian Pacific countries. As the Asian region is interlocked, the Japanese financial system was also affected by the Asian crisis. The Japanese model of growth involves lending to handpicked companies at low interest rates in cooperation with the government. In 1997, bad debt in Japan was estimated to be in the range of $624 to $800 billion. By 1998 the yen had fallen to 147 to the US dollar compared to 80 to the US dollar in mid-1995.

Japan suffered a financial and real estate bust but has warded off an industrial one. The Japanese banks and insurance companies were ridden with bad debt. Tokoyo City Bank, the 40th largest in Japan, and Sanyo Securities, among others, filed for bankruptcy in late 1997. The Japanese government, pressured by the crisis, had to open up its financial sector, and outside financial companies are helping to upgrade the financial industry. Fidelity Investments partnered with three Japanese banks to sell mutual funds. Citibank is taking a big share of Japanese retail banking. GE Capital entered into a joint venture with an almost bankrupt Toho Mutual Life. Meanwhile, Merrill Lynch acquired a 2,000-branch network from one of Japan's largest brokerage firms, Yamaichi Securities, which went out of business during the crisis.

For their part, Japanese financial institutions are also changing their ways. Nomura Securities of Japan was considering selling off its huge portfolio of bank shares, thereby dismantling a traditional system of cross-share ownership that has defined business in Japan. Meanwhile, the Long-Term Credit Bank of Japan has cut its board of directors by two-thirds and its staff by 20 per cent for savings of $1.6 billion. The liberalization is expected to make Japan's financial sector as free as that of Britain by the year 2001. After this shake-up things will never be the same in Japan.

1. How has the Asian financial crisis affected the Japanese banking system?

2. What was the role of Japanese banks in the keiretsu system?

3. Why are western financial institutions investing in Japan?

Source: Adapted from "Asia's Fall from Grace," *The Economist*, April 12, 1997, pp. 32–36; Joshua Cooper Ramo, "When Currencies Collide," *Time.com*, August 24, 1998, vol. 152, no. 8; Alan M. Rugman and Rory Knight, "A Regional Fix for Multinationals," *Global Finance*, vol. 12, no. 2, December 1998, p. 30.

ENDNOTES

1. For more on this subject, see *Doing Business in Japan* (Japan: Price Waterhouse, 1998).
2. Also, see Robert Neff, William J. Holstein, and Amy Borrus, "Japan: Who's in Charge?" *Business Week*, April 25, 1994, pp. 48–49.
3. David E. Sanger, "Tokyo's Tips for New York," *New York Times Magazine*, February 6, 1994, p. 29.
4. Noboru Yoshimura and Philip Anderson, *Inside the Kaisha* (Boston: Harvard Business School Press, 1997).
5. James C. Morgan and J. Jeffrey Morgan, *Cracking the Japanese Market* (New York: Free Press, 1991), p. 20.
6. Ibid., p. 68.
7. Much of this loyalty is not a result of culture but, rather, a result of guaranteed employment, as explained in Jeremiah J. Sullivan and Richard B. Peterson, "A Test of Theories Underlying the Japanese Lifetime Employment System," *Journal of International Business Studies*, First Quarter 1991, p. 94.
8. For an interesting comparative view, see John E. Rehfeld, "What Working for a Japanese Company Taught Me," *Harvard Business Review*, November–December 1990, pp. 167–176.
9. Jonathon Sapsford, "Japan's Banks Are Awash in Red Ink," *Wall Street Journal*, May 26, 1998, p. A14.
10. David E. Sanger, "Japan's Bad Debt is Now Estimated Near $1 Trillion," *New York Times*, July 30, 1998, pp. A1, 8.
11. Yumiko Ono and Jacob M. Schlesinger, "Sign of Changed Times: Japan's Jobless Rate Rises to the US Level," *Wall Street Journal*, December 28, 1998, pp. A1, 8.
12. Lisa Schuchman, "Mitsubishi Motors Announces Overhaul," *Wall Street Journal*, November 9, 1998, p. A20.
13. Bill Spindle, "Japan's Weak GDP Suggests Little Hope Soon," *Wall Street Journal*, September 14, 1998, p. A24.
14. Larry Holyoke, William Spindle, and Neil Gross, "Doing the Unthinkable," *Business Week*, January 10, 1994, pp. 52–53.
15. Robert S. Greenberger and Laura Johannes, "US Urges Japan to Further Open Its Film Market," *Wall Street Journal*, August 20, 1998, p. A4.
16. Also see Bill Spindle, "Japanese 'Big Bang' Is Leading to Big Boon for US High-Tech," *Wall Street Journal*, September 16, 1997, pp. A1, 13; Asra Q. Nomani and Douglas A. Blackmon, "How Maneuvering By Airlines Shaped US–Japan Accord," *Wall Street Journal*, February 2, 1998, pp. A1, 19; Martin Crutsinger, "Japan at Forefront in Deal to Lower Trade Barriers," *The Miami Herald*, November 16, 1998, p. 6a.
17. Robert Steiner, "Tokyo Regains Its Place as a Finance Hub," *Wall Street Journal*, May 29, 1997, p. A12.
18. *Handy Facts on US–Japan Economic Relations* (Tokyo: Japan External Trade Organization, 1998).
19. Also, see Nagami Kishi, "How Foreign Firms Can Succeed," *Journal of Japanese Trade & Industry*, no. 6, 1990, pp. 12–14.
20. Also, see Mark Mason, "United States Direct Investment in Japan: Trends and Prospects," *California Management Review*, Fall 1992, pp. 98–115.
21. Also, see Gale Eisenstadt, "Information Power," *Forbes*, June 21, 1993, pp. 171–172.
22. Sheryl WuDunn, "Japan Braces For Arrival of 'Big Bang'," *New York Times*, June 4, 1998, pp. C1, 6.
23. Maki Tanikawa, "Shareholder Rights? In Japan?" *Business Week*, November 9, 1998, p. 70 E12.
24. Also see Andrew Pollack, "Mazda Shows Improvement Under Ford's Leadership," *New York Times*, May 24, 1997, p. 22.
25. Morgan and Morgan, op. cit., p. 187.
26. *Investment in Japan: Facts and Figures* (Tokyo: JETRO, 1998).

ADDITIONAL BIBLIOGRAPHY

Abegglen, James C. and Stalk, George. *Kaisha, the Japanese Corporation* (New York: Basic Books, 1985).

Balassa, Bela and Noland, Marcus. *Japan in the World Economy* (Washington, DC: Institute for International Economics, 1988).

Black, J. Stewart. "Work Role Transitions: A Study of American Expatriate Managers in Japan," *Journal of International Business Studies*, vol. 19, no. 2 (Summer 1988).

Brouthers, Lance Eliot and Werner, Steve. "Are the Japanese Good Global Competitors?" *Columbia Journal of World Business*, vol. 25, no. 3 (Fall 1990).

Burton, F. N. and Saelens, F. H. "Japanese Strategies for Serving Overseas Markets: The Case for Electronics," *Management International Review*, vol. 27, no. 4 (Fourth Quarter 1987).

Campbell, John Creighton; Pucik, Vladimir; Yu, Chwo-Ming J.; and Ito, Kiyohoko. "The Japanese and the US Tax Systems: Implications for Japanese Auto Exports," *Management International Review*, vol. 27, no. 4 (Fourth Quarter 1987).

Cole, Robert E. "Work and Leisure in Japan," *California Management Review*, vol. 34, no. 3 (Spring 1992).

Cutts, Robert L. "Capitalism in Japan: Cartels and Keiretsu," *Harvard Business Review*, vol. 70, no. 4 (July/August 1992).

Czinkota, Michael R. and Woronoff, Jon. *Unlocking Japan's Markets* (Chicago: Probus Publishing Co., 1991).

Daniel, Shirley J. and Reitsperger, Wolf D. "Management Control Systems for JIT: An Empirical Comparison of Japan and the US," *Journal of International Business Studies*, vol. 22, no. 4 (Fourth Quarter 1991).

Dyer, Jeffrey H. and Ouchi, William G. "Japanese-Style Partnerships: Giving Companies a Competitive Edge," *Sloan Management Review*, vol. 35, no. 1 (Fall 1993).

Fahy, John and Taguchi, Fuyuki. "Reassessing the Japanese Distribution System," *Sloan Management Review*, vol. 36 (Winter 1995).

Friedman, George and Lebard, Meredith. *The Coming War with Japan* (New York: St. Martin's Press, 1991).

Gundling, Ernest. "Ethics and Working with the Japanese: The Entrepreneur and the 'Elite Course'," *California Management Review*, vol. 33, no. 3 (Spring 1991).

Hanssens, Dominique M. and Johansson, John K. "Rivalry as Synergy? The Japanese Automobile Companies' Export Expansion," *Journal of International Business Studies*, vol. 22, no. 3 (Third Quarter 1991).

Helper, Susan R. and Sako, Mari. "Supplier Relations in Japan and the United States: Are They Converging?" *Sloan Management Review*, vol. 36 (Spring 1995).

Johansson, Johny K. and Nonaka, Ikujiro. "Market Research the Japanese Way," *Harvard Business Review*, vol. 65, no. 3 (May/June 1987).

Johnson, Chalmers. "Comparative Capitalism: The Japanese Difference," *California Management Review*, vol. 35, no. 4 (Summer 1993).

Johnson, Jean L.; Sakano, Tomoaki; and Onzo, Naoto. "Behavioural Relations in Across-Culture Distribution System: Influence, Control and Conflict in US–Japanese Marketing Channel," *Journal of International Business Studies*, vol. 21, no. 4 (Fourth Quarter 1990).

Kaikati, Jack G. "Don't Crack the Japanese Distribution System – Just Circumvent It," *Columbia Journal of World Business*, vol. 28, no. 2 (Summer 1993).

Kearns, Robert L. *Zaibatsu America* (New York: Free Press, 1992).

Kotabe, Masaaki and Omura, Glenn S. "Sourcing Strategies of European and Japanese Multinationals: A Comparison," *Journal of International Business Studies*, vol. 20, no. 1 (Spring 1989).

Kriger, Mark P. and Solomon, Esther E. "Strategic Mindsets and Decision-Making Autonomy in US and Japanese MNCs," *Management International Review*, vol. 32, no. 4 (Fourth Quarter 1992).

Majumdar, Badiul A. "Industrial Policy in Action: The Case of the Electronics Industry in Japan," *Columbia Journal of World Business*, vol. 23, no. 3 (Fall 1988).

Mason, Mark. "United States Direct Investment in Japan: Trends and Prospects," *California Management Review*, vol. 35, no. 1 (Fall 1992).

McKinney, Joseph A. "Degree of Access to the Japanese Market: 1979 vs. 1986," *Columbia Journal of World Business*, vol. 24, no. 2 (Summer 1989).

McMillan, Charles J. *The Japanese Industrial System* (Berlin: Walter de Gruyter, 1984).

Mirza, Hafix; Buckley, Peter J. and Weir, David T. H. "European Direct Investment in Japan," *Management International Review*, vol. 35 (1995/1).

Morita, Akio. "Partnering for Competitiveness: The Role of Japanese Business," *Harvard Business Review*, vol. 70, no. 3 (May/June 1992).

Mowery, David C. and Treece, David J. "Japan's Growing Capabilities in Industrial Technology: Implications for US Managers and Policymakers," *California Management Review*, vol. 35, no. 2 (Winter 1993).

Nishiguchi, Toshihiro and Brookfield, Jonathan. "The Evolution of Japanese Subcontracting," *Sloan Management Review*, vol. 39 (Fall 1997).

Rehfeld, John E. "What Working for a Japanese Company Taught Me," *Harvard Business Review*, vol. 68, no. 6 (November/December 1990).

Rose, Peter S. "Japanese Banks Inside the US: Dynamic Changes in Their Sources and Uses of Funds," *Columbia Journal of World Business*, vol. 24, no. 4 (Winter 1989).

Rugman, Alan M. and Anderson, Andrew. "Japanese and Canadian Direct Investment in the United States." *Singapore Economic Review*, vol. 26, no. 2 (October 1991).

Rugman, Alan M.; Brown, Lee; and Verbeke, Alain. "Japanese Joint Ventures with Western Multinationals: Synthesizing the Economic and Cultural Explanations of Failure," *Asia-Pacific Journal of Management*, vol. 6, no. 2 (April 1989).

Rugman, Alan M. and Verbeke, Alain. "Trade Policy for the Asia-Pacific Region: A US–Japan Comparison," *Journal of Business Administration*, vol. 17, no. 1–2 (1987/88).

Ryans, Adrian B. "Strategic Market Entry Factors and Market Share Achievement in Japan," *Journal of International Business Studies*, vol. 19, no. 3 (Fall 1988).

Taylor, Sully and Napier, Nancy. "Working in Japan: Lessons from Women Expatriates," *Sloan Management Review*, vol. 37 (Spring 1996).

Tezuka, Hiroyuki. "Success as the Source of Failure? Competition and Cooperation in the Japanese Economy," *Sloan Management Review*, vol. 38 (Winter 1997).

Tyson, Laura D'Andrea. "Who's Bashing Whom?: Trade Conflict in High Technology Industries," Washington, DC: Institute for Research in International Economics, 1992.

Webber, Alan M. "Japanese-Style Entrepreneurship: An Interview with Softbank's CEO, Masayoshi Son," *Harvard Business Review*, vol. 70, no. 1 (January/February 1992).

Westney, D. Eleanor. *Imitation and Innovation* (Cambridge, Mass.: Harvard University Press, 1987).

Yoshino, M.Y. and Lifson, Thomas B. *The Invisible Link* (Cambridge, Mass.: MIT Press, 1986).

CHAPTER 18

Doing Business in
North America

OBJECTIVES OF THE CHAPTER

The United States, Canada, and Mexico constitute a thriving economic bloc. Almost 30 per cent of all US trade is with Canada and Mexico; both of these countries conduct well over 60 per cent of their international trade with the United States (see Tables 18.1, 18.2, and 18.3). Yet Canada and Mexico are very different from the United States and both have distinctive business practices. Doing business in these countries requires just as much research and attention to institutional detail as doing business in the EU or Japan. The specific objectives of this chapter are to:

1. **Examine** the nature of the Canadian and Mexican political and economic systems and their implications for business strategy.

2. **Review** the business environment with primary attention on the industrial, regulatory, banking and finance, and labor relations areas.

3. **Investigate** major economic opportunities that exist in Canada and Mexico and some of the ways of conducting business in these nations.

4. **Consider** specific institutional arrangements, namely, the Canada–United States Free Trade Agreement (FTA) and the North American Free Trade Agreement (NAFTA), which play an important role in shaping opportunities and the business environment in North America.

ACTIVE LEARNING CASE

Getting ready for the competition with NAFTA

The United States–Canada Free Trade Agreement (FTA) of 1989 is having a dramatic effect on the strategies of many companies in both countries. One of the most common developments is a consolidation of operations. For example, the Inglis Ltd unit of Whirlpool has stopped making washing machines in its 108-year-old Toronto factory and now imports washers with newer technology from the Whirlpool facility in Clyde, Ohio. In another move Molson Brewery and Carling O'Keefe Breweries merged. The result of these strategic decisions is a series of companies that are better positioned to take advantage of the US–Canadian market. In particular, these mergers and acquisitions will increase the efficiency of the firms and, in many cases, strengthen their competitive position.

Some Canadians worry that Canada will be unable to take advantage of the benefits of free trade between the two countries, and that US business will dominate the market. Canadian unions, in particular, are strongly opposed to the FTA; they attribute plant closings and layoffs caused by the recession of 1990 to 1992 solely to the FTA. On the other hand, many individuals argue that these are only short-run setbacks and that in the long run the economies of both countries will benefit from free trade. They also point out that most people are relatively immobile and will continue to buy goods made in their own country. Thus the likelihood of US firms dominating the Canadian economy is remote. Additionally, they point out that the market for Canadian goods in the United States is much larger than the market for US goods in Canada. So Canadians have more to gain than to lose from the FTA.

The signing of the North American Free Trade Agreement (NAFTA) in 1993 has extended the FTA to include Mexico and Chile will be next. The NAFTA will help Mexico to continue to open up its markets to free trade and help to increase its rate of economic growth. The country is also doing well in attracting outside investment by such major firms as General Motors and Chrysler which have collectively invested well over $500 million there.

Over the past five years triad countries have been setting up operations in Mexico to tap a growing local market. The Mexican middle and upper classes are spending more, especially on big ticket items. US autos, which often cost three times as much as they do in the United States, are a popular purchase. Moreover, although Japanese cars sell well in most places, many Mexicans prefer US-made products; Japanese are seen as lower status in Mexico. Sales growth has been so strong in Mexico that one Ford Motor executive speculated that the country could be a 1 million-car market by the millennium. Many other retail businesses such as clothing and home appliances are seeing equal growth.

Sources: Adapted from Todd Mason, "That Howling Up North Is Canada," *Business Week*, February 12, 1990, p. 43; Chuck Hawkins, William J. Holstein, and Mary J. Pitzer, "The North American Shakeout Arrives Ahead of Schedule," *Business Week*, April 17, 1989, pp. 34–35; Stephen Baker, Elizabeth Weinger, and Mike Zellner, "Can Latin America Move from the Third World to the First'?" *Business Week*, October 21, 1991, pp. 54–56; Louis R. Richman, "How NAFTA Will Help America," *Fortune*, April 19, 1993, pp. 95–102; John Urquhart, "Canada Pursues Latin American Trade," *Wall Street Journal*, November 7, 1997, p. A15; Jonathan Friedland and Joseph B. White, "GM Is Leading an Investment Boom in Mexico," *Wall Street Journal*, December 24, 1998, pp. A5–6.

1. How can the Free Trade Agreement help the Canadian economy?

2. Why are mergers and acquisitions taking place in Canada? Is this a good move for the firms involved?

3. How are new mergers affecting union membership in Canada?

4. Will the millennium see an increase in exports between the United States and Canada? Why or why not?

5. In what way is Mexico's economic progress creating a market for US products?

Table 18.1 Direction of US Trade

| | Exports to | | | | | Imports from | | | | |
| | 1987 | | 1996 | | | 1987 | | 1996 | | |
Country/region	(billions of US $)	% of total	(billions of US $)	% of total		(billions of US $)	% of total	(billions of US $)	% of total	
Canada	59.8	23.6	132.6	21.3		71.5	16.9	159.7	20.7	
Mexico	14.6	5.8	56.8	9.1		20.5	4.8	74.1	9.6	
Japan	28.2	11.2	67.5	10.8		88.1	20.8	118.0	15.3	
EU*	60.2	23.8	127.5	20.5		84.9	20.0	147.5	19.1	
All others	90.1	35.6	238.6	38.3		159.1	37.5	318.5	41.3	
Total	252.9	100.0	622.9	100.0		424.1	100.0	817.8	106.1	

*EU refers to the European Economic Community for 1987 and the European Union for 1996.

Source: IMF, *Direction of Trade Statistics Yearbook*, 1991, and IMF, *Direction of Trade Statistics Quarterly*, June 1997.

Table 18.2 Direction of Canada's trade

	Exports to				Imports from			
	1987		1996		1987		1996	
Country/region	(millions of US $)	% of total	(millions of US $)	% of total	(millions of US $)	% of total	(millions of US $)	% of total
United States	71.5	72.9	164.8	82.3	59.6	65.9	114.6	67.4
EU*	7.2	7.3	10.8	5.4	10.2	11.3	16.7	9.8
Japan	5.3	5.4	7.4	3.7	5.7	6.3	7.6	4.5
Triad	83.5	85.1	183.0	91.4	75.5	83.5	138.9	81.7
Mexico	0.4	0.4	0.9	0.4	0.9	1.0	4.3	2.5
All others	14.2	14.5	16.2	8.1	14.0	15.5	26.8	15.7
Total**	98.1	100.0	200.1	100.0	90.4	100.0	170.0	100.0

*EU for 1987 refers to 12 countries in the EC; EU for 1996 includes Sweden, Finland and Austria, which joined in 1995.

** Percentages might not add up to 100 due to rounding.

Sources: IMF, *Direction of Trade Statistics Yearbook*, 1991.

Table 18.3 Direction of Mexico's trade

Country/region	Exports to				Imports from			
	1987 (millions of US $)	% of total	1996 (millions of US $)	% of total	1987 (millions of US $)	% of total	1996 (millions of US $)	% of total
United States	13,265	63.5	80,663	84.0	7,574	62.3	67,624	71.9
Canada	312	1.5	1,181	1.2	214	1.8	1,744	1.9
North America*	13,577	65.0	81,844	85.3	7,788	64.1	69,368	73.8
Western Hemisphere**	1,629	7.8	5,855	6.1	364.77	3.0	2,350	2.5
EU***	2,997	14.3	4,543	4.7	2,050	16.9	7,732	8.2
Japan	1,347	6.4	1,363	1.4	837	6.9	3,901	4.2
Other Asia	376	1.8	1,094	1.1	168	1.4	4,014	4.3
All others	961	4.6	1,292	1.3	951.23	7.8	6,628	7.1
Total	20,887	100.0	95,991	100.0	12,159	100.0	93,993	100.0

* Excluding Mexico.

** Excluding Mexico, Canada and the US.

*** EU for 1987 refers to 12 countries in the EC; EU for 1996 includes Sweden, Finland and Austria, which joined in 1995.

Sources: IMF, Direction of Trade Statistics Yearbook, 1991, and IMF, Direction of Trade Statistics Quarterly, June 1997.

INTRODUCTION

In Chapter 15 we saw that governments and the various institutions through which they wield their powers are important external factors in the international business environment. This chapter will focus on institutional factors in the North American market that must be considered when looking at the Canadian and Mexican markets. The North American Free Trade Agreement (NAFTA) has not abolished all trading barriers between the United States, Canada, and Mexico. There are still major impediments to trade and investment. Furthermore, each of the partners retains its own trade laws. A legal mechanism to appeal trade decisions exists, but this is a compromise position. In contrast, EU member states cannot use trade laws against their partners. So although NAFTA is a step toward trade liberalization, business decisions should not assume that "free trade" makes Canada and Mexico identical to the United States.

CANADA

Canada, with a land area of almost 3.6 million square miles, is second in size only to Russia. The country is divided into ten provinces and two territories (see accompanying map). Canada is so large that it encompasses four time zones. The French and British fought over the country, with control passing into British hands in 1763. Canada became a separate nation in 1867, although it did not fully repatriate its constitution until 1982. Today it remains a leading member of the British Commonwealth.

Canada's economy

Canada's 31 million people enjoy one of the highest standards of living in the world. Consumer tastes and disposable wealth in Canada are very similar to those in the United States. Approximately two-thirds of all families own their own homes, and large percentages own durable goods such as radios (99 per cent), refrigerators (99 per cent), telephones (97 per cent), washing machines (77 per cent), and videocassette recorders (25 per cent).

Gross domestic product in 1996 was about $721 billion, in US dollars. The rate of economic growth during the 1980s was in the 3 to 4 per cent range for most years, although the economy hit a major recession in the early 1990s. Canada has typically had a positive balance of payments, thanks to its food, energy, and motor vehicle exports. Canada's primary trading partner is the United States, which provided 67 per cent of Canada's imports and accounted for 82 per cent of the country's exports in 1996 (see Table 18.2 which is in millions, compared to Table 18.1 which is in billions).

Canada's economic growth has been historically based on the export of agricultural staples, especially grains, and on the production and export of natural resource products such as minerals, oil, gas, and forest products. However, major secondary industries have also emerged; Canada now ranks as one of the top ten manufacturing nations of the world. The service industry is also expanding rapidly, especially financial services in Toronto. However, the country still faces a major productivity challenge. Recent studies show that Canada's productivity growth is threatening to draw down the nation's standard of living for decades to come.[1]

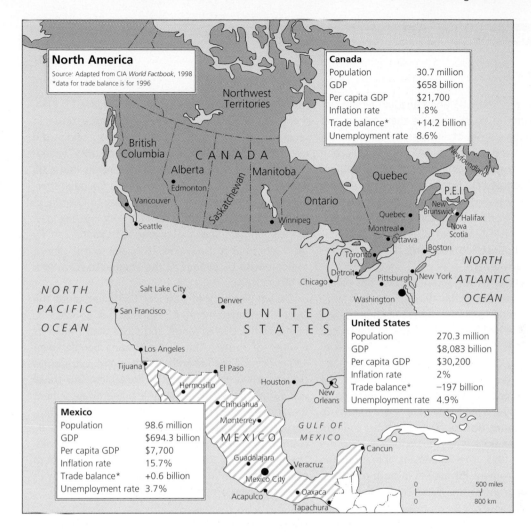

North America
Source: Adapted from CIA *World Factbook*, 1998
*data for trade balance is for 1996

Canada	
Population	30.7 million
GDP	$658 billion
Per capita GDP	$21,700
Inflation rate	1.8%
Trade balance*	+14.2 billion
Unemployment rate	8.6%

United States	
Population	270.3 million
GDP	$8,083 billion
Per capita GDP	$30,200
Inflation rate	2%
Trade balance*	−197 billion
Unemployment rate	4.9%

Mexico	
Population	98.6 million
GDP	$694.3 billion
Per capita GDP	$7,700
Inflation rate	15.7%
Trade balance*	+0.6 billion
Unemployment rate	3.7%

Almost 80 per cent of manufacturing activity is located in Ontario and Quebec, including the entire motor vehicle industry, which is Canada's largest segment, while Calgary has now become a major high technology center.[2] Almost one-third of all Canada's manufactured exports (and imports) are in autos and auto-related products. The Canada–United States autopact encouraged this two-way trade over the last 30 years. This provided free trade in autos assembled in Canada or the United States, provided there was 50 per cent value added in Canada. (Under the NAFTA the content provision is to be increased to 62.5 per cent.) Financial institutions and other business service industries are also concentrated in central Canada. The eastern and western areas of the country are more dependent on primary industries: fishing, forestry, and mining in the east; agriculture, ore, and mineral fuels in the west. Canada's growth was helped by large inflows of FDI; today 40 per cent of the primary and secondary industries are foreign-owned. Yet Canada is wealthy enough now, and its economy is sufficiently mature, to have substantial outward FDI, particularly in the United States.

INTERNATIONAL BUSINESS STRATEGY IN ACTION

Open Skies

Over the past few years US and Canadian airline carriers have begun to try to improve their competitive positions through a series of alliances. For example, Air Canada has become part of Star Alliance, a collection of six international airlines including United Airlines from the United States. Similarly, Canadian Airlines has joined American Airlines and its code-sharing partners around the world to form the Oneworld alliance. This is a result of a trend that is grouping the international airline business into four large alliances to compete against each other.

For the North American Airline market this means an increase in efficiency. In 1993 US carriers were authorized to serve only 44 routes in Canada, and Canadian carriers had a mere 28 routes in the United States. A study at the time revealed that if the skies between the two countries were allowed to open up, air traffic would double within the next few years. The study also estimated that the resulting increase in tourism and trade would generate $10.3 billion in additional economic activity. These statistics indicate why a new Open Skies treaty between the countries was enacted in 1995. The agreement liberalized the regulatory environment for airlines in both countries.

As the North American Free Trade Agreement (NAFTA) also came into effect on January 1, 1994, there was a further incentive to liberalize trade in services such as airline travel. However, under the restricted transportation provisions of NAFTA, national treatment does not apply. This means that a US airline can only do business across the Canadian borders on a point-to-point basis, from, say La Guardia in New York, to Toronto. It cannot pick up any passengers within Canada. Similarly, Air Canada can fly from Montreal to New York to Miami, but it cannot compete with US airlines on the internal US New York to Miami route.

Despite the lack of national treatment, since the Open Skies agreement, Air Canada has doubled its flights to the United States and more than tripled its number of routes. Today, Air Canada handles over 42 per cent of the Canada–US traffic and it attributes close to 3,000 new jobs to the agreement. Air travel was further eased in 1998 by a bilateral agreement to facilitate preclearance of customs and immigration services. This will reduce double inspections by customs and immigration officers in both countries. The large success of these agreements has led both governments to negotiate similar agreements with other countries around the globe.

Sources: Adapted from William C. Synods and Seth Payne, "Clear the Air Between the US and Canada," *Business Week*, June 21, 1993, p. 59; Randall Litchfield, "Sacred Cows of Nationhood," *Canadian Business*, January 1993, p. 13; Claude I. Taylor, "Critical Mass, Competitiveness and the New Economic Order," *Canadian Business Review*, Spring 1992, pp. 38–40; Alan M. Rugman, *Foreign Investment and NAFTA* (Columbia, SC: University of South Carolina Press, 1994); *http://www.aircanada.ca.*

The United States has more FDI in Canada than in any other country, including Great Britain. Since 1960 this investment has increased fivefold, and today it stands at about Canadian $80 billion. At the same time Canada has invested more money in the United States than in any other country. We can see these relationships within individual industries. For example, many US airlines, including American, Delta, and Northwest, fly to Canada, and Air Canada and Canadian Airlines, which recently merged, among others, have US routes. So part of the US international airline strategy involves competing with Canadian carriers that are vying for the US market (see the box "International Business Strategy in Action: Open Skies"). There are many other examples of Canadian investment in the United States. Canadian Pacific has purchased the Delaware & Hudson Railway and Bombardier Inc. bought the Learjet Corporation of Wichita, Kansas. Many other acquisitions are even larger.

Review your answer to Active Learning Case question 1 and make any changes you like. Then compare your answer to the one below.

1. How can the Free Trade Agreement help the Canadian economy?

The Free Trade Agreement will eliminate tariffs and make it easier for efficient Canadian firms to operate competitively in the United States. At the same time the Agreement will allow efficient US firms to ship their goods into Canada without paying any tariffs and, in the process, will help to drive down prices. So the Free Trade Agreement can help the Canadian economy by encouraging efficiency, lowering prices, and opening up new markets in the United States.

Differences in the business environment

Although there are many similarities between the business environments of the United States and Canada, there are also some important differences.

Canada's industrial climate The Canadian economy is characterized by private enterprise. However, some industries, such as broadcasting and public utilities, are government owned or subject to substantial government regulation.[3] Over the last decade the trend has been toward privatization and deregulation. In fact, there is a federal government minister who oversees privatization; this individual has been responsible for selling companies that the government feels are no longer essential to meet public policy goals. Firms that have been privatized in recent years include Canadair, the deHavilland Aircraft Company, Canadian National Railway's trucking division, Fisheries Products International, and Air Canada.

Small business is a major part of the economy and accounts for almost 80 per cent of all new employment in manufacturing. The service and retail trade industries are characterized by a large number of companies that vary in size. Seventy per cent of Canadians work in service industries.

Canada's regulatory environment Commerce and industry in Canada is regulated at every level of government: federal, provincial, and municipal. Many of these regulations are similar to those in the United States.

Competition Regulation of competition is under the jurisdiction of the federal Parliament. Legislation in this area was revised in the late 1980s in order to eliminate restrictive trade policies, to stimulate production, and to promote the international competitiveness of Canadian business. Although there are no price controls in Canada, there is regulation to review monopolies, acquisitions, and mergers. The regulation of anticompetitive practices is handled under the **Competition Act**. This Act prohibits individuals and companies from practices that will substantially lessen or prevent competition in the marketplace. The Act outlaws bid-rigging, price discrimination, or conspiring to unduly lessen competition. It also provides for regulation of acquisitions and mergers. If the purchase price is $400 million or more, the parties must refrain from completing the transaction for a time period ranging from seven to 21 days. During this time the government will review the situation and decide if the purchase will prevent or lessen competition (using international comparisons) and thus be noncompetitive in nature. A ruling will then be made.

ACTIVE LEARNING CHECK

Review your answer to Active Learning Case question 2 and make any changes you like. Then compare your answer to the one below.

2. Why are mergers and acquisitions taking place in Canada? Is this a good move for the firms involved?

Mergers and acquisitions are occurring because Canadian firms need to increase their international competitiveness. This is being accomplished in two ways. First, companies are looking for ways to become more efficient so that they can reduce overhead and lower prices. Second, companies are trying to strengthen their assets and market positions and thus prepare themselves for the increased competition that is being generated by the FTA. This is particularly true since Canadian firms are smaller, on average, than those of the United States. Canadian firms, on average, will have difficulty competing with larger US firms unless they expand in size or pursue niche strategies. By merging or acquiring the resources of other companies in the industry, Canadian firms hope to be able to weather the competitive storm that is likely to occur during the millennium. These mergers and acquisitions are necessary for the firms involved.

Exports and imports   Export permits are required for the shipment of goods having strategic value, such as uranium. They are also required to implement the provisions of various international agreements into which Canada has entered. Import documentation is also required, as well as payment of a goods and sales tax (GST).[4] This tax, which went into effect on January 1, 1991, is a value-added tax. On imports, this tax is collected by Canadian Customs. The GST was set at 7 per cent of the value of the goods plus any import duties.[5]

Francization in Quebec   The Canadian federal government has a bilingual policy.[6] But in the province of Quebec, French is the official language for business and education. All firms employing 50 or more employees in Quebec must use French at all levels of the organization. Other regulations related to the use of French in Quebec are that (1) all product labels must be in French; translations cannot be given greater prominence than the French portion, (2) company names and signs must be in French, but a version of the firm's name in another language may accompany the French version for use outside Quebec, and (3) all signs on the outside of stores must be in French only.[7] In addition, all education, health services, and all other services under provincial jurisdiction are delivered in French. Some exceptions to the French language and sign law policies accommodate the one-fifth of the Quebec population that speaks English. For example, McGill University and Concordia University can operate in English, and English signs can be displayed inside stores, provided they are smaller than French signs.[8]

Banking and finance   Banks in Canada offer a full range of financial services. There are six large Canadian chartered banks, with extensive national branch networks, and many smaller (often foreign-owned) banks. These banks respond to the actions of the central bank, the Bank of Canada. This federal government institution is directly responsible for the nation's monetary policy, including (1) regulating credit and currency, (2) controlling and protecting the external value of the Canadian dollar, and (3) regulating the general level of production, trade, prices, and employment, within the scope of monetary policy.

In carrying out its functions, the Bank of Canada buys and sells foreign exchange and sets the interest rate that is charged to commercial banks. These functions are similar to those carried out by the Federal Reserve in the United States, which helps to monitor the US monetary system. The Bank of Canada is also responsible for issuing the country's notes and coins and for managing the federal debt. Canadian interest rates and its exchange rate closely follow those set in the United States, especially in relation to non-North American interest and exchange rates.

Banks operate within the confines of the Bank Act. There are two types of banks: Schedule A and Schedule B. Schedule A banks are Canadian-owned and no shareholder has more than 10 per cent of the voting stock. Schedule B banks are closely held Canadian-owned or foreign banks. These are allowed to carry on normal banking activities. However, foreign-owned banks cannot, as a group, own more than 16 per cent of the total domestic assets of the Canadian banking system. Subsidiaries of US banks are not subject to this restriction because of the Canada–United States Free Trade Agreement. In addition, Canadian banks are allowed to operate across the country.

There is also a host of specialized financial institutions that provide limited services throughout the provinces. Examples include savings banks, cooperative credit unions, loan companies, mortgage companies, and insurance companies. Investment bankers provide short-term funds to companies for acquisition or reorganization purposes.

Canada has four major stock exchanges: Toronto, Montreal, Vancouver, and Calgary. Toronto is the major exchange; it accounts for approximately 80 per cent of dollar trading volume. Toronto is also the financial center of the country.

Labor relations Labor relations are governed by both federal and provincial labor legislation. The **Canada Labor Code** is the federal law that covers such matters as wages, employment practices, work safety, and conciliation in the event of a labor dispute. Province governments have similar laws to cover employer–employee relations at the local level.

Unions With the exception of farmers, domestic help, and white-collar workers, the work force is heavily unionized. Approximately 35 per cent of the total labor force are union members, in contrast to approximately 17 per cent in the United States. In some instances the workers are free to choose or reject union membership. In other cases they must become members in order to keep their jobs. The labor–management contract determines these conditions.

As in the United States, once a union has been certified to represent the workers, management must bargain in good faith. The result of such bargaining is a labor–management agreement that determines wage rates, fringe benefits, working conditions, and management rights. Economic nationalism is a strong component of Canadian unionization, and the unions have been major opponents of the FTA and other economic and political relationships with the United States.

ACTIVE LEARNING CHECK

Review your answer to Active Learning Case question 3 and make any changes you like. Then compare your answer to the one below.

3. How are new mergers affecting union membership in Canada?

New mergers to make Canadian firms more competitive in the global economy are hurting union membership. The primary reason is that as companies merge their operations, they cut back the number of people on the payroll. For example, if two airlines merge, they are unlikely to need two people to head the Human Resources Management Department. They can also trim the number of people in support areas, such as accounting, legal, and public relations. In fact, this is one of the primary reasons for the merger – to try to run two companies more efficiently than either has been operated alone. In Canada, public sector unions – that is, in services – are just as large as private sector unions, but even more militant and resistant to globalization. Since the Canadian work force is heavily unionized, mergers are much more likely to hurt union membership than would be the case in the United States, where the percentage of unionized employees is significantly lower.

Working conditions All provinces have legislated minimum wage rates and they are periodically adjusted. However, in most sectors wages and salaries are similar to US levels.

There is a national compulsory contributory pension plan that provides retirement benefits to contributors, generally at the age of 65. This age limit varies, however, and there is growing pressure to relax mandatory retirement rules.[9] In addition, many private pension plans are in effect. Other benefits include group life insurance, medical insurance, and subsidized food and housing. Most provincial legislation limits daily or weekly working hours, with mandatory overtime pay for hours worked in excess of these limits. The government also mandates minimum annual paid vacations in almost all industries. This typically is two weeks following one year of employment and increases up to three or four weeks after longer employment. There are also legislated holidays which, depending on the city and the province, usually vary between eight and 12 days.

All provinces prohibit employment discrimination on the basis of race, religion, national origin, color, sex, age, or marital status. There are also equal pay for equal work provisions, which vary across provinces. They are designed to prevent gender bias in pay levels, and in recent years Canada has taken significant strides in reducing the earnings gap between men and women who do the same types of work.[10] For example, Ontario has specific "pay equity" legislation that requires employers to remove gender bias in pay levels; salary adjustments were phased in starting in 1990. Similar legislation has been enacted in a number of other provinces, including Quebec and Saskatchewan.

Investments The **Investment Canada Act (ICA)** came into effect on June 30, 1985 and is designed to create a welcome climate for foreign investment by significantly loosening previous restrictions. At the same time, however, some regulations still remain in effect. As noted earlier, investments in certain industries are restricted. For example, a licence to operate a broadcasting station can be granted only to a Canadian citizen or corporation whose stock is 80 per cent owned by Canadian citizens or Canadian-controlled corporations. Generally, nonresidents cannot hold more than 25 per cent of the issued and outstanding shares of a chartered bank, a life insurance company, a sales finance company, a loan company, or a trust company. Nor can a single non-resident together with his or her associates hold more than 10 per cent of the issued and outstanding shares of these types of companies. Limits are much less stringent in the securities industry, but the government must be kept apprised of such ownership.

Under the ICA a non-Canadian wishing to acquire a Canadian firm must make an application to the ICA for review and approval, if the assets are valued at more than $5 million or the business relates to Canada's cultural heritage or national identity. In the case of US firms buying Canadian operations, under the provisions of the Free Trade Agreement, the ICA review takes place at the $150 million level. So the investment climate is much more conducive to US investors than to any others. When the ICA does conduct a review, a number of factors are considered in determining whether the investment will benefit Canada. These include employment, technological benefits, and product innovation.

In addition, there are numerous provincial statutes that place restrictions on foreigners seeking to invest in particular industries or activities. For example, in most provinces individuals have to be Canadian residents for at least a year in order to be registered securities dealers. Similarly, foreigners who are registering ownership of land must disclose their citizenship. In Alberta, British Columbia, Manitoba, Ontario, and Saskatchewan, a majority of the board of directors of corporations must be resident Canadians. However, an indirect takeover of a foreign-owned publisher will require that the firm be sold to a Canadian owner, according to the "Baie Comeau policy."

Canada's multinationals

It is useful to identify Canada's major companies against the background of global competition and triad power. Some larger Canadian companies like Northern Telecom and Seagram are well known in the United States.

Table 18.4 ranks the 20 largest Canadian-owned companies in decreasing order of size measured by their sales in 1997. The largest firm, BCE, with sales of over $33 billion, owns Northern Telecom, which is widely recognized as being one of Canada's most successful multinationals. It also owns Bell Canada, whose sales are about as large as Northern Telecom's. Other well-known Canadian industrial multinationals at the top of the list are Alcan, Noranda, and Seagram.

Table 18.5 lists the 20 largest foreign-owned firms in Canada. These firms also contribute to the performance of the country, creating jobs and wealth for Canadians. However, all foreign-owned firms must be examined in terms of their relationship to their parent firms. A high degree of autonomy, or development of world-class products in Canada, is necessary for a foreign-owned firm to provide sustained benefits to Canada. The Big Three auto firms have not done this. However, some energy firms, such as Imperial Oil (owned by Exxon), have a history of Canadian development, whereas others such as IBM Canada already operate divisions in Canada on a global basis. Others, such as Asea Brown Boveri (ABB), have a decentralized organizational structure with a large degree of local autonomy. These smaller (ABB is not on the list) but more autonomous Canadian firms have learned to survive within the global networks of their parent organizations, and their managers can help to provide leadership to Canadians.

Table 18.4   The largest Canadian-owned companies by size

Rank	Firm	Industry	1997 sales (in millions of Canadian $)	F/T
1	BCE	Telecommunications	33,191	0.58
2	The Seagram Co.	Conglomerates	17,161	0.97
3	TransCanada Pipelines	Gas/electrical utilities	14,243	0.55
4	George Weston	Conglomerates	13,921	0.11
5	The Thomson Corp.	Publishing and printing	12,137	0.95
6	Onex Corp.	Conglomerates	11,212	0.96
7	Alcan Aluminum	Mining	10,768	0.85
8	Imasco	Conglomerates	10,008	0.19
9	Canadian Pacific	Conglomerates	9,560	0.40
10	Power Corp. of Canada	Conglomerates	8,612	n.a.
11	Bombardier	Information technology	8.509	0.88
12	Magna International Inc.	Motor vehicles and parts	7,691	0.55
13	Westcoast Energy	Gas/electrical utilities	7,312	0.03
14	Quebecor Inc.	Publishing and printing	7,013	0.76
15	The Oshawa Group Ltd.	Food stores	6,813	n.a.
16	Hudson's Bay Co.	Merchandisers	6,447	n.a.
17	Noranda	Conglomerates	6,407	0.80
18	Petro-Canada	Oil and gas	6,017	0.10
19	Provigo Inc.	Food stores	5,956	n.a.
20	EdperBrascan Corp.	Conglomerates	5,886	0.35
Average			10,443	
Total			208,864	

F/T refers to foreign exports and sales divided by total sales.

Source: Adapted from "The Financial Post 500," *The Financial Post,* 1998.

Another indicator of the nature of international expertise among these firms comes from the degree of their exports. Table 18.4 also reports data on the foreign sales of the largest 20 Canadian-owned firms. Exports from Canadian sales of subsidiaries in the United States and others offshore (excluding the United States) are shown. According to the table, these large companies sell approximately 50 per cent of their output abroad. The foreign-owned firms in Canada (Table 18.5) also sell abroad, but they have fewer exports on average (17 per cent of output). This is partly because several distributors and retailers included in the list (Sears, Safeway, A & P) sell only within Canada.

Table 18.6 shows Canadian-based firms ranked according to overseas sales. The largest, the Potash Corporation exports virtually everything. Additionally, most of Seagram's sales are outside Canada, as are those for Onex, Thompson, Moore, and Laidlow. Two foreign-owned firms (Ford Motor of Canada and Mitsui) also make this list. For these large 20 firms the average ratio of foreign to total sales is 81 per cent, with 49 per cent of sales to the United States and 44 per cent to other foreign markets. This demonstrates the tremendous attraction of foreign markets for larger companies in

Table 18.5 The largest foreign-owned companies in Canada, by size

Rank	Firm	Industry	1997 sales (in millions of Canadian $)	F/T	Ownership
1	General Motors of Canada	Autos	34,249	n.a.	US (100)
2	Ford Motor of Canada	Autos	27,912	0.68	US (100)
3	Chrysler Canada	Autos	16,688	n.a.	US (100)
4	Imperial Oil	Oil and gas	9,512	n.a.	US (70)
5	IBM Canada	Information technology	7,400	n.a.	US (100)
6	Amoco Canada Petroleum	Oil and gas	6,177	n.a.	US (100)
7	Shell Canada	Oil and gas	5,445	0.11	Netherlands (78)
8	Canada Safeway Ltd.	Food stores	4,719	n.a.	US (100)
9	Sears Canada Inc.	Merchandisers	4,583	n.a.	US (55)
10	Canadian Ultramar	Oil and gas	4,175	n.a.	US (100)
11	Honda Canada	Autos	3,794	n.a.	Japan (100)
12	Mitsui & Co.	Import/Export	3,581	0.51	Japan (100)
13	Mobil Oil Canada	Oil and gas	3,307	0.51	US (100)
14	Cargill Ltd.	Agriculture	3,088	n.a.	US (91)
15	Anglo-Canadian Telephone Co.	Telecommuniations	3,058	n.a.	US (100)
16	Price Costco Canada Inc.	Merchandisers	2,653	n.a.	US (100)
17	Toyota	Autos	2,639	n.a.	Japan (100)
18	General Electric Canada	Manufacturing	2,537	0.35	US (100)
19	Great Atlantic & Pacific Co.	Food stores	2,457	n.a.	US (100)
20	SHL Systemhouse Co.	Information technology	2,400	n.a.	US (100)
Average			7,519		
Total			150,374		

F/T refers to foreign exports and sales divided by total sales.

Source: Adapted from "The Financial Post 500," *The Financial Post*, 1998.

a relatively small market like Canada's. This provides further evidence that access to a triad market (in this case the United States) is critical for success in a global market.

Multilateral Agreement on Investment (MAI)

Canada will benefit from any type of multilateral agreement on investment. An attempt to negotiate an MAI was made in Paris at the Organization for Economic Cooperation and Development (OECD) over the 1995 to 1998 period. The draft MAI was based on the lines of the North American Free Trade Agreement (NAFTA). The millennium round of the WTO may take up the need for an MAI.

An MAI will include the principle of national treatment, i.e., equal access for foreign investors to the host country's market (but according to host country rules). A number of sectors will be exempted from the national treatment principle. Canada, in the same spirit of the FTA and NAFTA, insists on exemptions on health care, education, social services, cultural industries, and transportation. All regulations on investment will be identified as will be all exemptions to the principle of national

Table 18.6 The largest Canadian-based firms, by degree of multinationality

Rank	Company	1997 (in millions of Canadian $)	% Sales Outside of Canada
1	Potash Corp. of Saskatchewan	3,220	98
2	The Seagram Co.	17,161	97
3	Onex Corp., Toronto	11,212	96
4	The Thomson Corp., Toronto	12,137	95
5	Moore Corp. Ltd., Toronto	3,643	93
6	Laidlaw	4,148	90
7	Abitibi-Consolidated Inc.,	3,747	90
8	Inco	3,277	89
9	Bombardier Inc., Montreal (Ja98)	8,509	88
10	Alcan Aluminium Ltd., Montreal	10,768	85
11	Noranda	6,407	80
12	Quebecor Inc.	7,013	76
13	Ford Motor Co. of Canada	27,912	68
14	BCE Inc., Montreal	33,191	58
15	MacMillan Bloedel	4,521	58
16	TransCanada PipeLines	14,243	55
17	Magna International Inc.,	7,692	55
18	Mitsui & Co. (Canada)	3,582	51
19	Mobil Oil Canada	3,307	51
20	Canadian Pacific Ltd., Calgary	9,560	40

Note: The data for foreign sales is limited and companies that might otherwise be in the list might be excluded.

Sources: Adapted from *Financial Post*, Top 50 Companies, *http://www.nationalpost.com*.

treatment. Additionally, dispute settlement mechanisms will be put in place, to allow individual investors (and companies) to appeal against government regulations and bureaucratic controls. The MAI will help countries to harmonize their regulations, although, in the areas of competition policy and tax policy, not much progress can be expected (no progress was achieved in NAFTA).

The need for an MAI arises because foreign investment has become an important part of the global economy. Today, the majority of international business is not done by traded goods, but through services and investments. Over 70 per cent of North Americans work in the service sector, with only 30 per cent in manufacturing. So the new agenda for international agreements is to negotiate rules for trade in services and investment.

Canada's outward stock of FDI is only 60 per cent in the United States, with which it already has national treatment through the FTA and NAFTA. Thus, its exporting businesses will go for an MAI with transparent rules.

Business opportunities in Canada

Although the Canadian economy began to slow down during the early 1990s, the country still offers excellent investment and trade opportunities for foreign investors. This is particularly true for US firms, thanks to the Free Trade Agreement of 1988 and its extension, the **North American Free Trade Agreement (NAFTA)**, which includes Mexico.[11]

The **United States–Canada Free Trade Agreement (FTA)** is designed to eliminate tariffs and most other barriers to trade between the two countries.[12] Some specific provisions of the FTA are:

1. All tariffs on US and Canadian goods were to be eliminated by 1998.

2. Most import and export quotas were to be eliminated by 1998.

3. Use of product standards as a trade barrier is prohibited and national treatment of testing labs and certification bodies is established.

4. Many restrictions on agricultural products, wine and distilled spirits, auto parts, and energy goods have been sharply reduced, if not totally eliminated.

5. The size of the government procurement markets that will be open to suppliers from the other country is slightly increased.

6. Travel by business visitors, investors, traders, professionals, and executives transferred intracompany is facilitated.

7. The opportunity to make investments in each other's country is facilitated and encouraged through the adoption of national treatment.

8. A binational commission to resolve disagreements that may arise from the enforcement of the FTA has been established and dealt with some 20 cases in the first three years of the Agreement.[13]

Marketing in Canada   Companies doing business in Canada need to know distribution practices and advertising and promotion channels. In many cases these are similar to those in other countries, but there are some important differences.

Distribution practices   Despite the country's vast size, sales to Canadian industries are characterized by short marketing channels with direct producer-to-user distribution. Many Canadian industries are dominated by a few large-scale enterprises that are highly concentrated geographically. It is not unusual for 90 per cent of prospective customers for an industrial product to be located in or near two or three cities.

The consumer goods market is more diffused than the industrial market, and the use of marketing intermediaries is often necessary. In many cases complete coverage of the consumer market requires representation in a number of commercial centers across the country. Firms having only one representative or distribution point typically choose Toronto. If the country is divided into two major markets, the other is often Calgary or Vancouver. If the market is divided into three areas, distributors are frequently put in Montreal, Ontario, and Vancouver.[14]

Direct selling is another growing area. This includes the sale of goods from manufacturing premises, by mail, through home delivery, through personal selling, and through other nonretail channels. Today direct selling accounts for over $2 billion annually in Canada.

Wholesale and retail trade are also important forms of distribution. Because of the wide dispersion of customers, wholesale trade is critical. However, retail trade is even more important and accounts for over $100 billion in sales annually. About 60 per cent of this is earned by independent stores, and the other 40 per cent is made by chain stores. In recent years the number of independent stores has been declining, and chain stores have begun gaining important footholds in some areas such as clothing, shoe, and general merchandise. Quebec and Ontario account for about 63 per cent of all retail sales, and the western provinces make up approximately 29 per cent of the total. Department stores and supermarkets constitute a large percentage of retail sales. However, as in the United states, they are facing increased competition from discount food stores, showroom retailing, and other forms of self-service retailing. There are also specialized markets for recreation and leisure equipment and associated services. There is also a growing demand for consumer durables. These trends are likely to continue well into the millennium.

Advertising and promotion   Media used for advertising in Canada include television, radio, newspapers, and magazines. Television and radio advertising are particularly popular because 97 per cent of all Canadian households have at least one television, and 99 per cent have at least one radio. Hundreds of private firms operate cable television and major broadcasting stations in metropolitan areas, and there are over 1,300 television stations and 550 cable television systems in the country, with over 50 per cent of the population hooked into a cable system. In addition, the Canadian Broadcasting Corporation (CBC) operates two national television networks, one in English and one in French. There are 1,400 licensed AM and FM radio stations.

Over 100 daily newspapers are published in Canada, and they are widely used by advertisers, as are trade magazines that are directed at specific industries such as computers, real estate, banking, and retailing. General interest Canadian magazines such as *Reader's Digest, L'actualité,* and *Quest* have raised their share of net advertising expenditure in Canadian periodicals to about 30 per cent, approaching the advertising of national newspapers. Two business newspapers, *The Financial Post* and *The Report on Business* of *The Globe and Mail* also are widely read in the business and financial community. There are over 450 advertising agencies in Canada that can be of assistance in developing advertising and promotion campaigns.

Exporting   One of the most popular ways of doing business in Canada is through exports. As noted earlier, Canada is the United States' largest foreign market. Every year Canadians buy as much US goods as do all the member nations of the EU combined.[15] In fact, over 20 per cent of all US exports go to Canada. In recent years the Canadian government has simplified the process for shipping goods into the country. This is particularly true for products coming from the United States since duties have been greatly reduced or eliminated, thanks to the FTA and NAFTA.

ACTIVE LEARNING CHECK

Review your answer to Active Learning Case question 4 and make any changes you like. Then compare your answer to the one below.

4. Will the millennium see an increase in exports between the United States and Canada? Why or why not?

The millennium will see an increase in exports between the two countries. Three reasons can be cited. First, the elimination of all tariffs under the FTA is going to encourage exports. Second, under the FTA arrangements both countries are more likely to produce those goods and services for which they have a competitive advantage and to buy the others from their neighbor. Third, as the economies of the two countries grow, so will the amount of trade as each begins to adapt operations to the desires of the other and starts to tap this market further.

Franchising

Canada is the dominant foreign market for US franchisors. Currently there are over 300 US franchise firms operating approximately 10,000 franchise units in Canada. A recent report by *Entrepreneur* magazine rated over 1,100 US franchises. Of those rated in the top 10, eight indicated that they were seeking to establish franchises in Canada, so there is a great deal of opportunity for those who want to do business in Canada via the franchise route.

Additionally, in recent years Canadian banks have become more responsive to the needs of franchised operations. Various loan and repayment plans for franchises are now offered by Canadian chartered banks. In some cases these financial institutions also offer payroll and cash management services. So there is considerable opportunity in international franchise operations in Canada.

MEXICO

Mexico, with a land area of approximately 760,000 square miles, is equal in size to almost 25 per cent of the contiguous United States. It is the third largest nation in Latin America and has a population of over 95 million. The country is a federal democratic republic divided into 31 states and the Federal District (Mexico City). Although the country endured political turmoil early in this century, since World War II the government has been stable,[16] and during the presidencies of Carlos Salinas (1988–94) and Ernests Zedillo (1994–2000) relations with the United States have been particularly cordial.

Mexico's economy

The country's economy is currently in a state of flux, which has been brought on by new economic relations with the United States. Today Mexico has the strongest economy in Latin America. One of the primary reasons has been the economic policies of Carlos Salinas, who, after becoming president in 1988, introduced liberalization rules regarding foreign investment and privatization. These changes have dramatically improved the economy; gross domestic product growth in 1996 was 5.1 per cent, but inflation continued to remain in the range of 25 per cent. The country has also vigorously promoted exports, especially to the United States, which now counts on Mexico for 25 per cent of all imported fruit and vegetables. The *maquiladora* industry (see Chapter 15) is another growing source of economic strength for the country.[17] At the same time Mexico has become a major region for international investment.

MNE investment The climate for foreign investment in Mexico has grown increasingly favorable in recent years. Although there were strict controls on foreign investment during the 1970s, regulations introduced in 1989 reversed many of these restrictions. As a result, an increasing number of MNEs are investing in Mexico. Ford Motor invested $700 million in expansion of an automotive plant in Chihuahua; Nissan put $1 billion in a new assembly plant to produce cars for export to both the United States and Japan; Volkswagen invested $950 million to expand its plant; McDonald's earmarked $500 million to open 250 new restaurants by the year 2000;

Sears Roebuck put $150 million into new stores and malls throughout the country, in addition to renovating older units; and PepsiCo expanded its snack business by purchasing a majority stake in Gamesa, Mexico's largest cookie maker.

One of the major reasons for the increase in FDI is the privatization campaign that began in 1982 and which has picked up speed since then. While the government continues to play a major role in the economy, primarily through state-owned entities such as Pemex, the giant oil firm, there has been significant reduction in its ownership. These sales have been made to both foreign companies and Mexican investors.

Another reason has been the changes in investment laws that now permit foreigners to hold major equity positions. In the past, foreign ownership in auto parts companies had been limited to 40 per cent of equity, but a new decree now sharply reduces the number of firms that are subject to this law by creating exemptions based on percentages of export sales and sales to individuals. Today approximately 75 per cent of the economy is open to full foreign ownership.

Labor   Labor is relatively plentiful and inexpensive. However, although there are numerous engineers, MNEs report a serious shortage of skilled labor and managerial personnel, particularly at the middle and upper levels of the organization. Worker absenteeism in recent years has declined, but turnover remains a serious problem, even in the *maquiladora* sector.

Approximately 40 per cent of the total work force is unionized. In industrial operations with more than 25 workers, about 80 per cent of the work force is unionized. Union control over the members has weakened in recent years, and this trend is likely to continue. However, strikes are not uncommon.

There is a three-tier minimum wage structure in Mexico, but increases have not kept up with the cost of living. Minimum wage in US dollars in Mexico City and major towns in 1992 was approximately $4 per day, whereas it was $3.60 in many other large cities and $3.25 in the rest of the country.

Government regulations require that at least 90 per cent of a firm's skilled and unskilled workers be Mexican nationals, and employers must favor Mexicans over foreigners and union personnel over nonunion personnel. On the other hand, these regulations are unlikely to limit investment by MNEs since hiring exceptions are permitted by the government.

Mexico and the North American Free Trade Agreement

In conjunction with their privatization policies, Presidents Salinas and Zedillo sought to motivate business through increased exposure to international competitive forces and access to the dynamic US market.[18] To this end, the government opened negotiations with the US and Canadian governments in Toronto on June 12, 1991 to create the North American Free Trade Agreement (NAFTA). This marked the first time that a less developed country entered into an agreement with two wealthy countries to create a free trade area. The NAFTA started in January, 1994 has had a major impact on Mexico's trade and investment.

Trade in several sectors has experienced considerable growth. In the textile and apparel sectors, quotas on Mexican products will be phased out and customs duties on all textile and apparel products will be completely eliminated over a ten-year period.

For automotive products, Mexico immediately reduced its tariffs on cars and light trucks by 50 per cent and pledged to eliminate the remaining duties over ten years. In agriculture, tariff restrictions were lifted on a broad range of goods when the Agreement went into effect on January 1, 1994.

The investment climate in Mexico has also been affected by the NAFTA. In the automotive sector, all investment restrictions are to be eliminated over a ten-year period. In transportation, Mexico allowed 49 per cent ownership of cars and trucking companies three years after the Agreement went into effect, 51 per cent after seven years, and 100 per cent after ten years. Similar liberalization approaches are planned for the finance and insurance sectors.[19] All these changes will open up Mexico even more to FDI and in turn lead to the growth of the Mexican economy and two-way flows of trade and investment with the United States in the future.

As with the Canada–United States FTA, binational panels will play an important role in resolving trade disputes. Under the NAFTA, panels will continue to contribute toward resolution of disputes in trade and now also investment matters. Where investments are concerned, complainants may also take their cases to binding investor–state arbitration.

Regional trade agreements

Other developments involving Mexico as a leader in the movement toward free trade and privatization have included the efforts to create and sustain regional trade agreements based on the NAFTA. One of the major regional integration efforts has been the creation of the **Latin American Integration Association (LAIA)**, a free trade group that was formed in 1980 to reduce intraregional trade barriers and to promote regional economic cooperation. Argentina, Bolivia, Brazil, Chile, Colombia, Ecuador, Mexico, Paraguay, Peru, Uruguay, and Venezuela are all members. The primary objective of LAIA is to create a Latin American common market. In recent years the association's slow process toward economic integration has led some members to create subregional groups. For example, in the southern cone, Argentina, Brazil, Paraguay, and Uruguay have established a common market called **Mercosur**, which was operational by 1996. In the north, Mexico, Colombia, and Venezuela have a similar agreement, and via NAFTA Mexico is likely to be a key bridge between Latin American countries and the United States. The NAFTA has a clause permitting accession of other countries. A second major integration effort is the **Andean Common Market (Ancom)**, a subregional free trade compact that is designed to promote economic and social integration and cooperation.[20] Bolivia, Colombia, Ecuador, Peru, and Venezuela are all members.

In 1990 President Bush launched his **Enterprise for the Americas**, which is aimed at creating an all-American free trade area from Alaska to Argentine Antarctica. If such an idea comes to fruition, it will eliminate the need for LAIA, Ancom, and similar Latin American trade agreements. The United States is aware of the need for reducing, and then eliminating, trade barriers in the Americas if it hopes to establish a viable world market that can compete against the EU and the Pacific Rim. The idea is also appealing to Latin American countries that see the opportunities associated with linking into the North American diamond and profiting from the economic growth that it creates. This development will bring about a "Western hemisphere" trading bloc and may well become a reality by the early twenty-first century.

INTERNATIONAL BUSINESS STRATEGY IN ACTION

Four common approaches in Mexico

Doing business in Mexico can take a number of different forms. Four strategies have proven particularly profitable.

One is to establish a wholly owned subsidiary. This can be an expensive strategy, but it gives the company total control and allows management to make decisions quickly and efficiently. Quite often the subsidiary is run by a local manager and almost always the majority of the management team are locals. However, headquarters exercises key control.

A second approach is to become part of the *maquiladora* program. This strategy works best for firms aiming to export most of their output back to the United States. The *maquiladora* arrangement allows manufacturing, assembly, and processing plants to import materials, components, and equipment duty-free, complete the work with Mexican labor, and then ship the finished products back north. Under recent changes in the arrangement, if the company wants, it can sell up to one-third of the output in Mexico and still participate in the program.

A third approach is the so-called shelter program. Under this arrangement local contractors assume responsibility for all aspects of the manufacturing operation from site selection to recruitment of personnel

to running the factory. After a predetermined time, however, the US company can buy out the shelter operator at a preset price and take over the business.

A fourth approach is a joint venture with a local partner. This combines a foreign company with financial and manufacturing know-how and a local partner who knows how to market the output. A number of US firms have opted for this approach, including Ford, DuPont, and General Electric (GE). In the latter case GE formed a joint venture with MABE, one of Mexico's largest appliance manufacturers. Since then the two have opened a gas range plant that now produces 800,000 units annually for the US, Canadian, and Mexican markets.

In most cases US MNEs will decide in advance which of these four strategies to implement. However, some firms have discovered that the need for such a decision is unanticipated. Take the example of Pace Foods, which went to Mexico City to film commercials for its Pace Picante Sauce. Since the crew did not want to carry back the jars of Pace's hot sauce that they used in the filming, they told a local store manager to keep the jars and to try to sell them. A few weeks later the company got a call from the manager. He had sold all 350 jars and wanted to know what he should do now. Today Pace has a thriving business selling products in Mexico.

Sources: Adapted from Nancy J. Perry, "What's Powering Mexico's Success," *Fortune,* February 10, 1992, pp. 109–115; Louis Uchitelle, "US Discounters Invade Mexico," *New York Times,* March 12, 1993, pp. C1–C2; Louis S. Richman, "How NAFTA Will Help America," *Fortune,* April 19, 1993, pp. 95–102; Joel Millman, "Nafta Motivates Asian Companies to Invest in Mexico," *Wall Street Journal,* August 14, 1998, p. A13; Joel Millman, "High-Tech Jobs Transfer to Mexico With Surprising Speed," *Wall Street Journal,* April 9, 1998, p. A18; Laurie P. Cohen, "With Help From INS, US Meatpacker Taps Mexican Work Force," *Wall Street Journal,* October 15, 1998, pp. A1, 8.

Doing business in Mexico

A number of strategic approaches are being used to conduct business in Mexico. (See the box "International Business Strategy in Action: Four Common Approaches in Mexico.") Two primary reasons for the success of these approaches are the high quality of the work force and the dramatic improvement in the economy over the early 1990s. MNEs operating in Mexico report that the quality of the work force is excellent. For example, senior-level executives at firms such as Caterpillar, Ford, General Electric, IBM, and Procter & Gamble all report that their Mexican work forces produce high-quality output. Moreover, a Massachusetts Institute of Technology study has named Ford's Mercury Tracer plant in Hermosillo the highest-quality assembly plant in the world. The head of IBM Mexico has stated that "for every dollar you pay a Mexican engineer, you get more from him or her than you'd get in other societies around the world."[21]

At the same time the market for goods and services is growing rapidly. Many MNEs admit that they are not in Mexico because of the low wage rates but because of rapidly growing demand. Despite a high inflation rate and loss of purchasing power, people want to buy consumer goods and to live more like their neighbors to the north. Mexicans are also expressing an interest in high-quality merchandise, resulting in US companies now reducing their reliance on agents and dealers and, instead, opening sales subsidiaries and warehouses to provide direct technical assistance. A good example is Compaq, which opened its first subsidiary in Mexico City in 1990 and was able to double personal computer sales the next year. With a burgeoning population of 99 million and an economy that is growing even faster, Mexico promises to be a major target area for MNEs during the millennium.[22] At the same time, these developments help Mexico to link itself to the triad via the United States.

ACTIVE LEARNING CHECK

Review your answer to Active Learning Case question 5 and make any changes you like. Then compare your answer to the one below.

5. In what way is Mexico's economic progress creating a market for US products?

Mexico's progress under the NAFTA will create a market for US goods in that as the middle and upper classes in the country increase their purchasing power, they will turn more and more to the purchase of US-made goods. From cars to television sets to home appliances, Mexican consumers will be buying products sold by US MNEs. Additionally, the sale of these goods will create increased interest in Mexico by US multinationals, and this will mean even greater opportunities for US firms – and Mexican consumers. The elimination of tariffs under the NAFTA ties Mexico into the North American triad.

Mexico and the double diamond   In order to maintain its economic growth, Mexico must continue developing international competitive strength.[23] This is currently being done by linking to the US market.[24] In particular, MNEs must view this market not just as a source for export, but also as part of the home market (see Figure 15.7). Specifically, this requires:

1. Developing innovative new products and services that simultaneously meet the needs of US and Mexican customers, recognizing that close relationships with demanding US customers should set the pace and style of product development;

2. Drawing on the support industries and infrastructure of both the US and Mexican diamonds, realizing that the US diamond is more likely to possess deeper and more efficient markets for such industries; and

3. Making free and full use of the physical and human resources in both countries.[25]

Mexico is doing this by relying heavily on a series of strategic clusters. The six major ones, in order of importance, are petroleum/chemicals, automotive, housing and household, materials and metals, food and beverage, and semiconductors and computers. The two that are most internationally competitive and provide the best insights into how the Mexican double diamond is used are the petroleum and automotive clusters.

Petroleum cluster   Mexico's petroleum industry accounted for 28 per cent of all exports and 15 per cent of GDP in 1991. The largest firm is state-owned Petroleos Mexicanos (Pemex), which is the world's fifth largest major crude oil producer and fifty-seventh largest firm. The company has a work force of 168,000 employees and assets of $45 billion, including pipelines, refineries, tankers, aircraft, and rail cars. This huge asset base helps to explain why Mexico is a net exporter of energy, principally oil, natural gas, hydraulic power, nuclear and geothermal power, and coal.

The country also has strong petroleum-related industries and infrastructure. At present there are 175 companies operating 490 basic and secondary petrochemical plants throughout the country and employing approximately 130,000 people.

Domestic demand of oil-related products in Mexico has been increasing sharply, forcing Pemex to become considerably more productive. The export market for this oil is expected to remain at current levels for the foreseeable future. The United States will remain Mexico's largest customer as US conservation measures and depressed prices will continue to create demand for oil imports. Moreover, although energy was excluded from NAFTA, recent discussions have centered on US access to Mexican oil through imports and increased opportunities for US technologies in the energy sector. Major US companies such as Arco, Chevron, and Phillips are selling off some of their domestic properties and are looking for exploration opportunities outside the United States, and Mexico is likely to prove a very attractive location. At present turnkey exploration contracts are being used to integrate US expertise and to improve Mexican drilling efficiency, thus reducing the cost of oil. This trend will make Mexico one of the lowest-cost producers in the world.

The commodity nature of the energy business provides little opportunity for Mexico to insulate itself from the cyclical changes of both pricing and demand in this cluster. The real opportunities for Mexico lie in trying to improve efficiencies through (1) liberalizing exploration programs by allowing more efficient foreign drilling contractors to carry out turnkey operations, (2) reducing the cost base by working with the unions to rationalize jobs that are not required, (3) using foreign technologies in areas where Mexican expertise is lacking, (4) allowing greater participation of foreign firms in producing petrochemicals to expand capacity and competitiveness of commodity products to meet domestic and export demand, (5) using foreign MNEs to bring in technology to produce advanced petrochemicals to be used in the US market, and (6) developing alternative, cleaner-burning fuels, such as natural gas and unleaded fuels to reduce reliance on US imports and to comply with international environmental standards.

The potential of this cluster looks promising, even though in recent years Mexican proven reserves have fallen slightly and the international benchmark price for crude oil has dropped to the $20 to $25 per barrel range. The vast unexplored areas of Mexico provide long-term opportunities to continue a strong hydrocarbon-based cluster. Additionally, the proximity of the United States, with its declining proven reserves and increased dependence on imports, will provide Mexico with an export base for improving economies of scale and generating funds for reinvestment in drilling and exploration activities. Thus Mexico's economic progress will be closely linked to the US diamond.

Automotive cluster   The global auto industry is currently undergoing worldwide restructuring. In this process Mexico is emerging as a major car and truck producer.

Since 1986 the industry has grown rapidly. In 1990 total unit production was 820,000, with exports of 276,800, and unofficial figures for 1991 put total output over 1 million units. Now that the North American Free Trade Agreement is a fact, production is expected to top 3 million units by the year 2000. Over the last decade the Big Three US automakers have been expanding their capacities in Mexico while closing plants in the United States and Canada. At the same time European and Japanese firms are investing in Mexico, in an effort to tap such benefits as low-cost labor, low capital cost, proximity to the largest auto market in the world, growth of domestic demand, and accessibility to related support industries.

Mexico has a strong, rich resource base supporting its automotive cluster. More than half the population is under the age of 20, and there is an abundance of young, skilled, adaptable labor. Foreign auto firms are finding that these workers are particularly effective after they have been given training in total quality management, just-in-time inventory, and related concepts. In addition, unions in Mexico are much more cooperative with management than their counterparts to the north. As a result, this resource base is now producing some of the highest-quality cars and trucks in North America, and the Hermosillo plant is widely regarded as the number one auto factory on the continent.

There are also strong supporting industries and a well-developed infrastructure in the automotive cluster. The auto parts industry consists of approximately 400 firms that employ 125,000 workers and supply about 51 per cent of the country's auto parts market. These companies produce for both the domestic and export markets, and many are a result of foreign direct investment by US-based auto part firms. For example, General Motors has component plants in the country as well as financial participation with Mexican auto part companies. Ford Motor has similar arrangements, as do Volkswagen, Nissan, and a host of other foreign firms.

The primary customers for auto output in Mexico are in the local market. However, the percentage of this output that goes for export is increasing every year. In particular, with the signing of the NAFTA, Mexico's accessibility to the largest auto market in the world will increase sharply. This accessibility is especially critical to the country since US protectionism is now threatening to raise import barriers. At the same time Mexican acceptance of US cars manufactured in Mexico is at an all-time high. The same is true in the United States, where the quality reputation of Mexican assembly plants is being felt at the dealer showroom.

The market potential of the automotive cluster is extremely high. There are some problems, however, that will have to be dealt with if the country is to continue increasing its competitiveness.[26] Foremost among these is the need for greater technology. One of the major reasons that Mexican autos are cost efficient is the lack of high automation and robotics. It is unlikely that this trend can continue. In addition, as more and more US and Canadian auto business is shifted to Mexico, it will put major pressure on the NAFTA to ensure that these two countries benefit handsomely from this strategy and that other foreign producers, such as the Japanese and Europeans, do not.

Overall, Mexico's economic future is closely linked to that of the United States and North America. When analyzed in terms of the Porter diamond, some of the country's strategic clusters have already developed worldwide competitive strength. During the 1990s the petroleum and automotive clusters have proven to be highly competitive. It is likely that before the turn of the century Mexico will have effectively linked these industries into the North American market and will be a major economic force in energy and automotive products. It is equally likely that the country will begin making major inroads into other areas such as semiconductors and computers. As in its automotive success, this development is less a result of technological prowess than of favorable factor conditions, related and supporting industries, demand conditions, and the structure and rivalry of the firms. As a result, Mexico will find that it can link its diamond framework with that of the United States and in the process become a worldwide competitor in still other areas. Porter's diamond framework will prove to be a useful paradigm.[27]

SUMMARY

Key points

1. Canada, with approximately 31 million people and a gross domestic product of about $721 billion annually, is the single largest trading partner of the United States. There has been a move toward privatization in the past few years as well as toward deregulation. As in the United States, the government attempts to promote competition, and in recent years the Free Trade Agreement (FTA) between the United States and Canada has recognized the high degree of trade between the two countries.

2. Financial institutions are similar to those in the United States, as are labor relations practices. However, a much larger percentage of Canadian employees are unionized, and the unions have been major opponents of the FTA.

3. The FTA will eventually eliminate most trade barriers between the United States and Canada. This should help to open up Canada to more economic development. At the same time the government welcomes foreign investment, and there are a wide variety of incentive programs that are designed to encourage such investments.

4. The approaches to doing business in Canada are similar to those in the United States. However, there are some important regulatory differences. The chapter identified and discussed both.

5. Mexico has the strongest economy in Latin America and its close business ties to the United States, as reflected by imports, exports, and US FDI, bode well for its future. The potential of the free trade agreement between the two countries and the growth of the *maquiladora* industry are helping Mexico to link its economy to that of the United States. Mexico's petrochemical and automotive clusters are key industries in this linkage and are likely to become world-class competitors in their respective areas.

Key terms

- Competition Act
- Canada Labor Code
- Investment Canada Act (ICA)
- North American Free Trade Agreement (NAFTA)
- United States–Canada Free Trade Agreement (FTA)
- Latin American Integration Association (LAIA)
- Mercosur
- Andean Common Market (Ancom)
- Enterprise for the Americas

Review and discussion questions

1. How high is the Canadian standard of living? Of what value is this information to a company that is interested in doing business in Canada?

2. Is the Competition Act of any concern to US firms, given that the FTA has eliminated most trade restrictions? Explain.

3. What do companies seeking to set up businesses in Canada need to know about labor relations in that country? Identify and discuss three areas of importance.

4. What are the most important provisions of the Free Trade Act and how do they affect US firms doing business in Canada?

5. Are there any restrictions on foreign investments in Canada? Identify and describe two of them.

6. What should a firm seeking to enter the Canadian market know about marketing practices there? Identify and describe three practices.

7. How good are franchise opportunities in Canada? Explain.

8. Why is Mexico doing so well economically? Identify two developments that have been particularly helpful in bringing this about.

9. What is the purpose of the LAIA? Of what value is the organization to its members?

10. How might the creation of an "Enterprise for the Americas" impact on the LAIA and Ancom? Give an example.

11. How is Mexico using its petroleum cluster to link itself to the North American triad?

12. How is Mexico using its automotive cluster to link itself to the North American triad?

13. Why are these linkages to the North American triad likely to be economically advantageous to Mexico? Cite two reasons.

REAL CASES

BOMBARDIER'S PLANES AND TRAINS

In 1942 the dreams of a budding young Quebec entrepreneur came true with the incorporation of L'Auto-Neige Bombardier, the world's first snowmobile manufacturer. Although the mechanic-turned-industrialist Joseph Armand Bombardier had great plans for his innovative transportation inventions, he could never have foreseen the course his company would take in the next 50 years.

Today Bombardier is one of the world's top manufacturers of transportation products with yearly revenues of over $5 billion and 30,000 employees. Having begun with snowmobile production, Bombardier is now among the world leaders in commuter and general transportation trains, as well as transport vehicles for industrial and military use, sailboats, motorcycles, and, more recently, smaller aircraft. This extension into numerous other industries has transformed Bombardier from a once small-town Quebec company into a global market competitor and leader with 90 per cent of its total business now conducted outside of Canada.

Bombardier's success is mostly due to the industrious and timely business instincts of company CEO Laurent Beaudoin, who in the past 30 years has followed a strategy of market entry and product improvement through acquisition, instead of relying strictly on R&D. As a result, the company has managed to produce the most technically advanced, innovative and reliable products

▶

on the market, thereby gaining substantial market share in many industries, especially with its rubberwheeled subway car, sold to New York City in the 1980s.

This strategy has been exemplified with Bombardier's entry into the aerospace industry with the acquisition of Canadair in 1986, 12 years after diversifying into the transportation equipment business. The Canadair purchase brought the company a large pool of human resources and technical expertise which has been applied to develop such "in-house" products as the twin-engine Challenger Business Jet. As a result, Bombardier all of a sudden held lead positions in numerous niche markets which ensured ongoing relations with such manufacturing giants as Boeing and MacDonnell-Douglas. This acquisition quickly resulted in numerous contracts for CF-18 fighters from the Canadian government and contracts for Airbus components from both British Aerospace and France's Aerospatiale.

Further acquisition was a logical step for the company, and by acquiring Northern Ireland's Short Brothers, Bombardier extended itself firmly into the European market as a supplier and manufacturer of aerospace technology. Then at the outset of the 1990s purchases of both Learjet out of Wichita, Kansas and Boeing's deHavilland, propelled diversification into regional jets, and turboprop aircraft. Finally, production of the first-of-its-kind 50-passenger Canadair Regional Jet signified Bombardier's full-fledged entry into the airline industry. With already the bulk of its profit coming from this industry and the shared knowhow, technology, resources and markets of all of these companies pooled under one roof, Bombardier is ripe to become a major player in the aerospace industry through the millennium.

1. How would you describe Bombardier's strategic approach to the aerospace industry and why?

2. The purchase of Canadair opened Bombardier up to a whole new market. Explain why the actions the company has taken since then have been wise business decisions.

3. Where do you foresee Bombardier in the future of the aerospace industry?

Sources: Rita Kolselka, "Let's Make a Deal," *Forbes*, April 27, 1992, pp. 62–63; Brenda Dalglish, "Tycoons in Progress," *Maclean's*, July 6, 1992, pp. 64–65; Christopher J. Chipello and G. Pierre Goad, "Bombardier, Bolstered by Acquisition, Enters New Phase," *The Wall Street Journal*, September 17, 1992, p. B4; Clyde H. Farnsworth, "Bombardier Snares DeHavilland," *The New York Times*, January 26, 1992, p. 12; Clyde H. Farnsworth, "Bombardier Returns to Earth," *The New York Times*, December 28, 1991, pp. L33, L35.

SOUTH OF THE BORDER, MEXICO WAY

Many opponents of NAFTA argued that the agreement would lead to the export of US jobs to Mexico, with a resulting decline in gross national product (GNP). Economists, however, reported that the agreement would help to save US jobs and GNP would rise by $30 billion annually once the treaty was fully implemented. Recent research also found that the first five years of NAFTA had improved growth and efficiency in all three members of NAFTA. Certainly, MNEs in the motor vehicle and parts industry and the telecommunications industry agreed with the economists and have already formulated strategies to address these impending changes.[27]

The US motor vehicle and parts industry expects to see some jobs go to Mexico. Moreover, the export of vehicles from foreign-owned factories in Mexico doubled in the three years after NAFTA. However, prior to NAFTA, Mexican government regulations forced US automakers to buy Mexican parts, which in many cases did not meet global standards. This led Mexican subsidiaries of US automakers to run plants at less-than-maximum efficiency levels. The government also forced the Big Three car companies to export more than they imported into Mexico. NAFTA has allowed companies to act regionally instead of on a country-by-country basis and to reorganize more production efficiently across North America. In an unexpected surge of events, some of the manufacturing previously assigned to Mexico is being brought back into the United States. For example, Ford relocated its production of Thunderbirds and Mercury Cougars from Cuautitlan to its assembly plant in Lorain, Ohio. At the same time US auto suppliers are doing better since the NAFTA requires 62.5 per cent of a vehicle's content to originate in North America. This means that foreign suppliers in Asia and Europe are losing out to regional, high-quality firms such as TRW and Dana. So NAFTA is proving to be a boon to the US motor and auto parts industry.

Telecommunications is another industry where US firms are doing very well. Annual US telecommunications exports to Mexico are now in excess of $961.2 million, and Telmex, the previously state-owned phone company, is 10 per cent owned by Southwestern Bell. By the year 2000 Telmex will have 35 million phones wired in an all-digital network, up from 12 million in 1993, and US companies are likely to supply much of this new equipment. At the same time some business customers in Mexico feel that it is taking too long for Telmex to provide them the service they need. So they are purchasing private networks that carry voice, data, and images by satellite. Scientific-

Atlanta, a Georgia-based firm, is the market leader in this area and has been able to land a series of large contracts for installing communication systems, including those for Cifra, the country's largest retailer, and for the Mexican Navy. Other companies that are likely to benefit from the growing market include McCaw, Cantel, and Motorola. As a result, US telecommunications firms appear to have found a lucrative market just south of the border.

1. Why is the NAFTA likely to be of benefit for US MNEs doing business in Mexico? Identify and describe one reason.

2. How might the NAFTA help the United States to deal with its own unemployment problem?

3. Can linking its trade to the US market help Mexico's economic growth? Why or why not?

Sources: Adapted from Louis S. Richman, "How NAFTA Will Help America," *Fortune*, April 19, 1993, pp. 95–102; Stephen Baker, Geri Smith, and Elizabeth Weinger, "The Mexican Worker," *Business Week*, April 19, 1993, pp. 84–92; Geri Smith and Douglas Harbrecht, "The Moment of 'Truth' for Mexico," *Business Week*, June 28, 1993, pp. 44–45; Alan M. Rugman and John Kirton, "Multinational Enterprise Strategy and the NAFTA Trade and Environment Regime", *Journal of World Business*, vol. 33, no. 4, December 1998, pp. 438–454; Alan M. Rugman, John Kirton and Julie Soloway, *Environmental Regulations and Corporate Strategy* (Oxford: Oxford University Press, 1999); http://www.ford.com; http://www.telmex.com.mx/.

ENDNOTES

1. Christopher J. Chipello and Roger Ricklefs, "Low Productivity Clouds Canada's Competitiveness, Living Standards," *Wall Street Journal*, February 9, 1999, p. A19.

2. Tamsin Carlisle, "Calgary Becomes Outpost On High-Tech Frontier," *Wall Street Journal*, March 24, 1998, p. A19.

3. Also see Rosanna Tamburri, "Canada Considers New Stand Against American Culture," *Wall Street Journal*, February 4, 1998, p. A18; Roger Ricklefs, "Canada Fights to Fend Off American Tastes and Tunes," *Wall Street Journal*, September 24, 1998, pp. B1, 8.

4. Barbara Wickens, "Getting the GST of It," *Maclean's*, September 10, 1990, pp. 40–43.

5. For more on the GST, see Joseph E. Payne, Jr., "Canada's New Goods and Services Tax Has Implications for US Exporters," *Business America*, August 13, 1990, p. 12.

6. See Rosanna Tamburri, "Canadians Clash Over Cost of Diversity," *Wall Street Journal*, April 1, 1998, p. A15.

7. For additional insights into the role of Quebec in US–Canadian economic ties, see Thane Peterson and William J. Holstein, "How a Freer Quebec Could Reshape the Continent," *Business Week*, July 9, 1990, pp. 40–43.

8. For a contrast see Christopher J. Chipello, "Francophones Struggle Outside Quebec," *Wall Street Journal*, February 26, 1998, p. A12.

9. E. Kaye Fulton and Nancy Wood, "A 'Reasonable Limit,'" *Maclean's*, December 17, 1990, pp. 20–21.

10. Shona McKay, "Narrowing the Gap," *Maclean's*, January 8, 1990, pp. 31–32.

11. Todd Mason, "Now Tariffs Can't Fall Fast Enough," *Business Week*, October 23, 1989, p. 80.

12. *Summary of the US–Canada Free Trade Agreement* (Washington, DC: US Department of Commerce, International Trade Administration, 1988), p. 12.
13. Ibid., pp. 10–11.
14. *Marketing in Canada* (Washington, DC: US Department of Commerce), International Marketing Information Series, Overseas Business Reports, OBR 88–05, May 1988, p. 8.
15. Ibid., p. 5.
16. Also, see Stephen Baker, "Mexico: Can Zedillo Stem the Tide of Crisis?" *Business Week*, April 18, 1994, p. 60.
17. Also, see Bob Ortega, "Some Mexicans Charge North in NAFTA's Wake," *Wall Street Journal*, February 22, 1994, pp. B1, B5.
18. Len J. Trevino, "Strategic Responses of Mexican Managers to Economic Reform," *Business Horizons*, May–June 1998, pp. 73–80.
19. Keith Bradsher, "US Trade Official Talks Tougher on Pact," *New York Times*, March 17, 1993, pp. C1, C2.
20. Some of the material in this section can be found in "Latin American Introduction," *ILT Latin America*, July 1991, pp. 1–13.
21. "The Business of the American Hemisphere," *Economist*, August 24, 1991, pp. 37–38.
22. Also see Rick Wartzman, "In the Wake of Nafta, A Family Firm Sees Business Go South," *Wall Street Journal*, February 23, 1999, pp. A1, 10.
23. Jonathan Friedland, "Mexico Is Hit Despite Belt-Tightening," *Wall Street Journal*, September 14, 1998, p. A27.
24. Richard M. Hodgetts, "Porter's Diamond and Framework in a Mexican Context," *Management International Review*, vol. 33, Special ed., 1993, pp. 41–54.
25. J. R. D'Cruz and Alan M. Rugman, *New Concepts for Canadian Competitiveness* (Toronto: Kodak Canada, 1992).
26. Elisabeth Malkin, "Holding Off Asia's Assault," *Business Week*, April 13, 1991, pp. 44–45.
27. Alan M. Rugman and Michael Gestrin, "The Strategic Response of Multinational Enterprises to NAFTA," *Columbia Journal of World Business*, vol. 28, no. 4, 1993, pp. 18–29.

ADDITIONAL BIBLIOGRAPHY

Averyt, William F. "Canadian and Japanese Foreign Investment Screening," *Columbia Journal of World Business*, vol. 21, no. 4 (Winter 1986).

Batres, Robertos E. "A Mexican View of the North American Free Trade Agreement," *Columbia Journal of World Business*, vol. 26, no. 2 (Summer 1991).

Beamish, Paul W.; Craig, Ron; and McLellan, Kerry. "The Performance Characteristics of Canadian Versus UK Exporters in Small and Medium Sized Firms," *Management International Review*, vol. 33, no. 2 (Second Quarter 1993).

Birkinshaw, Julian and Hood, Neil. "An Empirical Study of Development Process in Foreign Owned Subsidiaries in Canada and Scotland," *Management International Review*, vol. 37, no. 4 (1997).

Crookell, Harold. "Managing Canadian Subsidiaries in a Free Trade Environment," *Sloan Management Review*, vol. 29, no. 1 (Fall 1987).

Eden, Lorraine (ed.) *Multinationals in North America.* Calgary: University of Calgary Press, 1994.

Finnerty, Joseph E.; Owers, James; and Creran, Francis J. "Foreign Exchange Forecasting and Leading Economic Indicators: The US–Canadian Experience," *Management International Review*, vol. 27, no. 2 (Second Quarter 1987).

Gillispie, Kate, and Teegen, Hildy J. "Market Liberalization and International Alliance Formation: The Mexican Paradigm," *Columbia Journal of World Business*, vol. 30, no. 4 (Winter 1995).

Globerman, Steven and Walker, Michael (eds.). *Assessing NAFTA: A Trinational Analysis.* Vancouver, BC: The Fraser Institute, 1993.

Hecht, Laurence and Morici, Peter. "Managing Risks in Mexico," *Harvard Business Review*, vol. 71, no. 4 (July/August 1993).

Hodgetts, Richard. "Porters's Diamond Framework in a Mexican Context," *Management International Review*, vol. 33, no. 2 (Second Quarter 1993).

Hufbauer, Gary Clyde and Schott, Jeffrey J. *North American Free Trade: Issues and Recommendations*, Institute for International Economics, Washington, DC, 1992.

Hufbauer, Gary Clyde and Schott, Jeffrey J. *NAFTA: An Assessment.* Washington, DC: Institute for International Economics, 1993.

Hung, G. L. "Strategic Business Alliances Between Canada and the Newly Industrialized Countries of Pacific Asia," *Management International Review*, vol. 32, no. 4 (Fourth Quarter 1992).

Janisch, H. N. "Canadian Telecommunications in a Free Trade Era," *Columbia Journal of World Business*, vol. 24, no. 1 (Spring 1989).

Kamath, Shyam J. and Tilley, J. Roderick. "Canadian International Banking and the Debt Crisis," *Columbia Journal of World Business*, vol. 22, no. 4 (Winter 1987).

Kaynak, Erdener. "A Cross Regional Comparison of Export Performance of Firms in Two Canadian Regions," *Management International Review*, vol. 32, no. 2 (Second Quarter 1992).

Martinez, Zaida L. and Ricks, David A. "Multinational Parent Companies' Influence over Human Resource Decisions of Affiliates: US Firms in Mexico," *Journal of International Business Studies*, vol. 20, no. 3 (Fall 1989).

Neale, Charles W.; Shipley, David D.; and Dodds, J. Colin. "The Countertrade Experience of British and Canadian Firms," *Management International Review*, vol. 31, no. 1 (First Quarter 1991).

Nichols, Nancy A. "The Monterrey Group: A Mexican Keiretsu," *Harvard Business Review*, vol. 71, no. 5 (September/October 1993).

Rugman, Alan M. *Multinationals in Canada: Theory, Performance and Economic Impact* (Boston: Martinus Nijhoff, 1980).

Rugman, Alan M. "The Role of Multinational Enterprises in US–Canadian Economic Relations," *Columbia Journal of World Business*, vol. 21, no. 2 (Summer 1986).

Rugman, Alan M. *Outward Bound: Canadian Direct Investment in the United States* (Toronto: Canadian–American Committee, and Prentice-Hall of Canada, 1987).

Rugman, Alan M. *Multinationals and Canada–United States Free Trade* (Columbia: University of South Carolina Press, 1990).

Rugman, Alan M. "A Canadian Perspective on NAFTA," *The International Executive*, vol. 36, no. 1 (January–February 1994).

Rugman, Alan M. (ed.) *Multinationals and NAFTA* (Columbia, SC: University of South Carolina Press, 1994).

Rugman, Alan M. and D'Cruz, Joseph R. "The 'Double Diamond' Model of International Competitiveness: The Canadian Experience," *Management International Review*, vol. 33, no. 2 (Second Quarter 1993).

Rugman, Alan M. and Gestrin, Michael. "The Investment Provisions of NAFTA," in Steven Globerman and Michael Walker (eds.) *Assessing NAFTA: A Trinational Analysis* (Vancouver, BC: The Fraser Institute, 1993).

Rugman, Alan M. and Gestrin, Michael. "The Strategic Response of Multinational Enterprises to NAFTA," *Columbia Journal of World Business*, vol. 28, no. 4 (Winter 1993).

Rugman, Alan M., Kirton, John and Soloway, Julie A. *Environmental Regulations and Corporate Strategy: A NAFTA Perspective* (Oxford: Oxford University Press, 1999).

Rugman, Alan M. and Verbeke, Alain. "Multinational Corporate Strategy and the Canada–US Free Trade Agreement," *Management International Review*, vol. 30, no. 3 (Third Quarter 1990).

Rugman, Alan M. and Verbeke, Alain (eds.) *Research in Global Strategic Management: Vol. 1: International Business Research for the Twenty-First Century; Canada's New Research Agenda* (Greenwich, Conn.: JAI Press, 1990).

Rugman, Alan M. and Verbeke, Alain. "Foreign Subsidiaries and Multinational Strategic Management: An Extension and Correction of Porter's Single Diamond Framework," *Management International Review*, vol. 33, no. 2 (Second Quarter 1993).

Sanderson, Susan Walsh and Hayes, Robert H. "Mexico – Opening Ahead of Eastern Europe," *Harvard Business Review*, vol. 68, no. 5 (September/October 1990).

Seringhaus, F. H. Rolf and Botschen, Guenther. "Cross-National Comparison of Export Promotion Services: The Views of Canadian and Austrian Companies," *Journal of International Business Studies*, vol. 22, no. 1 (First Quarter 1991).

Solocha, Andrew; Soskin, Mark D.; and Kasoff, Mark J. "Determinants of Foreign Direct Investment: A Case of Canadian Direct Investment in the United States," *Management International Review*, vol. 30, no. 4 (Fourth Quarter 1990).

Spencer, William J. and Grindley, Peter. "SEMATECH After Five Years: High Technology Consortia and US Competitiveness," *California Management Review*, vol. 35, no. 4 (Summer 1993).

Ulgado, Francis M. "Location Characteristics of Manufacturing Investments in the US: A Comparison of American and Foreign-based Firms," *Management International Review*, vol. 36, no. 1 (1996).

Willard, Kristen L. "Do Taxes Level the Playing Field? How US Tax Policy Affects the Investment Decisions of Foreign Affiliates in the United States," *Columbia Journal of World Business*, vol. 29, no. 4 (Winter 1994).

CHAPTER 19

Doing Business in Non-Triad Nations

OBJECTIVES OF THE CHAPTER

More than 100 nations in the world are not triad members. How do they conduct international business? In order to build a global operation from the base of a smaller country, there must be access to the markets of at least one of the triad blocs. This chapter develops a general framework on the need for such market access. It also examines a number of representative non-triad countries as examples of how these general principles apply to any non-triad country. The specific objectives of this chapter are to:

1. **Discuss** why all non-triad countries need market access to a triad bloc in order to build a global business.

2. **Explain** the general principles of triad market access and relate this to the international business needs of non-triad countries.

3. **Describe** the major steps being taken in non-triad countries to develop successful global industries, especially in terms of the double diamond framework.

4. **Relate** how well select non-triad nations are doing in their attempts to establish economic linkages to triad countries.

ACTIVE LEARNING CASE

Economic progress among the smaller players

Economic growth in the millennium will not be limited to triad countries. A number of smaller nations, including those in Latin America, Eastern Europe, and Asia, are developing strong trade and investment ties to triad nations and are beginning to correct many of their economic problems.

Mexico is a good example. Over the past five years the economy has done so well that triad countries such as the United States and Japan are setting up operations there in order to tap the local market. Other Latin American countries such as Chile and Brazil are emulating the success of the Mexicans by privatizing industry and encouraging foreign investment in industries such as airlines, banks, oil companies, electric firms, copper mines, steelmaking, and communications. China is following a similar pattern of promoting economic development. In the southeast provinces of the country the economy is booming. Although only 1.5 per cent of the people live here, the area accounts for nearly 5 per cent of total industrial output and 10 per cent of exports. In fact, the economy in this region is so competitive that businesspeople in other Pacific countries, as well as the United States, are having goods manufactured here for sale back home. For example, Tomei International Ltd of Hong Kong, one of the world's largest producers of low- and medium-end audio equipment, has 90 per cent of its output produced in southeast China. These products are sold to such well-known firms as Emerson Radio, Panasonic, Philips, Radio Shack, Wal-Mart, K-Mart, and Sears. Factory wages in China, which run $60 to $80 monthly, are but one-tenth of that paid in Hong Kong.

Multinationals are also turning to non-triad countries in order to tap intellectual talent. Countries such as South Korea, Taiwan, and Singapore are turning out an increasing number of engineers and technically trained people, who are quickly snapped up by MNEs. Not only are the costs of hiring and retaining these people less than they are in triad countries, but these individuals are proving to be very effective in designing and carrying out complex engineering tasks. China is having similar success.

In Russia and Eastern European countries such as Poland, economic progress is being promoted through privatization. This is taking two routes. One is that of turning state-owned firms over to the employees, who in turn now both own and manage the enterprises. The other is bringing in foreign investors as part of joint venture arrangements. In both cases inefficient government operations are being run by private interests that are often linked to triad countries.

Sources: Adapted from Ford S. Worthy, "Where Capitalism Thrives in China, *Fortune*, March 9, 1992, pp. 71–75; Andrew Tanzer, "Cantonese Conquistadores," *Forbes*, March 2, 1992, pp. 56–58; Stephen Baker, Elizabeth Weinger, and Mike Zellner, "Can Latin America 'Move from the Third World to the First'?" *Business Week*, October 21, 1991, pp. 54–56; Ford S. Worthy, "Tapping Asia's Brainpower," *Fortune*, October 7, 1991, pp. 163–165; Stephen Baker and S. Lynne Walker, "The American Dream Is Alive and Well – In Mexico," *Business Week*, September 30, 1991, pp. 102, 105; and John Pearson et al., "Many Third World Players Are Going World-Class," *Business Week*, July 12, 1993, p. 56.

1. **How are Chile and Brazil using foreign investment to link themselves to triad countries?**

2. **In what way is China linking itself to the triad and other industrially developing countries?**

3. **Why is Asian brainpower so attractive to multinational investors from the West?**

4. **How is Russia promoting privatization? How can triad MNEs help in this process?**

5. **How is Poland moving toward privatization? Describe two developments that have been beneficial in this process.**

INTRODUCTION

Many countries are relatively small and depend on international trade and investment to maintain their economic growth. As seen in Chapters 3 and 15, countries that are not members of the triad must develop connections to these trading blocs if they hope to prosper internationally. A non-triad country that fails to do this will find itself uncompetitive and be forced to erect inefficient trade barriers or to see its industry overwhelmed by foreign imports. In this chapter select non-triad nations are considered, including Chile, Brazil, China, India, South Korea, Singapore, Australia, India, Russia, and Poland.

Although each country's performance reflects a unique response to a particular set of conditions, a number of common developments pervade the economies of these non-triad nations. Privatization,[1] the attracting of foreign investment, and strategies that are designed to help the country link to the triad are three of the most important. These are the reasons that they were chosen for consideration.

MARKET ACCESS TO THE TRIAD

International business operations in the twenty-first century are going to be even more challenging than in the past. One reason is the emergence of the three strong trade and investment blocs. These are complex arrangements with varying degrees of economic trade liberalization and protectionism that are inherent in their institutional and political structures. Both globalization and sovereignty dimensions are represented by the triad. The EU is the most politically integrated, in terms of institutional structures, and the Japanese-based bloc is the least. The NAFTA is a free trade agreement, not a common market, but the NAFTA contains provisions for the accession of Latin American and Caribbean and Central American nations, and it may then evolve into stronger political linkages like the EU model.

To develop global industries, non-triad nations need both trade and investment from the triad nations and also access to the markets of at least one of the triads. This implies that the focus of business strategy in a smaller, non-triad, nation should be to secure inward triad investment and market access for exports to a triad bloc. This can be done by direct business contact, but it is helped and reinforced by formal linkages arranged by the governments. As demonstrated in the last chapter, both Canada and Mexico have already gone this route.

In Chapter 2 we identified "clusters" of nations that are making such arrangements with triad blocs. In general, the NAFTA is the basis for a trading bloc of the Americas; the EU is the locus for Eastern European and African nations; Japan is the hub for many Asian businesses. Some smaller, non-triad nations may attempt to open the doors to two triad markets. For example, both South Korea and Taiwan have equal trade and investment with the United States and Japan. Australia still has a large amount of trade with Britain and the EU, but its trade with Japan and other Asian nations is increasing rapidly. Indeed, the geographical basis of the triad serves to reinforce the dependence of neighboring nations on their dominant regional economic partner. We begin our consideration by examining countries in the closest proximity to the United States.

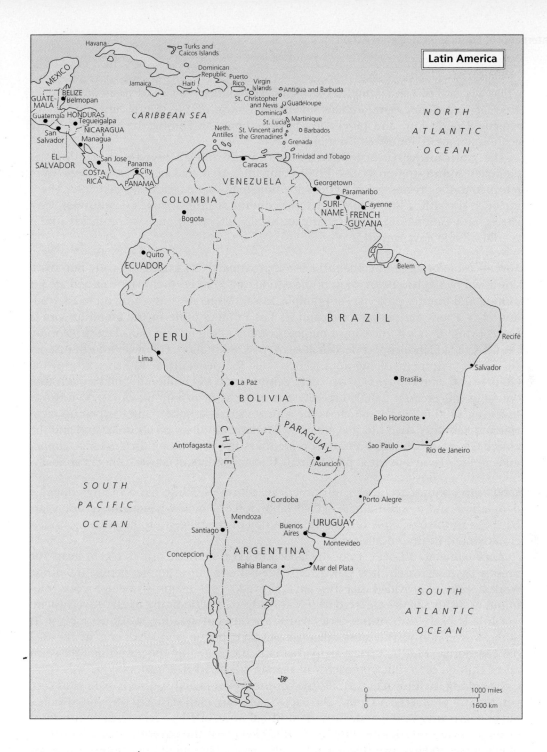

LATIN AMERICA

Latin America (see accompanying map) is a rapidly growing region. Mexico's linkage to the North American triad via the NAFTA will be extremely helpful, and other Latin American countries will also be following this lead. Chile and Brazil are examples.

Chile

Chile has one of Latin America's strongest economies. The gross domestic product grew at a 4–5 per cent annual rate during most of the 1980s, unemployment remained fairly low, and purchasing power improved. During the early 1990s the economic picture improved even more.

The government has a positive attitude toward foreign investment. During the Pinochet administration (1974–1990) companies that had been nationalized were returned to the private sector. At the same time many state businesses were sold. These included the airline LAN-Chile, Entel (telecommunications), Enaex (explosives), CAP (steel), and Laboratorio Chile (pharmaceuticals). Privatization has continued under the Ruiz-Tagle government.

MNE investment   FDI in Chile had been approximately $1 billion annually but saw a slowdown by the late 1990s. Most of these funds are from US multinationals and are for mining and forestry projects. For example, Exxon Minerals is investing up to $1.2 billion over a ten-year period to expand its Los Bronces mine in the mountains near Santiago and to boost fine-copper output. Cominco Resources of Canada is developing the Quebrada Blanca copper deposit at a cost of $280 million. Foresta e Industrial Santa Fe, a joint venture involving Royal Dutch Shell (60 per cent), Scott Paper Worldwide (20 per cent), and Citicorp (20 per cent), is investing $350 million to build a plant that annually will produce 250,000 metric tons of eucalyptus pulp for export. PepsiCo is investing $100 million to purchase the country's largest bottler and to open up Pizza Hut and Kentucky Fried Chicken outlets in Santiago. Outokumpo Oy of Finland and the Luksic Group of Santiago and London are investing $60 million in the Lince copper mine in the Atacama desert to produce 20,000 metric tonnes of copper cathodes annually.

Labor   In contrast to other Latin American countries, Chile has a highly educated population and a well-trained, skilled labor force. Unemployment in recent years has been in the 6 to 7 per cent range, with one of the biggest problems being under-employment in the middle class.

Approximately 12 per cent of the labor force is unionized, and in recent years the unions have increased their power. New regulations, for example, permit indefinite work stoppages, provided that they are approved by the majority of employees. Minimum monthly salaries are fixed by law and adjusted periodically by the government.

Chile is likely to continue as a favorite investment area for MNEs because of its attractive economy. The gross domestic product for the mid-1990s was in the 6–7 per cent range. Multinationals are particularly motivated by the government's assurances that its economic approach will remain free-market driven.

In linking itself to triad nations, the country relies heavily on such exports as copper, forestry products, and fruit.[2] The nation's primary markets are in the United States, Japan, Germany, Brazil, and the United Kingdom. Chile also relies heavily on most of these same countries for imports. So it is likely that the government will continue to encourage foreign investment and to nurture a market-oriented economy as it works to link itself to all three triad members.[3]

Brazil

In recent years the government of Brazil has launched sweeping economic liberalization and reform.[4] Most nontariff import barriers have been removed and the country is speeding efforts toward trade integration, most notably with Argentina. Additionally, the government's attitude toward free enterprise has been stronger than that in most developing countries.

At the same time, however, the economy has been encountering a host of problems.[5] In particular, Brazil has been running a trade deficit and the 1999 decision to devalue the currency[6] has produced many negative results including high interest rates and a slowing of economic growth. Firms such as Volkswagen, Fiat, Mercedes-Benz, and General Motors have sharply cut back their auto production because of the difficulty of competing with a weakened currency.[7] In turn the country's problems are now having a impact on its Mercosur partners: Argentina, Paraguay, and Uruguay.[8]

MNE investment   There have been hundreds of new investments and expansions in Brazil in recent years. Mercedes-Benz has completed a five-year, $500 million investment in new lines of trucks and buses. Ferruzi of Italy spent $250 million to buy a large local cleaning products company. Michelin put $140 million into tire plant expansions. The Bank of Boston invested $75 million in computerization and telecommunications. MNE-controlled firms dominate a number of manufacturing sectors, including automobiles, electrical and communications products, large computers, pharmaceuticals, and nonferrous metals.

Labor   Multinationals report that the quality of the Brazilian labor force is quite good. However, many firms find that they have to offer remedial education as well as regular training because of the country's poor educational system. A shortage of managerial talent has increased the competition for hiring at the management level and thus has driven up salaries. However, labor costs are low in comparison to those of industrial nations.

The 1988 constitution gives workers freedom to strike, restricted only by requirements such as protection of essential services and minimum quorums for strike votes. Many trade unions are highly politicized and work stoppages have become common.

The government has been slow to reduce inflation, the deficit, and the size of the federal bureaucracy. Yet because of its huge market, the country continues to be of interest to MNEs. At the same time it is particularly interested in linking itself to both the United States and the EU markets via increased trade.

ACTIVE LEARNING CHECK

Review your answer to Active Learning Case question 1 and make any changes you like. Then compare your answer to the one below.

1. How are Chile and Brazil using foreign investment to link themselves to triad countries?

Both countries are attracting foreign investors by allowing them to buy local companies as well as to set up their own operations for doing business locally. In both cases the countries are establishing a linkage by promoting an inflow of capital and other investments. This is different from the strategy of creating industry clusters that are capable of developing world-class companies. Chile and Brazil are doing the next best thing: attracting foreign investment into their own countries.

INTERNATIONAL BUSINESS STRATEGY IN ACTION

Looking for new opportunities in Asia

Asia is becoming a favorite target for many US multi-nationals. Between 1987 and 1999 US investment in East Asia skyrocketed to nearly $6 billion. DuPont intends to invest $3 billion here during the current decade, and after only five years onsite, Apple Computer has established ties with over 100 Asian software developers, including a host of firms in Hong Kong that are providing programming for its product line. Colgate-Palmolive has moved into Thailand and taken 40 per cent of the shampoo market away from the Japanese while Pizza Hut and Kentucky Fried Chicken are signing up dozens of local franchisees in the region. Sheraton, Hyatt, and Holiday Inns are expanding into the area, and Citibank is offering a wide variety of services, including automated teller machines, credit cards, and home equity loans; and Starbucks is planning a major expansion into China.

Motorola has gone further than most. The company has a $400 million complex in Hong Kong, in addition to a dozen other factories in nine countries, including China and Singapore. It is also the region's leading supplier of high-end walkie-talkies and digital cordless phones. No firm in this geographic market can rival its lead in cellular-communication subscribers.

Motorola's success story began a decade ago when the company realized that Asia would be critical to its growth. Management split its regional semiconductor headquarters in Tokyo, moving the base for the rest of Asia to Hong Kong. At the same time Singapore became the primary area for most of Motorola's telecommunications business. This restructuring helped the firm to focus on its primary competitors in Taiwan, South Korea, and Hong Kong. The company uses local talent in important positions. The result of this policy has been some major breakthroughs. For example, engineers in the firm's Malaysia factory designed the Handi-Talkie, a miniature two-way radio that has now sold over 1.5 million units. Meanwhile, personnel in the Hong Kong factory are developing chips for palmtop computers and pocket organizers about the size of a calculator and that cost less than $300. At the present time Sony, Sharp, and Casio dominate this market, but Motorola hopes to leap over their technology and to offer a better quality, less expensive unit. If the company continues its progress, Motorola will be one of the top few competitors in east Asia and is likely to increase its annual sales far above the $1 billion that it currently generates here.

Sources: Adapted from Amy Borrus, Pete Engardio, and Teresa Albor, "Carving Out a Place in the Pacific Century," *Business Week*, November 11, 1991, pp. 64–68; Pete Engardio et al., "How Motorola Took Asia by the Tail," *Business Week*, November 11, 1991, p. 68; Sally Stewart, Michael Tow Cheung, and David W. K. Yeung, "The Latest Asian Newly Industrialized Economy Emerges: The South China Economic Community," *Columbia Journal of World Business*, Summer 1992, pp. 30–37; Sheryl WuDunn, "Booming China Is a Dream Market for West," *New York Times*, February 15, 1993, pp. 1, 6; Pete Engardio, "Motorola in China: A Great Leap Forward," *Business Week*, May 17, 1993, pp. 58–59; Joanne Lee-Young, "Starbucks' Expansion in China Is Slated," *Wall Street Journal*, October 5, 1998, p. A27C.

ASIA AND THE PACIFIC

Pacific nations constitute a huge geographic area and, in some cases, a rapidly growing market.[9] This helps to explain why, despite the economic slowdown in Asia that began in the late 1990s, many US firms are targeting these markets. The box "International Business Strategy in Action: Looking for New Opportunities" provides some examples of firms that are finding that joint ventures and deals with Asian partners can help them to weather the strong competition they are facing from other foreign competitors.

In establishing successful operations, MNEs use guidelines that are similar to those employed in Japan. These include (1) have a local partner and get to know the

individual,[10] (2) put a strong and enduring emphasis on the quality of output, (3) tailor output to the specific needs of the local market, (4) rely heavily on nationals to market the product, and (5) have a solid understanding of local service requirements.[11]

China

China (see accompanying map) has the largest population in the world, and in recent years the nation's economy has done much better than casual observers realize.[12] Exports have outpaced imports and inflation, which at the beginning of the 1990s stood at over 20 per cent, dropped to 10 per cent by 1999.[13] At the same time annual GDP growth slowed from its rapid 10 per cent annual rate in the mid-1990s, but still remained a healthy 7.8 per cent.[14] Today the country's GDP is approximately $4 trillion and GDP per capita is in the range of $3,000.

At the same time the government has been moving toward privatization and encouraging greater entrepreneurial efforts.[15] Additionally, the International Monetary Fund estimates that China's GDP is far greater than commonly believed. Today the country's economy is just slightly smaller than Japan's and approximately half that of the United States. Clearly, China is a major economic power.[16]

In particular, southern China is proving to be one of the world's booming economies, although this geographic region has begun to slow down somewhat in the last four years.[17] Many companies, especially those in nearby Hong Kong, now have their production handled in provinces directly across from Hong Kong on the mainland because of the low wage rates in China. In addition, China is becoming an important area for MNE investment.

MNE investment   Multinationals have made a large number of investments in China. Occidental Petroleum has put over $180 million into a coal mining project. Motorola has invested $120 million to produce semiconductors and mobile phones, and General Motors has a $1.3 billion joint venture with a Shanghai automotive company to build Buick Century and Regal cars in China.[18] Dow Chemical has a $25 million joint venture in a polyurethane plant. H. J. Heinz has a majority interest in a $10 million baby-food plant. Procter & Gamble has put $10 million into a joint venture factory to produce laundry and personal care products, and Hewlett-Packard has a similar amount in an electronics joint venture. RJR Nabisco has a $9 million venture to manufacture Ritz crackers. Seagram has put up $6 million to make whiskey and wine products. Babcock and Wilcox have put $6 million into a joint venture boiler factory. Mitsubishi has invested $4.3 million in a venture to build elevators. Other firms on this growing list include Bell Telephone, Chrysler, General Bearing, Gillette, Lockheed, Pabst Brewing, Peugeot, Squibb, Volkswagen, and Xerox, to name but ten.

There are a number of reasons that MNEs want to do business in China. One is the growing market for both industrial and consumer goods. A second is the rapid growth of the economy, which is increasing the country's purchasing power as well as the desire to modernize its roads, communications system, and other aspects of its infrastructure. At the same time MNEs must be cautious.[19] The Tianamen Square massacre showed multinationals how quickly the government can change position and subsequently increase a firm's political risk.[20] Similarly, the annual debate in the United States over according favored-nation trade status to China helps to illustrate the potential problems faced by foreign firms doing business in China.[21]

Labor   One of the primary reasons that China is becoming a focal point for multinational investment is its low labor costs. The average factory wage ($100 per month) is about 10 per cent of that in more industrialized Pacific Rim countries such as Taiwan. On the other hand, the country has come under severe criticism for using prison labor to manufacture goods for export. This has caused Congress to back curbs on the country's access to markets in the United States. During the Bush administration China's support at the White House had been sufficient to blunt these measures and to ensure its most-favored nation status, and this has continued under President Clinton's administration. A number of changes are now taking place regarding the country's human rights program, and China is hoping for admission to the World Trade Organization.[22] However, there is great skepticism in many quarters regarding China's willingness to make changes.[23]

Doing business The business environment in China is different from that of many other Pacific Rim countries because of its communist government. In recent years the government has often changed its approach to dealing with MNEs, resulting in confusion regarding both rules of operation and assessment of risk.[24] In dealing with this environment, one of the first important steps is to find an appropriate domestic partner.[25] It is more common in China for multinationals to use intermediaries in the process than elsewhere in the Pacific Rim. Among other sources, the China International Trust and Investment Corporation and the Ministry of Foreign Trade and Economic Cooperation offer such assistance. It is important to note that the government has a priority list of desired investments. Ventures involving advanced technology, exports, or the generation of foreign exchange are given the highest priority.

In a joint venture the local partner is typically responsible for providing the land and buildings and for carrying out local marketing. The MNE is expected to contribute the equipment, technology, and capital and to be responsible for export marketing. In those cases where the multinational is manufacturing for sales in China, high-quality products, excellent service, and good promotional efforts are critical to success. Researchers have found that outstanding service and effective promotion can often make up for some lack of quality. However, price reductions and special sales terms are unlikely to offset poor quality. Similarly, while customer relations are important, they are often not enough to make up for poor quality or poor service. The Chinese want to buy the best quality available.

Additionally, it is important to remember that China still has a predominantly planned economy. Imports and exports are determined by the government, and these decisions can have strong consequences for MNEs doing business here. For example, China has been running a large trade surplus with the United States in recent years, and there is every reason to believe that unless this situation is corrected, the US government will limit Chinese imports. This could result in a backlash against US MNEs in China. In addition, the Clinton administration is planning on creating a new trade policy toward China and other Southeast Asian countries that will require more open markets. So there are important political/economic risks that must be weighed when planning a joint venture here.

ACTIVE LEARNING CHECK

Review your answer to Active Learning Case question 2 and make any changes you like. Then compare your answer to the one below.

2. In what way is China linking itself to the triad and other industrially developing countries?

China is linking itself to the triad and other industrially developing countries by providing low-cost output for businesses in these countries. In fact, many triad-based multinationals are setting up operations in China so that they can maximize this advantage. In turn the goods are being shipped back to triad home markets for sale by well-known firms throughout the world, including Sears, K-Mart, and Wal-Mart. This trading relationship is helping China to link itself to the large and growing triad economies and helps to increase the likelihood of China continuing a great economic leap forward.

India

India (see earlier map) encompasses an area of approximately 1.3 million square miles and has a population of almost 1 billion. Prior to 1990 the government had done little to promote multinational interest. Politics often prevailed over economic interests and many MNEs found their dealings with the government to be time-consuming and frustrating. For example, both IBM and Coca-Cola left India in the late 1970s rather than accede to the government's demand that they reduce their majority holdings to 40 per cent. And when PepsiCo sought permission to invest in India in 1986, the company's request had to be reviewed by 15 committees and was subjected to a host of parliamentary debates as well as to thousands of unfavorable newspaper articles. In recent years, however, the political climate has changed and the government is now trying very hard to attract foreign investment, although there are still many pitfalls facing investors.[26]

MNE investment   Since the early 1990s India has been the focus of new attention by MNEs. The primary reason is that there is now greater operating freedom for foreign investors than at any time since the country gained its independence in 1947. Total FDI in 1990 was less than $100 million, but today it is more than $2 billion and is continuing to increase with US MNEs leading the way. Coca-Cola has returned and invested $20 million to set up a wholly owned subsidiary. IBM is back and has joined a $20 million 50/50 joint venture with India's Tata group to make computers and to develop software. Mission Energy, a Los Angeles-based company, has signed a memorandum of understanding to build a $900 million power plant near Bombay. J. P. Morgan, the investment banking firm, has a 40 per cent equity interest in a joint venture to trade securities, to underwrite new stock issues, and to handle related financial activities in addition to managing the India Magnum Fund, which has an investment value of $400 million. General Electric has formed a $40 million joint venture to make refrigerators and washing machines. Other firms doing business in the country include Gillette, BMW, DuPont, General Motors, Fujitsu, Kellogg's, and Texas Instruments.

Potential and problems   One of the primary attractions of India is the large middle class. Estimates place this group at over 100 million, a sizable market with the potential to generate billions of dollars of sales for MNE investors. The lower middle class, estimated at 200 million, is another significant market niche. A second attraction is the government's recent efforts to make things easier for foreign investors. The government has now eased restrictions on the repatriation of dividends by foreign MNEs and has begun sharply to reduce tariffs on imported goods. One of the major reasons behind these policy changes is that India realizes that the vigorous growth of its economy depends heavily on foreign capital, and in the past the country has failed to exploit this avenue. A good example is the major power plant built by Enron, a Houston-based corporation. The project was initially approved by the local government but when it lost power to the opposition party, the latter canceled the contract. Over the next three years both Enron and the new government eventually worked out their differences, clearly indicating the importance of MNEs learning to work effectively with local political groups.[27]

At the same time MNEs remain cautious. If the government were to change its policies, as it has so often in the past, these firms could end up losing millions of dollars.[28] On the other hand, many countries in Asia are making giant economic strides, most notably China, and India does not want to fall behind. For this reason, the country is likely to keep its doors open to MNEs. At the same time the nation will have to continue pushing its exports and creating more market links to Japan and the triad nations. To the extent that it can maintain strong relations with MNEs, India's chances of doing this will increase.[29]

South Korea

South Korea has experienced rapid economic growth over the last two decades. The free enterprise system is well entrenched and the private sector dominates business, although government influence is considerable. GDP grew by 6.9 per cent in 1996, but since then the economy has been having problems. Interest rates have been rising and bankruptcies are up sharply.[30]

MNE investment   Despite the same type of resistance to foreign firms that is present in Japan, multinationals continue to invest in South Korea. Some major investments in recent years have come in chemicals, electronics, and machinery. Glaxo, the British pharmaceutical firm, is working with Lucky, a local pharmaceutical manufacturer, to develop and market antibiotics. Clerical Medical International, a British insurance group, has a joint venture with Coryo, a Korean firm, to sell insurance in that country. BASF, the German chemical firm, has bought three Korean operations, and GE Capital has purchased a controlling interest in Korea First Bank.[31] Other major investors include BP Amoco, Corning Glass, General Motors, Hewlett-Packard, IBM, Monsanto, Philips, Siemens, and Unilever.

Some major advantages of doing business in South Korea include a growing economy and increasing disposable income. Some major disadvantages include the difficulty of breaking into the market and of developing alliances that can effectively compete with the local conglomerates.

Labor   Labor unrest has been a problem, although this may be subsiding. MNEs face labor shortages, and there are basic labor laws that provide for minimum working conditions, collective bargaining, and labor arbitration disputes. In recent years labor unrest has pushed wages up dramatically, and fringe benefits add as much as 80 per cent to the basic cost of the wage package. This has resulted in an increase in the cost of exported goods and thus some firms have seen their overseas sales drop sharply.

At present Korean companies and their workers are trying to put aside their differences and to regain productivity ground that was lost in the late 1980s. Many firms are cutting executive jobs, streamlining operations, and emphasizing high-tech output. These efforts are designed to protect local markets and to generate exports. As a result, South Korea will continue to be a competitive market for MNEs, and the country is likely to continue linking strongly to the United States and EU parts of the triad as well as to Japan.[32]

Singapore

Singapore has seen strong economic growth but in recent years has felt the impact of recession. Some of this is the economic downturn in Asia which is affecting all of the local economies. At the same time the government has been encouraging foreign investment, and restrictions on equity, licensing, and joint ventures are negligible.

MNE investment   Singapore has been a major target for investment by MNEs in recent years, especially for US firms which have invested more over the last five years than either the Japanese or the Europeans. DuPont is spending $100 million to build a fiber plant, which is part of a $1.1 billion investment planned for the country. Texas Instruments is building a $185 million plant to upgrade its memory-chip assembly facility and testing center. Matsushita is investing $330 million in a factory to make high-precision automatic insertion equipment. Sony is putting $200 million in a cathode-ray tube manufacturing plant.

Labor   Productivity has been rising rapidly in Singapore, and this has put a strain on the country to recruit the needed personnel. Unemployment is extremely low and the tight market has been producing average wage increases of 7 to 8 per cent annually. Most workers in industrial plants and offices are unionized, but there has been little labor unrest in recent years. There is talk of paying new hires a lower wage than those currently in the work force, resulting in two-tiered compensation. The country is also looking to increase its manufacturing and research and development expertise, and to let others handle the low-skill work.

Singapore's geographic size and limited labor force require that the country pick the right business niches. High-tech manufacturing, transportation, and financial services are primary targets of interest, and MNEs in these areas are finding the government prepared to help create the necessary environment to attract their investment. This strategy should also be useful in ensuring Singapore's continued success among US and EU triad members.

Australia

Australia is the only continent occupied by one country. Australia has a two-party political system and a legal framework that was developed from British law. There are approximately 19 million people in the country. The economy is strongly based on private enterprise, and the government's stated industry goal is to encourage the development of internationally competitive manufacturing and service sectors. In particular, this is resulting in government action to upgrade industrial science and technology, to promote and encourage the processing of local resources, and to assist in the diffusion of new management and production techniques.

The recession of the early 1990s hit Australia hard. Economic activity slumped, unemployment rose, and exports weakened as prices for major commodities on the world market began to soften. In addition, the manufacturing sector has continued to remain uncompetitive in international markets. One of the biggest challenges facing the nation is that of attracting capital to finance growth.

MNE investment   Australia has been working very hard to attract FDI. Manufacturing has been receiving the largest share of new investment, followed by finance and real estate. The Japanese and Americans have been the major investors in recent years. Mitsui and Nippon Shinpan have purchased the remaining 50 per cent of the Mirage Resort Trust, investing a total of $390 million in the process. Chevron, Shell, and BP Amoco have continued their $9 billion gas development on the North

INTERNATIONAL BUSINESS STRATEGY IN ACTION

Unilever in Asia and Latin America

The second largest consumer goods business in the world, Unilever employs 270,000 people worldwide. It has production plants in 70 countries and sells its products in 158 countries. With annual revenues of $48 billion, it is considered one of the world's 50 largest MNEs. Its products include food and home and personal care products. The company's success can be attributed to two things: its long history of global presence and its decision in the 1990s to restructure its operations to better suit emerging markets.

Unilever was founded in 1929 through the merger of Margarine Unie (Dutch) and Lever Brothers (UK). Lever Brothers already had operations in Africa and Asia, so that when Unilever was created, it was already a multinational enterprise with 20 per cent of its profits originating outside of Europe. By 1980, this number had doubled, mainly due to expansions in Africa, South America, and Asia.

Today, the company sees itself as a multicultural multinational with a global strategy. This strategy includes the development of its operations in five key selected regions: Southern South America, Central and Eastern Europe, India, China, and Southeast Asia. Unilever understands that it has an advantage in national responsiveness against its main competitors in many of these regions. It has been in South America since the company was founded, with operations in Chile (1928), Argentina (1928), and Brazil (1929). In 1927 it started operations in the Philippines, followed by Thailand in 1932 and India and Indonesia in 1933. The company started operations in China in the 1920s and when the government opened up in the 1980s Unilever was quick to sign joint ventures to re-enter the market. Today it has sales of $300 million in China.

Unilever's success in emerging markets is a result of its regional perspective. To sell to consumers from different cultures and economic means, it must comprehend their specific needs. The company recognizes this need for adapting to local tastes and is committed to assuring that managers understand the special needs of their diverse customers. Differences in taste, culture, and income must all be taken into account. In India, one of their most profitable regions, future managers are required to live with a family in a remote village for six months. This is to remind them of who their customers are. In Brazil, the largest economy in South America, the company has developed a special cheap shampoo to cater to the poorest and the largest social group. Furthermore, the company hopes to increase the amount of local innovation in emerging markets and is expected to finish a program to institute innovation centres in key regions.

Emerging markets require a long-term approach. The majority of the world's growth potential is in these markets, but the short-term risks are high. Economic situations like the Asian crisis of 1998 and the Mexican peso devaluation of 1994 can cause large setbacks in the short run. A multinational can reduce risk by having operations in different areas of the world. Bad times in one region are offset by good times in another region. Unilever's global presence certainly allows it to reduce risk in this way, but the company goes a step further. It produces a variety of products to cater to different income levels. In one country it may sell a cheap shampoo and an expensive shampoo. If the country goes into a recession, operations are shifted to produce more of the cheap shampoo, reducing the impact.

Sources: Adapted from Deborah Orr, "A Giant Reawakens," *Forbes*, January 25, 1999, pp. 52–54; "Munching on Change – Unilever's Food Business," *The Economist*, January 6, 1996, pp. 56–61; *http://www.unilever.com*.

West Shelf. Mobil has purchased oil refining and marketing operations from another oil company. Coca-Cola has bought 59 per cent of a local soft-drink manufacturer for $500 million.

Most foreign investments are not subject to specific equity rules; they simply need to be approved on a case-by-case basis. However, foreign investment is prohibited in utilities, radio, television, daily newspapers, and some parts of the civil aviation industry. There are also specific regulations governing foreign participation in the development of natural resources such as oil, coal, gas, and uranium, and real estate investments are examined to ensure that they clearly benefit the national interest. In the case of acquisitions and takeovers there are a series of basic rules which must be followed, including full knowledge of who is making the acquisition and providing the shareholders with reasonable time to consider the offer.

Labor   The work force consists of 8 million people, who, in contrast to some other Asian and Pacific countries, are educated and well trained. As a result, there is an abundance of professionally skilled people but a shortage of skilled manual laborers. The government has attempted to address this problem through an aggressive immigration program in which skilled workers are given priority. Average weekly earnings vary from state to state, but companies must pay men and women equal wages for the same work. Worker salaries generally have three components: a minimum wage, a margin for skill, and a market premium offered by the employer and established by collective bargaining. Many workers are unionized, but unions are organized according to job function or trade rather than according to industry. As a result, there may be as many as ten unions in a particular company and the power of any one of them is small. Moreover, wage and labor conflicts are traditionally settled by an arbitrator so that the union has less chance of "flexing its muscle" than it does in many other countries.

Australia has strong trading ties to Japan, which in recent years has purchased about 25 per cent of all exports. The United States and the EU together purchase a similar percentage, but this is slowly declining. So as the twenty-first century unwinds, Australia is fashioning increased ties to the Japanese segment of the triad and is likely to find its economic future closely intertwined with that of Pacific Rim countries, rather than with traditional Anglo nations.

ACTIVE LEARNING CHECK

Review your answer to Active Learning Case question 3 and make any changes you like. Then compare your answer to the one below.

3. Why is Asian brainpower so attractive to multinational investors from the West?

There are three reasons that Asian brainpower is attractive to multinational investors from the West. One is the low cost of hiring and retaining highly educated personnel. A second is the level of education and technical training that many of these people have, thus helping the MNEs to design and manufacture high-tech products. A third is that with the assistance of these people, MNEs are able to set up overseas operations and to staff them with local talent.

EASTERN EUROPE

The difficulty of moving from a communist to a market system has plunged much of Eastern Europe into economic turmoil. National currencies such as the Russian ruble have lost much of their value, and because many administered prices have been eliminated, the purchasing power of the average citizen in Eastern Europe has declined. So too have the GNP and the industrial and agricultural outputs declined, while unemployment has risen. Simply put, the economic picture in this geographic region is bleak. The region needs triad-based investment and access to the rich markets of the triad countries for its exports.

The move toward a free-market economy carries with it a host of short-term problems. Yet if these countries continue their efforts toward privatization, with the encouragement of foreign investment, they can turn the corner and begin developing more prosperous economies.[33] The major challenges that these countries must be prepared to face include (1) resisting the temptation to move back toward centralized planning in order to control current inflation and unemployment and (2) accepting the fact that the inflow of foreign capital, technology, and managerial expertise often brings with it social and political pressures to do things that up to now have been anathema, such as allowing foreign ownership and control of local operations. This is the type of environment in which the countries of Eastern Europe now find themselves. Because of its size and economic conditions, the country that faces the greatest challenge is Russia.

Russia

On December 8, 1991 the leaders of Russia, the Ukraine, and Byelorussia declared that the Soviet Union had ceased to exist and proclaimed a new "Commonwealth of Independent States."[34] The accompanying map shows Russia both before and after the breakup of the Soviet Union. Currently there are numerous changes being introduced as the Russian government works to right the nation's economic "ship." This will be a major challenge for a number of reasons, including the fact that the country faces far more problems than do most other eastern European nations.

Price and economic reform   The Russians are currently undertaking price reform. In many areas administered prices and subsidies are being eliminated and free-market forces are taking over. These developments have had a major effect on the economy. During the first six months of 1991 GNP declined by 10 per cent, agricultural output went down by 11 per cent, and industrial output sank by 6 per cent. On the positive side, these developments were not unexpected, given the experiences of other countries that have moved from command to market economies. For example, Poland's industrial output declined by 29 per cent in the year following the transition to a free-market economy.

Since then, however, things have gone from bad to worse. By the end of the 1990s the economy was reeling.[35] Russia's foreign debt, which stood at around $115 billion in 1992, had risen to $145 billion by 1998.[36] In addition, annual debt payments were a whopping $17 billion and some analysts were predicting that the government would default on its foreign debt.

At the same time the Yeltsin government was having political problems and a majority of Russians wanted to see him resign before his term of office was up.[37] The

International Monetary Fund has tried to help, but the conditions set down by the Fund were considered too severe by many Russian politicians. As a result, many of the promised reforms never took place.[38] Moreover, the government considered a Soviet-style economic plan that called for imposing tight control on the flow of foreign currencies.[39] This proposal resulted in some MNEs reevaluating their investments in Russia.[40] There was also concern about the possibility of a devaluation of the ruble. These developments all resulted in Russia's hard currency debt being rated as the riskiest in the world.

The West continues to work with Russia in providing monetary and economic assistance. Meanwhile inside the country many businesses have turned to bartering because there is a lack of money to buy goods. For example, businesses will trade their products to local utilities in exchange for electric power and the utility, in turn, will use these products to pay their own personnel and to acquire the resources needed to keep the company afloat. The bartering system is widely used and fairly sophisticated. The head of one of Russia's regional departments recently remarked that someone should write a book on how the system works. "It will be more interesting than a horror film" he said.[41]

Privatization   Another major undertaking is the privatization of industry. There are thousands of state-owned factories in Russia and privatization is critical because without it the government is unlikely to stimulate a broad industrial recovery. Private ownership is the key to economic growth. However, progress in this area is difficult since management skills and capital are lacking.

Privatization is taking a number of different forms. One is that of turning 25 to 35 per cent of the state-run businesses over to the workers and managers, who then assume managerial responsibility and also set up a board of directors to oversee the operation. A second is to attract private investors both inside and outside the country.

Table 19.1 Major US firms doing business in Russia

Abbott Laboratories	Johnson & Johnson
American Express	Lilly (Eli)
Andersen (Arthur)	Litton Industries
Archer-Daniels-Midland	McDermott*
AT&T	McDonald's*
BankAmerica Corp.	Minnesota Mining & Manufacturing
BP Amoco*	Mobil*
Cargill	Monsanto
Caterpillar	Occidental Petroleum
Chase Manhattan Corp.	PepsiCo
Chevron*	Pfizer
Coca-Cola	Philip Morris
Conoco*	Polaroid
Control Data	Procter & Gamble
Cooper Industries	Radisson Hotels*
Corning*	Ralston Purina
CSX*	RJR Nabisco Holdings
Dow Chemical	Strauss (Levi)*
Dresser Industries	Texaco*
DuPont	Union Carbide
Emerson Electric	United Telecomm.*
Ernst & Young	Upjohn & Pharmacia
Exxon*	US West*
FMC	Xerox
General Motors	Young & Rubicam
Hewlett-Packard	
Honeywell	
IBM	

* Established business in Russia after 1986.

Business dealings in Russia Despite the economic turbulence, some MNEs are doing business in Russia and others have plans to do so. (Table 19.1 provides a list of major US firms in Russia.) For example, IBM is providing 40,000 personal computers for Russian schools; Daimler-Benz of Germany has a contract for a $140 million plant to build buses; the Carroll Group of Britain is constructing a $250 million hotel/trade center; Alcatel, the giant French telecommunications company, has a $2.8 billion contract to supply advanced digital telephone switches; McDonald's plans to construct an office building in downtown Moscow and to open 20 additional restaurants throughout the country; and United Technologies is installing the first-ever data communications switching center to handle fax and electronic mail. But this foreign direct investment is still relatively small (on a triad perspective), and it will remain so until profits can be repatriated at a rate commensurate with the political risk in Russia.

Other examples are provided by US soft-drink companies. Coca-Cola is investing more than $50 million over a three-year period to build a soft-drink production plant in St Petersburg. This plant will replace reliance on importing the soft drink from Coke plants in Western Europe. PepsiCo has agreed to spend more than $1 billion to increase to 50 the number of bottling plants in the Soviet Union, allowing it to produce 2 billon 8-ounce containers annually. The company has also received government permission to introduce disposable, lightweight aluminum cans and plastic containers to replace the heavy $11\frac{1}{2}$-ounce bottles that must be returned and which limit distribution to 20 kilometers around each bottling plant. In return for the soft-drink products PepsiCo takes payment in the form of Stolichnaya vodka and has received transfer title to ten Soviet-built ocean-going ships. This barter agreement is important to PepsiCo because the ruble is currently worthless in the international market. However, by selling vodka, the company can earn a substantial profit on its investment.

Coca-Cola recently followed its main competitor to Russia and is now opening a subsidiary that will operate a plant in Moscow and has a network of 2,000 kiosks that will sell Coke and Fanta orange soda throughout the capital. The new company, Coca-Cola Refreshments-Moscow, plans to have well over 500 kiosks in operation by the millennium.

Another development is the rise in joint ventures. Bankers Trust, J. P. Morgan, Boeing, and Pennzoil also have joint ventures, and other firms such as Archer-Daniel-Midland, Dresser Industries, Eastman Kodak, General Electric, Johnson & Johnson, Pratt & Whitney, and RJR Nabisco are working on deals of their own.

Another interesting development is the increase in joint ventures between Russian businesses and foreign partners. Aeroflot, the giant Russian airline, has 42 joint ventures and is looking to establish even more as management seeks to make the company a major player in the international airline industry. The box "International Business Strategy in Action: Aeroflot, The Body Shop and Customer Service" describes some of the latest developments.

ACTIVE LEARNING CHECK

Review your answer to Active Learning Case question 4 and make any changes you like. Then compare your answer to the one below.

4. How is Russia promoting privatization? How can triad MNEs help in this process?

Russia is promoting privatization in a number of ways. One is by turning state-owned firms into stock and limited liability companies with outside capital participation. Another way is by selling businesses to private groups. MNEs can help in this process by purchasing these firms either outright or as part of a joint venture. Multinationals can also help by investing capital in the country and by bringing in high technology and management expertise so that state-owned firms can be turned into efficient, competitive companies. These companies would then be able to export their products and thus generate profit and hard currency for the economy.

INTERNATIONAL BUSINESS STRATEGY IN ACTION

Aeroflot, The Body Shop and customer service

Aeroflot – Russian International Airlines – flies to about 150 destinations in 94 countries and controls about 70 per cent of the international travel by Russian airlines. The most important of Aeroflot's assets is landing rights in various international airports. However, to be truly competitive it must improve service. In 1996 it carried 3.9 million passengers, just a fraction of the 138 million passengers it carried in 1991.

The airline has been notorious for delayed and canceled flights. In fact, flight schedules are so frequently missed that the president of a London-based airline consulting firm recently noted that: "Aeroflot is never quite sure of where its planes are." Since the gradual collapse of the economy, jet fuel shortage has led to the closing of more than half the country's airports; 40 per cent of the fleet has been grounded due to a shortage of spare parts and most flights to the Ukraine, the Caucasus and Kazakhstan have been eliminated. Customers' complaints about the service include everything from the state of the audio equipment to the meals. Perhaps worst of all is the fact that the airline has the poorest safety record in the world. In 1994 the number of crashes reached a record number, leading the US embassy in Moscow to direct its workers to use alternative means of transportation. In that same year, a flight to Hong Kong crashed after the pilot let his 13-year-old son fly the plane, killing 75 people. One Russian newspaper concluded that: "Flying Aeroflot is now about as safe as playing Russian roulette."

The good news is that most of the airline's problems were with its internal flights. Most of these have been consolidated into other companies while Aeroflot concentrates on international flights. The company is modernizing its fleet with purchases from Boeing and Airbus. New landing rights have been established in Anchorage, Chicago, Miami and San Francisco. The company is also working to position itself to provide services between Europe and Asia, since the trans-Siberian route can save four to six hours over traditional polar routes.

In order to become a first-class airline company, Aeroflot has started frequent-flyer programs and formed joint ventures with international competitors. However, Aeroflot will be unable to capture and retain international markets if it does not upgrade its service. Most other successful western companies, such as The Body Shop and 3M are responsive to the needs and social values of their customers. The Body Shop was the first manufacturer of personal products to use animal rights as their marketing strategy. 3M was a visionary of environmental management that instituted the Pollutor Pays Program, along with other environmental programs, to target a growing concern among its customers. Aeroflot must sensitize itself to the needs of its customers if it expects to maintain a large share of the Russian market and expand into other markets.

Sources: Adapted from *http://www.aeroflot.org/e_aero.html*; *http://www.bodyshop.com/*; *http://www.3m.com/*; Paul Kebnikov, "The day they raided Aeroflot," *Forbes*, March 22, 1999, pp. 106–10; G. Bruce Knecht, "Aeroflot Takes Aim at the Post Communist World," *New York Times*, January 12, 1992, p. F7.

Poland

Poland encompasses an area of approximately 121,000 square miles, the size of Wyoming, and has a population of almost 40 million. The country's borders were reconfigured at the end of World War II, and in the decade that followed Poland was ruled by Stalinist communists. By the late 1950s, however, a more independent Polish Communist party began to emerge – collectivization of farms was ended and religious freedom was permitted. During the 1980s the powerful, noncommunist labor unions wrested major concessions from the government, and despite the use of martial law and the imprisonment of union leaders, at the end of the decade there were free elections and economic policies that were designed to privatize industry and to bring about free-market conditions. In the process the country encountered major price inflation.[42] By the 1990s, however, the GDP was starting to post a modest growth, and legislation to promote an open and liberal investment environment was beginning to generate results.

Business dealings in the country A number of MNEs have invested in Poland and many others are looking to do so.[43] Pilkington, the world-renowned glass manufacturer, has put $150 million into HSO Sandomierz, a local company in the same industry. Asea Brown Boveri has bought Zamech, a turbine manufacturer, for $50 million. One factor that lures investors is the low hourly wage in industries such as manufacturing. This makes Poland an attractive locale for manufacturers. Other investors are being lured by the opportunity to apply their technology and management expertise in improving Polish businesses and making them competitive in the local and regional markets. This is particularly important because of the major privatization effort that is now under way by the government. Although it will take years to privatize the economy totally, given that there are over 8,000 large state-owned enterprises, rapid strides have been made and free enterprise is beginning to take a strong foothold. The government is encouraging small business formation, and today there are over 750, 000 new businesses in Poland, accounting for 40 per cent of the GNP. Additionally, both throughout the country and abroad Polish-owned firms are developing and increasing their business operations.

Like the other Eastern European countries examined in this section, Poland faces a myriad of economic challenges.[44] However, the nation's vigorous growth in the private sector and its determination to close the gap in living standards between itself and western neighbors will continue to make the country attractive to MNEs during the millennium.

ACTIVE LEARNING CHECK

Review your answer to Active Learning Case question 5 and make any changes you like. Then compare your answer to the one below.

5. How is Poland moving toward privatization? Describe two developments that have been beneficial in this process?

Poland is taking a number of steps in moving toward privatization. One of the most helpful has been legislation that is designed to promote an open, liberal investment environment and thus attract foreign businesspeople to buy local companies as well as to participate in joint ventures. A second is the encouragement of new small business formation.

SUMMARY

Key points

1. Non-triad countries need investment from, and access to, a triad bloc in order to develop global industries. Current trends such as privatization and legislative changes that are designed to encourage foreign direct investment (FDI) are helping these countries to tap their economic potential. A number of factors will influence their success during this decade, including privatization, attraction of foreign capital, and intraregional trade agreements that can be helpful in creating mini-common markets. Additionally, each non-triad nation will continue trying to establish markets in triad countries.

2. Countries in Latin America are beginning to follow Mexico's lead and more closely to link their economies to triad nations. Chile and Brazil, for example, are now encouraging FDI and have privatized many state-owned businesses. As a result, their economies are beginning to improve.

3. Asia has some of the fastest growing economies in the world. China has been doing extremely well in recent years, as labor costs are so low that more and more companies in the Asian region are transferring their manufacturing to China. The government, however, will have to take steps to deal with the country's large trade surpluses with triad countries such as the United States. There is likely to be strong pressure for continued improvement in human rights or many industrialized countries will take trade action against China.

4. Other Asian countries that are of interest to MNEs include India, South Korea, and Singapore. India is now trying to attract foreign investment and the government's new policies are designed to make it easier for MNEs to set up operations there. The government is also interested in linking the country's trade to triad partners. Korea and Singapore have had strong economic growth in the past but are currently facing economic downturns. Both are looking to establish stronger ties to the EU and North American triads. Australia is following a slightly different strategy, becoming more economically intertwined with Asian countries like Japan and relying less on the triads of the EU and the United States as their primary markets.

5. Russia is currently undergoing major economic changes. One way that the country is trying to improve its economy is through privatization. This development is taking a number of different forms, including turning control over to the workers and managers and entering into joint ventures with foreign MNEs. Poland has over 8,000 large state-owned businesses, and foreign investment banks and accounting firms are acting as advisors in helping to privatize them. At the same time many Poles have started their own businesses.

Review and discussion questions

1. Why is it critical for Latin American countries such as Chile and Brazil to link with the triad, in most cases the United States? Why do these countries not simply create their own economic union and compete directly with triad members?

2. How well has the Chinese economy done in recent years? What has helped to account for this? Cite and describe two factors.

3. China currently faces a number of problems that could lead to an economic slowdown. What are two of them? Identify and describe both.

4. Why does China want to link its trade to nations such as the United States? Why not simply trade with Pacific Rim countries?

5. What guidelines must MNEs follow when doing business in China? Identify and briefly describe each.

6. Why is India now becoming a focal point of interest for multinationals? Identify and describe two reasons.

7. Why do South Korea and Singapore want to link their economies to those of Japan and other triad members? Based on what you have learned in other chapters, as well as in this one, explain the logic of this international business strategy.

8. How well has the Australian economy done in recent years? Why is it critical for Australia to link its economy with the triad? Which triad members would be of most value? Explain.

9. How is privatization taking place in Russia? Identify and describe two different approaches.

10. How successful has Russia been in attracting foreign investment? What accounts for this?

11. How well is privatization progressing in Poland? What are the major stumbling blocks?

12. Where has Poland had the greatest business success in the transition to a free-market economy? How likely is it that this development will continue? Explain.

REAL CASES

DOING BUSINESS IN KOREA

In many cases government policies for Pacific nations are designed to promote exports, not imports. Because this thwarts competitive pricing, local companies can charge consumers premium prices and make hefty profits. Until the 1980s South Korea fell into this category. In response, people who could afford to travel would fly to Hong Kong and buy everything from clothes to food to consumer goods at far less than they were paying locally. Now, thanks to a program introduced by the government in the 1990s to reduce inflation, many protected markets have been opened. The government also hoped that this policy would make its giant competitors more competitive.

Foreign firms responded with interest. Citibank has opened a number of branches and offers 24-hour banking service, something previously unseen in Korea. Merrill Lynch already has operations and a seat in the Korean stock market. Ford and Christian Dior have opened outlets, while companies like Whirlpool continue to export products. The biggest winners are the Korean consumers who cannot afford costly imported goods and have been unable to travel abroad to purchase them. Goldstar, the country's second largest electronics firm, has cut the price of various products in order to meet competition, and Korean banks are offering round-the-clock services in order to meet the challenge from Citibank.

The new government policy also means that the Korean chaebols – big family owned conglomerates that had dominated the economy – are being scrutinized for the first time. Business leaders and government officials have been imprisoned for corruption. The arrests were symbolic but the message was clear: no longer would the government look the other way in favor of its domestic companies. The chaebols' problems intensified when the Asian Flu hit South Korea in 1998. Not only was the domestic economy in which they operated faced with a large recession, but they were also being blamed for it. For the top 30 chaebols, the debt-to-equity ratio was at 802 per cent in the middle of the 1998 crisis. The government has identified chaebol companies that are insolvent. The objective is to reform and consolidate Korea's companies so that they can compete internationally. Many international economists believe that opening up the Korean market to foreign MNEs will help the country to reform its own industrial system and perhaps to get a jump on others, such as the Japanese, who in many areas continue to discourage imports and allow local firms to garner much larger profits at home than they can earn abroad.

1. How can Korea's new trade policy help the country? Be specific in your answer.

2. Is Korea making a mistake by allowing foreign manufacturers and retailers into country? Why or why not?

3. How can the reform of Korea's chaebols help the country to become more competitive in foreign markets? Explain.

Sources: Adapted from Laxmi Nakarmi, "Korea Throws Open Its Doors," *Business Week*, July 29, 1991, p. 46; Laxmi Nakarmi and Patrick Oser, "The Korean Tiger Is Out for Blood," *Business Week*, May 13, 1993, p. 54; The Chaebols That Ate Korea," *The Economist*, November 14, 1998, pp. 67–68; *http://www.ford.com*.

KIWIFRUIT: A NEW ZEALAND SUCCESS STORY

New Zealand farmers invented the name "Kiwifruit" in 1959 for their famous green version of the Chinese gooseberry, a fruit first developed by horticulturalist Hayward Wright. In the winter months for Europe and North America, New Zealand accounts for 70–80 per cent of world sales of Kiwifruit, although it only has a one-third annual share of the world market. Other large producers are Italy, France, Greece, and the United States.

One of the advantages of improved sea transportation in refrigerated containers is that perishable fresh fruit can be produced in Southern Hemisphere countries like New Zealand and Chile and marketed through the Northern Hemisphere winter. Fruit is a low value, bulky product that can only be transported by ship in a cost-effective manner. This contra-seasonal production works both ways. New Zealand actually imports from California in its winter months. Competing with New Zealand for the winter contra-seasonal market is Chile.

In both New Zealand and Chile the many small fruit farmers face a problem in transporting and selling their products. One solution has been to form producers' cooperatives and export marketing boards. In 1988 the New Zealand Kiwifruit Marketing Board was formed to coordinate exports and in 1997 this was privatized to become Kiwifruit New Zealand (KNZ). This company launched a brand product "Zespri" to differentiate the high-quality New Zealand product from competitors and to provide a better customer focus.

Kiwifruit is a speciality fruit in a niched world market with few rivals, so the major management issues are logistical ones of developing an effective internal supply chain plus reliable export marketing. In contrast, New Zealand also produces apples, pears and other "pipfruit." These are now commodity products, with many large producers all over the world. Here New Zealand is an insignificant participant, with under 1 per cent of the world market and no power to manage industry pricing, as it can with Kiwifruit. For small, open, trading economies like New Zealand and Chile, market access to triad regions is essential to build a business, whether it be in a niche or in a commodity.

1. How does New Zealand gain access to large foreign markets?

2. What is the role of the KNZ?

3. What global strategy is being followed for Kiwifruit?

Sources: Trade New Zealand, *Monthly Export Statistics*, January 1999 *http://www.tradenz.govt.nz/nz/stats/monthly/199901MKT.html*; *The Economy of New Zealand* (*www.treasury.govt.nz/pubs/nzdmo/ EFO_98*); *New Zealand Treasury's Assessment of the Impact of Asian Economies on the NZ Economy*, January, 1998 (*www. treasury.govt.nz/briefing.asia.html*); *External Sector* (*www.treasury. govt.nz/pubs/nzdmo/EFO_98*); *Key Facts and Figures about FDI in New Zealand* (*www.oic.govt.nz/invest/brief/ appenda.html*).

ENDNOTES

1. Ravi Ramamurti, "Why Are Developing Countries Privatizing?" *Journal of International Business Studies*, Second Quarter, 1992, pp. 225–249.

2. Craig Torres, "Chilean Firms Suffer Pain of a Japanese Recession," *Wall Street Journal*, February 25, 1999, p. A14.

3. See also "All Good Things Must Slow Down," *Economist*, March 7, 1998, pp. 35–36.

4. Seth Schiesel, "Brazil Sells Most of State Phone Utility," *New York Times*, July 30, 1998, pp. C1, 5.

5. Peter Fritsch and Pamela Druckerman, "Brazil's Falling Currency Stirs Concern Over Its Ability to Keep Up with Debt," *Wall Street Journal*, January 28, 1999, pp. A13, 15; Peter Fritsch, "Brazil's Currency Falls Further as Nerves Fray," *Wall Street Journal*, February 1, 1999, pp. A15, 18.

6. Peter Fritsch and Michael M. Phillips, "Brazil's Devaluation Reignites Global Fears Of Spreading Malaise," *Wall Street Journal*, January 14, 1999, pp. A1, 8.

7. Craig Torres, "Brazilian Turmoil Threatens Argentine Car Exports," *Wall Street Journal*, February 1, 1999, pp. A15, 17; and Diana Jean Schemo, "Global Crisis Hits Brazil's Auto Industry," *Miami Herald*, September 29, 1998, p. 7B.

8. "Brazil Rocks the Mercosur Boat," *Economist*, February 13, 1999, pp. 35–36.

9. See, for example, Earl F. Cheit, "A Declaration on Open Regionalism in the Pacific," *California Management Review*, Fall 1992, pp. 116–130.

10. In most cases the interface will be with male managers, but there is an increasing number of Asian businesswomen who manage large enterprises. For more on this, see Louis Kraar, "Iron Butterflies," *Fortune*, October 7, 1991, pp. 143–154.

11. For more on this, see Bernard P. Zwirn, "Operating a Manufacturing Plant in Indonesia," *The Investment Executive*, September/October 1991, pp. 37–39; and Joseph D. O'Brian, "Focusing on Quality in the Pacific Rim," *The International Executive*, July/August 1991, pp. 21–24.

12. Joyce Barnathan et al., "China: Birth of a New Economy," *Business Week*, January 31, 1994, pp. 42–48.

13. *Wall Street Journal Almanac*, 1999, p. 399.

14. "China Just Misses GDP Goal, But Data Signal New Trouble," *Wall Street Journal*, December 31, 1998, p. A6.

15. Ian Johnson and Leslie Chang, "China Offers an Array of Reforms," *Wall Street Journal*, March 25, 1999, pp. A18, 23.

16. Joyce Barnathan, Pete Engardio, and Lynne Curry, "China: The Emerging Economic Powerhouse of the 21st Century," *Business Week*, May 17, 1993, pp. 54–68.

17. Karby Leggett, "China's Economic Zones Losing Luster," *Wall Street Journal*, December 29, 1998, p. A10.

18. Kathy Chen and Hilary Stout, "Boeing, GM Obtain China Agreements," *Wall Street Journal*, March 25, 1997, pp. A3, 4.

19. Joyce Barnathan, Michael Weiss, and Dave Lindorff, "All the Tea in China Might Not Put Out this Fire," *Business Week*, January 17, 1994, p. 47.

20. Also, see "Colliding with China," *Economist*, March 12, 1994, p. 37.

21. Edward A. Gargan, "Gauging the Consequences of Spurning China," *New York Times*, March 21, 1994, pp. C1, C3.

22. Ian Johnson, "WTO Talks Between US, China Turn Serious," *Wall Street Journal*, March 5, 1999, pp. A9, 11.

23. Richard Tomlinson, "China's Reform: Now Comes the Hard Part," *Fortune*, March 1, 1999, pp. 156–164.

24. Helene Cooper and Dean Takahashi, "GOP's China Bashing Finally Worries Business," *Wall Street Journal*, March 16, 1999, p. A28; Jane Perlez, "Hopes For Improved Ties with China Fade," *New York Times*, February 12, 1999, p. A6; Ian Johnson, "China Fosters Price-Fixing Cartels As Economy Crimps Firms' Profits," *Wall Street Journal*, December 3, 1998, p. A17; Seth Faison, "China Applies Brakes on Move Toward Market Economy," *New York Times*, September 30, 1998, p. C3; Ian Johnson, "China's Venture Ban Could Cost Foreign Firms," *Wall Street Journal*, September 23, 1998, pp. A14, 17.

25. Michael Y. Hu, Chen Haiyang, and Joseph C. Shieh, "Impact of US–China Joint Ventures on Stockholders: Wealth by Degree of International Involvement," *Management International Review*, vol. 32, no. 2, 1992, pp. 135–148.

26. Manjeet Kripalani, "Investing in India Is Not For The Fainthearted," *Business Week*, August 11, 1997, pp. 46–47.

27. Jonathan Karp and Kathryn Kranhold, "Enron's Plant in India Was Dead; This Month, It Will Go on Stream," *Wall Street Journal*, February 5, 1999, pp. A1, 6.

28. Manjeet Kripalani, "Why India's Ruling Party is Flirting with Disaster," *Business Week*, August 10, 1998, p. 42.

29. Also see Jonathan Karp, "India Unveils Reform Plan for Telecom Industry," *Wall Street Journal*, March 29, 1999, p. A19.

30. Moon Ihlwan, "It's Not Just the *Chaebol* That Are Squeezed," *Business Week*, February 16, 1998, p. 54.

31. Stephanie Strom, "Korea to Sell Control of Bank to US Investors," *New York Times*, January 31, 1999, pp. C1, 3.

32. Stephanie Strom, "Korea Places 55 Companies On 'Death List,'" *New York Times*, June 19, 1998, pp. C1–2; Louis Kraar, "Korea's Comeback . . . Don't Expect A Miracle," *Fortune*, May 25, 1998, pp. 120–126; Jane L. Lee, "Mobile-Phone Companies Target Korea," *Wall Street Journal*, November 9, 1998, p. 13B.

33. See Cacilie Rohwedder, "For Hugo Boss, 'It's Time to Leave Home'," *Wall Street Journal*, April 15, 1994, p. A5.

34. Serge Schemann, "Declaring Death of Soviet Union, Russia and Two Republics Form New Commonwealth," *New York Times*, December 9, 1991, pp. 1, 4.

35. Michael R. Sesit, "Investors' Confidence in Russia Fades Further," *Wall Street Journal*, July 8, 1998, p. A11–12.

36. Timothy O'Brien, "Horrific Debt, Devastated Economy," *New York Times*, September 15, 1998, p. A12.

37. Patricia Kranz et al., "Who Will Lead Russia?" *Business Week*, November 9, 1998, pp. 62–64.

38. "Russia's Crisis Isn't Over," *Economist*, June 27, 1998, pp. 49–50.

39. Betsy McKay, "Russia Considers Limiting Access to Foreign Currency," *Wall Street Journal*, October 2, 1998, p. A12.

40. Patricia Kranz, "Will the Ruble Bring Down the Banks?" *Business Week*, June 29, 1998, p. 50.

41. Andrew Higgins, "Lacking Money to Pay, Russian Firms Survive On Deft Barter System," *Wall Street Journal*, August 27, 1998, pp. A1, 6.

42. *New York Times*, October 25, 1991, p. C4.

43. Also, see James B. Treece et al. "New Worlds to Conquer," *Business Week*, February 28, 1994, pp. 50–52.

44. See "Solidarity v Solidarity," *Economist*, April 25, 1998, pp. 51–52.

ADDITIONAL BIBLIOGRAPHY

Ali, Abbas J. "Middle East Competitiveness in the 21st Century's Global Market," *The Academy of Management Executive*, vol. 13, no. 1 (February 1999).

Beamish, Paul W. "Joint Ventures in LDCs: Partner Selection and Performance," *Management International Review*, vol. 27, no. 1 (First Quarter 1987).

Beamish, Paul W. and Wang, Hui Y. "Investing in China via Joint Ventures," *Management International Review*, vol. 29, no. 1 (First Quarter 1989).

Bugajski, Janusz. "Eastern Europe in the Post-Communist Era," *Columbia Journal of World Business*, vol. 26, no. 1 (Spring 1991).

Capon, Noel; Christodoulou, Chris; Farley, John U.; and Hulbert, James M. "A Comparative Analysis of the Strategy and Structure of United States and Australian Corporations," *Journal of International Business Studies*, vol. 18, no. 1 (Spring 1987).

Cartwright, Wayne R. "Multiple Linked 'Diamonds' and the International Competitiveness of Export-Dependent Industries: The New Zealand Experience," *Management International Review*, vol. 33, no. 2 (Second Quarter 1993).

Chao, Paul. "Export and Reverse Investment: Strategic Implications for Newly Industrialized Countries," *Journal of International Business Studies*, vol. 20, no. 1 (Spring 1989).

Clegg, Jeremy; Kamall, Syed and Leung, Mary. "European Multinational Activity in Telecommunications Services in the People's Republic of China: Firm Strategy and Government Policy," *Management International Review*, vol. 36 (1996/1).

Geier, Philip H., Jr. "Doing Business in Brazil," *Columbia Journal of World Business*, vol. 31, no. 2 (Summer 1996).

Hertzfeld, Jeffrey M. "Joint Ventures: Saving the Soviets from Perestroika," *Harvard Business Review*, vol. 69, no. 1 (January/February 1991).

Hu, Michael Y.; Haiyang, Chen; and Shieh, Joseph C. "Impact of US–China Joint Ventures on Stockholders' Wealth by Degree of International Involvement," *Management International Review*, vol. 32, no. 2 (Second Quarter 1992).

Hung, C. L. "Strategic Business Alliances Between Canada and the Newly Industrialized Countries of Pacific Asia," *Management International Review*, vol. 32, no. 4 (Fourth Quarter 1992).

Johnson, Simon and Loveman, Gary. "Starting Over: Poland After Communism," *Harvard Business Review* (March–April 1995).

Kao, John, "The Worldwide Web of Chinese Business," *Harvard Business Review*, vol. 71, no. 2 (March/April 1993).

Krawczyk, Marek and Lopez-Lopez, Jose A. "The Role of Government in Poland's Economic Transition: Ideas and Experience from the Recent Past," *Columbia Journal of World Business*, vol. 28, no. 1 (Spring 1993).

Lane, Henry W. and Beamish, Paul W. "Cross-Cultural Cooperative Behavior in Joint Ventures in LDCs," *Management International Review*, vol. 30 (1990).

Lawrence, Paul and Vlachoutsicos, Charalambos. "Joint Ventures in Russia: Put the Locals in Charge," *Harvard Business Review*, vol. 71, no. 1 (January/February 1993).

Leung, Hing-Man. "The China–Hong Kong Connection: The Key to China's Open-Door Policy," *Journal of International Business Studies*, vol. 24, no. 1 (First Quarter 1993).

Luders, Rolf J. "The Success and Failure of State-Owned Enterprise Divestitures in a Developing Country: The Case of Chile," *Columbia Journal of World Business*, vol. 28, no. 1 (Spring 1993).

Luo, Yadong. "Strategic Traits of Foreign Direct Investment in China," *Management International Review*, vol. 38, no. 2 (1998).

McCarthy, Daniel J. and Puffer, Sheila M. "Strategic Investment Flexibility for MNE Success in Russia: Evolving Beyond Entry Modes," *Journal of World Business*, vol. 32, no. 4 (Winter 1997).

Milosh, Eugene J. "Breaking Down Barriers to US–Soviet Trade with Soviet Market Access for Small and Medium Size US Companies," *Columbia Journal of World Business*, vol. 23, no. 2 (Summer 1988).

Mokkelbost, Per B. "Financing the New Europe with Participating Debt," *Management International Review*, vol. 31, no. 1 (First Quarter 1991).

Molz, Richard. "Privatization in Developing Countries," *Columbia Journal of World Business*, vol. 25, nos. 1, 2 (Spring/Summer 1990).

Nigh, Douglas and Smith, Karen D. "The New US Joint Venture in the USSR: Assessment and Management of Political Risk," *Columbia Journal of World Business*, vol. 24, no. 2 (Summer 1989).

Olivier, Maurice J. "Eastern Europe: The Path to Success," *Columbia Journal of World Business*, vol. 26, no. 1 (Spring 1991).

Prahalad, C. K. and Lieberthal, Kenneth. "The End of Corporate Imperialism", *Harvard Business Review*, vol. 76, no. 4 (July–August 1998).

Puffer, Sheila M., McCarthy, Daniel J. and Naumov, Alexander I. "Russian Managers' Beliefs about Work: Beyond Stereotypes," *Journal of World Business*, vol. 32, no. 3 (Fall 1997).

Quelch, John A.; Joachimsthaler, Erich; and Nueño, Jose Luis. "After the Wall: Marketing Guidelines for Eastern Europe," *Sloan Management Review*, vol. 32, no. 2 (Winter 1991).

Rabino, Samuel and Shah, Kirit. "Countertrade and Penetration of LDC's Markets," *Columbia Journal of World Business*, vol. 22, no. 4 (Winter 1987).

Ramamurti, Ravi. "Why are Developing Countries Privatizing?" *Journal of International Business Studies*, vol. 23, no. 2 (Second Quarter 1992).

Rondinelli, Dennis A. "Resolving US–China Trade Conflicts: Conditions for Trade and Investment Expansion in the 1990s," *Columbia Journal of World Business*, vol. 28, no. 2 (Summer 1993).

Rosten, Keith A. "Soviet–US Joint Ventures: Pioneers on a New Frontier," *California Management Review*, vol. 33, no. 2 (Winter 1991).

Rugman, Alan M. "Strategies for Canadian and Korean Multinational Enterprises," in Dalchoong Kim and Brian L. Evans (eds.), *Korea and Canada: New Frontiers in the Asia-Pacific Era* (Yonsei University: Seoul, Korea, 1989).

Sabi, Manijeh. "An Application of the Theory of Foreign Direct Investment to Multinational Banking in LDCs," *Journal of International Business Studies*, vol. 19, no. 3 (Fall 1988).

Schroath, Frederick W.; Hu, Michael Y.; and Chen, Haiyang. "Country-of-Origin Effects of Foreign Investments in the People's Republic of China," *Journal of International Business Studies*, vol. 24, no. 2 (Second Quarter 1993).

Siddharthan, N. S. and Safarian, A. E. "Transnational Corporations, Technology Transfer and Imports of Capital Goods: The Recent Indian Experience," *Transnational Corporations*, vol. 6, no. 1 (April 1997).

Stewart, Sally; Cheung, Michael Tow; and Yeung, David W. K. "The South China Economic Community: The Latest Asian Newly Industrialized Economy Emerges," *Columbia Journal of World Business*, vol. 27, no. 2 (Summer 1992).

Tallman, Stephen B. and Shenkar, Oded. "International Cooperative Venture Strategies: Outward Investment and Small Firms from NICs," *Management International Review*, vol. 30, no. 4 (Fourth Quarter 1990).

Tatoglu, Ekrem and Glaister, Keith W. "Western MNCs' FDI in Turkey," *Management International Review*, vol. 38, no. 2 (1998).

Vasconcellos, Geraldo M. "Factors Affecting Foreign Direct Investment in the Brazilian Manufacturing Sector: 1955–1980," *Management International Review*, vol. 28, no. 4 (Fourth Quarter 1988).

Vernon-Wortzel, Heidi and Wortzel, Lawrence H. "Globalizing Strategies for Multinationals from Developing Countries," *Columbia Journal of World Business*, vol. 23, no. 1 (Spring 1988).

Von Glinow, Mary Ann and Clarke, Linda. "Vietnam: Tiger or Kitten," *The Academy of Management Executive*, vol. 9, no. 4 (November 1995).

Welfens, Paul J. J. "Foreign Investment in the East

European Transition," *Management International Review*, vol. 32, no. 3 (Third Quarter 1992).

Wells, Louis T. Jr. "Multinationals and Developing Countries," *Journal of International Business Studies*, vol. 29, no. 1 (First Quarter 1998).

Williams, Christopher. "New Rules for a New World: Privatization of the Czech Cement Industry," *Columbia Journal of World Business*, vol. 28, no. 1 (Spring 1993).

PART FIVE

INTERNATIONAL BUSINESS HORIZONS

PART ONE: THE WORLD OF INTERNATIONAL BUSINESS

Chapter 1 Introduction	Chapter 2 MNEs	Chapter 3 Triad

PART TWO: THE ENVIRONMENT OF INTERNATIONAL BUSINESS

Chapter 4 Political Environment	Chapter 5 Cultural Environment	Chapter 6 Economic Environment	Chapter 7 Financial Environment

PART THREE: INTERNATIONAL BUSINESS STRATEGIES

Chapter 8 Strategic Planning	Chapter 9 Organizing Strategy	Chapter 10 Production Strategy	Chapter 11 Marketing Strategy
Chapter 12 Human Resource Strategy		Chapter 13 Political Risk/Negotiation	Chapter 14 Financial Strategy

PART FOUR: INTERNATIONAL BUSINESS STRATEGIES IN ACTION
To do Business in International Markets Including:

Chapter 15 Corporate Strategy/National Competitiveness	Chapter 16 EU
Chapter 17 Japan	Chapter 18 North America	Chapter 19 Non-Triad Nations

PART FIVE: INTERNATIONAL BUSINESS HORIZONS

Chapter 20 Future of International Business

CHAPTER 20

Future Challenges in International Business

OBJECTIVES OF THE CHAPTER

Over the course of this text we have seen how much the world of international business has changed in the last decade. Germany is now one nation, the Soviet Union has broken up into many independent republics, the EU has emerged as a full-fledged economic union, the European Union (EU), and Japan now dominates in many areas, from autos to electronic goods. These dramatic changes will continue, but it may be hard to predict the direction that the world economy will take. The United States is proving its economic resilience; despite a recession in the early 1990s and a growing national deficit the US economy began to recover in 1993 and by the turn of the century had the strongest economy in the world. Moreover, US exports are increasing every year, US businesses are downsizing and eliminating inefficiencies, and new world markets are being created and developed. At the same time Japan and the EU find their economies stagnating. Of course, this trend will not continue unabated. For example, Japan and Germany are working to regain ground lost to US business,[1] and they are opening up new markets of their own as well.[2] Developing countries are playing more important roles on the international scene and will probably continue to offer good opportunities for business investment.

The specific objectives of this chapter are to:

1. **Examine** how these changing developments will create both challenges and opportunities for MNEs over the next decade.
2. **Examine** some ways that MNEs will cope with their changing political and economic environments.
3. **Relate** the importance of the changing global work force composition on multinational strategies.
4. **Explain** why research will continue to be of critical importance to the field of international business.

American steel is back on top

For a number of years the US steel industry had been in the doldrums. Foreign competitors with lower wage rates and more efficient equipment had been able to dominate the world market. They found eager customers in the United States, and between 1980 and 1984 the import share of this market rose from 16 to 27 per cent. At the same time US steel exports declined sharply from 4 million tons in 1980 to 1 million tons in 1984. Since then, however, US steelmakers have been making a slow but steady comeback.

A number of developments have contributed to this recovery. The falling value of the dollar makes US exports more attractive and foreign imports more costly. The industry has also seen slower wage increases in the United States than in other industrial countries. For example, US wages during the 1980s went up an average of about 3 per cent annually, whereas they rose over 10 per cent a year in Japan and over 9 per cent annually in Germany. By 1992 US steel firms had increased their exports to over 6 million tons. At the same time the import share of the US steel market fell to under 20 per cent.

A second major development has been the replacement of old equipment with new, state-of-the-art machinery. In Gary, Indiana, for example, USX used to operate a giant mill that employed 27,000 people, produced steel from ingots, and manufactured a wide array of products, from nails to railroad tracks to sheets for automobile hoods. Today the firm's 8,000 employees use a cost-efficient continuous casting method to turn out a much smaller number of products, including sheet metal for cars and appliances, tin for food and beverage cans, and plates for construction and shipbuilding. It now takes the factory 2.7 hours of labor to produce a ton of steel, compared to 7.1 hours ten years ago. In the industry at large it takes US steelmakers 5.3 hours to produce a ton of steel, compared to 5.4 in Japan, 5.6 in Germany and Britain, 6.4 in South Korea, 7.2 in Taiwan, and 8.9 in Brazil. New efficient machinery and equipment

have also helped to drive down the cost of a ton of sheet steel from $504 in 1980 to $440 by the mid 1990s.

A third development has been the rise of minimills, which are small, efficient steel companies. In the past minimills produced only items for which quality was not a critical factor. This includes reinforcement bars for concrete used in highways and bridges, and material for fences, wires, and nails. However, today the minimalls have moved toward the more profitable product lines of the big companies, including flat rolled steel used in autos and appliance parts. As a result, the big steel firms now regard the minimills as a much more competitive threat than foreign steel, and this local competition is forcing both groups to become even more efficient.

A fourth development has been the dramatic change in company-union relations. Many plant rules have been altered drastically so that workers are no longer confined to one specific job but, instead, can be assigned as needed. Workers often operate in teams and are asked to spend time brainstorming to determine more efficient operating methods. Much of this new attitude is a result of a young generation of steel managers, whose views have been shaped by global competition in the steel business and experience in joint ventures with foreign partners.

As a result of these developments, foreign steelmakers have not been using all their import quotas. They are finding the US market too competitive and less profitable than in the past. In turn the US government has now allowed quotas on imported steel to expire, although it continues to fight dumping by foreign steel firms that are trying to regain market share by selling steel cheaper in the United States than in their own market. After a decade of protection the US steel industry rivals, and in many cases outperforms, its competitors in Germany and Japan. In fact, Japanese automakers in the United States such as Honda, Subaru, and

Toyota are now using US steel in their cars. The US steel firms are on their way back to the top.

Sources: Adapted from Jonathan P. Hicks, "US Steelmakers Staging Comeback on World Market," *New York Times*, March 31, 1992, pp. 1, 13; Howard Banks, "The World's Most Competitive Economy," *Forbes*, March 30, 1992, pp. 84–88; Steven Greenhouse, "Punitive Tariffs Raised Against Foreign Steel," *New York Times*, June 23, 1993, pp. C1–C2; Chris Adams, "Steelmakers Complain About Foreign Steel; They Also Import It," *Wall Street Journal*, March 22, 1999, pp. A1, 8.

1. In what way has the political environment in the US steel industry recently changed? Does this hurt or help the industry? Explain.

2. In what way have personal work ethics and values in the US steel industry helped to increase US competitiveness?

3. How can international business research be of value to firms in the US steel industry?

INTRODUCTION

MNEs are finding that one of the major challenges they face is to develop effective strategies for coping with changing environments. The international microcomputer chip industry is a good example. During the 1980s the Japanese dominated this industry, pushing out many US and European competitors to gain the majority of the world market. In the early 1990s US firms (most notably Intel) counterattacked and regained the lead. Strategic countermoves can cause successful firms to be dislodged by competitors.[3] But this is an ongoing process of attack and counterattack, and today's victor could be dislodged by the competition tomorrow. This process explains development in many industries, from autos to computers to real estate.[4] It also helps to explain why continual innovation and strategy modification are necessary for MNEs to retain their competitive advantage. In doing so, multinationals will be focusing increased attention on strategies that are designed to cope with changing environments.

DEVELOPING EFFECTIVE STRATEGIES

There are a number of ways that MNEs are supplementing or supplanting their old strategies in order to compete more effectively worldwide.[5] Two of the most recent developments include going where the action is and developing new compacts with governments, suppliers, customers, and competitors.

Going where the action is

One strategy that is proving increasingly important is the need to go international in order to keep up with the competition.[6] Successful multinationals have operations in the home countries of their major competitors. For example, IBM's strongest competitors are located in the United States, Europe, and Japan. In turn the company has facilities in all three places, to monitor the competition as well as to conduct research. Moreover, the communication network among the company's facilities allows each to share information with the others and to provide assistance. This also helps the company to maintain a strong competitive posture.[7]

Another reason for locating near major competitors is that some markets develop faster than others and the experience and knowledge that is learned here can help in other markets. For example, in the US market IBM is now trying to develop a strategy of providing the best service in the industry. In the past the company had often referred service problems to its dealers. However, now the firm is attempting to address these issues directly, ensuring a higher level of service and taking back customers who were lured away by smaller firms with better service, support, and prices. If this strategy works well, the company is likely to use it in other worldwide locations where small firms have been gaining market share.[8]

Another important aspect of a location-focused strategy is that MNEs often establish a home base for each major product line, and a multiproduct-line company will have "centers for excellence" all over the world. These centers are responsible for providing global leadership for their respective product lines. For example, Asea Brown Boveri, a Swiss firm, uses Sweden as the home base for transmission equipment. Research, development, and production are centralized here. Nestlé, the giant food company, has the world headquarters for its confectionery business in Great Britain because this home base is more dynamic in terms of the marketing environment and the high per capita consumption of confectionery products. At the same time Nestlé has made its Italian company, Buitoni, the world center for pasta operations. Meanwhile, Siemens has designated the United States as the world home base for medical electronics because this is where the market is most dynamic and will provide the company with the best chance of developing and maintaining state-of-the-art products.

It is also important to realize that the degree of globalization will be dictated by the product line. For example, food companies in Europe tend to be less international and more regional in focus. Local tastes vary widely and there are only modest gains to be achieved through large-scale operations, so European food companies tend to have an extensive local presence. The same is true for home appliances, which are often produced for regional markets. On the other hand, when European companies have become truly global, they have tended to focus on products that do not require high levels of integration on a worldwide basis.

So some companies have a need for global centers throughout the world, whereas others tend to stay in closer geographic proximity because of the nature of their product lines. Still others combine both of these approaches, as seen in the box "International Business Strategy in Action: 3M."

Developing new compacts

During the millennium governments will become more selective in their approach to industrial policy, aware that in the past billions of dollars have been wasted by bureaucratic efforts to streamline and refocus economic efforts. This recent trend is likely to result in more government–business efforts. However, the success of international business firms will depend more heavily on the companies themselves than on the government. Some of these developments will include the forging of new business networks for competitive advantage and the development of new relationships with nonbusiness sector groups.[9]

Forging new business networks Increasingly, the relationship of successful MNEs with their suppliers, customers, and competitors is changing. New strategies based on trust

INTERNATIONAL BUSINESS STRATEGY IN ACTION

3M

The 3M Company is a major MNE that has over 50,000 products comprising everything from office supplies to construction and building maintenance to chemicals, employs over 73,000 people, and has operations in 60 countries. How does the firm manage such a large international operation? One way is by matching its global strategies with the needs of the local market. Some goods such as home videocassettes are standardized and are sold on the basis of price and quality. Culture and local usage are not important considerations. Other products are greatly influenced by local preferences or regulations; telecommunications is an example. Each country or region of the world has its own modifications for local application.

The company balances its global strategies and national responses on a region-by-region basis. For example, in Europe the company has set up a series of business centers to address local differences. The company also uses European management action teams (EMATs) to balance the needs of subsidiaries in responding to local expectations with the corporation's need for global direction. Today, 3M has 50 EMATs in Europe, each consisting of 8–14 people, most of whom are marketing personnel. These groups are charged with bringing the firm's global plans to life by helping their execution at the local level. EMAT meetings, which usually occur quarterly, are designed to create action plans for the European subsidiaries. When the meetings are over, the members then return to their respective subsidiaries and begin executing the plans. In Asia the company uses a different approach, relying heavily on its Japanese operation to provide much of the needed direction to the subsidiaries. At the same time there are regional centers in Singapore and South Korea that help subsidiaries to address their local markets. In Latin America, meanwhile, 3M uses a macro approach, conducting business on a national rather than regional basis.

The company also carefully identifies those products that it will sell in each geographic area while following two basic strategies: (1) try to be the first in the market with new offerings because this strategy puts the competition at a disadvantage, and (2) grow new markets gradually by picking out those products that address the country's most pressing needs and focus exclusively on them. Commenting on its worldwide strategy, a company executive said:

We don't believe in formulating a single global strategy for selling videocassettes in India and laser imagers in France and Post-it brand notes in Brazil. For each of 3M's 23 strategic business centers in each region the company's strategy is a blend of global, regional, and local companies and that will continue.

Sources: Adapted from Harry Mammerly, "Matching Global Strategies with National Responses," *Journal of Business Strategy*, March/April 1992, pp. 8–13; Kevin Kelly, "3M Run Scared? Forget About It," *Business Week*, September 16, 1991, pp. 59, 62; James Braham, "Engineering Your Way to the Top," *Machine Design*, August 22, 1991, pp. 65–68; http://www.3m.com; 3M, *Annual Report*, 1997.

and reciprocal support are replacing the old business–client relationship in which companies sought to dictate the terms and conditions of sales and services.

In the case of suppliers, the current trend is toward reducing this number to a small group of reliable, efficient, and highly responsive firms. These suppliers are then brought into a close working relationship with the MNE so that both sides understand the other's strategy and plans can be formulated for minimizing working problems. The multinational will detail its needs and the supplier will draw up plans that ensure timely, accurate delivery. Another trend is the increase in the amount of responsibility being given to suppliers. Previously they were charged only with manufacturing, assembly, and delivery. Now many MNEs use their network partners to develop new materials and components, to perform industrial engineering functions, and to assume liability for warranties.

Conventional System

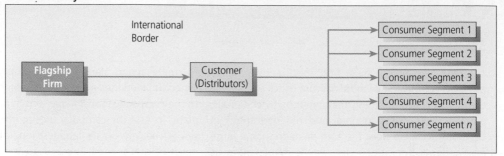

Network System

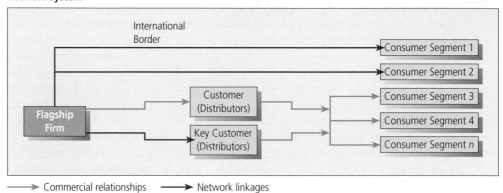

Figure 20.1   Network linkage and the changing shape of international distribution systems

Source: Adapted from Joseph R. D'Cruz and Alan M. Rugman, *New Compacts for Canadian Competitiveness*
(Toronto: Kodak Canada, 1992), p. 30.

In the case of customers, network linkages now involve changing the focus of the relationship from one in which sales representatives would work directly with MNE purchasing agents to one in which sellers interact more directly with their customers. D'Cruz and Rugman have explained this idea in the case of **flagship firms**, characterized by global competitiveness and international benchmarks.[10] In the conventional system the flagship firm and its customers maintain an arm's length relationship. However, new relationships are now being forged in which there is a direct link between the flagship firm and its most important customers (see Figure 20.1, segments 1 and 2), whereas traditional relations are maintained with some distributors to serve the firm's less important customers. At the same time network linkages are being developed with key distributors to serve other customers better. (Again see Figure 20.1, segments 3 and 4, etc.)

Network arrangements are also being created between international competitors in the form of joint ventures, technology transfers, and market sharing agreements such as a Japanese firm selling the product of a US firm in the Japanese market in return for a similar concession in the United States. Mazda and Ford Motor are excellent examples.

These strategic relationships among suppliers, customers, and competitors are becoming integral parts of MNE strategies, as are linkages to nonbusiness organizations such as unions with whom multinationals are now sharing their strategies in the hope of creating a working relationship that will save jobs and ensure company

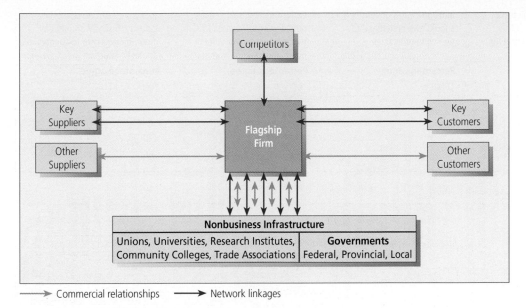

Figure 20.2   Network linkages for successful MNEs

Source: Adapted from Joseph R. D'Cruz and Alan M. Rugman, *New Compacts for Canadian Competitiveness* (Toronto: Kodak Canada, 1992), p. 47.

profitability. Partnerships are also being fostered with universities that can help to educate and train human resources, and research institutions that can provide scientific knowledge that is useful for helping organizations to develop and maintain worldwide competitiveness. Another group that is getting increased attention is government, since this institution can be particularly helpful in supporting legislation that will encourage the upgrading of the work force, development of state-of-the-art technology and products, exports, and the building of world-class competitors. Figure 20.2 provides an illustration of the basic structure of the "five partners" in an effective network. Notice how these relationships go beyond commercial transactions and involve network linkages to a wide variety of other groups. This is one of the waves of the future in international business.

COPING WITH CHANGING ENVIRONMENTS

The international environment of the millennium will continue to be one of rapid change, and MNEs will have to stay abreast of a number of developments. The political and economic environments will present the greatest challenges.

Political environment

As already seen, the political environment affects MNE activities in many ways. For example, all major triad groups have trade barriers that are designed to limit the sale of foreign goods in their countries. This in turn typically results in trade negotiations that are designed to open up these markets and/or to reduce trade deficits. Protectionism trends are particularly treacherous because they are psychological as

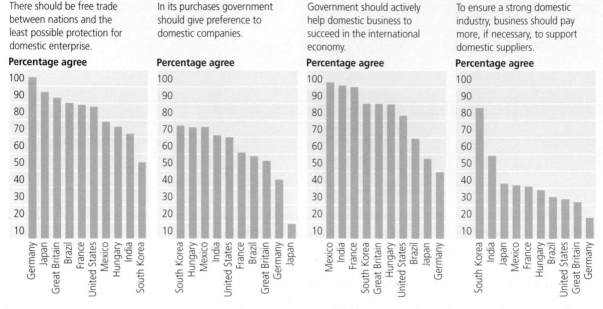

There should be free trade between nations and the least possible protection for domestic enterprise.

In its purchases government should give preference to domestic companies.

Government should actively help domestic business to succeed in the international economy.

To ensure a strong domestic industry, business should pay more, if necessary, to support domestic suppliers.

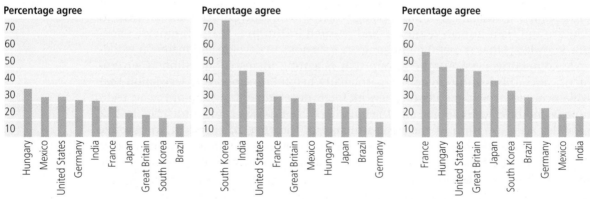

Businesses should be committed to their home country; it should not be easy for them to move facilities to another part of the world.

Government should limit the amount of foreign ownership of corporate assets.

It is acceptable for foreign companies to try to influence the laws and regulations of host countries.

Figure 20.3   Responses by international business executives to free trade and protectionism

Source: For more on this, see Rosabeth Moss Kanter, "Transcending Business Boundaries: 12,000 World Managers View Change," *Harvard Business Review*, May–June 1991, p. 156.

well as legislative.[11] That is, even when trade barriers are lowered, there is a tendency for people to be protectionist and to "buy local."

Many managers say that they favor open markets, but when questioned closely, they state strong support for protectionist strategies such as government assistance to domestic businesses and help for home-based firms that are seeking to go international.[12] In short, many businesspeople speak out for free trade but advocate policies that put foreign firms at a distinct disadvantage. A close look at Figure 20.3 reveals that the Japanese are some of the strongest supporters of free trade. However, research shows that these opinions are not translated into action. For example, Monroe shock absorbers hold 59 per cent of the US market and 28 per cent of the European market, yet the company (Tenneco Automotive) holds a scant 1 per cent of the Japanese market. Similarly, General Motors has approximately 35 per cent of the US market and 12 per cent of the European market, but it has less than three-tenths of 1 per cent of the Japanese market. Ford has similar statistics, holding 24 per cent of the US market and 11 per cent of the European market, but holds a mere one-tenth of 1 per cent of the Japanese market.

The ability of US firms to penetrate foreign markets will also be influenced by US government policies. The Clinton administration has been more vigorous than its predecessor in pushing for open markets in Asia.[13] Its formulation of a US government trade policy toward Japan and Southeast Asia includes guidelines for negotiations for open markets in the region, coupled with US aid to US high-tech industries, among others. The administration's objective is to increase the market share of US firms in this geographic region as well as to reduce the large trade deficit that the United States is running, most noticeably with Japan and China. The latter is likely to receive particular attention, given that in recent years China has sold far more to the US than it has purchased from them.

At the same time overseas companies are lobbying their governments to negotiate greater access to the US market. In Asia, for example, US air carriers such as United Airlines and Northwest Airlines can pick up passengers in one Asian locale and fly them to another locale. However, Asian airlines flying into the United States are limited in terms of market access. As a result, most of Asia's large airlines have now banded together to insist that they be given the same rights in the United States that US air carriers have in Asia. If they are successful, this will open new markets for such carriers as Japan Airlines, Singapore Airlines, Thai Airways, Cathay Pacific Airways of Hong Kong, and Qantas Airways of Australia.

Europe is also beginning to receive renewed attention. During the last few years of the Bush administration the United States had been running a trade surplus with these European countries. However, as Europe's economies began to slow down, there was growing talk on the continent about eliminating the trade deficit with the United States, and negotiations between the United States and Europe began taking on new dimensions.

A related issue is political risk. Many small countries are now embracing free-market concepts, privatizing state-owned businesses, encouraging foreign investment, and trying to get their economies moving. Will this trend continue? In some cases, such as Russia, the government has intervened and slowed down the move toward free markets in order to halt the short-term rapid inflation that accompanies such changes. This type of action is detrimental and merely increases the time needed to strengthen the economy. These changes also increase the risk to multinationals doing business there since any step back from the charted course toward free enterprise could herald the beginning of renewed state control. The US government and others are helping with financial and technical support. The goal of this aid is to ensure that the forces of democracy and free enterprise continue to progress. But the political climate in Russia and Eastern Europe remains uncertain.

Hong Kong also faces an uncertain political future. The former British colony was returned to China in 1997. The latter is now investing heavily in Hong Kong and has more total direct investment there than in any other country. At the same time two-thirds of foreign investment in China comes from Hong Kong Chinese. Yet relations between Hong Kong and China have sometimes been strained and have resulted in some Hong Kong firms diversifying their investments and moving funds to other geographic locales. Many Hong Kong businesspeople believe that relations with China will be worked out for the betterment of both sides. Certainly China needs Hong Kong and vice versa. Forty per cent of China's international trade passes through Hong Kong, and the latter provides China with a window to the West. At the same time China will eventually decide the political fate of Hong Kong. However, a great deal of concern continues to remain about what will happen over the next decade, thus increasing the political risk for MNEs doing business there.

Another region where political risk is being reevaluated is Vietnam.[14] Relations between the United States and Vietnam are now beginning to normalize, and the country is seeking business ties with US multinationals that can provide assistance in helping to rebuild the economy. President Clinton approved a renewal of lending to Vietnam by both the International Monetary Fund and the World Bank. These funds were necessary to allow critical highway and seaport projects to begin. At the same time, Vietnam has been trying to attract billions of dollars in manufacturing investment from European and Asian companies. Now that the US trade embargo has ended, Vietnam is also trying to lure US banks, aircraft, and power plant manufacturers to help in the rebuilding effort. One major reason that Vietnam is interested in rapprochement with the United States is that it sees America as a counterbalance to Japan and the growing military might of China. As relations between the two countries continue to thaw, political risk will decline and Vietnam will become an increasingly popular area for investment opportunities.

The continuing development of free trade agreements will also work to lessen political risk during the millennium. For example, the North American Free Trade Agreement (NAFTA) will bind Canada, the United States, and Mexico together into an interdependent market in which each nation will profit by working harmoniously with the others.[15] The same is true for members of the EU as well as for other economic unions, from those being fostered in Latin America to those in Africa and the former Soviet Union. Firms doing business in these geographic areas will find that the greatest ongoing challenge is more likely to be economic than political. There will also be further consolidation of the world's trade agreements into a triad-based system (see Table 20.1).

ACTIVE LEARNING CHECK

Review your answer to Active Learning Case question 1 and make any changes you like. Then compare your answer to the one below.

1. In what way has the political environment in the US steel industry recently changed? Does this hurt or help the industry? Explain.

The political environment has changed in that the government has allowed quotas on imported steel to expire. This will not hurt the industry, at least in the short run, because US productivity is increasing and many international competitors cannot match their prices. The decision will not help the industry, but as noted in the case, the government feels that further protection is not needed. Of course, if things change in the future and imports begin again to erode the domestic market share of US steelmakers, the government may again introduce quotas.

Table 20.1 The world's major trade agreements

EU (15)	EFTA (4)	OPEC (11)	NAFTA (3)	CARICOM (14)	CACM (5)	Council of Arab Economic Unity (7)	ASEAN (7)	MERCOSUR (4)	Andean Group (5)	LAIA (11)	ECOWAS (16)	SADC (14)
Austria	Iceland	Algeria	Canada	Antigua and Barbuda	Costa Rica	Egypt	Indonesia	Argentina	Bolivia	Argentina	Benin	Angola
Belgium	Liechtenstein	Indonesia	Mexico	Barbados	Guatemala	Iraq	Malaysia	Brazil	Colombia	Bolivia	Burkina Faso	Botswana
Denmark	Norway	Iran	United States	Belize	El Salvador	Jordan	Philippines	Paraguay	Ecuador	Brazil	Cape Verde	Dem. Rep. Congo
Finland	Switzerland	Iraq		Dominica	Honduras	Libya	Singapore	Uruguay	Peru	Chile	Cote d'Ivoire	Lesotho
France		Kuwait		Grenada	Nicaragua	Mauritana	Thailand		Venezuela	Colombia	Gambia	Malawi
Germany		Libya		Guyana		Syria	Brunei			Ecuador	Ghana	Mauritius
Greece		Nigeria		Haiti		Yemen	Vietnam			Mexico	Guinea	Mozambique
Ireland		Qatar		Jamaica						Paraguay	Guinea-Bissau	Namibia
Italy		Saudi Arabia		Montserrat						Peru	Liberia	Seychelles
Luxembourg		United Arab Emirates		St. Kitts and Nevis						Uruguay	Mali	South Africa
Netherlands		Venezuela		Saint Lucia						Venezuela	Mauritana	Swaziland
Portugal				St. Vincent and the Grenadines							Niger	Tanzania
Spain				Surinam							Nigeria	Zambia
Sweden				Trinidad and Tobago							Senegal	Zimbabwe
United Kingdom											Sierra Leone	
											Togo	

EU–European Union; EFTA–European Free Trade Agreement; OPEC–Organization of Petroleum Exporting Countries; NAFTA–North American Free Trade Agreement; CARICOM–Caribbean Community and Common Market; CACM–Central American Common Market; ASEAN–Association of Southeast Asian Nations; MERCOSUR–Mercado Comun del Sur; LAIA–Latin American Integration Association; ECOWAS–Economic Community of West African States; SADC–Southern African Development Community.

Sources: Adapted from *http://europa.eu.int/abc-en.htm; http://www.efta.int; http://www.opec.org; www.efta.int; http://www.caricom.org/; http://wellsfargo.com/nat//wr/da/mn//intro/other/; http://www.aladi.org/; http://www.sadc-usa.net/members/default.html; http://www.imf.org/external/np/sec/decdo/ecowas.htm. http://www.sice.oas.org/; http://www.aladi.org/;*

591

INTERNATIONAL BUSINESS STRATEGY IN ACTION

Volvo's success

Volvo makes 70 per cent of its cars in Sweden but has 90 per cent of its sales abroad. The firm has developed as a high-quality niche manufacturer of safe vehicles, and it does well against rivals such as Saab, BMW, Audi, and Mercedes.

The first Volvos produced in Gothenburg in 1927 were rugged cars designed to survive on the rough roads and in the winter cold of Sweden. This emphasis on durability has been transformed into a concern for passenger safety. Volvos are recognized as high-quality, well-built, and safe vehicles. Over the years Volvo has continuously invested in standard-setting safety improvements. These include side-collision protection, integrated child booster cushions, and the three-point passenger safety belt.

By the 1960s Volvos were out of favor as they were regarded as old fashioned, even if they were safe. So the top management team decided to change its design from "safe, but boxy" to "safe, but slinky." The

Volvo management also took on board lean production techniques (with robots and total quality management) which led to more efficient manufacturing. In the 1970s Volvo greatly improved worker participation and in the 1980s it helped set industry standards in green environmentalism. The latter was partly achieved by greater recycling features in its vehicles. Volvo has also reduced pollution and has, for example, the lowest paint solvent emissions in the industry.

Volvo's strategy is to be successful in a niche of high-end, safe, dependable, and well-engineered vehicles. Its brand name is globally recognized and reinforced by advertising emphasizing safety features and durability. Volvo attempted to have an alliance with Renault in the 1990s, but this failed. However, despite the mergers of Chrysler and Daimler-Benz, smaller vehicle producers like Volvo are proving successful in global niche markets. In 1998 Ford bought Volvo cars, mainly because of its high quality, niche positioning.

Sources: Volvo Annual Report; *http://www.Volvo.com;* Alex Taylor III, "Volvo and Saab," *Fortune,* July 21, 1997.

Economic environment

The economic environment of the millennium will be replete with opportunities for MNEs. (The box "International Business Strategy in Action: Volvo's Success" provides one example.) US multinationals, for example, will continue to be a dominant force in the export market, as seen by the fact that the United States again became the world's largest exporter in 1992. This is due, in no small part, to the growing competitiveness of US manufacturing and the fact that labor costs in the United States have risen more slowly than in other major economies.[16] Part of this development is a result of cooperative agreements between US management and labor unions, a trend that now appears to be shaping labor relations in Germany, where manufacturing labor wages far outdistance those anywhere else in the world.[17]

Economic opportunity will also be provided by the growing trend of privatization. In Western Europe, for example, governments are now seeking to sell many of their state-owned businesses. The governments collectively hope to raise approximately $150 billion from these privatization efforts. In an effort to stimulate economic development, nations in newly emerging markets are also employing this strategy. In Mexico, for example, privatization is attracting both new businesses and investment in local enterprises such as Anheuser-Busch's purchase of 18 per cent ownership in

Corona, the country's largest brewer. In Russia, Coca-Cola announced plans to invest more than $50 million over a three-year period to build a soft-drink production plant in St Petersburg. In China, a growing number of businesses are finding markets for their goods, as seen by such recent examples as AT&T's contract to provide over $1 billion worth of telecommunications equipment, Boeing's $800 million order for six 777 jets, General Electric's contract for $150 million of aircraft engines, and Motorola's order for $120 million of pagers, cellular phones, and semiconductors. Investor attention is also being directed to smaller countries such as Estonia, Latvia, and Lithuania. Although the total population of all three former Soviet republics is less than 8 million, these nations have natural resources such as oil shale, peat, timber, and amber, in addition to their warm-water ports on the Baltic Sea. The GDP per capita is in the neighborhood of $6,000 and the governments of these nations are trying to build bridges of free enterprise with the West. Similar opportunities are likely to evolve in other countries that currently are finding themselves falling further and further behind and will want to take action before the standard of living gap becomes any greater.

New goods and services will help to create new markets. An example is the tiny, portable personal computers (PCs) that are now entering the marketplace. These PCs are small, lightweight, and cost less than $800. The machines rely on superchips that provide the same power as that of many desktop models and are likely to revolutionize the PC market. These products also lend themselves to a globalization strategy since purchasers buy them based primarily on performance characteristics and not on cultural requirements. As a result, computer industry MNEs are likely to find the millennium offering both new opportunities and new challenges. The opportunities will come in the form of emerging markets since sharp declines in PC prices tend to increase demand sharply. The major challenge will come in the form of increased competition since PC technology tends to be easy to emulate, and so the barriers to entry for new firms are often quickly surmounted.

An accompanying development is the rise of the Internet as a source of competition. Today a growing number of MNEs are becoming electronic companies, or e-corporations for short.[18] The Internet is driving down costs and helping companies reach thousands of new potential customers worldwide.[19] As a result, MNEs are now throwing out their old business models and creating new ones that will help them do business electronically with customers who in the past were not accessible to them.[20] One of the keys to this new development is the rapid rise of both businesses and households with Internet access. As recently as 1997 approximately 25 per cent of households in Europe and 46 per cent of those in the United States had personal computers. Moreover, 6 per cent of the European and 18 per cent of the American homes had Internet access.[21] In addition, 47 per cent of European and 61 per cent of American businesses had Internet access. As a result, e-commerce is now accounting for a growing percentage of GDP in these economies.[22]

Major MNEs that are finding themselves unable to compete in the everchanging international arena are restructuring[23] and realigning markets. A good example is IBM; by 1993 it was cutting over 25,000 jobs annually and trying to stem its loss of revenues and profits. The company's poor performance in the microcomputer market and the stagnation of sales growth in the mainframe market called into question the viability of IBM in the 1990s. The decision to bring in a chief executive officer from outside the computer industry helped to highlight the fact that the firm believed that it needed fresh leadership, and recent results show that the company's decision was a good one, as IBM has now begun to increase its profitability. The firm is not alone. Most large computer MNEs are finding it difficult to maintain market share. This same situation exists in a host of other international industries, including (1) aircraft manufacturing, where Boeing is having to scurry to meet competition from Airbus, (2) autos, where Volkswagen, General Motors, and Ford are trying to stave off the onslaught of Japanese competition, and (3) household electronics, where such well-known manufacturers as Sony, Panasonic, and Goldstar are finding that the markets for products such as videocassette recorders are now becoming saturated and the key to the future will be new product development.

Exporting is likely to gain popularity, especially among multinationals with operations in the United States. There are a number of reasons supporting this development. One is the low wage rates of the United States *vis-à-vis* other industrialized countries, which help to create a competitive edge. A second is the major retooling that is occurring in many US firms, helping to dramatically improve the companies' efficiency. A third is the continuing effort of the US government to open up foreign markets for US goods and services.

New strategies, carefully crafted to the specific market, will offer increased opportunities for MNEs. In Japan, for example, the success of firms such as Toys "R" Us, Spiegel, and Amway is a result of learning how to work within the system. Toys "R" Us set up its own retail stores by teaming up with McDonald's Japan for investment capital and by relentlessly pursuing its objective despite vigorous opposition from small, local merchants who opposed letting Toys "R" Us into the market. Thanks to its dogged determination, the company was eventually given permission to open a large retail store and has been very successful in the Japanese market. Spiegel, famous for its mail order business, formed a joint venture with Sumitomo Trading Company and introduced an upscale fashion catalog in Japan. The company directed its efforts at women 20 to 40 years of age. Catalog selling proved so successful that by the mid-1990s the joint venture was generating annual sales of over $160 million. Amway decided to penetrate the Japanese market by sidestepping the complex, costly distribution system used by many retailers and by setting up its own distribution system. The company began hiring independent distributors who sell household goods through catalogs, mainly to neighbors, friends, and relatives. Today there are over 700,000 part-time and full-time people working for Amway, covering virtually every part of the Japanese market. These efforts, which are characterized by strategies that are designed to circumvent problems in the distribution system rather than trying to meet them head on, are typical of those strategies that will be used in Japan and other foreign locations during the years ahead.

HUMAN RESOURCE CONSIDERATIONS

There are a host of human resource considerations that will be major focal points for MNEs' activity in the future.[24] Some of these discussed earlier in the text include the global search for human resource talent and the need to select, train, and support expatriate personnel who are able to lead a diverse work force. Table 20.2 provides a contrast of the leadership practices that will be needed in the millennium. The following sections examine other major issues, including the changing composition of the global work force and the importance of addressing cultural needs.

Table 20.2 Strategic leadership practices

Practices used in the twentieth century	Practices needed in the twenty-first century
Outcome focused	Outcome and process focused
Stoic and confident	Confident without being cocky
Sought to acquire knowledge	Seeks to acquire and leverage knowledge
Guided people's creativity	Seeks to release and nurture people's creativity
Work flows were determined by the hierarchy	Work flows are influenced by relationships
The importance of integrity was articulated	The importance of integrity is demonstrated through actions
Demanded respect	Earns respect
Diversity was tolerated	Diversity is sought
Reacted to environmental change	Acts to anticipate environmental changes
Served as the great leader	Serves as the leader and as a great group member
Viewed employees as a resource	Views organizational citizens as a critical resource
Operated primarily through a domestic mindset	Operates primarily through a global mindset
Invested in employees' development	Invests significantly in citizens' continuous development

Source: Adapted from R. Duane Ireland and Michael A. Hitt, "Achieving and Maintaining Strategic Competitiveness in the 21st Century: The Role of Strategic Leadership," *Academy of Management Executive*, February 1999, p. 54.

Work force 2000

A series of demographic changes have occurred over the last 20 years that are going to affect the world's work force significantly during the next decade. In particular, the growth rate in major industrial countries is slowing down, whereas the rate in developing countries is rising. This trend will bring about a number of important changes, including (1) massive relocations of people on a worldwide basis, as countries needing more workers begin to lower and eliminate their immigration barriers and those with a surplus of workers allow them to leave, (2) nations with large, educated labor forces becoming targets of foreign direct investment by MNEs, and (3) countries needing to attract people but unwilling to encourage immigration dramatically increasing labor productivity in order to avoid slower economic growth.

Some key demographics A number of key demographics support the above developments. One is the growth of worldwide work forces. Between 1985 and 2000 economically advanced countries such as Canada, France, Japan, Italy, Spain, the United Kingdom, and the United States all had labor force increases of 1 per cent or less, whereas Germany's work force rate declined by approximately 0.3 per cent. In contrast, developing countries such as China, India, South Korea, and Thailand had labor force growth rates in excess of 1 per cent; countries such as Brazil, Indonesia, the Philippines, and Turkey had growth rates in excess of 2 per cent; and Mexico had a 3 per cent growth. Since economic progress is partially accounted for by adding more productive people to the work force, the sheer growth of the population in non-triad countries will be increasingly important to MNE plans.

Women will continue to join the work force in increasing percentages. In developed countries such as Japan, Sweden, and the United States a large percentage of women is already working. However, in developing countries this percentage is low but is rising quickly, and in some cases there is room for significantly more growth. For example, in 1950 in Brazil, 10 per cent of women 15 to 64 years of age held paying jobs; by 1980 this number had risen to 20 per cent, and it is likely to go much higher during the millennium. Similarly, in Mexico, 8 per cent of women worked in 1950, 17 per cent in 1980, and today it is over 20 per cent and rising. Both of these countries can add large numbers of people to their work forces by taking advantage of an untapped labor pool.

The age distribution of the worldwide work force is another demographic factor that is changing. In developed countries lower birthrates and longer life spans are increasing the average age. By the millennium less than 40 per cent of the employees in the United States, Germany, and Japan were under the age of 34. This is in contrast to countries such as Thailand, China, and Pakistan, where well over half the work force is now less than 34 years of age. In fact, today more than 15 per cent of the work force of most industrialized countries is over the age of 65, in contrast to approximately 5 per cent for most developing countries (see Table 20.3 for still other statistics), so the work force of most triad countries is significantly older than those of many other nations. Additionally, the productivity of these older workers may be less than that of their counterparts in developing nations (unless companies are willing to invest heavily in new workplace technology), and certainly the wages and healthcare costs to support this older group are higher than elsewhere in the world. These demographic statistics help to explain why MNEs are likely to turn more and more to third world countries for additional, and less costly, sources of labor.

A final important demographic trend is the rising number of educated people in developing countries. In the past it was the industrialized nations such as the United States, the EU countries, and Japan that provided most of the world's educated work force. In 1970 almost 60 per cent of all college graduates came from these nations. By the mid-1980s, however, they accounted for only 42 per cent of all graduates, whereas developing countries were providing almost 50 per cent of the total. Today four of the six largest sources of college graduates are the developing countries: Brazil, China, the Philippines, and South Korea. In addition, developing countries are becoming important sources of new engineers and scientists. Brazil, China, Korea, Mexico, and the Philippines each turns out more engineers annually than does France or Great Britain. Also, China and Brazil rank third and fifth, respectively, in the number of science graduates, ahead of sixthplace Japan. Developing countries are also becoming fertile ground for MNEs seeking to recruit highly skilled personnel. One researcher has noted that Bell Laboratories physicists, for example, come from universities in England or India as well as from Princeton or MIT. At Schering-Plough's research labs the first language of biochemists is as likely to be Hindi, Japanese, or German as it is English.

These data reveal that the world's labor force is becoming globalized and MNEs can no longer depend on one country or region to supply their human resource needs. An international labor pool has emerged, and companies will increasingly tap this source.[25]

Addressing cultural needs

Another important human resource consideration will be the development of more effective selection techniques for ensuring that expatriate managers succeed in overseas cultures. In the past many people have been given such assignments because

Table 20.3   The aging of the world's work force population

Country/region	Share of work force under age 34 (%)		Share of population over age 65 (%)		Labor force participation of workers over age 65 (%)
	1985	2000	1985	2000	1985
World*	57.1	51.7	5.9	6.8	32.8
Developed regions**	46.9	40.7	11.2	13.3	9.0
United States	50.4	39.5	12.3	12.9	10.3
Japan	33.8	33.9	11.1	15.8	26.0
Germany	45.7	37.4	14.2	16.0	3.2
United Kingdom	43.6	38.8	15.5	15.4	4.6
France	47.0	41.5	13.6	15.6	3.0
Italy	48.0	44.6	14.0	16.7	3.9
Spain	49.9	49.0	9.1	11.5	3.8
Canada	50.9	39.7	11.1	13.1	7.1
Australia	50.7	44.4	10.7	11.6	5.1
Sweden	38.7	36.3	16.9	17.2	5.4
Developing regions**	60.7	54.9	4.2	5.1	26.3
China	63.7	53.3	5.5	7.3	16.0
India	55.6	52.0	3.4	4.1	40.1
Indonesia	55.7	52.7	2.8	4.2	38.3
Brazil	62.5	42.1	4.0	4.9	17.7
Pakistan	63.3	59.2	4.1	3.9	33.7
Thailand	62.8	55.2	3.9	5.2	27.2
Mexico	61.4	51.9	4.1	4.9	42.1
Turkey	59.6	54.4	4.3	5.2	10.9
Philippines	59.2	54.8	3.3	3.8	44.8
South Korea	54.7	44.2	4.5	5.9	26.5
Former USSR	50.2	42.9	9.3	11.9	4.4

*Totals include some countries that are not listed in the table.

**Developed and developing regions as defined by the International Labour Office.

Sources: Adapted from International Labour Office, Economically Active Population, 1950–2025 and Yearbook of Labour Statistics, 1988.

they requested them and had shown a high-performance level at the domestic location. MNEs believed that such personnel could repeat this performance internationally. This selection philosophy is known as the **practical school of international selection**, which is grounded in the assumption that leaders can be successful in any culture because effective managerial behavior is universal.[26] Today this thinking is coming under severe criticism from the **cross-cultural school of international selection**, which holds that the effectiveness of a particular managerial behavior is a function of the culture in which the behavior is performed.[27] Accordingly, these people believe that major consideration must be given to screening and matching expatriates carefully with their assignments.

A number of factors are helping to speed this development. As we saw in Chapter 12, it is much less expensive to use local management. Also, research shows that successful managerial behaviors are not universal; what works well in one country may be inappropriate or useless in another. A good example can be seen in the work of two researchers who examined managerial behavior among three groups: (1) US managers in Los Angeles, (2) US managers who had been assigned from Los Angeles to Hong Kong, and (3) Hong Kong Chinese managers who were working in Hong Kong. This researchers found that the two groups of Americans has similar managerial behaviors and that they were quite different from those of the local Hong Kong managers. Moreover, although these behaviors were successful in the United States, they were not related to successful job performance in Hong Kong. Commenting on the results of their investigation, the researchers concluded that the philosophy of the practical school of thought is open to question, and many US firms are choosing the wrong people for overseas assignments.[28]

An ongoing management challenge will be that of developing valid and reliable methods of both screening and selecting people for international assignments. This trend will be complemented by efforts to identify, recruit, train, and promote local talent. There are two reasons for this latter development. One is the increasing supply of talented, worldwide personnel that MNEs can tap to help manage local markets. The other is the need to immerse oneself in the local environment by using national managers, salespeople, agents, and so on. Japan provides an excellent example. Firms such as IBM Japan have succeeded in no small measure because of their willingness to use local people to manage most of this operation. Another successful US firm is Applied Materials Japan, whose chief executive officer has noted that there are six important human resource management steps in doing business here: (1) hire a strong Japanese leader and top management team, (2) demonstrate a long-term commitment to the employees, (3) develop strong relationships with university professors, since they play such an important role in recruiting graduates, (4) look outside the industry and in government for qualified personnel, (5) hire retiring executives from major Japanese companies and government ministries, and (6) seek out Japanese members for the board of directors and for advisory groups.[29]

National work ethics and values are changing, and this is another reason that human resource managers in multinationals will have to make adjustments. In the United States, for example, people are now working more hours per year than they did 20 years ago. The work force is also proving to be one of the best in the world as measured by both cost and quality. Because of this, more and more foreign MNEs are attracted to the United States. In countries where workers expect a shorter workweek and have a strong desire for more personal and family time, multinationals must be prepared to address these concerns. The box "International Business Strategy in Action: The Japan That Can Say No" provides some examples.

An accompanying challenge will be balancing legal and business interests in light of the Civil Rights Act of 1991 and the protections it affords to US female expatriates. The Civil Rights Act of 1964 granted workplace protections to women and other minorities. In 1991 Congress expanded this coverage by defining an employee to mean a US citizen employed in a foreign country by a US-owned or controlled company. As a result, many US expatriates now have the same equal employment protections as workers in the United States. The major exception to this law is that companies are not required to comply with Title VII of the Act, if such compliance violates the laws of the host country. Barring such eventualities, female expatriates, in particular,

INTERNATIONAL BUSINESS STRATEGY IN ACTION

The Japan that can say no

There are many misconceptions about how Japanese and US workers compare. For example, whereas working hours in Japan have declined by almost 13 per cent in the last 15 years, in the United States they have increased during this time period.

Work hours in Japan are going down for a number of reasons. Some Japanese workers want to spend more time with their families and to pursue leisure activities more than they have in the past. Also, work can be difficult and demanding. In assembly-line factories, for example, the pace of the line is very fast and the employees must continually be working. Rest breaks have been cut back and team members have been cross-trained so that everyone on the team can do each of the jobs. This means that if someone is slow in performing his or her tasks, the other members must join in and help out. A third reason is that many employees feel that they are not being appropriately rewarded with either sufficient pay and benefits or improved working conditions.

Some executives at major Japanese companies agree with many of these complaints. Akio Morita, the late chairman of Sony, raised a number of questions about how the workers are being treated. In particular, he challenged whether long work hours are good for the employees or whether they should be given more holidays and fewer work hours so that they can enjoy their lives. Morita also raised questions about the quality of life and whether Japanese firms are providing fair compensation to their employees. He believed that it is time for Japanese companies to start emulating the examples of their international competitors: US, German, and other EU companies, where workers have fewer hours and/or better pay and benefits.

Will the future see a continuing decline in work hours in Japan? More importantly, will it see its system of employment converging towards that of other developing nations? It might not have a choice. It might not only have to decrease its number of work hours, but it might also have to destroy a system of life-long employment that has come to symbolize the Japanese economic system. Workers were guaranteed their jobs until the end of their careers. However, for the first time since World War II, Japan is facing its first recession. The new demands for better working conditions might be coupled with large layoffs and fundamental changes to labor relations. Matsushita has reduced its workforce by 5,300 in the last five years and Kanebo, a cosmetics manufacturing company, cut 3,300 jobs in 1998. Sony and NEC, though reluctantly, have also begun to dismiss workers or offer them early retirement bonuses. This has caused severe social problems as older workers who had vowed loyalty to a company find themselves in the street.

Today the Japanese economy stands at around 4 per cent unemployment, the highest it has ever been. While many developed economies would like to have such an unemployment rate, it is forecasted that if layoffs continue unemployment could reach up to 10 per cent in the future. However, those who remain in their jobs, a new generation of young professionals, might have better working conditions.

Sources: Adapted from Akio Morita, "Why Japan Must Change," *Fortune*, March 9, 1992, pp. 66–67; Steven R. Weisman, "More Japanese Workers Demanding Shorter Hours and Less Hectic Work," *New York Times*, March 3, 1992, p. 6; *http://www.sony.com/*; Japan, Policy Planning and Research Department, Minister's Secretariat, *Monthly Labor Survey*, January 1998 (*http://www.jinjapan.org/stat/stats/09LAB41.html*); Citibase, *DRI Basic Statistics*, December 1998; Frank Gibney Jr., "Death of a Salaryman," *Time.com*, February 16, 1998, vol. 151, no. 6.

are entitled to consideration for overseas assignments despite the on-site problems that this may cause for the MNE. In dealing with this challenge, multinationals are now developing action plans for ensuring equal opportunity for female expatriates while minimizing the problems associated with posting them to overseas positions. Examples include special training programs to ensure proper uniform implementation of Title VII provisions; special training for women and other minorities, thus better preparing them for the unique challenges that they will face overseas; and the filling of multiple positions with women and other minorities, thus avoiding a show of company tokenism.

ACTIVE LEARNING CHECK

Review your answer to Active Learning Case question 2 and make any changes you like. Then compare your answer to the one below.

2. In what way have personal work ethics and values in the US steel industry helped to increase US competitiveness?

One way in which these ethics and work values have helped to increase US competitiveness is through the change that has occurred in company-union relations. Today in many plants workers do a variety of jobs, as opposed to just one, so that they can switch tasks and cover for each other should someone be out that day. Employees also work in teams and collectively try to determine more efficient ways of getting things done. Another way in which work values have changed is that union and management now listen to each other and try harder to work together. A third way is through the attitudes of the new generation of steel managers whose views have been shaped by global competition in the steel business and experience in joint ventures with foreign partners.

INTERNATIONAL BUSINESS RESEARCH

No study of international business would be complete without paying attention to the role and importance of research. Much of what has been discussed in this book is based on research findings. In many cases the data were drawn from government statistics, company records, and business reports on recent developments and strategies. In other cases the information was garnered from formal studies such as the one reported above, which examined managerial behaviors among US and Hong Kong managers. Collectively, research provides important input for building international business theories and for formulating and implementing future strategies. As a result, it is useful to both academicians and practitioners.

Unfortunately, research can be confusing and contradictory. For example, many studies are extremely limited in focus and thus cannot be generalized to a universal setting. The study of US and Hong Kong managers relates the importance of training expatriates before sending them to Hong Kong. However, if these people were being sent to England, would training be necessary, and, if so, how much? The research study provides insights into international business, but its scope is limited. Similarly, when research is broadly based, it is likely that the findings cannot be generalized to specific situations. The Porter diamond, for example, helps to explain how triad nations develop competitive advantage. However, its value to non-triad nations, as explained in Chapter 15, is limited and the findings must be revised and modified in order to apply them. Despite such shortcomings, however, international business research will continue to be of critical importance to the field. Such research will allow us to test theories and to refine their practical applications.

Theory testing

A great many theories have relevance to the study of international business. In some cases these are first constructed and then tested. A good example is Adam Smith's theory of labor specialization. Smith presented this concept over 200 years ago in his *Wealth of Nations*, and in recent years learning curve analysts have confirmed these findings. Of course, not all theories have had to wait centuries before being proven. However, this example does illustrate that international business research can be advanced through the formulation of useful theories.[30]

In other cases theories are being tested for the purpose of reconfirming earlier findings. This is particularly important in learning how well a theory stands the test of time. A good example is the theory of lifetime employment in Japan. For many years theorists have argued that lifetime employment creates a highly motivated work force and western organizations would be wise to copy this approach. More recent research, however, reveals that lifetime employment is less useful as a motivator than as a control tool for ensuring worker loyalty and performance. In return for guaranteed employment workers stay with the firm for their entire career, work hard, and are compliant with management's wishes. Even unions are employer-dominated and serve more to maintain harmony within the employee ranks than to represent the workers.

Based on an analysis of empirical data collected on this topic, two researchers recently concluded, "Lifetime employment is offered within a . . . context of loyalty and benevolence based on cultural values. Its impact, however, is to increase the control of Japanese employees by managers."[31] Moreover, these researchers found that lifetime employment was not widely used by firms in tight labor markets because it was not possible to control the workers, who could easily find jobs with other companies and who derived little motivation from such guarantees.

This type of research is also important because it generates new hypotheses for testing. For example, as workers in large companies with guaranteed lifetime employment near retirement (55 to 60 years of age), will management replace them with younger people who are not given such guarantees? As the competitive environment increases, will companies stop offering these guarantees because they reduce the firms' flexibility in responding to changing conditions? Will young workers entering the Japanese work force during this decade be motivated by such guarantees, or will they turn them down because they are unwilling to commit their career to one firm in return for job security? These types of questions will be focal points for future international business research efforts, since changing economic, cultural, and social environments are creating new conditions in which MNEs must compete. Research can help to shed light on the effect of these changes.

Practical applications

Research is also going to play an increasing role in helping to uncover how and why multinationals succeed. In particular, greater attention will be given to strategy research that is designed to explain why some firms do better than others and how these strategies are changing. For example, during the 1970s traditional international business strategy gave strong support to **strategic fit**, the notion that an organization must align its resources in such a way as to mesh with the environment. Auto firms had to design and build cars that were in demand, and this might mean a variety of models and accessories, depending on the number of markets being served. Similarly, electronics firms had to maintain state-of-the-art technology so as to meet consumer demand for new, high-quality, high-performance products. Today, however, successful multinationals realize that they must do much more than attempt to attain a strategic fit. The rapid pace of competitive change is requiring linkages between all segments of the business from manufacturing on down to point-of-purchase selling, and in every phase of operation there must be attention to value-added concepts.[32] So the basic strategic concepts of the past, once widely accepted, must be reconsidered and sometimes reformulated.

Other research areas likely to receive future attention will be cross-national collaborative research by individuals from two or more countries and joint efforts by international and noninternational researchers. The world of international business is getting larger every day, and it is critical that research be designed not only to help explain what is happening and why it is occurring, but also to help predict future developments and thus better prepare students and practitioners for the international challenges of the twenty-first century.

ACTIVE LEARNING CHECK

Review your answer to Active Learning Case question 3 and make any changes you like. Then compare your answer to the one below.

3. How can international business research be of value to firms in the US steel industry?

There are a number of ways that international business research can be of value to firms in this industry. One way is by finding out what international competitors are doing and determining if any of their successful ideas can be copied. A second way is by gathering information on supply and demand in overseas locations and by identifying market niches that can be served through exports.

APPENDIX: A FRAMEWORK FOR GLOBAL STRATEGIES

Much of the material in this book can be synthesized within a single analytical framework.[33] We will develop this here to help summarize our key points. There are two basic building blocks in an international business course, as illustrated in Figure 20.4.

First, there is a set of firm-specific factors which determine the competitive advantage of an organization. We call these firm-specific advantages (FSAs). An FSA is defined as a unique capability proprietary to the organization. It may be built upon product or process technology, marketing or distributional skills.

Second, there are country factors. These, of course, are unique to an international business course. They can lead to country-specific advantages (CSAs). The CSAs can be based on natural resource endowments (minerals, energy, forests) or on the labor force, and associated cultural factors.

In this book, Part One introduced a set of FSAs used by multinational enterprises (MNEs). Part Two was a survey of potential CSAs due to political, cultural, economic,

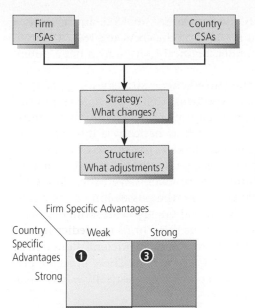

Figure 20.4   The basic components of international business

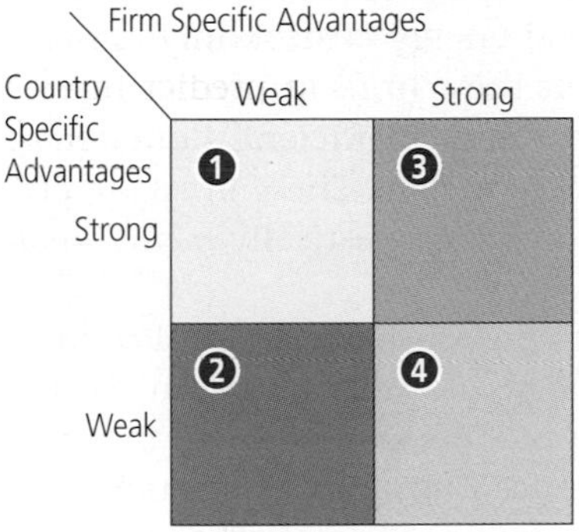

Figure 20.5   The competitive advantage matrix

and financial factors. Building upon the interaction of FSAs and CSAs, Part Three considered management strategies for MNE managers. Part Four then applied these strategies to the triad and smaller economies.

Managers of most MNEs use strategies which build upon the interactions of CSAs and FSAs. They do this so that they can be positioned in a unique strategic space. The CSAs represent the natural factor endowments of a nation; they are based on the key variables in its aggregate production function. For example, CSAs can consist of the quantity, quality, and cost of the major factor endowment, namely resources.

In Porter (1990) terminology, the CSAs form the basis of the global platform from which the multinational firm derives a home-base "diamond" advantage in global competition. CSAs are also influenced by tariff and non-tariff barriers to trade, and government regulation. Building on these CSAs, the firm makes decisions about the efficient global configuration and coordination between segments of its value chain (operations, marketing, R&D and logistics). The skill in making such decisions represents a strong, managerial firm-specific advantage (FSA).

The FSAs possessed by a firm are based ultimately on its internalization of an asset, such as production knowledge, managerial or marketing capabilities, over which the firm has proprietary control. FSAs are thus related to the firm's ability to coordinate the use of the advantage in production, marketing or the customization of services.

The competitive advantage matrix

To help formulate the strategic options of the MNE, it is useful to identify the relative strengths and weaknesses of the CSAs and FSAs they possess. Figure 20.5, the competitive advantage matrix, provides a useful framework for discussion of these issues.

It should be emphasized that the "strength" or "weakness" of FSAs and CSAs is a relative notion. It depends upon the relevant market and the CSAs and FSAs of potential competitors. A strong FSA implies that, under identical CSAs, a firm has a potential competitive advantage over its rivals.

Cells 1, 2 and 3 correspond broadly to the three generic strategies suggested by Porter (1980): cost leadership, differentiation, and focus. Cell 3 firms generally can follow any of the strategies. Firms in cell 4 are generally differentiated firms with strong FSAs in marketing and customization. These firms follow basically a differentiation strategy. In cell 4 the FSAs dominate, so in world markets, the home-country CSAs are not essential in the long run. Cell 1 firms are generally resource-based and/or mature, globally-oriented firms producing a commodity-type product. Given their late stage in the product life cycle, production FSAs flowing from the possession of intangible skills are less important than the CSAs of location and energy costs, which are the main sources of the firm's competitive advantage. Thus these firms are following low cost and price competition strategies. Cell 2 firms represent inefficient, floundering firms with no consistent strategy, nor any intrinsic CSAs or FSAs. These firms are preparing to exit or to restructure. Cell 2 can also represent domestically-based small and medium-sized firms with little global exposure.

In terms of business strategy, cells 3 and 2 are unambiguous in their implications. A cell 3 firm can benefit from strategies of both low cost and differentiation. Such a firm is constantly evaluating its production mix. As a product line matures and then declines it eventually graduates to cell 2. However, by adopting new product lines, developing dynamic organizational capabilities and maintaining an effective strategy, the firm can maintain its overall position in cell 3. In cell 2 there is no alternative but to restructure or to eventually leave the market.

Cells 4 and 1 are credible positions for different types of firms. For instance, a cell 4 firm which has strong FSAs in marketing (customization) can operate globally without reliance on its home-market CSA, or the CSAs of the host nation. For such a firm, cell 4 does not signal a CSA weakness; the CSA is not relevant. In contrast, cell 1 has mature multinationals or product lines determined more by CSAs than by FSAs. By improving potential FSAs in marketing or product innovation and increasing value added through vertical integration, the cell 1 firm can move to cell 3, where its profitability should be enhanced.

Although cells 1, 3, and 4 represent appropriate strategic positioning for some firms, there exists an asymmetry between cells 4 and 1. A cell 4 strategic choice may be a stable one for some firms; however, cell 1 firms should be able to aim for cell 3. The reason for this asymmetry is rooted in the fact that CSAs are for the most part exogenous to the firm, while FSAs are not. Even to the extent that CSAs can be influenced by government protection, there is always increased uncertainty associated with such strategies. For the firm in cell 4 already following an efficiency-based strategy there is no incentive, nor need, to move to cell 3.

It is useful to note the following two points. First, if the firm has a conglomerate structure it would be more useful to situate each division or product line individually, recognizing that different units of the diversified firm would use different generic strategies. Second, changes in the trading environment, such as the EU 1992 single market measures, or the EU 1999 single currency, or the Canada–US Free Trade Agreement and NAFTA, will affect the relative CSAs of the firms. To the extent that CSAs are improved, the firms will tend to move to cell 3, and to the extent that the CSAs are hampered, the firm or some of its product lines may move to exit, as in cell 2.

SUMMARY

Key points

1. Multinationals, as flagship firms, are beginning to develop new relationships with suppliers, competitors, governments, unions, universities, and a host of other external groups. This networking relationship is proving particularly helpful in increasing productivity, profitability, and overall competitiveness.

2. The two environments that will present the greatest challenges for MNEs during the millennium are the political and the economic. The rising tide of protectionism will require that multinationals deal astutely with foreign governments. They will also have to weigh carefully the political risk associated with investing in countries that are now beginning to shed their central planning systems and to move toward free enterprise economies.

3. Another major challenge and opportunity will be presented by the changing nature of the world's work force. Over the next 30 years triad nations will have growth rates of approximately 1 per cent, whereas developing countries will have rates in the range of 2 to 3 per cent. Developing countries will have younger work forces and an increasing share of the world's high school and college graduates. This means that MNEs will be able to tap this labor force to help meet overseas needs. It also indicates that these companies will have to be alert to the fact that local competition in these developing countries is going to become much stronger.

4. There will also be an increase in the amount of international business research that is being conducted. This will come in the form of both theory testing and the practical application of information. Both academicians and practitioners will find this development helpful.

Key terms

- flagship firms
- five partners model
- practical school of international selection
- cross-cultural school of international selection
- strategic fit

Review and discussion questions

1. In what ways are MNEs developing new compacts and networks? Give two examples and then explain why these developments are likely to help the companies maintain their competitive strengths.

2. How is the political environment likely to change during the millennium? Give one example and relate its significance for multinationals.

3. How is the economic environment likely to change during the millennium? Give one example and relate its significance for multinationals.

4. What are some of the demographic changes that have taken place in the international work force in recent years? Identify and describe three of them.

5. In what way have the demographic changes described in the above answer influenced multinational strategy? Give an example for each of the demographic changes.

6. How do supporters of the practical school of international selection differ from supporters of the cross-cultural school of international selection? Which group is correct? Why?

7. Why is theory testing of value to the field of international business research? What can be learned from such information?

8. In addition to theory testing, how is international business research of value to both scholars and practitioners? In your answer, give an example of how each group can benefit from such research.

REAL CASES

ENRON RECRUITS THE BEST

Working for Houston-based Enron, a US utility company producing and trading natural gas, was not seen as an exciting career move for top-quality MBAs. Indeed, in 1990 new CEO Kenneth Lang found that Enron did not even recruit from the top US business schools such as Harvard, Stanford, and Chicago. Instead, Enron went to second- and third-tier schools, as its experience was that these MBAs were more stable and it found that these graduates were very committed to careers in the gas utility business. However, Lang fired the human resource (HR) director who was failing to recruit top-class people. At the same he began injecting enthusiasm and vision into the company. In particular, he now spends a large amount of his time in recruitment, and he believes that to be a world-class company it is necessary to recruit world-class people. Today Enron competes with consulting firm McKinsey for MBAs from Harvard and other top business schools in the world.

When Enron was formed in 1985 in a merger of two US gas companies, it became the largest natural gas utility in the United States with the largest gas pipeline system and more gas-fired independent power plants than any other company in the world. In 1997, Enron's revenues were over $10 billion. At this time it owned and operated energy plants in 15 countries and had new projects in another 15. This represented 15 per cent of total sales. One of Mr Lang's strategies was to build up the international side of Enron's business, providing exciting opportunities and responsibilities for fast-track MBA recruits.

In 1992 Enron Development Corporation signed a contract for $2.8 billion to develop the Dabhol Project for a gas-fired power plant in the Indian state of Maharashtra. In 1995 this project was cancelled by the new BJP Socialist government of Maharashtra. The project was one-third complete at the time of cancellation and employed 2,600 people. The head of EDC, Rebecca Mark, renegotiated the project and Enron eventually offset this political risk.

Enron has also developed a new core competence (firm-specific advantage) in organizational learning and managing political risk. It has been one of the first firms in a stable and traditional energy-related sector to develop a knowledge-based business with skilled and well trained people. These individuals are managers rather than engineers. This gives Enron a competitive advantage compared to the average business in the energy field. The lesson to be learned is that even commodity-type utilities can become global businesses if they are willing to spend the time and effort needed to develop dynamic organizational capabilities.

Source: Enron Annual Reports; Andrew Inkpen, "Enron Development Corporation," in Paul W. Beamish, Allen Morrison, and Philip M. Rosenzweig, *International Management: Text and Cases* (Chicago: Irwin 1997); Sumantra Ghoshal and Christopher A. Bartlett, "Play the Right Cards to Fit the Aces in the Pack," *Financial Times*, July 28, 1998; Sumantra Ghoshal and Christopher A. Bartlett, *The Individualized Corporation* (New York: Harper Business, 1997); Jonathan Karp and Kathryn Kranhold, "Enron's Plant In India Was Dead; This Month, It Will Go On Stream," *Wall Street Journal*, February 5, 1999, pp. A1, 6.

HEWLETT PACKARD'S ENVIRONMENTAL MANAGEMENT POLICY

Today, like never before, MNEs have to be concerned about their public image. Consumers, employees, and shareholders all expect the corporation to behave responsibly and ethically towards the communities in which they operate. Some companies have learned the hard way that they are accountable. For instance, Royal Dutch/Shell had to apologize to its shareholders when the company's environmental and human rights report card did not measure up to their expectations. Today's MNEs are trying to get in line with the expectations of the stakeholders, and some companies, like 3M, Kodak, and Hewlett Packard, are outdoing themselves.

Hewlett Packard's Environmental Management Policy (EMP) oversees the environmental quality of its products through their life cycle. The company's EMP is complemented with an Environmental Management System (EMS). Through its EMS, Hewlett Packard audits its operations regularly with business managers being accountable to the CEO on their environmental standing. The system is based on the principles of total quality management. The quality of their products depends on their effect on the environment.

Environmental issues are an integral part of the planning and decision process. Hewlett Packard designs and constructs its facilities to minimize waste generation, and to promote energy efficiency and ecosystem protection. It pursues a strategy of pollution prevention to reduce the generation of chemical and solid waste and proactively addresses contamination resulting from its operations. It also encourages suppliers to adopt similar environmental principles.

In 1992 the company began a product stewardship program. The program maintains the following guidelines: to design products and packaging to minimize the energy they consume, to use fewer raw materials, and to use more recycled material; to develop products that are easier to reuse or recycle; and to reduce waste and emissions from the manufacturing process. The first priority is to avoid hazardous wastes. The company then finds proactive ways of recycling, treating, and disposing of these wastes. It is important to note that the company's EMS and EMP were found to be consistent with international standards set in the ISO 14001.

1. How can environmental innovation allow a company to gain a first-mover advantage against its competitors?

2. Governments constantly update their environmental regulations. How does the amount of flexibility allowed to a company influence the kinds of environmental investments it makes?

3. What kind of problems might make it difficult for an MNE to coordinate environmental strategies in different countries?

Sources: Adapted from Alan M. Rugman and Alain Verbeke, "Multinational Enterprises and Green Capabilities: Coping with Environmental Regulations" (Templeton College, University of Oxford, 1999); Alan M. Rugman and Alain Verbeke, "Corporate Strategies and Environmental Regulations: An Organizing Framework," *Strategic Management Journal*, vol. 19, no. 4, April 1998, pp. 363–376; *http://www.hp.com/abouthp/envrnmnt/*; "Shellman says sorry (Cor Herkstroter)," *The Economist*, May 10, 1997, p. 95.

ENDNOTES

1. Neil Gross, "Japan's Stimulus Plan Goes High-Tech," *Business Week*, April 5, 1993, p. 44.
2. Bill Spindle, "In Japan, New Policies Yet to Boost Economy," *Wall Street Journal*, March 31, 1999, p. A19.
3. See, for example, Dean Takahashi, "How the Competition Got Ahead of Intel In Making Cheap Chips," *Wall Street Journal*, February 12, 1998, pp. A1, 11.
4. Jeanne B. Pinder, "Japan's New York Realty Investing Plunges," *New York Times*, March 19, 1993, p. C10.
5. Shaker A. Zahra, "The Changing Rules of Global Competitiveness in the 21st Century," *Academy of Management Executive*, February 1999, pp. 36–42.

6. Also, see James B. Treece et al. "New Worlds to Conquer," *Business Week*, February 28, 1994, pp. 50–52.

7. Also see Howard Thomas, Timothy Pollock, and Philip Gorman, "Global Strategic Analyses: Frameworks and Approaches," *Academy of Management Executive*, February 1999, pp. 70–82.

8. Also see David Kirkpatrick, "Why the Internet Is Boosting IBM's Mainframe Sales," *Fortune*, January 11, 1999, pp. 148–149.

9. Joseph R. D'Cruz and Alan M. Rugman, *New Compacts for Canadian Competitiveness* (Toronto: Kodak Canada, 1992), p. 31; and Joseph R. D'Cruz and Alan M. Rugman, "Business Networks for International Competitiveness," *Business Quarterly*, vol. 56, no. 4, Spring 1992, pp. 101–107.

10. D'Cruz and Rugman, op. cit.

11. For an example of this psychological reaction, see David E. Sanger, "64 per cent of Japanese Say US Relations Are 'Unfriendly,'" *New York Times*, July 6, 1993, pp. A1, A6.

12. For more on this, see Rosabeth Moss Kanter, "Transcending Business Boundaries: 12,000 World Managers View Change," *Harvard Business Review*, May–June 1991, pp. 151–164.

13. See, for example, Keith Bradsher, "US Upset with Japan on Chip Pact," *New York Times*, March 4, 1993, pp. C1, C2.

14. Mark Landler, "Back to Vietnam, This Time to Build," *New York Times*, September 13, 1998, Section 3, pp. 1, 11.

15. See "Mexico: A Market That Is Ready for Services," *New York Times*, July 21, 1993, pp. C10–C15; and Bob Graham, "Free Trade Means Fair Trade," *Miami Herald*, July 22, 1993, p. 21A.

16. See, for example, John Templeman et al., "Germany Fights Back," *Business Week*, May 31, 1993, p. 48.

17. Brian Coleman, "German Union Sends a Warning With Series of Strikes for Pay Rise," *Wall Street Journal*, February 2, 1999, p. A19.

18. Gary Hamel and Jeff Sampler, "The E-Corporation," *Fortune*, December 7, 1998, pp. 80–92.

19. R. Duane Ireland and Michael A. Hitt, "Achieving and Maintaining Strategic Competitiveness in the 21st Century: The Role of Strategic Leadership," *Academy of Management Executive*, February 1999, pp. 43–57.

20. Heather Green and Linda Himelstein, "Throw Out Your Old Business Model," *Business Week E-Biz*, March 22, 1999, pp. EB 22–23.

21. Thane Peterson and Stephen Baker, "A High-Tech Europe Is Finally In Sight," *Business Week*, August 31, 1998, p. 122.

22. Robert D. Hof, Gary McWilliams, and Gabrielle Savers, "The 'Click Here' Economy," *Business Week*, June 22, 1998, pp. 122–128.

23. Claude H. Deutsch, "Digital Polish for Factory Floors," *New York Times*, March 22, 1999, pp. C1, 7.

24. Karen Roberts, Ellen Ernst Kossek, and Cynthia Ozeki, "Managing the Global Workforce: Challenges and Strategies," *Academy of Management Executive*, November 1998, pp. 93–106.

25. Also see Joseph A. Petrick, Robert F. Scherer, James D. Brodzinski, John F. Quinn, and M. Fall Ainina, "Global Leadership Skills and Reputational Capital: Intangible Resources for Sustainable Competitive Advantage," *Academy of Management Executive*, February 1999, pp. 58–69.

26. J. Stewart Black and Lyman W. Porter, "Managerial Behaviors and Job Performance: A Successful Manager in Los Angeles May Not Succeed in Hong Kong," *Journal of International Business Studies*, First Quarter, 1991, p. 101.

27. Ibid., p. 100.

28. Ibid., p. 111.

29. James C. Morgan and J. Jeffrey Morgan, *Cracking the Japanese Market: Strategies for Success in the New Global Economy* (New York: Free Press, 1991), pp. 188–189.

30. Otto Andersen, "On the Internationalization Process of Firms: A Critical Analysis," *Journal of International Business Studies*, Second Quarter 1993, pp. 209–231; and Sumantra Ghoshal and Nitin Nohria, "Horses for Courses: Organizational Forms for Multinational Corporations," *Sloan Management Review*, Winter 1993, pp. 23–35.

31. Jeremiah J. Sullivan and Richard B. Peterson, "A Test of Theories Underlying the Japanese Lifetime Employment System," *Journal of International Business Studies*, First Quarter, 1991, p. 79.

32. Richard M. Hodgetts, "A Conversation with Michael E. Porter," *Organizational Dynamics*, Summer 1999, pp. 25–26.

33. Alan M. Rugman, *Inside the Multinationals: The Economics of Internal Markets* (New York: Columbia University Press, 1981); Alan M. Rugman (ed.) *International Business in Canada: Strategies for Management* (Toronto: Prentice-Hall Canada, 1989), Chapters 8, 13; Alan M. Rugman, *The Theory of Multinational Enterprises* (Cheltenham: Edward Elgar, 1996).

ADDITIONAL BIBLIOGRAPHY

Auster, Ellen R. "International Corporate Linkages: Dynamic Forms in Changing Environments," *Columbia Journal of World Business*, vol. 22, no. 2 (Summer 1987).

Ball, Donald A., and McCulloch, Wendell H., Jr. "The Views of American Multinational CEOs on Internationalized Business Education for Prospective Employees," *Journal of International Business Studies*, vol. 24, no. 2 (Second Quarter 1993).

Brewer, Thomas L. and Young, Stephen. *The Multilateral Investment System and Multinational Enterprise* (Oxford: Oxford University Press, 1998).

Clarkson, Max B. E. "A Stakeholder Framework for Analyzing and Evaluating Corporate Social Performance," *The Academy of Management Review*, vol. 20, no. 1 (January 1995).

D'Cruz, Joseph R. and Rugman, Alan M. "Developing International Competitiveness: The Five Partners Model," *Business Quarterly* (Winter 1993).

D'Cruz, Joseph R. and Rugman, Alan M. "Business Networks, Telecommunications and International Competitiveness," *Development and International Cooperation*, vol. 9, no. 2 (December 1993).

D'Cruz, Joseph R. and Rugman, Alan M. "Business Network Theory and the Canadian Telecommunications Industry," *International Business Review*, vol. 3, no. 3 (1994).

Doyle, Frank P. "People-Power: The Global Human Resource Challenge for the '90s," *Columbia Journal of World Business*, vol. 25, nos. 1, 2 (Spring/Summer 1990).

Dunning, John H. *Multinational Enterprises and the Global Economy* (Reading, UK: Addison-Wesley, 1993).

Dunning, John H. *The Globalization of Business: The Challenge of the 1990s* (London and New York: Routledge, 1993).

Egelhoff, William G. "Information-Processing Theory and the Multinational Enterprise," *Journal of International Business*, vol. 22, no. 3 (Third Quarter 1991).

Emmerij, Louis. "Globalization, Regionalization and World Trade," *Columbia Journal of World Business*, vol. 27, no. 2 (Summer 1992).

Ghoshal, Sumantra; Arnzen, Breck; and Brownfield, Sharon. "A Learning Alliance Between Business and Business Schools: Executive Education as a Platform for Partnership," *California Management Review*, vol. 35, no. 1 (Fall 1992).

Ghoshal, Sumantra and Bartlett, Christopher A. "The Multinational Corporation as an Interorganizational Network," *Academy of Management Review*, vol. 15, no. 4 (October 1990).

Globerman, Steven. "Government Policies Toward Foreign Direct Investment: Has a New Era Dawned?" *Columbia Journal of World Business*, vol. 23, no. 3 (Fall 1988).

Guntz, Hugh P. and Jalland, R. Michael. "Managerial Careers and Business Strategies," *The Academy of Management Review*, vol. 21, no. 3 (July 1996).

Kim, W. Chan and Mauborgne, Renee A. "Effectively Conceiving and Executing Multinationals' Worldwide Strategies," *Journal of International Business Studies*, vol. 24, no. 3 (Third Quarter 1993).

Kimura, Yui. "Firm-Specific Strategic Advantages and Foreign Direct Investment Behaviour of Firms: The Case of Japanese Semiconductor Firms," *Journal of International Business Studies*, vol. 20, no. 2 (Summer 1989).

Kogut, Bruce and Zander, Udo. "Knowledge of the Firm and the Evolutionary Theory of the Multinational Corporation," *Journal of International Business Studies*, vol. 24, no. 4 (Fourth Quarter 1993).

Martinez, Jon I. and Jarillo, J. Carlos. "The Evolution of Research on Coordination Mechanism in Multinational Corporations," *Journal of International Business Studies*, vol. 20, no. 3 (Fall 1989).

Martinez, Jon I. and Jarillo, J. Carlos. "Coordination Demands of International Strategies," *Journal of International Business Studies*, vol. 22, no. 3 (Third Quarter 1991).

Miller, Kent D. "Industry and Country Effects of Managers' Perceptions of Environmental Uncertainties," *Journal of International Business Studies*, vol. 24, no. 4 (Fourth Quarter 1993).

Morita, Akio. "Partnering for Competitiveness: The Role of Japanese Business," *Harvard Business Review*, vol. 70, no. 3 (May/June 1992).

Morrison, Allen J. and Inkpen, Andrew C. "An Analysis of Significant Contributions to the International Business Literature," *Journal of International Business Studies*, vol. 22, no. 1 (First Quarter 1991).

Nehrt, Chad. "Maintaining a First Mover Advantage When Environmental Regulations Differ Between Countries," *The Academy of Management Review*, vol. 23, no. 1 (January 1998).

Ohmae, Kenichi. "Managing in a Borderless World," *Harvard Business Review*, vol. 67, no. 3 (May–June 1989).

Rosenzweig, Philip M. and Singh, Jitendra V. "Organizational Environments and the Multinational Enterprise," *Academy of Management Review*, vol. 16, no. 2 (April 1991).

Rugman, Alan M. "Multinationals and Trade in Services: A Transaction Cost Approach," *Weltwirtschaftliches Archiv*, vol. 123, no. 4 (December 1987).

Rugman, Alan M. and D'Cruz, Joseph R. "A Theory of Business Networks," in Lorraine Eden (ed.), *Multinationals in North America* (University of Calgary Press, 1993).

Rugman, Alan M., Kirton, John and Soloway, Julie. *Environmental Regulations and Corporate Strategy* (Oxford: Oxford University Press, 1999).

Rugman, Alan M. and Verbeke, Alain. *Research in Global Strategic Management: Volume 3: Corporate Response to Global Change* (Greenwich, Conn.: JAI Press, 1992).

Rugman, Alan M. and Verbeke, Alain. *Research in Global Strategic Management: Volume 4: Beyond the Three Generics* (Greenwich, Conn.: JAI Press, 1993).

Rugman, Alan M. and Verbeke, Alain. "Corporate Strategies and Environmental Regulations: An Organizing Framework," *Strategic Management Journal*, vol. 19 Special Issue (April 1998).

Scott, Bruce R. "Competitiveness: Self-Help for a Worsening Problem," *Harvard Business Review*, vol. 67, no. 4 (July/August 1989).

Shan, Weijian. "Environmental Risks and Joint Venture Sharing Arrangements," *Journal of International Business Studies*, vol. 22, no. 4 (Fourth Quarter 1991).

Sills, Charles F. "Draft-Horse, Not Dragon: Observations on Trade and the Environment," *Columbia Journal of World Business*, vol. 27, no. 3 (Fall/Winter 1992).

Vandermerwe, Sandra and Oliff, Michael D. "Corporate Challenges for an Age of Reconsumption," *Columbia Journal of World Business*, vol. 26, no. 3 (Fall 1991).

Westcott, William F., II. "Environmental Technology Cooperation: A Quid Pro Quo for Transnational Corporations and Developing Countries," *Columbia Journal of World Business*, vol. 27, no. 3 (Fall/Winter 1992).

Yip, George S. "Global Strategy . . . In a World of Nations?" *Sloan Management Review*, vol. 31, no. 1 (Fall 1989).

Zahra, Shaker A. "The Changing Rules of Global Competitiveness in the 21st Century," *The Academy of Management Executive*, vol. 13, no. 1 (February 1999).

Glossary

Acceptance zone. An area within which a party is willing to negotiate.

Ad valorem tariff. A tax which is based on a percentage of the value of imported goods.

Advertising. A nonpersonal form of promotion in which a firm attempts to persuade consumers of a particular point of view.

Aesthetics. The artistic tastes of a culture.

Andean common market (Ancom). A subregional free trade compact designed to promote economic and social integration and cooperation; Bolivia, Colombia, Ecuador, Peru, and Venezuela are all members.

Andean Pact. An economic union consisting of Bolivia, Colombia, Ecuador, Peru, and Venezuela.

Antidumping duties. Import tariffs intended to protect domestic producers from foreign products sold at less than their cost of production or at lower prices than in their home market.

Arm's length price. The price a buyer will pay for merchandise in a market under conditions of perfect competition.

Association of Southeast Asian Nations (Asean). An economic union founded in 1967 by Indonesia, Malaysia, the Philippines, Singapore, and Thailand; this economic bloc focuses not on reducing trade barriers among members but, rather, on promoting exports to other nations.

Attitude. A persistent tendency to feel and behave in a particular way toward some object.

Autonomous infrastructure. An infrastructure used by multinationals that compete in dissimilar national markets and do not share resources.

Backward integration. The ownership of equity assets used earlier in the production cycle, such as an auto firm that acquires a steel company.

Balance of payments (BOP). The record of all values of all transactions between a country's residents and the rest of the world.

Base salary. The amount of cash compensation that an individual receives in the home country.

Basic economic infrastructure. The primary economic industries, including transportation, communication, and energy.

Basic mission. The reason that a firm is in existence.

British Export Credits Guarantee Department. A governmental agency that lends money for export financing of British equipment.

Business managers. Managers responsible for coordinating the efforts of people in a corporate organization; for example, in a matrix structure.

Canada Labor Code. A federal law that covers areas such as wages, employment practices, work safety, and conciliation of labor disputes.

Capital account items. A balance-of-payments account that involves transactions which involve claims in ownership.

Capital expenditures. Major projects in which the costs are to be allocated over a number of years.

Caribbean Basin initiative. A trade agreement that eliminates tariffs on many imports to the United States from the Caribbean and Central American regions.

Cartel. A group of firms that collectively agree to fix prices or quantities sold in an effort to control price.

Centrally determined economy. An economy in which goods and services are allocated based on a plan formulated by a committee that decides what is to be offered.

Cluster analysis. A marketing approach to forecasting customer demand; it involves the grouping

611

of data based on market area, customer, or similar variables.

Codetermination. A legal system that requires workers and their managers to discuss major strategic decisions before companies implement the decisions.

Collectivism. The tendency of people to belong to groups who look after each other in exchange for loyalty.

Common market. A form of economic integration characterized by the elimination of trade barriers among member nations, a common external trade policy, and mobility of factors of production among member countries.

Communication. The process of transferring meanings from sender to receiver.

Communism. A political system in which the government owns all property and makes all decisions regarding production and distribution of goods and services.

Comparative advertising. The comparing of similar products for the purpose of persuading customers to buy a particular one.

Competition Act. A Canadian federal law which regulates anticompetitive practices and prohibits actions that will substantially lessen or prevent competition; it is similar to US antitrust laws.

Competitive scope. The breadth of a firm's target market within an industry.

Compound duty. A tariff consisting of both a specific and an *ad valorem* duty.

Concurrent engineering. The process of having design, engineering, and manufacturing people working together to create a product, in contrast to working in a sequential manner.

Confucian work ethic. A belief that people should work hard at their tasks.

Consolidation. The combining of the major financial statements of subsidiaries into composite statements for the parent firm.

Container ships. Vessels used to carry standardized containers that can be simply loaded onto a carrier and then unloaded at their destination without any repackaging of the contents of the containers.

Contract management. A process by which an organization (such as the government) transfers operating responsibility of an industry without transferring the legal title and ownership.

Controlling. The process of determining that everything goes according to plan.

Coordinated infrastructure. An infrastructure used when there is a high degree of similarity among national markets and business units share resources in an effort to help each other to increase overall sales.

Cost strategy. A strategy that relies on low price and is achieved through approaches such as vigorous pursuit of cost reductions and overhead-control, avoidance of marginal customer accounts, and cost minimization in areas such as sales and advertising.

Council for Mutual Economic Assistance (Comecon). An economic union of communist countries led by the former USSR and including most eastern bloc nations; today Comecon's role has been greatly diminished.

Council of Ministers. The major policy decision-making body of the EU; it consists of one minister from each of the 12 member states and is one of four major institutions of the EU.

Countertrade. Barter trade in which the exporting firm receives payment in products from the importing country.

Countervailing duties. Import tariffs intended to protect domestic producers from harmful subsidization by foreign governments.

Court of Justice. A court that has one judge appointed from each EU member country; this court serves as the official interpreter of EU law.

Cross-cultural school of international selection. A school of thought which holds that the effectiveness of a particular managerial behavior is a function of the culture in which the behavior is performed.

Cross rate. An exchange rate computed from two other rates, such as the relationship between Swiss francs and German marks.

Cultural assimilator. A programmed learning technique designed to expose members of one culture to some of the basic concepts, attitudes, role perceptions, customs, and values of another culture.

Culture. The acquired knowledge that people use to interpret experience and to generate social behavior.

Currency diversification. The spreading of financial assets across several or more currencies.

Currency option. An instrument that gives the purchaser the right to buy or sell a specific amount of foreign currency at a predetermined rate within a specified time period.

Current account. A balance-of-payments account that consists of merchandise trade, services, and unrequited transfers.

Customs. Common or established practices.

Customs union. A form of economic integration in which all tariffs between member countries are eliminated and a common trade policy toward nonmember countries is established.

Decision making. The process of choosing from among alternatives.

Delayed differentiation. A strategy in which all products are manufactured in the same way for all countries or regions until as late in the assembly process as possible, at which time differentiation is used to introduce particular features or special components.

Democracy. A system of government in which the people, either directly or through their elected officials, decide what is to be done.

Diet. The branch of the Japanese government in which legislative power is vested; it consists of a popularly elected House of Representatives and House of Councillors.

Differentiation strategy. A strategy directed toward creating something that is perceived as being unique.

Distribution. The course that goods take between production and the final consumer.

Divestiture. (Also see *Privatization*) A process by which a government or business sells assets.

Dumping. The selling of imported goods at a price below cost or below that in the home country.

Economic exposure. The foreign exchange risk involved in pricing products, sourcing parts, or locating investments to develop a competitive position.

Economic integration. The establishment of transnational rules and regulations that enhance economic trade and cooperation among countries.

Economic union. A form of economic integration characterized by free movement of goods, services, and factors of production among member countries and full integration of economic policies.

Embargo. A quota set at zero, thus preventing the importation of those products that are involved.

Empowerment. The process of giving employees increased control over their work.

Enterprise for the Americas. An idea launched by President Bush; the aim of this effort is to create the free trade area from Alaska to Argentine Antarctica.

Estimation by analogy. A method of forecasting market demand or market growth based on information generated in other countries, such as determining the number of refrigerators sold in the United States as a percentage of new housing starts and using this statistic in planning for the manufacture of these products in other world markets.

Ethnocentric predisposition. The tendency of a manager or multinational company to rely on the values and interests of the parent company in formulating and implementing the strategic plan.

Ethnocentric solution. An approach to determining parent–subsidiary relations; it involves treating all foreign operations as if they were extensions of domestic operations.

Ethnocentrism. The belief that one's way of doing things is superior to that of others.

Eurobond. A financial instrument that is typically underwritten by a syndicate of banks from different countries and is sold in countries other than the one in which its currency is denominated.

Eurocurrency. Any currency banked outside its country of origin.

Eurodollars. Dollars banked outside the United States.

European Bank for Reconstruction and Development. A bank created to promote democracy and free enterprise in Eastern Europe and to lend public and private money.

European Coal and Steel Community. A community formed in 1952 by Belgium, France, Italy, Luxembourg, the Netherlands, and West Germany for the purpose of creating a common market that would revitalize the efficiency and competitiveness of the coal and steel industries in those countries.

European Commission. A 12-member group chosen by agreement of member governments of the EU; the Commission is the executive branch of the EU.

European Free Trade Association. A free trade area currently consisting of Austria, Finland, Iceland, Liechtenstein, Norway, Sweden, and Switzerland; past members included the United Kingdom (before it joined the EU).

European monetary system. A system created by some major members of the EU which fixes their currency values in relation to each other (within a band) and floats them together against the rest of the world.

European Parliament. A group of 518 members elected directly by voters in each member country of the EU; the Parliament serves as a watchdog on EU expenditures.

European Research Cooperation Agency. A research and development alliance which emphasizes projects in the fields of energy, medicine, biotechnology, communications, information technology, transport, new materials, robotics, production automation, lasers, and the environment.

Exchange controls. Controls that restrict the flow of currency.

Exchange rate. The amount of one currency that can be obtained for another currency.

Exchange risk. The probability that a company will be unable to adjust prices and costs to offset changes in the exchange rate.

Exchange risk adaptation. The use of hedging to provide protection against exchange rate fluctuations.

Exchange risk avoidance. The elimination of exchange risk by doing business locally.

Expatriates. Individuals who reside abroad but are citizens of the parent country of the multinational; they are citizens of the home, not of the host country.

Export tariff. A tax levied on goods sent out of a country.

Exports. Goods and services produced by a firm in one country and then sent to another country.

Expropriation. The governmental seizure of private businesses coupled with little, if any, compensation to their owners.

External economies of scale. Efficiencies brought about by access to cheaper capital, highly skilled labor, and superior technology.

Factor conditions. Land, labor, and capital.

Factor endowment theory. A trade theory which holds that nations will produce and export products that use large amounts of production factors that they have in abundance and will import products requiring a large amount of production factors that are scarce in their country.

FDI cluster. A group of developing countries usually located in the same geographic region as a triad member and having some form of economic link to this member.

Femininity. The degree to which the dominant values of a society are caring for others and the quality of life.

Financial infrastructure. The monetary system of a country; it consists of the nation's banking, insurance, and financial services.

Firm specific advantages. Strengths or benefits specific to a firm and a result of contributions that can be made by its personnel, technology, and/or equipment.

Fisher effect. An international finance theory which describes the relationship between inflation and interest rates and holds that as inflation rises, so will the nominal interest rate.

Five partners. A business network consisting of five partner organizations: the flagship firm (a multinational enterprise), key suppliers, key customers, key competitors, and the nonbusiness infrastructure.

Flagship firms. Multinational firms characterized by global competitiveness and international benchmarks.

Focus strategy. A strategy that concentrates on a particular buyer group and segments that niche based on product line or geographic market.

Foreign bond. A bond sold outside the borrower's country.

Foreign direct investment (FDI). Equity funds invested in other nations.

Foreign exchange. Any financial instrument that carries out payment from one currency to another.

Foreign exchange arbitrageurs. Individuals who simultaneously buy and sell currency in two or more foreign markets and profit from the exchange rate differences.

Foreign exchange brokers. Individuals who work in brokerage firms where they often deal in both spot rate and forward rate transactions.

Foreign exchange hedgers. Individuals who limit potential losses by locking in guaranteed foreign exchange positions.

Foreign exchange traders. Individuals who buy and sell foreign currency for their employer.

Foreign investment controls. Limits on foreign direct investment or the transfer or remittance of funds.

Foreign investment review agencies. Agencies which review foreign investments to ensure that they benefit the local economy.

Foreign Sales Corporation Act. Legislation designed to allow US exporters to establish overseas affiliates and not pay taxes on the affiliates' income until the earnings are remitted to the parent company.

Foreign trade zones. Areas where foreign goods may be held and processed and then reexported without incurring customs duties (same as a free trade zone).

Forward exchange contract. A legally binding agreement between a firm and a bank that calls for the delivery of foreign currency at a specific exchange rate on a predetermined future date.

Forward integration. The purchase of assets or facilities that move the company closer to the customer such as a computer manufacturer that acquires a retail chain which specializes in computer products.

Forward rate. The rate quoted for the delivery of foreign currency at a predetermined future date such as 90 days from now.

Free trade area. An economic integration arrangement in which barriers to trade (such as tariffs) among member countries are removed.

Free trade zone. A designated area where importers can defer payment of customs duty while further processing of products takes place (same as a foreign trade zone).

Fronting loan. A funds positioning strategy that involves having a third party manage the loan.

Funds positioning techniques. Strategies used to move monies from one multinational operation to another.

Gaijin. A Japanese word which means "outsider"; it is used to refer to foreigners doing business in Japan.

Gairojin. A Japanese person who leaves his or her company to work for a foreign firm.

General Agreement on Tariffs and Trade (GATT). A major trade organization that has been established to negotiate trade concessions among member countries.

Geocentric predisposition. The tendency of a multinational to construct its strategic plan with a global view of operations.

Geocentric solution. An approach to determining parent–subsidiary relations; it involves handling financial planning and controlling decisions on a global basis.

Global area structure. An organizational arrangement in which primary operational responsibility is delegated to area managers, each of whom is responsible for a specific geographic region.

Global functional structure. An organizational arrangement in which all areas of activity are built around the basic tasks of the enterprise.

Global product structure. An organizational arrangement in which domestic divisions are given worldwide responsibility for product groups.

Global sourcing. The use of suppliers anywhere in the world, chosen on the basis of their efficiency.

Globalization. The production and distribution of products and services of a homogenous type and quality on a worldwide basis.

Hardship allowance. A special payment made to individuals posted to geographic areas regarded as less desirable.

Heckscher-Ohlin theory. A trade theory that extends the concept of comparative advantage by bringing into consideration the endowment and cost of factors of production and helps to explain why nations with relatively large labor forces will concentrate on producing labor-intensive goods, whereas countries with relatively more capital than labor will specialize in capital-intensive goods.

Hedge. A form of protection used against an adverse movement of an exchange rate.

Home country nationals. Citizens of the country where the multinational resides.

Horizontal integration. The purchase of firms in the same line of business such as a computer chip firm which acquires a competitor.

Host country nationals. Local people hired by a multinational.

Ideology. A set of integrated beliefs, theories, and doctrines that helps to direct the actions of a society.

Import tariff. A tax levied on goods shipped into a country.

Imports. Goods and services produced in one country and bought in another country.

Indigenization laws. Laws which require that nationals hold a majority interest in all enterprises.

Individualism. The tendency of people to look after themselves and their immediate family only.

Industrial democracy. The legally mandated right of employees to participate in significant management decisions.

Initial screening. The process of determining the basic need potential of the multinational's goods and services in foreign markets.

Integrative techniques. Strategies designed to help a multinational become a part of the host country's infrastructure.

Intermodal containers. Large metal boxes that fit on trucks, railroads, and airplanes and help to reduce handling cost and theft losses by placing the merchandise in an easy-to-move unit that is tightly sealed.

Internal economies of scale. Efficiencies brought about by lower production costs and other savings within a firm.

International Bank for Reconstruction and Development. (See World Bank)

International business. The study of transactions taking place across national borders for the purpose of satisfying the needs of individuals and organizations.

International division structure. An organizational arrangement in which all international operations are centralized in one division.

International finance. An area of study concerned with the balance of payments (BOP) and the international monetary system.

International Fisher effect (IFE). An international finance theory which holds that the interest rate differential between two countries is an unbiased predictor of future changes in the spot exchange rate.

International human resource management. The process of selecting, training, developing, and compensating personnel in overseas positions.

International joint venture. An agreement between two or more partners to own and control an overseas business.

International logistics. The designing and managing of a system to control the flow of materials and products throughout the organization.

International market assessment. An evaluation of the goods and services that the multinational can sell in the global marketplace.

International marketing. The process of identifying the goods and services that customers outside the home country want and then providing them at the right price and place.

International Monetary Fund. An agency that seeks to maintain balance-of-payments stability in the international financial system.

International monetary system. The multinational arrangement among the central banks of those countries that belong to the International Monetary Fund.

International product life cycle theory (IPLC). A theory of the stages of production of a product with new "know-how"; it is first produced by the parent firm, then by its foreign subsidiaries, and finally anywhere in the world where costs are the lowest; it helps to explain why a product that begins as a nation's export often ends up as an import.

International screening criteria. Factors used to identify individuals regarded as most suitable for overseas assignments.

International trade. The branch of economics concerned with the exchange of goods and services with foreign countries.

Investment Canada Act. An act designed to create a welcome climate for foreign investment by significantly loosening previous restrictions.

Japan Development Bank (JDB). A government-owned institution whose primary objective is to promote industrial development nationwide.

Japan External Trade Organization (JETRO). A nonprofit, government-supported organization dedicated to the promotion of mutually beneficial trade between Japan and other nations.

Just-in-time inventory. The delivery of parts and supplies just as they are needed.

Kaizen. A Japanese term which means continuous improvement.

Keiretsu. A Japanese term for a business group consisting of a host of companies and banks linked together through ownership and/or joint ventures.

Kinesics. A form of nonverbal communication which deals with conveying information through the use of body movement and facial expression.

Lag strategy. A hedging strategy that calls for delaying the receipt of foreign currency payment if this foreign currency is expected to strengthen and delaying foreign currency payables when the local currency is expected to weaken.

Large Retail Store Law. A Japanese law that limits the size of retail stores and requires that local competitors approve the opening of any facility that is more than 500 square meters.

Latin American Integration Association (LAIA). A free trade group formed to reduce intraregional trade barriers and to promote regional economic cooperation. Argentina, Bolivia, Brazil, Chile, Colombia, Ecuador, Mexico, Paraguay, Peru, Uruguay, and Venezuela are all members.

Lead strategy. A hedging strategy that calls for collecting foreign currency receivables before they are due if the currency is expected to weaken, and paying foreign currency payables before they are due if the currency is expected to strengthen.

Leontief paradox. A finding by Wassily Leontief, a Nobel prize economist, which shows that the United States, surprisingly, exports relatively more labor-intensive goods and imports capital-intensive goods.

License. A contractual arrangement in which one firm (the licensor) provides access to some of its patents, trademarks, or technology to another firm in exchange for a fee or royalty.

Licensee. A firm given access to some of the patents, trademarks, or technology of another firm in exchange for a fee or royalty.

Licensing agreement. An arrangement whereby one firm gives another firm the right to use certain assets such as trademarks, patents, or copyrights in exchange for a fee.

Licensor. A company that provides access to some of its patents, trademarks, or technology to another firm in exchange for a fee or royalty.

Lighter aboard ship (vessel) (LASH). Barges stored on a ship and lowered at the point of destination.

London Inter-Bank Offered Rate (LIBOR). The interest rate banks charge one another on Eurocurrency loans.

Macro political risk. A risk that affects all foreign enterprises in the same way.

Managerial development. The process by which managers obtain the necessary skills, experiences, and attitudes that they need to become or remain successful leaders.

Manners. Behaviors regarded as appropriate in a particular society.

***Maquiladora* industry.** A free trade zone that has sprung up along the US–Mexican border for the purpose of producing goods and then shipping them between the two countries.

Maquiladoras. (Also see *Twin factories*) Production operations set up on both sides of the US–Mexican border in a free trade zone for the purpose of shipping goods between the two countries.

Market coordination infrastructure. An infrastructure used by firms that compete in similar national markets but do little resource sharing among their businesses.

Market-driven economy. An economy in which goods and services are allocated on the basis of consumer demand.

Market growth. The annual increase in sales in a particular market.

Market indicators. Indicators used for measuring the relative market strengths of various geographic areas.

Market intensity. The richness of a market or the degree of purchasing power in one country as compared to others.

Market size. An economic screening consideration used in international marketing; it is the relative size of each market as a percentage of the total world market.

Masculinity. The degree to which the dominant values of a society are success, money, and material things.

Material culture. Culture which consists of objects that people make.

Materials handling. The careful planning of when, where, and how much inventory will be available to ensure maximum production efficiency.

Matrix structure. An organizational arrangement that blends two organizational responsibilities such as functional and product structures or regional and product structures.

Mercantilism. A trade theory which holds that a government can improve the economic well-being of the country by encouraging exports and stifling imports.

Merchandise trade. A balance-of-payments account that reports imports of goods from foreign sources and exports of goods to foreign destinations.

Mercosur. A subregional free trade group formed to promote economic cooperation; the group consists of Argentina, Brazil, Paraguay, and Uruguay.

Micro political risk. A risk that affects selected sectors of the economy or specific foreign businesses.

Ministry of International Trade and Industry (MITI). A Japanese ministry charged with providing information about foreign markets and with encouraging investment in select industries and, in the process, helping to direct the economy.

Mixed economies. Economic systems characterized by a combination of market and centrally driven planning.

Mixed structure. A hybrid organization design that combines structural arrangements in a way that best meets the needs of the enterprise.

Monetary exchange rate. The price of one currency stated in terms of another currency.

Multilateral netting. The process of determining the net amount of money owed to subsidiaries through multilateral transactions.

Multinational enterprise (MNE). A company headquartered in one country but having operations in other countries.

National responsiveness. The ability of MNEs to understand different consumer tastes in segmented regional markets and to respond to different national standards and regulations imposed by autonomous governments and agencies.

Nationalization. A process by which the government takes control of business assets, sometimes with remuneration of the owners and other times without such remuneration.

Nominal rate of interest. The interest rate charged to a borrower; it is called the "money" rate of interest to distinguish it from the "real" rate.

Nontariff barriers. Rules, regulations, and bureaucratic red tape that delay or preclude the purchase of foreign goods.

Organization for European Economic Cooperation. A group established to administer the Marshall plan and to help with the reconstruction of Europe after World War II. It now consists of 22 advanced economies, mostly in Western Europe, plus Japan, the United States, and Canada.

Overseas Private Investment Corporation. An organization that provides insurance of US foreign investment against blocked funds, expropriation and war, and revolution and insurrection.

Personal selling. A direct form of promotion used to persuade customers of a particular point of view.

Political risk. The probability that political forces will negatively affect a multinational's profit or impede the attainment of other critical business objectives.

Political union. An economic union in which there is full economic integration, unification of economic policies, and a single government.

Polycentric predisposition. The tendency of a multinational to tailor its strategic plan to meet the needs of the local culture.

Polycentric solution. An approach to determining parent–subsidiary relations; it involves treating the MNE as a holding company and decentralizing decision making to the subsidiary levels.

Portfolio investment. The purchase of financial securities in other firms for the purpose of realizing a financial gain when these marketable assets are sold.

Power distance. A cultural dimension which measures the degree to which less powerful members of organizations and institutions accept the fact that power is not distributed equally.

Practical school of international selection. A school of thought which holds that leaders can be successful in any culture because effective managerial behavior is universal.

Privatization. The process of selling government assets to private buyers.

Process mapping. A flow charting of every step that goes into producing a product.

Product managers. Managers responsible for coordinating the efforts of their people in such a way as to ensure the profitability of a particular business or product line.

Production system. A group of related activities designed to create value.

Promotion. The process of stimulating demand for a company's goods and services.

Protective and defensive techniques. Strategies designed to discourage a host country from interfering in multinational operations.

Protestant work ethic. A belief which holds that people should work hard, be industrious, and save their money.

Proxemics. A form of nonverbal communication which deals with how people use physical space to convey messages.

Purchasing power parity theory (PPP). An international finance theory which holds that the exchange rate between two currencies will be determined by the relative purchasing power of those currencies.

Quota. A quantity limit on imported goods.

Real interest rate. The difference between the nominal interest rate and the rate of inflation.

Regiocentric predisposition. The tendency of a multinational to use a strategy that addresses both local and regional needs.

Regional managers. In a geocentric matrix, managers charged with selling products in their geographic locale.

Regression analysis. A mathematical approach to forecasting which attempts to test the explanatory power of a set of independent variables.

Repatriation. The process of returning home at the end of an overseas assignment.

Repatriation agreement. An agreement which spells out how long a person will be posted overseas and sets forth the type of job that will be given to the person upon returning.

Resource managers. In a matrix structure, managers charged with providing people for operations.

Resource sharing infrastructure. An infrastructure used by firms that compete in dissimilar national markets but share resources such as R&D efforts and manufacturing information.

Return on investment (ROI). A percentage determined by dividing net income before taxes by total assets.

Ringsei. Decision making by consensus; this process is widely used in Japan.

Roll-on-roll-off (vessels) (RORO). Ocean-going ferries that can carry trucks that drive onto built-in ramps and roll off at the point of debarkation.

Scenario analysis. The formulation and analysis of events that are likely to happen; this strategic planning tool is used to help firms deal with future events.

Secular totalitarianism. A system of government in which the military controls everything and makes decisions which it deems to be in the best interests of the country.

Shinto work ethic. A belief that people should work hard at their tasks.

Single European Act. An act passed by the EU which contains many measures to further integrate the member states, along economic and political dimensions, and which allows the Council of Ministers to pass most proposals by a majority vote, in contrast to the unanimous vote that was needed previously.

Single European market. A market consisting of all members of the EU, bound together by a single currency, a special charter, complete harmonization of social and economic policies, and a common defense policy.

Social infrastructure. The societal underpinnings of an economy; they consist of the country's health, housing, and educational systems.

Special drawing right. A unit of value that has been created by the IMF to replace the dollar as a reserve asset.

Specific duty. A tariff based on the number of items being shipped into a country.

Speculator. In foreign exchange markets, a person who takes an open position.

Spot rate. The rate quoted for current foreign currency transactions.

Standardized training programs. Generic programs that can be used with managers anywhere in the world.

Strategic business units. Operating units with their own strategic space; they produce and sell goods and services to a market segment and have a well-defined set of competitors.

Strategic cluster. A network of businesses and supporting activities located in a specific region, where flagship firms compete globally and supporting activities are home-based.

Strategic fit. A strategic management concept which holds that an organization must align its resources in such a way as to mesh effectively with the environment.

Strategic management. Managerial actions that include strategy formulation, strategy implmentation, evaluation, and control and encompass a wide range of activities, including environmental analysis of external and internal conditions and evaluation of organizational strengths and weaknesses.

Strategic partnership. An agreement between two or more competitive multinational enterprises for the purpose of serving a global market.

Strategic planning. The process of evaluating the enterprise's environment and its internal strengths and then identifying long- and short-range activities.

Stragegy formulation. The process of evaluating the enterprise's environment and its internal strengths.

Strategy implementation. The process of attaining goals by using the organizational structure to properly execute the formulated strategy.

Tailor-made training programs. Programs designed to meet the specific needs of the participants, typically including a large amount of culturally based input.

Tariff. A tax on goods shipped internationally.

Tax havens. Low-tax countries that are hospitable to business.

Theocratic totalitarianism. A system of government in which a religious group exercises total power and represses or persecutes nonorthodox factions.

Theory of absolute advantage. A trade theory which holds that by specializing in the production of goods which they can produce more efficiently than any others, nations can increase their economic well-being.

Theory of comparative advantage. A trade theory which holds that nations should produce those goods for which they have the greatest relative advantage.

Third country nationals. Citizens of countries other than the one in which the multinational is headquartered or the one in which they are assigned to work by the multinational.

Time-to-market accelerators. Factors that help reduce bottlenecks and errors and ensure product quality and performance.

Totalitarianism. A system of government in which one individual or party maintains complete control and either refuses to recognize other parties or suppresses them.

Trade adjustment assistance. Assistance offered by the US government to US businesses and individuals harmed by competition from imports.

Trade creation. A process in which members of an economic integration group begin to focus their efforts on those goods and services for which they have a comparative advantage and start trading more extensively with each other.

Trade diversion. A process in which members of an economic integration group decrease their trade with nonmember countries in favor of trade with each other.

Trading-with-the Enemy Act. A law which disallows trade with countries judged to be enemies of the United States, including North Korea and Cuba.

Training. The process of altering employee behavior and attitudes in a way that increases the probability of goal attainment.

Transaction exposure. The risk that a firm faces when paying bills or collecting receivables in the face of changing exchange rates.

Transfer price. An internal price set by a company in intrafirm trade such as the price at which one subsidiary will sell a product to another subsidiary.

Transit tariff. A tax levied on goods passing through a country.

Transition strategies. Strategies designed to help smooth the move from foreign to domestic assignments.

Translation. The process of restating foreign financial statements in the currency of the parent company.

Translation exposure. The foreign exchange risk that a firm faces when translating foreign currency financial statements into the reporting currency of the parent company.

Transnational network structure. An organization design which helps MNCs take advantage of global economies of scale while also being responsive to local customer demands.

Trend analysis. The estimation of future demand by either extrapolating the growth over the last 3 to 5 years and assuming that this trend will continue or by using some form of average growth rate over the recent past.

Triad. The three major trading and investment blocs in the international arena: the United States, the EU, and Japan.

Twin factories. (Also see *Maquiladoras*) Production operations set up on both sides of the US–Mexican border for the purpose of shipping goods between the two countries.

Uncertainty avoidance. The extent to which people feel threatened by ambiguous situations and have created institutions and beliefs for minimizing or avoiding those uncertainties.

Unconventional cargo vessels. Vessels used for shipping oversized and unusual cargoes.

United States–Canada Free Trade Agreement (FTA). A trade agreement that eliminates most trade restrictions (such as tariffs) between these two countries and extends national treatment to foreign investment.

Unrequited transfers. A balance-of-payments account that reports transactions which do not involve repayment or performance of any service.

Value chain. The way in which primary and support activities are combined in providing goods and services and increasing profit margins.

Values. Basic convictions that people have regarding what is right and wrong, good and bad, important and unimportant.

Vertical integration. The ownership of assets involved in producing a good or service and delivering it to the final customer.

Work councils. Groups that consist of both worker and manager representatives and are charged with dealing with matters such as improving company performance, working conditions, and job security.

Working capital. The difference between current assets and current liabilities.

World Bank. A multigovernment-owned bank created to promote development projects through the use of low-interest loans.

Acknowledgements

CHAPTER 2

Appendix 2A adapted from *Fortune*, "The Fortune Global 500," August 3, 1998, copyright ©1998 Times Inc. All rights reserved.

Appendix 2B adapted from *Fortune*, "The Fortune Global 500," August 3, 1998, copyright ©1998 Time Inc. All rights reserved.

Appendix 2C adapted from *Fortune*, "The Fortune Global 500," August 3, 1998, copyright ©1998 Times Inc. All rights reserved.

Appendix 2D adapted from *Fortune*, "The Fortune Global 500," August 3, 1998, copyright ©1998 Times Inc. All rights reserved.

Appendix 2E adapted from *Fortune*, "The Fortune Global 500," August 3, 1998, copyright ©1998 Times Inc. All rights reserved.

Appendix 2F adapted from *Fortune*, "The Global 500," August 4, 1997, copyright ©1996 Times Inc. All rights reserved.

CHAPTER 3

Table 3.7 reported in *USA Today*, June 10, 1998, copyright ©1998, *USA Today*. Reprinted with permission.

CHAPTER 4

Table 4.1 adapted from *Fortune*, Special Issue, Spring/Summer 1991, copyright ©1991 Time Inc. All rights reserved.

CHAPTER 5

Figure 5.1 from Geert Hofstede, "The Cultural Relativity of Organizational Practices and Theories," *Journal of International Business Studies*, Fall 1983. Reprinted with permission.

Figure 5.2 from Geert Hofstede, "The Cultural Relativity of Organizational Practices and Theories," *Journal of International Business Studies*, Fall 1983. Reprinted with permission.

Table 5.2 from Alfred M. Jaeger, "Organizational Development and National Culture: Where's the Fit?," *Academy of Management Review*, January 1986, pp. 188–190.

Table 5.3 from Geert Hofstede, "The Cultural Relativity of Organizational Practices and Theories," *Journal of International Business Studies*, Fall 1983. Reprinted with permission.

Table 5.4 adapted from James R. Lincoln, "Employee Work Attitudes and Management Practice in the United States and Japan: Evidence from a Large Comparative Survey," the *California Management Review*, copyright ©1989, by The Regents of the University of California. Reprinted from the *California Management Review*, vol. 25, No. 1. By permission of The Regents.

Table 5.5 adapted from Itzhak Harpaz, "The Importance of Work Goals; An International Perspective," *Journal of International Business Studies*, vol. 21, no. 1, 1990. Reprinted with permission.

Table 5.7 from Rosalie L. Tung, "Selection and Training Procedures of US, European, and Japanese Multinationals," *California Management Review* copyright ©1882, by The Regents of the University of California. Reprinted from the *California Management Review*, vol. 25, No. 1. By permission of The Regents.

CHAPTER 6

Figure 6.1 from Raymond Vernon and Louis T. Wells, Jr., *The Manager in the International Economy*, 7th edition, copyright ©1996. Adapted by permission of Prentice-Hall, Inc., Upper Saddle River, NJ.

CHAPTER 8

Table 8.2 adapted from *International Dimensions of Management*, 2nd edition, by copyright ©1989. Reprinted with permission of South-Western College Publishing, a division of Thomson Learning. Fax 800 730 2215.

Figure 8.4 reported in Arnoldo C. Hax and Nicholas S. Majluf, *The Strategy Concept and Process: A Pragmatic Approach*, copyright ©1991. Reprinted by permission of Prentice-Hall, Inc., Upper Saddle River, NJ.

CHAPTER 10

Table 10.1 adapted from *Fortune*, Special edition, Spring/Summer 1991, copyright ©1991 Times Inc. All rights reserved.

Figure 10.2 reprinted by permission of *Harvard Business Review* 9 (an exhibit). From "Computers and the Coming of US Keiretsu," by Charles H. Ferguson, July-August, 1990. Copyright ©1990 by the President and Fellows of Harvard College, all rights reserved.

Figure 10.3 from Ford S. Worthy, "Japan's Smart Secret Weapon," *Fortune*, August 12, 1991, copyright ©1991 Time Inc. All rights reserved.

Table 10.5 adpted from *Fortune*, July 15, 1991, copyright ©1991 Time Inc. All rights reserved.

CHAPTER 12

Figure 12.1 reprinted from *Columbia Journal of World Business*, Summer 1973 Lawrence G. Franko, "Who Manages Multinational Enterprises?", p. 33, copyright ©1973, with permission from Elservier Science.

Table 12.1 from Geoggrey W. Latta, "Expatriate Incentives: Beyond Tradition," reprinted from *IIRFOCUS*, March 1998. Copyright ©1998. American Manage-ment Association International. Reprinted by permission of American Management Association International, New York, NY. All rights reserved. *http://www.amanet, org.*

Figure 12.2, 12.2 C. Reynolds, "Compensation of Overseas Personnel," in *Handbook of Human Resource Administration*, 2nd Edition, edited by J.J. Famularo, Copyright ©1986. Reproduced by permission of The McGraw-Hill Companies.

Table 12.3 adapted from Fred E. Fiedler, Terence Mitchell, and Harry C. Triandis, "The Cultural Assimilator: An Approach to Cross-Cultural Training," *Journal of Applied Psychology*, April 1971, copyright ©1971 by the American Psychological Association. Adapted by permission.

CHAPTER 13

Table 13.4 adapted from Richard M. Hodgetts and Fred Luthans, *International Management*, 4th Edition, copyright ©2000. Reproduced with permission of The McGraw-Hill Companies.

CHAPTER 16

Table 16.3 adapted from Maria Brindlmayer, "Comparing EC Investment Incentives and Getting the Best Deal," *Journal of European Business*, Novermber/December 1990, copyright ©Faulkner & Gray, Inc. Republished with permission.

Table 16.4 adapted from Maria Brindlmayer, "Comparing EC Investment Incentives and Getting the Best Deal," *Journal of European Business*, November/December 1990, copyright ©Faulkner & Gray, Inc. Republished with permission.

Table 17.2 adapted from *Fortune*, "The Fortune Global 500," August 3, 1998, copyright ©1998 Time Inc. All rights reserved.

Figure 20.3 reprinted by permission of the *Harvard Business Review* (an exhibit). From "Transcending Business Boundaries: 12,000 World Managers View Change," by Rosabeth Moss Kanter, May-June 1991. Copyright ©1991 by the President and Fellows of Harvard College, all rights reserved.

Whilst every effort has been made to trace the owners of copyright material, in a few cases this has proved imposs-ible and we take this opportunity to offer our apologies to any copyritht holders whose rights we may have unwittingly infringed.

Subject Index

Name Index